Principles of
Behavior Change

Understanding Behavior
Modification Techniques

Principles of Behavior Change

Understanding Behavior
Modification Techniques

Edward P. Sarafino
Trenton State College

John Wiley & Sons, Inc.
New York • Chichester • Brisbane • Toronto • Singapore

EXECUTIVE EDITOR   Christopher Rogers
ACQUISITIONS EDITOR   Karen Dubno
MARKETING MANAGER   Rebecca Herschler
PRODUCTION EDITOR   Deborah Herbert
TEXT DESIGN   Nancy Field
COVER DESIGN   Karin Kincheloe
MANUFACTURING COORDINATOR Dorothy Sinclair
PHOTO RESEARCHER   Lisa Passmore
ILLUSTRATION   Rosa Bryant
ILLUSTRATORS   Academy Artworks Inc.

This book was set in 10/12 New Baskerville by LCI Design and
printed and bound by R. R. Donnelley Crawfordsville. The cover was printed by Phoenix Color Corp.

Recognizing the importance of preserving what has been written, it is a
policy of John Wiley & Sons, Inc. to have books of enduring value published
in the United States printed on acid-free paper, and we exert our best
efforts to that end.

Library of Congress Cataloging-in-Publication Data:
Sarafino, Edward P., 1940–
    Principles of behavior change : understanding behavior
  modification techniques / Edward P. Sarafino.
      p.   cm.
    Includes bibliographical references and indexes.
    ISBN 0-471-10954-1

Printed in the United States of America

10 9 8 7 6 5 4 3 2 1

To Precious

Preface

"Now that's a book I could use," a nonpsychologist friend said when I told him about the book I was writing on techniques for changing behavior. I hope you will respond the same way as you examine what I have written. Psychologists have discovered a great deal of information about human behavior, but not all of the knowledge we have gained can be applied to improve the way people behave and function in everyday life. The field of behavior modification is unique in this respect, having developed a rich and varied system of techniques, based on established principles of learning, that have been applied effectively toward improving people's behavior. Applications of behavior change techniques have been successful in almost all areas of psychology and in a wide variety of settings.

My goal while writing this text was to create a clear and engaging teaching instrument that describes the techniques psychologists and other professionals use in helping people change their behavior. The book draws on research, theory, and my own experiences to explain and provide examples of the concepts and methods of behavior modification. I have endeavored to write a comprehensive text that is appropriate for several courses, especially *behavior modification, applied behavior analysis, behavior therapy,* and the *psychology of learning.*

I recognized that students who will use this text are likely to come from a variety of fields, such as psychology, education, counseling, social work, nursing, and allied medical areas including physical and occupational therapy. I tried to make the material interesting and relevant to all these readers. The content of the book is appropriate for upper-division students, especially juniors; the straightforward writing style also makes the material accessible to most sophomores. Students using the book will probably benefit from having taken an introductory psychology course, but this will not be essential for mastering the material.

The field of behavior modification is very exciting, partly because of its relevance to the lives of those who study it and to individuals the students know or will work with in the future. The field is also exciting because the techniques can be applied in so many different settings and can be used to change one's own behavior. Creating a book that is comprehensive and up-to-date in its coverage of behavior change principles and their applications was a challenge. I consulted over 1500 articles and books in the process of writing this text and have cited about 900 references.

Objectives and Distinctive Features of This Book

Several important objectives guided the content and organization of my writing. This text was designed to:

- Provide an understanding of the fundamental techniques of behavior modification by presenting concepts and procedures in a logical sequence and by giving clear definitions and examples of each technique.

- Teach students how to pinpoint and define the behavior to be changed and to learn how a response is determined by its antecedents and consequences.

- Teach usable, practical skills by specifically stating the purpose of each technique, describing how it is carried out, and presenting guidelines and tips to maximize its effectiveness.

- Describe why and how to design a program to change a behavioral deficit or excess by conducting a functional analysis and then selecting and combining techniques that can be directed at the behavior itself and its antecedents and consequences.

- Illustrate why and how to collect and analyze data.

- Give students an opportunity to design and carry out a self-management program to improve a behavior of their own choosing.

- Provide students with a handbook to use when they enter their careers and begin to design and conduct interventions to modify people's behaviors in various settings.

A main feature of this text that sets it apart from others is the use of end-of-chapter *application exercises* with *work sheets*. These exercises enable the students to generate solutions that can be drawn together to form the basis for self-management projects. At the same time, the exercises get the students actively involved in the chapter material. Because of the flexible design of these exercises, an instructor has the option of using them to create any of the following class assignments. The students can be asked to:

- Design a self-management project, execute it, analyze the data and submit a report.

- Design a project and submit a report, but not carry out the intervention or collect data.
- Complete the exercises and submit their work sheets as homework or extra credit assignments.
- Complete the exercises as in-class activities or as study guides for tests.

By the end of Chapter 8, students who carry out self-management programs will have *learned all the techniques* they will need to start their interventions and will have *begun collecting baseline data*. Interventions can begin at the end of Chapter 9 and last for 3 or 4 weeks while subsequent chapters are being covered. I have tested this process with my own classes, and the schedule works well in a semester format. For quarter-length formats, instructors might allow shorter intervention periods or use an option for the exercises where students do not actually carry out the self-management projects.

How This Text Is Organized

The chapters and material within them start with relatively simple concepts and techniques and build toward increasingly complex and specialized methods. The book is divided into 16 chapters in the following six parts:

- *Part One* introduces the student to the behavior modification approach, defines the basic concepts and processes, describes how behavior change principles have been applied effectively with a wide variety of behaviors in diverse settings, and provides some foundation skills for the design and assessment of behavior change programs.
- *Part Two* deals with modifying operant behavior. It discusses in depth what antecedents and consequences (reinforcement, punishment, and extinction) are and details methods for managing events to change operant behavior.
- *Part Three* examines basic respondent concepts and techniques, including overt and covert methods, and describes how to apply them to change emotional behavior and associations.
- *Part Four* focuses on program design and evaluation. It shows how to combine behavior modification techniques to form an effective program for changing behavior and describes ways to maintain behavior improvements and to evaluate a program's effectiveness. Students who are conducting a self-management program will be able to use the material in these chapters to start an intervention, evaluate it, and add techniques to improve its effectiveness and to maintain the target behavior when the intervention ends.
- *Part Five* examines specialized or advanced methods for changing behavior, such as token economies and clinical approaches professionals use in behavior therapy.
- *Part Six* consists of a chapter on concerns and future challenges for the field of behavior modification.

Learning Aids

This book contains many pedagogical features including a table of contents and a prologue at the beginning of each chapter. These give the student an overview of the chapter material and include and engaging, relevant vignette. The body of each chapter includes *figures*, *tables*, and *photographs* to clarify concepts or research findings. For example, special figures were created to show how second-order conditioning occurs and how to collect data for a functional analysis. Graphs illustrate the effects of behavior modification methods on performance. Important terms are printed in **boldface** type, and *italics* are used liberally for other terms and for emphasis.

Three types of boxed material are incorporated throughout the text:

 Concept Checks. These boxes enable students to apply concepts or techniques to specific questions or problems to check their basic understanding of the material they have just read. A question followed by a ⇔ identifies it as a critical thinking question. Because these questions are intended to promote students' analytical and critical thinking, more than one answer could be correct.

 Case Studies. This material describes actual cases in which behavior modification techniques were applied. Behavior problems and interventions are presented in rich detail, giving students an appreciation of how procedures are conducted, and their impact and utility.

 Close-Ups. This third type of box presents specific theoretical or controversial issues, in-depth conceptual topics and procedural steps, or important research.

Each chapter ends with a *summary*, a list of *key terms*, *review questions*, a list of *related readings*, and an *application exercise* with a *work sheet*. The key terms consist of all boldfaced items from the chapter and are redefined in the *glossary* at the back of the book.

Instructor's Manual

The instructor's manual contains a test bank and information to help instructors (1) organize and present the subject matter effectively and (2) design activities that enrich classroom discussion.

Acknowledgments

Writing this book has been a huge task. I am indebted first of all to the researchers whose important and creative work I have cited. There would be no field of behavior modification without their work. I also received a great deal of direct help and encouragement from a number of people whose contributions I gratefully acknowledge.

My heartfelt thanks go to Chris Rogers and Karen Dubno, the acquisitions editors at John Wiley & Sons, who saw merit in my plan and signed the book, and to the other Wiley staff who helped establish my writing schedule, oversaw the review process, coordinated the production process, and generated the marketing plan. I also appreciate the fine work of Lisa Passmore, Photo Research; Rosa Bryant, Illustration; Karin Kincheloe, Design Supervisor; Deborah Herbert, Production Editor; and Barbara Bredenko, Editorial Program Assistant.

The cover-to-cover review process generated many helpful suggestions that have made this a better book than it would have been otherwise. I thank the reviewers for reinforcing me for the work I did and prodding me to do still better. The resulting book has benefitted greatly from this process and the excellent perspectives of the following colleagues: *Henry Adams,* University of Georgia; *Gywneth Hill Beagley,* Alma College; *D. Wayne Mitchell,* Southwest Missouri State University; *Joseph Olmi,* University of Southern Mississippi; *Robert J. Presbie,* SUNY New Paltz; *Brian Rabian,* University of Southern Mississippi; *Donald Schupe,* California State Polytechnic University; *A. Robert Sherman,* University of California—Santa Barbara; *Nelson Smith,* University of Rhode Island; *John Steffen,* University of Cincinnati; *Richard Wesp,* Elmira College.

Many other individuals helped, too. I thank my very good friend and colleague, Jim Armstrong, who read and commented on many chapters before they went out for review and my students in the spring 1995 semester, who used a draft of the book as their text and gave me feedback. I am also grateful to my assistants, Erin Murphy, Margaret Paterson, and Tina Volpe, who photocopied hundreds of journal articles. The staff at the Trenton State College library were enormously helpful in acquiring needed materials, and the college accepted a grant for released time so that I could complete this work.

Very personal thanks go to the closest people in my life—family, friends, and colleagues—for encouraging and supporting my efforts to complete this book and for tolerating my preoccupation.

Edward P. Sarafino

To the Student

"I wish I could eat healthier," a student said when planning to change her behavior. But what does her statement mean? "Eating healthier" can be accomplished in many different ways. My student could choose to eat diets that are lower in calories, lower in saturated fats, higher in fiber, or just better balanced. What specifically should she do or not do? One of the first topics we will consider in this book is the importance of identifying and defining the behavior we wish to change. Once we've established how to define a problem behavior exactly, we'll examine the many techniques behavior modification has to offer in helping people change how they behave. You will find that these techniques have been used effectively in psychotherapy, education, parenting, business and industry, and health promotion.

When learning about principles of behavior change, you'll find two appealing features of the material that will probably make it interesting to you: (1) the material is *personally relevant* and (2) many of the things you learn can actually be *applied* in your everyday life. Although taking a course in behavior modification and reading this book will not make you an expert in changing people's behavior, you will learn some skills to use in your own lives and you will acquire an understanding of what behavior modification techniques are and how professionals use them. What you learn in this course will lay the foundation for gaining more training in behavior modification so that you may enter a career in which you can apply its techniques to help other people.

The Book

This book was designed for you, the reader. First and foremost, it provides a thorough and up-to-date presentation of the major issues, theories, concepts, and research in behavior modification. The material throughout the book is organized so that relatively simple concepts and techniques can be used and built on in the presentation of increasingly more complex and specialized methods. Because some of the concepts are complex and technical, I have made special efforts to write in a straightforward, clear, and engaging fashion.

A unique feature of this book is that each chapter ends with an *application exercise* that will have you use material from your reading to carry out a creative task of solving a series of applied problems and questions. A *work sheet* for each exercise is provided, with the questions and spaces for your answers and solutions. Most of the problems and questions in the work sheets will focus on designing a program you can implement to *change your own behavior*. The content and structure of the course you are taking will determine which of several options your instructor may choose for using the *application exercises*. For instance, the instructor may have you (1) design a program, execute it, analyze the data, and submit a report; or (2) design a project and submit a report, but not carry it out or collect data; or (3) complete the exercises and submit them as homework or extra credit assignments. Even if these exercises are not required activities for the course, you may use them as study activities for tests.

To help you master the material and remember it longer, the book includes the following learning aids.

- *Chapter Contents and Prologue.*   Each chapter begins with a contents list that outlines the major topics in the order in which they are covered. The prologue then introduces the chapter with a vignette that is relevant to the material ahead and gives an overview of the basic ideas you will read about.

- *Illustrations.*   The many figures and tables in each chapter are designed to clarify concepts and research findings and help them stick in your mind.

- *Concept Checks.*   Each chapter contains boxed quizzes at appropriate intervals to check your basic understanding of the material you have just read. The symbol ⇔ identifies a question as a "critical thinking" item for which more than one answer could be correct. These questions are intended to get you thinking analytically and creatively about the concepts and procedures you've read about.

- *Application Exercises.*   Toward the end of each chapter you'll find an application exercise that will have you apply the principles and concepts you've read about.

- *Summary.*   Each chapter has a substantial summary, which presents the most important ideas covered.

- *Key Terms and Review Questions.*   Following the summary are two features: a list of the most important terms in the chapter, arranged in order of their appearance, and a set of essay-type review questions.

- *Glossary.*   The glossary at the back of the book gives definitions of important terms and concepts. It will be useful when you are studying or reading and are not sure of the exact meaning of a term.

Study Hints

There are many ways you can use the features of this book to learn and study well, and you may want to "experiment" to find the best way for you. I will describe one method that works well for many students.

Survey the chapter first. Read the contents list and browse through the chapter, examining the displayed material (figures and tables,). (Some students also find it useful to read the summary first, even though it contains terms they may not yet understand.) Then read the prologue. As you begin each new section of the chapter, look at its title and turn it into a *question*. Thus, the heading early in Chapter 1, "Acquiring and Changing Behavior Through Learning," might become "How can learning help us to acquire and change behavior?" Doing this helps you focus on your reading. After reading the section, *reflect* on what you have just read. Can you answer the question you asked when you reworded the title?

When you have finished the body of the chapter, *review* what you have read by reading the summary. Next, define the items in the list of key terms. If there is an item you do not understand, look it up in the chapter or glossary. Then develop in your mind an answer for each of the review questions. Last, *reread* the chapter at least once, concentrating on the important concepts or ideas. You may find it helpful to underline or highlight selected material now that you have a good idea of what is important. If your exam will consist of "objective" questions, such as multiple choice, using this approach intensively should be effective. If your exam will have essay items, you will probably find it helpful to answer the review questions carefully, completely, and in writing.

I hope that you enjoy this book, that you learn a great deal from it, and that by the time you finish the course, you will have come to share my enthusiasm and fascination for behavior modification.

E. P. S.

Brief Contents

Contents

Part Two · **Methods of Changing Operant Behavior**   **101**

Part One

Overview and Basic Issues

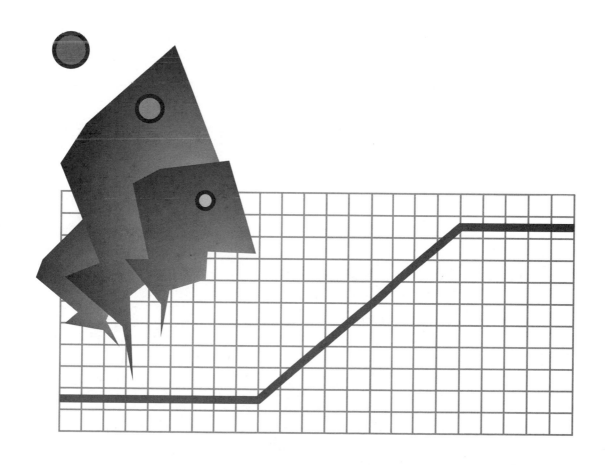

1 *What Is Behavior Modification?*

Prologue

"What do you think this study was about, Karen?" Joel asked a student who had participated in his psychology experiment. "I don't know—nothing much happened," she replied. Her tone suggested that she was very curious to know the answer. Actually something important happened, but she didn't realize it. When she arrived at the laboratory an hour ago, Joel had her sit in a chair and instructed her simply to "say all the words you can think of. Say them individually. Do not use sentences or phrases. Do not count. Please continue until I say stop." Joel sat behind her and said nothing, except the sound "mmm-hmm" occasionally, while she recited words for 50 minutes. (The sound Joel made was pronounced, "mmm-HMM," the way an English speaker might simply acknowledge something a person said.)

What happened that was so important? Joel was very careful about when he said "mmm-hmm." He only said it when Karen said a plural noun, such as "chairs" or "books." He never said it when she said anything else. Within just a few minutes, her behavior changed dramatically: she began saying lots of plural nouns and kept on saying them as long as Joel said "mmm-hmm"! But she didn't realize that she was doing this or that Joel's behavior was linked in any specific way to what she said.

This story, composed on the basis of a classic experiment by Joel Greenspoon (1955), illustrates that environmental events can modify specific behaviors substantially. This is true for almost all behaviors people perform, not just reciting plural nouns. Our behavior in everyday life occurs in the context of *external* events, such as the behavior of other people in our environment, and *internal* events, such as our thoughts and physiological processes. These are naturally occurring events that influence how we behave, regardless of whether we are aware of their effects. By using organized and systematic methods to regulate these events, we can help people change their behavior.

This chapter introduces the field of *behavior modification*—the well-established and exciting approach to understanding and changing behavior. We will first examine what behavior is and how it is acquired. Then we will look at some basic characteristics and techniques of behavior modification, chart the history of the field, and briefly consider how to use data and do research on human behavior. Finally, we will introduce you to the prospect of using principles of behavior change to modify your own behavior.

Behavior: What It Is and What It Isn't

Because this book focuses on ways to change behavior, we need to be very specific about what behavior is and is not. The term **behavior** refers to anything a person does, typically in response to internal or external events. When Karen answered "I don't know" to Joel's question about the study's purpose, her verbal behavior was in response to an external event. When you feel hungry and go to the kitchen to eat, you are responding to an internal event: feeling hungry. In each case, we can describe the individual's specific *actions* or *responses*. Sometimes the behavior we want to change is fairly simple, such as raising one's hand when a teacher asks a question, and sometimes it involves a sequence of actions, as in making a sandwich.

External and Internal Behaviors

The behaviors we have considered thus far have been external or *overt*, open to view or observation. There are two types of overt behaviors, verbal and motor. *Verbal behaviors* are actions that require the use of language. Karen's answering Joel's question and reciting words are examples of verbal behavior. *Motor behaviors* involve body movement, without requiring the use of language. Grasping a doorknob is a motor behavior; and swinging a baseball bat, getting dressed, and walking up a flight of stairs are other examples. Some activities, such as working a crossword puzzle, require both verbal and motor components. Overt behaviors have been and continue to be the main focus of behavior modification.

But not all behaviors we can change are overt (Homme, 1965; Scott et al., 1973). Some behaviors are internal or *covert*, not viewable or openly shown. Suppose you hear a "special" song on the radio, which leads you to think about a romantic date you had with your boyfriend or girlfriend. Thinking about that date is a response to an event, but the response is not viewable. Suppose hearing that song also produces inside you some emotions, such as happiness or sadness, and physiological changes, such as increased heart rate. These responses are also covert. You may show some outward signs—for example, facial or verbal expressions—of what's happening internally, but people's outward signs do not always reflect their covert behaviors accurately. An important difference between overt and covert behaviors is that overt behaviors can be measured directly, whereas covert behaviors must be measured either indirectly, perhaps through self-reports, or with special equipment.

What Is Not Behavior?

If I asked you to describe your best friend's behavior, what would you say? Chances are, you wouldn't describe specific behaviors. You'd probably focus on the friend's prominent *traits*, or broad and stable characteristics. You might answer, for instance, "Oh, Nancy's really nice. She's considerate, friendly, honest, smart, and creative. But she's not very conscientious." We tend to focus on broad characteristics to describe a person's behavior because they provide a convenient and efficient way of communicating a lot of information. Although you may have decided Nancy is smart because of specific behaviors you've observed, "smart" is not a behavior. In fact, none of the adjectives in the answer describes a behavior.

One problem with using broad characteristics as if they were behaviors is that they can be misleading and inconsistent. For example, you may have decided that

Nancy is "honest" because you've seen her return money that didn't belong to her and "considerate" because you've heard her lie to protect other people's feelings. Aren't these observations inconsistent? Or are the terms "honest" and "considerate" misleading? Another problem with using broad characteristics is that they are imprecise—they don't tell us specifically what we would need to change to improve a person's behavior. Consider Nancy's frequent lack of conscientiousness. Perhaps she almost always keeps promises to friends and gets to her part-time job promptly, but she rarely cleans her room and often fails to finish her college assignments and studying on time. If we wanted to help improve her conscientiousness, we would focus on specific behaviors involved in cleaning her room and doing her school-work. The more precise we are in describing the behavior to be changed, the more successful we are likely to be in measuring and improving the behavior.

In clinical practice, therapists generally use *diagnoses* to classify clients. One client is diagnosed as severely depressed, and another client is schizophrenic. One child is mentally retarded, and another is autistic. The advantages and problems associated with using diagnoses are similar to those associated with using traits: diagnoses are efficient for communicating, but they can be imprecise, and they do not always indicate what specific behaviors need to be changed. Therapists make diagnoses on the basis of behaviors that are common to individuals who display the condition. For example, children receiving the diagnosis of autism tend to have several of the following behavioral characteristics (Lovaas, 1977):

- Absence of speech or severely impaired speech with unusual patterns, such as echoing the speech of others.
- Lack of awareness of salient sounds and objects around them.
- Indifference to being liked; little or no affection.
- Frequent behaviors that seem to provide only self-stimulation: children rocking back and forth incessantly, for example, or fluttering their hands in front of their eyes.
- Absence or severe impairment of self-help behaviors, such as grooming and dressing themselves, and inability to protect themselves from physical danger.
- Frequent and severe self-injurious behaviors, such as biting their arms.

But most autistic children have only some of these characteristics and differ in the severity of the specific deficits they show. Knowing simply that a child is autistic does not tell therapists how to help the child. They must assess and try to improve the child's specific behaviors.

Last, the *outcomes of behavior* are not behaviors. Students who apply behavior change techniques on themselves to produce an outcome of, say, losing weight or improving their grades, often misdirect their focus toward the outcome rather than the behavior change needed to reach the outcome. In the example of losing weight, the behavior involves (1) what and how much people eat and (2) how much physical exercise they get—not how much they weigh, which is the outcome of their behavior. Individuals who focus their efforts toward the outcome often fail to identify and deal effectively with the specific behaviors they need to change.

How Behavior Develops

Human babies come into the world with only a small number of well-formed, inborn behaviors. These inborn behaviors are called *reflexes*. Several reflexes have obvious survival value for infants because they are useful in feeding, maintaining physiological functioning, and protecting the baby against injury (Sarafino & Armstrong, 1986). For example, two reflexes that are important for feeding are the *rooting reflex*, in which the baby turns its head toward an object that lightly touches its cheek, and the *sucking reflex*, in which the baby starts to suck when its lips are touched with any small rounded object, such as a nipple or finger. Inborn reflexive responses are inherited.

Virtually all other behaviors develop after birth, and their development depends on two processes: heredity and experience. Heredity affects behavioral development in at least two ways (Sarafino & Armstrong, 1986). First, it charts the course of the individual's *maturation*, or physical growth, including growth of the muscle and nervous systems. In the earliest years, physical growth is fastest in the head and upper trunk of the body; it speeds up later in the lower trunk, arms, and legs. This is why a 3-year-old's head is large relative to the legs, as compared with the bodies of older children and adults. Growth and coordination of the muscle and nervous systems follow the same pattern, showing the fastest advances in the head and upper body in the earliest years and spreading down the arms and legs later. This is why typical 3-year-olds can put on a pullover sweater but cannot tie their shoelaces. Maturation determines when motor actions become possible. Second, hereditary factors provide the foundation for or tendency toward developing behaviors of certain types. For instance, studies have found that people's inheritance influences the likelihood that they will develop a wide variety of behavioral problems, including stuttering (Scarr & Kidd, 1983), severe anxieties (Torgersen, 1983), autism (Cantwell & Baker, 1984), and alcoholism (Goodwin, 1986). The influence of heredity in developing some behaviors is moderately strong, but it is fairly mild for many other behaviors. Experience plays an important role—and is usually the dominant factor—in the development of almost all human behaviors. This role occurs through the process called *learning*. (Go to ✔ —as described in the Preface, this instruction prompts you to read the nearby boxed material that has the same icon.)

Acquiring and Changing Behavior Through Learning

People talk a lot about learning things. They say, for instance, "Ginny learned to brush her teeth a few months ago," or "Morry learned the multiplication tables in school," or "I learned to use my new computer software last week," or "I learned to like Japanese food when I was an exchange student in Tokyo." We decide that individuals have learned things when we see changes in their behavior—assuming we can rule out other influences on behavior, such as an injury that causes a person to walk differently. But what exactly do we mean by the term *learning*? A definition is

✔ **Concept Check 1.1**

• •

Pause now to check your understanding of the concepts you've just read about. Below are five statements about people. In the space following each statement, write the appropriate code: OB for a statement describing an overt behavior; CB for a covert behavior; T for a trait; or O for an outcome of behavior.

1. Elly was a very dependable student. _____
2. Jim laughed at the joke. _____
3. Joe developed strong biceps muscles at the gym. _____
4. Dolores dreamed about a spider last night. _____
5. Tony was a motivated employee. _____

_____

Answers: 1. T 2. OB 3. O 4. CB 5. T

• •

difficult to frame because learning is an internal process that applies to such a wide range of behaviors, and people don't always display what they have learned. The definition we will use takes these difficulties into account: **learning** is a relatively permanent change in behavioral tendency as a result of experience.

In the next sections, we'll see how different varieties of experiences lead to relatively permanent changes in behavior. The types of learning we will consider are discussed briefly here and examined in more detail in later chapters. We'll begin with the type of learning called *respondent* (or "classical") *conditioning.*

Respondent Conditioning

Let's first take an example of respondent conditioning in your life. Sit back, relax, and concentrate on the *name* of your favorite food. Does the name remind you of eating that food? If so, fine—you may let your imagination take over. Enjoy how tempting it looks and smells. Savor the delectable taste and allow it to linger in your mouth. . . . Are you salivating more now? If so, this illustrates your learned reaction to the *name* of a food. The flow of saliva is the result of prior respondent conditioning.

This example is a lot like the first laboratory demonstrations of respondent conditioning, reported in 1927 by Ivan Pavlov, the Russian Nobel prize–winning physiologist. Pavlov was studying the role of salivation in dogs' digestive processes when he noticed that the dogs began to salivate before the food was actually in their mouths. From this observation he correctly concluded that the association between the *stimulus,* such as the sight of food, and the salivary *response* must be a learned one. Moreover, he proposed that this learned relationship was formed through its association with the *reflexive,* or automatic, connection between food in the mouth and salivation. Pavlov later showed that virtually any stimulus, such as a light or tone, regularly associated with this reflexive connection could produce the salivary response.

In our demonstration you salivated in response to the *name* of your favorite food—say, "chocolate." In the past, the name of that food has been frequently associated with eating it: "Oh, that's to-die-for chocolate," you'd think while eating it. The presence of food in one's mouth *elicits* or produces salivation reflexively, or *without prior conditioning*. Thus, food in the mouth is an example of an **unconditioned stimulus** (US)—an event that automatically produces a specific response— and the automatic response to that stimulus is called the **unconditioned response** (UR). Although this reflexive association was not learned, your associating salivation to the *name* of the food was learned through the experience diagrammed in Figure 1.1. We know it was learned because you surely didn't salivate to the word "chocolate" before you had ever eaten any. Because you learned the name–salivation association, the learned stimulus—that is, the food's name—is called the **conditioned stimulus** (CS). And since there was no food in your mouth (that is, there was no US) in our demonstration, the salivation elicited by the name of the food is called a **conditioned response** (CR). Notice that the UR and CR are the same behavior. They are classified as *respondent behaviors* because they are elicited involuntarily by stimuli.

From this example, we can formulate the following definition: **respondent conditioning** is a learning process in which a stimulus (the CS) gains the ability to elicit a response through repeated association with a stimulus (the US) that already elicits that response. Did you notice how broadly this definition is phrased? Its breadth suggests that we can learn many things through respondent conditioning, and we do. For example, at one of Barbra Streisand's concerts in 1967, she forgot the words to three songs in front of a hugh audience. She developed severe stage fright from this experience. "I was terrified. It prevented me from performing for all these years," she said in an interview (Seligmann, Namuth, & Miller, 1994). Performing on stage became a CS that began to elicit intense fear as a CR. Emotions, often negative ones, are some of the most important things we learn through respondent conditioning. Negative emotions are not necessarily problematic, and they can be quite beneficial. For instance, a mild fear of heights leads us

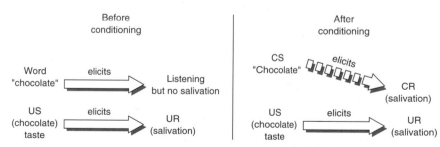

Figure 1.1   The respondent conditioning events. *Before conditioning*, the first couple of times your parents gave you chocolate, their saying "Here's some chocolate" elicited some listening behavior, but no salivation. You didn't yet associate the word "chocolate" with the US, the taste of chocolate. *After conditioning*, you began to associate the word "chocolate," now a CS, with having the taste in your mouth. The CS could then elicit salivation as a CR. Note that the dashed arrow indicates a learned association. Once conditioning has occurred, the CS can elicit the CR without the US being present, as we showed in our demonstration.

to be cautious when using a ladder. We probably also learn positive emotions and to like things through respondent conditioning. As an example, by watching comedian Bill Cosby tell funny jokes, you probably learned to like him.

Operant Conditioning

In the story about Karen at the beginning of the chapter, why do you suppose her output of plural nouns increased? It was because of the consequences of her behavior. Each time she said a plural noun, but not other words, Joel said "mmm-hmm." As long as he did this, Karen continued to say lots of plurals. Notice that Joel's saying "mmm-hmm" was *contingent* on—that is, depended on—Karen's saying plural nouns, and her saying plurals was affected by the contingent consequence of that behavior. This story gives an example of operant (or "instrumental") conditioning. **Operant conditioning** is the learning process by which a given behavior is changed by the *consequences* of that behavior. The responses we acquire through this type of learning are called *operant behaviors*. The term "operant" reflects the view that these behaviors *operate* on the environment, thereby producing consequences.

Consequences in Operant Conditioning

The scientist most prominently associated with operant conditioning is B. F. Skinner, who established the basic techniques and terminology for the study of operant behavior. Skinner (1938, 1953) distinguished between two types of behav-

B. F. Skinner (1904–1990)

Dennis the Menace
By HANK KETCHAM

"How'm I gonna learn Joey anything if I can't give him a little award when he DOES it?"

Dennis knows that the consequences of behavior are important.

DENNIS THE MENACE ® used by permission of Hank Ketcham and © by North America Syndicate

ioral consequence: reinforcement and punishment. In **reinforcement**, a consequence causes an *increase* in the performance of the behavior on which it is contingent. We saw an example of reinforcement in the story about Karen: her output of plural nouns increased in frequency as a result of Joel's saying "mmm-hmm," which was the consequence of her behavior. Reinforcement typically involves a consequence the person wants or finds pleasant, and perhaps Karen found Joel's "mmm-hmm" pleasant because she "unconsciously" thought it meant "That's good." In most cases, the consequence in the process of reinforcement is obviously desirable, something we would call a *reward*, such as praise, money, or candy. But our knowing *why* a particular consequence has an effect on behavior is irrelevant to the process. If the frequency of a behavior increases when it is followed by a consequence, we can conclude that reinforcement occurred.

In **punishment**, a consequence causes a *decrease* in the performance of the behavior on which it is contingent. In the experiment on which the story about Karen was based, Greenspoon (1955) tested other subjects using exactly the same procedure as we've seen, but the consequence of saying plural nouns was the researcher's saying "huh-uh" (pronounced "huh-UH," in a somewhat noncommittal way). For these subjects, the output of plurals *decreased*. Thus, "huh-uh" served to punish saying plurals. Punishment generally involves a consequence the person does not want or finds unpleasant, and perhaps Greenspoon's subjects interpreted "huh-uh" to mean "That's wrong." (If so, they were unaware of it. They, like the subjects who received "mmm-hmm," didn't realize that their behavior changed or that it was linked to what the researcher had said.) Once again, it isn't necessary to know *why* a particular consequence has an effect on behavior. If a behavior decreases in frequency when it is followed by a consequence, we can conclude that punishment occurred. When people try to apply punishment, they generally use events—such as spankings, reprimands, or reducing the person's privileges—that they *think* will work, but their thinking is not always correct. The best way to determine whether events punish a behavior is to observe the behavior when we apply the consequence: if it decreases, punishment has occurred.

Antecedents in Operant Conditioning

When you drive a car, traffic signals provide cues that have a strong influence on your behavior. You see the light before you act: if it is red, you depress the brake pedal; if it is green, you depress the gas pedal. Making these distinctions leads to reinforcement and helps you avoid punishment, such as traffic tickets or accidents. Stepping on the gas pedal when the light is red is likely to lead to unpleasant consequences. Clearly, behavior is influenced not only by the consequences that follow it, but also by the events and circumstances that precede it. Because these cues precede and set the occasion for your action, they are called **antecedents**. An important learning task in people's lives involves finding and learning cues that help us determine the type of consequence our behavior will bring.

We can now diagram the process of operant conditioning, using the letters A, B, and C to stand for *antecedents*, *behavior*, and *consequences*:

$$A \Rightarrow B \rightarrow C$$

The boldly printed, solid arrow between the B and C means *produces*: that is, behavior produces consequences. All behaviors we perform produce consequences, regardless of whether we notice them. When you write a word correctly in your notes, the consequences of this behavior include being able to move on. You don't really notice this reinforcing event, but it is there. The open arrow between the A and B means *sets the occasion for*: that is, antecedents set the occasion for behavior. Whether the behavior occurs depends on many factors, including the strength of the link between the antecedent and the behavior. Being in a place of worship presents a very strong antecedent for certain behaviors, such as whispering rather than talking loudly. At home, on the other hand, you have more latitude in how loudly you can talk and what you can say.

Operant conditioning can influence virtually any human behavior, verbal or motor, overt or covert. In subsequent chapters, we will see that programs to alter antecedents and consequences have been applied successfully to change essentially any behavior one can think of in people of all ages and with widely different backgrounds and abilities. (Go to 📖 .)

Case Study 1.1

Reinstating a Schizophrenic Man's Speech Using Operant Conditioning

• •

This case involves the use of operant conditioning to reinstate speech in an institutionalized 40-year-old man who had not spoken for 19 years (as described in Isaacs, Thomas, & Goldiamond, 1960). He had been diagnosed as schizophrenic, a condition characterized by major disturbances in thought, emotion, and behavior.

The therapist decided to try using chewing gum as a reward for speaking because of the interest the client had shown toward a package of gum that had fallen out of the therapist's pocket. The procedure progressed through five steps, each lasting a week or two, with three meetings a week:

1. The therapist held a stick of gum in front of the client and waited. When the client looked at the gum, the therapist gave it to him. After several of these episodes, the client looked at the gum as soon as it appeared.

2. The therapist held up a stick of gum and waited until the client moved his lips before

giving him the gum. After a few of these episodes, the client looked immediately at the gum and moved his lips.

3. The therapist held up the gum and gave it to the client if he made a vocal sound. After a few episodes, the client quickly looked at the gum and vocalized. The client's vocal sounds resembled "a croak."

4. The therapist held up the gum; said, "Say *gum, gum*"; and gave the treat to the client if his vocalizations progressed toward sounding more like gum.

Finally, at a session in the sixth week, the therapist said, "Say *gum, gum*," and the client responded, "Gum, please." He also gave his name and age when asked. At the time this case was written for publication, the client had received very little additional therapy for his speech, which continued to be very limited. Still, this case provides a fascinating demonstration of the utility of operant conditioning.

• •

Relating Respondent and Operant Conditioning

When books or instructors discuss learning, respondent and operant conditioning are usually presented as if they are separate, independent processes. To use looking at photographs as an analogy, you're being told: "Here's respondent conditioning in this picture, and here's operant conditioning in this other picture. See how separate and different they are?" Students often get the idea that respondent and operant conditioning function separately or independently—as discrete units—in real life. Although the two types of conditioning are to some extent separate and different, they almost always happen together in real life, with one flowing into the other. In terms of our analogy, real life is more like a videotape than a series of separate pictures. Let's consider a couple of examples of the two types of conditioning occurring together.

The first example is of a newborn baby named Vicki who was being fed. Her behavior involved the UR of sucking on a nipple that provided milk. This was a situation in which respondent conditioning was likely to occur. That is, when the nipple touched Vicki's lips, she would begin to suck reflexively. Stimuli, such as the bottle or breast she noticed at the time her lips were touched (the US), were potential CSs. But the feeding sequence did not stop here. There was an operant com-

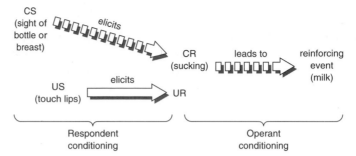

Figure 1.2   Respondent and operant conditioning functioning together in real life, using an example of a newborn infant's feeding experience. (Adapted from Sarafino & Armstrong, 1986, Figure 4.13.)

ponent, too, because a baby's sucking behavior is not just a UR, it's also an operant motor behavior. Vicki's sucking produced a consequence, milk, which reinforced that behavior. This sequence is diagrammed in Figure 1.2. In real life, the two components happen together.

Another real-life example of the two types of conditioning occurring together has the operant component preceding the respondent component. Ten-year-old Jim was playing with some small firecrackers. He lit one (an operant motor behavior) and it exploded early, burning his hand (punishment for his behavior). For the respondent conditioning part, he was watching the lit fuse (the CS) when he heard and felt the firecracker explosion (the US), which caused him to scream out in fear and pain (the UR). From that time on, whenever Jim saw a lit fuse (CS) or even a lit match, he felt very frightened (CR).

These are just two examples of operant and respondent conditioning happening together. In real life, it's quite unlikely that experiences involving one type of conditioning would not include the other, too.

Modeling

Four-year-old Jo watches her father tie his shoelaces and tries to copy his movements. Jo is learning through the process of **modeling**, or learning by watching the behavior of other people. This method of learning involves at least two participants, the *observer* and the *model*. Because of these characteristics, this learning method is frequently called "social," or "observational," or "vicarious" or "imitative" learning. Modeling is a very useful and efficient way to acquire and change behavior because we can learn actions without actually having to perform them. As we are about to see, we can learn both operant and respondent behavior through modeling.

One type of operant behavior people can learn through modeling is aggression, as classic research by Albert Bandura (1965) demonstrated with children. The children first saw one of three films showing a model performing a series of unusual aggressive acts, such as hitting a Bobo doll with a mallet and shouting "Sockeroo."

The consequences the model received for these acts were different in the three films: the model received either punishment, rewards, or no consequences for the acts. The children were then taken individually to a room that had a Bobo doll and the other objects they had seen in the film. They were told they could play with the toys in any way they wished, with *no consequences* promised or threatened for their actions. As expected, they copied the model's behavior, but the children who had observed the model being punished for aggression performed fewer of the model's aggressive acts than the other children did. Later, *all* the children were promised very attractive rewards if they would reproduce the aggressive behaviors they had seen the model do. Under this contingency, the children performed the same number of acts, regardless of the consequences they had seen in the film. These results indicate that children learn models' punished and rewarded aggressive acts equally. Seeing models punished for their acts merely *suppresses* the children's performance of those behaviors. These and other similar findings support the large body of research showing that watching violence on TV increases children's aggressive behavior (Friedrich-Cofer & Huston, 1986).

Modeling is an effective learning method for acquiring and changing a wide variety of operant behaviors, including simple responses, such as pulling a drawer open or shaking a tambourine, and complex behavioral sequences, such as those needed in preparing scrambled eggs (D. M. Baer, Peterson, & Sherman, 1967; Griffen, Wolery, & Schuster, 1992). Research has also shown that modeling affects the rate at which people drink alcoholic beverages. Individuals increase their drinking rates when others around them are drinking more than they are, and decrease their drinking rates when others are drinking less (Caudill & Lipscomb, 1980; DeRicco & Niemann, 1980).

People also learn respondent behaviors—such as fears—through modeling. One study had children, with their parents' permission, watch a short film that portrayed

These photos show a child in Bandura's research modeling the behaviors she saw the adult in the film perform (see top row).

"*THAT'S* A GOOD GIRL!"

Dennis probably learned this behavior of providing praise through the process of modeling.

DENNIS THE MENACE ® used by permission of Hank Ketcham and © by North America Syndicate

a 5-year-old boy screaming and withdrawing when his mother showed him a plastic figure of a cartoon character, Mickey Mouse; but when the mother showed the child a plastic figure of Donald Duck, he responded in a calm and undistressed manner (Venn & Short, 1973). After the children had watched this film, they participated in a task that involved the Mickey Mouse and Donald Duck figures. At this time they tended to avoid the Mickey Mouse figure (the one feared in the film) in favor of the Donald Duck. Initially the fear was pronounced—but a day or two later, the children showed no avoidance of or preference for either figure. What's more, the researchers had measured the children's physiological reactions while they watched the film. The children showed greater reactions during the Mickey Mouse (fearful) episode than during the Donald Duck. Although these effects were temporary, it is clear that observing fear in other people affects both internal and external behavior.

Cognition

The term **cognition** refers to mental activity, particularly thinking and reasoning. In the process of *thinking*, we use mental representations of the knowledge we have acquired and stored in memory, mostly in the form of language or images, which are mental pictures. If you see someone perform a behavior you'd like to do, you can "practice" it in your head by describing the actions in words or by forming mental pictures of the actions you would make. In *reasoning*, we apply logic in our thinking processes, usually to make plans and solve problems. If you feel sick, you try to plan the best course of action to take for your illness. Thinking and reasoning are involved in generating mental units we call plans, ideas, expectations, beliefs, and rules—and these units are basically statements we make to ourselves that serve as *covert antecedents* to our behavior. If you decide to see your physician for your illness, your plan initiates an action: you call to make an appointment.

Covert antecedents can influence our behavior in very important and broad ways. Let's consider the role of beliefs or expectations. We generate many beliefs about ourselves and our behavior, including beliefs regarding our ability to perform behaviors effectively. **Self-efficacy** refers to a belief about our ability to succeed at a specific activity we want to do (Bandura, 1977, 1986). We estimate our chances of success or failure on the basis of prior experience with similar activities. For example, if you wanted to play the piano but believed that you had very poor ability to learn this skill, you would not be likely to try. Research has shown that self-efficacy does influence people's behavior. Cigarette smokers who believe they cannot kick the habit typically don't try, but smokers who believe they can quit often make the attempt and succeed (DiClemente, Prochaska, & Gilbertini, 1985). Similarly, medical patients with chronic lung diseases who believe they can perform a prescribed program of physical exercise, such as walking certain distances, are more likely to carry out the program than equally ill patients with less self-efficacy (Kaplan, Atkins, & Reinsch, 1984).

To illustrate another kind of belief we generate, consider this example: a friend throws a football while you're not looking, it hits you in the head, and you wonder, "Did he mean to hurt me?" We generate beliefs about other people's actions, motives, and intentions—and we're more likely to respond aggressively to being hit if we think a given act was intentional. Interestingly, individuals who often behave aggressively tend to believe other people's injurious acts are intentional. This was demonstrated in a series of studies with elementary school boys whose behavior was regularly either aggressive or nonaggressive (Dodge & Frame, 1982). In one study, each boy described his beliefs about stories in which he was the victim. An example story had him "sitting at a lunch table and having a peer's milk carton spill milk all over his back." The stories did not indicate why the events happened. The aggressive boys were far more likely than the nonaggressive boys to decide that the acts had been intentional and to say that they would react aggressively. In another of these studies, the boys were observed playing freely in a large room. Aggressive boys not only initiated more unprovoked aggressive acts than nonaggressive boys, but they *received* more as well. The finding that aggressive boys received more aggression suggests that their tendency to believe that others intend to hurt them may be rooted in actual experience. (Go to ✔ .)

Defining Behavior Modification

Now that we have seen what behavior is and how people can acquire and change it, we should be able to define behavior modification. We will do that, but you should recognize that there is no "official" or fully agreed upon definition. This is because behavior modification has evolved over many years, but not all the field's experts

Concept Check 1.2

· ·

Check your understanding of the preceding concepts. Question 1 is followed by a ⇔, which means that the answer can vary somewhat or take different directions. As explained in the Preface, this symbol identifies a "critical thinking" item, one that encourages you to think analytically and creatively about what you've read and to apply the material to your life. The answers the book gives to critical thinking items are only suggestions; you may come up with different responses that are equally correct.

1. The text mentions that you may have come to like Bill Cosby by watching him tell jokes. What might be the **a.** US, **b.** UR, **c.** CS, and **d.** CR? ⇔
2. Anita's literature professor announced that a wonderful play was being performed on campus, and students who saw it and wrote a brief review would receive extra credit toward their final grades. Anita went to see the play and wrote a review, and she got the extra credit. Identify the **a.** antececent, **b.** behavior, and **c.** consequence.
3. Learning by watching other people's behavior is called _____.
4. People use thoughts as covert _____ for behavior.

Answers: **3.** modeling **4.** antecedents
                                        2a. professor's announcement, **2b.** see play and write review, **2c.** extra credit
                    1a. funny joke, **1b.** laugh/feel happy, **1c.** Cosby's face/name, **1d.** feel happy

· ·

have seen eye to eye on incorporating each major new idea and method within the discipline. Keeping this in mind, we will define **behavior modification** as the field of study that focuses on *using principles of learning and cognition to understand and change people's behavior.*

Behavior modification has several defining characteristics that make its approach unique (Kazdin, 1978; Wixted, Bellack, & Hersen, 1990). These characteristics, which are accepted by most experts in the field, apply when factors that affect behavioral development are studied in research and when principles of behavior change are used to modify behavior. We'll begin with the general focus on behavior.

Focus on Behavior

We have seen that the behavior modification approach focuses on behavior. As a result, professionals who use behavior change techniques place a strong emphasis on (1) *defining people's current status and progress in terms of behavior* rather than traits or other broad characteristics, (2) being able to *measure the behavior* in some way, and (3) *whenever possible, assessing covert behaviors, such as fear, in terms of overt actions* the person makes when afraid so that objective and reliable measurements can be made. The behavior modification approach considers emotional and cognitive events to be accessible to study and change in much the same way as overt behaviors. However, assessing covert behaviors with subjective measures only, such as having people simply rate their feelings of fear, provides relatively weak evidence that efforts to change the behavior are succeeding.

Efforts to change a behavior can be directed toward increasing it or decreasing it, depending on whether the problem being addressed involves a deficit or an excess of the behavior. When a **behavioral deficit** exists, the person does *not* perform a specific appropriate behavior often enough, long enough, well enough, or strongly enough. Examples of behavioral deficits include not initiating conversations often enough, not spending enough time studying, and not exercising vigorously enough. When a **behavioral excess** exists, the person performs a particular behavior too frequently, too strongly, or for too long. Examples of behavioral excesses are smoking cigarettes, spending too much time socializing, and experiencing too much fear when taking tests.

Importance of Learning and the Environment

For the most part, human behavior is *learned* behavior. We discussed earlier that genetic factors can influence behavior and its development, but learning and cognition provide the most substantial and pervasive processes by which people acquire and change almost everything they do. As a result, the application of behavior change techniques assumes that behavior is generally malleable and can be modified by providing appropriate new experiences.

The new experiences used in modifying behavior involve altering aspects of the individual's *environment*, mainly by changing the antecedents and consequences of the behavior. Suppose a teacher wants to reduce a behavioral excess, such as students being out of their seats too much. If an antecedent condition leading to the behavior was the children's being very far from one another while working on group projects, for instance, the teacher could rearrange the seating. If the consequences of students being out of their seats were more attractive than the consequences of being in their seats, the teacher could introduce rewards for students who stayed in their seats for appropriate amounts of time. The antecedents and consequences addressed in behavior change programs are usually in the person's external environment, but altering covert antecedents and consequences can also be effective in changing behavior.

Although providing new learning experiences has been highly successful in changing behavior, we need to keep four limiting factors in mind. First, the antecedents and consequences altered or introduced must be chosen and applied very carefully. If they are not, the effort to change the behavior will be hampered. Second, the body of knowledge used in behavior modification is still far from complete and continues to grow. Behavior that is difficult to change now may be easier to change in the future. Third, in some cases, the existing antecedents and consequences for a behavior are rooted in a person's social or cultural environment. These environmental factors often exert very strong influences on behavior and may be very difficult or impossible to alter substantially or to override. Last, some behaviors are so severely disordered or have such strong physiological bases that behavior modification methods may not be sufficient to change them, at least initially. In these circumstances, medication may be prescribed by a physician and used as a adjunct to environmental changes (W. H. Wilson & Simpson, 1990). The goal in using principles of behavior change in these cases often includes reducing or eliminating the use of medication over time.

Scientific Orientation

Behavior modification has a strong scientific orientation—its core is the knowledge revealed through the methods of science. The *scientific method* basically involves conducting research by (1) carefully gathering data *empirically*—that is, by direct observation or measurement, (2) analyzing and interpreting the data, and (3) specifying the precise methods used to gather and analyze the data so that other researchers will know exactly what was done and can repeat the procedures. A hallmark and essential feature of research on principles of behavior change and their application is the careful and precise measurement of behavior. Using the scientific method, researchers have discovered ways by which learning and cognition influence behavior.

Pragmatic and Active Methods to Change Behavior

Behavior modification takes a pragmatic approach in the methods it uses to change behavior (D. M. Baer, Wolf, & Risley, 1968). The term *pragmatic* means "practical, rather than theoretical or idealistic." Thus, professionals who use behavior change techniques emphasize finding and using *methods that work* to change behavior, regardless of whether the techniques fit into a particular theory or ideal. By taking this view, the discipline has incorporated and enhanced the effectiveness of many new and creative methods for changing behavior. Behavior modification today includes behavior change techniques in two broad categories: behavioral methods and cognitive methods (Sweet & Loizeaux, 1991). **Behavioral methods** apply principles of operant conditioning, respondent conditioning, and modeling, particularly toward changing overt behaviors. **Cognitive methods** focus on changing overt and covert behaviors by modifying people's thought processes—for example, by helping individuals recognize and alter illogical beliefs. Although these categories appear to be separate and distinct, in practice there is considerable overlap. Some behavior change techniques make use of elements of both, as you would do if you practiced a modeled behavior in your mind. In addition, efforts to change behavior often include techniques from each category. When the methods overlap, the techniques sometimes are called "cognitive–behavioral."

The last characteristic of behavior modification we will consider is that its techniques for changing behavior often require that clients or subjects be *active* participants in the process of modifying their behavior. In contrast to other approaches in which clients or subjects just talk about their difficulties, behavioral and cognitive methods have clients or subjects *do* things to help. Such help may take the form of deciding which techniques to use and how to implement them, by performing the methods under supervision, or by applying some techniques on their own as "homework."

How Behavior Modification Developed

Although the discipline of behavior modification developed only a few decades ago, practical applications of behavioral and cognitive methods to influence behavior are by no means new in human history. For instance, psychologists were not the first to realize that rewarding a behavior tends to increase its frequency. What psychologists and other professionals did was to examine these methods, clarify what they are, and determine how to apply them most effectively. In this section, we will outline the highlights in the history of behavior modification. (Go to 🔍 .)

 Close-Up 1.1
Buddhism and the Principles of Behavior Change
• •

Buddhism is an Eastern religion with the basic view that people can liberate themselves from life's inevitable suffering by practicing methods of mental and moral self-purification. Many of the self-purification methods recommended have a lot in common with behavior modification techniques. Buddhism is taught from texts based on anecdotes and teachings passed down from the Buddha's life, about 2500 years ago. Let's look at some examples Padmal de Silva (1984) described from Buddhist texts.

• *Antecedents:* A monk was having difficulty maintaining a committment to monastic life: he kept leaving the monastery to return to his old life as a farmer. Each time he left, he would plant seed beans—and when they were ripe, he would harvest them and consume all but a pint of beans, which he would save with his spade when he returned to the monastery. At last, "determined to break his attachment to lay life, he threw away what he saw to be the crucial items that lured him" (p. 667). That is, he threw away the seed and spade, which served as antecedents for leaving.

• *Modeling:* The Buddha recognized the influence of social learning on people's behavior when he taught that "he who has bad men as friends, and does not make friends with the good, he behaves like bad men" (p. 665).

• *Behavioral consequences:* When a king who had been overeating regularly and had become lazy asked the Buddha why, he was told: "King, overeating causes problems. Anyone who lives indolently, eats large quantities of food, sleeps all the time, so that he rolls around like a pig fed on grain, such a man is a fool because it is bound to lead to suffering. . . . King, one should observe moderation in eating because that leads to comfort." (pp. 666–667).

• *Rewards:* A father who wanted his unwilling son to learn from the Buddha said, "There is no living being here in the world who may not be influenced by rewards. I shall therefore try to influence my son with rewards" (p. 668). He did so, and it worked—the son listened to the Buddha and was converted!

The approaches in these examples involve behavioral methods. Later in this book we'll see that Buddhist texts also give anecdotes and recommendations that involve cognitive methods that are used in behavior modification.

• •

Theory and Research Leading Toward Behavior Modification

During the first half of the twentieth century, the dominant *theories*—or systematic explanations—of why people behave the way they do proposed that behavior resulted from various internal "forces," such as drives, motives, conflicts, and traits. Some of these theories grouped several forces together, with the resulting constellation being called the *personality*. The well-known *psychoanalytic theory* of Sigmund Freud (1933, 1949), for example, views a person's behavior as an expression of his or her personality and its component forces, such as drives and conflicts. According to this theory, each personality develops through a maturationally determined series of stages, is profoundly affected by early experiences, and becomes fairly entrenched in childhood. Freud believed that changing an individual's problem behavior required that the person talk with a therapist to arrive at a comprehension of the behavior's underlying forces, such as conflicts and unresolved childhood experiences.

A different perspective called behaviorism began to emerge in the early 1900s, with psychologists John B. Watson (1913, 1930) and B. F. Skinner (1938, 1953) as two of its main proponents. **Behaviorism** is the theoretical orientation that emphasizes the study of observable and measurable behavior and proposes that nearly all behavior is the product of experience. As a result, behavior can be explained by principles of learning, particularly operant and respondent conditioning. This theory developed from two sources: philosophy and science. Certain philosophical views, which had been proposed more than 200 years earlier, had become widely accepted in England and the United States. For instance, the British philosopher

John B. Watson (1878–1958)

John Locke had proposed that a baby's mind has no innate ideas and is essentially a blank tablet (called *tabula rasa* in Latin) on which experience "writes." At the time behaviorism was introduced, psychology was already becoming a separate discipline from philosophy, and the scientific method was seen as the main feature permitting a distinction between the two fields. As a result, early behaviorists rejected philosophy's unobservable concepts, such as mind, consciousness, and soul. Instead, they used the scientific method to examine learning principles. Two lines of research were especially important: Ivan Pavlov (1927) demonstrated the process of respondent conditioning, and Edward Thorndike (1898, 1931) studied how "satisfying" and "annoying" consequences—reinforcement and punishment—affect learning.

Two other studies set the stage for applying learning principles to change behavior. In one of these studies, John Watson and Rosalie Rayner (1920) conditioned an 11-month-old boy they called Little Albert to fear a white rat. Albert was not afraid of the rat before conditioning began. On the contrary, his behavior (reaching toward it and giggling) suggested that he liked it. During conditioning, the researchers presented the rat along with a loud noise (the US) made by striking a steel bar with a hammer, which elicited distress (the UR) in Albert. After several of these episodes in a week's time, the rat (now a CS) elicited distress and efforts to escape. This was an important demonstration: Albert had *learned* to fear the rat through respondent conditioning. Although Watson and Rayner had planned to reverse the conditioning, using methods later shown to be effective in reducing fear, Albert's mother's job change made the child unavailable for this plan. [Note: A study like this one probably could not be conducted today; the American Psychological Association developed guidelines in 1973 that restrict using potentially harmful procedures in research, as we shall see in Chapter 16.]

A few years later Mary Cover Jones (1924) described how she reduced the fear a toddler named Peter developed in his everyday life. Peter's fear was a lot like Albert's—he was intensely afraid of white furry objects, such as rabbits. The procedure Jones used to reduce the fear involved bringing a rabbit closer and closer while Peter ate favorite foods in the presence of a research assistant whom he liked. After many episodes of this procedure in the course of several weeks, Peter no longer showed signs of fear in the presence of the rabbit and would seek it out, pat it, and play with it. This dramatic change in Peter's fear response demonstrated clearly the potential value of using learning principles to modify behavior.

The next 35 or 40 years witnessed four important historical events (Bandura, 1969; Kazdin, 1978). First, psychology and philosophy became clearly separate disciplines, as illustrated by the humorous poem:

> *Alas, poor psychology, sad is her Fate!*
> *First she lost her Soul, and then she lost her Mind,*
> *And then she lost Consciousness.*
> *Now all that's left to her is her Behavior—*
> *And the less said of that, the better!*

(Anonymous, cited in Goldiamond, 1974, p. 38)

Second, researchers showed that principles of operant and respondent conditioning could be used effectively in many different settings to change a wide variety of behaviors. The case study we saw earlier of reinstating speech in a mute schizophrenic man is an example. Third, a research area called the *experimental analysis of behavior* developed to study basic theoretical processes in learning, usually without an emphasis on application. Fourth, psychologists became increasingly dissatisfied with the lack of scientific evidence to demonstrate that traditional therapies, such as psychoanalysis, were effective in treating problem behaviors.

Emergence and Growth of Behavior Modification

The 1950s and early 1960s saw the emergence of an academic discipline to study and apply learning principles as an approach for changing people's behavior (Kazdin, 1978). B. F. Skinner continued to have a profound impact on the development of this approach, mainly through his creative descriptions of ways to apply principles of operant conditioning in the modification of behavior in education, business, government, and therapy. Many other scholars contributed ideas and research findings that furthered the discipline during its emergent years, but two deserve special mention.

Joseph Wolpe developed respondent conditioning therapy techniques that were soon shown to be highly effective in helping people reduce strong fears and anxieties. And Hans Eysenck published the results of a series of investigations indicating that patients who received traditional types of psychotherapy, especially psychoanalysis, were no more likely to show improved psychological functioning than individuals who received no treatment at all. Although Eysenck's conclusions somewhat exaggerated the futility of trying to change behavior with traditional methods, they formed the basis for professionals to question the utility of traditional approaches in treating psychosocial problems, and they stimulated a search for new approaches. Some of these new approaches involved the application of behavioral methods.

By the late 1960s, behavior modification had become a formal discipline, journals to publish research articles in the discipline had become established, and an area of research called *applied behavior analysis* had been formed to focus on ways to apply behavioral methods to socially important problems, such as those relating to education, child rearing, crime, and mental illness (D. M. Baer, Wolf, & Risley, 1968, 1987; Kazdin, 1978). Also by this time, psychotherapeutic approaches in clinical psychology included a category called *behavior therapy*, which applies principles of behavior change to treat clients' problems. The treatment techniques used in the early years of behavior therapy were based almost entirely on behavioral methods, but the scope of techniques began to incorporate more and more cognitive methods in the 1970s (Mahoney, 1977; Wixted, Bellack, & Hersen, 1990).

Principles of behavior modification are widely applied today. For example, they are used by psychotherapists, teachers in regular and special education classrooms, parents of "normal" children, supervisors in business and industry, personnel in institutions for juvenile delinquents, and personnel working with mentally retarded and emotionally disturbed children. A major reason for the wide acceptance of behavioral and cognitive methods is that professionals who use them, in both research and applied settings, measure the behavior they are trying to change and examine the data collected. Using these data, they can see and show others how well the methods work.

Using Data and Doing Research in Behavior Modification

You may be thinking, "Sure, it's important to see if your efforts to change a behavior worked. But why do you need to collect and examine data? If your efforts work, won't it be obvious?" Occasionally it is, but usually it's not—an example comes from teachers' efforts at a preschool to stop a boy named Davey from pinching adults. They tried at first just to ignore this unpleasant habit, but Davey pinched

> hard enough to produce at least an involuntary startle. Teachers next decided to develop a substitute behavior. They selected patting as a logical substitute. Whenever the child reached toward a teacher, she attempted to forestall a pinch by saying, "Pat, Davey," sometimes adding, "Not pinch," and then strongly approving his patting, when it occurred. Patting behavior increased rapidly to a high level. The teachers agreed that they had indeed succeeded in reducing the pinching behavior through substituting patting. Then they were shown the recorded data [which] showed clearly that although patting behavior was indeed high, pinching behavior continued at the previous level. (Harris, Wolf, & Baer, 1964, pp. 16–17)

It may be that the teachers were so focused on the increase in patting that they didn't notice the pinching so much anymore; but whatever the reason, they wrongly evaluated the success of their efforts. Later in this book we'll see that there are other reasons for collecting data that are important, too. Whenever behavior modification techniques are used, data must be collected and evaluated.

Using Data

Suppose you were a teacher, had a "Davey" in your class, and decided to start an *intervention*—a program of behavior change methods—to stop his pinching. What data would you collect, and what would you look for to decide whether the intervention had worked? You'd probably want to keep track of exactly how often Davey pinched, perhaps by having the people he pinched record each instance on index cards they would carry all day. What would you look for in the data they collect?

At the very least, you'd want to see that the frequency of pinching decreased during the intervention, compared to what it was before you tried to change it. This means that you'd need to collect "baseline" data *before* starting the intervention. The term **baseline** has two meanings: it can refer to the *data* collected before the intervention begins or to the *period of time* during which those data were collected. If your

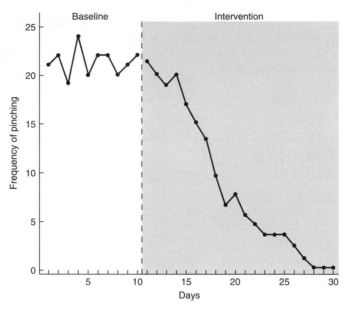

Figure 1.3   How your graph of "Davey's" pinching behavior might look in the case of a successful intervention. Although the graph assumes that the baseline period lasted 10 days and the intervention lasted 20, these periods can vary in duration.

intervention worked, the frequency of pinching during intervention would decline from its baseline level. You could see this pattern best in a graph, like the one in Figure 1.3. Occasionally, behavior modification data are presented with a *cumulative graph* in which the data are summed from one point to the next. For example, if the mute schizophrenic man in Case Study 1.1 had said 2 words on the first day he talked, 3 words on the second day, and 3 words on the third, a cumulative graph of words spoken would have shown 5 words for day two and 8 words for day three.

Doing Research

When scientists do research in behavior modification, they try to determine whether certain methods affect behavior and which ones do so most effectively. Typically, such research can be classified into one of three designs: intrasubject, between-subjects, and within-subjects. In *intrasubject designs*, researchers evaluate behavior and look for changes *within* individual subjects across time, while interventions are either in effect or absent, as we did in the Davey example. Because the focus is on one subject, this type of research is often called the "single-subject design." Intrasubject designs usually assess behavior in a sequence of four phases—baseline, intervention, reversal, and intervention—rather than just the first two. In a *reversal phase*, the intervention is withdrawn or altered to see whether the behavior will revert toward baseline levels. Alternating the presence and absence of the intervention allows us to see systematic changes in the person's behavior that occur with the presence of the intervention.

Between-subjects designs use many subjects who are separated into two or more groups. Data on their behaviors are combined and compared to see whether the groups differ. The researchers usually give the groups different treatments—for instance, if one group receives a particular intervention, another group will not—and comparisons of their behavior are intended to determine whether any differences found are linked to the treatments administered. The study we've mentioned of people's saying plural nouns is an example: when subjects in one group said plurals, the researcher said "mmm-hmm"; when subjects in the other group said plurals, the researcher said "huh-uh." The subjects' output of plurals differed depending on which response the researcher made to their words (Greenspoon, 1955).

Within-subjects designs use many subjects and test all of them in more than one treatment condition. In research on the principles of behavior change, these designs usually resemble intrasubject designs, with each subject's behavior being tested in baseline and intervention phases. But instead of focusing on individual subjects, the data are combined. The researcher then evaluates whether the grouped data changed systematically with the presence and absence of the intervention. For our purposes, you may think of within-subjects designs as intrasubject designs with many subjects.

This discussion of using data and doing research provides only the most basic concepts, to prepare you for the material in the next several chapters. More information on collecting data and research methods will appear later, especially in Chapters 3, 10, and 12. (Go to ✔ .)

✔ Concept Check 1.3

Pause again to answer the following fill-in-the-blank questions.

1. An example of a behavioral deficit one of your friends has is _____ .⇔
2. The four defining characteristics of behavior modification are _____
   _____
   _____
   _____ .
3. A behavior change technique that uses operant conditioning would be classified as a _____ method.
4. The Buddhist monk's spade and bean seeds in the anecdote related in Close-Up 1.1 were the _____ to his behavior of returning to the farm.
5. "Little Albert" learned to fear a white rat by the process of _____ conditioning.

Answers: 1. not exercising enough 2. focus on behavior, importance of learning and environment, scientific orientation, and pragmatic and active methods to change behavior 3. behavioral 4. antecedents 5. respondent.

Application Exercise

"Nobody's perfect," you've surely heard people say—and that includes us! If you're like I am, you've probably thought many times about improving certain aspects of your overt or covert behavior. You may have thought you should exercise more, swear less, be less anxious, or think more highly of yourself, for example. You may even have tried to change aspects of your behavior, succeeding at some but not others. If you didn't succeed, why do you suppose you didn't? Think about this for a moment.

Did your thinking result in the answer, "I failed because I don't have enough willpower"? Lots of people blame their "willpower" when they can't change their old habits, such as smoking cigarettes or socializing instead of studying. To some degree they may be right if they were not very motivated to change—they tried to change because they knew it was the "right thing to do," but they really didn't want to change. But the term *willpower* often implies more than motivation for a specific task. When we say we lack willpower, we usually mean two additional things. First, we imply a broad trait: we cannot control our behavior in most tempting situations. But that's neither fair nor true. No one has perfect willpower, and you've controlled your behavior pretty well to be where you are in life. Second, we imply that we should be able to control our behavior even in the face of high temptation. But few people actually manage this. Many people who seem to have lots of willpower find ways to *avoid highly tempting situations*.

People who can control their behavior have the *skills* to do so. These skills often involve knowing how to influence the antecedents and consequences of their behavior. If they want to change their behavior, they deploy the appropriate behavior modification skills to make the plan work. Research comparing people who succeed at changing their behavior with people who don't has shown that those who succeed apply *more* of these skills and use them *longer* (Heffernan & Richards, 1981; O'Neill, Sandgren, McCaul, & Glasgow, 1987; Perri & Richards, 1977). These findings indicate that the skills work. *People who fail at changing their behavior generally don't have the skills to help them succeed or don't use ones they know.*

This book has two purposes. Its primary purpose is to teach you *methods by which people's behavior can be changed*. Although this text is not sufficient to train you to do psychotherapy or to help individuals with serious behavior problems, knowing about the methods it describes will enable you to understand the basic methods psychologists and other professionals use in helping people function better in their everyday lives. The book's secondary purpose is to show you how to use behavioral and cognitive methods *to improve your own behavior*! Applying principles of behavior change to modify one's own behavior is called **self-management** or "self-modification." The *application exercises* near the end of each chapter and the corresponding *work sheets* are designed to promote both purposes of this book. Because these exercises have you apply concepts from the chapter, doing them will help you *master the material*—like a creative study guide. And since the exercises for the first nine chapters guide you through designing *your own self-management program*, you can apply the program before the end of the course to change your own behavior. Thus, the *application exercises* can constitute a study guide, a guide to designing a program, and an opportunity to do a self-management project. You should check with your instructor to find out how these exercises will be used in the course and whether you will need to submit *work sheets* or any other materials as part of your course requirements.

I encourage you to design and carry out a self-management program, regardless of the requirements for the course. Having this experience will help you learn effective principles of behavior change and benefit you for the rest of your life. I've taught a course for many years in which students do—and *enjoy* doing—self-management projects. They get to apply concepts from the course, modify behaviors they want to change, and learn useful skills. Their projects are also very effective—the vast majority of the students succeed in making substantial behavioral changes. Designing and carrying out a program is challenging, but you can do it.

Why not browse over some of the *work sheets* now. They're at the very end of their corresponding chapters. Fill out the one for Chapter 1 soon; it gets you started in designing a program by having you generate a list of possible *outcome goals*, or broad results, you'd like your self-management program to help you achieve.

Summary

Behavior is anything people do, usually in response to internal or external events. Behaviors can be overt actions that are open to view or covert activities that are not openly shown. People's traits—broad and stable characteristics—are not behaviors, nor are psychological diagnoses or the outcomes of behavior, such as becoming more physically fit. Both heredity and experience affect behavioral development.

Experience affects behavior through learning. We acquire and change behaviors through respondent conditioning, operant conditioning, modeling, and cognition. In respondent conditioning, a potential conditioned stimulus (CS) gains the ability to elicit a conditioned response (CR) by being associated repeatedly with an unconditioned stimulus (US) that already elicits an unconditioned response (UR). The UR and the CR are the same behavior. In operant conditioning, behavior is affected by the consequences it produces and the antecedents that set the occasion for it. There are two broad types of consequence: reinforcement increases the behavior's frequency; punishment decreases its frequency. Respondent and operant conditioning occur together in everyday life.

Modeling is the process of learning by observing other people's behavior. We can learn both operant and respondent behaviors in this way. Cognition is mental activity, especially thinking and reasoning, by which we generate plans, ideas, expectations, beliefs, and rules that serve as covert antecedents to our behavior. Self-efficacy is our belief concerning our ability to succeed at a particular activity.

Behavior modification is a discipline that uses principles of learning and cognition to understand and change behavior. The discipline has four defining characteristics: (1) it focuses on behavior, trying to modify behavioral deficits and excesses; (2) it considers learning and the environment to be the main sources by which behaviors can be changed; (3) it has a strong scientific orientation; and (4) its approach to changing behavior is pragmatic and active, using both behavioral and cognitive methods.

Although the principles of behavior change developed from the perspective called behaviorism and associated research, the roots of these methods go back at least to the beginnings of Buddhism. These techniques are widely accepted and used today, partly because professionals who have studied and applied them also collected data and conducted research showing their utility. Behavioral and cognitive methods are highly effective in changing people's behavior and can be applied to change your own behavior in a self-management program.

Key Terms and Review Questions

Key Terms

behavior
learning
unconditioned stimulus
unconditioned response
conditioned stimulus
conditioned response
respondent conditioning
operant conditioning
reinforcement
punishment
antecedents

modeling
cognition
self-efficacy
behavior modification
behavioral deficit
behavioral excess
behavioral methods
cognitive methods
behaviorism
baseline
self-management

Review Questions

1. Describe the research by Greenspoon (1955) on modifying verbal behavior and tell why its results are important.

2. What is behavior? Give three examples each of overt and covert behaviors.

3. Why are traits, diagnoses, and outcomes of behavior not behaviors?

4. How is heredity involved in behavioral development?

5. Describe the structure of how respondent conditioning occurs and give an example from your own life.

6. Define the terms reinforcement and punishment and give two examples of each from your own life.

7. What are antecedents? Give two examples from your life.

8. How was reinforcement used in the case study of reinstating speech in a schizophrenic man?

9. Describe the research and findings of Bandura (1965) on the role of consequences on modeling.

10. Give two examples each of modeling and cognition affecting your behavior.

11. Describe the four defining characteristics of behavior modification.

12. What are behavioral deficits and excesses? Give two examples of each in people you know.

13. Define behavioral methods and cognitive methods.

14. Define the terms applied behavior analysis and behavior therapy.

15. Describe the four phases you would use in an intrasubject design to study how reinforcement can be used to reduce hitting behavior in 4-year-old Janet.

16. When people say they don't have any willpower, what do they usually mean?

Related Readings

Baum, W. M. (1994). *Understanding behaviorism: Science, behavior, and culture.* New York: HarperCollins.

Karoly, P., & Kanfer, F. H. (Eds.) (1982). *Self-management and behavior change: From theory to practice.* New York: Pergamon Press.

Kazdin, A. E. (1978). *History of behavior modification: Experimental foundations of contemporary research.* Baltimore: University Park Press.

Ormrod, J. E. (1990). *Human learning: Theories, principles, and educational applications.* New York: Macmillan.

Skinner, B. F. (1974). *About behaviorism.* New York: Knopf.

Name _____

Date _____

Day & time
class meets_____

Chapter 1: Work Sheet 1.1

1. The following alphabetized list gives a variety of potential *outcome goals* for your program, and you may add some others at the bottom. My students have used almost all these goals. Do the following. (a) Look through the list carefully and mark a small dot in the space preceding any *ten* goals you might consider, at least remotely, as "possibles" for your program. (b) Narrow these "possibles" down to six "in-the-running" goals by placing a check mark over the corresponding dots, making sure that *at least* one of the six involves an overt and one a covert behavior, and *at least* one involves a behavioral deficit and one a behavioral excess. (c) Rate each of the six in-the-running goals on a nine-point scale, where 1 = "not very important to change," 5 = "important to change," and 9 = "enormously important to change." Place each rating to the right of the goal.

_____ Anger, reduce

_____ Anxiety/stress, reduce

_____ Anxiety in tests, reduce

_____ Asserting rights/opinions, increase

_____ Biting nails/cuticles, reduce

_____ Cleaning room/apartment, increase

_____ Creative works, increase

_____ Drinking alcohol, reduce

_____ Fears, reduce

_____ Fitness, increase

_____ Gossiping, reduce

_____ Healthful diet (not to lose weight), increase

_____ Money managing/saving, increase

_____ Practicing musical instrument, increase

_____ Procrastinating in general, reduce

_____ Procrastinating in schoolwork, reduce

_____ Saying "um" or "like," reduce

_____ Self-esteem, increase

_____ Sleeping, increase

_____ Sleeping, reduce

_____ Smoking, reduce

_____ Social relations quality (family), increase

_____ Social relations quality (friends, romantic, etc.), increase

_____ Speaking in public/class, increase

_____ Studying time/concentration, increase

_____ Sulking/unhappiness, reduce

_____ Swearing, decrease

_____ Time management, increase

_____ Vocabulary, increase

_____ Weight, reduce

_____ Other: _____

_____ Other: _____

_____ Other: _____

_____ Other: _____

2. For *each* of the six in-the-running outcome goals you selected, identify the overt or covert behavior involved *and* state whether the behavior involves a deficit or excess.

3. In connection with any of the above outcome goals, think back to two fairly recent resolutions you made to change your behavior without succeeding in changing. For each resolution, answer these questions: Did you make an effort to change the behavior? If not, why? If you tried, specifically how could you improve on the effort you made?

NOTE: If you will be submitting work sheets to your instructor or to a fellow student, make a copy of each sheet before submitting it.

2 Effective Applications of Behavior Modification

Prologue

Have you often encountered two traffic signals in succession that have long waits at the red lights? If so, was it also the case that if you drove fast from the first to the second signal, you could make it through before the light turned red? If you did this, did you feel "victorious"? This traffic situation is not uncommon in urban areas, and it can lead to dangerous behavior, such as speeding between the signals or zipping through the second signal when it is yellow or has just turned red. Can traffic engineers use principles of behavior change to prevent this dangerous behavior?

Traffic lights are antecedents to behavior. Making it through a signal without having to stop is a consequence most drivers find reinforcing, and having to stop for a long time is unpleasant, or punishing. To influence drivers' behavior, traffic engineers would need to alter the antecedents and/or the consequences. Researchers did this at an intersection in Chicago after collecting baseline data showing that more than half of the drivers approaching yellow or red lights at that intersection went through without stopping (Jason, Neal, & Marinakis, 1985). By altering the timing sequence of the two signals so that the second signal's yellow light came on sooner and the red stayed on for a shorter period, the researchers made driving safer: over 90% of the drivers now stopped for the yellow or red lights, and the accident rate at that intersection declined by more than 36%. This example describes a clearly successful application of principles of behavior change.

In this chapter, we look at commonly used, effective behavior modification applications. Conducted by psychologists and other professionals in many settings, such as public schools and psychiatric hospitals, these applications have focused on a wide variety of individuals and behaviors. As you read this chapter, you'll notice three things. First, the potential for applying behavioral and cognitive methods is almost limitless. The traffic engineering problem we just described illustrates the broad possibilities for using principles of behavior change. Second, some details of how applications in this chapter were conducted were left out so you could see an overview of each program. We will examine the details of behavior change programs in later chapters. Third, behavior change techniques have a promising future built on solid research support. Our overview begins with a look at how these methods can improve parenting and parent–child relationships.

Parenting and Parent–Child Relationships

Suppose 7-year-old Ken's mother will not buy the junk food he wants while they're shopping, so he sasses her. How will she respond? She can either react constructively to dampen his hurtful behavior or she can aggravate it. She can dampen it by explaining calmly why she won't buy the food and why disrespectful behavior is unacceptable, or she can escalate the encounter by responding in a *coercive*, or dominating, manner—such as by snapping, "You really are a brat today." Coercive acts often fuel a chain reaction of increasingly hostile coercive exchanges by both parties. In the latter case, the encounter between Ken and his mother might end with her hitting or yelling at him and dragging him to her car, or it might end with her giving in, when he has a nasty tantrum. If this kind of interchange becomes more and more common in a family, the members may develop a *coercive pattern* in their interactions with one another (Patterson, 1982). That is, mutual escalations in hostility may come to characterize their responses to everyday unpleasant behaviors. This pattern can lead to serious outcomes, such as abuse and neglect of children (Burgess & Richardson, 1984).

There are many potential pitfalls in parenting, and when parents lack the skills they need to deal with the everyday problems that are common in all families, the social functioning of their families deteriorates over time. The coercive pattern is one of many forms this deterioration can take. How can parents acquire the skills they need to promote constructive family environments?

Training in General Parenting Skills

Teaching parents behavioral and cognitive skills can help change their behavior, which, in turn, fosters improvements in their children's behavior. Parents who learn how to use behavioral methods, such as reinforcement and modeling, are often surprised at how effective these techniques can be. Adults tend to overlook the small, appropriate behaviors a child shows, perhaps because we expect them. So, when a young child looks both ways before crossing the street, we rarely say, "That's very good. You looked both ways." We often think these actions are so simple that they don't need to be pointed out and praised. And sometimes praising a child sounds silly to adults. For instance, you might feel odd saying, "Gee, Bobby, I'm glad to see you haven't hit Kim today. That's really good." But Bobby might not think it sounded silly at all. It wasn't easy for him to reduce his hitting, and he wants his success appreciated, not ignored. Research has shown that training parents in behavioral methods is effective in helping them deal with a variety of childrearing concerns, such as getting children to do household chores or reduce TV watching (Christophersen et al., 1972; Wolfe, Mendes, & Factor, 1984).

Modeling and discussion are useful approaches for teaching parents general behavioral and cognitive methods to improve their childrearing practices. Carolyn Webster-Stratton (1982a, 1982b) demonstrated this with mothers and their 3- to 5-year-old children. First she observed each mother and child interact for half an hour in a playroom to determine baseline levels of their positive social behaviors, such as smiling and praising, and negative social behaviors, such as frowning, ridiculing, and slapping. Then the mothers received parent training for 4 weeks, with four 2-hour sessions each week. The training sessions consisted of watching and discussing short videotaped vignettes of parent models who portrayed either positive or negative social behaviors toward children. Assessments through direct observations and surveys soon after the training revealed substantial improvements in mother–child social interactions and in the children's general behavior compared with baseline data and with another mother–child group that had not yet received the training. Additional assessments a year after each group received the training showed that the gains had persisted.

Another parent training program was designed to teach neglectful parents how to think through and plan solutions to everyday parenting problems (Dawson et al., 1986). For example, one of the three parents in the program had a history of leaving her children unattended in potentially dangerous situations. All the parents showed serious deficits in their ability to solve everyday child care problems, such as handling unexpected events that conflict with child care responsibilities or making sure they have enough money for food and medicine by not buying unnecessary items. In the several weekly sessions the mothers attended, the trainer modeled how to think through specific problem situations and asked the parents to think of several ways to deal with each problem; then the parents were asked to explain how they would carry out the solutions and what the likely outcomes might be. The trainer next asked the parents to choose the best solution and discussed the choice with them, particularly if it would produce undesirable consequences. The parents were also asked to do homework assignments each week, consisting of bringing in for discussion examples of actual problems they experienced in the preceding week. Comparisons of data collected before, during, and after training indicated that the parents' abilities to solve child care problems improved dramatically as a result of the training—and so did their actual parenting performance, as rated by social workers.

Training to Deal with a Child's Existing Difficulties

"How can we get Jason to stop being so hostile?" Jason's parents asked the therapist they decided to consult when their son's hostility got him suspended from school. Parents often postpone getting professional help until their child's behavior has become a serious problem. Parent training in behavior change techniques often occurs as part of an effort to correct specific behavioral difficulties children have already developed. We will consider parent training approaches with well-established effectiveness in dealing with difficulties of two different types: children's oppositional behavior and bed-wetting (TFPDPP, 1993).

Correcting Oppositional Behavior

Oppositional behavior refers to acting in a hostile and contrary manner, such as a child's frequent ignoring of rules, failure to comply with parents' requests, and habitual fighting or arguing (Wahler & Dumas, 1984). Parents find oppositional behavior very distressing and frustrating.

One of the first studies to show that parents trained in behavior modification methods could reduce their children's oppositional behavior was conducted by Robert Wahler and his coworkers (1965). The children were three boys with various behavior problems serious enough to motivate their parents to seek professional help. Although parent training had positive results in all three cases, we'll focus on a 4-year-old named Eddie whose behavior was clearly oppositional. According to Eddie's mother, the child generally either ignored her requests or did the opposite. She would react with pleas, threats, or spankings, all of which seemed to be ineffective in changing this behavior. Baseline observations during four 20-minute play sessions with his mother at a psychology clinic confirmed the mother's account of these interactions: Eddie exhibited over 200 oppositional responses and only about 30 cooperative responses per session! What's more, the mother reacted negatively to oppositional responses but tended to ignore cooperative behavior. The researchers suggested several behavioral methods to use in changing Eddie's behavior. The most effective intervention was to combine a smiling enthusiastic response to episodes of cooperating with isolation in an empty room for a few minutes each time Eddie showed oppositional behavior. Isolation is a punishment technique called "time-out," which we will examine in Chapter 6. When this combination was used in several play sessions, Eddie showed over five times as many cooperative responses as oppositional ones.

Subsequent research has shown that parents can apply principles of behavior change—rewarding appropriate acts and ignoring or punishing those that are inappropriate, for example—to correct oppositional behavior effectively at home. What's more, the benefits of doing so appear to be broad and durable. For instance, studies have found that when parents used behavior change methods to reduce disruptive behavior at home, the children behaved better in other settings, too—when shopping, visiting relatives, or in school (McNeil et al., 1991; Sanders & Glynn, 1981). Other findings suggest that the broad benefits of parent training to reduce oppositional behavior can last for many years. One study compared two groups of individuals in late adolescence: (1) adolescents whose parents used behavioral methods to correct their oppositional behavior in early childhood and (2) adolescents selected from the general community (Long et al., 1993). Assessments of delinquent behavior, emotional adjustment, academic achievement, and relationships with parents revealed no differences between these groups in adolescence. The finding that the two groups were functioning equally well suggests the possibility that parent training to reduce young children's oppositional behavior may help these children develop and function normally in later years. (Go to the nearby box with the icon $\mathbb{Q}$.)

Bed-wetting

Bed-wetting—technically, *nocturnal enuresis*—is defined as wetting the bed at least twice a month after reaching 5 years of age (Houts, Berman, & Abramson, 1994). About 7% of American 8-year-olds and as many as 3% of adolescents have bed-wetting problems. Normally, people awaken from sleep when bladder tension exceeds a certain limit. If a physical examination of a bed-wetting child shows nothing organically wrong, the enuresis is usually assumed to result from a failure to learn the response of awakening to the antecedent, bladder tension. How can parent training in the principles of behavior change help correct a child's bed-wetting problem?

Two behavior modification approaches appear to be effective in helping parents eliminate their children's bed-wetting (Doleys, 1977; Houts, Berman, &

Close-Up 2.1
Are Rewards Bribes?

Many people think that providing reinforcement for performing appropriate behavior is "bribery." But two arguments can be made against this view. First, dictionary definitions of *bribery* either imply or state that the behavior thus rewarded is unethical or illegal. As psychologists John and Helen Krumboltz have noted:

> Our language contains many words to represent the exchange of services, products, or money. Wage, salary, commission, honorarium, fee, prize, reward, reparation, bribe, ransom, tip, blackmail, pay, and compensation all refer to the

exchange of one valuable for another. However, each different word connotes different circumstances. Only if you wish to pervert the judgment of a child or corrupt the conduct of a child could it be said that you are bribing him by offering him some reinforcer. (1972, p. 25)

Second, the reinforcers we apply are not necessarily material things, such as money, that we usually think of as bribes. They can be praise, smiles, or fun activities, too. The cartoon in Figure 2CU.1 nicely illustrates the distinction between rewards and bribes.

Reprinted with special permission of North America Syndicate

Figure 2CU.1   The "good grade incentive money" promised to Funky Winkerbean (striped shirt) was intended as a *reward*, probably for studying hard. Funky is proposing to use part of that money as a *bribe* to get Monroe to help him cheat, which is unethical behavior. Note also that the "good grade incentive money" was contingent on reaching *outcome goals* (grades), not on performing the appropriate behavior for achieving good grades (studying). This illustrates why it is important to make reinforcers contingent on the behavior you're trying to change.

Abramson, 1994). One approach uses a **urine alarm apparatus** consisting of a water-sensitive sheet electrically connected to a loud battery-powered bell or buzzer (Mowrer, 1938). No shock is involved. When urine is released, the bell rings, waking up the child. This technique incorporates both operant and respondent conditioning components, as Figure 2.1 diagrams. Treatment success using this apparatus without any other behavioral methods is fairly high: positive results were reported in about two-thirds of treated cases in dozens of studies aimed at doing away with bed-wetting (Houts, Berman, & Abramson, 1994).

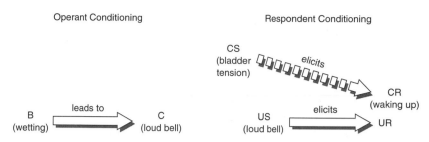

Figure 2.1   Operant and respondent principles applied in a urine alarm apparatus to reduce bedwetting. In the *operant conditioning* component, wetting the bed leads to the sound of the loud bell, which is an aversive consequence that punishes the release of urine. Parents can also provide praise and other rewards for improvement. In the *respondent conditioning* component, the child learns to wake up (the CR) when the bladder is tense (the CS), but *before* urine is released. Responding to the CS prevents wetting and enables the child to avoid the aversive bell. (Adapted from Sarafino & Armstrong, 1986, Figure 7.10.)

The second approach for eliminating bed-wetting uses a program of operant conditioning techniques, in which the child is an active participant with the parents in the process (Azrin, Hontos, & Besalel-Azrin, 1979; Azrin & Thienes, 1978). In the operant program, the parents awaken the child periodically in the first few hours of sleep during the first week or two to prevent "accidents." They reward the child for successes, but make sure that he or she remakes the bed and changes pajamas in the event of an accident. As Figure 2.2 shows, this approach can be quite effective in helping enuretic children stop wetting the bed. There is some evidence that com-

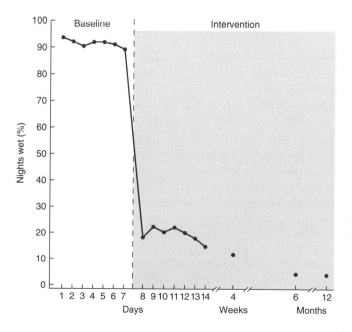

Figure 2.2   Bedwetting by 44 enuretic children in baseline and after an operant conditioning intervention was introduced. The percentage of nights in which wetting occurred dropped dramatically in the week when the intervention was introduced and continued to decline at 4 weeks, 6 months, and 12 months. (Adapted from Azrin, Hontos, & Besalel-Azrin, 1979, Figure 1.)

bining operant methods and the urine alarm apparatus may be more successful than using either approach alone (Doleys, 1977; Houts, Berman, & Abramson, 1994).

Education

Principles of behavior change have been applied effectively in educational settings to improve instructional methods and classroom conduct. Let's see how.

Enhancing Instructional Methods

Angela was sitting at a computer in her kindergarten class and wrote the following story: "I like sprang. Sprang brangs flowers. Berds seng in sprang. I git days off. That is wi I like sprang" (Asbell, 1984). Not a perfect job, but quite remarkable for a 5-year-old! Computers are being used to teach kindergartners language skills, usually by showing them how to spell sounds or syllables, put these together as words, and combine the words into sentences.

The use of computers in classroom instruction has its roots in B. F. Skinner's (1954) concept of **programmed instruction**, a self-teaching process in which students actively learn material presented step by step as a series of discrete items in textbooks or with mechanical devices. Each item presents some information, asks a related question, and gives feedback on the student's answer. The items build toward overall learning goals, such as being able to spell a body of words or to recite multiplication tables. Since students advance at their own pace in small steps, they are unlikely to give wrong answers and likely to get reinforcement—that is, positive feedback—for their efforts. A newer and more advanced form of programmed instruction, called **computer-assisted instruction** (CAI), uses a computer to coach students through a series of lessons, much as a human tutor might do. CAI programs explain concepts, give examples, ask questions, give feedback for students' answers, and provide additional explanations if needed. Studies have shown that these teaching methods are about as effective in teaching students as traditional instruction is, and often CAI is superior (Ormrod, 1990).

Psychologist Fred Keller (1968) applied behavior modification principles to develop an alternative approach to teaching students at the college level. This approach, called the **personalized system of instruction** (PSI, sometimes called the Keller Plan), divides the course content into units called "modules," has students study independently the modules presented in textbooks and guides, tests students on each unit when they feel ready, and gives immediate feedback on test performance. Before moving to the next module, students must master the material for each module, getting a high score—such as 80% correct—on the test. If they score lower, they must restudy the material and take another test. Advanced students called "proctors" provide tutoring, administer tests, and give feedback. An instructor oversees the process and may provide supplemental "enrichment" experiences, such as lectures or films. Because students advance at their own pace, they may complete the course before the end of the semester.

These students are learning academic skills through the method of computer-assisted instruction.

Using students as tutors is an important innovation of the PSI approach that has been used effectively in primary and secondary school classrooms (Kohler & Strain, 1990). Teachers who use peer tutoring generally see it as a practical way to give extra help to specific students, individualize the focus of instruction, and

In the personalized system of instruction approach, advanced students provide tutoring for other students, as this girl is doing.

enhance children's social skills (Greenwood, Carta, & Kamps, 1990). Compared with traditional methods of instruction, peer tutoring results in students spending more time engaged in learning, having more opportunities to make active responses, and getting more feedback to facilitate the correction of errors. But using peer tutors can present problems as well. The teacher must train the tutors, monitor the quality of their work and coverage of course material, and make certain that both the tutee and tutor are benefiting from the tutoring experience and want to take part in it. How do tutors benefit? Some evidence indicates that being a tutor increases a child's academic achievement and enhances the development of social skills (Greer & Polirstok, 1982).

Improving Classroom Conduct

Children do all sorts of things in school that disrupt the class and upset the teacher. Conduct problems include students being out of their seats without permission, making noises, fighting, name calling, swearing, refusing to follow a teacher's request, and daydreaming. What can a teacher do about conduct problems? The answer can be seen in the operant sequence of antecedent, behavior, and consequence.

Patricia Krantz and Todd Risley (1977) examined the role of antecedents on kindergartners' on-task behavior at a preschool during story reading and demonstration activities. "On-task behavior" was essentially paying attention to the activities and not being disruptive. Two antecedent conditions were studied: the amount of activity the children had in the periods preceding the activities and the degree of crowding in the seating arrangements during the activities. The researchers found that on-task behavior was far lower when the activities followed a vigorous play period instead of a rest period and when seating during the activities was crowded rather than uncrowded. Antecedents are not always obvious events that appear suddenly before the behavior. Teachers need to watch carefully for antecedents in the classroom that lead to off-task and disruptive behavior so that they can try to alter those antecedents.

Consequences also have strong effects on behavior, and teachers can deploy them quite effectively. One consequence that teachers can employ easily is social attention to students. Early studies of behavior change techniques in classroom settings found that teachers could increase students' on-task behavior by praising or paying attention to it, and they could decrease disruptive behavior by simply ignoring it (Becker et al., 1972; Madsen, Becker, & Thomas, 1968). These types of behavior are linked: if students increase one, they're very likely to decrease the other. Another kind of reward teachers can use effectively to improve classroom conduct is the opportunity to engage in free-choice activities, such as playing with toys or crafts (Wasik, 1970).

Using principles of behavior change to reduce classroom misconduct enhances the school environment and makes teaching and learning more pleasant. It also has some positive side effects. First, teachers who use behavioral methods come to provide more reinforcement and less punishment than other teachers do, and their students show greater gains in academic achievement (Rollins et al., 1974). Second,

✔️ Concept Check 2.1

Check your understanding of the preceding concepts by answering the following fill-in-the-blank questions. Remember that the symbol ⇔ means various answers can be correct.

1. When it becomes usual for a family to deal with an unpleasant behavior by saying or doing increasingly hostile things to each other, a _____ pattern exists.

2. An example of a child's oppositional behavior is _____ . ⇔

3. When oppositional Eddie's mother played with him in baseline, she almost completely ignored his _____ behavior.

4. The urine alarm apparatus uses _____ conditioning to stop children's bed-wetting.

5. A behavior modification instructional approach that divides class material into small units and gives immediate feedback on test performance is called _____ . ⇔

_____

Answers: 1. coercive 2. disobeying rules 3. cooperative 4. operant and respondent 5. programmed instruction, CAI, or PSI

students with conduct problems who participate in a behavior modification program to improve their conduct continue in school longer than those who do not (Heaton & Safer, 1982). (Go to ✔️ .)

Training for Mentally Retarded and Autistic Individuals

Young people who are classified as mentally retarded or autistic have disorders that impair essentially all their developmental processes, making them very unlikely to become well-functioning adults. People with these disorders share many characteristics, particularly a great difficulty in learning almost all skills—motor, cognitive, language, and social. As a result, these individuals need highly structured and well-planned training to learn even simple tasks. Beginning in the 1960s, behavioral methods have provided this kind of training for mentally retarded and autistic people of all ages. Behavior modification is currently the only psychological intervention with well-established success for treating individuals with these disorders (TFPDPP, 1993).

Training Mentally Retarded People

The American Association of Mental Retardation defines mental retardation on the basis of two major characteristics: very low general intelligence and deficiencies in

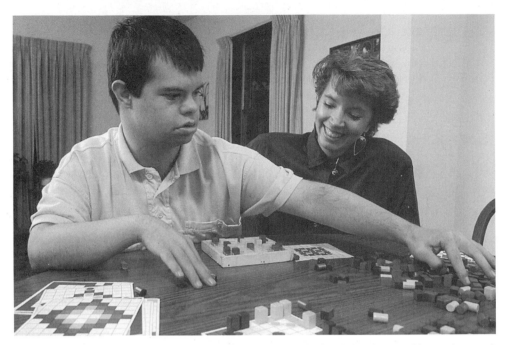

This mentally retarded male student is receiving individual training in matching colors and shapes from his teacher.

adaptive behavior. In actual practice, people are most often classified as retarded on the basis of IQ—"intelligence quotient"—scores and clinical judgment because there are no adequate tests of adaptive behavior (Davison & Neale, 1994; M. Hamilton & Matson, 1992). People's IQ scores are determined by their performance on a standardized intelligence test, usually either the *Wechsler Intelligence Scale for Children* or the *Stanford-Binet Intelligence Scale*. The average IQ score is 100.

About 2.5% of the United States population consists of mentally retarded individuals, that is, persons classified in one of the following four levels of retardation:

- *Mild* (IQ from about 53 to 69): This category includes the vast majority—about 85%—of retarded individuals. They are labeled "educable" because they can benefit greatly from special education programs and are usually able to function at about a sixth-grade academic level in adulthood and maintain unskilled jobs.

- *Moderate* (IQ from about 38 to 52): These individuals make up about 10% of retarded people and are described as "trainable." They often have poor motor coordination, however, and are unlikely to advance beyond the second-grade academic level by adulthood.

- *Severe* (IQ from about 22 to 37): Severely retarded people can learn only very simple tasks and often have serious physical handicaps, too. Although they are likely to remain very dependent on the help of others throughout life, many acquire habits of personal cleanliness and learn to perform simple self-help skills.

- *Profound* (IQ below about 22): These individuals usually have severe physical deformities as well; they require life-long care and have short life spans.

Many factors can lead to mental retardation. The more serious levels of retardation often stem from abnormal brain development due to genetic disorders, prenatal damage, or diseases. At the less serious levels, particularly among the mildly retarded, there is no detectable brain damage. Intellectual problems usually become apparent after the mildly retarded children enter school, encounter academic difficulties, and do poorly on an IQ test. In many cases retardation results mainly from environmental deprivation, which frequently is found in the homes of neglectful and socially immature parents.

Training the mentally retarded requires intensive effort, particularly at the more serious levels of retardation. The teacher must break down tasks into small steps, introduce the antecedents, monitor each student's performance carefully, and provide rewards for correct responding. Using these behavioral methods, each mentally retarded individual can learn tasks that are appropriate to his or her age and level of ability (M. Hamilton & Matson, 1992). For example, profoundly retarded children can be toilet trained (Azrin & Foxx, 1971), and severely retarded children can learn how to pluralize nouns (Guess et al., 1968) and perform simple social behaviors (Whitman, Mercurio, & Caponigri, 1970). And mildly retarded adult mothers can learn basic child care skills, such as bathing their babies, cleaning baby bottles, and treating diaper rash (Feldman et al., 1992). (Go to 📖 .)

Training Autistic Children

For autistic children like Sam inCase Study 2.1, behavior modification training begins with the simplest of tasks and builds from one task to the next (Lovaas, 1977). Autistic children learn slowly and with great difficulty. Tasks must be presented many, many times. Individual instruction, a great deal of structure, and immediate feedback with rewards for correct performance are necessary.

In Sam's case, training for his many behavioral deficits started with the application of strategies for developing eye contact with the teacher (Oltmanns, Neale, & Davison, 1991). A teacher might have begun by saying, "Look at me," and rewarding a good response. After Sam had learned eye contact, his training during his first year involved imitation of simple behaviors ("Sam, stretch your arms up like this."), pointing to named objects in pictures ("This is an orange. Point to the orange."), imitation of simple speech sounds ("Say this, *ah*."), using the toilet, and dressing and undressing himself. Progress with autistic children usually is very slow. By the end of the first year, Sam could point correctly to only 38 named objects when presented in pairs, such as an orange and a cat.

Autistic children also exhibit many behavioral excesses that must be reduced or eliminated to make the children accessible to treatment (Schreibman, Charlop, &

Case Study 2.1
Sam—An Autistic Child

Sam was born in 1974 to middle-class parents, and his first couple of years seemed fairly normal (as described in Oltmanns, Neale, & Davison, 1991). But by his second birthday, his parents were becoming concerned for several reasons— for instance, Sam's motor development was slow (his sister's had been more rapid), and it

> seemed uneven. He would crawl normally for a few days and then not crawl at all for awhile. Although he made babbling sounds, he had not developed any speech and did not even seem to understand anything his parents said to him. Simple commands such as "Get the ball," "Come," or "Do you want a cookie?" elicited no response. (p. 248)

At first, the parents thought Sam might be deaf. They consulted his pediatrician, who suggested mental retardation as a possibility. When Sam was nearly 3 years old, his

> parents also began to notice him engaging in more and more behavior that seemed strange and puzzling. Most obvious were his repeti-

tive hand movements. Many times each day he would suddenly flap his hands for several minutes. Other times he rolled his eyes around in their sockets. He still did not speak, but he made smacking sounds and sometimes he would burst out into laughing for no apparent reason. (pp. 248–249)

Sam's social and play behavior were also worrisome to his parents. For instance, he would let them hug him, but acted indifferently to the attention and wouldn't look at them. He didn't play with his sister, and his solitary play also seemed deviant. If he had a toy car, for example, he wouldn't pretend to drive it around, as other children do. He'd turn it over and spin its wheels incessantly.

A physical and neurological examination had not revealed any detectable defect, and next a psychiatrist examined Sam, diagnosed him as autistic, and recommended that he attend a special school for treatment. Like many schools for severely disordered children, the school that was selected used principles of behavior change to provide training.

Kurtz, 1992). One of these is called *self-stimulation*, which may consist of rocking back and forth, flapping the hands, twirling objects with the fingers, and similar motor activities. The reason for these behaviors is unknown, but one possibility is that they produce internal perceptual stimuli that are reinforcing to the persons so behaving (Lovaas, Newsom, & Hickman, 1987). Behavioral methods have been successful in reducing self-stimulation in autistic children (Lovaas et al., 1973).

Adolescent and Adult Behavior Therapy

Up to now, we have discussed applications that focus mainly on using principles of behavior change with children. In this section we switch our focus to examine the use of behavior therapy to treat psychological problems in adolescents and adults. Behavior therapy is a therapeutic approach that is clearly effective in treating several adolescent and adult disorders—including depression, sexual difficulties, and severe fears and anxieties—and useful in programs to treat many other problems, such as substance abuse, eating disorders, and schizophrenia (Bellack & Hersen, 1990; TFPDPP, 1993; Turner, Calhoun, & Adams, 1992; G. T. Wilson, 1982). Many children experience some of these problems, too—especially severe fears and anxieties—and they can benefit from behavior therapy, as we will see later in this book.

The Setting and Structure for Therapy

Behavior therapy techniques are used in a variety of settings: institutions and clinics (for people with mental problems), medical hospitals (for patients who are having difficulty adjusting to their illnesses), college and school counseling offices (for students who have emotional difficulties), and private practice offices (for individuals from the general community who have psychological problems). Many behavior therapists use the full range of behavior modification techniques, including behavioral methods to alter the antecedents and consequences of problem behaviors and cognitive methods to alter thought patterns (Swan & MacDonald, 1978). Although behavior therapy is usually conducted with individual patients, it can also be applied with groups of clients (Davison & Neale, 1994). We'll examine the techniques and structure of behavior therapy in greater detail later, particularly in Chapters 14 and 15.

Examples of Behavior Therapy Applications

To give you an idea of how behavior therapy can be applied effectively to help people overcome some of the disorders just mentioned, we'll look briefly at applications of behavior change techniques for depression, sexual dysfunctions, and substance abuse.

Depression

We all feel depressed at times, although we may call the feeling something else—perhaps "sad," or "blue," or "unhappy." Occasional feelings of depression are normal and differ from the disorder we are discussing here. Basically, *depression* is considered to be a clinical disorder when the person's feelings of sadness or loss of interest and pleasure are very severe, frequent, and long-lasting (Craighead, Evans, & Robins, 1992; Davison & Neale, 1994).

Behavior therapy for depression often includes both cognitive and behavioral methods (Craighead, Evans, & Robins, 1992; Freeman, 1990). Depressed people typically have distorted beliefs, such as "Everything I do turns out wrong," or "They all think I'm incompetent, and they're probably right," or "I can't live without a mate." Cognitive methods are designed to alter these thought patterns by questioning the evidence the person uses to support these beliefs, for example, or by showing that "the worst thing that could happen" really wouldn't be so terrible (Freeman, 1990). People who are depressed also tend to be inactive and listless, often because they feel they lack necessary social skills. Behavioral methods can help clients acquire the needed skills by showing them how to perform the behavior and giving them feedback as they practice it. The overall treatment for depressed clients usually includes medication as well, particularly if their disorder is so severe that participation in psychotherapy would be out of the question otherwise (Freeman, 1990).

Sexual Dysfunctions

The term *sexual dysfunction* means impaired or abnormal sexual response, such as might be seen in a person's degree of interest in having sex, extent of arousal during sexual activity, or timing or occurrence of orgasm. Sexual dysfunctions are fairly common in adults, and behavioral and cognitive methods are very effective in treating them (Beck, 1992; Morokoff & LoPiccolo, 1982; TFPDPP, 1993). We will consider two of these methods, one for treating women's difficulties in reaching orgasm and one for treating men's problems with premature ejaculation.

According to psychologist J. Gayle Beck (1992), the most effective method for treating inhibited female orgasm involves *directed masturbation*, by which the woman can explore her body and sensations with a high likelihood of reaching orgasm. This approach:

> leads the woman through a guided series of activities designed to increase her awareness of genital sensations, expand her range of erotic imagery, and help her to identify types of stimulation that are arousing. At the outset, these activities are done alone, with introduction of the sexual partner in later stages. (p. 164)

For men who experience premature ejaculation, a highly effective treatment is the *stop-go/squeeze technique* (Beck, 1992, p. 165). This method involves having the man reach a high level of arousal with his partner before they either (1) squeeze "beneath the coronal ridge of the penis, effectively reducing arousal and postponing ejaculation" or (2) stop activities with the penis, "engage in nongenital pleasuring," and return to activities with the penis.

Substance Abuse

People voluntarily use many illegal or unhealthful substances, including tobacco, alcohol, and drugs. Stopping these behaviors is often very difficult to do, but some research evidence indicates that behavior modification techniques can help (Sobell, Toneatto, & Sobell, 1990; Tucker, Vuchinich, & Downey, 1992). Keep in mind, however, that quitting using a substance is more easily achieved than staying quit for good. Many people return to using tobacco, alcohol, or drugs weeks or months after quitting.

To illustrate how behavior therapy has been applied to substance abuse problems, we will focus on the abuse of alcohol and describe just one of dozens of behavioral and cognitive methods that have been used with some degree of success. The technique we'll describe involves respondent conditioning and is called **emetic**

therapy because the person takes an *emetic*—that is, a drug that produces nausea as an unconditioned response (UR) when alcohol is later consumed. Usually this therapy is administered in a hospital, on an inpatient basis. In a typical half-hour session, the person first receives an injection of the drug and then repeatedly drinks an alcoholic beverage, each time quickly becoming nauseated and vomiting (Miller & Hester, 1980). After having several of these treatments, usually the person receives occasional "booster" sessions as an outpatient. Many studies have found that emetic therapy can be effective in treating alcohol abuse (Elkins, 1991). But one critic of this approach has noted that emetic therapy "has not been shown to be more effective than alternative, less costly methods" in behavior modification for treating alcohol abuse (G. T. Wilson, 1991, p. 415). (Go to ✔ .)

Health and Medicine

If you became really sick, what would you do to get better? One thing you'd probably do is see your physician—that certainly would be a good idea. We typically think of illness as an affliction of the body that results from injury, biochemical imbalances, or bacterial or viral infection. And we know that physicians can prescribe treatments that usually will attack the cause and correct the problem.

But in recent years, we have become aware that psychological and behavioral circumstances can also affect whether we get sick and how quickly we recover from an illness. For instance, we know that our health can be harmed by experiencing long-term intense stress, smoking cigarettes, having a physically inactive lifestyle,

 Concept Check 2.2

Pause now to answer the following questions.

1. Mental retardation is defined on the basis of _____
   _____ and deficiencies in adaptive behavior.
2. The _____ level of retardation is described as "trainable."
3. A behavioral deficit and a behavioral excess in the case study of Sam that might
   have suggested he was autistic are _____ and
   _____ . ⇔
4. A person who no longer gets aroused when trying to have sex may have a disorder
   called sexual _____ .
5. In the respondent conditioning technique of emetic therapy, what might be the (a)
   US, (b) UR,(c) CS, and (d) CR? ⇔

Answers: **5c.** seeing a bottle of liquor or a drink   **5e.** nausea.
5b. nausea   **5c.** seeing a bottle of liquor or a drink
self-stimulation behavior (spinning wheel)   **4.** dysfunction   **5a.** emetic drug
1. very low general intelligence   **2.** moderate   **3.** no speech at age 3 [and]

eating diets that are high in fat and low in fiber, having unsafe sex, failing to get immunized, driving when intoxicated, and failing to carry out treatments prescribed by a physician. As these examples show, health and illness result from the interplay of the biological, psychological, and social aspects of life. This perspective is called the *biopsychosocial model* of health and illness (Engel, 1977, 1980).

The recognition that medicine and psychology are related led to a joining of these two disciplines within three similar fields of study (Sarafino, 1994):

- **Psychosomatic medicine** is a field introduced to study connections between people's symptoms of illness and their emotions, but its focus broadened later to include all relationships within the biopsychosocial model. Most members of this field are physicians, but many are psychologists.

- **Behavioral medicine** is a field introduced to study relationships between health and behavior and apply behavior change methods to enhance health. Its members come from many disciplines, including psychology, medicine, nursing, and public health.

- **Health psychology** is a field of psychology introduced to examine the causes of illness and to study ways of promoting and maintaining health, preventing and treating illness, and improving health care systems. Its members are mainly psychologists.

As the descriptions of these fields suggest, psychologists have become increasingly involved in promoting health and treating illness. Although behavior change techniques are most strongly emphasized in behavioral medicine, professionals in all three fields commonly use behavioral and cognitive methods in their work.

Promoting Health

Principles of behavior change have been applied effectively to promote health and prevent illness or injury in an enormous variety of ways. The traffic engineering application at the beginning of the chapter is an example. Let's look at a couple of other applications to promote health.

We all know that smoking can harm our health, but did you know that a pregnant woman who smokes may be harming her baby's health? Babies of mothers who smoke tend to have low birth weight compared with other babies (Cook, Petersen, & Moore, 1990). Thomas Burling and his coworkers (1991) used health warnings as antecedents to reduce smoking among pregnant women. Of the pregnant smokers attending a clinic for prenatal care, half received special antismoking materials. These materials included a letter stating that blood tests had revealed "abnormalities in the chemistry of your blood [that] indicate you are probably a cigarette smoker." The materials also urged each smoker to give up the habit for her own health and that of her baby. Although most of the women who received these materials did not quit smoking, they were more than twice as likely to quit during pregnancy than those who did not receive the materials.

The second application we will consider is a behavior change program to reduce the risk of contracting AIDS through infection with the human immunodeficiency virus (HIV). The subjects were gay men whose sexual practices placed them at relatively high risk of infection (J. A. Kelly, St. Lawrence, Hood, & Brasfield, 1989). The program had components for training in four areas.

1. *AIDS risks.* Trainers provided information about behaviors that put people at risk of infection.

2. *Self-management techniques.* Trainers led group discussions to identify antecedents for high-risk behaviors, such as the men's moods when these behaviors occurred in the past, the places at which these behaviors tended to occur, or the intoxicating substances the men had used. The group then discussed how to alter or eliminate these antecedents by means of such strategies as avoiding sexually oriented settings.

3. *Assertiveness.* Discussion and modeling were used to train the men to talk to partners about safer sex practices and to refuse to engage in high-risk behaviors if the partner insisted.

4. *Social problem-solving skills.* Discussion was used to find solutions to problems the men had experienced in developing stable relationships and becoming involved in the gay community.

Compared with similar men who were waiting to receive the same program, these men dramatically decreased their frequency of high-risk behaviors, especially with regard to having anal intercourse without using a condom.

Another AIDS prevention program produced an enormous increase in nurses' use of protective gloves in high-risk hospital situations (DeVries, Burnette, & Redmon, 1991). The intervention involved showing the nurses data regarding when they had and had not worn the gloves in the preceding 2 weeks, praising them for glove use, and urging them to use gloves more often.

Many other behavior modification interventions for health promotion have also been successful—for example, people have been helped to improve their diets, exercise more, use seat belts, and reduce stress in their lives (Sarafino, 1994).

Enhancing Medical Treatment

Not only can behavior change techniques help in promoting health when people are well, they also can enhance the effectiveness of medical treatments patients receive when they are ill. We'll describe two of the many ways behavioral methods can help.

If your physician prescribed a medication, would you always use it exactly as directed? Or if your physician advised some painful exercises to help your injured knee heal, would you follow the program? Many patients do not adhere to physicians' recommendations as closely as they should, and behavioral methods have been applied effectively to increase patients' *adherence* to, or *compliance* with, medical treatment (Sarafino, 1994). Some of these methods involve altering the antecedents to the behavior—for instance, patients are more likely to continue taking medication if they have reminders or cues, such as an alarm, and if taking medicine coincides with existing habits and rituals, as is the case when pills are to be taken at meals. Adherence to treatment also improves when rewards are contingent on performing the behavior. Behavioral methods have improved treatment adherence in patients with many different medical conditions, including asthma (Sarafino, 1995a), diabetes (Lowe & Lutzker, 1979), kidney disease (Mosley et al., 1993), and severe burns (Hegel et al., 1986).

Principles of behavior change can enhance medical treatment, as well, by reducing the anxiety of hospitalized patients who are awaiting surgery. People with high preoperative anxiety tend to stay in the hospital longer and to use more medication for pain during recovery than patients with less preoperative anxiety (Anderson & Masur, 1983). A study by Barbara Melamed and Lawrence Siegel (1975) evaluated the possible benefits of modeling techniques for children who were awaiting surgeries that were not life threatening. One group of children saw a film that was relevant to having surgery, and the other group saw a film about a boy going on a trip to the country. The relevant film showed a 7-year-old hospitalized boy named Ethan being initially apprehensive but then coping well with typical presurgical events, such as having a blood test and being separated from his mother. The children who saw the film about Ethan experienced less anxiety before and after surgery than those who saw the other film. Other research has shown that children who receive this kind of intervention before surgery recover more quickly than children who do not (Pinto & Hollandsworth, 1989).

Athletic Performance and Skills

Researcher Brent Rushall (1993) described the case of a champion female rower who was training to enter an international competition. To be eligible to compete, she had to take fitness tests twice a month and report the results to the governing body to show that she was maintaining her fitness and motivation for the sport. The young athlete had become very concerned that even though she was training harder, her fitness scores were showing a declining trend and she had started to feel weak and a little ill for a couple of days prior to her testing dates. Cognitive methods were applied during fitness testing to help her overcome her problem: she was instructed both to *concentrate* her thoughts on each segment of the motor actions she needed to make during testing and to *distract* her thoughts from her pain and effort. This approach worked. The rower's fitness scores improved markedly and her confidence was restored.

Behavior change techniques are also useful in helping less accomplished athletes improve their sports skills, using modeling and reinforcement for progress in performing the skills (Donahue, Gillis, & King, 1980; Whelan, Mahoney, & Meyers, 1991). These behavioral methods require the athletes' close attention to details of the behavior, both when it is modeled and when they perform it themselves.

Technological advances in video and computer equipment can make these methods more precise (Franks & Maile, 1991). Athletes can watch the action performed well on a video monitor, try to copy the action while being videotaped, view their own tapes, and then make moment-by-moment comparisons between their actions and the model's.

Employment Settings

Edward Feeney (1972) was working for the Emery Air Freight Corporation as a vice president, having worked his way up from being a freight agent, when he introduced some behavioral methods into the company's operations. For instance, he arranged to have employees observe employee activities that were previously identified as inefficient, suggest ways to improve those activities, implement the more efficient behaviors, and receive praise and other rewards for good performance. The use of behavioral methods saved the company millions of dollars. Applying behavior modification principles in organizations—such as business and industrial firms and human service agencies—is called **organizational behavior management** (Frederiksen & Lovett, 1980).

Organizational behavior management focuses on changing behavior by altering its antecedents and consequences and by teaching new actions through instructions and modeling (P. L. Brown, 1982; Luthans & Kreitner, 1985). These methods can be effective in achieving many different goals. One frequent goal is to save money, either by reducing losses or by increasing productivity. For example, a large grocery store used behavioral methods to reduce thefts (Carter et al., 1988), a consulting firm reduced the miles employees drove their cars on workdays (Foxx & Schaeffer, 1981), and factories reduced tardiness (Hermann et al., 1973) and absenteeism (Pedalino & Gamboa, 1974). Improving worker safety is another common goal organizational behavior management has addressed successfully by modifying employee behavior to cut down on accidents and exposure to toxic chemicals (Hopkins et al., 1986; Komaki, Barwick, & Scott, 1978).

Self-Management: Changing Your Own Behavior

Do you wish you could study more, eat a healthier diet, stop biting your nails, or stop complaining so much? If you have tried to change these or other behaviors in the past and failed, you probably lacked the needed skills. We learned in Chapter 1 that it is possible to apply behavior change techniques in a *self-management* program to change your own behavior, and we saw that people who don't succeed when they try to change their behavior generally lack the needed skills. Learning self-management techniques will give you these skills, thereby strengthening two general abilities:

- **Self-control** is the ability to *exercise restraint* over our emotions, impulses, or desires. For instance, people with self-control can to resist temptation or delay gratification when they want something. Young children typically have poor self-control; they want things—toys, snacks, and so on—"right now." Adults often can persevere for months or years to obtain some objectives.

- **Self-regulation** is the ability to *direct* and *modulate* our own actions, behaving appropriately even when we are not being monitored by someone else.

Chances are, you called your lack of these two abilities "no willpower" when you didn't succeed in changing your behavior in the past. The abilities often overlap, with self-regulation involving a broader set of skills that may require the person to have strong skills in self-control. Although the terms self-control, self-regulation, and self-management sometimes are used interchangeably in books, they really have somewhat different meanings (Brigham, 1982).

By learning self-management techniques, you'll gain the self-control and self-regulation skills you need to improve whatever behavior you set out to change. How can I be so sure you can succeed? There are two reasons. First, self-management has been applied extensively in behavior therapy with considerable success. When this approach is used, therapist and client work together to design a self-management program, which usually involves altering the antecedents and consequences of a target behavior. The client then carries out the program under the therapist's supervision. In one of the earliest examples of this approach, a husband decreased his sulking and bickering behaviors (Goldiamond, 1965). In a more recent example, several men with the hard-driving behavior pattern called *type A* used self-management successfully to decrease the frequency with which they acted impatiently in social situations and increase the amount of time they spent relaxing after dinner (Nakano, 1990). Having someone with training in behavior modification to supervise the program—even for just a few minutes a week by phone—seems to be useful in helping clients stick with their self-management programs and improve their behaviors (Marshall, Presse, & Andrews, 1976; Zeiss, 1978). It seems likely, too, that individuals who have used self-management successfully before will be better able to use the techniques independently to modify their behavior.

The other reason I think you'll succeed in changing your behavior is that I and other instructors have seen the great majority of our self-management students apply the techniques successfully in college courses for many years. What's more, research on student success in self-management projects has confirmed these observations. For instance, Scott Hamilton (1980) found that his students met their preestablished goals in 83–86% of their self-management projects. Manuel Barrera and Russell Glasgow (1976) found that 85% of their students were satisfied with the behavioral change they achieved: although the extent of behavior improvement over baseline varied widely, on average the behavior was 96% better at the end of the month-long program than it was in baseline. The behaviors students choose to change in self-management projects are quite diverse, from very common problems, such as exercising and studying too little, to less common ones, such as grinding one's teeth a lot or failing to meet savings goals. Commonness is probably not a factor in whether students succeed—researchers have reported students marked-

Concept Check 2.3

• •

1. Of the three fields of study that join medicine and psychology, the one that focuses most on applying behavior modification techniques is _____ .

2. The text discusses how principles of behavior change can increase patients' adherence to doctor-prescribed behaviors, such as taking medicine and exercising. A prescribed behavior not discussed in the text that you think might respond to behavioral methods is _____ . ⇔

3. Applying behavior modification principles in business and industry is called _____ .

4. A 16-year-old's behavior that would be an example of self-control is _____ _____ . ⇔

5. True or false: Research has found that the great majority of students' self-management projects succeed in changing their behavior. _____

_____

Answers: 5. true

mother. ⇔   2. reducing dietary fat   3. organizational behavior
management   4. refusing to have sex, particularly without using a condom
1. behavioral medicine

• •

ly increasing exercising (Kau & Fischer, 1974) and reducing tooth grinding (Pawlicki & Galotti, 1978), for example. (Go to ✔ .)

Application Exercise

This application exercise takes the next step in designing a self-management project. Our main task will be to narrow down and refine the list of potential outcome goals you generated in the Chapter 1 Work Sheet 1.1. We will do this by reducing your six in-the-running goals to three *finalists* and identifying the behaviors involved in these three goals. Once we know what these behaviors are, we can begin to consider each corresponding *behavioral goal*—the level of the behavior you hope to achieve by the end of your behavior change program. Keep in mind, however, that *the outcome and behavioral goals may be the same.* If your outcome goal is to stop smoking, the behavioral goal would be the same; but if your outcome goal is to lose weight, the behavioral goal would be different—it would be stated in terms of your eating and physical activity.

We'll start this application exercise by narrowing down the goals to your three finalists, using another work sheet. We are trying to create a project with outcome and behavioral goals you believe will be:

• Interesting and reasonably important to achieve.

• Fairly challenging for you, with a good possibility of success.

Now, turn to Work Sheet 2.1 at the end of this chapter and fill it out.

Summary

Behavior modification principles can be applied effectively to improve behavior in many spheres of everyday life. For instance, parents can be trained in behavioral and cognitive methods to improve their parenting skills, thereby enhancing their relationships with their children and preventing the development of coercive patterns in family interactions. Parents can also learn and apply skills to reduce problems their children may have, by altering antecedents and consequences to reduce children's oppositional behavior, for example, or by using a urine alarm apparatus and operant conditioning techniques to decrease bed-wetting.

In educational settings, behavioral methods can make instruction more effective through the techniques of programmed instruction, computer assisted instruction (CAI), and the personalized system of instruction (PSI). These educational approaches divide course material into small units and give immediate feedback on test performance. To a large degree, they allow each student to progress at his or her own pace. Behavioral methods are also useful in helping teachers decrease class disruptions and increase students' attention to class activities.

Behavior modification is currently the most effective approach for training children whose ability to acquire skills is markedly impaired. Many of these children are classified into one of the four levels of mental retardation: mild, moderate, severe, and profound. Other children with markedly impaired learning abilities are classified as autistic. The training autistic and mentally retarded children receive stresses the use of behavioral methods to help these individuals acquire basic self-help skills, language and social behaviors, and, sometimes, vocational skills.

Behavior therapy applies behavioral and cognitive methods to help individuals overcome serious behavioral or emotional difficulties. It is effective with people of all ages, and it has been used successfully in treating several adolescent and adult disorders, especially depression, sexual dysfunctions, and severe anxieties and fears. It is useful also in programs to treat substance abuse and eating disorders. Behavior therapy for depression usually focuses on helping clients correct distorted beliefs. The sexual dysfunction of inhibited orgasm in females can be treated very effectively with programs that include directed masturbation. Premature ejaculation in males can be treated successfully with the stop-go/squeeze technique. In programs to treat substance abuse, the method of emetic therapy has had some success.

After it became clear that physical health and illness result from the interplay of biological, psychological, and social factors in people's lives, the disciplines of medicine and psychology were joined to form the fields of psychosomatic medicine, behavioral medicine, and health psychology. Professionals from these three fields, particularly behavioral medicine, have begun to apply behavioral and cognitive methods successfully toward the promotion of human health by such means as helping people to stop smoking, encouraging them to use safer sex methods, and enhancing medical treatment.

Three other effective applications of behavior change techniques can be mentioned: athletes use behavioral and cognitive methods to improve performance and skills, employers use behavioral methods in organizational behavior management programs, and you can use behavioral and cognitive methods to change your own behavior and improve your self-control and self-regulation.

Key Terms and Review Questions

Key Terms

urine alarm apparatus

programmed instruction

computer-assisted instruction

personalized system of instruction

emetic therapy

psychosomatic medicine

behavioral medicine

health psychology

organizational behavior management

self-control

self-regulation

Review Questions

1. Describe an example of a coercive pattern that you saw in a movie or on television, or witnessed in your own life.

2. In the study we cited on oppositional behavior, a boy named Eddie performed about seven times more oppositional than cooperative responses when playing with his mother (Wahler et al., 1965). In terms of operant conditioning, why did he do this?

3. How are rewards and bribes different?

4. In terms of operant and respondent conditioning, how does the urine alarm apparatus reduce bed-wetting?

5. Describe the process and characteristics of programmed instruction.

6. Suppose you were teaching one of your current courses. Outline how you might structure the course to use the PSI approach.

7. Name five classroom conduct problems you've seen in school and describe the likely antecedents leading to those behaviors.

8. Describe the four levels of mental retardation.

9. Name five self-help skills a 7-year-old autistic or moderately retarded girl would probably need to learn if she had received little special training.

10. What three types of disorder in adolescence and adulthood are most successfully treated with behavior therapy?

11. What are psychosomatic medicine, behavioral medicine, and health psychology, and how are they different?

12. Describe three types of reminders or cues, other than alarms, patients could use as antecedents to improve adherence to prescribed medication.

13. What is organizational behavior management?

14. Your author believes you will be able to design and carry out a successful self-management program for two reasons. What are they?

Related Readings

Krumboltz, J. D., & Krumboltz, H. B. (1972). *Changing children's behavior.* Englewood Cliffs, NJ: Prentice-Hall.

Luthans, F., & Kreitner, R. (1985). *Organizational behavior modification and beyond: An operant and social learning approach.* Glenview, IL: Scott, Foresman.

Orlick, T. (1986). *Psyching for sport: Mental training for athletes.* Champaign, IL: Leisure Press.

Sarafino, E. P. (1994). *Health psychology: Biopsychosocial interactions* (2nd ed.). New York: Wiley.

Sulzer-Azaroff, B., Drabman, R. M., Greer, R. D., Hall, R. V., Iwata, B. A., & O'Leary, S. G. (Eds.)(1988). *Behavior analysis in education.* Lawrence, KS: Society for the Experimental Analysis of Behavior.

Turner, S. M., Calhoun, K. S., & Adams, H. E. (Eds.) (1992). *Handbook of clinical behavior therapy* (2nd ed.). New York: Wiley.

Name _____   Day & time
                                      class meets_____
Date _____

Chapter 2: Work Sheet 2.1

1. Using Work Sheet 1.1 from Chapter 1, list the six *outcome goals* that are still in the running and their *ratings*. Also indicate about *how long* you've known you'd like to address each goal.

In-the-Running Goals	*Ratings*	*How Long*
_____	_____	_____
_____	_____	_____
_____	_____	_____
_____	_____	_____
_____	_____	_____
_____	_____	_____

2. To help you reduce the list of in-the-running goals to three finalists, make notes in the margins of the list using the following guidelines:

- Try to retain at least one goal involving an overt behavior and one involving a covert behavior.

- Make sure that each of the three finalists involves behavior that clearly represents either (a) a *deficit* (it *should* occur often or for a long time on most days, but doesn't) or (b) an *excess* (it *already occurs* often or for a long time on most days).

- Make sure each of the finalists involves behavior you are willing to let other students and your instructor know about. Don't address or describe in your project behaviors that are either illegal (your instructor could be required by law to turn you in!) or very embarrassing.

- Consider the *ratings* and *how long* data to decide how difficult it will be to change your behavior. For your first self-management project, it's best not to choose a behavior that will be very hard to change—as might occur if the rating is 9 and you've tried to deal with the problem for years without success. At the same time, you want the project to be challenging and interesting for you, and goals you rated 1 or 2 probably are trivial.

3. List the three outcome goal *finalists* below, along with their ratings in the parentheses. In the remaining space provided for each goal, (a) make the goal as specific as possible (e.g., "I want to lose 10 pounds," or "I want to increase my self-esteem so that I feel good about myself almost every day") and (b) describe the overt or covert behavior(s) you'll need to change to reach the goal.

- _____ (rating points)

- _____ (rating points)

- _____ (rating points)

4. _SELF-MANAGEMENT NOTICE:_ Read the following notice about doing a self-modification project and fill out the bottom portion after you have read it.

- _Confidentiality issues:_ All students and the instructor should keep information about any student's project confidential, unless required by law to do otherwise.

- _Therapy issues:_ Doing a self-management project in a college course is an educational activity and is _not_ meant to be a form of or to take the place of psychotherapy. _Do not try to do a project as therapy_ entailing a goal such as reducing clinical depression or extreme anxieties or fears. You could do more harm than good. Students who have serious psychological problems should consult the college counseling office. If you are _already receiving psychotherapy_ and your project relates in any way to the psychological problem being addressed in therapy, you _must consult your therapist regularly for help and supervision_ in designing and carrying out your self-management project.

- _Physical health issues:_ You should not design a project that could conceivably harm your physical health, as exemplified by the following cases: (a) you want to lose a great deal of weight quickly, (b) you want to lose weight but are already within the standard healthful weight range for your height, or (c) you have a serious medical disorder—such as heart disease or asthma—that could be affected by your project behavior, say, exercise. If there is any possibility of physical harm, your physician must approve your design.

I have read the self-management notice and will follow its recommendations.

Your Signature _____ Date _____

Your Printed Name _____

NOTE: If you will be submitting work sheets to your instructor or to a fellow student, make a copy of each sheet before submitting it.

3 Specifying and Assessing What You Want to Change

Prologue

The year was 1980: counselors in the junior high and high schools in a medium-sized American city became alarmed when they realized that drug use among their students had skyrocketed in the last decade and was approaching the levels seen in larger cities. The counselors felt they must do something about the increasing magnitude of this problem, so they decided to design a drug prevention program and request permission to implement it from the superintendent of schools.

Through many hours of meetings, the counselors decided that the way to prevent drug use was to attack two problems: (1) the students' lack of knowledge about many of the negative effects of using drugs and (2) the students' low levels of self-esteem, which made them vulnerable to the appeal of drugs. The counselors then designed a program to address these two problems. They identified numerous readings and videos showing how various drugs can cause health problems or even death, lead to addiction, destroy a user's motivation, lead to other criminal behavior, and ruin the user's life. They also contacted former drug users who agreed to come to the schools and give testimonials, confirming these negative effects. To deal with the self-esteem problem, the counselors decided to have discussion groups in which the students could talk about themselves and things that were bothering them. It was believed that these groups would serve to increase students' self-esteem by helping them dispel negative ideas about themselves and having them share their feelings with one another. Because drug use in the community almost never began before ninth grade, the counselors decided to administer their prevention program to eighth-graders.

The superintendent liked the program and decided to conduct it in half the city's junior high schools in the fall semester and the remaining schools in the spring. This way, the counselors could use personnel more efficiently, and they could compare drug use on the part of students who received the program in the fall with the behavior of those who would receive it later. When the program was completed, the counselors and the superintendent were elated by the results. The fall comparisons of students who had received the program and those who had not and before-and-after comparisons of students showed consistent outcomes: after receiving the program, the students reported higher levels of self-esteem, scored much higher on knowledge about drugs, and reported much more negative attitudes toward drugs, drug use, and drug abusers. A news release concluded that the program "was a complete success and accomplished everything the school officials had hoped for."

Was this conclusion correct? We'll answer that question in this chapter, and we'll learn how to specify and assess behaviors to be changed in ourselves and in other individuals. We saw in Chapter 1 that behavior change programs focus on behavior and use data about a person's responses to decide whether it has changed. The first steps in this process include identifying and defining the goals and behaviors to focus on in the program.

Goals and Target Behaviors

Suppose you are a human resources expert working in a large organization and a supervisor comes to you for help in dealing with a problem employee. The first thing you ask is "What's the problem?" The supervisor answers, "Well, Al's lazy, he doesn't have much initiative, and he's so negative all the time. He just doesn't seem to care about his work." This sounds bad, but the description doesn't help you decide what to do about the problem. Why? So far all you have are broad characteristics of Al's behavior. As we saw in Chapter 1, broad characteristics don't specify the behaviors that need to change. The behaviors to be changed in a behavior modification program are called **target behaviors**.

Without knowing what the specific problem behaviors are, you can't identify the goals the program should have. You also can't determine the behavior's antecedents and consequences or devise ways of altering them. You need to get the supervisor to be more specific—to pinpoint the behaviors. **Pinpointing** is the process of converting broad characteristics into specific, objective, and measurable actions (P. L. Brown, 1982). There are several ways to pinpoint the behaviors. For instance, you can observe Al's performance directly, or you can prod the supervisor to describe examples, such as:

- Almost always when I talk to Al about a new project, he complains about his workload and looks only for difficulties in doing the project rather than trying to find solutions to these difficulties.

- He's come to work late in the morning and after lunch several times this month and acts as if I shouldn't think it's a problem when I call him on it.

- He turned in several reports late—2 or 3 days late—this month, and they were poorly prepared. One of them, for instance, contained data for the wrong month.

- When we have staff meetings, Al rarely contributes ideas that help move a project along. Instead, he verbally abuses the others, calling their ideas "stupid" or "silly," and distracts our work with jokes or irrelevant comments.

Now we can see what some of the target behaviors need to be: some involve *behavioral deficits*, such as late and poorly prepared reports, and some involve *behavioral excesses*, such as inappropriate joking at staff meetings.

Pinpointing is a critical process in all behavior change programs and is used in each type of application we discussed in Chapter 2, including self-management. Once the target behaviors are clear, you can identify and define the behavioral goals of any program you design.

Identifying and Defining Behavioral Goals

We saw in earlier chapters that we can identify broad results we might want to achieve—the so-called **outcome goals**—by applying a behavior change program. In Al's case, the outcome goals might be to help this man be a more conscientious, cooperative, and productive employee.

Outcome goals in behavior modification programs usually are very obvious and straightforward, relating directly to the broad characteristics we've noticed about the person. And the need for or value in achieving these goals is usually clear and not widely disputed, as in Al's case and in the following examples:

- Reducing children's excessive oppositional behavior.
- Improving children's mastery of academic material.
- Enabling autistic children to acquire self-help skills.
- Preventing substance abuse.
- Preventing the spread of AIDS.

But sometimes the goals or the behaviors targeted to achieve the goals are strongly disputed. In education, for instance, some parents may disagree with schools' goals of having children learn about sex or moral values. And although most educators agree that students should learn to think critically about information they encounter, they sometimes disagree on which specific behaviors or skills should be taught to achieve this goal. Disputes about goals and target behaviors typically are based on differences in values or beliefs. For now, we will defer discussing appropriate goals of behavior change programs until later chapters, especially Chapter 16.

In Chapter 2 we saw that a **behavioral goal** is the level of the target behavior a person should achieve by the end of a program. We also saw that outcome and behavioral goals sometimes are the same—for instance, both goals may involve quitting a particular behavior, such as smoking or drinking. Very often, outcome and behavioral goals are different, with outcome goals being broader or less directly tied to the specific behaviors. An example of the difference between goals of these types comes from an application of behavior change techniques to reduce cash register shortages in a small restaurant (Marholin & Gray, 1976). The outcome goal was to have the cash in the register equal the register tape totals at the end of each day, and the consequences introduced to change behavior were contingent on the cashiers' meeting that goal. If a shortage existed that was greater than 1% of daily sales, the cashiers' salaries were docked to cover the loss. Although the program succeeded in achieving the goal, as Figure 3.1 shows, no target behavior or behavioral goal was identified. Is this OK? Probably not, because the cashiers might have met the goal in many different ways, including shortchanging customers and underringing sales on the register. To change behavior in a particular way, such as making cashier transactions more precise, you must identify the target behavior and the behavioral goal, and then make appropriate consequences contingent on the behavior.

People who try to lose weight often focus on the outcome goal—losing weight—rather than the behaviors that enable them to meet the goal. Most people know that the "best" way to lose weight combines two behaviors: eating lower calorie diets and exercising. But there are many other ways to lose or control weight, some of which are dangerous. For example, *bulimia nervosa* is an eating disorder characterized by recurrent episodes of binge eating, followed quickly with purging by self-induced vomiting, laxative use, or other means to prevent the food from

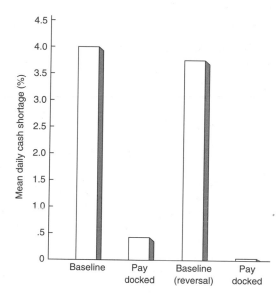

Figure 3.1 Mean daily percent of cash shortages as compared against cash register records during baseline and intervention (pay-docked) phases. (Data from Marholin & Gray, 1976.)

being digested. Individuals who develop this disorder usually diet normally before beginning to use more extreme methods (Polivy & Thomsen, 1988). It may be that because people who diet are frequently so focused on the outcome goal, the behaviors that enable them to lose weight begin to diverge across individuals, with some people trying increasingly desperate methods and becoming convinced that these methods help them meet the goal. Somewhere in this process, they lose the ability to resist tempting foods (self-control) and to direct and modulate their eating behavior (self-regulation). The development of bulimia nervosa is much more complex than this tentative outline suggests, but it may well include these events.

Once you have identified behavioral goals for a behavior modification program, you need to *define* them very clearly. In trying to change Al's work performance, it wouldn't be enough to say, for instance, "By the end of the program, Al will come late to work much less than in the past." This goal is too vague. How will you know whether he achieves it? You must specify the level you want exactly, for example: "By the end of the program, Al should reduce his coming to work late from about 10 instances to fewer than 3 per month, with each lateness being less than 10 minutes." It's a good idea to indicate the baseline level, "about 10 instances," in stating the behavioral goal.

Another good idea in defining behavioral goals is to identify **behavioral subgoals**—intermediate levels of the behavior to be achieved during the program. So, if you were to allocate 3 months for Al's program, you might set the following subgoals for his lateness behavior: fewer than 7 latenesses in the first month, 5 in the second, and 3 in the third. Setting subgoals will make the program seem reasonable, and as Al achieves each subgoal, he will gain self-efficacy and motivation for reaching the behavioral goal.

To modify behaviors effectively, we must *define the behaviors clearly, completely, and in measurable terms.* If we fail to do this, we will sometimes think the behavior

🔍 Close-Up 3.1
Deciding Whether a Program to Prevent Substance Abuse Worked

At the beginning of this chapter we looked at a program school counselors designed and administered to prevent drug abuse, and we asked whether the program was a success. Let's see why we asked this question.

The program focused on preventing substance abuse through drug education. This approach has been widely used in schools, and dozens of studies have been done to assess its effectiveness. In 1988 Robert Bangert-Drowns published an evaluation of these studies' findings, using a research technique called *meta-analysis*, which pools the results of prior research to create an integrated overview of the findings. Meta-analyses are useful in clarifying research results and arriving at an overall conclusion when the effects found in various studies have differed, as has occurred in the field of sub-

stance abuse education. Bangert-Drowns's meta-analysis revealed that "typical substance abuse education had its most positive effects on knowledge and attitudes, but was *unsuccessful in changing the drug-using behaviors* of students" (p. 243, italics added).

Did the counselors' program work? Probably not, since its purpose was to reduce drug use—the target behavior—but the counselors didn't measure this, and indeed, most similar programs have failed to reduce drug use. As in most other programs, the counselors documented desirable changes only in the students' knowledge and attitudes about drugs. To tell whether a program to change behavior worked, we need to measure the target behavior and compare it against a specified behavioral goal.

occurred when it actually didn't, or we won't realize it occurred when it actually did. As a result, the data will be inaccurate and the techniques we apply to change the behavior will be directed frequently toward the wrong actions. These circumstances obviously are not desirable, and they will make the task of changing the target behavior harder and less successful. Decisions about whether a behavior change program has succeeded must be based on whether the behavioral goals have been met. (Go to 🔍 .)

Defining Operant Target Behaviors

To illustrate the importance of defining target behaviors clearly, completely, and in measurable terms, let's suppose you decided to change your personal diet, stating your target behavior as "to eat healthy." Some of my students have begun in this manner. In prodding them to be more precise, I would ask, "What does 'eat healthy' mean? Does it mean you'll now eat three meals a day, or eat more vegetables and less fat, or chew your food to a certain consistency, or consume fewer calories?" Eating is an operant behavior, and to change it, you'll need to alter its antecedents and consequences. If you define a target behavior vaguely, you'll be uncertain when, where, and how to introduce appropriate antecedents and consequences.

How much detail your definition of the target behavior must have depends on exactly what you're trying to achieve—the definition must match the goal. If your behavioral goal states or implies certain details of the behavior, such as the specific

"Yes, dammit! I was a good boy today. Now give me my vodka Martini!"

Although it's nice that this man was "a good boy" today, his target behavior should have been defined more clearly.

snacks you will or will not eat, your definition of the target behavior must reflect those details. For instance, some evidence indicates that obese individuals who lose the most weight in a behavior change program chew each bite of food more slowly than those who are less successful in losing weight (Spiegel, Wadden, & Foster, 1991). If you wanted to modify how fast you chew each bite of food, you'd need to define "bite" and "slower."

Overt and Covert Behaviors

In Chapter 1 we saw that behaviors can be overt or covert and that applications and research on principles of behavior change tend to focus on overt behavior. This is true because we can usually define external behaviors more clearly and measure them more objectively than internal behaviors.

Think about the overt behavior of playing a guitar—you could define and measure its occurrence very accurately, couldn't you? Although you may have to work a little harder to define some other external behaviors, such as whining and bickering, it can be done. In a program to improve children's behaviors at home, Edward Christophersen and his coworkers (1972) defined *whining* as a "verbal complaint conducted in a sing-song (wavering) manner in a pitch above that of the normal speaking voice" and *bickering* as a "verbal argument between any two or all three of the children conducted in a degree of loudness above the normal speaking voice." Having these definitions makes it easier to recognize the behaviors when they occur.

The tasks of defining and measuring covert behaviors—thoughts, feelings, and physiological changes—are more problematic, but still possible. Suppose you were a therapist and wanted to help a client reduce her output of negative thoughts about herself. The two of you probably could generate useful definitions of these covert behaviors, perhaps including some typical words or phrases she uses in her thoughts, such as "dumb" or "fat." This would help her recognize negative thoughts when they occurred. Since only she can know for sure when a negative thought has occurred, however, measuring the behavior will be a very subjective process. Without some independent way of substantiating her self-reports, any progress the client makes will be unclear (D. M. Baer, Wolf, & Risley, 1968). This situation is less than ideal, but we will see later that there are ways to make self-reports more convincing.

Defining and measuring internal changes in physiology, such as increases in blood pressure or the secretion of adrenaline, often require special apparatus or biochemical analyses. Professionals in research or therapy may be able to make these assessments. One physiological measure you can make easily and fairly accurately is heart rate: when you take your pulse, you are counting heartbeats.

Task Analyses of Complex Behaviors

Sometimes the operant target behavior we want to teach or improve involves a complex set of responses. If so, it is useful to determine what these responses are and whether they need to be performed in a certain sequence, as when we put on a pair of slacks or brush our teeth. A motor activity that consists of a sequence of responses is called a **chain**, and the responses that make up the chain are called *links* (Gagné, 1985). For instance, putting on a shirt with buttons consists of the sequence:

1. Holding the shirt upright with one hand, with the front facing you.
2. Inserting the free arm in the corresponding sleeve.
3. Reaching the other arm behind the back to locate the corresponding sleeve hole.
4. Inserting that arm in the corresponding sleeve.
5. Pulling the front of the shirt together.
6. Inserting the first button into its buttonhole.
7. Inserting the next button, etc.

To perform a chain correctly, the links must be done pretty much in a particular order. Learning to perform a chain or other complex set of responses can be very difficult, especially if the task is extremely complicated or the person's learning abilities are very limited, as they are if the learner is a young child or has a learning disorder. Once the component responses of a complex task have been identified, a program can be designed to train the person to perform each component and put all the links together.

The process of identifying the responses and any required sequences that make up a complex set of behaviors is called **task analysis**. Stephen Fawcett and L. Keith Miller (1975) conducted a task analysis of public speaking behavior to design and carry out a program to train people in this complex skill. Their task analysis broke the skill down into two types of behavior—(1) *eye contact* and *gesturing*, which should occur continuously during a speech, and (2) a series of *speaking behaviors* that should occur: the speaker should start by standing in an appropriate position, next scanning the audience briefly while smiling, thanking the host for the introduction, greeting the audience with a statement while smiling, and introducing the topic of the speech. The final speaking behaviors should include a final eye sweep of the audience while smiling and a request for questions. The trainees received feedback on each behavior for each of several speeches, and they improved quickly and dramatically during training. A very different complex skill is *cardiopulmonary resuscitation* (CPR), which individuals can learn and apply to save heart attack victims' lives. Table 3.1 presents a task analysis of this skill. CPR is a very intricate skill to use and should be learned with formal instruction, practiced often, and maintained by taking refresher courses (AMA, 1989).

Response Generalization

Suppose a boy behaves very aggressively toward classmates in school, and his teacher begins introducing consequences to reduce the target behavior of hitting. Do you think the child would decrease making other aggressive behaviors, such as pushing or kicking, too? Chances are, he would. The effects of interventions to modify a target behavior frequently *generalize*, or spread, to *other behaviors* that the interventions *did not specifically address* (Carr, 1988). In the phenomenon of **response generalization**, altering one behavior leads to similar changes in another, unaddressed response—usually one that is similar or related to the target behavior. This is an important phenomenon because it can enhance the efficiency of behavior modification programs: if we design a program for someone with many behavioral deficits or excesses, we may be able to produce desirable changes in many behaviors even though the program focuses on a few target behaviors.

This potential efficiency sounds very helpful—and often it is—but we can't always predict whether and to what degree response generalization will occur. Some evidence indicates that generalization occurs more readily to responses that are similar or related to the target behavior (Carr, 1988; Kimble, 1961). For instance, the aggressive behaviors of hitting and pushing are *similar* in that in both cases the hands are used to apply force against another person, and they are *related* in that they often occur together and can be used to achieve the same reward, such as getting to use a toy another child does not want to give up. But response generaliza-

Table 3.1   *Analysis of Tasks (Lettered) and Subtasks (Numbered) of the American Heart Association's Single-Rescuer CPR Procedure*

A. *Establish unresponsiveness*
  1. Place hands on patient and shake or tap gently. Ask "Are you okay?" or "Can you speak?"
B. *Call for help*
  2. Call out loudly, "Help!"
C. *Open patient's airway*
  3. Place hand nearest patient's head upon forehead and hand nearest feet around back of neck near base of skull.
  4. Elevate neck gently while pushing forehead downward (chin should point nearly straight upward).
D. *Establish breathlessness*
  5. Place ear over patient's mouth while looking at patient's chest. Look for chest movement, listen for air exchange, and feel for air movement.
E. *Ventilate patient*
  6. While maintaining the opened airway, extend index finger and thumb of hand upon forehead and pinch patient's nostrils closed.
  7. Seal mouth around patient's mouth and give 4 quick breaths while observing for chest expansion. Remove mouth between breaths to get air.
F. *Establish pulse*
  8. Remove hand from behind patient's neck and use fingertips to feel for pulse on the near side of neck for a minimum of 5 s.
G. *Activate EMS system*
  9. Call loudly for someone to call an ambulance. Shout the EMS telephone number, if known.
H. *Acceptable time lapse for preceding steps:* 15–30 s.

I. *Perform cardiac compressions*
  10. Bare patient's chest; use middle and index finger of hand nearest patient's feet to trace edge of ribs up to the notch where ribs meet sternum. Place middle finger in notch with index on top of sternum.
  11. Place heel of other hand on patient's sternum, just next to and touching the index finger.
  12. Remove middle and index fingers (on sternum's tip) and place that hand on the back of the hand on patient's lower sternum.
  13. With shoulders directly above sternum, elbows locked, and fingers off patient's chest, depress sternum downward (1.5 to 2 inches) by bending from the hips. Without bouncing or losing hand contact with sternum, count compressions as follows: 1&2&3&4&5 & 1&2&3&4&10 & 1&2 . . . 15.
J. *Ventilate patient*
  14. Open airway as in steps 3 and 4. Ventilate as in steps 6 and 7, two times.
K. *Complete 4 compress/ventilate cycles (steps 10–14). Follow compressions by two ventilations.*
L. *Pulse check*
  15. After fourth comp/vent cycle, remove hand from behind patient's neck and use fingers to feel for pulse on near side of patient's neck.
M. *Breathing check*
  16. Maintain open airway and place ear over patient's mouth while looking at chest. Look for chest movement, listen and feel for air exchange.
N. *Acceptable elapsed time for preceding steps:* 72–101 s.

Source: Seaman, Greene, & Watson-Perczel (1986).

tion sometimes occurs among behaviors that are not similar or clearly related, as you will see in the following list of examples of response generalization in interventions. The addressed and unaddressed behaviors that changed seem to show more similarity or relatedness in the examples at the beginning of the list than in the ones toward the end.

- Three 4-year-old girls who were rewarded for changing the forms they made out of blocks in a preschool began to construct forms they never made before (Goetz & Baer, 1973).

- A 5-year-old boy whose oppositional behavior at home was reduced with behavioral methods showed a corresponding reduction in bedwetting (Nordquist, 1971).

- Pizza delivery drivers who participated in an intervention to increase their use of seat belts also improved their use of turn signals (Ludwig & Geller, 1991).

- Four retarded 3- to 5-year-olds who were rewarded for complying with therapists' simple requests—for instance, "Touch your nose" and "Open the door"—increased their compliance; at the same time, the children decreased certain inappropriate behaviors, such as being aggressive toward the therapist, disrupting training sessions, and destroying property (Parrish et al., 1986).

- A 7-year-old retarded boy whose excessive talking to his teacher was reduced by having the teacher stop rewarding it with her attention showed associated increases in disruptive behavior and in talking and playing with other children (Sajwaj, Twardosz, & Burke, 1972).

What's more, a study by Robert Wahler (1975) found that the behaviors that are related to each other and change together can differ from one individual to the next.

Although we don't yet know all the factors that affect response generalization and can't always predict when and how much it will occur, we have enough knowledge to use the phenomenon to increase the efficiency of some program designs. For instance, if a client has many behavioral deficits or excesses, we can focus the program on target behaviors we think are similar or related to unaddressed problem behaviors, monitor for changes in the unaddressed behaviors, and revise the program later to cover problem behaviors that do not show response generalization.

Defining Respondent Target Behaviors

We saw in Chapter 1 that respondent behaviors include unconditioned and conditioned responses. People learn through respondent conditioning to associate two previously unrelated events—a conditioned stimulus (CS) and a conditioned response (CR)—so that the CS gains the ability to elicit the CR. Because CRs are learned behaviors, they often are targets of behavior change programs. Emotions, feelings, and likes and dislikes are CRs that are common respondent target behaviors.

Like operant behaviors, respondent behaviors can be internal or external. Often they are both. For example, when we are anxious or afraid, we may show overt signs of fear in facial expressions or in efforts to escape the situation, and we may experience covert behaviors, such as negative thoughts and increased physiological arousal. When designing a program to change a respondent behavior, we need to define the behavior in terms of its internal or external responses, or both.

Some programs may need a dual focus to be fully successful. For instance, in behavior change programs to reduce fear of public speaking, successfully reducing people's subjective feelings of fear while giving a speech does not necessarily generalize to such overt signs of fear as frequently moistening the lips or pacing (Marshall, Presse, & Andrews, 1976). To reduce these overt signs of fear, programs probably need to include training in public speaking skills, too.

From the example on public speaking, you may be wondering whether response generalization occurs with respondent behaviors. There is evidence that it can (Kimble, 1961). But, as in the case of operant behavior, we do not have enough knowledge yet to predict accurately how much, if any, generalization will occur when respondent behaviors are modified. It's possible that programs to reduce one type of fear, such as fear of snakes, may help people to cope better with other fears that were not addressed in the intervention. An adult whose fear of snakes was reduced in a behavior modification program reported that the greatest benefit of the "treatment was the feeling that if I could lick [my fear of] snakes, I could lick anything. It gave me the confidence to tackle, also successfully, some personal stuff" (Bandura, Jeffery, & Gajdos, 1975).

Alternative or Competing Responses

Can you feel anxious and calm at the same time? Can you bite your fingernails if you put your hands in your pockets? Probably not. Each of these situations involves two incompatible or interfering behaviors, making them difficult to do at the same time. Actions that interfere or are incompatible with other behaviors are called **alternative responses** or "competing responses." A useful technique for reducing a target behavior is to encourage the person to replace it with an alternative response. One way to encourage someone to make an alternative response is to reward it. So, if we want to reduce a child's oppositional behavior, we might reinforce cooperative behavior. If we choose to use alternative responses in a program, we should *define them*, just as we would define target behaviors.

From the examples of alternative responses we've mentioned, you can see that alternative responses can involve operant or respondent behaviors and can be overt or covert behaviors. Some other examples of alternative responses are:

- Praising people instead of criticizing them.
- Thinking "I can do it" instead of "I'll never do well at this."
- Smiling instead of frowning.
- Saying "darn" instead of "#@*$%."
- Exercising instead of lying on the sofa.
- Taking a deep breath and "counting to ten" instead of getting angry.

As you look at these examples, you will probably see that there may be several possible alternative responses for each undesirable behavior. (Go to ✔ .)

✓ Concept Check 3.1

• •

1. Converting a trait, such as honesty, into specific target behaviors is called _____ .

2. A behavioral goal a college student might choose when modifying how much study-ing he or she does is _____ . ⇔

3. To tell whether a behavior change program was successful, you need to assess the target behavior and compare it against a specified _____ .

4. A link in a chain you might perform when starting your car is _____ _____ . ⇔

5. You would do a _____ to break down a complex skill into its component responses.

6. If behavioral methods were used to increase the time children's clothes stayed clean, a likely example of response generalization might be their _____ _____ . ⇔

7. If you were trying to reduce eating junk foods and begin eating carrot sticks instead, eating carrot sticks would be an _____ response. _____

Answers: **1.** pinpointing **2.** studying 20 hours a week **3.** behavioral goal **4.** inserting the key in the ignition **5.** task analysis **6.** washing their hands **7.** alternative

• •

How to Assess Behavior

A student of mine named Dave was planning a self-management project to decrease his swearing behavior when he announced in class, "I've got a big problem. All of a sudden, I don't swear much anymore." Although he hadn't yet collected any data, he believed his swearing had declined markedly. We discussed the problem, and Dave agreed to ask his roommates to help him keep track of his swearing for a few days. As you probably suspect, the roommates' data showed a considerable amount of swearing. Assessing behavior requires that you collect data, and there are sever-al types of data you can use.

Types of Data

The data you collect must measure the target behavior and reflect any progress that has been made toward the behavioral goal. Behavior can change across several dif-ferent dimensions—including how *often*, how *long*, how *soon*, how *well*, and how strongly it occurs. Each type of data reflects a different dimension, and you need to select the type(s) of data that will best reflect the dimension(s) of target behavior you want to change (Dowrick, 1991). For example, if the behavioral goal is to increase the time a student spends studying per week, the data must involve a mea-sure of time. As this example suggests, you can express data as a *rate*—that is, per unit of time—as in "how long a student studies *per week*." Let's look at the different types of data you can use to assess behavior, beginning with how frequently it occurs.

Frequency

Probably the most common type of data collected in behavior modification programs is **frequency**—the number of times a behavior occurred. Frequency is an appropriate measure when (1) the target behavior is *discrete*—that is, each instance has a clear start and end; (2) performing each instance takes a *fairly constant amount of time*; and (3) the *behavioral goal* involves *changing how often* the behavior occurs. Dave's project to reduce his swearing qualified on all three of these criteria, so he assessed this behavior in terms of its frequency.

Collecting frequency data is relatively easy to do, and most target behaviors can be appropriately assessed with frequency data. For example, the frequency of a boy's oppositional behavior was assessed in a behavior change program to reduce how often that behavior occurred (Nordquist, 1971). In another case, the number of arithmetic problems computed correctly by underachieving fifth-graders was assessed after the children had participated in a program to increase their arithmetic skills (Pigott, Fantuzzo, & Clement, 1986). Other target behaviors that can be assessed appropriately with frequency data are attending classes, biting nails, paying bills on time, taking medication on schedule, smoking cigarettes, doing specific rehabilitation exercises, hitting classmates in school, and thinking unpleasant thoughts. You can keep track of response frequencies in several different ways, including marking on a sheet of paper, moving a coin from one pocket to another, or advancing a golf score counter each time the response occurs.

Duration

Duration refers to the length of time each instance of the target behavior lasts, from beginning to end. This type of data is appropriate for assessing instances of behavior that are *ongoing activities*, lasting or continuing for *varying periods of time*, and for behavioral goals that involve either *increasing or decreasing that time*. For instance, the duration of social interaction was assessed in a program to increase the time two severely withdrawn, mentally retarded children spent in simple social activities, such as rolling balls to each other (Whitman, Mercurio, & Caponigri, 1970). Other examples of target behaviors that can be assessed in terms of duration are studying, watching television, exercising, sleeping, sitting in one's seat, having a tantrum, talking on the telephone, spending time with one's children, and feeling anxious or "blue."

Magnitude

In a program to reduce someone's anxiety, wouldn't it be important to assess *how strong* the anxiety is? This would involve a measure of the behavior's **magnitude**—its intensity, degree, or size. Assessing the target behavior's intensity, degree, or size is useful if the magnitude *can or does vary* and the *behavioral goal* involves *changing the magnitude.* For example, the magnitude of a retarded girl's speech was assessed in a behavior change program to increase the loudness at which she spoke, measured with an electronic device (Jackson & Wallace, 1974). Before the program, her speech had been almost inaudible. In another example, college students participated in a program to increase the intensity with which they did aerobic exercise; magnitude was assessed by means of charts that take into account the type of activity, such as jogging or swimming, and its duration (Wysocki et al., 1979). Other ways to assess exercise intensity include taking one's pulse or recording the weights of barbells lifted, as a student named Marc did in the weight-lifting self-management program he designed for my course.

Magnitude can be an appropriate measure for many other target behaviors—increasing the degree of concentration in studying, for example, or decreasing the amount or caloric content of foods in a diet. Measuring intensity is usually important when one is trying to change emotional behaviors, such as overt and covert expressions of anger, jealousy, anxiety or fear, depression, love, and happiness. The most common method for measuring emotion magnitude is to use a *rating scale* with discrete numerical values. In measuring stress, for example, a student named Rose used a 10-point scale ranging from 0 to 9, where 0 equaled "no stress" and 9 equaled "extreme stress." Similar approaches can be used to assess the magnitude of other behaviors.

Data of Other Types

Several other types of data are also useful in assessing behavior, and we will describe a few of them briefly. One type is *latency,* or the amount of time a person takes to respond appropriately to an antecedent. Measuring the quickness with which a child complies with a teacher's or parent's request would be an example of using latency to assess a target behavior. Another example comes from the treatment of insomnia: the effectiveness of a behavior modification intervention was evaluated on the basis of people's latencies in getting to sleep after going to bed (Puder et al., 1983).

Sometimes a program's behavioral goal involves improving the *quality* of a target behavior—that is, how well it is performed. For instance, a behavior change program was used to improve the quality of students' classroom discussions (B. M. Smith et al, 1982). After the students had been trained to use reasons, examples, and comparisons as discussion skills, their statements in discussions were rated for quality on the basis of the use of these skills. Other target behaviors for which quality may be an appropriate measure include playing a musical instrument, taking photographs, drawing pictures, and performing sport skills.

The last type of data we'll consider for assessing behavior is the *percentage*—the proportion of behaviors, or individuals performing behaviors, that meet some criterion, multiplied by 100. Percentages are especially useful measures when people have *many opportunities to respond* or when the *opportunities to meet a behavioral criterion vary* across time or circumstances. For example, people's driving over the speed limit probably varies with many conditions, such as the weather, time of day, and day of the week. As a result, a good way to evaluate the effectiveness of a program to reduce speeding would be to look for a reduction in the percentage of cars observed speeding, rather than the number of cars speeding. One study found that the percentage of cars speeding was reduced by posting the percentage of cars that did *not* speed during the day before and during the best day to date (Van Houten, Nau, & Marini, 1980).

There are two other issues to keep in mind about collecting data. First, it is often necessary to collect more than one type of data to reflect changes in a target behavior. For instance, in a behavior change program to reduce someone's feelings of depression, the behavioral goal might include reducing the frequency of these feelings as well as their duration and magnitude. If so, three types of data should be collected. Second, it is typically useful to design and record data on carefully structured *data sheets*, like the one presented in Figure 3.2. Other data sheets can be simpler—mere lists providing spaces for tick marks for frequency data, or they can be more detailed—incorporating a lengthy checklist of behaviors to be assessed with two or more types of data. Using data sheets makes recording and evaluating data much easier and faster. When designing a data sheet, try it out by collecting some sample or "pilot" data so you can correct any design flaws before using this tool in a program.

DATA SHEET: Exercise

Student: Bonnie   Observer: Mr. Armstrong

Date	Starting Time	Duration (entire session, in minutes)	Magnitude (pulse beats/min., while jogging)	Comments
9-7-94	3 00	30	120	She hasn't exercised before.
9-9-94	3 30	35	125	
9-12-94	3 15	40	130	
9-14-94	3 15	40	130	Feeling a little achy.
9-16-94	3 00	45	140	Feeling better.

Figure 3.2   Data sheet for use in an exercise program at school, with a physical education teacher as the observer. Each session includes general calisthenics and jogging, and is assessed with two types of data: *duration* of the entire session and *magnitude*, as measured by the student's pulse rate taken for 1 minute during jogging.

Strategies for Assessing Behavior

All methods for assessing behavior involve some form of *observation,* but we can "observe" behavior in two ways: *directly,* through seeing or hearing the actual behavior, for example, or *indirectly,* through interviews, questionnaires, or comparable means. Observers can be almost anyone—therapists, teachers, coworkers, relatives, or even the person whose behavior is being changed. When individuals assess their own target behaviors, the strategy is called **self-monitoring**, or self-observation. Direct observation strategies should be used to collect data whenever feasible. Overt target behaviors almost always can be assessed directly, but covert behaviors often must be assessed indirectly. (Go to .)

Direct Assessment Methods

Direct assessment methods measure instances of the actual target behavior in a straightforward manner; the responses of interest are usually seen or heard. For instance, a teacher may assess a student's hand-raising behavior by watching for instances of it and keeping a record of those instances. When using direct assessment methods, observers may measure the behavior (1) while in the same room or setting as the subject, (2) by watching secretly from an adjacent room, perhaps through a one-way mirror, or (3) by recording the behavior on videotape or audiotape and scoring it later (Dowrick, 1991; Foster & Cone, 1986).

Sometimes direct assessments are taken in a *structured test* of the behavior (D. A. Bernstein, Borkovec, & Coles, 1986; Wixted, Bellack, & Hersen, 1990). In one example, a client who is extremely afraid of snakes might be tested by having a ther-

 ## Case Study 3.1
Reducing Bob's Self-Talk

An institutionalized 31-year-old schizophrenic man named Bob had a history of talking to himself frequently and at varying levels of loudness (as described in Wong et al., 1987). Many mental patients exhibit self-talk, which is one of several fixed patterns of speech called *stereotypic vocalizations.* In this case study, Bob's self-talk was defined and measured in the following way:

Self-talk, defined as any vocalization not directed at another person, excluding sounds associated with physiological functions (e.g., coughing), was the target response for Bob. Stereotypic vocalizations were monitored with a microcassette recorder (Sony model no. M-203) carried in a shirt jacket worn by the patient. The recorder received input from a tie-clip microphone (Radio Shack catalog no. 33-1058) attached to the jacket lapel. Microcassette tapes were later rated by observers who recorded the duration of self-talk with stopwatches. (p. 78)

Bob's therapists reduced his self-talk by about 60% simply by providing recreational activities that would serve as antecedents for alternative behaviors. Because the study's observers heard and scored Bob's self-talk from tape recordings, the method they used involve a *direct assessment* of the target behavior.

Direct assessment methods are sometimes conducted by watching the behavior through a one-way mirror and/or videotaping the behavior

apist move a caged snake gradually closer. When the client feels uncomfortable, the test ends and the distance between the snake and the client is measured and recorded. In another type of structured test, anxious or assertive behaviors might be tested by having the client role-play at being in specified situations, perhaps giving a speech or requesting a refund in a store, while the therapist rates the performance for specific behaviors, such as stammering or facial tension.

Direct assessment methods often use devices to measure physical characteristics or dimensions of behavior. Tape measures are routinely used to determine how close a client can get to a feared object, how high an athlete can jump, and so on. In therapy or rehabilitation settings, the devices used can be quite specialized. For instance, medical patients with severe burns on their arms or legs must perform physical therapy exercises to stretch their limbs as far as they can so that they will regain their range of motion. The degree of stretching can be measured with a *goniometer*, which has two arms joined by a pivot—one arm has a pointer and the other has a protractor scale (Hegel et al., 1986). When the limb is stretched, the physical therapist positions the device on the limb and records the angle the limb forms. In behavior therapy for male sexual dysfunctions, the diameter, rigidity, and duration of the penile erections can be measured with a small computerized device called the RigiScan (Ackerman et al., 1991, 1993).

Because direct assessment methods are used in a straightforward manner, they have traditionally been the preferred approaches for collecting data in behavior modification research and applications. But these methods have some drawbacks (Wixted, Bellack, & Hersen, 1990). For one thing, they can be very time-consuming and expensive to use if it is necessary to train and employ paid observers. Also, these methods sometimes assess only a sample of the behavior you are trying to change, and that sample may or may not be representative of the person's behavior in everyday life. One purpose of the indirect assessment methods we are about to examine is to document the occurrence of or change in a given behavior in everyday life.

Indirect Assessment Methods

Indirect assessment methods use abstract or roundabout ways to measure the target behavior: we might ask the person to describe instances of the behavior or how it has changed, for instance. Because these methods do not assess the actual behavior directly, they are sometimes inaccurate or misleading—for example, people may misperceive or misremember details of the behavior or whether it occurred at all. Not all these methods rely on people's memories, however. We will consider four indirect assessment methods: interviews, self-report instruments, nonclient ratings of the client's behavior, and physiological measures.

Interviews   Interviews are the most widely used assessment procedures in behavior therapy (Swan & MacDonald, 1978). Therapists use initial interviews with the client and significant people in his or her life—such as relatives, friends, and teachers—to accomplish three things (Ciminero, 1986; Davison & Neale, 1994; Gross, 1984; Turkat, 1986). First, interviews can help identify the client's behavioral deficits and excesses, as well as appropriate alternative responses, existing antecedents and consequences for the problem behaviors, and potential consequences to use in treatment. Second, interviews may also help in assessing related issues, such as important cultural norms that exist in the client's life and persons who will be affected by changes in the client's behavior. Third, therapists try to establish with interviewees a relationship of mutual trust, called *rapport*. People who are interviewed in the therapy process are often under a great deal of stress and may be unwilling to reveal important information about the client.

Interviews can vary in their degree of structure (Davison & Neale, 1994; Turkat, 1986; Wixted, Bellack, & Hersen, 1990). When interviews are highly structured, the therapist asks a set of questions in a specific order, usually with the goal of identifying or diagnosing the client's problem in a prescribed way. When interviews are unstructured, the therapist has considerable leeway in posing questions and must rely on clinical experience and intuition in deciding the direction questions should take and how to interpret the answers. Because interview assessments are retrospective—that is, the person looks back at behaviors that have already occurred—therapists must watch for inconsistent answers that may reflect errors in memory.

Self-Report Instruments   Clients can report large amounts of clinically important information very efficiently by filling out questionnaires and rating scales (Jensen & Haynes, 1986; Wixted, Bellack, & Hersen, 1990). Some self-report instruments are constructed by individual therapists for specific purposes, but many others have been developed for general use and are available to therapists through professional sources. Some therapists have clients fill out a packet of instruments prior to the first session to expedite the assessment process.

Some self-report instruments provide information about the client's background, while other instruments are designed to help diagnose the problem and identify target behaviors (Jensen & Haynes, 1986). Questionnaires and rating scales are available to help therapists assess many specific behavioral deficits or excesses, including:

- Anger (Novaco, 1976).
- Assertiveness (Rathus, 1973).
- Binge eating (Gormally et al., 1982; Hawkins & Clement, 1980).
- Depression (Beck et al., 1961; Carson, 1986)
- Fears and anxieties (Bernstein, Borcovec, & Coles, 1986; Cautela, 1981; Ollendick, 1983)
- Parent–child conflicts (Cautela, 1981; Frankel, 1993).
- Sexual dysfunctions and skills (Ackerman & Carey, in press; Malatesta & Adams, 1986).
- Substance abuse (Correa & Sutker, 1986).

When used along with other assessment methods, data from self-report instruments can help guide the selection of target behaviors and treatment approaches.

Nonclient Ratings of the Client's Behavior   Useful information about an individual's behavior can be obtained by having the person's teacher, therapist, parents or spouse, or coworkers fill out rating scales or checklists. For instance, Lynn McClannahan and her colleagues (1990) developed a checklist that teacher-therapists can use to assess 20 dimensions of developmentally disordered children's personal appearance and care. Checklist items include whether a child's nose is clean and whether the socks match. Totaling across dimensions gives an overall rating of the child's appearance. Other ratings scales are very simple and involve only a single class or dimension of behavior, such as in rating how effective psychiatric patients' social skills are (Frederiksen et al., 1976). Figure 3.3 presents a simple rating scale a student named Chris used to measure jealousy/anger.

Physiological Measures   Many different physiological measures can be used to assess internal events, and most of these measures require special equipment or biochemical tests. Taking physiological measures can be useful in behavior change programs under two main circumstances (Bernstein, Borkovec, & Coles, 1986; Kallman & Feuerstein, 1986). First, the target behavior itself may be an internal physiological response, such as high blood pressure. Second, the target behavior may have a consistent physiological component to it, as in the heightened heart rate characteristic of people experiencing anger or anxiety. In this case, measurments of heart rate can be used to confirm clients' self-reports that their feelings have changed.

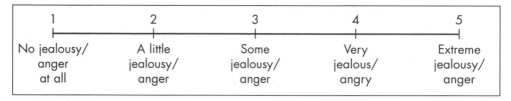

1	2	3	4	5
No jealousy/ anger at all	A little jealousy/ anger	Some jealousy/ anger	Very jealous/ angry	Extreme jealousy/ anger

Figure 3.3 A rating scale to measure the magnitude of jealousy/anger experienced in various situations.

Using physiological measures is the only objective approach available for assessing covert events, and these assessments can produce data on frequency, duration, and magnitude. But physiological measures are often expensive to use and don't necessarily give a clearer picture of the current status of the covert behavior than self-reports do (Kallman & Feuerstein, 1986).

Timing and Accuracy in Behavioral Assessments

If you were going to assess a person's responses, when exactly would you take your measures and how would you try to make sure that the data you collect accurately reflect the status of the behavior? These are the issues we examine next.

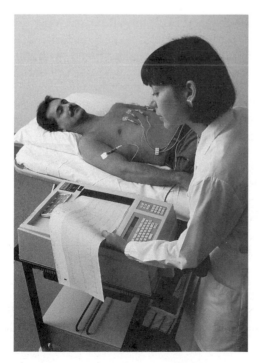

Physiological measures can be taken to assess internal events.

Timing Behavioral Assessments

A very common approach to collecting data involves designating a specific period of time—such as a one-hour therapy session, a recess period at school, an entire day at work, or an entire month anywhere—and attempting to assess every instance of the target behavior during that time. The assessment and recording of all instances of a behavior during a specific time period is called **continuous recording**. This approach can be difficult to use if the behavior occurs at extremely high rates, if measuring each instance requires special equipment or a lot of time, or if the observer must simultaneously monitor other events, such as other students' classroom activities.

Another way to time behavioral assessments is to designate specific observation periods (say, 30 minutes each), divide each period into fairly short intervals of equal length (say, 15 seconds), and record whether the target behavior occurs in each interval. This approach is called **interval recording**. The record for each interval is essentially yes/no, and only one instance of the behavior is recorded for a particular interval even if there were actually many more. Knowing when the intervals start and end is a problem that must be solved, perhaps by having a beeper sound every 15 seconds through an earphone. The data used to evaluate the behavior would be either the number or the percentage of intervals in which the behavior occurred. For example, in a study of children's distracting behavior on shopping trips with their parents, observers followed the family through a store and recorded on audiotape whether distracting behaviors occurred in each 15-second interval (Clark et al., 1977). A program of behavioral methods markedly reduced the percent of intervals in which distractions occurred.

A third approach for timing assessments, called **time sampling**, involves designating one or more observation periods of equal length, dividing each period into subperiods of equal length (say, 1 minute), and designating a short interval (say, 10 seconds) at the start of each subperiod for collecting data. There is quite a bit of flexibility in the type of data that can be collected during these intervals. For instance, researchers in one study assessed the frequency and duration of an employee's in-seat behavior, recording whether she was in her seat for all, part, or none of each interval (Powell, Martindale, & Kulp, 1975). In a study of infant and toddler social behavior, researchers collected a continuous record of nine social behaviors during each interval by jotting down a code for each response (Sarafino, 1985). As in interval recording, the observer using time sampling needs to have a signal for the start and end of each interval. Figure 3.4 gives an example of a data sheet that could be used to make time-sampling assessments of a child's disruptive behavior.

Accuracy and Validity of Behavioral Assessments

Assessments must be reasonably accurate and valid if they are to be useful. What does "valid" mean? Assessments have *validity* to the degree that they reflect what they are intended to measure. We consider the accuracy and validity of direct and indirect assessment methods briefly in this section, and we'll return to these issues again in Chapter 12.

| DATA SHEET: TIME SAMPLING ASSESSMENT OF DISRUPTIVE BEHAVIOR | | | | | |

Student _____ Observer: _____

Start time: _____   Day/date:_____ / _____

Intervals

	1	2	3	4	5
First 10 min	A O Y	A O Y	A O Y	A O Y	A O Y
Second 10 min	A O Y	A O Y	A O Y	A O Y	A O Y
Third 10 min	A O Y	A O Y	A O Y	A O Y	A O Y

A = aggression, O = out of seat, Y = yelling, making loud noises

Figure 3.4   Data sheet for time-sampling assessment of a student's disruptive behavior. In this example, the complete observation period lasts 30 minutes, with fifteen 2-minute subperiods. During the short interval (say, 10 seconds each) at the start of each subperiod, the observer would circle the letter representing any of the three target behaviors that occurred in that interval. In this case, we would evaluate the data in terms of the number or percentage of intervals in which each type of behavior occurred.

Direct assessment methods generally measure the actual target behavior they are intended to examine—for example, if the target behavior is stuttering, you might count instances of it in a person's speech. How accurate these assessments are depends on how carefully the behavior has been defined, how thoroughly the observers have been trained, and how sensitive or precise are the measurements obtained from any assessment devices used. If the direct assessments are accurate and measure the actual behavior they are intended to examine, these measures usually have a high degree of validity. But sometimes direct assessments are used to infer internal events. In such circumstances—for example, when people's willingness to approach a feared object is used to reflect their fear—the validity of the measure is not as clear because there may be some other reason for the degree of approach behavior observed. For instance, a child who was feeling intense fear might be willing to get near a big spider if other children were watching.

Indirect assessment methods often involve very subjective estimates and rely on people's memories, as happens when clients are interviewed or fill out self-report instruments. Thus validity and accuracy may be high or not. One way to enhance the validity of such instruments is to consider the data they produce in the context of data from several assessment approaches—interviews with or ratings by family members to corroborate the client's data, for example. Family members' assessments can be fairly accurate if they know exactly what the target behavior is and have opportunities to observe it (McMahon, 1984). If these conditions don't exist—as they will not if parents don't see their child's target behavior, such as truancy—the related assessments are likely to be inaccurate (Schnelle, 1974). Many other factors can also affect the accuracy of indirect assessment methods—for example, accuracy is enhanced when interview or rating questions are asked and answered clearly and when the person is who administers interviews or physiological tests is highly trained.

A phenomenon that can reduce the accuracy and validity of direct and indirect assessment methods is **reactivity**—the process by which people's behavior tends to change when they know they are being observed (Bornstein, Hamilton, & Bornstein, 1986; Monette, Sullivan, & DeJong, 1990). As an example of reactivity, consider trying to assess store customers' everyday stealing behavior if they can see you are watching them intently. If no one steals anything during your observation, the behavior might reflect the subjects' reactivity rather than their honesty. Or suppose a third-grade teacher started keeping records on a pad of students' in-seat behavior and announced this new procedure to the class. Chances are, the students would stay in their seats longer than usual, at least for a while. Reactivity generally brings people's behavior into line with their values or their ideas about socially acceptable conduct. The effects of reactivity on behavior can be short-lived if the observee "gets used to" being observed, doesn't want to behave in the new way, and finds that there are no new consequences for behaving that way. Keep in mind that the observee and the observer are the same person when *self-monitoring* strategies are used. Behavior therapists often have clients use self-monitoring techniques to capitalize on the beneficial effects of reactivity on target behaviors (Bornstein, Hamilton, & Bornstein, 1986).

Developmental and Normative Comparisons

Do people at 2, 10, 30, and 70 years of age behave the same? Of course not, and they're not expected to behave alike. What is "normal" and acceptable behavior changes with age. The strategies we use in assessing behavior and the way we interpret the data must be sensitive to the individual's developmental level (Edelbrock, 1984; Evans & Nelson, 1986; Ollendick & Hersen, 1984). We'll focus on development in childhood because of the rapid and enormous changes that occur in children's motor, cognitive, and social abilities.

The strategies used in assessing children's behavior must be appropriate to each child's abilities, and we'll consider three examples. First, children below 10 years of age or so may have difficulty filling out self-report instruments on their own, especially if a questionnaire or rating scale requires strong verbal or reading abilities. Sometimes these problems can be reduced by designing rating scales that use nonverbal symbols, such as happy faces, instead of words. Also, self-report instruments must ask questions that are appropriate to the child's age—for instance, it wouldn't make sense to ask a 5-year-old about the stresses of dating. Second, children below the age of 6 or so appear to lack the ability to judge and record the occurrence of a target behavior, making self-monitoring an inappropriate strategy for preschoolers.

Third, many young children are fearful or wary of strangers, which may increase the effects of reactivity. This problem usually can be overcome by having observers spend time playing with the children before trying to assess their behavior.

When interpreting assessment data or setting behavioral goals, we must consider what behavioral characteristics are normal for a child's age. We should not expect a child's motor, language, or social abilities to be greater than those of most other children at the same age. We also need to be aware that certain behavior problems are more common at some ages than others. For instance, fears and whining are common in early childhood and decline sharply by adolescence—and certain specific fears, such as fears of animals, are very common at early ages but not later. On the other hand, truancy and substance use occur very rarely before early adolescence.

Analyzing the Functions of Behavior

An essential part of designing a program to change behavior is answering the question, "What functions does the behavior serve?" (Groden, 1989; O'Neill et al., 1990). To obtain a proper answer, we must know the times and situations in which the behavior does or does not occur and how the person benefits from his or her current pattern of behavior. Often, when people try to change behavior without analyzing its functions, they make the situation worse without realizing it. (Go to .)

 ## Case Study 3.2
The Functions of a Boy's Temper Tantrums

An 11-year-old boy of normal intelligence and with no apparent organic disorder often showed disruptive classroom behavior that was unusual for a child his age (as described in Zimmerman & Zimmerman, 1962). He would speak baby-talk, voice irrelevant comments and questions, and have several temper tantrums each week. For instance, when he refused to go to class, school staff would drag him down the hall as he

screamed and buckled his knees. On several of these occasions, the boy threw himself on the floor in front of the classroom door. A crowd of staff members inevitably gathered around him. The group usually watched and commented as he sat or lay on the floor, kicking and screaming. Some members of the group hypothesized that such behavior seemed to appear after the boy was teased or .

frustrated in some way. However, the only observable in the situation was the consistent consequence of the behavior in terms of the formation of a group of staff members around the boy. (p. 60)

This description suggests two possible reasons for this boy's tantrums: the *antecedents*— being frustrated or teased—and the *consequences*, receiving attention. The possible role of the tantrums' consequences was based on observations of the actual situation. When the staff were instructed not to attend to the boy's tantrums, these behaviors disappeared gradually over several weeks. Because the staff hadn't realized that the function of the tantrums was to get their attention, they had been rewarding the behavior unknowingly. Determining the functions of behavior usually requires careful observation.

What Is a Functional Analysis?

A **functional analysis** is an assessment of the connections between a behavior and its antecedents and consequences (R. E. O'Neill et al., 1990). Functional analyses vary in the rigor and completeness in which they are carried out. They can be highly detailed and exhaustive, as they often are in carefully conducted research (for example, Cooper et al., 1982; Iwata et al., 1992; Johnson et al., 1995; Sasso, et al., 1992; Wacker et al., 1990). At the other end of the spectrum, they can be very informal—as they are in our everyday, casual observations of why people behave the way they do (R. E. O'Neill et al., 1990). For most behavior change programs, moderately rigorous and complete functional analyses are sufficient and should have three outcomes. They should (1) define the target behavior exactly and clearly, (2) determine which antecedents function to produce the behavioral excess or deficit, and (3) explain how the person's behavior functions to produce reinforcement. Although the antecedents, behaviors, and consequences in functional analyses are usually overt, they can be covert, too.

We saw in Chapter 1 that *operant behavior* follows a standard A-B-C sequence in which *antecedents* lead to *behaviors*, which produce *consequences*. It is evident that functional analyses apply straightforwardly in programs to change operant behaviors. In the case of *respondent behavior*, the CS is the antecedent, and CRs in everyday life function to produce consequences, as we saw in Chapter 1 (see Figure 1.2). Suppose, for instance, a child who is afraid of dogs comes across a dog (a CS), which arouses the CRs of fear and running away. What's the consequence of escaping? The child's feeling of fear decreases.

Functional analyses of respondent behavior include the consequences produced by respondent behaviors (Bernstein, Borkovec, & Coles, 1986; Emmelkamp, Bouman, & Scholing, 1992). Interventions to reduce fears and anxieties need to address the consequences for individuals of escaping or avoiding the situations that arouse these emotions. When people escape or avoid the antecedents that elicit fear or anxiety, they retain their inability to cope effectively with the situations and often increase the chances that these antecedents will arouse the same emotions in the future.

Recording Data for a Functional Analysis

In conducting a functional analysis, we maintain records of our assessments of the behavior. These records are kept on a series of forms; often there is a separate form for each of the following: (1) interview data, (2) the target behavior observational data, (3) a summary of the observational data, and (4) an overall analysis and plan for changing the behavior. Gerald Groden (1989) and Robert O'Neill and his coworkers (1990) have written excellent guides for conducting functional analyses and developing forms to record and organize the data. I used these guides as main sources in preparing the material for this section and constructing the two forms we will examine.

When the program will address a *behavioral excess,* observations of the target behavior in a functional analysis must be made until the behavior has occurred often enough to reveal patterns in the relationships between the behavior and its antecedents and consequences. Useful patterns generally emerge after about 2 to 5 days of observation, with *at least a dozen or so instances* of the behavior recorded. Figure 3.5 presents an **A-B-C log**—a chronological record of the target behavior, along with the antecedents and consequences of each instance of the behavior. This form has been filled out with data on 4-year-old Ray's tantrum behaviors. When you do a functional analysis, the A-B-C log is the form to use to record observational data regarding the target behavior. For each instance of the behavior, record its *day, date, time,* and *place.* Specify the place as precisely as you think necessary—for example, if the behavior tends to occur in certain rooms in the house, such as the bedroom or kitchen, you should devise and use special codes for those places.

The A-B-C log also includes three other sets of codes that you should record for each instance of the behavior. One of these sets of codes indicates the *type of data* you recorded. Another set describes the *types of consequences* the behavior produced. The final set specifies the conditions that preceded the behavior, classified into seven *antecedent types:*

- *Activity:* what the person was doing immediately prior to the behavior. Be specific, such as by indicating the name of a game the person was playing, or otherwise identifying the activity.
- *Social:* which people were in the environment, and what specifically they did or said immediately before the behavior occurred.
- *Covert:* what the person was thinking or imagining just before the behavior. Sometimes this can be determined by asking the person or noticing what he or she said prior to the behavior.
- *Emotion:* the type of emotion the person seemed to experience just prior to the behavior.
- *Physical events:* any nonsocial stimuli that occurred or the person noticed, such as a loud noise or an object that came in view, immediately before the behavior.
- *Other:* any immediate antecedents that do not belong to the preceding categories.
- *Distant:* any conditions or events that happened "several minutes to 24 hours or more before the behavior occurred and which you feel may be related to the occurrence of the behavior" (Groden, 1989, p. 165). An example might be an argument that occurred earlier in the day. Distant antecedents' relationships to behavior are usually speculative, but sometimes they can be useful in functional analyses.

After having observed at least a dozen instances of the behavior during a period of a few days or more, the data collected are used to fill out a **summary record** form. This form organizes, collates, and summarizes the data, allowing us to see patterns among the factors examined and the behavior. Figure 3.6 presents a summary

A-B-C Log: _Tantrum_ Behavior

Person: _Ray_   Age: _4_   Observer(s): _Ms. Ashcroft, Mother, Father_

Day/ Date/ Time	Place[1]	Antecedents		Behaviors		Consequences		Thoughts/ Comments
		Description	Type[2]	Description	Data[3]	Description	Type[4]	
Mon/ 9-26-94/ 11 50 AM	H	Drawing trees, Ashcroft told him favorite food on table for lunch, parents had big argument before leaving for work, Ray sulked	A, S, D, E	Screaming, crying, hitting	11 min. D	Ashcroft made Ray another lunch	+	Ray had been upset all morning
Mon/ 9-26/ 7 00 PM	H	Watching TV, mother told Ray it was time to take bath, Ray seemed anxious at dinner	A, S, E	Screaming, crying, kicking	15 min. D	Parents let him watch TV longer	+	
Tues/ 9-27/	H			No tantrum				No family problems
Wed/ 9-28/ 9 30 AM	H	Ray and Ashcroft reading picture book, she told him it was time to practice his printing (he dislikes)	A, S	Screaming, crying	4 min. D	Ashcroft said maybe he would print later, continued reading	− +	No family problems. Ray seemed OK before.

[1] Place: C = classroom, H = home, __ = ____ , __ = ____ , __ = ____
[2] Type: A = activity, S = social, C = covert, E = emotion, P = physical events, O = other, D = distant
[3] Data: record with F = frequency, D = duration, M = magnitude, Q = quality, or L = latency
[4] Type: + = get or obtain desirable or wanted object or activity
        − = escape, avoid, or reduce something unpleasant
        U = unpleasant consequence

Figure 3.5   An A-B-C log. Use this format to keep a chronological record of the behavior(s) in a functional analysis. This log is for tantrum behavior, with the boy's babysitter and parents as the observers. Although the format used in this log would work well for many behaviors, it can be modified to accommodate others. Codes are provided for place, antecedents, behaviors, and consequences; other codes can be added as needed.

Functional Analysis

SUMMARY RECORD: A-B-C Log of ___Tantrum___ Behavior

Person: _Ray_   Period covering: _9-26 to 10-9-94_   Observer(s): _Ms. Ashcroft, Mother, Father_

Factors Examined	Behavior Frequency (Duration)	Factors Examined	Behavior Frequency (Duration)
Day		**Immediate antecedents** (cont.)	
Monday	4 (12 min avg)	Social (describe):	
Tuesday	2 (6 min avg)	Asking him to do something he dislikes	8 (7.25 min avg)
Wednesday	1 (8 min)	Asking him to do something he likes or is neutral	4 (11 min avg)
Thursday	3 (7 min avg)		
Friday	0 —		
Saturday	1 (3 min)		
Sunday	1 (10 min)	Covert (describe): none clear	
Time AM / PM		Emotions (describe): Upset	4 (12 min avg)
12:00 - 1:59	1 (6 min) PM	Physical events (describe):	
2:00 - 3:59	2 (9 min avg) PM	Other (describe):	
4:00 - 5:59	1 (9 min) PM		
6:00 - 7:59	1 (4 min) AM 3 (12 min avg) PM		
8:00 - 9:59	3 (6 min avg) AM		
10:00 - 11:59	1 (11 min) AM		
Place		**Distant antecedents** (describe):	
Home	12 (8.5 min avg)	Parent arguments	3 (11 min avg)
Other places	never		
Immediate antecedents		**Consequences**	
Activities when behaviors occur (describe):		+ (describe):	
Playing	2 (10 min avg)	Got food he wanted 2 times	
Watching TV	3 (11 min avg)	Got to continue playing, reading, or watching TV 7 times	
Reading	1 (4 min)		
Awakening from nap	2 (45 min avg)	– (describe):	
Printing or other academic training	4 (9 min avg)	Avoided academic training 5 times	
Activities when it doesn't occur (describe): Seems to happen regardless of activities he's doing		U (describe): Scolded at each tantrum, but that didn't help	

Figure 3.6   A functional analysis summary record sheet for summarizing the A-B-C log data to permit patterns to emerge more clearly. This form can be modified to suit the needs of other programs.

record of Ray's tantrum behavior during a 2-week period, during which time he had 12 tantrums. As you examine this summary record, you'll probably notice several patterns, the clearest of which is that after a tantrum, the boy always got his way.

If the program will address a *behavioral deficit*, we'll need to look for instances when the behavior *could have* or *should have* occurred, but didn't. If the behavior was physically possible to perform and/or the types of antecedent that usually work for other people were present, we can assume that the person could have or should have performed the behavior. To do the functional analysis, we simply use *nonoccurrences* of the behavior rather than occurrences in the A-B-C log.

How to Use a Functional Analysis

The patterns in a functional analysis summary record should give us information about three important relationships. First, they should enable us to predict when the behavior is likely to occur—that is, the days and times, the places, and the immediate and distant conditions that are associated with an increased likelihood that the behavior will happen. Second, we should be able to see how different consequences relate to the behavior. And third, we should be able to examine the situations in which the behavior does *not* occur and discover *why* it doesn't. All this information will be useful in designing a program to change the behavior. If the patterns of relationships are clear, we can proceed to design the program.

What if the relationships are not clear? If we conduct a functional analysis and the summary record of a dozen instances of the behavior does not reveal sufficiently clear patterns, we should do two things (R. E. O'Neill, et al., 1990):

1. Check the data collection process for flaws, such as poorly defined behaviors, and determine whether the observers carried out the observation and recording correctly. If we find problems with the process, we'll need to correct the problems and collect another set of data.

2. If there were no problems in the data collection, observe another dozen or so instances of the behavior. Doing so probably will clarify the patterns.

If the summary record still contains no clear patterns, the next step would be to conduct *systematic environmental manipulations*—that is, to introduce or alter antecedents or consequences of the target behavior. For example, we could make certain requests of the person, place the individual in particular settings, give him or her access to certain objects or activities, or withhold social attention when the person performs the behavior. We can choose which specific manipulations to try by looking at interview and observational data and then generating hypotheses about why the behavior does or does not occur. By manipulating selected events, we can test whether they change the behavior—and if they do, we will know how these events influence the behavior.

Researchers have used systematic environmental manipulations in functional analyses to discover why autistic children repeatedly perform behaviors that cause severe injury to themselves—for example, biting their arms hard enough to draw blood. These studies have found that performing self-injurious behavior often functions to gain *escape* from certain activities, such as toothbrushing or learning a new skill (Carr, Taylor, & Robinson, 1991; Sasso et al., 1992; Steege et al., 1990). It may be that the children dislike these activities, or just find them unpleasant momentarily—for instance, a child may feel overwhelmed by the cognitive demands of a task. Studies have also used systematic environmental manipulations to find out how self-injurious behaviors can be stopped. A study by Mark Steege and his coworkers (1990) found that self-injury can be reduced by identifying and rewarding a noninjurious alternative behavior that allows the children to escape from disliked activities for brief periods of time.

Performing a careful functional analysis is a critical step in designing a program to change behavior. It is carried out before or during the *baseline phase* of behavior modification. Once we have identified the antecedents and consequences for doing or not doing the target behavior, we can select the most appropriate behavioral and cognitive methods to use in the *intervention phase* of a program designed to improve a person's behavior. Ideally, the program also should have a *follow-up phase* to determine the degree to which improvements in the target behavior are maintained after the intervention ends. The follow-up phase usually extends for several months; but sometimes it may cover only a few weeks, and sometimes it continues for years. (Go to ✔.)

✔ Concept Check 3.2

1. A behavior not mentioned in the book that qualifies for using frequency data in its assessment is _____ . ⇔
2. Rating your degree of self-esteem is an example of the type of data called _____ .
3. When opportunities to meet a behavioral criterion vary across time, it is useful to convert the data to _____ .
4. Assessing your own target behavior is called _____ .
5. An example of an indirect assessment method is _____ . ⇔
6. The only objective approach to assess covert events involves using _____ _____ measures.
7. The method of collecting data during a short segment of time at the beginning of each observation subperiod is called _____ .
8. An example of reactivity that students might show when they know they're being observed in school is _____ . ⇔
9. A chronological record of antecedents, behavior, and consequences is called a(n) _____ .

Answers: 1. saying "like" in your speech 2. magnitude 3. percentages 4. self-monitoring 5. interviews 6. physiological 7. time sampling 8. not cheating on a test 9. A-B-C log.

Application Exercise

At this point, you have narrowed down your potential outcome goals for a self-management program to three finalists, specified each goal carefully, and described the overt or covert behavior(s) you'll need to change to reach the goal. The main tasks in this application exercise will be to select one outcome goal for your project, arrive at a detailed definition of the target behavior, decide how to assess it, and outline the format for an A-B-C log you can use.

Most of the application exercises from this point on will contain a section giving a set of tips on how the techniques discussed in the text are usually applied by professionals when they design or conduct behavior change programs. These tips also apply to designing self-management programs. Here's the first Tips section.

Tips on Specifying and Assessing Behavior

As you read and carry out the tasks in this application exercise, you'll want to keep in mind the following helpful tips on specifying and assessing behavior.

1. Define your target behavior very carefully, giving details of where and when it occurs more than it should or doesn't occur as much as it should. Students often think, "I know what the behavior is," and define it unclearly. Specifying the behavior is the foundation for your program. Make the foundation strong.

2. For most projects, once you have selected a reasonable and specific behavioral goal, you should set some subgoals that will allow you to advance toward the goal gradually. Trying to achieve too much in too short a time will be discouraging and will undermine your motivation.

3. If the target behavior is covert, look for overt signs to assess, too. If you think you don't show any signs of the covert behavior, find out whether close friends or family members agree.

4. If your project will address a behavioral excess, find an alternative behavior to strengthen in its place. If the project will address a behavioral deficit, such as not exercising, you may need to decide how you'll make time for the desired behavior in your schedule.

5. If at all possible, use at least one direct assessment method.

6. Some operant behaviors, such as smoking and studying, can be closely tied to your emotional state—being bored or being under stress, for example. Keep track of your emotional behaviors if they apply.

7. Before using a data sheet or an A-B-C log, compose a draft of it and try it out to find "bugs" to correct.

8. You'll probably have enough time in the course you're taking to carry out baseline and intervention phases in your program. When the course is over, you

may want to continue the intervention or conduct a follow-up assessment of your target behavior.

The Next Steps in Your Program Design

The first task in this application exercise involves selecting one outcome goal for your project. The next step will be to fine-tune the definition of the target behavior you composed for the last application exercise. To do these tasks, you'll need to consult your answers on Work Sheet 2.1 from Chapter 2. Then we'll decide how to assess the behavior and outline the format for an A-B-C log for your project. Turn now to Work Sheet 3.1 and fill it out.

Summary

Target behaviors to be changed in behavior modification programs must be defined in terms of specific, objective, and measurable actions. Using pinpointing to define the behavior in this way makes it possible to specify a behavioral goal to be achieved by the end of the program and behavioral subgoals to be reached along the way. By achieving the behavioral goal, the person should accomplish the broad outcome goals that were selected for the program.

Three aspects of target behavior should be considered in designing a program to change behavior. First, some target behaviors are very complex, often requiring a sequence of response links to be performed as a chain of behavior. Because learning to perform complex behaviors can be very difficult, it may be necessary to conduct a task analysis to identify the component responses. Second, changing a target behavior sometimes produces response generalization in which similar changes occur in another behavior that was not specifically addressed in the intervention. It may be possible to use this phenomenon to make behavior modification programs more efficient. Third, an effective way to reduce a target behavior involves encouraging the person to replace it with an alternative response.

Assessments of a target behavior use one or more type of data, including frequency, duration, and magnitude. Observations of the behavior can be conducted through self-monitoring or can involve any of several direct and indirect assessment methods. Different approaches for timing of behavioral assessments can also be used, including continuous recording, interval recording, and time sampling. If people know their behavior is being observed, the accuracy and validity of behavioral assessments may be reduced by reactivity. Functional analyses consist of observing target behaviors and recording data in A-B-C logs and summary records; these data are then examined to identify connections between the behavior and its antecedents and consequences.

Key Terms and Review Questions

Key Terms

target behaviors

pinpointing

outcome goals

behavioral goal

behavioral subgoals

chain

task analysis

response generalization

alternative responses

frequency

duration

magnitude

self-monitoring

direct assessment methods

indirect assessment methods

continuous recording

interval recording

time sampling

reactivity

functional analysis

A-B-C log

summary record

Review Questions

1. What is pinpointing, and how is it used in defining target behaviors?

2. What are outcome goals and behavioral goals, and how are they different?

3. Define "behavioral subgoals" and give two examples. Why are subgoals useful?

4. What is a meta-analysis?

5. Describe the task analysis reported by Fawcett and Miller (1975).

6. Construct a task analysis of making a peanut butter and jelly sandwich, identifying any chains and links within them.

7. Give two examples of alternative responses that were not described in the text, and list the behavioral excesses they might be helpful in reducing.

8. Define the three main types of data—frequency, duration, and magnitude—one can use in assessing behavior.

9. Distinguish between direct and indirect assessment methods and give two examples of each.

10. Define and give an example of continuous recording.

11. Define and give an example of interval recording.

12. Define and give an example of time sampling.

13. What is a functional analysis, and what does it tell you?

14. How are A-B-C logs and summary records used in functional analyses?

15. Describe the types of antecedents that can be assessed with an A-B-C log.

Related Readings

Ciminero, A. R., Calhoun, K. S., & Adams, H. E. (Eds.) (1986). *Handbook of behavioral assessment* (2nd ed.). New York: Wiley.

Groden, G. (1989). A guide for conducting a comprehensive behavioral analysis of a target behavior. *Journal of Behavior Therapy and Experimental Psychiatry, 20,* 163–169.

Gross, A. M., & Drabman, R. S. (1982). Teaching self-recording, self-evaluation, and self-reward to nonclinic children and adolescents. In P. Karoly & F. H. Kanfer (Eds.), *Self-management and behavior change: From theory to practice.* New York: Pergamon Press.

Ollendick, T. H., & Hersen, M. (Eds.) (1986). *Child behavioral assessment: Principles and procedures.* New York: Pergamon Press.

O'Neill, R. E., Horner, R. H., Albin, R. W., Storey, K., & Sprague, J. R. (1990). *Functional analysis of problem behavior: A practical assessment guide.* Sycamore, IL: Sycamore.

Name _____   Day & time
                                      class meets_____

Date _____

Chapter 3: Work Sheet 3.1

1. Look over the three outcome goal finalists you selected in your Chapter 2 work sheet and do two things. First, check to see whether any of these goals involves changing *more than two different types of behavior,* such as smoking, exercising, and dieting. If so, either eliminate those goals or alter them so that you do not have to change more than two behaviors. Having one or two different types of behavior is OK, but more than two will be very difficult for your first self-management project. Second, reconsider the *ratings* and *how long* data in the Chapter 2 work sheet to select your outcome goal. Keep in mind that we're trying to identify for your first project one outcome goal that you'll find interesting, important to achieve, and fairly challenging.

The outcome goal you selected for your self-management program is:

2. Give a detailed definition of the target behavior(s). If the behavior involves a long chain or several discrete parts—as exercising often does, for instance—include a *task analysis* in your definition.

If you are planning to change a *behavioral excess,* think about the behavior and list when and where it occurs most often. If the behavior is covert, also describe a few actual instances.

If you are planning to change a *behavioral deficit,* list when and where you think the behavior should or could occur—for instance, when and where might you be able to study or exercise.

3. To decide how you might assess the target behavior, answer the following items:

State your specific *behavioral goal*(s):

Examine the following aspects of the target behavior(s). Circle any aspects that fill in the blank in the statement, "I'd like to change instances of the behavior in terms of their _____ ."

- Frequency

- Duration

- Intensity, degree, or size

- Latency

- Quality

For any aspects you did *not* circle, write next to them *why* they are not needed. For example, you could write next to latency, "My behavioral goal involves only the number of cigarettes I smoke."

4. Answer the following questions. (a) What *direct* and *indirect* assessment methods can you use to measure the target behavior? (b) If you haven't included direct methods, why not? (c) Which approach will you use to time your assessments: continuous recording, interval recording, or time sampling?

5. In the space provided, outline the columns and headings you might use for an A-B-C log in doing a functional analysis of your target behavior. You may find that the format in Figure 3.5 will work well for you.

NOTE: If you will be submitting work sheets to your instructor or to a fellow student, make a copy of each sheet before submitting it.

Part Two

Methods of Changing Operant Behavior

4 Identifying, Developing, and Managing Operant Antecedents

Prologue

"I feel like such a social klutz. How is it you get so many dates, Dina, and I haven't had one for weeks?" Kim asked. "I don't know," Dina replied, "I guess I just go places where there are guys, and I flirt. When I flirt, guys ask me out." Dina has just described in casual terms that her flirting is an antecedent to guys' behavior of asking for a date. Most men and women look for cues or signs that the person they find attractive is interested in them. OK, but what exactly is flirting—What are the cues people look for, which set the occasion for them to show interest? When Kim asked Dina what she did to flirt, Dina said, "Well, I guess I just show an interest in the guy— what he says and what his interests are. Stuff like that."

Dina's right, but her answer is incomplete and a bit vague. A study by Charlene Muehlenhard and her colleagues (1986) with male college students identified 36 flirting cues men look for to indicate that a woman would be interested in dating them. These men's ratings of videotaped male–female interactions showed that some of the strongest cues they perceived as indicating a woman's interest included her:

- Complimenting the man.
- Asking him questions about himself.
- Making it clear that she has noticed him in the past—for example, by recalling something he wore on another occasion.
- Mentioning an activity they could to do together—pointing out, for example, that a movie she's interested in seeing will be playing at a local theater.
- Looking at him almost constantly during a conversation.
- Touching him briefly.
- Stopping what she is doing if he talks to her.

Both men and women behave in ways that can set the occasion for another person to respond with interest, and they learn to use their behavior as antecedents to increase their chances of getting the consequences they want, such as being asked out on dates. One objective in behavior therapy for individuals with poor dating skills is to teach them how and when to behave in ways that serve as cues for other people to respond with interest (Conger & Conger, 1986).

This chapter focuses on the role of antecedents in producing operant behavior. We will study how antecedent cues set the occasion for behavior to take place, how we acquire these cues, what kinds of event can serve as cues, and how we can manage antecedents to increase or decrease operant behavior.

Setting the Occasion for Behavior

Antecedents tend to "push" or "pull" us toward doing, thinking, or feeling something. If you notice *hunger pangs* when you see a *restaurant* and know that it is *supper time*, these three antecedent cues set the occasion for you to go into the restaurant and have supper. In the past, going into restaurants when these antecedents were present led to pleasant outcomes, such as tasty food. We learn the cues that tell us when and where to perform or not perform certain responses by linking the cues with the behaviors and the consequences that follow.

What Stimuli Can Be Antecedents

People's behavior happens in a *context* that includes objects or other people, and anything in the context that arouses behavior is a *stimulus*. Almost any stimulus—any event, person, object, or place—can serve as an antecedent for operant behavior. For instance, we saw in the story about Kim and Dina that the things people do—in this case, flirting—can set the occasion for other people to behave in certain ways. Some other examples of antecedents influencing behavior are:

- A teacher asking a question sets the occasion for students to raise their hands.
- Seeing some friends leads you to wave and call to them.
- Tasting a friend's ice cream persuades you to order some of your own.
- Hearing someone yell, "Fire!" gets you to leave a building.
- Feeling someone you like caress your neck leads you to hug him or her.
- Being in a bar sets the occasion for ordering a drink.
- Thinking about an argument you had makes you act like a grouch.
- Saying to yourself, "I hate this book," makes you stop reading.
- Feeling tired induces you to take a nap.
- Friends' asking you to go to the gym with them leads you to get some exercise.

As you can see in this list, antecedents can be overt or covert and can involve any of our senses. You also may be wondering whether a stimulus that serves as an antecedent for one person can have a different effect for other people. The answer is yes—the effects of particular antecedents can differ from one person to the next (Wahler & Fox, 1981). For instance, some students never raise their hands when a teacher asks a question, and some students raise their hands only when they are sure they know the answer. We learn when and when not to respond.

Most antecedents are present shortly before the behavior and are called *immediate antecedents*—imagine yourself heading quickly toward an exit after hearing someone in the building yell, "Fire!" (Groden, 1989; Wahler & Fox, 1981). Most immediate antecedents are less dramatic but they can also be very useful to learn. For instance, Susan Ziegler (1987) trained beginning tennis players to use cues to

. Identifying, Developing, and Managing Operant Antecedents

help them hit balls projected from a machine. She first found that simply saying "Concentrate" and "Keep your eye on the ball" brought no improvement. But skills in hitting the balls—with both forehand and backhand strokes—improved substantially when the would-be tennis players were taught to give themselves four verbal cues: saying "Ready" when the machine was about to project the next ball, "Ball" when the ball shot out of the machine, "Bounce" when the ball hit the surface of the court, and "Hit" when they saw the racquet meet the ball. Training can help people learn the cues they fail to perceive on their own.

Immediate antecedents don't have to be discrete events, such as saying a word. They can be continuing or ongoing conditions, too. For example, a study found that elderly patients in a mental institution communicated more frequently with each other and with staff when the institution made two environmental changes: they rearranged the furniture on the wards so that the patients sat around small tables rather than along walls, and they presented meals and snacks buffet style, so that the patients served themselves rather than being given their food on individual trays (Melin & Götestam, 1981). Another study found that having children play organized outdoor games while they waited for school to open in the morning reduced their aggressive acts by more than half (Murphy, Hutchison, & Bailey, 1983).

Antecedents that precede the behavior by several minutes, hours, or much longer amounts of time are called *distant antecedents* (Groden, 1989; Wahler & Fox, 1981). Distant antecedents often continue to affect behavior for a long time after the occurrence of the actual antecedent because they have strong emotional components; thus, the behavior of a child who is a witness to or a victim of violence at home might be influenced hours or days later by such events. (Go to 📖 .)

Identifying Antecedents

Not all stimuli that precede a behavior set the occasion for the person to respond. Some stimuli may just happen now and then to coincide in time and place with the actual antecedents. To get a reliable picture of the relationships between behavior and the stimuli that precede it, we will need to make systematic observations in a functional analysis of the behavior. Although it's useful to have hunches about which stimuli are antecedents for the target behavior, hunches should serve only as hypotheses, not conclusions. We should do a functional analysis, looking for patterns in relationships between the behavior and its preceding stimuli, to confirm or disconfirm our hypotheses.

In programs to reduce behavioral excesses, antecedents that are *overt and immediate* are usually fairly easy to identify in a functional analysis because they are present and observable just before the target behavior occurs. But sometimes overt, immediate antecedents are not easily noticed. For instance, we saw in Chapter 2 that children in a classroom become distracted from their studies when they are seated too close together. This antecedent is overt and immediate, but might be overlooked. Antecedents that are *covert* or *distant* can be relatively difficult to identify. Covert antecedents are not directly observable and consist of thoughts, feel-

Case Study 4.1
The "Betrayed" Husband

Israel Goldiamond (1965) described the case of a 29-year-old male graduate student. He began behavior therapy in an effort to save his marriage 2 years after his wife had committed the "ultimate betrayal" with his best friend. This event was especially distressing to him because he

> had suggested that the friend keep his wife company while he was in the library at night. Since that time, whenever he saw his wife, [he] screamed at her for hours on end or else was ashamed of himself for having done so and spent hours sulking and brooding. (p. 856)

The antecedents that set the occasion for his behavior were probably both immediate—seeing his wife—and distant—the betrayal. Part of the therapy program to change this behavior involved altering the cues. For instance, to decrease the activity of sulking, the husband was told to sulk as much as he wanted, but not in the rooms at home where he usually sulked, and not in the presence of his wife. When he finished sulking, he could leave his sulking place and join his wife. This method helped decrease his sulking duration to about half an hour per day for the first couple of weeks, after which it stopped entirely. Similarly, individuals who worry chronically can successfully restrict their worrying to certain times or places (Borkovec et al., 1983).

ings, and physiological states. Often the person whose target behavior is to be changed isn't aware of these cues. Careful direct observations, along with well-chosen and properly administered indirect assessment methods, such as interviews, are needed to discover covert and distant antecedents.

© 1994 Washington Post Writers Group. Reprinted with permission.

Covert antecedents can have powerful effects on people's behavior.

What if we want to correct a behavioral deficit—how do we identify cues to responses that rarely or never happen? We saw in Chapter 3 that functional analyses of behavioral deficits look for antecedents and consequences for *nonoccurrences* of responses that could have or should have occurred. Knowing what cues usually precede people's *not* performing the behavior when they could or should do so can help us decide how to alter those antecedents to make the behavior occur more frequently. For instance, individuals who could and should exercise may fail to do so partly because they think, "But it's so boring," each time they consider exercising. They might begin exercising if they could change their thinking and find exercises that are more fun.

How We Learn Antecedents

Wouldn't it be wonderful if children knew how to behave correctly and maturely in all situations? In school, for instance, if a substitute teacher were to take over their class, they would sit politely and attentively, waiting to carry out the teacher's instructions. But often that's not what happens. Instead, students recognize from past experience that things will be different now—the rules and consequences established by their regular teacher are no longer in effect. How do they know this?

Learning a Discrimination

Learning to distinguish between different stimulus conditions and respond differently toward them is called **discrimination learning**. For example, we learned as toddlers to say "Mommy" when we saw our mothers, but not when we saw other women or our fathers. In early childhood, we learned to say "ess" when we saw the letter *S*, but not when we saw the number *8* or the letters *J* and *Z*. And we learned later to step on the brake pedal of a car we're driving when a traffic light is red, but not when it is green. The stimulus conditions in these examples are antecedents for our behavior.

We learn to discriminate through the process of **differential reinforcement** in which responding in a certain way (such as by saying "Mommy") to a particular stimulus (mother) leads to a rewarding consequence (in this case, lavish attention and praise), but responding in the same way to other stimuli (father, uncles) does not. This process is called *differential* reinforcement because the consequence of making that response is different for different stimuli. Thus, differential reinforcement involves antecedent stimuli of two types (Michael, 1982):

- A stimulus that is associated with reinforcement of a particular response is called a **discriminative stimulus**, or S^D (pronounced "ess-DEE"). Thus an S^D becomes a cue for performing the behavior, which probably will lead to reward.

- A stimulus that is associated with *not* being reinforced for a particular response is called an **S-delta**, or S^Δ (Δ is the fourth letter in the Greek alphabet). Thus the S^Δ becomes a cue for *not* performing the behavior.

For children in school, the regular teacher is usually an S^D for paying attention, and a substitute teacher is an S^Δ, all too often! Another example of an S^D from everyday life is a person's smile, because we've learned that a pleasant interaction is likely to follow, whereas a frown tends to serve as an S^Δ.

A study by William Redd and J. S. Birnbrauer (1969) demonstrated how people who dispense rewards can become discriminative stimuli (S^Ds) for the behavior of others. The subjects in this study were mentally retarded 12- to 15-year-old boys who received praise and sweets (candy, bites of ice cream, or sips of cola) every minute or so in a playroom in which there were toys and other boys. Two adults, who provided the praise and sweets as rewards, served as the stimuli. One adult was a woman who dispensed the rewards to the boys only when they engaged in cooperative play, moving or manipulating a toy with another boy. The other adult, a man, provided the same rewards, but at regular intervals of time that had no relation to what the boys were doing. Because the man's rewards were not contingent on any particular behavior, playing cooperatively was unlikely to receive rewards very often from him. In later tests, the children showed much more cooperative play when the woman entered the playroom than when the man entered, indicating that the woman had become an S^D for cooperative play and the man had not. Then when the adults switched modes of giving rewards, the man became the S^D for cooperative play and the woman lost her influence on the boys' play behavior.

Another study showed a similar effect when the consequence was punishment (Rolider, Cummings, & Van Houten, 1991). Two teachers were present during training sessions, but only one reprimanded the subjects for misbehaviors. Later tests showed that the subjects' misbehaviors decreased only when the reprimanding teacher was present. These findings indicate that teachers and other authority figures can also become antecedents for the withholding or suppression of inappropriate behaviors. The effect of antecedents on behavior depends on the consequences with which they have been associated in the past.

In our discussion of discrimination learning thus far, you may have gotten the impression that we learn to respond only to the particular, exact S^D we experienced in our learning. This is not the case. As we learn to make a particular response to a specific S^D, we also learn to respond in the same way to other stimuli that are similar to it. This phenomenon is called **stimulus generalization**. For example, children who have learned to say "dee" whenever they see the letter *d* may also say "dee" when they see a *b* or even a *p*. These letters are similar, and we may be tempted to think that generalization simply reflects a failure to discriminate carefully (Rilling, 1977). But stimulus generalization seems to be more than that, since when children learn to raise their hands to ask questions in kindergarten, they continue to use this convention when they enter first grade; similarly, when they learn to say "please" to request something from their parents, they tend to do the same with other people. These behaviors probably aren't mistakes, but they show stimulus generalization.

In a related phenomenon called *stimulus equivalence*, two or more physically different stimuli come to serve the same purposes and can be used interchangeably (Sidman & Tailby, 1982). For instance, suppose no one told you the numbers *4* and *IV* represent the same quantity, but you had the following two experiences in childhood. First, when your father taught you about numbers, he showed you four dots and wrote next to them, "There are *4*." Then, when your teacher taught you about Roman numerals, she drew four dots on the board and wrote next to them, "There are *IV*." If you remembered both experiences, wouldn't you have assumed that, or at least wondered whether, *4* and *IV* are interchangeable? If someone at that time asked you count out *4* fingers on one hand and *IV* fingers on the other hand, you'd have counted four on each hand. Stimulus generalization and stimulus equivalence involve learning processes that allow us to connect a variety of antecedent stimuli to a single response without actual training for each stimulus.

Stimulus Control

After people have learned to discriminate between different stimuli and have associated a response with an S^D as an antecedent, this cue comes to exert stimulus control over the behavior. **Stimulus control** refers to the ability of an antecedent to influence the individual's performance of the behavior (Albin & Horner, 1988; Rilling, 1977). When an antecedent exerts a high degree of stimulus control, the behavior tends to occur mainly or always in the presence of the cue, and when the cue is present, the response is highly likely to occur.

Our everyday lives contain many examples of cues that have a high degree of stimulus control. For instance, when we hear a telephone ringing, we're very likely to answer it, even if we have an answering machine. And our answering the phone—that is, picking up the receiver and saying, "Hello"— happens only when the phone rings. We don't go around answering the phone when it hasn't rung! Another example is found when someone greets us, saying, "Hi. How are you?" Even if we're not feeling all that well, we're likely to reply, "Fine, thanks. How are you?" Many behaviors for which antecedents have a high degree of stimulus control are habitual and automatic—we give them very little thought, or no thought at all. All habitual, automatic behaviors happen in response to antecedents with high stimulus control.

The everyday examples of antecedents we've considered were generally simple, involving only one stimulus. But our everyday lives often have much more complex antecedents, consisting of several relevant stimuli. For example,

> if you are driving on a two-lane road and you come up behind a slow-moving vehicle, you only pass when the center line is broken on your side *and* there are no oncoming cars in the opposite lane. [The antecedent] consists of at least three elements: (1) the slow-moving vehicle ahead, (2) the broken center line, and (3) the clear opposite lane. If any one of those elements were absent, you would be unlikely to pass. The combination sets the *context.* (W. M. Baum, 1994, p. 89, italics added)

Oftentimes the antecedent is the overall context, rather than a collection of stimuli (D. M. Baer, Wolf, & Risley, 1987; Michael, 1982; Wahler & Fox, 1981). When this is the case, stimulus control is described as *contextual control* (Haring & Kennedy, 1990).

✓ Concept Check 4.1

1. An example of a fragrance or smell as an antecedent that leads to a behavior is _____ . ⇔

2. Antecedents are relatively easy to identify in a functional analysis if they are _____ and _____ .

3. We learn to respond differently to different stimuli through _____ learning.

4. An example of differential reinforcement in learning a sport skill is _____ . ⇔

5. In your last answer, the S-delta (S^Δ) might be _____ . ⇔

6. A child who uses a key to open a padlock after having learned only how to open a door lock is showing stimulus _____ .

7. An example of an antecedent with a high degree of stimulus control in a high school classroom might be _____ . ⇔

Answers: 1. the smell of food gets you to go to the kitchen 2. overt, immediate 3. discrimination 4. rewarding a baseball batter for swinging at a "strike" pitch 5. a pitch that is "high and outside" 6. generalization 7. the end-of-class bell

Behavior therapists have used principles of stimulus control in treating people with insomnia. One intervention was conducted with men and women who were over 60 years of age and had experienced insomnia for at least the past 6 months (Puder et al., 1983). The treatment consisted of teaching these individuals to reassociate the bed and bedroom with going to sleep quickly by having them (1) go to bed only when sleepy, leave the bed if they are awake for 10 minutes, and return to bed only when drowsy again, and (2) go to another room to engage in activities that are incompatible with sleep, such as reading, watching TV, and worrying. This treatment was effective for most of the clients, and the data across all clients showed that the average latencies in getting to sleep declined from over an hour per night to about half an hour. (Go to ✓ .)

Shortcut Stimulus Control Methods

Using differential reinforcement methods alone to teach someone when, where, and how to perform behaviors can be very time-consuming because the person doesn't know what responses to make. You would present the cues (the S^Ds) that should lead to the behavior, but the person would not respond correctly very often.

Fortunately, we can shortcut this process by capitalizing on the learning and cognitive abilities that develop in early childhood. These abilities enable people to use antecedents with existing stimulus control to help them learn or perform new or infrequent responses. You would still need to present the appropriate S^Ds, monitor the person's responses, and make sure reinforcement follows the correct behavior, but the person would be more likely to respond correctly. These shortcut methods are ones we commonly use in everyday life. Let's see what they are.

Prompting and Fading

A **prompt** is a stimulus that *reminds* us to perform a behavior we already know how to do or *helps us perform* a behavior we don't do often or well. Our everyday lives contain many prompts, such as the sound a car makes to remind us to use our seat belts and the description a coach gives of how to perform a sport or dance movement. Using prompts to remind or help people to perform a behavior is called *prompting*. In behavior modification interventions, each prompt is presented along with S^Ds that should themselves set the occasion for the initiation of the behavior, minus the prompt, in the future. The purpose of prompting is to enable stimulus control to "shift" from the prompt to the S^D. Several types of prompt are used in behavior modification.

Physical Guidance Prompts

Suppose you were trying to help 3-year-old Cecily print the first letter of her name. You'd probably grasp her hand and guide her printing with your own hand. Manually moving part of the person's body through the desired action or sequence is called *physical guidance*.

This prompting method is often used in teaching simple tasks to children who have not yet developed very much language. For instance, infants who are physically guided to shake a rattle and hear its sound soon learn to perform that behavior on their own to produce the reinforcing sound. Older children who are retarded, autistic, or otherwise learning-impaired also benefit from manual prompts for basic tasks, such as using a toilet or rolling balls to one another (Kazdin & Erickson, 1975; Lovaas, 1977; Strain, Shores, & Kerr, 1976).

Physical guidance is also very useful with older children and adults who are trying to learn or improve complex skills, such as swimming, playing a violin, or dancing. A violin teacher might put the violin in the playing position and manually move the child's head so that the chin clamps the instrument in place, position the left hand to grasp the fingerboard correctly, position the right hand to grasp the bow, and move the bowing arm back and forth. Elderly people can also benefit from physical guidance prompts. For example, individuals in nursing homes are often unoccupied, even when recreational activities are available. Placing recreational equipment in their hands and helping them to use it can increase their involvement in these activities, as Figure 4.1 depicts (McClannahan & Risley, 1975).

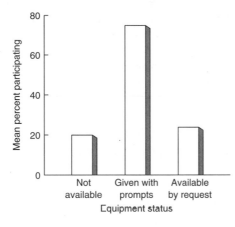

Figure 4.1 Mean percent of nursing home residents participating—that is, being engaged with recreational equipment, materials, or other people—while in a communal lounge. Data were taken on days when recreational material was either not available, given directly to individuals with prompts to encourage participation, or available only by request. (Data from McClannahan & Risley, 1975.)

Verbal Prompts

"Look at the doggie," parents might say to get their child to pay attention to what the animal is doing. Words that are spoken or written to induce a specific behavior, called *verbal prompts*, are useful with individuals who can understand the words; they can be very helpful when teaching new speaking skills and material. For instance, the director of a dramatic play might provide the first few words of an actor's lines in rehearsal when the actor can't recall them. In such a case, the actor usually hasn't mastered the lines fully yet and simply needs a reminder.

SHORT RIBS reprinted by permission of United Features Syndicate, Inc.

Verbal prompts must be clearly stated so that the learner can use them effectively.

Verbal prompts function as reminders and statements of the behavior to be performed and have been used effectively in many different ways, for instance:

- Researchers had a passenger in a car flash a sign that read, "Please buckle up— I care" to drivers of stopped cars who were not using their seat belts (Geller, Bruff, & Nimmer, 1985). Of the nearly 900 drivers who looked at the sign, 22% buckled up before driving on.
- Four brain-injured adults were able to modify their behavior to avoid accidents at home by using checklists that described such potential hazards as a drinking glass near the edge of a table and presented steps to eliminate each hazard (O'Reilly, Green, & Braunling-McMorrow, 1990).
- Customers at an employee cafeteria were given the opportunity to play a game to make their diets healthier (Zifferblatt, Wilbur, & Pinsky, 1980). Each time they stood in the serving line, they got cards to collect that had verbal prompts, such as "The idea is valid—have a salad." At the end of 6 weeks, each customer had a collection of cards to be used to win prizes. Even though winning prizes did not depend on the foods the customers bought, their diets improved during the intervention.

Verbal prompts don't have to be as direct as those we've considered thus far. Sometimes they're less direct, as in the question, "What is the next thing you need to do?" Notice that the question doesn't say what the specific behavior should be, but it still serves to encourage the hearer to make the appropriate response.

Pictorial, Gestural, and Auditory Prompts

The knobs and buttons on the dashboards of new cars are stamped with icons representing the function of each knob. These icons make it easier to learn how to operate the car. *Pictorial prompts* consist of pictures—for example, drawings, paintings, photographs, or video images. Sometimes a pictorial prompt is just an element in the picture that is accentuated to make it more distinctive so that the discrimination is easier to learn, as Figure 4.2 illustrates (Gibson & Levin, 1975). Although pictorial prompts usually consist of a single picture to induce a person to perform a specific response, they can also show a sequence of pictures to prompt each link in a complex behavioral chain. Programs to teach the life-saving technique of cardiopulmonary resuscitation (CPR) usually provide pictorial prompts to help people learn the complex, step-by-step procedure.

Figure 4.2 A pictorial prompt designed to accentuate the feature that distinguishes two stimuli children often find hard to discriminate. In this case, the distinctive feature is the diagonal leg of the *R*. Similar prompts can be made to help children discriminate between other letters, such as *F* and *E, c* and *e,* and *b* and *d.*

The hand signals of this traffic officer provide clear gestural prompts.

Gestural prompts are physical motions that were previously learned S^{D}s for specific behaviors. For example, a frown in certain contexts means "Stop that." An orchestra conductor signals to musicians to play louder by using gestures, such as turning his or her palms up and moving the hands in a high and upward direction. And teachers use pointing as a gesture to direct students' attention toward material on the chalkboard or in a diagram, to enable them to learn the material and study it better on their own.

Auditory prompts are sounds other than words that can serve as S^{D}s for particular behaviors. An alarm beeping on your wristwatch during the first week or two of a semester to remind you to check your class schedule for the time and place of an upcoming class would be an example. An intervention demonstrated that auditory prompts can help incontinent children who are moderately to severely retarded learn toileting behaviors (K. Mahoney, Van Wagenen, & Myerson, 1971). The procedure involved presenting an auditory signal through an electronic device repeatedly with each link the children practiced in the chain of toileting responses (walking to the toilet, lowering their pants, and so on). Once each child had learned to perform the chain in response to the signal, that same sound was used in a urine alarm apparatus, like the one we described in Chapter 2, that was placed in the child's pants. When the child released urine during regular activities, such as playing, the first drops triggered the signal, thereby prompting the child to perform the chain of toileting responses. This toilet training procedure was effective in eliminating "accidents" for four of the five retarded children.

Fading

We saw earlier that prompts are useful because they already have a high degree of stimulus control to remind or help individuals to perform specific behaviors. If a prompt is presented along with one or more S^Ds that normally are antecedents for that behavior, stimulus control for the behavior will "shift" from the prompt to the S^Ds. When this shifting develops, we can reduce the person's reliance on the prompt through a process called **fading** in which the prompt is gradually removed or changed so that it becomes increasingly like the normal antecedent for the behavior (Deitz & Malone, 1985; Demchak, 1990; Rilling, 1977).

Prompts can be faded in several different ways (Demchak, 1990). In one of the more commonly used fading approaches, *decreasing assistance*, the frequency or magnitude of the prompt's presentation is gradually reduced. To reduce its frequency, you would simply present the prompt with the S^D less and less often until the person responds reliably to the S^D alone. For instance, a program that used physical guidance and other prompts to train profoundly retarded women to stamp return addresses on envelopes faded the prompts by gradually reducing the number of occasions on which the trainer helped the women perform parts of the task (Schepis, Reid, & Fitzgerald, 1987).

Reducing the magnitude of a prompt can be accomplished in two ways. First, you can change the type of prompt from one that is very direct, such as physically guiding a child's printing the letter *C* on a sheet of paper, to one that is less direct, such as gesturing the shape of a *C* on the paper. Second, you can weaken the prompt's completeness or strength. If you were physically guiding a child's printing with your entire hand, you could reduce this prompt by (1) beginning to guide with only two fingers, (2) then using only one finger, and (3) eventually following, or "shadowing," the child's actions with your hand but not touching the child. If the prompt were pictorial, such as a drawing of the letter the child was to trace, you could weaken the lines in the drawing, as Figure 4.3 illustrates. Teachers in a school for retarded children used this fading approach to help 8-year-old Danny match digits he could already name, such as *5*, with the number of objects each digit represented (Murrell, Hardy, & Martin, 1974). A digit and its corresponding number of circles were printed on a page, and Danny had to identify the digit and place circle cutouts on the printed circles. The lines of the circles were weakened over time

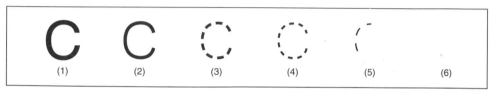

Figure 4.3   Illustration of fading a pictorial prompt. The child would start with the drawing that is darkest and most complete (level 1), tracing the letter with a marker pen. Once the child has mastered that level of prompt magnitude, he or she can progress to level 2, and so on to level 6, where no pictorial prompt is given.

until no circles were on the page, but Danny could still place on the page as many circles as were represented by the digit.

You may have noticed that progressing from one level to the next is fairly easy when decreasing assistance methods are used in fading prompts. This is done to promote *errorless learning*—fading that is introduced so gradually that the person makes few or no errors while learning the task (Deitz & Malone, 1985; Rilling, 1977). Another commonly used fading technique, called *increasing assistance*, takes a very different approach (Demchak, 1990). For each instance of the target behavior, the trainer starts by giving a minimal prompt to encourage the person to respond correctly. If the individual does not respond correctly, the trainer gradually introduces stronger prompts until the correct response occurs. For each subsequent instance of that behavior, the trainer starts again with a minimal prompt and uses stronger prompts only when necessary. Although the level of assistance increases when individuals do not respond correctly, they require less and less assistance as they learn the task. This is why the method of increasing assistance is considered a fading technique.

In the last method we will consider for fading prompts, *delayed prompting* (or *time delay*), a normal antecedent for the behavior and the prompt are presented together initially, but the prompt is delayed for increasing lengths of time as the person learns the task (Demchak, 1990; Touchette & Howard, 1984). If a delayed prompting procedure is designed appropriately, the person will begin to respond correctly during the delay period, before the prompt occurs, and will make few or no errors in learning the task. Technically, delayed prompting is not really a fading method because the prompt is not actually changed or removed (Deitz & Malone, 1985).

Designing an effective and efficient fading procedure for a particular person is more an art than a "science" and requires some experience and skill. One of the most important concerns is the choice of "steps"—where a *step* is the movement from one level to the next—particularly with respect to the *sizes of the steps*. When the steps are too large, the person will make many errors, and the usefulness of the prompts will be impaired. But when the steps are too small, the person may become too dependent on the prompts, and the learning process will become inefficient and tedious. Psychologist O. Ivar Lovaas, who has worked extensively with autistic children, has recommended that the rate of fading be determined by the child's ability.

> In some cases, very rapid, almost sudden, fading is appropriate and possible. In other cases, for certain children performing certain behaviors, fading is a slow process. The rule is to use the minimal number of prompts necessary to obtain the desired response. (1977, p. 20)

The same recommendation probably applies to all fading methods with all individuals. We can cite a few guidelines for the design of fading procedures:

- List the steps you plan to use in the fading procedure and the criteria for advancing from one step to the next.

- Keep the steps small enough to ensure a minimum of errors, even when increasing assistance methods are used.
- Monitor the person's performance carefully. When errors begin to occur, try going back to the preceding step for a while and then advance again to the step at which errors occurred. If more errors occur at that step, you may need to revise the size of that step, and perhaps others, you had planned to use.

Therapists and teachers who help individuals acquire new skills typically intend for their clients or students to function without prompts in their everyday lives. Fading is the best way to remove these cues.

Modeling and Instructions

Modeling and instructions are also shortcut methods by which we can use antecedents with a high degree of stimulus control to help a person learn and perform new or infrequent responses. We saw in Chapter 1 that **modeling** is a process by which people learn behaviors by watching what other individuals do. In modeling, the antecedent is the modeled action, which *demonstrates how* to perform the behavior. For example, a woodshop teacher might show a student how to install a new sheet of sandpaper in an electric sander. **Instructions** are oral or written information designed to *describe how* to perform the target behavior. For instance, a VCR owner's manual describes how to set the device to record a program you won't be there to watch. Modeling and instructions occur very frequently in our everyday lives because they are easy to use and enable people to learn behavior with few or no errors. When these shortcut stimulus control methods are used in behavior change programs, they also indicate *when* to perform the behavior and *what consequences* are likely to follow it.

Applying Modeling and Instructions

Modeling and instructions often exert a high degree of stimulus control over behavior and can be thought of as "elaborate prompts." They're prompts because they help the person perform a new or infrequent behavior; they're elaborate because they provide so much information: how to perform the behavior, and often when to do it and what the payoff will probably be. Having people know the likely consequences is an important element in getting them to perform a behavior. In many cases, there are built-in or "natural" rewards for behavior—for example, we may want to learn to play a musical instrument because we enjoy the activity or see some utility in it. When strong natural rewards exist, modeling or instructions can lead to improved performance without the need to provide additional rewards. But many behaviors people need to learn have inadequate or no natural rewards. For instance, researchers showed that second-graders' frequent classroom misbehavior didn't improve when the teacher simply wrote instructions on the chalkboard: "We sit in our seats," "We raise our hands to talk," "We face the front of the room," and "We keep our desks clear" (O'Leary et al., 1969). But the students misbehaved only about half as often when the teacher specified and administered rewards for following the rules.

Instructions have been used effectively in changing a wide variety of behaviors. Charlotte Patterson and Walter Mischel (1975) used instructions to help preschoolers keep working on a task of copying *X*s and *O*s on a sheet of paper when they could be distracted by a Clown Box that contained a tape recorder that invited the children to play a game. Two of the instructions the children received to resist the invitations were:

> When Mr. Clown Box says to look at him and play with him, you can just look at your work, not at him, and say, "No, I can't; I'm working." And when you say it, do it. That's Number One: he says "look" and you say, "No I can't; I'm working." The second thing you can do is . . . say to yourself, "I'm going to keep working so I can play with the fun toys and Mr. Clown Box later" (p. 371)

Not all children were given instructions on how to resist the invitations, but all were promised that they could play with the fun toys and the Clown Box if they finished their work quickly while the researcher was out of the room; otherwise they could play only with broken toys. Children who were given instructions on how to resist the invitations worked far longer on the task than the other children. Other researchers have shown that some cartoonists of well-known comic strips, such as *Blondie* and *Dennis the Menace*, increased their depiction of people in cars wearing seat belts after receiving letters from an advocacy group explaining the importance of modeling this behavior (Mathews & Dix, 1992).

Models and instructors who help to improve children's behavior do not need to be adults. Studies have found that children can provide very effective modeling and instructions to help other children learn and perform appropriate behaviors (Kohler & Strain, 1990; Lancioni, 1982; Strain, Shores, & Kerr, 1976). How practical it is to use children as models and tutors depends on the circumstances. For example, if students in a classroom will serve as models or tutors to teach specific skills to certain classmates, they will need to be trained to do this and monitored to see that they are applying the methods correctly (Kohler & Strain, 1990). And if the classroom has, say, 20 or 30 students and only one teacher, it can be very difficult or impossible for the instructor to monitor and provide feedback for several models or tutors. But modeling sometimes can be applied in less formal ways and still be reasonably effective. For instance, Marcia Broden and her coworkers (1972) were able to improve the conduct of two disruptive boys who sat next to each other in class by having the teacher reward with her attention and praise *one* boy's on-task behavior. The one who was rewarded improved more than the other—and when the second boy later received rewards for on-task behavior, his conduct showed further improvements.

Behavior modification interventions often combine modeling and instructions in a single program. For example, three moderately retarded 10- to 13-year-old students were trained to prepare foods, such as scrambled eggs, by having instructions provided to one student, the model, while the others watched (Griffen, Wolery, & Schuster, 1992). The teacher provided instructions to the model verbally and with a printed recipe with words and pictures. The teacher also provided rewards to the model for correctly performing the response links making up each food preparation chain and to the other students for paying attention and for performing actions they had seen the model do. The model learned the instructed skill, and the observers learned most of the links they had seen. Other researchers have combined instructions and videotaped modeling to help adults reduce their verbally abusive behavior (Frederiksen et al., 1976) and to assert themselves in social situations, such as having someone cut ahead of them in a checkout line or receiving a poorly prepared meal in a restaurant (Hersen, Eisler, & Miller, 1974). Professional videotapes are available to conduct modeling in behavior therapy for such problems as sexual dysfunctions and social skills deficits (Dowrick & Jesdale, 1991).

Guidelines for Effective Modeling and Instructions

Several guidelines can be given to make modeling and instructions effective. First, because modeling and instructions are elaborate prompts, behavior change programs that use these methods often include *fading* procedures to eliminate clients' reliance on them. Second, the modeled behavior or instructions should be *matched to the abilities* of the individuals who must learn from them. If the methods are too hard, the learner will make many errors; if they are too easy, the learner may lose interest. Third, if there are no adequate natural rewards to strengthen the behavior, the modeling and instructions should *describe the consequences* for performing or not performing the behavior, and the consequences should be applied as specified. Fourth, whenever possible, the instructor should *describe reasons* for the behavior in terms of natural consequences ("If you share your toys with her, she'll be nice to you," or "If you play with matches, you may get burned."). Fifth, if the target behavior is complex, it should be *broken down into smaller tasks* that can be trained roughly in a sequence from easiest to most difficult.

In addition, we can use the following ways to enhance the effectiveness of modeling techniques:

- Provide rewarding consequences for the model.
- Reward the observer for paying attention to what the model does.
- Use models who can perform the responses reasonably competently—but keep in mind that if the model appears too competent, the observer may think learning the behavior will be too difficult.
- Use models who are similar to the observer, perhaps in age and gender, and have enough status to be admired by the observer.
- Use more than one model, and make sure that all perform the target behavior in a consistent manner and show positive attitudes about the behavior.

✔ **Concept Check 4.2**

. . . .

1. A father who manually moves his daughter's fingers to help her learn to tie her shoelaces is using a _____ prompt.

2. An example of a verbal prompt you could use to remind yourself to take medicine before going to bed might be _____ _____ . ⇔

3. Examples of pictorial prompts that are often used to designate men's and women's restrooms are _____ _____ . ⇔

4. The process of gradually removing or changing a prompt to reduce someone's reliance on it is called _____ .

5. Beth's special education teacher had trained her with prompts to use a spoon to eat. To fade the prompts, he first pointed to the spoon—and when this didn't work, he asked her to use the spoon. Then he placed it in her hand. He was using the fading method called _____ .

6. Modeling and instructions often indicate how to perform a target behavior, when to do it, and what the _____ will be for doing it.

7. A model's characteristic that usually enhances the effectiveness of the modeling process is _____ _____ . ⇔

. . . .

We will see later in this book that modeling is a frequently used technique in behavior therapy and is effective in reducing a wide variety of behavioral deficits, fears, and anxieties. (Go to ✔)

Using Cognitive Antecedents

We saw in Chapter 1 that our cognitive activities of thinking and reasoning allow us to generate plans, ideas, expectations, beliefs, and rules that can serve as antecedents to our behavior. For instance, we generate self-efficacy beliefs about our abilities to learn or perform specific behaviors. Individuals whose sense of self-efficacy for a task is low are not likely to try to perform it. These cognitive antecedents usually take the form of covert statements we make to ourselves, and often we are not aware of them. To some extent the Patterson and Mischel (1975) study we discussed earlier, in which preschoolers tried to resist attractive invitations to play involved the children's using cognitive antecedents. But virtually all the children who were instructed on how to decline the invitations did so aloud with no other people present, and may well have been talking to Mr. Clown Box rather than to themselves.

Self-Instructions

"Watch the curb there—don't fall," 2-year-old Paul's mother shouted too late, and the toddler tripped over the curb. As she soothed her son's scraped knee, she said gently, "You need to watch for curbs, or you'll fall." At the next street they crossed, Paul said to himself aloud, "Watch the curb—don't fall." A **self-instruction** is a statement people make to themselves that describes, directs, or guides the behavior they will perform. *Positive self-instructions* lead us to perform appropriate or desirable actions, as in the example with Paul. But we can also have *negative self-instructions* that lead us into undesirable behavior and prevent us from performing appropriate actions. Some negative self-instructions people commonly use are "They won't like me," "I'm not good at this," "I'm too tired to exercise," "This reading is boring," or "I really shouldn't have dessert, but it looks so good."

When very young children, like Paul, use self-instructions, they usually say them aloud, and the statements are ones adults have said to them. As children get older, their self-instructions become more and more covert (Luria, 1961; Vygotsky, 1962). The speech young children use spontaneously to direct their behavior tends to be very simple, like verbal prompts, rather than elaborate, like full-scale instructions. For instance, Richard Roberts and Roland Tharp (1980) tape recorded first-graders' speech as they worked on a task in school. The task required them to choose from a list words to complete partial sentences they were given, then copy the words onto a sheet of paper. Although the children verbalized a lot, they rarely stated instructions that specifically referred to themselves or described the behavior they were to perform. More than three-quarters of the things they said involved "sounding out" the words they were writing, as they had been taught to do in school. Similarly, researchers who studied what children of different ages think during stressful experiences, such as going to the dentist or giving a speech in school, found that younger children tend to focus on their negative feelings, such as thinking "I'm scared," but older children are much more likely to give themselves instructions that can help them cope, such as thinking "I can take this" or "Be brave" (Brown et al., 1986).

How well do children learn and use self-instructions to improve their behavior? Researchers have examined this issue but found inconsistent results. Some studies were conducted to improve perceptual and motor skills in hyperactive, impulsive children, who today would be classified as having attention deficit hyperactivity disorders (Davison & Neale, 1994; Meichenbaum, 1986; Meichenbaum & Goodman, 1971). These children have great difficulty keeping still, paying attention, and performing motor tasks that require fine coordination. In one of these studies, a trainer modeled the use of self-instructions to copy drawings in the following way:

> Okay, what is it I have to do? You want me to copy the picture with the different lines. I have to go slowly and carefully. Okay, draw the line down, down, good; and then to the right, that's it; now down some more and to the left. Good, I'm doing fine so far. Remember, go slowly. Now back up again. No, I was supposed to go down. That's okay. Just erase the line carefully. . . . Good. Even if I make an error I can go on slowly and carefully. I have to go down now. Finished. I did it! (Meichenbaum, 1986, p. 351)

After the children mastered using the self-instructions aloud, the overt statements were faded to become covert. For comparison, other hyperactive children spent time with a trainer but did not receive training in self-instructions. Compared with the children who received no training, those who were trained to use self-instructions showed markedly improved performance on a variety of perceptual and motor tasks, and this improvement continued when testing was repeated a month later. Another study found increased on-task behavior in hyperactive preschoolers who received self-instructions training (Bornstein & Quevillon, 1976).

But other studies with hyperactive children and with students having difficulty learning arithmetic skills have found that training in self-instructions produced little or inconsistent improvement in academic skills and on-task behavior (Billings & Wasik, 1985; Bryant & Budd, 1982; R. N. Roberts, Nelson, & Olson, 1987). Although the reasons for these inconsistent findings are unclear, it is likely that the children in some studies failed to use the self-instructions they were taught when their academic skills or on-task behaviors were tested. One study found support for this possibility with preschoolers whose on-task behaviors and independent work skills were deficient (Guevremont, Osnes, & Stokes, 1988). After being trained to use overt and covert self-instructions with a procedure like the one just quoted for hyperactive children, the preschoolers were given work sheets to complete in their classroom. At first the children didn't use the self-instructions they had been taught. But when the teacher specifically prompted them to use the self-instructions, they did so, and the percentage of correct items on the work sheets improved substantially. (Go to .)

Case Study 4.2
Betty's Self-Instructions for Studying

A 19-year-old college student named Betty had a problem with studying (as described in R. Cohen, De James, Nocera, & Ramberger, 1980). By talking on the phone, snacking, conversing with roommates, or listening to music, she often got sidetracked or distracted from studying. She decided to try to increase the percentage of time she actually studied during her regular study hours simply by using self-instructions. Before starting to study, she would read a card that stated:

> It's important to study to get good grades. I need to study to understand new material. I'm not going to talk to my roommates because it's important that I learn this material. . . . I will not talk on the phone. I will remain studying even though I feel the urge to eat or drink something. Because listening to music distracts me and it's important that I learn this material I will not play the stereo. (pp. 447–448)

Every 15 minutes during studying she would read a similar statement.

Betty collected data during baseline and intervention phases using the time sampling method: every 5 minutes during her study hours she recorded whether she was studying. The data in her graph indicate that her studying increased from about 60% of the time during baseline to over 80% of the time during intervention.

Rules, Strategies, and Logical Thinking

Many human behaviors require using higher order cognitive activities as antecedents; this is true, for example, when it is necessary to plan the most efficient way to solve an intellectual or academic problem. Suppose you are mixing a chemical solution and need only half as much of it as the directions would make. How would you know exactly what to do? To solve a problem like this one, you would need to understand concepts about measuring liquids and arithmetic rules. Robert Gagné (1985) has proposed that learning is a cumulative process in which acquiring complex intellectual skills, such as using arithmetic rules, requires mastery of relevant simpler skills, such as operant behaviors and discriminations. To mix the chemical solution, you would also need to discriminate the numbers on a measuring beaker, and you would have to be able to pour liquid from a bottle into the beaker. All these skills would be needed to *plan* how to mix the solution.

Young children typically lack most of the complex, logical skills and many of the simpler skills they would need to solve complex intellectual problems (Sarafino & Armstrong, 1986). For instance, preschoolers' abilities to count or use numbers are very limited, and they don't understand the concept of time very well. Because young children haven't acquired the necessary cognitive skills, they have a harder time solving logical problems than older children do. As an example, look at the

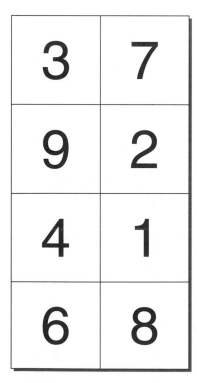

Figure 4.4   A matrix for studying children's strategies in solving problems. (From Sarafino & Armstrong, 1986, Figure 8.4.)

two-by-four matrix in Figure 4.4. Suppose I were to present this challenge: determine which number from the matrix I am thinking of by asking me the fewest possible questions, which I will answer only "yes" or "no." How would you solve this problem? The most efficient strategy would be to use three questions, each of which pares the potentially correct cells in the matrix by half. Thus, you might ask, "Is the number in the bottom half?" And then, "Is it in the right two remaining cells?" This would leave two remaining cells, and you could simply guess, knowing that even if you guess wrong, you have found the correct number. Peter Eimas (1970) presented this problem to children and found that the older they were, the more logical were their strategies. At about 8 years of age, they simply guessed haphazardly; at age 11, they tried systematic strategies but usually partitioned the matrix unevenly; at age 13, the children used very efficient strategies. The conclusion from this section is that if a behavior you want to change requires the individual to construct plans or strategies as cognitive antecedents, you must be sure the individual has the skills to construct them. (Go to .)

Close-Up 4.1
Can Young Children Think Logically?

Try this task with a preschooler, as one of my students did with her 5-year-old nephew. She mixed together seven same-sized writing instruments (you could use other items): two red felt-tipped pens and five red pencils. She had the boy separate the "things to write with" into the pens and the pencils, and then asked five questions: (1) "How many things to write with are there?", and he answered seven. (2) "How many pencils are there?", and he said five. (3) "How many pens are there?", and he said two. (4) "Are there more pencils than pens?", and he said yes. (5) "Are there more pencils than things to write with?"—to her amazement, he answered "More pencils." Why did the child answer the last question incorrectly? Is it because 5-year-olds can't think logically?

Theorist and researcher Jean Piaget (1929, 1952, 1970) conducted tasks like this one and found similar outcomes. From children's performance he came to believe that their thinking and reasoning abilities progress through a sequence of *stages*. He called the stage when children are from 2 to 7 years of age *preoperational* because he believed that children could not

acquire the "operations," or logical mental actions, needed to think through the solution of a cognitive problem. According to Piaget's view, preoperational thinking is "intuitive"—it does not apply logic effectively and is determined largely by what they currently see or hear. Is young children's thinking really so intuitive?

Research has shown that Piaget's theory greatly underestimates the cognitive abilities of preschool-aged children (Sarafino & Armstrong, 1986). Although it is true that young children have more difficulty than older ones in reasoning through logical problems, they are capable of acquiring and using logic for many tasks and situations. Children's thinking seemed so intuitive to researchers several decades ago mainly because the youngsters had not received training in the skills needed to solve the problems Piaget presented to them. But we know today that preschoolers can learn many logical operations with modest amounts of relevant training and apply these skills to new problems they have not been trained on before (Dasen & Heron, 1981; Field, 1981; Gelman & Baillargeon, 1983).

Altering Antecedent Chains

Suppose you wanted to stop smoking cigarettes. Smoking a cigarette requires a chain of antecedent responses, such as reaching into a pocket, pulling out the pack, pulling out a cigarette, putting it in the mouth, reaching for a lighter, and lighting the cigarette. In a *behavioral excess*, it becomes harder and harder to stop yourself from performing the final, undesirable behavior with each advance through the antecedent chain. It is easier to stop yourself as you reach into your pocket than as you are about to light the cigarette.

One of the best ways to reduce the likelihood of performing an undesirable act that occurs after an antecedent chain is to alter the chain of events in some way. This approach, called **altering antecedent chains**, is especially effective if it is used *early* in the chain. Two basic methods can be used to alter antecedent chains. First, you can build *pauses* into the chain. For instance, in trying to reduce the amount of snacks you eat, you can pause before going to get the snacks. What's more, you can use an early pause in the antecedent chain to assess the behavior you're about to do, marking the data in your records. Recording the behavior may help you to stop at that time (and you can cross out the data!). Pauses can also help while you're eat-ing—at meals, for example, you can pause after cutting pieces of food, delay putting the food in your mouth, and put your utensils down. The second method for altering antecedent chains is to *reorder the links*. For instance, in smoking a ciga-rette, you can reach for a lighter before reaching for the pack of cigarettes. Doing this can help break down the antecedent chain's stimulus control.

When the target response following an antecedent chain is a *behavioral deficit*, you'll need to increase the stimulus control of the chain. This can be accomplished in any of the ways we've already considered—by using prompts, modeling, or instructions. As an example, suppose a medical patient frequently failed to take the pills recommended by a physician. Putting a pill in one's own mouth is a step that occurs at the end of an antecedent chain. If you could get the chain started, the patient probably would take the pill. An effective way to accomplish this is to pro-vide an auditory prompt, such as an alarm tone, to initiate the chain (Azrin & Powell, 1969). The alarm can turn off in a few seconds automatically or it can be built into the pill box and programmed to stay on until the box is opened. In either case, the prompt can be faded later.

We have examined a wide variety of shortcut stimulus control methods to improve people's operant behavior. You may have noticed that some of these meth-ods seem to overlap, and to some degree this is true. For instance, if gestural prompts are fairly detailed, at what point do they become modeling? In a similar vein, at what point do verbal prompts become instructions? And couldn't self-instructions sometimes serve as part of a complex chain of behavior rather than as antecedents? There isn't any clear way to establish dividing lines between these phe-nomena. The purpose in separating these methods is to organize them in a way that will allow you to see the many different methods we can use, categorize most instances of methods we encounter, and describe efficiently most methods we apply.

Managing Antecedents to Increase or Decrease Behavior

We have discussed many behavior modification techniques by which we can introduce or alter antecedent events to increase an operant target behavior when a deficit exists and to decrease a target behavior when an excess exists. To use these techniques effectively, we must first conduct a functional analysis to identify the antecedents for the current behavior pattern. When designing a behavior change program to modify your own or someone else's behavior, there's no substitute or shortcut for keeping an A-B-C log and filling out a summary record. Sometimes you'll be tempted to skip or abandon careful record keeping, thinking "I know what the behavior is and when and why it happens. Keeping records is just a waste of time." But my students often discover important aspects of the antecedents, behavior, and consequences that they had overlooked before doing their functional analyses. Keeping records forced them to pay closer attention to what was going on. And don't forget that some factors that lead to a behavior are distant antecedents, which are very hard to identify without paying close attention.

The title of this section begins with the words "managing antecedents." To manage antecedents you must select the most appropriate stimulus control techniques and administer them carefully to change existing antecedents or introduce new ones. A few additional methods we've not yet considered can be useful in changing existing antecedents.

- *Reducing or avoiding antecedents.* Sometimes it's possible to reduce or avoid the antecedents that lead to behavioral excesses or deficits. For instance, if a person drinks too much alcohol, staying away from bars would help a lot. Similarly, someone who must eat in restaurants often but consumes too much fatty food there can reduce the temptations inherent in these situations by snacking on low-fat foods before going out to eat. If a college student fails to study because there are too many distractions in the dorm, it might be a good idea to study in the library.

- *Narrowing antecedent control.* It may be possible to limit an undesirable behavior to a smaller range of antecedents—a technique called **narrowing**. If someone watches too much TV, gradually reducing the times or places that TV watching may occur can help.

- *Using cognitive strategies.* Several cognitive strategies can help change existing antecedents, such as negative self-instructions. For instance, when we are tempted to perform an undesirable behavior, we can think about the *benefits of not doing it,* try to *distract* ourselves from the antecedents, or try to *reperceive the antecedents* we notice. When our perceptions of antecedents involve "hot" cognitions, such as "Oh, that chocolate looks so delicious," the unwanted behavior becomes very enticing and hard to resist (Mischel, 1981). We can reperceive the antecedents by substituting "cool" cognitions about them, such as "That candy is the same color as my belt and is about 1 1/2 inches long, 1 inch wide, and 1 inch high." Reperceiving antecedents for a short while, sometimes just for several seconds, can be enough to get us past the temptation successfully. In people's efforts to quit smoking, combining cognitive and behavioral methods appears to more effective than using methods of either approach alone (Shiffman, 1984).

- *Turning an S^D into an S^Δ.* One way to change existing antecedents (S^Ds) is to present them while preventing them from being associated with rewards, thereby turning them into S^Δs. For instance, seeing or smelling alcoholic beverages can be strong antecedents for drinking. Some research has found that presenting the stimuli that heavy drinkers of alcohol associate with drinking and simultaneously preventing them from consuming alcohol can help them quit drinking (Blakey & Baker, 1980).

Introducing new antecedents can be accomplished with the methods we've already seen, such as prompting and instructions. In most cases, these antecedents will be used only temporarily to build stimulus control to normal antecedents; then they will be faded. In other cases, the new antecedents can become a permanent part of the normal ones, especially if the person cannot perform appropriately without them. When managing antecedents in an intervention, it is important to keep in mind that the desirable behavior the S^Ds elicit must be reinforced. (Go to ✔ .)

Application Exercise

The Chapter 3 work sheet activities gave your self-management project a concrete focus by having you define in detail your outcome goal, target behavior(s), and behavioral goal(s). Those activities also had you consider how you will assess your behavior and what form your A-B-C log might take. The main objective of the present application exercise will be to form the foundation for conducting your functional analysis, which you'll begin after reading Chapter 5. We will also list some tips you can use in trying to manage the antecedents you discover as you collect data in your A-B-C log and complete your summary record.

Tips on Managing Antecedents

As you carry out the tasks in this application exercise, keep in mind the following tips on managing antecedents in behavior change programs. You'll want to refer to these tips, as well, when you conduct your functional analysis and begin thinking about how you might deal with the antecedents you discover for your behavior.

1. Look for immediate and distant antecedents carefully. Don't leave out information about particular stimuli in immediate antecedents simply because you

✔ Concept Check 4.3

....

1. One sentence in the self-instructions you might use when planning to run some errands is _____
   _____ . ⇔

2. Self-instructions, rules, and strategies are examples of _____ antecedents.

3. Research has found that Piaget's theory greatly _____ preschool children's abilities to learn and use logic.

4. An example of building in a pause to alter the antecedent chain for smoking is
   _____ . ⇔

5. The portion of an antecedent chain for a behavioral excess during which it becomes especially difficult to stop oneself from performing the behavior is
   _____ .

6. An example of narrowing antecedent control for snacking might be _____
   _____ . ⇔

_____

Answers: 1. Buy some gas. 2. cognitive 3. underestimates 4. delaying pulling out a cigarette from the pack 5. near the end 6. eat snacks only in the kitchen

....

think such points are not important. Remember that your preconceived "hunches" are useful, but they can be misleading.

2. Look for both overt and covert antecedents.

3. If possible, ask friends and relatives to help monitor your behavior—for instance, they can signal you when the response occurs or keep their own data, which can be compared with yours.

4. You'll need to take special measures to collect data if you have chosen to reduce a behavioral excess but are usually unaware of your own responses because you do them absentmindedly or habitually. Biting fingernails and swearing are two behaviors people often perform absentmindedly. One way to help you pay attention to these responses is to use a technique called **negative practice**, that is, to deliberately perform the behavior over and over while paying close attention to every sensation it produces, such as the sounds you make or the exact position of your fingers. You can also use *prompts* to remind you to pay attention to the behavior and record each instance.

5. Make sure you can *record data immediately* or very close in time to the occurrence of the behavior. The accuracy of your data will decline with each second or minute you wait. Your record-keeping instruments—data sheets, pencil or pen, or even a watch or device to count frequency (such as a golf counter)—must be easy to use and accessible when the behavior occurs.

6. If the target behavior occurs in social situations, you'll need to be ready to deal with questions about your record keeping or any other changes people may

notice in your behavior. Telling the truth is fine. If you don't want anyone to know what you're doing, you'll need to find a nonobvious way to record your data.

7. After you have identified the antecedents to your behavior, go through this chapter and look at *all* the methods by which we learn and by which we can change the stimuli that set the occasion for our behavior. Tentatively decide which methods you might and might not be able to use for your program. (You'll need to do a similar survey of material for the next several chapters, so keep this in mind as you read each chapter.)

8. If your antecedents for a behavioral deficit include your thinking "I don't have the time," look in your usual schedule for times and occasions when you either waste time or spend "free" time, so you can plan to decrease those activities to make room for the time you'll need to make your project work.

The Next Steps in Your Program Design

The first task for this chapter's work sheet will be to examine your hunches about the antecedents that currently support your behavioral excess or deficit. Then we will finalize the procedures and materials you'll use in assessing the target behavior(s) and the antecedents and consequences. Doing these tasks will require that you consult your Work Sheet 3.1 from Chapter 3. Turn now to Work Sheet 4.1 and fill it out.

Summary

Almost any stimulus can serve as an antecedent for operant behavior. Immediate antecedents are present shortly before the behavior occurs, distant antecedents precede the behavior by at least several minutes, and stimuli of both types can be overt or covert.

We learn to respond differently to different stimulus conditions through the process of discrimination learning, which involves differential reinforcement in which responding to a discriminative stimulus (S^D) is regularly associated with reinforcement and S-delta (S^Δ) stimuli are not. In this way, people who are regularly associated with reinforcement of particular behaviors can become antecedents for those behaviors. Although individuals can learn to make fine discriminations and to make a certain response only when specific stimuli are present, the behavior often shows some degree of stimulus generalization. Some antecedents exert a great deal of stimulus control, having considerable influence on one's performance of a particular behavior. When the antecedent involves the overall context in which behavior occurs, the stimulus control is called contextual control.

Many shortcut stimulus control methods can be used in modifying behavior. These methods include a variety of prompts (physical guidance, verbal, pictorial, gestural, and auditory) that are typically faded once the discrimination has been learned. Fading can be done through decreasing assistance, increasing assistance, and delayed prompting. Modeling and instructions are essentially elaborate gestural and verbal prompts that demonstrate or describe how to perform the behavior. One type of cognitive antecedent consists of self-instructions, which can be either positive or negative, according to whether they lead to desirable or undesirable behavior. Other cognitive antecedents include the rules and logic people use to plan what they will do. Children's ability to learn and use cognitive antecedents improves with age and is stronger than Piaget's theory suggested. Antecedent chains can be altered by building in pauses between links and by reordering the links.

Behavior modification programs can manage antecedents by helping people reduce or avoid them, narrowing antecedent control, using cognitive strategies, and turning discriminitive stimuli into S-deltas. If individuals often perform the target behavior absentmindedly, with the result that not noticing instances of the behavior impairs their data collection, negative practice can be used to draw their attention to the problem.

Key Terms and Review Questions

Key Terms

discrimination learning	fading
differential reinforcement	modeling
discriminative stimulus	instructions
S-delta	self-instructions
stimulus generalization	altering antecedent chains
stimulus control	narrowing
prompt	negative practice

Review Questions

1. Describe the antecedents that might set the occasion for the following behaviors: calling the police, recycling trash, and cooking a gourmet dinner.

2. What is differential reinforcement, and how is it involved in children's learning to discriminate letters of the alphabet?

3. Define and give the abbreviations for the terms discriminative stimulus and S-delta.

4. Describe the study by Redd and Birnbrauer (1969) on how people can become discriminitive stimuli.

5. Define "stimulus generalization" and give an example of it in the names children use for different flowers.

6. What is stimulus control? Give two examples of it from your current life.

7. A father complains to you that "Prompts don't work. I remind my kid all the time to clean up his room, and he never does." If you did a functional analysis of the boy's behavior, what reasons do you think you'd find for the failure of these prompts?

8. Describe how you might use physical prompts to teach a dog to respond correctly to the command, "Give me your paw."

9. Describe two gestural prompts a baseball coach might make.

10. Define "fading," and give an example of how you might fade (a) a verbal prompt to improve first-graders' classroom conduct and (b) a pictorial prompt to help a child discriminate between the numbers *3* and *8*.

11. Define "modeling" and "instructions" and describe how you might use each method to teach an elementary school student how to use scissors to cut paper triangles.

12. Define positive and negative self-instructions and give an example of each from your own life.

13. What rules or other cognitive skills would be needed to play a card game, such as poker or gin rummy?

14. Describe an example of narrowing antecedent control from Case Study 4.1.

15. Describe in detail how negative practice might be used to help a girl stop twirling her hair with her fingers.

Related Readings

Demchak, M. (1990). Response prompting and fading methods: A review. *American Journal on Mental Retardation, 6,* 603–615.

Gibson, E. J. (1969). *Principles of perceptual learning and development.* New York: Appleton-Century-Crofts.

Kohler, F. W., & Strain, P. S. (1990). Peer assisted interventions: Early promises, notable achievements, and future aspirations. *Clinical Psychology Review, 10,* 441–452.

Rilling, M. (1977). Stimulus control and inhibitory processes. In Honig, W. K., & Staddon, J. E. R. (Eds.), *Handbook of operant behavior.* Englewood Cliffs, NJ: Prentice-Hall.

Shiffman, S. (1984). Coping with temptations to smoke. *Journal of Consulting and Clinical Psychology, 52,* 261–267.

Name _____   Day & time
                                   class meets_____

Date _____

Chapter 4: Work Sheet 4.1

1. Your self-management target behavior(s): _____

2. In my students' functional analyses for their self-management projects, they have identified a great variety and number of antecedents to the behaviors they planned to change. Some examples of the more common antecedents for operant behaviors they discovered can be grouped into five categories:

- *Internal physical stimuli:* being hungry, feeling tired, and feeling overly aroused from having caffeine.
- *External physical stimuli:* seeing a tempting food, seeing a vending machine for snacks, being in a bar, driving a car, talking on the phone, and hearing or seeing a television.
- *Social stimuli:* seeing friends socializing, being invited by friends to go to a fast-food restaurant, and seeing friends smoking or drinking.
- *Emotional stimuli:* feeling angry, anxious, "stressed out," or lonely.
- *Cognitive stimuli:* thinking "I'll never do this right," "No one likes me," "I don't have enough time," "I'm fat," or "I'm too tired."

Do you think some of these antecedents are involved in your target behavior? My students discovered dozens of other antecedents as well. Do you think there are other antecedents to your behavior? Describe the hunches you have about what antecedents will turn out to be important precursors to your behavioral excess or deficit.

3. How will you make sure you will record your data immediately or very soon after each instance of the target behavior? What will your record-keeping instruments be, and where will you keep them?

4. Go back to your Work Sheet 3.1 and do two things: (a) *Circle* the type(s) of data you plan to collect for your target behavior—frequency, duration, magnitude, latency, and quality. (b) *Circle* the approach you will use to time your assessments—continuous recording, interval recording, or time sampling. Now, for each type of data you circled, describe exactly what you will be measuring and how you will structure the timing of the assessments.

5. Refer back to Work Sheet 3.1 and compose a final draft of the format for the A-B-C log you plan to use in the functional analysis of your target behavior.

NOTE: If you will be submitting work sheets to your instructor or to a fellow student, make a copy of each sheet before submitting it.

5 *Using Reinforcement to Increase Operant Behavior*

Prologue

Some years ago, the newspaper printed a letter to "Dear Abby" describing how a woman got her teenaged stepson to keep his room neat. According to the letter, the room had been so messy that sometimes the teen had to "jump" from the door to his bed. The stepmother's program provided a nicely designed, moderately structured set of specified rules regarding the behavior needed to keep the room neat and consequences of doing so. She enforced the following rules:

- If his bed was made, he got breakfast.
- She would launder *only* the clothes he placed in a clothes basket in his closet.
- She would place anything left on the floor in a "mess box" located in the garage. If he wanted any of these items, *he* had to retrieve it or them.
- If his room was vacuumed on his "day for the car," he received the keys.

This letter was written in response to Abby's suggestion to an earlier letter writer: the mother of very untidy teenagers had been advised to close the bedroom doors and "rake" their rooms weekly.

I don't know whether the stepmother had received training in behavioral methods, but, as you can see, much of her program involved creative common sense in making important consequences contingent on the boy's behavior. Three further points about this story should be mentioned. First, the boy initially "fought" the program, but eventually gave in. Second, once his room was consistently neat, he became proud of it and would take friends there. Third, it is instructive to contrast the stepmother's approach with the advice Dear Abby had given, which, if carried out, would in fact have *rewarded messy behavior* if the teens happened to want their doors closed and rooms "raked."

This chapter and the next focus on the role of consequences—reinforcement and punishment—in operant conditioning. In this chapter, we will concentrate on the process of *reinforcement*, the cornerstone and most reliable process in changing operant behavior. We will examine what reinforcement is, consider its many different types, and learn how to identify and administer reinforcers effectively in behavior change programs.

What Is Reinforcement?

To reinforce means to make stronger or more pronounced. In operant conditioning, **reinforcement** is a process whereby a consequence strengthens the behavior on which it is contingent. Increases in the strength of a behavior are reflected in its reduced latency or its increased frequency, duration, or magnitude. Of course, these measures may not improve much when reinforcement occurs for well-established behaviors—ones the person already performs very frequently or intensely, for instance. The term *reinforcer* refers to a stimulus that is introduced or changed when the behavior occurs; its introduction or change is the consequence in the process of reinforcement. Loosely speaking, reinforcers are things or events the person "wants" or finds "pleasant" or "satisfying." These are subjective qualities, but we will see later that it is sometimes possible to assess them objectively.

We have used the terms *reward* and *reinforcer* as synonyms, which they are for the most part. But "reward" is an everyday word and has some excess meanings that can make it a less precise term. For instance, a prize or special payment for doing something unusual, like returning a wallet or performing a job especially well, often is called a reward. We don't usually think of rewards as subtle stimuli, such as casual praise or a warm smile, which are extremely frequent and very important reinforcers in our lives. What's more, the term "reward" tends to imply that *most* people find the stimulus pleasant or satisfying, but this isn't true of all reinforcers. For instance, masochists find pain very reinforcing, at least under some conditions, but most people do not. Thus, a reinforcer can be any stimulus that will strengthen an individual's behavior. For these reasons, we will use the term "reward" less frequently.

Keep this rule in mind: when reinforcement occurs, it *always* strengthens the behavior on which it is contingent. This means that if you provide a consequence for a behavior and find that the person subsequently does not perform the response at least as frequently, intensely, quickly, or persistently as in the past, reinforcement has not occurred.

Positive and Negative Reinforcement

The process of reinforcement involves a pattern of events in which the behavior results in a consequence: a reinforcing stimulus being introduced or changed. This pattern of events can happen in two ways. In **positive reinforcement** the consequence involves introducing or *adding* a stimulus after the individual has performed the behavior. As we have seen, this consequence typically is something the person wants or finds pleasant or satisfying. Virtually all the reinforcing consequences we have mentioned so far in this book have been examples of positive reinforcement. For one example of positive reinforcement, recall the Dear Abby story in which a boy got the keys to the car if he vacuumed his room. We've seen other examples of positive reinforcement, too: receiving money, praise, and attention from parents or teachers for behaving appropriately.

But the pattern of events in reinforcement can happen in another way. For example, suppose you have a splitting headache, which is an *aversive stimulus*—that is, a painful, unpleasant, or injurious event. What could you do about it? One thing you could do is take a painkiller, such as aspirin. Performing this behavior changes the aversive stimulus: it reduces the pain. In this pattern of events, which is called **negative reinforcement**, the consequence of the behavior—in this case, taking aspirin—involves *reducing* or *removing* an aversive circumstance. To the extent that the aspirin reduces the headache, you are more likely to take aspirin when you have a headache. The headache is the antecedent, and its reduction is the reinforcing consequence that strengthens aspirin taking. (Go to 🔍 .)

Reward Value

The likelihood that a particular consequence will reinforce a response depends on the degree to which the person *values* it. Our preferences for particular reinforcers differ from one person to the next and can change from one time to the next. Suppose a fitness program offered tickets to a Whitney Houston concert in exchange for jogging. This consequence might be very reinforcing for you, but a friend who jogs with you might consider tickets to the Philadelphia Orchestra a more attractive reward. And these preferences can change, given the "right" circumstances. If you are "in the mood" for classical music, Whitney Houston might be less appealing. The greater the value a consequence has, the more likely it will reinforce behavior.

What aspects of a reward determine its value? Reinforcers can vary in their *quantity*—for example, the amount of candy a child receives for good behavior—and their *quality*, or character—for instance, different candies have different flavors. To understand how these factors affect reward value, we need to consider positive and negative reinforcement separately. In positive reinforcement, the quantity and quality of a reinforcer determine its value. A large piece of chocolate candy generally has more reward value than a small piece, and chocolate candy may have more reward value than the same amount of licorice candy. Studies of positive reinforcement have found that reinforcers with greater value produce stronger responding than lesser reinforcers do, as reflected in the frequency or magnitude of the behavior (Crespi, 1942; Flaherty & Caprio, 1976; Green et al., 1991). In negative reinforcement, reward value seems to be determined mainly by the quantity factor—that is, the amount by which the aversive situation is reduced (Campbell & Kraeling, 1953). For instance, we are more likely to take aspirin to relieve a headache in the future if doing so in the past relieved most or all of the pain rather than just a little of it.

By permission of Johnny Hart and Creators Syndicate, Inc.

When we try to predict the reward value of specific reinforcers, the saying "different strokes for different folks" applies.

🔍 Close-Up 5.1
Confusions About Negative Reinforcement

Many students and some professionals have difficulty understanding the concept of negative reinforcement (Kimble, 1993; McConnell, 1990). A common problem results from *incorrectly equating* negative reinforcement and punishment. We saw in Chapter 1 that punishment *decreases* the behavior on which it is contingent, and we've just learned that negative reinforcement does the opposite.

To help clarify the distinction between punishment and negative reinforcement, let's look at an example of both processes happening in an everyday sequence of events. Suppose 9-year-old Sandra hits her younger sister Cheryl in an argument over what to watch on TV. The girls' father punishes Sandra's behavior by sending her to her room, where she has no TV to watch. But he also tells her she can come back to the TV room after half an hour *if* she writes Cheryl a note of apology. He has made Sandra's gaining release from her room contingent on her producing an apology, thereby setting the stage for her to receive negative reinforcement for apologizing.

Why do people confuse negative reinforcement and punishment? One reason is that both circumstances involve aversive situations, which people associate with punishment. But in punishment the unpleasant event occurs *after* the behavior on which it is contingent, whereas in negative reinforcement the aversive situation is present *before* the behavior that reduces it. Another reason for confusing these terms is that Skinner (1953) called negative reinforcement's aversive stimulus a "negative reinforcer," which makes it seem that the consequence occurred

before the behavior. A third reason for confusion about negative reinforcement is the tendency to think that the word "negative" refers to the unpleasantness of the aversive stimulus. It doesn't. In describing reinforcement, the words "positive" and "negative" refer to the arithmetic terms for *adding* (+) and *subtracting* (-): in negative reinforcement, a stimulus is *subtracted* from the situation if the appropriate behavior occurs; in positive reinforcement, a stimulus is *added* when the behavior occurs. Actually, *both types of reinforcement result in a relatively desirable state of affairs* following the behavior on which they are contingent.

With all this confusion, you'd think someone would propose changing the terms to describe the patterns by which reinforcement happens. In 1975 a noted behavior modification researcher named Jack Michael proposed dropping the words "positive" and "negative" entirely and retaining the term *reinforcement* to refer to consequences of both types. He argued that it isn't very meaningful to distinguish between patterns of reinforcement in which stimuli are subtracted versus added, since the end result is pleasant in both patterns. What's more, a single reinforcer can provide both types of reinforcement. For instance, we can probably agree that eating food can reinforce preparing meals, but is the reinforcement positive or negative? Eating tasty food is a pleasant activity that occurs after preparing a meal, but it also reduces hunger. Perhaps dropping the distinction between positive and negative reinforcement would be a good idea, but these terms still persist in the literature.

Unconditioned and Conditioned Reinforcers

Some consequences can serve as reinforcers because of innately determined processes. These consequences are called **unconditioned reinforcers** (or *primary reinforcers*) because little or no learning is needed for them to be reinforcing. Examples include satisfying basic physiological needs by eating food or scratching an itch. Unconditioned reinforcers are associated with internal stimuli, such as feelings of hunger, and the reward value they have depends on the individual's current physiological state—in this case, whether the person is or is not hungry. The reward value for an unconditioned reinforcer increases when the person has been deprived of it for a sufficient period of time. Other examples of unconditioned reinforcers include water, oxygen, normal body temperature, and sleep.

Other stimuli become reinforcing through learning and are called **conditioned reinforcers** (or *secondary reinforcers*). For instance, an infant who is given a hundred-dollar bill probably would not be very impressed. In fact, if the bill were brand new, the baby might even find it aversive because of its stiffness and sharp, prickly edges. Making receipt of a hundred-dollar bill contingent on some behavior, say, head turning, would not strengthen the baby's head-turning behavior. The baby hasn't learned to value money. But chances are you have, and you might suffer whiplash if someone offered you $100 to turn your head! Some evidence indicates that non-reinforcing stimuli can become reinforcers through respondent conditioning (Ormrod, 1990). The procedure generally involves pairing the stimulus that is non-reinforcing with one that is already able to strengthen behavior. Money probably became a reinforcer for you by being associated with many other stimuli that were already reinforcing, such as food and clothing.

Why Are Reinforcers Reinforcing?

Reinforcing consequences have certain properties that enable them to strengthen behavior. One of these properties involves the ability to *reduce drives*. Learning theorist Clark Hull (1943) proposed that biological needs produce unpleasant internal drives, such as hunger, that can be reduced directly by performing behavior that leads to a relevant unconditioned reinforcer, in this case, food. This reduction in drive and biological need strengthens the connection between the successful behavior and its antecedents. Conditioned reinforcers, such as money, work indirectly through their associations with unconditioned reinforcers, such as food.

Although reducing drives seems to be an important property that enables some consequences to reinforce behavior, not all reinforcers reduce drives. As you read the following research examples with animal subjects, ask yourself whether the reinforcer could have reduced any *biologically based drive* directly or indirectly:

- *Visual exploration as a reinforcer.* Robert Butler (1954) placed a series of monkeys in individual cages; each cage was surrounded by a box, preventing the monkeys from seeing out. There was a small door in the box, however; and Butler trained the monkeys to open it. Each time they did so, they could see an empty laboratory room for a short time. The monkeys learned this behavior with no other reinforcers given. In later tests, opening the door allowed the monkeys to see the laboratory either empty or containing different stimulus conditions, such as an array of food, a moving toy train, or another monkey in a cage. Door opening occurred frequently under each of the stimulus conditions, but it was highest for a glimpse of another monkey or the train.

- *Saccharin as a reinforcer.* Saccharin is a sweetener that has no calories or nutritional value. Researchers examined saccharin as a reinforcer with rats that had been fed in the past on an unsweetened grain mash with water always available in their home cages (Sheffield, Roby, & Campbell, 1954). The subjects, which were hungry but not thirsty, were trained three times a day for 2 weeks to run from one end to the other in a runway; some got plain water for running and others got a water–saccharin solution. Comparisons of the subjects' runway performance for the last few days revealed that those trained with the water-saccharin reinforcer ran six times faster than those that trained with just the plain water.

- *Sex without ejaculation as a reinforcer.* Ejaculation is the release of semen by males at orgasm, which appears to reduce the sex drive. Researchers trained sexually inexperienced male rats twice a day for 2 weeks to run a runway and cross a 4-inch high hurdle to enter a large, circular chamber that contained a female rat in heat (Sheffield, Wulff, & Backer, 1951). In each training session, the male was allowed to copulate with the female, which typically occurs as a series of a dozen or more mountings and dismountings before ejaculation occurs. To prevent drive reduction, the researchers removed the female after several mountings before the male could mount her again and eventually ejaculate. During the last few days, the males were running more than twice as fast down the runway than they had during the first few days. What's more, a comparable group of males that were trained in the runway with a *male* rat in the chamber increased their running speed across sessions, too, but to a much lesser degree.

- *Brain stimulation as a reinforcer.* James Olds and Peter Milner (1954) implanted very thin electrodes deep in rats' brains to deliver tiny pulses of electrical current to specific locations. The researchers then trained the subjects to press a lever and receive an electrical pulse to the brain with each press. Not only did the subjects learn this operant task, but they would then perform the response at extremely high rates if the pulses were to a particular region (the septal area)—for instance, one rat made 1920 responses in a 1-hour period.

Although the reinforcing effects of at least some of these reinforcers may seem intuitively reasonable, the problem is that reinforcement occurred without reducing a biologically based drive directly or indirectly. This means that other properties of consequences must also enable the reinforcers to strengthen behavior.

Many reinforcers provide *sensory stimulation,* and this is another important property (Baldwin & Baldwin, 1981; Fiske & Maddi, 1961; D. D. Schultz, 1965). If you are at home alone, you might feel you have nothing to do and become bored. On the other hand, sometimes the events around you become too stimulating, and you feel overwhelmed. Both feelings are unpleasant. The reward value of sensory stimulation is greatest between these extremes, when there is enough going on to keep your interest and when the stimulation has some variety and meaning to it. The third property that makes some consequences reinforcing is that they involve performing *high-probability behaviors* (Premack, 1959, 1965). High-probability behaviors are responses the person performs frequently or for long periods of time when

✔ Concept Check 5.1

1. Reinforcement always _____ the behavior on which it is contingent.
2. In positive reinforcement, the consequence is _____ after the behavior occurs.
3. If you stubbed your toe, a behavior you could perform that would produce negative reinforcement might be _____ . ⇔
4. The terms "positive" and "negative" to describe reinforcement refer to _____ and _____ in arithmetic.
5. A reinforcer with high reward value for a typical child might be _____ . ⇔
6. Another term for primary reinforcer is _____ .
7. One property reinforcers often have that enables them to strengthen behavior is

_____ .

_____

Answers: 6. unconditioned reinforcer.   7. reducing drives

1. strengthens   2. added   3. rub the toe   4. adding, subtracting   5. candy

free to choose what he or she will do. Some common high-probability behaviors are eating, watching TV, having sex, dancing, and playing games. For the most part, these behaviors are ones the person enjoys doing. (Go to ✔ .)

Types of Positive Reinforcers

Choosing the reinforcers to change operant behavior is a pivotal consideration in any program to change behavior because reinforcers can have a very powerful impact on what people do. To make our choices carefully, we need to know what reinforcers we may have at our disposal. This section describes several different but somewhat overlapping categories of positive reinforcers. Most potential rewards belong to one or more of these categories. Knowing the reinforcers from which we can choose and examples of each type will help us in making our choices.

Tangible and Consumable Rewards

When asked to give examples of reinforcers, many things people think of first are items that are *tangible*—that is, material objects we can perceive, such as toys, clothing, or musical recordings—or *consumable*—that is, things we can eat or drink, such as candy, fruit, or soft drinks. Tangible and consumable rewards have a strong influence on our everyday actions and include both unconditioned and conditioned reinforcers. When you go to a store to buy a new pair of jeans, the jeans are a tangible reinforcer for your shopping behavior. When children in school obey their teacher's instructions to line up in a quiet and orderly fashion before they may go to the lunch room, food is the reinforcer for their behavior.

Although food can be a useful reinforcer, it isn't used very often in human behavior modification interventions for at least three reasons. First of all, food is most effective as a reinforcer when the clients or subjects are hungry, and making people hungry by depriving them of food against their will can raise ethical and legal concerns. Of course, you could reserve using food until just before mealtime, but it would still have limited value to reward many instances of the target behavior because hunger will weaken as the subjects or clients consume their rewards. Second, consumable reinforcers are often difficult and messy to carry around and dispense in everyday life situations, such as shopping with children or teaching them in classrooms. This problem is compounded by the great differences in food preferences from one person to the next and for the same person from one time to the next. Thus, to use food effectively as a reinforcer, we would need to have a sufficient variety of foods with us at all times when the target behavior could occur. Third, a person who receives and consumes food as a reward for each instance of a target behavior is likely to be distracted from an ongoing behavior we're trying to train. For example, suppose we were trying to improve children's concentration while studying. Giving them food rewards every several minutes would disrupt their efforts.

Still, using food reinforcers is sometimes reasonable and practical. For instance, a parent or teacher could use food rewards for children who meet specifically identified behavioral goals. An example of this approach would be a teacher providing snacks at specified times if students keep their disruptive behavior below a certain level. For another example, recall the woman in the Dear Abby story who gave her teenaged stepson breakfast if he made his bed. Food rewards often are used, as well, when few or no other reinforcers are effective. For instance, some moderately retarded children may respond only to edible reinforcers in the early phases of an intervention (Lancioni, 1982). In another intervention, highly preferred foods were used as reinforcers to get children to eat a wider range of foods; these children, however, had become malnourished because of their refusal to eat almost all other foods (Riordan et al., 1984).

Activities

"You may watch TV after you finish your homework," your parents may have promised. They were using an activity as a reinforcer for your doing homework. Watching TV is probably one of many activities you enjoy and do frequently when you have a free choice. We saw earlier that such activities are called high-probability behaviors. David Premack (1959, 1965) proposed that consequences are reinforcing because they involve performing high-probability behaviors, and these activities will work as reinforcers only for less frequent behaviors. This rule is known as the **Premack principle**.

Studies have shown that the Premack principle has some validity—having the opportunity to engage in high-probability behaviors can increase people's performance of infrequent behaviors. Here are some example research results:

- Mentally retarded adults increased the number of repetitions they performed of physical exercises, such as knee bends and toe touches, when researchers made the opportunity to participate in games contingent on increased exercising (L. D. Allen & Iwata, 1980).
- Toothbrushing at a summer camp increased when the opportunity to go swimming was contingent on the campers' brushing their teeth (Lattal, 1969).
- Children's classroom conduct improved when a teacher made the opportunity to play with toys, games, and crafts contingent on increasing desirable behaviors and decreasing undesirable ones (Wasik, 1970).
- Female college students who were trying to lose weight by changing their eating habits were trained to think of undesirable aspects of being overweight and desirable aspects of losing weight. Some of the subjects were instructed to engage in a high-probability noneating activity, such as sitting in a frequently used chair, only if they practiced these thoughts. These subjects reported practicing the positive and negative thoughts more often and lost more weight than subjects who were not instructed to use activity rewards to increase these thoughts (Horan & Johnson, 1971).

An important implication of the Premack principle is that we can identify existing and potential reinforcers by looking for high-probability behaviors in people's naturally occurring activities, as we do in functional analyses. This approach is usually effective and easy to use, but deciding how to assess and compare different behaviors can be tricky (Allison, 1989). For instance, suppose you wanted to determine whether reading novels and drinking soft drinks are high-probability behaviors. Would you measure the frequencies or durations of the activities? Suppose you chose durations. Now, when assessing drinking, would you include the time between sips such as while the person swallows or can still taste the drink? And how would you determine whether one activity involves a higher probability behavior than another if you decided that frequency is the best measure for one behavior and duration is the best measure for the other? Measurement decisions like these generally do not present serious problems in applying the Premack principle, but they make using this approach a little harder than you might have suspected.

Although using high-probability behaviors, such as playing a game, usually works to reinforce performing low-probability behaviors, we're not entirely sure why this is true. William Timberlake and James Allison (1974) have proposed an explanation called the *response deprivation hypothesis*: using a high-probability behavior (playing a game) as a reward makes that activity contingent on performing an infrequent behavior, such as doing chores, thereby restricting or depriving the person of his or her usual opportunities to perform the high-probability behavior. And so, if you used activities to reinforce a person's doing chores, the person would increase doing chores to overcome the restricted opportunities to do the restricted behavior, playing a game. A number of studies have found evidence supporting this explanation (Konarski et al., 1981).

Social Reinforcers

Do you know what "moshing" is? It's a dance craze that began in the early 1990s. To the outsider, it looks like a riot or street fight—as Paul Tough (1993) describes it:

> torsos slam into one another, chests collide, heads recoil, noses bleed; clothing is ripped off, trampled underfoot, forgotten; bodies fall and disappear, sucked into the sweaty undertow. Occasionally a warrior is tossed above the crush and passed along from hand to hand. It's unspeakably hot, often painful, certainly claustrophobic. (p. 53)

What reinforces such behavior? The rewards are probably social, for the most part. We learn to value social reinforcers through conditioning.

Social reinforcers are consequences of behavior that involve interpersonal acts, such as smiling, nodding, praising, and giving attention or affectionate touches. These acts can be given directly to the person or indirectly, such as in a letter of appreciation or commendation at work. Social reinforcers usually are very subtle in our everyday lives, but they have very powerful effects on people's actions and often strengthen undesirable behaviors without our realizing it. For example, a parent or

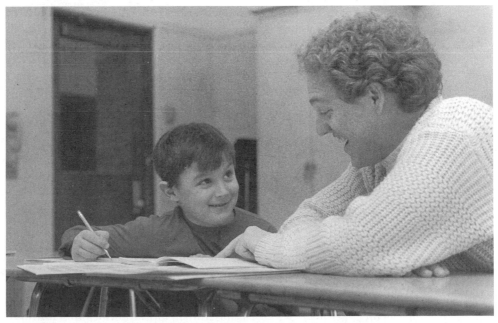

This teacher is using social reinforcers to help his student learn.

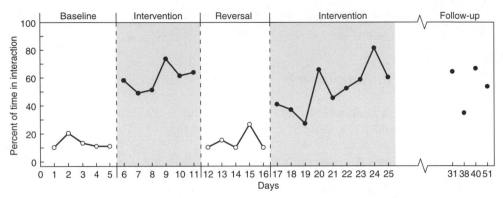

Figure 5.1   Daily percentages of time a 4-year-old socially retarded girl spent in social interaction with other children during 2-hour morning sessions. In the intervention phases, she received social reinforcement from teachers for playing with other children in her nursery school. The follow-up data indicate that the increased social interaction was durable. (Adapted from Harris, Wolf, & Baer, 1964, Figure 2.)

teacher who pays attention to children's misbehavior by trying to correct or "punish" it—saying, "Stop that," for instance—without attending to their desirable acts often increases their conduct problems (Harris, Wolf, & Baer, 1964; Madsen et al., 1970; Wahler et al., 1965). In one study, researchers discovered that preschool teachers had been unknowingly reinforcing children's excessive crying, whining, and solitary play activities (Harris, Wolf, & Baer, 1964). The teachers then were instructed to ignore such behaviors but to give social reinforcers for alternative responses, such as playing with other children. Figure 5.1 presents the substantial effect the teachers' attention had on a 4-year-old girl's social interactions with other children.

   Using social reinforcers to improve people's behavior has four main advantages over other rewards. First, social reinforcers can be administered easily and quickly in almost any setting. Second, they can be given immediately after an instance of the target behavior, thereby enhancing their effectiveness. Third, social reinforcers, such as praise or a pat on the back, generally disrupt ongoing behavior very little. Fourth, rewards like these occur "naturally" in people's everyday lives for most kinds of behavior. As a result, social consequences may continue to reinforce a target behavior after the intervention ends. (Go to 📖 .)

Feedback

Feedback refers to information that assesses or corrects people's performance. We get feedback continuously about our motor actions: as you reach to grasp an object, your senses give you information about how the movements are progressing. When we receive "positive" feedback, the information indicates that our behavior was correct or is being performed well. Feedback generally is implicit in many of the other

Case Study 5.1

Using Social Reinforcers to Overcome a Man's "Pain Behavior"

People in pain behave in characteristic ways, such as by moaning, grimacing, moving in a guarded or protective manner, or stooping while walking. These actions are called *pain behaviors.* Regardless of why these behaviors start, they often have reinforcing consequences, such as receiving attention and care from family and friends and getting certain benefits, called "secondary gains," like not having to go to work or do chores around the house. If the reinforcing conditions persist too long, the person who was in pain may continue to show pain behaviors when little or no pain exists, being caught in a vicious circle of others' solicitous behavior leading to more pain behavior, which elicits more solicitousness, and so on. But don't misunderstand this phenomenon: the person and his or her family and friends probably are not aware this is happening.

This phenomenon may have led to the condition of a 42-year-old man who was admitted to a medical center in a wheelchair after having experienced years of medical treatment, including surgery, for back pain that had no medically detectable cause (as described in Kallman,

Hersen, & O'Toole, 1975). The patient had retired from work 5 years earlier, and his wife was supporting the family. At admission, he was unable to walk or straighten his body, which was bent at the waist. The behavior modification treatment he received was very simple: a female assistant paid three 10-minute daily visits to his room, each time chatting with him and then asking him to stand and walk as far as possible. She assessed these behaviors and provided social reinforcers, saying, for instance, "You're standing straighter now," and "I'm very proud of you." During the first few days, the social rewards had little noticeable effect, but soon standing and walking began to improve. After 18 days, the patient was walking normally and was discharged from the center. A month later, he was readmitted to the center, showing severe pain behaviors again. Because his family had socially reinforced these behaviors, they received training to ignore his pain complaints and praise his motor activities. Follow-up assessments in the 12 weeks after he was discharged from the center revealed no further problems.

types of reinforcer we receive. If we receive praise or a gift for something we did, the reward also tells us we performed well. Using feedback has essentially the same advantages as using social reinforcers: feedback occurs naturally in people's lives, doesn't interrupt ongoing behavior, and can be administered easily, quickly, and immediately in almost any setting.

Although feedback alone sometimes is sufficient to strengthen or maintain a behavior, combining feedback with other rewards, such as praise, usually works better. The greater reinforcing effect of feedback plus praise was demonstrated in an intervention to decrease home heating-oil consumption (Seaver & Patterson, 1976). Heating-oil customers were divided into three groups. A feedback group received a form giving information about their rate of oil use during the current delivery period, their rate for a comparable period in the preceding year, and what the difference in these rates means in dollars a family had saved or lost. A feedback/praise group got the same type of feedback, but if their rate of oil use had declined, the information form was accompanied by a decal that read, "We are saving oil," in red letters and a note commending their efforts. The third group got no special information at all. Assessments at the next oil delivery revealed that the feedback/praise group had used 10% less oil than either of the other groups, which did not differ.

A special technique called *biofeedback* helps people gain voluntary control over body processes by giving them continuous and very specific information about the current functioning of a physiological process, such as heart rate or muscle tension. This technique has been used effectively in helping individuals reduce chronic headaches and asthma attacks (Sarafino, 1994). We will examine biofeedback in greater detail in Chapter 14.

Tokens

Tokens are symbolic rewards that represent or resemble money because they can buy or be traded in for goods or privileges. The tokens themselves can be tickets, small chips or buttons, check marks or stars on a chart, or points recorded in a log. The goods or privileges are called *backup reinforcers*, which are generally some form of tangible, consumable, activity, or social rewards. So, for example, someone who has earned enough tokens can buy a candy bar or the opportunity to watch TV as a backup reinforcer. Receiving stars or stickers for good performance, without being able to trade them in for backup reinforcers, would just be feedback or social reinforcement.

To use token reinforcers, we must determine the specific behavioral criteria to earn the tokens, what the backup reinforcers will be, and how many tokens will be needed to buy each backup reinforcer. For example, a simple token system was used as part of program to reduce the frequent tantrums of an 8-year-old elementary school student named Diane (Carlson et al., 1968). The teacher gave

> Diane a star (on the board) for each half-day of non-tantrum behavior. When four stars *in a row* were received there would be a little class party, with Diane passing out the treats. The latter provision was designed with the thought of increasing Diane's acceptance by her peers. (p. 118)

Although the little girl had several tantrums in the first couple of weeks of the program, she had only three more in the remaining 2 1/2 months before summer recess. Having the tokens buy a backup reinforcer that Diane and her classmates could share seemed to be a useful approach. Another study found that children's earning tokens to provide backup reinforcers for all students in the class is more effective than earning tokens to buy rewards for themselves alone (Kazdin & Geesey, 1977).

Token reinforcement systems can be much more complicated than the one used with Diane. They can involve more than one behavior, offer different numbers of tokens for different behaviors or levels of performance, and present a wide variety of backup reinforcers from which to choose. Using tokens as reinforcers has many of the advantages we've seen for social and feedback reinforcement. In addition, tokens have the advantages of (1) bridging the delay between performing the target behavior and getting tangible, consumable, or activity reinforcers for it and

(2) offering the possibility of a variety of backup reinforcers, to maintain the reward value of the tokens at a consistently high level. Tokens have no reinforcing value of their own—they become reinforcers because of the backup reinforcers they can buy. Simply explaining the token system is sufficient for most people to establish the link to the backup reinforcers. But individuals who either are very young or have severe learning impairments may need a little training to establish the value of the tokens.

One thing to keep in mind in designing a token reinforcement system is that the criteria for earning tokens should be neither too easy nor too difficult, and the number of tokens needed to buy backup reinforcers should be reasonable. Individuals should get attractive backup reinforcers when they perform at acceptable levels. In Chapter 13, we will discuss in detail how token reinforcement systems can be used with many individuals, for example, in institutional settings.

Covert Reinforcers

Covert reinforcers are consequences individuals experience for their behavior through imagination (Cautela, 1993a). These reinforcers are used in the following way: after you perform the target behavior, you might imagine a pleasant scene or engaging in a pleasant activity. For instance, the scene might involve your feeling proud and self-satisfied at having behaved correctly and saying to yourself, "Way to go! I knew you could do it" (Krop & Burgess, 1993). Or the scene might involve imagining how nicely proportioned your body will be because of the exercise routine you've begun. Covert reinforcers are different from other rewards because they are not actually or directly experienced when they occur, and it seems unlikely that they would have as much reward value as their actual counterparts. But they have the advantage of always being available and easy to use. Like all other rewards, covert reinforcers work best if they are invoked soon after the target behavior.

Identifying and Strengthening Reinforcers

"Different strokes for different folks" is the rule for selecting and applying reinforcers to change operant behavior. Because people differ in their reinforcer preferences, we must choose reinforcers with high reward values from the point of view of the individual whose problem behavior we're trying to help change. We must also determine through a functional analysis the consequences already existing in the person's life that strengthen or maintain the problem behavior (Groden, 1989; Iwata et al., 1982; O'Neill et al., 1990). In other words, we need to know what reinforcers we should apply in our program and what existing reinforcers we must overcome or eliminate to change the behavior. Sometimes the actual consequences that reinforce behavior are surprising and probably would not be discovered if we simply asked the person or someone else. For example, a study found evidence indicating that placing self-injurious children in arm splints to restrain them from repeatedly harming themselves sometimes serves as a reinforcer. For instance, a profoundly retarded woman named Peg learned the behavior of placing a marble in a box when prompted to do so. The only reinforcer used in teaching this response was placing her arms in splints for 30 seconds after each correct response. When this consequence was discontinued, Peg's performance deteriorated sharply; and when the reinforcer was reintroduced, her performance improved quickly and dramatically (Favell, McGimsey, & Jones, 1978).

Identifying Potential Reinforcers

Generating hunches about what consequences are likely to have high reward value can be a useful *first step* in identifying potential reinforcers for a particular individual. We develop these hunches through our everyday observations, noticing, for instance, that many of the things people seem to like are related to broad demographic factors, such as gender and age. As an example, research by Sam Witryol (1971) found that reinforcer preferences change during childhood. Kindergarten children tend to prefer tangible reinforcers, such as candy or trinkets, over social reinforcers, such as praise, but this preference is reversed by third grade. Hunches are not sufficient, however, to decide what reinforcers to use in changing a person's behavior. To the extent that the everyday connections we observe between demographic factors and reward value are valid, they reflect overall trends and not necessarily what a *particular person* will value. How can we assess what consequences will serve as strong reinforcers for a given individual?

Direct Assessment Methods

One way to determine what consequences will reinforce a person's behavior is through *direct assessment methods*: observing and recording the individual's reactions toward the stimuli when they occur or are available. Direct assessment methods can be carried out in two ways. First, we can use *naturalistic observations*—observing the person in his or her natural environments and recording the frequency and duration of each behavior displayed. This is essentially the approach Premack (1959, 1965) proposed using to identify high-probability behaviors to serve as activity reinforcers. The activities the person engages in most frequently or for the longest amounts of time are likely to be good reinforcers. Second, we can conduct *structured tests*, presenting a previously selected set of stimuli and assessing those the person prefers. The stimuli can be presented in two ways: (1) one at a time, with data collected on how soon the person approaches or reaches for them, or (2) two or more at a time, with data collected on which ones the person chooses (Green et al., 1988, 1991; Neef et al., 1992; Pace et al., 1985; Wong et al., 1987). The 1988 study by Carolyn Green and her coworkers demonstrated that reinforcers identified through structured tests are more effective in changing children's behavior than rewards identified by asking staff who work with the children. Structured tests are especially useful when trying to identify reinforcers for individuals who have severe learning or motor handicaps.

Indirect Assessment Methods

A simple but indirect way to identify potential reinforcers is to ask individuals what items or experiences they like or find pleasurable. This can be done by asking probing questions in an interview or by having the person fill out a questionnaire, such as the one presented in Figure 5.2. This questionnaire provides some flexibility to the assessment process by allowing the person to add potential reinforcers that were not listed and clarify the information he or she gives. A much more detailed and extensive questionnaire called the Reinforcement Survey Schedule is also available (Cautela & Kastenbaum, 1967).

Using indirect assessment methods to identify reinforcers has some limitations. First, like all self-report measurements, they may be less accurate than direct methods might be. Second, young children, mentally retarded people, and others whose verbal abilities are very limited may be unable to answer the questions. And third, people who are extremely depressed may feel that nothing gives them pleasure. When the latter two limitations arise, people who know the individual may be able to answer some of the questions, but it would be better to use direct assessment methods.

Enhancing Reinforcer Effectiveness

It is sometimes useful to strengthen the effectiveness of potential reinforcers, as in the case of token reinforcers that have no value in their own right. Individuals who cannot understand an explanation of a token reinforcement system will need to have the tokens associated repeatedly with the backup reinforcers. We can do this by giving out the tokens either for desirable behaviors already performed readily or for no particular behavior at all, and then exchanging the tokens immediately for backup reinforcers.

Another way to enhance reinforcer effectiveness involves presenting a small or brief sample of the consequence *before* the behavior occurs, to increase the likelihood that the person will make the response and get the reinforcer. This method is called **reinforcer sampling** (Ayllon & Azrin, 1968a). For instance, to encourage a mentally retarded child to repeat a word you say, you might show the child a small bit of candy he or she will receive after saying the word. Stores selling food sometimes use a similar method, allowing customers to sample items they can buy in larger quantities.

Modeling is another technique by which we can increase the effectiveness of reinforcers. Individuals who see others receiving and enjoying pleasant consequences for their behavior tend to increase the value they place on these consequences and to copy the behavior they saw the other people do. Alan Kazdin (1973) demonstrated this effect with mildly retarded children in an elementary school. He

PREFERRED ITEMS AND EXPERIENCES QUESTIONNAIRE (PIEQ)
FOR ADOLESCENTS AND ADULTS

Name _____ Age _____ Sex _____ Date _____

This questionnaire is designed to find out how much you like or get pleasure from various *items and experiences* in your life. The questionnaire contains lists of items and experiences many people enjoy, and each list has spaces in which you may add other things you like that the list left out. You may write on the questionnaire to clarify any information you give. For each item or experience, rate how much you like *to receive, have,* or *do it.* Use the following scale:

0	1	2	3	4
Not at all	A little	A fair amount	A lot	Very much

Items/Experiences	Ratings	Items/Experiences	Ratings
1. Tangible items:		**5. Friends'/relatives' actions toward you:**	
New clothes	_____	Praising your	
Sports equipment	_____	appearance	_____
Games	_____	competence	_____
Tools	_____	personality	_____
Beauty supplies	_____	Giving affection	_____
Music recordings	_____	Socializing with you	_____
Video recordings	_____	Inviting you for	
Other:	_____	a date	_____
Other:	_____	dinner	_____
Other:	_____	a party	_____
		Other:	_____
2. Foods:		Other:	_____
Ice cream	_____		
Candy	_____	**6. Leisure activities (passive)**	
Fruit	_____	Watching TV	_____
Pastry	_____	Watching movies	_____
Cookies	_____	Attending performances of	
Popcorn	_____	sports	_____
Potato chips	_____	music	_____
Other:	_____	drama	_____
Other:	_____	dance	_____
Other:	_____	Listening to music	_____
		Lying in the sun	_____
3. Beverages:		Taking leisurely bath	_____
Milk	_____	Other:	_____
Soft drinks	_____	Other:	_____
Juices	_____	Other:	_____
Coffee			
Tea	_____	**7. Leisure activities (active)**	
Other:	_____	Hobbies/crafts	_____
Other:	_____	Gardening	_____
		Hiking/camping	_____
4. Outcomes for work, chores, or skills		Playing athletics	_____
at work, school, or home:		Exercising	_____
Money	_____	Playing games	_____
Praise/feedback	_____	Reading	_____
Input in decisions	_____	Socializing	_____
Flexible duties	_____	Other:	_____
Special privileges	_____	Other:	_____
Other:	_____	Other:	_____
Other:	_____		

Figure 5.2   (left) The Preferred Items and Experiences Questionnaire (PIEQ) for adolescents and adults to identify potential reinforcers. (From Sarafino, 1995b.)

had the teacher praise some children in the classroom when they were in their seats and paying attention to their work. Reinforcing attentive behavior in these children increased the attentive behavior of the children who were praised *and* of classmates who were sitting near them. (Go to ✔ .)

How to Administer Reinforcement

Once we have decided which reinforcers to use in changing someone's behavior, we need to consider exactly how and when to provide them. In this section we will look at many different procedures for administering reinforcement, beginning with the process of shaping behavior.

Shaping a Behavior

In **shaping**, an individual's behavior gradually improves because the criteria or standards for successive instances of reinforcement become more and more rigorous. This means that for the individual to keep receiving reinforcement, his or her behavior must advance through a series of successively better approximations to the behavioral goal. For example, suppose 3-year-old Erin is learning to print the first letter of her name, with her father giving social reinforcers. Even though the child's first attempts are likely to be very distant or primitive approximations to a well-

✔ **Concept Check 5.2**

· ·

1. A favorite consumable reward of people you know is _____ . ⇔
2. Parents saying to a teenager, "You can go out tonight if you finish your chores," is an example of using a(n) _____ as a reinforcer.
3. An advantage of using feedback or social reinforcers is _____ _____ . ⇔
4. Providing continuous information about the functioning of a person's physiological processes is called _____ .
5. A backup reinforcer for tokens might be _____ . ⇔
6. A means of identifying reinforcers by presenting different stimuli to the person and seeing which he or she prefers is _____ .

Answers: **1.** chocolate **2.** activity **3.** they are administered immediately/easily and quickly **4.** biofeedback **5.** watching TV **6.** structured tests

· ·

formed *E*, those initial attempts would receive praise. But then the father's standards would begin to increase, and Erin would be required to make successively better approximations to receive praise. Although shaping is usually used to train a behavior the person doesn't presently perform, it can also be applied to improve an existing skill—making a very good tennis backhand stroke excellent, for example.

Types of Shaping

Shaping can be applied to improve qualitative and quantitative features of the behavior. In *qualitative shaping* (or "topographic" shaping) the successively higher standards for performance pertain to the degree to which the responses look, sound, or feel like the well-formed behavior. Erin's printing better and better *E*s is an example of qualitative shaping. *Quantitative shaping* refers to setting criteria for reinforcement to increase or decrease the quantity of the behavior, perhaps by changing its frequency, duration, or magnitude. An example of quantitative shaping is provided by a study that used biofeedback methods to increase a 20-year-old man's heart rate by 17 beats per minute above baseline levels (Scott et al., 1973). The subject could hear the audio portion of television programs at all times during the intervention, but the video portion remained on only if he kept his heart rate at certain levels. The initial criterion was 5 beats above baseline to keep the video portion on, but the criterion was raised once each level had been achieved. An older man's heart rate was decreased by 16 beats per minute in a similar fashion. These changes were temporary, of course. Another study used shaping to induce a retarded girl, who rarely spoke at an audible level, to talk louder and louder (Jackson & Wallace, 1974).

Shaping "Steps"

Shaping advances the behavior through a series of levels, and movement from one level to the next is a *step*. Because the behavior that undergoes shaping is new to the person, it generally starts as a very primitive approximation to the desired action—and it often is so primitive that its relationship to the desired behavior may be hard to see. Erin's first attempt to print an *E* might be a squiggle that has little resemblance to the letter. But as a first approximation, it's probably worth reinforcing.

How big should the steps be? There's no hard and fast answer to this question because step sizes depend on the difficulty of the task and the learner's abilities. But a very general rule can be given: shaping steps should be large enough to produce some challenge and fairly quick progress, but small enough to allow the person to succeed. If a step is too large, the person will fail. Here are three guidelines to follow:

- Do not try to advance to the next step until the person has mastered the current one. If you do, the required degree of change is likely to be too big.

- If the person's behavior begins to deteriorate because you tried to advance too quickly, reinforce an earlier approximation to build from there again.

- Try not to make the steps too small, either. If you do, the task may become boring, the training will be inefficient and unnecessarily expensive, and the person may become "stuck" at a level of behavior that has produced inordinate reinforcement.

Perhaps the best advice in shaping behavior is to *be flexible* enough to speed up or slow down the shaping process as needed. Being able to shape behavior effectively is a skill that requires knowledge of the person's abilities and experience in training different people to perform various tasks. Computer programs are now available that simulate important features of the shaping process and help train the skills needed to administer reinforcement effectively (Acker, Goldwater, & Agnew, 1990).

Shortcuts to Shaping

As you read the material on shaping, you may have recognized that there are ways to shortcut the process of shaping. Four of the approaches we discussed in Chapter 4 to shortcut stimulus control can be used to speed shaping, too. One way to shortcut shaping is to use *physical guidance,* manually moving the person's body through the desired movements. Another method involves using *pictures* of the behavior or its product, such as a printed letter. The third approach is *modeling* the behavior. And the fourth way to shortcut shaping is to use *instructions* to describe how to perform the responses. Only the last approach requires good language skills on the part of the learner.

Timing and Schedules of Reinforcement

When we are helping someone change an existing behavior or learn a new one, we can maximize the effect of reinforcement by delivering it *immediately after each and every correct response* (Chung, 1965; Michael, 1986). This is an important rule. The longer we delay giving the reinforcer, the less effective it will be in strengthening the behavior—even if the delay is just a matter of several seconds. Suppose that the reinforcers cannot be given immediately—for instance, we are using prizes for improved performance throughout a whole school day? We should find ways to *bridge the delay* in time between the behavior and the reinforcer. The best way to bridge the delay is to use additional reinforcers that can be delivered immediately, such as tokens or praise, being sure to describe instances of the target behavior when we give the prizes.

Thinning the Schedule of Reinforcement

During an intervention to change or teach behaviors, we monitor a person's responses and try to time or "schedule" reinforcement for each and every correct response—a pattern called a **continuous reinforcement** (CRF) schedule. This

Dennis the Menace
By HANK KETCHAM

"That's where my Mom pastes a gold star on the days I'm good."

DENNIS THE MENACE ® used by permission of Hank Ketcham and © by North America Syndicate.

One reason Dennis's behavior has not been good enough to earn a star may be that no reinforcers are given immediately after his good behavior. There is probably too much delay in the procedure of giving a star at the end of the day, particularly if that is the only reinforcer provided.

approach is ideal and produces the fastest progress in modifying behavior. But we cannot monitor people's behavior and provide continuous reinforcement forever. Fortunately, it isn't necessary to do this. We can actually help individuals maintain the target behavior and strengthen their self-regulation by phasing out our use of reinforcement after the behavioral goal has been achieved and the target behavior is well established.

How can we phase out reliance on reinforcers? By gradually changing the **schedule of reinforcement**—that is, the rule that determines which instances of a response, if any, will be reinforced. Most of our behaviors do not receive reinforcers from others each time they occur; sometimes they are reinforced, and sometimes they are not. If you clean your room, sometimes people notice and praise you, and sometimes they don't. At the end of behavior change programs, we try to copy everyday life by employing a procedure called **thinning**, in which we gradually reduce the *rate* at which the behavior receives reinforcement. For example, we might start by reinforcing, say, 80% of correct responses for a few days, and then slowly reducing the rate to 60%, 40%, 20%, and 10%. These gradual reductions make the schedule of reinforcement progressively "thinner." Reinforcing only some instances of a behavior is called **intermittent reinforcement** or *partial reinforcement*. There are several types of reinforcement schedule, and we will discuss them in detail in Chapter 11.

Research by Frank Kirby and Frank Shields (1972) provides an example of thinning a schedule of reinforcement in an intervention to improve the arithmetic skills of a 13-year-old boy named Tom. Each day, the researchers gave Tom a set of 20 math problems to do in 20 minutes. They reinforced Tom's correct arithmetic answers with simple statements of praise, such as "Good work" or "Great, you got 14 right today." Every couple of days they doubled the number of problems Tom needed to complete to receive praise, eventually requiring 16 correct problems. By the end of this program, the speed at which the student correctly computed math problems tripled compared with his baseline performance. What's more, Tom's on-task behavior increased during the intervention, even though that aspect of his conduct was not specifically reinforced.

Probably the simplest schedule of reinforcement is to stop rewarding a behavior entirely. **Extinction** is the condition in which a behavior no longer receives reinforcement, making the person less likely to perform it in the future. One of the main benefits of thinning the reinforcement schedule at the end of an intervention is that the *target behavior usually becomes even stronger*—that is, it occurs at a higher rate than under continuous reinforcement and persists longer when reinforcement is discontinued entirely. This is one of several ways to help maintain appropriate behavior after an intervention ends. In Chapters 6 and 11, we will discuss in detail the effects of extinction on behavior and ways to maintain improved behaviors.

Delaying Reinforcement

Another way to phase out a person's reliance on reinforcers and maintain the target behavior after the intervention ends is to increase the delay between the occurrence of the response and its reinforcer. As in thinning schedules of reinforcement, delaying reinforcement is begun when the behavior is well established, and it proceeds in gradual "steps." This approach was used in an intervention to increase elementary schoolers' adherence to rules of good classroom conduct, such as working quietly on assignments and following the teachers' instructions (Greenwood et al., 1974). The students received continuous feedback regarding their conduct during reading and mathematics sessions, and activity reinforcers were given immediately after each session if their behavior met certain criteria. When the students' good conduct was well established, the activity reinforcers were delayed more and more, obliging the students to behave well for longer periods of time before engaging in the reinforcing activities. Follow-up assessments taken a few weeks after the intervention ended showed that the children's good conduct remained at high levels.

Using Reinforcers to Develop Behavior Chains

When teaching a complex series of responses that forms a behavior chain, we often need to identify its links by doing a task analysis, as we saw in Chapter 3. Suppose we wanted to help a young retarded boy learn to dress himself, and we were teaching him to put on his sock while seated. This chain consists of four links, each containing an antecedent cue (an S^D) and a response. The responses are: (1) *grasp* a sock with one hand, making sure the heel points down; (2) *spread* the hole with the fingers of both hands; (3) *position* the foot up at the hole; and (4) *insert* the foot into the sock. Seeing each response completed serves as the cue for the next link, as depicted in the following diagram:

$$S^{D1} \rightarrow R_{(1)} \rightarrow S^{D2} \rightarrow R_{(2)} \rightarrow S^{D3} \rightarrow R_{(3)} \rightarrow S^{D4} \rightarrow R_{(4)} \rightarrow \textbf{Reinforcer}$$

see   *grasp*   see   *spread*   see   *position*   see   *insert*
sock   grasp   spread   position

Once we know what the links are, we can teach the chain using one of three main methods:

- **Forward chaining** involves teaching one link at a time in sequence, beginning with the first. In our example, the child would first learn to grasp the sock correctly, and the reinforcer would be given just for that response. After the first link has been mastered, the child must add the second link (spread the hole with the fingers) to the first to get the reinforcer. Then the next link is added, and so on, until all links have been performed and the chain must be completed before the reinforcer is administered.

- **Backward chaining** consists of teaching one link at a time in the reverse sequence, beginning with the last one. Referring again to the diagram above, the child would first learn to insert the foot correctly, $R_{(4)}$, and the reinforcer would be given for that response. Then the child would need to add the next-to-last link ($R_{(3)}$—position the foot at the hole) to the last link to get the reinforcer. This reverse sequence continues until the chain is complete.

- **Total-task presentation** is teaching all the links together as a full sequence. From the start of training, the child would be required to make the entire series of links from beginning to end to receive the reinforcer.

In each of these training methods, the teacher may use prompts of all kinds, as they are needed to perform each link. Is one of these methods best? Studies with retarded people have compared these methods and found that the total-task presentation method teaches behavior chains at least as quickly as backward or forward chaining methods (Kayser, Billingsley, & Neel, 1986; Spooner, 1984; Yu et al., 1980). But two reservations about this conclusion should be mentioned. First, some evidence suggests that individuals who are severely retarded show more disruptive behavior, such as aggression, when trained with total-task methods than with methods that break the task down (Weld & Evans, 1990). Second, for chains in which the last link is particularly difficult, backward chaining methods may offer the best approach (Ash & Holding, 1990).

Regardless of which method we use to teach a behavior chain, a few guidelines should be followed to enhance training effectiveness. First, be sure that all the links the task analysis identifies are simple enough for the person to learn without too much difficulty. Second, design the approach to ensure that to receive reinforcement, the person must perform all the links he or she has learned, and always in the correct order. Third, apply and then fade shortcut stimulus control methods—prompts, modeling, and instructions—to help the person learn the links. Last, we should use shaping and give reinforcement liberally as we begin to teach each link.

Using Group and Individual Contingencies

Most of the interventions we have seen so far in this book have involved *individual contingencies*—that is, the reinforcers received were contingent on the learner's own behavior and did not depend on what anyone else did. But it is possible to arrange contingencies in ways that involve the performance of groups of people. We will discuss some of these approaches in this section.

Reducing Extraneous Counterproductive Reinforcers

Picture this scenario. Almost every day for the past month Miss Jones, the teacher of a sixth-grade class, has shown her displeasure when one student, Jeff, has come to class late, disrupting ongoing activities. When he arrives, the other students giggle, which reinforces Jeff's behavior of arriving late. Miss Jones will need to stop that reinforcement if she is to eliminate Jeff's lateness.

Two approaches can stop a group from reinforcing a person's inappropriate behavior. One way is to *reinforce them for not reinforcing* the person. This approach was used in the program we discussed earlier to reduce the classroom tantrums of a girl named Diane (Carlson et al., 1968). In addition to giving Diane tokens for non-tantrum behavior, the teacher attempted to reduce the social reinforcers the child might receive from her classmates for disruptive behavior. If Diane had a tantrum, she was taken to the back of the room so her classmates couldn't watch her, and the other children were given candy treats if they didn't turn around. The second approach involves having the *other people share in the rewards* the individual earns for improved behavior. In the intervention reported by Carlson and coworkers, the whole class would have a party if Diane did not have a tantrum for four half-days in a row. A similar approach was used effectively on a much larger scale to reduce classroom conduct problems of 48 third- to sixth-grade students (Walker & Buckley, 1972). The backup reinforcers in this token reinforcement program included watching cartoons and taking field trips.

Lotteries

A **lottery** is a procedure in which all eligible individuals are entered in a drawing to determine one or more prizewinners on the basis of chance. In behavior change programs, eligibility to enter lotteries is based on people's behavior; as a rule, a token system is used to keep track of participation. Entering individuals into a lottery is often as simple a process as giving one entry to each person whose behavior meets a certain criterion. But other methods to enter people can be more complicated—for example, by allowing more than one entry per person on the basis of the number of points he or she earned and whether the behavior has improved since the last lottery (Sarafino, 1977).

Lotteries can be used in many different settings, including schools, psychiatric hospitals, and workplaces. For instance, a lottery intervention by Michael Johnson and Stephen Fawcett (1994) was introduced to improve the courteousness of human service staff when they interacted with clients. The staff first received training in such specific forms of courtesy as addressing clients by name and stating reasons for requesting information. In the lottery, assessments of the staff members' courteousness determined how many entries they had in a weekly drawing for a $10 cash prize. As Figure 5.3 shows, the training alone increased courteous behavior substantially, and the lottery increased it a good deal more and made it more consistent. Other lottery interventions in workplaces have reduced employee absenteeism and unnecessary use of automobiles (Foxx & Schaeffer, 1981; Pedalino & Gamboa, 1974).

Group Contingencies

In an intervention that uses a **group contingency**, the performance of *all members of the group* determines the consequences that befall its members. An intervention that used a group contingency for reinforcement was conducted with boys whose prior behavior indicated that they were at risk of becoming habitual delinquents (Alexander, Corbett, & Smigel, 1976). The boys were living at a treatment center and were supposed to go to a high school during the day, but they skipped nearly half of their classes. To increase class attendance, lunch money was used as a reinforcer. The boys had been accustomed to receiving lunch money from the center with no strings attached. But a few weeks before the intervention began, the center started packing sack lunches for the boys instead. Then the boys were told that they could get lunch money instead of sack lunches if they attended all their classes. At first this reinforcer was on an individual contingency: if a boy attended all his classes for the day, he received the money for the next day. Later, the lunch money was offered on a group contingency: the boys would receive money only if *all* the boys attended *all* their classes for the preceding day. Under the individual contingency, attendance increased to an average of about 80% of the classes; but with the group contingency, the boys' average attendance increased to nearly 100%.

Another way group contingencies can be used is to divide the individuals into *teams* that compete for reinforcers. An intervention used this approach to improve first- and second-grade children's toothbrushing (Swain, Allard, & Holborn, 1982). Each class was divided into teams to play the "Good Toothbrushing Game" in which four children from each team were chosen at random each day to have their oral hygiene assessed with a standardized procedure. All members of the class team with the best oral hygiene score got "scratch 'n' sniff" stickers and had their names post-

Figure 5.3 Performance of courteous behaviors by three subjects (staff members) during interactions with clients, as reflected in the percentage of the 30 trained behaviors they were expected to use in the courtesy training intervention phase. The data for the baseline, courtesy training, and lottery phases were collected over a 5-month period. (From Johnson & Fawcett, 1994, Figure 1.)

ed. The children's oral hygiene scores improved markedly during the intervention and remained quite good at a follow-up assessment 9 months later.

Group contingencies have three main advantages over individual contingencies in behavior modification programs. For one thing, programs with group contingencies are easier to administer—it is simpler to monitor and keep records on behavior and to dispense reinforcers for a group as a whole than to carry out these tasks for each individual in a group. Second, group contingencies have built-in incentives to prevent members of the group from reinforcing one another's inappropriate responses. Third, group contingencies often promote desirable side effects in the social behaviors of the group members (Greenwood & Hops, 1981). For example, Frank Kohler and Charles Greenwood (1990) implemented a program in which elementary school classmates were assigned to teams that were divided into pairs of students to tutor each other in spelling. After the children had received training in tutoring, they earned points for practicing these skills. The only reinforcer the teacher provided for tutoring was announcing at the end of each day which team, having earned the most points that day, was the winner. With this contingency, the children not only performed the tutoring skills they were trained to do, but some students added helpful techniques they had not been trained to use, such as spelling the word more than once when correcting a teammate's errors. In a similar vein, another study found that among elementary school children, group contingencies for candy rewards produced greater cooperation than individual contingencies (Williamson et al., 1992). But one caution should be pointed out: group contingencies sometimes lead to negative peer-pressure tactics, such as threats or scolding (Greenwood & Hops, 1981). Although it isn't entirely clear why these negative tactics occur, they are probably more likely when the program consequences include group *punishment* if behavioral criteria are not met. (Go to 🔍.)

Who Will Administer Reinforcement?

In most of the interventions we have discussed so far, reinforcement was administered by teachers, therapists, or parents. But many behavior change programs have used peer-administered or self-administered reinforcement. How well do these approaches work?

Peer-Administered Reinforcement

Studies have shown that children can monitor other children's behavior and provide reinforcement for correct responses. As an example, an intervention was introduced to improve the arithmetic skills of underachieving fifth-grade students, with classmates serving as tutors (Pigott, Fantuzzo, & Clement, 1986). The tutors' jobs included keeping score of the number of math problems each student completed correctly, comparing that number with the current goal, and deciding whether the tutee had earned any backup reinforcers. During baseline, the students who were to receive the intervention had averaged only about half as many

Q Close-Up 5.2
Can Rewards Undermine Behavior?

In the early 1970s a study with preschool children produced surprising and provocative results suggesting that giving children rewards for a behavior they like to do may reduce their performance of that behavior in the future (Lepper, Greene, & Nisbett, 1973). Children who were already interested in drawing pictures with Magic Markers were asked to draw some pictures. Some of the children were shown a Good Player Award and told they would get that prize for drawing pictures. Other children got the same opportunity to draw pictures without being told about a prize. After doing the drawings, the children who expected the reward received it, and the others did not. Several days later, the researchers secretly observed the children while materials for drawing and other activities were freely available, with no prizes offered to anyone. At this time, the children who received the reward for drawing spent less time using the drawing materials than those who had not gotten the reward. Similar effects have been reported for older individuals, using a variety of tangible rewards (Sarafino, 1984). Does getting a reward for doing a preferred activity reduce people's interest in that activity?

The idea that rewards can reduce our interest in activities we enjoy contradicts common sense.

After all, many people get paid for work they enjoy and continue to work hard despite receiving paychecks. Research since the 1970s has clarified the effects of rewards on preferred activities. First of all, many studies have found no decrease in interest after people got rewards for performing enjoyable activities (Dickinson, 1989; Flora, 1990). Second, the conditions under which reduced interest sometimes occurs are very limited: the person's interest before being rewarded must be very high, the reward must be *tangible or consumable*, and the person must expect that people are *not normally given rewards* for the activity (Sarafino, 1984). Third, when reduced interest does occur, these

decrements are *transient* if the individual continues to perform the task following the reward, and are not likely at all if individuals *meet or exceed specified performance standards*, or if rewards *increase the frequency* of the behavior and are delivered *repetitively*. (Dickinson, 1989, p. 12, italics added)

So, it appears that rewards can undermine people's interest in enjoyable activities, but the likelihood and durability of these effects are minimal.

correct math problems as their classmates. But their performance improved dramatically, equaling that of their classmates by the end of the 3-week intervention and during the next 12 weeks of follow-up assessments. Other studies have shown that programs with same-aged children serving as tutors and administering reinforcement can improve ninth-graders' reading skills and retarded children's social skills (Greer & Polirstok, 1982; Lancioni, 1982).

Using peers as tutors and administrators of reinforcement has some advantages. For one thing, the individuals requiring the intervention can receive more frequent and individualized help than is available with standard teaching procedures. Second, the peers who serve as tutors often gain from the experience themselves. For instance, the target behaviors they are helping others improve, such as socialization with classmates, also tend to improve in themselves (Dougherty, Fowler, & Paine, 1985; Fowler et al., 1986). In addition, the general social relationships among the tutors and tutees also tend to improve as a result of the intervention experiences (Fantuzzo & Clement, 1981; McGee et al., 1982; Pigott, Fantuzzo, & Clement, 1986; Sanders & Glynn, 1977). A potential disadvantage of using peer-administered reinforcement with children is that they appear to be much more liberal than teachers in giving reinforcers. A study found that although children correctly gave reinforcers that were earned, they often provided reinforcers that were *not* earned, too (L. K. C. Smith & Fowler, 1984). When children administer reinforcement, the professional who supervises them should monitor their decision making periodically and try to improve it when needed.

Self-Administered Reinforcement

Administering reinforcement to oneself is the cornerstone of self-management programs and is often used as a supplemental method in behavior therapy. This technique has been used in a variety of settings and has been applied to change many different behaviors, such as college students' studying and psychotherapy patients' feelings of anxiety (Gross & Drabman, 1982; R. T. Jones, Nelson, & Kazdin, 1977).

Several studies have examined the use of self-administered reinforcement in classroom settings. In an intervention to improve third-graders' story writing, the children wrote a story in class each day and assessed it for number of sentences, verb variations, and modifying words (adjectives and adverbs) it contained (Ballard & Glynn, 1975). The children had been taught how to use verbs and modifying words, and these features were listed on a chart they could see while they scored their stories to determine the number of points earned. These points could be exchanged later for backup reinforcers of choice, such as having their stories displayed publicly or being allowed to play games or read. Self-reinforcement more than doubled the stories' numbers of sentences, verb variations, and modifying words over baseline levels. What's more, ratings of the stories by English instructors who knew nothing about the study revealed that the stories written when self-reinforcement procedures were in effect were of higher quality than those written during baseline.

One problem with using self-administered reinforcement is that sometimes people take unearned rewards (Gross & Drabman, 1982; McReynolds & Church, 1973; Santogrossi et al., 1973). It is difficult to know how deliberate such errors are. Although it sometimes appears that individuals must know they have not performed the behavior, oftentimes these reinforcement errors seem to result from the subjects' use of very lenient standards in assessing their behavior. Three approaches can help reduce these errors. First, training by using modeling and instruction methods can show how more rigorous or accurate standards can be applied to personal behavior (Gross & Drabman, 1982; O'Brien, Riner, & Budd, 1983). Second, having the person make his or her target behavior and goals public appears to increase accuracy in self-reinforcement (Hayes et al., 1985). Third, using an accuracy checking procedure in a behavior change program increases the person's accuracy, especially if there are consequences for inaccuracies (Hundert & Batstone, 1978; McLaughlin, Burgess, & Sackville-West, 1982).

Negative Reinforcement in Escape and Avoidance

If you were to ask cigarette smokers why they smoke, chances are many of them would implicate the role of negative reinforcement, saying, "It relieves my tension." We've seen that negative reinforcement strengthens behaviors we perform that reduce aversive circumstances in our lives. Tension is aversive, and the nicotine in cigarette smoke triggers in just a few seconds the release of chemicals that reduce feelings of tension, anxiety, and pain (Pomerleau & Pomerleau, 1989). Using other substances, such as alcohol, appears to have similar effects. The aversive stimuli we try to reduce can be *covert*, as in anxiety or depression, or *overt*, as when someone is physically hurting us. In these situations, we learn to perform behaviors that help us escape from the aversive stimuli.

Escape and Avoidance

In **escape conditioning**, we learn to make responses that reduce or eliminate aversive stimuli we are currently experiencing. If these responses succeed, they are strengthened through the process of negative reinforcement. Escape conditioning is clearly useful when the aversive stimuli we experience can harm us and when the behaviors we learn enable us to adapt well in our lives.

But escape conditioning can lead to maladaptive behaviors, too. For example, children may learn that lying can help them escape from teachers' or parents' threatening accusations or that being disruptive in school can help them escape from a class they don't like. A series of studies by Brian Iwata and his colleagues

PEANUTS reprinted by permission of United Features Syndicate, Inc.

Charlie Brown's failing to raise his hand suggests that he has learned through avoidance conditioning not to volunteer for potentially aversive events.

(1990) examined this process in developmentally disabled children who frequent-ly performed self-injurious behaviors, such as banging their heads or biting their arms. Part of the research essentially entailed a functional analysis of the self-inju-rious behaviors by means of systematic environmental manipulations—that is, introducing various antecedents and consequences to see whether they affected the behavior. Two findings from this research are relevant here. First, self-injurious behaviors were especially frequent when the children were asked to perform a behavior they were being trained to do, such as a self-help skill. Second, self-injuri-ous behavior became more frequent when it resulted in the trainer stopping the training activity, removing the training materials, and turning away from the child. These findings indicate that training procedures can be unpleasant to children with developmental disabilities and that stopping the training when self-injury occurs negatively reinforces the escape behaviors.

How can we eliminate maladaptive escape behaviors? One way uses the process of extinction—that is, terminating the negative reinforcement. In another part of the research by Iwata and his coworkers, they provided physical guidance in doing the task when self-injurious behavior occurred, instead of stopping the training. This approach almost entirely eliminated the self-injurious behavior during train-ing sessions. Another way to eliminate maladaptive escape behaviors is to use escape to negatively reinforce adaptive alternative responses. This was done with children who were very disruptive during dental treatment (Allen et al., 1992; Allen & Stokes, 1987). Their disruptive behavior decreased markedly when the dentist praised them and gave them "a little rest break" for being quiet and still but did not stop the treatment when disruptive behavior occurred.

What do people do if they can predict that an aversive event is likely to happen? They do something to try to avoid the unpleasant experience. In **avoidance condi-tioning**, we learn to respond in ways that prevent us from experiencing aversive events. For instance, we learn to carry an umbrella when rain is likely and to give an excuse if asked to do something we find threatening, such as giving a speech. When I was a child, I learned to predict that I'd be in deep trouble if I didn't get home immediately when I heard my mother call, "Edward *Paul* Sarafino!" The mid-dle name signaled future trouble, which I learned to avoid by going home right away.

Learning to avoid aversive events appears to be a two-step process. According to O. H. Mowrer's *two-factor theory* (1947), the first step is to learn the signal as a con-ditioned stimulus in respondent conditioning. When my mother first used my mid-dle name to call me, I didn't know what it meant, dallied a while, and encountered the "trouble"—the unconditioned stimulus—when I finally got home. The uncon-ditioned response was feeling distress. Soon the signal (the CS) gained the ability to elicit distress, a covert aversive stimulus I could reduce by going right home. Thus, the second step involves operant conditioning: in my case, avoidance behav-ior (going home immediately) received negative reinforcement by reducing my feeling of distress.

A good deal of evidence supports the combined roles of respondent and oper-ant conditioning in learning to avoid aversive events (Stasiewicz & Maisto, 1993).

But two-factor theory does not fully explain avoidance behavior. For instance, people often learn to avoid events of which they have no direct experience, as children do when they stay away from a house they've heard is "haunted." In addition, research has shown that avoidance behavior that was learned by direct experience can be extremely persistent even though the aversive event has not occurred since the original experience (Solomon, Kamin, & Wynne, 1953; Herrnstein, 1969).

To explain such features of avoidance behavior, some researchers have proposed that cognitive factors are also involved. For instance, it may be that when people learn avoidance behaviors, they also learn two *expectancies*: (1) "If *I make* the avoidance response, *I will not experience* the aversive event," and (2) "If *I do not make* the avoidance response, *I will experience* the aversive event" (Seligman & Johnston, 1973). By making the avoidance response consistently thereafter, individuals confirm the first expectancy and *fail to disconfirm* the second one. Although incorporating cognitive factors to explain avoidance behavior has some appeal, many researchers disagree that such factors are necessary or useful (Pear & Eldridge, 1984).

Factors Affecting Negative Reinforcement Effectiveness

Several factors can contribute to the effectiveness of negative reinforcement in our learning to escape or avoid aversive events. One factor is the *reward value* of the negative reinforcement, which appears to be determined by how much the escape or avoidance behavior reduces the aversive stimulus. The greater the degree to which the behavior removes the aversive event, the more effective the negative reinforcement is (Campbell & Kraeling, 1953). Thus, your behavior of taking aspirin when you have a headache is more strongly reinforced if it reduces the headache by 90% than by only 50%. Another factor is the strength of the aversive stimulus: negative reinforcement is more effective when the behavior reduces a very aversive stimulus than when it reduces a milder stimulus (Piliavin et al., 1981). The last factor we'll consider is the delay of reinforcement: the more quickly the behavior results in removing the aversive stimulus, the more effective the negative reinforcement will be (Weiss, Cecil, & Frank, 1973).

Although negative reinforcement occurs very frequently in our everyday lives and influences much of our behavior, it isn't used very often in behavior modification programs. Professionals who design and administer interventions to change behavior typically try to minimize the use of aversive events, partly because of undesirable side effects in the person's behavior. Often when aversive events are used, the subject becomes physically aggressive and makes efforts to escape or avoid the program and the staff involved in it. In addition, the behaviors rewarded through negative reinforcement are often "superficial." For example, a child may apologize verbally for having been bad, thereby escaping or avoiding punishment, but the apology may be insincere. If it is, insincere behavior is reinforced. When negative reinforcement must be used, the person should receive clear instructions about the link between making the escape or avoidance response and reducing the aversive stimulus, and positive reinforcement should be provided for performing the target behavior. (Go to ✔ .)

Application Exercise

The Chapter 4 work sheet laid the foundation for conducting a functional analysis of your target behavior(s). You determined your hunches about the antecedents to your behavior, made plans for collecting data and keeping records regarding your behavior, and designed your A-B-C log. Now that we've defined reinforcement and examined the forms it can take, you have enough information to begin analyzing the functions of your behavior in relation to its antecedents and consequences. The main objectives of this application exercise are to get started on data collection for your functional analysis, to design a summary record format, and to identify possible reinforcers for use in your self-management program.

Tips on Using Reinforcement

Most of these tips on using reinforcement have been applied by professionals in a wide variety of behavior change interventions. You'll find them useful in designing your self-management program, particularly as you finalize the design of your program in Chapter 9.

1. Be sure to select reinforcers with strong reward value and apply them consistently for performing operant target behaviors. If the target behavior is a respondent behavior, such as an emotional response, apply the reinforcers for performing the behavior modification activities to change that response.

2. Don't use reinforcers that could work against the behavioral or outcome goals. For instance, it's not a good idea to use sweets as a reward for meeting subgoals in a diet program to reduce caloric intake. This may seem obvious, but I've had students propose such rewards for their self-management projects.

3. Make sure the person whose behavior is to be changed is aware that the reinforcers are contingent on and consequences for the target behavior.

4. Use a variety of reinforcers whenever possible. One good idea is to allow the person to select from a menu the reinforcer he or she wants when it has been earned.

5. Be sure to maintain a high degree of reward value during the intervention. If you are using consumable reinforcers, be careful not to let the person become satiated on them before a training session is over. To prevent this problem, you can either switch reinforcer types periodically or give small portions of the food or drink for each instance of reward.

6. Use naturally occurring reinforcers, such as praise, whenever possible.

✔ Concept Check 5.3

1. A voice coach who reinforces gradual improvements in the "feeling" a students' voice projects is using _____ shaping.

2. A reinforcer you could use to bridge a delay between the target behavior and its main reinforcer is _____

   _____ . ⇔

3. Gradually reducing the rate at which a behavior is reinforced is called _____ .

4. An example of a behavior chain is _____ ; if you were teaching that chain using backward chaining, the first link you would train would be _____ . ↔

5. An employer who gives special privileges to an entire department if all members come to work on time is using a _____ contingency for reinforcement.

6. Having classmates monitor and provide reinforcement for other students' behavior is called _____ .

7. According to two-factor theory, the first step in learning to avoid an aversive stimulus involves _____ conditioning.

_____
Answers: respondent **7.** peer-administered reinforcement **6.** group **5.** doorknob
1. qualitative **2.** praise/tokens **3.** thinning **4.** open a locked door; push the

7. Make sure that some kind of reinforcement can be presented immediately after the appropriate behavior and that it will not disrupt ongoing desirable responses very much.

8. Give reinforcement on a CRF schedule initially, and thin the schedule when the behavior has become well established.

9. Watch for and try to eliminate counterproductive extraneous reinforcers.

10. Be wary of using reinforcers that are social activities, such as going to a concert with a friend. If the target behavior doesn't meet the criteria for earning the reward, what happens to tickets bought in advance? And what about the problems that now arise with the friend?

11. Check the behavior periodically to make sure the reinforcer is improving it.

12. Go through this chapter and consider all the reinforcer types and the methods for administering them that we discussed. Identify the ones that might work in the intervention you design.

The Next Steps in Your Program Design

In this application exercise, the first task toward your program design will be to get your functional analysis started. Some of you may need to obtain feedback on your plans from your instructor or fellow students before starting to collect data. If you need to get feedback, wait to start the functional analysis until you have it. When you have the feedback, do two things:

- Get your A-B-C log ready to use. Revise your A-B-C log design as needed, type up the log as a form on a single sheet of paper, and make several copies of it to fill in with numerical and written information as shown in Figure 3.5.
- Reread the Chapter 3 material in the section entitled "Analyzing the Functions of Behavior" to refresh your memory on how to do a functional analysis.

Once you've done the rereading, you should be ready to begin collecting data for your A-B-C log. Follow the Chapter 3 instructions carefully.

For the remaining tasks in this application exercise, we will identify several reinforcers you can use in your program, make some tentative plans on how you might administer reinforcement, and design a summary record to organize the data from your A-B-C log. Turn now to Work Sheet 5.1 to complete these tasks.

Summary

Consequences that provide reinforcement strengthen the behaviors on which they are contingent. This rule is true for positive and negative reinforcement. Unconditioned reinforcers satisfy basic physiological needs without having to be learned, but we learn to value conditioned reinforcers as they become associated in our lives with stimuli that are already reinforcing. Evidence suggests that reinforcers can strengthen behavior for three reasons: they reduce biologically based drives directly or indirectly; they provide sensory stimulation; and they involve performing high-probability behaviors.

Positive reinforcers include tangible or consumable items, Premack principle activities, social reinforcers, feedback, tokens, and covert reinforcers. We can identify potential reinforcers for an intervention by using direct assessment methods, such as naturalistic observations and structured tests, and indirect assessment methods, such as self-report instruments like the Preferred Items and Experiences Questionnaire (Figure 5.2). The effectiveness of reinforcers can be enhanced by the technique of reinforcer sampling, in which a small or brief sample of the consequence is presented before the behavior.

Many different procedures are available for administering reinforcement. Shaping is a technique in which behavior improves because the standards for receiving reinforcement are increased gradually. Interventions generally apply a continuous reinforcement schedule initially. When the behavior is well established, the schedule of reinforcement undergoes a procedure called thinning; that is, the rate at which the behavior is reinforced is reduced within schedules of intermittent reinforcement. In the condition of extinction, reinforcement is terminated. When teaching chains, reinforcers can be administered within forward chaining, backward chaining, and total-task presentation procedures. Reinforcement also can be administered with individual and group contingencies and by using peer- and self-administered reinforcement methods. Negative reinforcement is involved in escape and avoidance conditioning.

Key Terms and Review Questions

Key Terms

reinforcement

positive reinforcement

negative reinforcement

unconditioned reinforcers

conditioned reinforcers

Premack principle

tokens

reinforcer sampling

shaping

continuous reinforcement

schedule of reinforcement

thinning

intermittent reinforcement

extinction

forward chaining

backward chaining

total-task presentation

lottery

group contingency

escape conditioning

avoidance conditioning

Review Questions

1. Define positive and negative reinforcement, indicating how they are different. Give two examples of each.

2. What determines the reward value in positive and negative reinforcement?

3. What is the difference between unconditioned and conditioned reinforcers?

4. Describe two research examples suggesting that not all reinforcers directly or indirectly reduce biologically based drives.

5. What are tangible and consumable reinforcers? Give two examples of each.

6. Describe two examples of the use of the Premack principle in your life.

7. Give two examples each of teachers using social reinforcement and feedback in the classroom.

8. What are tokens and backup reinforcers?

9. Describe how direct and indirect assessment methods can be used to identify potential reinforcers.

10. Define and give examples of qualitative and quantitive shaping.

11. Describe a thinning procedure you might use to reduce the rate of reinforcement you give in an intervention.

12. Compare the procedures of forward chaining, backward chaining, and total-task presentation.

13. What are the advantages of using group contingencies for reinforcement?

14. What are the advantages and disadvantages of using peer- and self-administered reinforcement?

15. Describe the two-factor theory of avoidance conditioning, and give an example of how these processes may have happened in your own escape and avoidance behavior.

16. Describe three factors that determine the effectiveness of negative reinforcement.

Related Readings

Bellamy, G. T., Horner, R. H., & Inman, D. P. (1979). *Vocational habilitation of severely retarded adults: A direct service technology.* Baltimore: University Park Press.

Dickinson, A. M. (1989). The detrimental effects of extrinsic reinforcement on "intrinsic motivation." *Behavior Analyst, 12,* 1–15.

Jones, R. T., Nelson, R. E., & Kazdin, A. E. (1977). The role of external variables in self-reinforcement. *Behavior Modification, 1,* 147–178.

Michael, J. (1975). Positive and negative reinforcement, a distinction that is no longer necessary; or a better way to talk about bad things. *Behaviorism, 3,* 33–44.

Premack, D. (1965). Reinforcement theory. In D. Levine (Ed.), *Nebraska Symposium on Motivation.* Lincoln: University of Nebraska Press.

Name _____   Day & time
                                      class meets_____
Date _____

Chapter 5: Work Sheet 5.1

1. Your self-management target behavior(s): _____

2. To identify potential reinforcers you might use in your program, complete the Preferred Items and Experiences Questionnaire (PIEQ) presented in Figure 5.2. Then use your ratings on the PIEQ to pick *10 to 15 items or experiences you like most* to receive, have, or do. List these potential reinforcers below, along with the ratings you gave them:

3. Look through your list of potential reinforcers carefully. Are any of these items or experiences things you can't be sure you can receive, have, or do even if you earn them, such as a weekend trip you probably can't afford? Would any of your potential reinforcers work against your goals, as described in tip number 2? Are any of your potential reinforcers social activities you think will lead to difficult and unresolvable problems, like those described in tip number 10? If your answer to any of these questions is *yes*, the items or experiences involved should be *eliminated or modified.*

4. Most of the potential reinforcers you listed above either cannot be given *immediately* after each instance of the behavior you want to reinforce or would *disrupt* the behavior. Although these items or experiences don't qualify for tip number 7, they *can be used as distant or backup reinforcers.* List below some other reinforcers you can include in your program to receive *immediately* after the behavior:

5. If your program involves changing an operant target behavior, outline the "steps" you might use in *shaping* the behavior.

6. Outline a tentative *token reinforcement system* you might use in your program, indicating (a) the behavioral criteria you might require to earn the tokens, (b) the number of tokens you think you might earn in a week, and (c) the number of tokens you would need to buy some possible backup reinforcers.

7. Refer back to Figure 3.6 and compose a draft of a *summary record* form you could use to organize the data you collect in your A-B-C log.

NOTE: If you will be submitting work sheets to your instructor or to a fellow student, make a copy of each sheet before submitting it.

6 *Methods for Decreasing Operant Behavior*

Prologue

Helen was a psychiatric patient who had been hospitalized for several years before a simple behavior modification intervention was conducted by Teodoro Ayllon and Jack Michael (1959) to reduce a problem behavior of hers. That behavior was "psychotic talk," which refers to making statements based on delusional (false) beliefs. Helen would talk mainly about an illegitimate child she claimed to have and men who supposedly pursued her constantly. She had been doing this for 3 years or more. Her psychotic talk was a serious problem because it constituted almost all of her speech—91% of her baseline talking—and it

> had become so annoying during the last 4 months prior to treatment that other patients had on several occasions beaten her in an effort to keep her quiet. . . . Some of the nurses reported that, previously, when the patient started her psychotic talk, they listened to her to get to the "roots of her problem." A few nurses stated that they did not listen to what she was saying but simply nodded and remarked, "Yes, I understand." (p. 327)

Observations of Helen's behavior suggested that people's seeming to pay attention to the psychotic talk was reinforcing it.

So the intervention simply consisted of *extinguishing* the psychotic talk by having the nurses stop paying attention to delusional statements and *reinforcing* appropriate speech by paying attention whenever Helen made sensible statements. After 2 days of these new consequences, the patient's psychotic talk constituted only about 50% of her speech, and after another week, the undesirable behavior declined to 25%. Interestingly, Helen's psychotic talk began to increase again, probably because others at the hospital began to reinforce it: once when Helen wasn't getting attention from a nurse, she said, "Well you're not listening to me. I'll have to go and see [a social worker] again, 'cause she told me that if she would listen to my past she could help me."

In this chapter, we will focus on methods to decrease behavioral excesses. We will examine extinction and punishment, their advantages and disadvantages, and the factors that affect their effectiveness in decreasing undesirable behavior. And we will discuss several other methods for changing unwanted operant behavior.

What Is Extinction?

When discussing operant behavior, the term **extinction** actually has two meanings. It is a *procedure* or *condition* in which reinforcement is terminated for a previously reinforced response, and it is a *process* whereby the likelihood and vigor of performing the no-longer-reinforced response decrease. The verb form for extinction is *to extinguish*. So, we talk about a teacher or therapist extinguishing a child's disruptive behavior; and after the behavior rarely or no longer occurs, we say that it has been extinguished. In reducing Helen's psychotic talk, the nurses used the procedure of extinction when they stopped paying attention to her delusional statements, thereby extinguishing the unwanted behavior.

Extinction can apply to behaviors that have received either positive or negative reinforcement. In either case, reinforcement is terminated and the behavior on which reinforcement was contingent declines. If the consequence of the behavior was *positive reinforcement*, such as receiving tangible or social reinforcers, the extinction procedure consists of ceasing to provide those reinforcers. But if the consequence of maintaining the behavior was *negative reinforcement*, the extinction procedure involves preventing the individual from escaping or avoiding the unpleasant situation he or she is in. Because reducing the unpleasant situation provides negative reinforcement, that consequence must be stopped if extinction is to be used to decrease the behavior. For example, children who do not want to be in school sometimes develop tantrums when they arrive there, leading their parents to take them home (Sarafino, 1986). Extinguishing the tantrums requires that these children not be allowed to get out of being in school.

We know that behavior declines when reinforcement is terminated, but does extinction "erase" the original learning? No, it doesn't. After the response has been extinguished, the individual's memory retains at least part of what was learned in the original conditioning and in extinction (Bouton & Swartzentruber, 1991). Whether the person does or does not perform the behavior after extinction seems to depend on which memory is activated by antecedent stimuli. For instance, people who have quit smoking are much more likely to start smoking again if antecedents occur that are like those that were present during conditioning. These antecedents can be overt, such as seeing a pack of cigarettes, or covert, such as feeling tense. This means that programs designed to change behavior need to prevent the return of an extinguished behavior by incorporating stimulus control techniques to modify the impact of antecedents. And so, programs to stop smoking need to make the antecedents associated with extinction as strong as possible, and the antecedents associated with smoking must be weakened or avoided when the program ends.

Extinction can occur as a haphazard condition in everyday life or as a careful and deliberate procedure in an intervention. In everyday life, for example, if children have parents who are quite indifferent toward or uninvolved in their parenting roles, many of the appropriate social behaviors children observe in school and elsewhere may not receive sufficient reinforcement to be maintained. At the same time, negative social behaviors, such as aggression, may produce quick rewards. These reinforcement patterns help to explain why children with indifferent, uninvolved parents tend to be aggressive, disobedient, and disagreeable (Sarafino & Armstrong, 1986). In contrast, extinction procedures in interventions are planned to accomplish certain behavioral goals. To start an extinction procedure for a target behavior we must identify the reinforcer and be able to control its source. If we don't control the source of reinforcement very carefully, extraneous reinforcers may occur and reinstate the behavior.

Identifying and Controlling Reinforcement for Extinction

The first step in using extinction is to conduct a functional analysis to identify what the reinforcers have existed for the behavior we want to eliminate. Although the reinforcers may seem obvious in some cases, often they are unclear or even surprising. Gary Sasso and his colleagues (1992) conducted a functional analysis to determine the reinforcers for aggressive behavior toward adults by a 7-year-old autistic girl named Molly. They discovered that her aggression was reinforced when the teacher allowed her to escape classroom activities she didn't like and engage in activities she did like. They also found that social attention, such as saying "Please don't do that," did not affect Molly's aggression. This is surprising because attention is a common reinforcer for aggressive behavior. Molly's aggression was reduced with a program that centered around eliminating the negative reinforcement the behavior had been getting.

Similarly, other researchers have found that escaping from academic and self-care training sessions can reinforce self-stimulation and self-injurious behavior, but preventing escape in these circumstances extinguishes the behavior (Iwata et al., 1990, 1994; Repp, Felce, & Barton, 1988). Self-injurious and self-stimulation behaviors were very puzzling for many years because their reinforcers were unknown. Functional analyses allow therapists to identify the reinforcers and eliminate them when it is possible to control them. Sometimes the reinforcers for self-injury or self-stimulation are the sensations the behavior produces in the individual (Iwata et al., 1994; Lovaas, Newsom, & Hickman, 1987). When this is so, eliminating the reinforcement for self-stimulation behaviors may be possible—for example, by blindfolding the person (Rincover & Devany, 1982). But such measures are not always feasible.

Controlling the sources of reinforcement is essential in extinguishing a target behavior. If other sources reinforce the behavior, extinction may not occur. This is often a problem in classrooms when classmates socially reinforce undesirable behavior in fellow students. What's more, if reinforcers appear for behavior that has already been extinguished, it will be reinstated. This is what happened in Helen's case when the social worker paid attention to her psychotic talk. A similar situation happened in an extinction procedure that was applied to eliminate a 21-month-old boy's tantrums at bedtime (C. D. Williams, 1959). These outbursts had been reinforced by the child's having one of his parents or his aunt stay with him for up to 2 hours each night until he went to sleep. To extinguish the tantrums, the adults put him to bed in a relaxed and pleasant fashion, left the room, closed the door, and did not reenter the room regardless of any screaming. Although the tantrum on the first night of extinction lasted for 45 minutes, the episodes declined rapidly in the following nights and were absent a week later. Several days later the boy began to scream again one evening, and his aunt returned to the bedroom and stayed with him as in the past. This reinforcement reinstated the tantrums, which had to be extinguished again. Follow-up assessments during the next 2 years revealed no recurrence of this behavior.

Interventions using extinction to reduce an undesirable behavior often apply other techniques as supplements. A commonly used supplement to extinction is positive reinforcement to increase a desirable, alternative response. For example, extinction and reinforcement were combined in a program to reduce the pain behaviors of a young woman who suffered from migraine headaches (Aubuchon, Haber, & Adams, 1983). It appeared that such pain behaviors as complaining of pain were being reinforced by the enormous amounts of attention those actions generated from her family, physician, and nurses. These individuals were then instructed to ignore the pain behaviors and reinforce alternative responses, such as exercising and doing household chores. The frequency of pain behaviors dropped markedly in the first month from an average of almost 8 per day in baseline to less than 1 per day, and remained below 1 per day at 6- and 12-month follow-up assess- ments.

An interesting combination of extinction and reinforcement was used in an intervention to reduce 3 1/2-year-old Cain's aggressive behavior toward his class- mates in preschool (Pinkston et al., 1973). These behaviors included choking, bit- ing, pinching, hitting, and kicking. The teacher had been dealing with Cain's aggression by reprimanding him ("Cain, we don't do that here," or "Cain, you can't play here until you're ready to be a good boy.") But such commonsense statements seemed to be reinforcing the behavior. During the intervention, the teacher ignored Cain when he was aggressive and, instead, gave attention and activity rein- forcers to his victim, for example, by saying "I'm sorry that happened to you. Why don't you play with this nice truck?" In addition, the teacher began to give Cain social reinforcement for alternative responses: interacting appropriately with other children. The intervention reduced the child's aggressive behavior in a couple of weeks or so from about 30 instances per day in baseline to about 5 per day, and his positive interactions with peers increased substantially, too.

The Process and Characteristics of Extinction

Picture this scene: you're running late on your way to class one morning and have skipped breakfast. You expect from the many other times this has happened in the past that you'll be able to buy a snack from a conveniently located vending machine, to take the edge off your hunger. You get to the machine, insert the cor- rect change, and pull the lever for the snack you want, but nothing comes out. How will you react to not having your behavior reinforced? Chances are, you'll react ini- tially by pulling the lever once again. When that produces the same result, you might pull the lever several times in rapid succession and very strongly. And when that doesn't work, you might kick the machine or pound on it.

This example illustrates two aspects of the extinction process. First, when rein- forcement fails to occur, the response often increases temporarily in its frequency and magnitude, as in pulling a vending machine lever rapidly and strongly (Skinner, 1938). This phenomenon is called an **extinction burst**. Figure 6.1 gives an example of an extinction burst for the first night in an intervention to decrease the

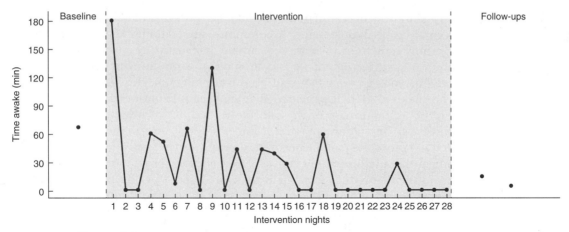

Figure 6.1   Number of minutes an infant was awake after having gone to sleep at night. Each data point for baseline and follow-up periods represents the average time awake across 14 nights for one infant (child 1). The intervention was conducted with seven 8- to 20-month-old infants who had been referred by nurses for treatment because of long-term sleep disturbances. The sole technique used in the intervention was extinction: the parents put the child to bed but did not return if the infant woke up unless the child was sick or might be injured. The infant whose awake time is presented in the graph was sick only on night 9 of the intervention. (Data abstracted from France & Hudson, 1990, Figure 2.)

amount of time an infant was awake after having gone to sleep at night (France & Hudson, 1990). On that night, the infant was awake almost three times longer than the baseline average. People's responding in extinction does not always show an extinction burst (Lerman & Iwata, 1995). But when an extinction burst happens, people who want to change the behavior but don't expect a burst may think that extinction does not work. Second, extinction often increases the individual's aggression and other emotional behaviors (F. A. Kelly & Hake, 1970; Kimble, 1961; Todd, Morris, & Fenza, 1989). If these two characteristics occur when you are trying to extinguish an undesirable behavior, there may be problems in carrying out an extinction procedure, particularly if someone is harmed physically as a result or if the behavior is very annoying, such as the screaming of a child in a tantrum. An effective way to reduce these problems is to provide reinforcement for alternative responses, instructing the person of the new contingencies in advance.

Extinction has two other characteristics that are quite typical of the process. For one thing, the behavior tends to decline gradually or irregularly rather than immediately and smoothly. You can see this in Figure 6.1: notice how the infant's awake time had a generally decreasing trend but fluctuated a lot during the first couple of weeks of the intervention. Although the awake times of the seven infants treated in that intervention didn't all show so much fluctuation, they all declined in a fairly gradual pattern, with some being extinguished in just a few days (France & Hudson, 1990). The other characteristic of the extinction process is that an extinguished behavior can reappear temporarily—a phenomenon called **spontaneous recovery**.

This reappearance may happen partly because antecedents that were present when the behavior had received reinforcement in the past are present again (Bouton & Swartzentruber, 1991). When an extinguished response "recovers" without being reinforced, its strength—as reflected in its frequency, duration, or magnitude—usually is weaker than it was before extinction. Referring again to Figure 6.1, the infant's fairly brief durations of being awake during the follow-up assessments probably reflect spontaneous recovery.

What Factors Affect Extinction Effectiveness?

Several factors affect how quickly and completely extinction procedures will extinguish a behavior. We've already discussed some of these factors. That is, extinction is especially effective in stopping a target behavior when we have (1) carefully and fully identified the reinforcers that maintained the response in the past, (2) withheld all these reinforcers when the behavior occurs, and (3) supplemented these procedures by giving reinforcement for desirable, alternative responses. When any of these conditions is lacking in an extinction program, the behavior will be more *resistant to extinction*—or harder to extinguish.

The reinforcement history of the target behavior can also affect its resistance to extinction in three ways. First, the more often the behavior was reinforced in the past, the longer it is likely to take to extinguish the response (P. S. Siegel & Foshee, 1953). Second, the greater the reward value of the reinforcers the behavior produced in the past, the harder extinguishing the response is likely to be (Lewis & Duncan, 1957). Third, behavior that was reinforced on an intermittent reinforcement schedule generally takes longer to extinguish than behavior reinforced on a continuous reinforcement schedule (Kimble, 1961; Lewis, 1960; Lewis & Duncan, 1956). For instance, an intervention was conducted in which two retarded male adults were instructed that they could earn token reinforcers if they conversed with other individuals (Kazdin & Polster, 1973). During a 5-week period, one man received tokens on a continuous schedule for conversing and the other man received tokens on an intermittent schedule. Later, when token reinforcement was withdrawn, conversing during the next 5 weeks continued at a high rate in the man who had received intermittent reinforcement; in contrast, conversing declined rapidly in the man who had received continuous reinforcement.

Another factor that can affect how quickly extinction procedures will eliminate a behavior is instruction in the new contingencies. Behavior often extinguishes much faster when people are told that their responses will no longer be reinforced than when reinforcement simply ceases to appear (Weiner, 1970). The factors that affect the effectiveness of extinction lead to a couple of basic rules about using extinction procedures. Remember that the behavior we want to reduce may show an extinction burst and may fluctuate early in the process. If we have identified the reinforcers carefully and eliminated them, we shouldn't conclude from the burst and/or fluctuation in behavior that the extinction process isn't working. Behaviors sometimes get worse for a while before they get better. By stopping the extinction

✔ Concept Check 6.1

1. Terminating reinforcement for a previously reinforced response is called _____ .

2. Before introducing an extinction procedure, we should identify the reinforcers by conducting a(n) _____ .

3. Suppose a teacher terminated the social reinforcement that had maintained a child's habit of blurting out questions in class. An alternative response the teacher might reinforce is _____ . ⇔

4. A temporary increase in a target behavior at the start of extinction is called _____ .

5. A relatively weak recurrence of an extinguished response is called _____ _____ .

6. Behaviors that have been reinforced intermittently rather than continuously tend to show greater _____ to extinction.

_____

Answers: 6. resistance 5. spontaneous recovery
1. extinction 2. functional analysis 3. hand raising 4. extinction burst

procedure and allowing the behavior to receive reinforcement again, however, we'll reinforce the behavior's getting worse—that is, we'll fuel the burst. Also keep in mind that most behaviors in everyday life receive reinforcement intermittently, making them harder to extinguish. As a result, we'll need to be patient when using extinction. (Go to ✔ .)

What Is Punishment?

"Punishment doesn't work with Brian," the boy's parents told a neighbor who complained of the child's daily racket. "We've scolded him and spanked him for making so much noise. That stops him for the moment, but he starts making noise again in a while." Did Brian's parents punish his making noise when they scolded and spanked him? Probably not. Let's see why we should doubt it.

In operant conditioning, **punishment** is a process whereby a consequence *suppresses* the behavior on which it is contingent, decreasing its frequency, duration, or magnitude. The consequence that suppresses the behavior in this process is called a *punisher.* Punishers are aversive stimuli or conditions—loosely speaking, the person finds these consequences "undesirable" or "unpleasant." Brian's behavior didn't seem to be affected by the consequences his parents applied. If a consequence must suppress behavior to be considered a punisher, it isn't likely that scolding or spanking punished Brian for making noise. The best way to determine whether a consequence is a punisher is to *apply it and assess carefully* whether the behavior declines. In cases like Brian's, we can't be sure whether a given behavior declined because parents typically don't assess their children's behavior carefully, and their impressions may be wrong.

You may be thinking, "But scolding and spanking *are* punishers. Everyone finds these things unpleasant!" Well, maybe Brian doesn't agree. If we're going to define punishers loosely as "consequences people find unpleasant," we must be sure to assess the unpleasantness from the *point of view of the person who will receive these consequences.* We've seen in earlier chapters that stimuli or conditions parents and teachers ordinarily think of as punishers, such as scolding, can actually *reinforce* the behavior they're supposed to decrease. What's more, we know that some people dislike stimuli or conditions that most other people like, and vice versa. For instance, some people seem to like pain—at least under some, usually sexual, situations—and are called *masochists.* It may be that pain becomes a conditioned reinforcer for these people through the process of respondent conditioning—that is, by participating in or viewing activities that associate pain with pleasure in a sexual context (Wincze, 1977).

There are two other reasons for not being certain whether scolding and spanking are punishers for Brian. First, the parents may have applied these consequences poorly, thereby severely weakening the punishing effects of these stimuli. We will see later that several factors affect how effective punishment is likely to be. Second, scolding and spanking may be punishers for Brian, but the reinforcement he gets from making noise may be so much stronger than the punishment being applied that the undesirable behavior fails to change much after the scolding or spanking. The problems we have discussed in identifying punishers underscore, once again, the needs for conducting a functional analysis in designing a behavior change program and collecting data carefully to assess the program's effects. Hunches are helpful, but not sufficient.

Types of Punishment

We saw in Chapter 5 that reinforcement can be delivered in two ways: when we give positive reinforcement, our *adding* a consequence strengthens the behavior on which such reinforcement is contingent; when we give negative reinforcement, our *subtracting* or taking away an aversive circumstance is the consequence, and it strengthens the behavior on which the reinforcement is contingent. The same "adding" versus "subtracting" distinction exists in punishment. As Figure 6.2 outlines, punishment can also be delivered in two ways.

- In **positive punishment**, an aversive stimulus or condition is *added* as a consequence of the behavior. This is the kind of punishment noisy Brian's parents tried to apply.
- In **negative punishment**, a stimulus or condition the person already has at the time the behavior occurs is *subtracted* as a consequence of performing the behavior. This stimulus or condition typically is something "pleasant" or valued—that is, receiving it for doing something would reinforce that behavior.

	Positive	Negative
Reinforcement	"Pleasant" stimulus or condition **added**	Aversive stimulus or condition **subtracted**
Punishment	Aversive stimulus or condition **added**	"Pleasant" stimulus or condition **subtracted**

Figure 6.2   Four types of behavioral consequences: positive reinforcement, negative reinforcement, positive punishment, and negative punishment. Notice that "positive" and "negative" refer to whether the stimulus or condition is *added* to or *subtracted* from the situation following a response.

An example of negative punishment is having to pay money as a fine for a traffic violation. The money is something the person already has, and probably it was obtained as reinforcement for an earlier behavior, such as working.

We discussed in Chapter 5 that many people confuse the processes of punishment and negative reinforcement. An example may help you distinguish between these types of consequence. Suppose 2-year-old Fran is curious about electrical outlets and keeps trying to pull plugs out of and stuff things into the little holes. This behavior justifiably frightens Fran's parents, and they scold her each time. Scolding has helped—the child stops immediately and has been doing less and less plug pulling. Scolding in this case is positive punishment for Fran's behavior, but it is also an *escape* behavior for her parents, since it stops her behavior, thereby reducing their fright. Scolding is negatively reinforced by reducing their fright.

All sorts of stimuli and conditions can serve as punishers to suppress behavior (Azrin & Holz, 1966; Matson & Taras, 1989; Van Houten, 1983). Most punishers can be classified into several categories that may overlap somewhat. The first few types we will consider involve positive punishment, and the last types involve negative punishment.

Physically Aversive Stimuli

I visited a stop-smoking clinic years ago and tried out a device that gave a mild electric shock to my finger. The idea was to punish cigarette smoking to help people quit. The shock didn't hurt, but it produced a very unpleasant sensation, and I wanted it to stop. **Physically aversive stimuli** are events that cause physical pain, discomfort, or other unpleasant sensations. To be punishers, they must suppress behavior.

Physically aversive stimuli are very common consequences of behavior in our everyday lives. These consequences are often provided deliberately, with the intention of correcting behavior—for example, when parents and other adults hit children and animals in response to some inappropriate or undesirable action. But physically aversive stimuli can also be "naturally occurring events" that happen in our environments as consequences of our behavior (Azrin & Holz, 1966). Naturally occurring punishers that come to mind most easily involve careless behavior, such as bruising your head by bumping into a post because you were looking at a physically attractive person, burning your hand by spilling hot coffee because you moved too quickly, and getting scratched by a pet because you played with it too roughly.

Using physically aversive stimuli as punishers in therapy is usually avoided for humanitarian reasons and because of their side effects on behavior, which will be described later in this chapter. When the stimuli are strongly aversive, their use is controversial. One very controversial form of punishment is strong, painful electric shock (Goodman, 1994). The use of painful electric shock as a punisher in behavioral methods was pioneered in the 1960s in interventions with developmentally disabled children, mainly to eliminate self-injurious and self-stimulatory behaviors (Corte, Wolf, & Locke, 1971; Lovaas, Schaeffer, & Simmons, 1965; Lovaas & Simmons, 1969). Although this method had some success, it is rarely used today and is reserved for those cases in which all other approaches have failed and the behavior must be suppressed quickly, as in cases of self-injury. Other approaches to stop self-injury and self-stimulation that often are successful include using *mild*, brief electric shock as punishment (Linscheid et al., 1990) and withdrawing negative reinforcement for these behaviors while giving positive reinforcement for alternative behaviors (Iwata et al., 1990, 1994; Repp, Felce, & Barton, 1988).

Milder forms of physically aversive stimuli are less controversial punishers. *Mild* electric shock as punishment was used effectively to eliminate a life-threatening behavior in a 9-month-old infant named Mark (Cunningham & Linscheid, 1976). The behavior is called chronic ruminating, and it consists of vomiting repeatedly after feeding. This behavior resulted in Mark's being hospitalized for malnutrition, dehydration, and severe weight loss. The shocks decreased his ruminating from 36 instances a day in baseline, to 4 instances on the first day of the intervention, and only occasional instances after about a week. Other relatively mild, physically aversive punishers include tasting a bitter or sour substance such as unsweetened lemon juice, having water sprayed into the face, and smelling a pungent odor, such as ammonia (Altman, Haavik, & Cook, 1978; Dorsey et al., 1980; Sajwaj, Libet, & Agras, 1974; Singh, Watson, & Winton, 1986; Vargas & Adesso, 1976). (Go to 🔖 .)

Reprimands

Reprimands are negative verbal statements or feedback—such as "No! That's bad!"— sharply criticizing a behavior. When used in behavior modification, these statements are given with a fixed stare and, often, a firm grasp (Van Houten, 1983). Because these statements are added after the behavior, they provide positive punishment when they reduce operant behavior. Reprimands are very common, naturally occurring events in everyday life. Studies have found that teachers use reprimands more than praise with their students, particularly after second grade (Thomas et al., 1978; White, 1975).

Reprimands can be administered easily and quickly, and sometimes they are more effective than other punishers that are more time-consuming to use (Doleys et al.,

Case Study 6.1
Lemon Juice Therapy to Stop Public Masturbation

A severely retarded 7-year-old boy had begun masturbating publicly when he was living in an institution and continued to display this behavior for nearly 2 years since returning to live at home (as described in Cook et al., 1978). The behavior would occur at school and at home, causing his parents such embarrassment that they were considering reinstitutionalization. Prior to the intervention, the boy's parents or teachers had tried to stop his public masturbating by shouting "No!" and spanking his hand, but this didn't seem to be working. Because the parents were not concerned with his private masturbation in his bedroom or a bathroom, the intervention focused only on the target behavior's occurrence in all other places.

The lemon juice punishment was carried out in the following way. Whenever the boy "put

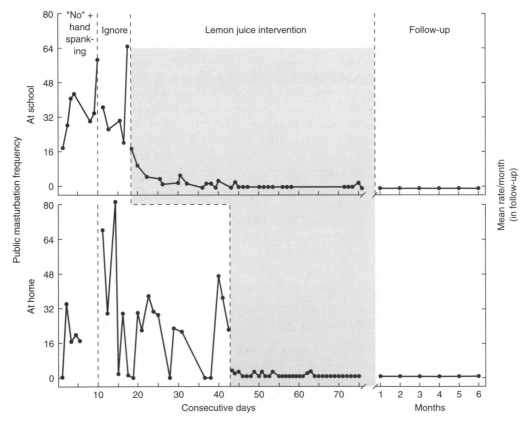

Figure 6.3 Public masturbation frequency at home and at school during four phases: "No" plus hand spanking, ignoring, lemon juice punishment intervention, and follow-up. Assessments were taken during six 5-minute observation periods in a day. For the first three phases, the data represent daily frequencies during the observation periods. For the follow-up phase, the data represent the mean frequency per day for each of 6 months. (From J. W. Cook et al., 1978, Figure 1.)

either hand inside his pants and directed toward his penis," his parent or a teacher would squirt unsweetened lemon juice

> into his mouth with a plastic squirt bottle. . . . During the early stages of treatment the subject was under nearly constant observation, and the treatment procedure was always implemented as soon as possible after the target behavior occurred. The subject's mother carried the lemon juice in her purse when she took her son to public places. (p. 132)

Data on the boy's target behavior were collected at school and at home during four phases of the treatment: a baseline in which the prior method ("No!" plus hand spanking) was continued, a second baseline in which the target behavior was simply ignored, the intervention with lemon juice punishment, and a follow-up period. As Figure 6.3 shows, the boy's masturbatory behavior occurred at very high rates during both baseline periods, was almost completely eliminated quickly when the lemon juice intervention was used, and was totally absent in 6 months of follow-up assess-

1976). Their effectiveness is enhanced when the person receiving them is nearby and the statements are accompanied by a fixed stare and firm grasp, such as of the person's arm or shoulders (Van Houten et al., 1982). Their effects can also be enhanced by pairing them with other punishers, such as mild physically aversive stimuli (Dorsey et al., 1980). Reprimands that suppress responses are *conditioned punishers*—that is, they gain their ability to suppress behavior by being paired with other punishers.

The photo of this infant boy on the left shows him when his chronic ruminating had reduced his body to skin and bones (the tape on his face was used for holding a tube to feed him through his nose). After punishment was used to suppress his ruminating, his weight increased by 26% in less than 2 weeks and his face, body, arms, and legs had filled out, as shown on the right.

One problem with using reprimands alone to change behavior is that their effects appear to be more variable than those of other consequences. For instance, we've seen in earlier chapters that parents' and teachers' scoldings often serve as reinforcers for children's undesirable behavior, *increasing* the behavior instead of decreasing it. Sometimes using reprimands creates an illusion of being effective: the misbehavior stops immediately, but only for a short time, and the frequency of the behavior actually increases later. If their effects are assessed periodically, however, reprimands can still be very useful as a part of programs to change behavior.

Aversive Activities

An 11-year-old boy named Mark who lived in a residential institution during the week used swear words nearly 11 times per dinner period (Fischer & Nehs, 1978). He went home on weekends. His "cottage parents" at the institution had been unsuccessful in trying to induce him to stop swearing, so they conducted an intervention requiring him to spend 10 minutes washing windows for each instance of swearing during dinner. His swearing declined sharply within a few days and remained infrequent during follow-up assessments taken in the 15 days after the intervention ended.

This example illustrates that aversive activities can serve as positive punishers. When we discussed the Premack principle and reinforcement in Chapter 5, we saw that engaging in high-probability behaviors can reinforce the performance of infrequent responses. Using aversive activities as punishers is essentially the other side of this coin—that is, being required to engage in a *low*-probability behavior as a consequence of performing a target response that occurs too frequently, such as Mark's swearing, can reduce the person's performance of the frequent response. As we saw in Mark's case, the low-probability behavior does not have to be related to the target behavior. Researchers found, for instance, that requiring grade school children to perform arbitrarily chosen motor activities, such as repeatedly standing up and sitting on the floor, can serve as punishers to reduce their aggressive behavior (Luce, Delquadri, & Hall, 1980).

Of course, the aversive activities selected as punishers in interventions may be related to the behavioral excesses we're trying to reduce. A punishment approach called **overcorrection** requires the person to engage in aversive activities that correct or are the opposite of the undesirable target behavior when that misbehavior occurs (Foxx & Azrin, 1972). For this approach there are two methods, restitution and positive practice, which can be used together or separately (Axelrod, Brantner, & Meddock, 1978; Ollendick & Matson, 1978). **Restitution** refers to correcting the effects of the misbehavior and restoring the environment, usually to a condition better than it had had before the misbehavior. For example, a person who wrote graffiti on a wall might be required to paint the entire wall. In **positive practice**, when the misbehavior occurs, the person must repeatedly perform an appropriate or useful alternative or opposite response to that of the misbehavior. For instance, a girl who pushes her little brother down to get the toy he was playing with might have to practice over and over asking him nicely for the toy and offering to give him another toy in exchange.

An intervention to reduce stealing by institutionalized mentally retarded adults used restitution as punishment for the target behaviors (Azrin & Wesolowski, 1974). These 34 individuals stole from one another very frequently, taking mainly food, at mealtimes and at snack times. No baseline assessment was made because this would have required an ethically indefensible condition: the staff would not have been able to intervene when they became aware of victims losing their property. Instead, the first few days of the intervention used a "simple correction" procedure in which staff required only that the thief return the food (or the part remaining, if some had been consumed). Because thefts often occurred as a "sudden grasping-biting movement," this procedure seldom restored the original condition, and thefts continued at a high rate. The intervention used an overcorrection restitution method that included the simple correction procedure *and* the requirement that the thief go to the food display area with a staff member, get an identical item, and give it to the victim. Nearly 20 thefts occurred each day when simple correction was the only consequence, but the thefts declined rapidly with the restitution method and were completely eliminated in a few days, as Figure 6.4 shows.

Positive practice was used in an intervention to reduce mentally retarded adults' sprawling—that is, sitting or lying about—on the floors instead of sitting in available

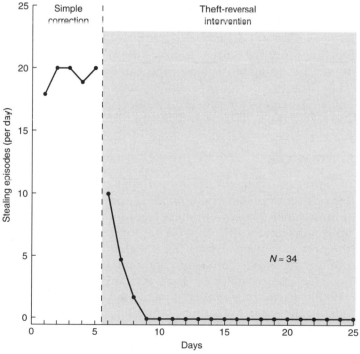

Figure 6.4 Frequency of stealing episodes each day by 34 retarded adults during two phases: simple correction and an overcorrection theft-reversal intervention. (From Azrin & Wesolowski, 1974, Figure 1.)

chairs at the institution where they were residents (Azrin & Wesolowski, 1975). The behavior was not just unsightly; it also created a hazard that had caused injuries. Other behavioral methods had been tried without success to change this behavior. Positive practice was conducted in the following way: residents who sat on the floor were told they could not do that and were required to get up, go to a nearby chair, sit there for about a minute, and then go and sit for a minute on each of several other chairs. They were left sitting on the last chair. Verbal prompts were given for each step in the sequence, and physical guidance prompts were used initially and then faded. This method eliminated floor sprawling in about 10 days, and a follow-up assessment found that the residents continued to use the chairs 6 months later.

Research has shown that overcorrection methods can be effective in reducing a variety of problem behaviors in hospital, classroom, and home settings (Axelrod, Brantner, & Meddock, 1978; Ollendick & Matson, 1978). And some research results indicate that overcorrection may be effective in classrooms even when the punishment, positive practice, is delayed until a lesson or the class is over (Azrin & Powers, 1975; E. J. Barton & Osborne, 1978). An advantage of overcorrection methods is that they have built-in alternative responses, thereby providing opportunities to learn appropriate behaviors instead of just suppressing misbehavior (Carey & Bucher, 1981). But these methods have some disadvantages as well—for example, they are complicated and very time-consuming to administer (J. A. Kelly & Drabman, 1977; MacKenzie-Keating & McDonald, 1990). In addition, problems may arise with any punisher that involves an aversive activity if the person being punished refuses to engage in the activity. Suppose the retarded people who were stealing food had refused to make the required restitution. What then? Although sometimes using physical prompts can help move a person into a given activity, if such measures don't work, making other consequences contingent on engaging in the activity may have the desired effect. If not, however, we may have to abandon the use of the aversive activity as a punisher.

Time-Out

Most of us have heard the parental command, to "Go to your room!" If being in your room is not very stimulating and does not provide many opportunities for reinforcement, being sent there from someplace more reinforcing constitutes negative punishment. The method of punishing misbehavior by converting or moving the person's environment from one that is relatively reinforcing to one that is less reinforcing is called **time-out** (Brantner & Doherty, 1983; Van Houten, 1983).

How long should the time-out last? Jennie Brantner and Michael Doherty (1983) reviewed the results of many studies and found that effective time-out periods usually can be fairly short, lasting a matter of minutes rather than hours or days. Usually periods of between 1 and 15 minutes work well. One study compared the punishing effects of three time-out period lengths: 1, 15, and 30 minutes (G. D. White, Nielsen, & Johnson, 1972). The time-out procedures were applied with institutionalized retarded individuals to reduce their deviant behaviors, such as aggression and tantrums. The results indicated that the 15- and 30-minute time-out peri-

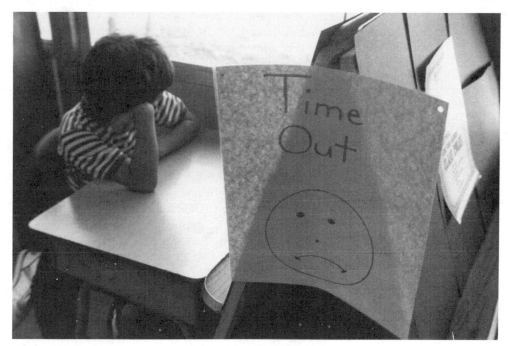

Time-out punishment is often used to discourage misbehavior in school.

ods reduced deviant behavior the most, but these two lengths were equally effective. In general, time-out periods should be as short as possible while still reducing the target behavior substantially. Sometimes just a minute or two is enough.

Brantner and Doherty (1983) have described three types or levels of time-out. In the most restrictive level, called *isolation time-out,* the person is removed from the relatively reinforcing environment and placed in a separate, substantially less reinforcing environment. Being sent to your room would be an example of isolation time-out if it is a less reinforcing environment. Some schools or institutions have set up special "time-out rooms" where individuals are sent or taken when they misbehave (Barton et al., 1970). But using isolation time-out can have some disadvantages and is inadvisable in some cases. For instance, individuals who might harm themselves if left unattended may require a staff member to monitor their behavior in isolation. And isolating developmentally disabled children may provide them with opportunities to perform self-stimulating or self-injurious behaviors that are undesirable and dangerous.

Exclusion time-out involves removing the individual from opportunities for reinforcement without isolating him or her. A common way of using exclusion time-out is to move the person to a separate part of the same environment and not allow him or her to participate in ongoing reinforcing activities. Researchers used this method in a day-care center to reduce such disruptive behavior as being aggressive or damaging toys and other objects (Porterfield, Herbert-Jackson, & Risley, 1976).

When an instance of disruptive behavior occurred, the caregivers described to the child both the misbehavior and an alternative behavior. "No, don't take toys from other children," the caregiver might say. "Ask me for the toy you want." Then the time-out would be started: the child had to sit on the floor, with no toys, at the periphery of the play and learning activities and watch how the other children interacted. After the child had watched quietly for about a minute, he or she was allowed to rejoin the other children. Although misbehavior occured during the intervention with this time-out punishment, the rate was only about 37% of the rate resulting when the children were simply told the behavior was wrong and given another activity to do.

Similar exclusion time-out procedures have been applied in interventions that effectively reduced oppositional behavior in preschoolers and disruptive behavior in retarded adults (Bostow & Bailey, 1969; M. W. Roberts, Hatzenbuehler, & Bean, 1981). Exclusion time-out also can be applied by having the person stay in the same environment while the materials or stimulation normally used for reinforcement are taken away for a short period. For example, toys might be removed and the radio or TV might be turned off for a few minutes. This exclusion time-out approach was applied effectively to reduce an autistic child's spitting and self-injurious behaviors (Solnick, Rincover, & Peterson, 1977).

In *nonexclusion time-out*, the person who misbehaves is not removed from the ongoing activities at all, but receives a signal indicating a period in which he or she cannot earn reinforcers that would have been available if the misbehavior hadn't occurred. An intervention using a nonexclusion time-out procedure was conducted with five retarded boys in a special education class to reduce disruptive behaviors, such as aggression and yelling (Foxx & Shapiro, 1978). During the usual classroom activities, the boys could earn social and consumable reinforcers every few minutes for working quietly. Each child who was eligible for these reinforcers wore a colored ribbon around his neck to signify this status. When a boy misbehaved, the teacher removed the ribbon from his neck for 3 minutes. Thus, when the teacher distributed the next round of reinforcers, he could not receive any. This procedure reduced disruptive behavior in all the boys, and the two boys who had been most disruptive during baseline were misbehaving only about 5% as often by the end of the intervention.

Time-out punishment appears to be effective in reducing unwanted behavior and may be a very good alternative to punishers of other types, especially those that apply physically aversive stimuli (Brantner & Doherty, 1983). Exclusion and nonexclusion time-out methods seem to be as effective as isolation time-out procedures in most situations, while having fewer disadvantages. Time-out punishment is likely to be most effective in suppressing behavior if the amount of reinforcement in the original environment is much greater than that in the time-out environment (Solnick, Rincover, & Peterson, 1977; Van Houten, 1983).

Response Cost

Response cost refers to a negative punishment procedure in which misbehavior results in the person who is punished losing something valued—an item or privilege that probably was a reinforcer for an earlier behavior (Van Houten, 1983). Although the stimulus is usually something the person already has, it can also be a reinforcer he or she has earned but not yet received. Everyday examples of response cost include having to pay money as a fine for a traffic violation or as a penalty for writing a check that bounces, or for failing to pay a bill on time. The lost stimulus can also be an item the person owns, such as a favorite article of clothing or videotape, or a privilege he or she ordinarily has, such as watching TV. Of course, losing something of value in this procedure occurs only when the unwanted target behavior is performed.

Interventions usually apply response cost with fines in the form of money or tokens. In one example, Peter Miller (1972) applied response cost in behavior therapy to treat a man's alcohol abuse. The client and his wife agreed that he should limit his drinking to no more than three drinks per day and that he must consume all drinks in her presence, whether they were at home or out. Through discussion, the couple mutually agreed to use a response cost procedure: if he drank outside the aforementioned constraints—as determined by her smelling liquor on his breath or seeing him drink or appear drunk—he had to pay her $20 that she would spend very frivolously. What's more, the wife's behavior was included in the program, too: if she criticized her husband for drinking, she had to pay him $20. Each spouse reported that having to pay the fine would be very unpleasant. The man's drinking decreased from a baseline average of about 7 1/2 drinks a day to 3 or fewer in less than 2 weeks and remained at that level throughout follow-up assessments over the next 6 months. Although this simple approach effectively reduced this man's drinking, it would not be sufficient by itself to control drinking in most alcohol abusers.

Response cost has been applied very effectively in classrooms. One intervention used response cost to reduce off-task, distracted behaviors in children with conduct and learning problems (Sullivan & O'Leary, 1990). In this program, teachers would scan their classes periodically, checking to see whether individual children were working on class activities or performing off-task behaviors. In some classes, response cost was used in a way that punished the performance of *off*-task behavior during the scan with the loss of a token, which was worth 1 minute of recess. In other classes, reinforcement was used instead of punishment; thus performing *on*-task behavior was reinforced with a token that was worth 1 minute of recess. Both conditions improved the children's working on class activities, and using response cost was at least as effective as using reinforcement. Other classroom interventions have used response cost methods in token programs that effectively reduced off-task behavior in hyperactive children, stealing in second-graders, and disruptive behavior in fourth- to sixth-graders (Barrish, Saunders, & Wolf, 1969; Harris & Sherman, 1973; Rapport, Murphy, & Bailey, 1982; Swizer, Deal, & Bailey, 1977). The interventions for stealing and disruptive behaviors gave the consequences on the basis of group contingencies.

Response cost punishment is fairly easy to apply, especially when it is part of a token reinforcement program. One thing to keep in mind about the response cost approach is that taking away something of value contingent on misbehavior is not the same as withholding reinforcement until appropriate behavior occurs. Many students confuse the two circumstances. The former applies when the person *has performed* an unwanted response in a program designed to modify a behavioral excess, and the latter applies when the person *has not yet performed* the wanted response in a program aimed at modifying a behavioral deficit. (Go to .)

The Process and Characteristics of Punishment

We've seen that there are many varieties of punishers and that punishment can suppress behavior effectively. But using punishment is very controversial, especially when the punisher is a physically aversive stimulus. The issues in these controversies focus on the advantages and disadvantages of using punishment in all applications of behavioral methods—in behavior therapy interventions, everyday parenting, education, business and industry, and so on (P. L. Brown, 1982; Singh, Lloyd, & Kendall, 1990; Walters & Grusec, 1977). Let's see what these issues are.

Advantages of Punishment

Punishment techniques achieve *rapid results* in suppressing the undesired behavior. This advantage is especially important if the behavior is dangerous, as in the cases we discussed earlier of self-injurious behavior and infant ruminative vomiting. Electric shock has been applied to stop these behaviors, and *mild* shock is frequently sufficient to suppress them very quickly, sometimes with just a few applications (Cunningham & Linscheid, 1976; Linscheid et al., 1990). These effects are especially impressive because the target behaviors in these interventions had

Case Study 6.2
Response Cost to Stop "Lady Mary's" Blurting Out

A 29-year-old retarded woman who worked in a sheltered workshop had a habit of blurting out statements that were either false or nonsensical in the context (as described in Kazdin, 1971). For instance, she would suddenly say "You can't take that away from me," when no one had tried to take anything, or "My name is Lady Mary," which it wasn't.

A response cost intervention was designed to reduce the frequency of "Lady Mary's" blurting out. To implement this intervention, a response cost procedure was added to a token reinforcement system that had already been in effect for 6 months to increase her job production rate, which was only 20% of the minimum industrial rate. The woman was informed that her blurting out now would cost her tokens. But during the first week, to see whether the threat alone would be sufficient to reduce the target behavior, no tokens were taken to punish incidents of blurting out. The blurting out continued, however, at the baseline rate of about 40 instances a week. Once the response cost was actually in force, blurting out plummeted to about 3 instances per week. What's more, it remained at that level during the 4-week follow-up period when the response cost consequences were no longer applied.

occurred for months or years before shock was applied, and other methods had been tried to stop the behaviors without success.

Rapid results are also important when the target behavior is very embarrassing, as in the case we considered earlier of a boy who masturbated in public. Using lemon juice as a punisher dramatically reduced this boy's public masturbation in just a few days and eliminated it almost completely in a couple of weeks (J. W. Cook et al., 1978). Interventions using time-out and overcorrection punishment methods have quickly and substantially decreased aggressive and self-stimulation behaviors, too (Marholin & Townsend, 1978; C. C. Wilson et al., 1979). Although speed in reducing these two behaviors may be less critical, it is certainly desirable.

Another advantage in using punishment is the *positive side effects* sometimes produced in nontarget behaviors. In the mild shock intervention Thomas Linscheid and his colleagues (1990) applied to decrease the long-standing self-injurious behaviors of retarded and autistic individuals, not all such behaviors the subjects performed were actually punished. Specific assessments, however, indicated that several of these nontarget behaviors improved, too. And anecdotal information suggested that social behaviors and independent feeding improved in some individuals. Other studies using other kinds of punishment have found positive side effects on such nontarget behaviors as individuals' greater attentiveness when aggressive behavior was suppressed and in increased play behavior when self-stimulation was suppressed (Van Houten, 1983).

The last advantage in using punishment we'll consider is that it often leads to a *complete suppression* of the unwanted response (Van Houten, 1983). For most of the studies of punishment effects we have examined, the data presented verbally in the text or in graphs (see Figures 6.3 and 6.4) depict long-lasting, complete or near-complete suppression of the target behaviors. This durability is an important advantage for two reasons. First, when the target behavior is dangerous, the most appropriate behavioral goal is to stop it entirely. Although other behavioral methods frequently can reduce dangerous responses substantially, they may not eliminate them. Second, behaviors that have been strongly suppressed are less likely to recover and become problems again in the future.

Disadvantages of Punishment

Researchers have described several negative side effects punishment sometimes produces. We will examine these disadvantages within three broad categories: emotional and escape/avoidance reactions, aggressive behaviors, and future use of punishment.

Emotional and Escape/Avoidance Reactions People don't like to be punished—they don't like to receive unwanted or unpleasant consequences for their behavior. Understandably, being punished sometimes produces negative emotional reactions, causing the person to cry or have tantrums, for instance. These reactions are not limited to punishment techniques that involve physically aversive stimuli, such as painful events, but may also occur with other methods, such as overcorrection (Axelrod, Brantner, & Meddock, 1978; Carey & Bucher, 1981). We might be concerned about causing negative emotions for many reasons, but one relates to the likely success of our intervention: negative emotions interfere with therapy and learning processes.

A related side effect of punishment is that the unpleasantness of the aversive stimuli may cause the individual to try to escape from the situation, even when the punisher is fairly mild (Azrin & Holz, 1966). What's more, associations the person is likely to make between the aversive stimuli and the therapy or training situation may lead him or her to try in the future to avoid the situation or the people dispensing the punishment (E. K. Morris & Redd, 1975).

Aggressive Behavior Sometimes individuals become physically aggressive toward the people who dispense punishment or toward other individuals in the environment (Azrin & Holz, 1966; Hutchinson, 1977; Mayhew & Harris, 1978; Oliver, West, & Sloane, 1974). In therapy sessions, this response may take the form of hitting, kicking, or throwing objects at the therapist—behavior that disrupts the session, at least temporarily. To the extent that the person's aggression leads to escape from the therapy or training session, that behavior will be negatively reinforced by virtue of the reduction of the discomfort associated with the aversive situation.

Future Use of Punishment I remember seeing a cartoon years ago depicting a boy across his father's lap, being spanked. The caption read, "This will teach you to hit your sister." Although the father was using punishment to reduce the boy's physical aggression, he was also modeling the undesired type of behavior for his son to learn. Children often imitate the punishing acts they see, and the punishment can be physical, as in hitting, or nonphysical, as in response cost (Gelfand et al., 1974; Walters & Grusec, 1977).

A dramatic example of the likely role of modeling in children's using physical punishment comes from a study of disadvantaged toddlers in four day-care centers that focused on helping battered children and nonabused children from "families under stress" (Main & George, 1985). The researchers observed the children for incidents in which a child showed distress by crying or behaving fearfully and assessed the reactions of the other children toward the distressed child. How did the abused and nonabused children react? Nonabused children tended to respond in a concerned or sad manner. In contrast, not one of the abused boys and girls showed concern—instead, they often reacted with physical attacks or anger. The following example describes one such episode:

> Martin [an abused boy of 32 months] tried to take the hand of the crying other child, and when she resisted, he slapped her on the arm with his open hand. He then turned away . . . and began vocalizing very strongly, "Cut it out! CUT IT OUT!", each time saying it a little faster and louder. He patted her, but . . . his patting became beating, and he continued beating her despite her screams." (p. 410)

Although these observations can't pinpoint the source of this behavior on the part of abused children, the similarity to their parents' abusiveness is both disturbing

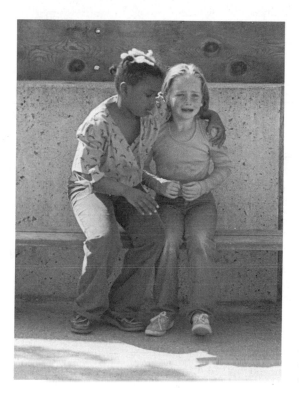

Children normally comfort and show concern toward another child who is distressed. Physically abused children are less likely to do this.

and provocative, suggesting a role of modeling. We know also that abusive parents often were themselves abused or neglected as children (Kempe, 1976).

But the recipient of punishment is not the only person in the aversive situation who can learn to use punishment more in the future—the person dispensing it can, too. For example, parents or teachers who use punishment are likely to find that it stops the current misbehavior immediately and tends to reduce future instances of the response rapidly. When this happens, their punitive acts are reinforced, and they become more likely to use aversive consequences in the future.

The negative side effects of using punishment in changing behavior are serious concerns when they occur, but they don't appear to happen very often (Linscheid & Meinhold, 1990; Matson & Taras, 1989; Van Houten, 1983). For instance, children are not likely to become abusive individuals from having received punishment occasionally, even if some of it was fairly intense and physically aversive. The more excessive the punishment is in its frequency, duration, and intensity, the more likely it is that long-lasting negative side effects will develop. Still, whenever we consider using punishment in interventions to change behavior, we should move cautiously and examine the likely advantages and disadvantages carefully. And if we don't begin to see improvements in the target behavior fairly quickly—usually in a matter of hours or days—we should reassess the situation and, perhaps, discontinue the aversive consequences. (Go to ✔ .)

✓ Concept Check 6.2

1. Punishment is a process whereby a consequence _____ the behavior on which it is contingent.

2. An example of positive punishment from your life is _____
   _____ . ⇔

3. An example of negative punishment from your life is _____
   _____ . ⇔

4. Washing out a child's mouth with soap for swearing is an example of using a(n)
   _____ stimulus as a punisher.

5. Overcorrection consists of two methods: (a) _____ and
   (b) _____ .

6. The length of time-out periods usually doesn't need to exceed _____
   to be effective.

7. Having a student sit facing a rear corner of the classroom is an example of
   _____ time-out punishment.

8. An advantage of using punishment is _____ . ⇔

9. A disadvantage of using punishment is _____ . ⇔

Answers:

9. aggressive reactions
6. 15 minutes   7. exclusion   8. undesirable behavior declines rapidly
4. physically aversive   5a. restitution   5b. positive practice
1. suppresses   2. a scolding   3. interest charged for not paying a credit card bill on time

When to Consider Using Punishment

Wouldn't it be nice if punishment never occurred in life? To prevent it, we would need to control everyone's antecedents carefully and monitor the behavior of each person constantly to make sure it is sufficiently reinforced. This is not a scenario that's likely to happen, nor is it one most people want. Instead, we encounter individuals whose prior behavior and reinforcement history is unknown. And if we try to influence antecedents and consequences deliberately at all, we generally intervene haphazardly. But as psychologist Paul Brown (1982) has pointed out, sometimes just "catching people doing well" and then "accentuating the positive" with reinforcement isn't enough. Sometimes we need to consider using punishment.

When is using punishment a good idea? We will look at some issues that can help us judge whether to use punishment and what types of punisher to apply. The first issue to consider is whether *other behavior modification methods have been tried.* Other behavioral methods worth trying include modifying antecedents, providing reinforcement for alternative responses, and using extinction procedures to eliminate the reinforcers that maintain the undesirable behavior. If such methods to decrease the target behavior were applied unsuccessfully upon completion of a careful functional analysis, we may want to consider using punishment (Axelrod, 1990; Guess, Turnbull, & Helmstetter, 1990). Unfortunately, functional analyses are not always conducted to help select the behavioral methods to use in interventions (Lennox et al., 1988).

The second issue we need to examine in deciding whether to use punishment relates to *characteristics of the person's behavior.* An important characteristic of the behavior is its likelihood of causing injury to the person or others. The greater the likelihood of injury, the more acceptable is the use of punishment (T. Smith, 1990). Self-injurious behavior, severe aggression, and ruminative vomiting are three kinds of behavior for which punishment typically can be justified. In addition, behaviors that are highly embarrassing or bizarre, such as self-stimulation, have the effect of isolating the individual socially. For that reason, punishment may be an acceptable approach if other behavioral methods have not been successful. Many professionals have substantial reservations about using punishment even when injury is likely if the behavior is allowed to continue (Donnellan & LaVigna, 1990; Luiselli, 1990). But if other methods have failed to decrease behaviors that are dangerous or severely impair intellectual and social development, professionals who are trying to change the behaviors may find it necessary to consider using punishment.

The third issue in deciding on using punishment entails our ability *to control extraneous, counterproductive reinforcers* of the undesirable behavior. As researcher Ron Van Houten (1983) has pointed out, some behaviors may have intrinsic, or "built-in," reinforcers, as in cases of self-stimulation and public masturbation. Other behaviors, such as stealing or speeding, may receive naturally occurring reinforcement in the environment. And some behaviors may receive reinforcement from individuals over whom we have little control. When we cannot control extraneous reinforcement, nonpunitive methods may not be sufficient to decrease the behavior very much, and punishment may be necessary.

Our last issue relating to the making of decisions on using punishment focuses on the *types of punisher* available. Punishers that produce strong pain or tissue damage are precluded or restricted by professional guidelines or law in many locations (Hamilton & Matson, 1992; Singh, Lloyd, & Kendall, 1990). In addition, the general public may have a voice in the choice of punishers that can be applied, particularly in schools. One study had adults rate different types of punisher for use in school and at home (Blampied & Kahan, 1992). Response cost and reprimands were rated as the most acceptable types, followed by time-out, overcorrection, and physical punishment. Although this order of acceptability held for both school and home, overcorrection and physical punishment were rated as more acceptable at home than at school. What's more, these acceptability ratings may be related to a punisher's likelihood of leading to negative side effects. For instance, studies have found relatively fewer negative side effects in using response cost than physical punishment methods (Kazdin, 1972). Of course, an important consideration in choosing a punisher is that it must be effective in decreasing the target behavior. But regardless of the type of punisher selected, its degree of severity or restrictiveness should be as mild as possible while still allowing the intervention to succeed in reducing the undesirable behavior. (Go to 🔍 .)

Close-Up 6.1
The "Gentle Teaching" Approach

Controversies over the use of aversive stimuli with developmentally disabled people have led to the design of a training approach called *Gentle Teaching* (McGee et al., 1987; J. J. McGee & Gonzalez, 1990). This approach assumes that teachers or therapists, called "caregivers," and the disabled person must develop a social "bonding" as a prerequisite to training. To encourage bonding, caregivers try to show that other people are safe and that participating in training leads to rewards, not punishment.

Gentle Teaching uses no aversive consequences, and the only consequences the caregiver applies are social reinforcers—such as praise, hugs, and smiles. Inappropriate behaviors are seen as examples of a failure to bond. When they occur, the caregiver attempts to extinguish them by withholding social reinforcers and tries to redirect the behaviors toward a desirable activity by giving the person new task materials. If self-injurious behavior begins, the caregiver acts to prevent harm by blocking the response, perhaps by deflecting the person's arm in the act of hitting, and then conveys calming messages, such as "Everything's fine. No one will hurt you."

Research on the effectiveness of the Gentle Teaching approach with individuals who are developmentally disabled has yielded mixed results. One study found that Gentle Teaching increases appropriate behaviors, such as participating correctly in training activities, and decreases inappropriate behaviors, such as making errors and performing disruptive acts (J. J. McGee & Gonzalez, 1990). But other studies have found that Gentle Teaching either fails to decrease inappropriate behaviors, such as self-injury or self-stimulation, or is less effective in decreasing them than behavioral methods that include a wider range of reinforcers and some mild punishers, such as *visual screening*, in which the teacher covers the person's eyes briefly with a hand or piece of cloth when misbehavior occurs (Barrera & Teodoro, 1990; L. J. Jones, Singh, & Kendall, 1990; Jordan, Singh, & Repp, 1989). Gentle Teaching offers some creative methods that can be tried in interventions before resorting to punishment, but the evidence does not yet support total reliance on its methods in the training of developmentally disabled individuals.

How to Use Punishment Well

If we decide to use punishment in changing behavior, we'll want to maximize its effectiveness. The more carefully we apply punishment, the less we'll need to use it because the behavior will decline faster. The most basic rule in applying consequences if to be *systematic.* To apply punishment well, we'll need to use behavioral criteria consistently to determine when to apply a punisher, instead of waiting until we've "had enough" of the misbehavior (Hall et al., 1971). We should also eliminate or reduce as much as possible extraneous reinforcers that maintain the target behaviors. We'll turn now to examining several aspects of the application of punishment that can influence the effectiveness of the approach selected.

Reinforcing Alternative Responses

It's rarely a good idea to design an intervention that uses punishment by itself, without providing reinforcement for alternative responses. There are three reasons to reinforce alternative responses if we use punishment. First, punishment teaches only what *not* to do. It doesn't teach new, more appropriate behavior to take the place of the undesirable actions (Brown, 1982). Second, combining reinforcement of alternative responses with punishment for undesirable behaviors is more effective in decreasing target behaviors than punishment is alone (Van Houten, 1983). This approach can make relatively mild punishers more useful. For instance, a study used positive practice of alternative responses to decrease self-stimulation behaviors in retarded adults (Carey & Bucher, 1986). When the activity in positive practice was reinforced, the positive practice method became more effective in suppressing undesirable behavior than when it was not reinforced. Third, the occasional negative side effects of punishment are less likely to appear if alternative responses are reinforced (Van Houten, 1983).

Using Instructions

Punishment appears to work best in suppressing unwanted behavior when the person receives specific instructions describing both the target behavior and the consequences. An intervention that used instructions was introduced to decrease negative social behaviors among unpopular boys in the first to third grades in school (Bierman, Miller, & Stabb, 1987). The program operated by describing the undesirable acts and applying response cost when they occurred. What's more, some of the boys also received instructions on and reinforcement for performing positive social behaviors as alternative responses. Only the boys who received instructions on positive and negative behaviors along with a description of the consequences for each type of behavior became more popular among their classmates.

Punisher Magnitude

In general and within limits, the more intense a punisher is, the more effective it is likely to be in suppressing the target behavior (Van Houten, 1983). But this relationship doesn't mean that it's a good idea to use highly aversive consequences as punishers. Intense punishers tend to produce more negative side effects than milder ones, and mild punishment is often quite effective when used in combination with reinforcement for alternative responses. To restate the rule we developed earlier with respect to applying punishment: we should use the mildest level we can to achieve the behavioral goals of the program (Brantner & Doherty, 1983).

The Timing of Punishment

Punishment is most effective in suppressing undesirable behaviors when it is delivered *immediately after every instance* of the behavior (Van Houten, 1983). Its effects are weakened when it is delayed or when it occurs only occasionally, particularly at the beginning of an intervention. Sometimes after the behavior has declined substantially, the punishment can be thinned to an intermittent schedule and eventually eliminated. For instance, studies have found that delivering time-out punishment intermittently after the behavior has been decreased to a low frequen-

"HOW'S THE LIFE OF THE PARTY
FEELING THIS MORNING?"

A hangover is an unpleasant consequence of the prior night's life-of-the-party behavior. But that consequence is too delayed to be a very effective punisher, especially when life-of-the-party behavior receives immediate, powerful social reinforcers.

cy does not lead to an increase in the behavior (Calhoun & Lima, 1977; Clark et al., 1973). If the behavior involves a chain of responses, it's probably best to punish it as early in the sequence of responses as possible.

Varying the Punishers

We saw in Chapter 5 that reinforcement tends to be more effective when a variety of reinforcers is available to be given for appropriate behavior. A similar phenomenon exists for punishment—that is, varying the punishers applied for misbehavior appears to suppress the behavior more effectively than using the same punisher all the time. This phenomenon was demonstrated with three developmentally disabled 5- and 6-year-olds in an intervention to decrease specific deviant behaviors, such as aggression and self-stimulation (Charlop et al., 1988). During some training sessions, the children received one of four punishment methods: reprimands, overcorrection, time-out, and a loud noise. During other training sessions, the trainer alternated using three of the four punishers when misbehaviors occurred. The results revealed that each of the punishers suppressed the deviant behaviors when presented singly in the sessions. But the children engaged in deviant behaviors even less often during sessions when the trainer varied the punishers. It may be that people adapt to the same punisher over time and that varying the punishers prevents this adaptation.

Self-Administering Punishment

An option in using punishment is to have people administer punishers to themselves, especially in self-management approaches. Will people do it? Yes, but probably not as reliably as they should. We saw in Chapter 5 that individuals often become lenient in giving reinforcers to themselves. The same problem seems to arise if punishment is to be self-administered. For instance, Jack James (1981) had a young man try to reduce his stuttering by using self-punishment. When the client stuttered, he was to take a very brief time-out period (about 2 seconds) from speaking. Although the intervention reduced his stuttering from baseline levels, he applied the time-out in less than half of the appropriate instances, as reflected in periodic assessments. But later his accuracy in administering time-out was improved substantially by adding the following response cost procedure: each time he failed to apply the time-out when he should have, he lost a small amount of money.

Using procedures to monitor the use of self-administered punishment is likely to increase its accuracy. Thus in a program to help a man reduce his smoking, the subject's wife kept collateral records of the smoking for verification (Belles & Bradlyn, 1987). When the man exceeded agreed-upon smoking limits, he had to apply response cost by writing a $25 check to a charity he disliked and sending it to the researcher, who would then forward it to the charity. Other factors to consider in weighing an individual's likely accuracy in administering self-punishment are characteristics of the punishers selected for use in the intervention. It seems likely that people's accuracy decreases as punisher magnitude increases. As we have seen, sometimes very mild punishers can help suppress behavior. One way to reduce the severity of a punisher is to make it covert. For instance, the person can imagine an aversive consequence, such as getting caught or being fined, for performing the undesirable behavior (Cautela, 1993a). Of course, we cannot verify that covert punishers have been applied, but we can assess whether the behavior changed.

Other Strategies for Decreasing Behavior

Other strategies that do not eliminate reinforcers or apply punishment can be included in programs to decrease undesired operant behaviors. The first of these strategies we will examine is called differential reinforcement.

Differential Reinforcement to Decrease a Behavior

It is possible to use reinforcement to decrease an undesirable behavior, and we will look at three ways to do this. We've discussed one method before without giving it a specific name: **differential reinforcement of incompatible behavior** (DRI, pronounced by spelling "d-r-i") is the systematic provision of reinforcers for performing an alternative response. An effective approach in using DRI involves doing a functional analysis to identify the reinforcing functions of the target behavior and making sure that the alternative response receives the same reinforcers as the undesirable behavior. This approach was used in an intervention to decrease developmentally disabled children's deviant behaviors, such as aggression and self-injury (Carr & Durand, 1985). After it had been determined that the function of these behaviors was to communicate the children's need for help or feedback from their teachers, the intervention had the teachers provide attention for communicating the needs verbally, such as by saying, "I don't understand" or "Am I doing good work?" DRI methods can also be used by parents at home to decrease their children's disruptive behaviors and sibling conflicts (Friman & Altman, 1990; Leitenberg et al., 1977).

The second way to use reinforcers to decrease a target behavior is to give them if the behavior occurs less and less often. In this approach, called **differential reinforcement of low rates of responding** (DRL), reinforcement is given only when instances of the undesirable behavior fall below certain rates. For example, a teacher might decide to reinforce students for being out of their seats fewer than three times in an hour. Although technically, DRL methods could reinforce the first instance of the behavior after a minimum period of time in which it did not occur at all, DRL procedures are rarely used in this way in applied settings (Rolider & Van Houten, 1990). Interventions using DRL methods have successfully decreased a wide variety of inappropriate behaviors, including sleeping and talking out in class and eating too quickly (Deitz, Repp, & Deitz, 1976; Lennox, Miltenberger, & Donnelly, 1987).

The third way to use reinforcers to decrease operant behaviors is a variation on the DRL approach called **differential reinforcement of other behavior** (DRO). In the DRO procedure, reinforcement is given when the target response, such as whining, does *not occur at all* during a certain time period—perhaps for a whole day. In a sense, reinforcement is given for doing anything except the target response, which is why the name of the method mentions "other behavior." DRO methods are very effective and have successfully reduced many different target behaviors, including sibling conflict at home, classroom misconduct, and thumb-sucking (Leitenberg et al., 1977; Repp, Deitz, & Deitz, 1976).

Habit Reversal

A strategy called **habit reversal** includes several methods to decrease operant behavior, particularly repetitive motor "nervous" habits, such as muscle tics (Azrin & Nunn, 1973). One of its chief methods is called *competing response practice*, in which the person engages for a few minutes in a response that is the opposite of the target behavior. For example, to reduce thumb-sucking or nail-biting, clients are instructed to place their hands by their sides and clench their fists for 3 minutes when they find that the target behavior has begun or is about to happen. This method is like that of positive practice, which we saw earlier, but it is designed to "minimize any aversiveness of the required practice" (Azrin & Nunn, 1973, p. 623). The other methods in habit reversal include training the person to be more aware of the target behavior's occurrence and having family members reinforce improvements in the behavior at home. Several studies have found that habit reversal procedures often can eliminate highly frequent habits almost entirely (Azrin & Nunn, 1973; Azrin, Nunn, & Frantz, 1980; Azrin & Peterson, 1990; Finney et al., 1983; Miltenberger, Fuqua, & McKinley, 1985).

Self-Monitoring and Self-Instructions

Sometimes simply using *self-monitoring* and *self-instructions* may help to decrease operant behaviors. For example, Clarke Harris and William McReynolds (1977) had college students self-monitor their nail-biting by marking each instance of it on a card. Other students also self-monitored their nail-biting, but some were instruct-

✓ **Concept Check 6.3**

••

1. An example of the type of punishment people generally find least acceptable to use in school or at home is _____ . ⇔

2. The approach for training developmentally disabled children by having teachers "bond" with the child and use only social reinforcers is called _____ _____ .

3. The most effective timing pattern for punishment is to deliver it _____ _____ of the behavior.

4. Rewarding someone for smoking fewer than five cigarettes a day is an example of the strategy called differential reinforcement of _____ _____ .

5. The strategy for decreasing operant behavior that includes having the person practice a competing response is called _____ .

_____

Answers: 1. spanking 2. Gentle Teaching 3. immediately after each and every instance 4. low rates of responding 5. habit reversal

••

ed to say to themselves "Don't bite" periodically during the day and others were instructed to say "Don't bite" each time they found themselves doing so. The students' nail-biting behavior was assessed by measuring their fingernail lengths. Individuals in all these conditions showed greater gains in nail length than other students who did not receive an intervention. The individuals who were told to say "Don't bite" contingent on nail-biting had the greatest gains, which suggests that the statement may have served as a punisher. Another study found that self-monitoring by itself helped a woman reduce her frequent upsetting thoughts about the possibility of developing cancer (Frederiksen, 1975). (Go to ✓ .)

Application Exercise

By now you should have collected all or most of the data for your A-B-C log. The main objectives of this application exercise will be to prepare and complete your summary record form, prepare a draft of a data sheet for the collection of baseline data, and consider how you might use methods to decrease an operant behavior in a self-management program.

Tips on Using Extinction and Punishment

The following tips on using extinction and punishment methods can be applied to decrease operant behavior in any behavior modification program to correct a behavioral excess. You'll want to refer back to these tips when you complete the design of your self-management program (Chapter 9).

1. Make sure the person whose behavior is to be modified is aware of the changes in consequences and exactly what the target behavior is.

2. If at all possible, identify an alternative response to prompt and reinforce when methods are used to decrease the target behavior.

3. Think carefully about the reinforcers that maintain the behavioral excess and what you can do to eliminate them. After the behavior has started to decline, watch for new sources of reinforcement that may cause the behavior to recover.

4. If you will use extinction, remember that extinction bursts sometimes occur at the beginning of the process.

5. If you will use a punisher, select the weakest one that you believe will be effective.

6. Make sure a punisher you use can be applied immediately after every instance of the target behavior you want to decrease.

7. When using response cost punishment, you should make sure there is always a supply of things to lose. If the supply of things to lose is exhausted, you will not have any punishing consequence to use.

8. Don't present punishment at about the same time as reinforcement. If you do, you may weaken one or both. This could happen, for example, if you comfort a person who has just been punished because he or she now looks sad.

9. It's a good idea to precede instances of punishment with a warning cue, such as saying "No!" By doing this, you may strengthen the ability of the cue to suppress unwanted behavior.

10. Go through this chapter and consider all the methods we discussed to decrease behavior. Identify ones that might work in the intervention you design.

The Next Steps in Your Program Design

The first task in this application exercise will be to finalize and fill out your summary record form. Some of you may need to obtain feedback from your instructor or fellow students on the draft you prepared on Work Sheet 5.1 before revising it to construct the final summary record form. If so, wait to do the revision until you have the feedback and then do two things:

• Get your summary record form ready to use. Revise your draft as needed, type up the form, and fill it in with the numerical and written information as shown in Figure 3.6.

• Reread the section of Chapter 3 entitled "How to Use Your Functional Analysis," to refresh your memory on using the summary record information.

Follow the Chapter 3 instructions carefully.

The other tasks in this application exercise will involve preparing a data sheet for collecting your baseline data and examining how you might use extinction, punishment, or other methods to decrease a behavioral excess. Turn now to Work Sheet 6.1 to complete these tasks.

Summary

In the procedure or condition of extinction, the reinforcers that maintained an operant behavior are withdrawn, and the behavior eventually declines. To conduct extinction effectively, a functional analysis should be done to determine what reinforcers to terminate. At the beginning of extinction, the behavior may increase temporarily in an extinction burst, and sometimes behaviors that have been extinguished show spontaneous recovery. The target behavior's reinforcement history can affect its resistance to extinction.

Punishment suppresses the behavior on which it is contingent. In positive punishment, an aversive stimulus or condition is added after the behavior; in negative punishment, a valued stimulus or condition is taken away after the behavior. Some types of punishment involve physically aversive stimuli or reprimands. Other punishers consist of aversive activities, as in the procedure of overcorrection, which includes the methods known as restitution and positive practice. And other punishers involve imposing a time-out from opportunities for reinforcement or applying response cost.

Using punishment has several advantages and disadvantages that influence selection decisions as well as the decision to use this method at all. To be very effective, punishment should be applied systematically, an alternative response should be identified and reinforced, and the person should be instructed about the target behavior and the new consequences. The suppressive effects of punishment are affected by its magnitude, its timing, and the variety of aversive stimuli. Self-punishment can work, but people do not always administer punishers to themselves very reliably.

Strategies other than extinction and punishment that also are able to decrease operant behavior include differential reinforcement of incompatible behavior, differential reinforcement of low rates of responding, and differential reinforcement of other behavior. Habit reversal, self-monitoring, and self-instructions are additional strategies that can reduce undesirable behavior.

Key Terms and Review Questions

Key Terms

extinction   punishment
extinction burst   positive punishment
spontaneous recovery   negative punishment

physically aversive stimuli

reprimands

overcorrection

restitution

positive practice

time-out

response cost

differential reinforcement of incompatible behavior

differential reinforcement of low rates of responding

differential reinforcement of other behavior

habit reversal

Review Questions

1. What is extinction? Describe how it is conducted when the behavior has been maintained with positive and negative reinforcement.

2. Why is it important to conduct a functional analysis before using extinction?

3. Describe an undesirable behavior of someone you know and its likely reinforcers. Outline how you could or why you couldn't extinguish that behavior.

4. Define and give examples of an extinction burst and spontaneous recovery.

5. What is punishment, and how does positive punishment differ from the negative form?

6. What are physically aversive stimuli? Give four examples.

7. How could you determine whether a stimulus, such as a reprimand, is a punisher for a specific person?

8. Define "overcorrection" and give an example of how a parent might use this method to decrease a child's misbehavior.

9. Describe the procedure and findings of the research by Azrin and Wesolowski (1974) on using restitution as punishment.

10. Distinguish among the three types of time-out punishment.

11. Define and give an example of response cost punishment from your own life.

12. What are the advantages and disadvantages of using punishment?

13. Describe five aspects of the way punishment is applied that influence its effects and what the effects of each aspect are.

14. Define and distinguish among DRI, DRL, and DRO procedures for reducing undesirable behavior.

15. Describe the strategy of habit reversal.

Related Readings

Axelrod, S., & Apsche, J. (Eds.)(1983). *The effects of punishment on human behavior.* New York: Academic Press.

McGee, J. J., Menolascino, F. J., Hobbs, D. C., & Menousek, P. E. (1987). *Gentle Teaching: A nonaversive approach for helping persons with mental retardation.* New York: Human Sciences Press.

Repp, A. C., & Singh, N. N. (Eds.)(1990). *Perspectives on the use of nonaversive and aversive interventions for persons with developmental disabilities.* Sycamore, IL: Sycamore.

Walters, G. C., & Grusec, J. E. (1977). *Punishment.* San Francisco: Freeman.

Name _____   Day & time
                                        class meets_____
Date _____

Chapter 6: Work Sheet 6.1

1. Your self-management target behavior(s): _____

2. Briefly describe the revisions you decided to make to construct your final summary record form.

3. After filling out the summary record, look through your record for the kinds of pattern described in the Chapter 3 material. If the patterns in your data are not clear, take steps to clarify them. When the patterns are clear, describe below exactly what patterns you found.

4. Refer back to Figure 3.2 and compose a draft of a *data sheet* you could use to collect your baseline data in an organized format. To do this, you'll need to consult the information in Work Sheets 3.1 and 4.1.

5. If your self-management program deals with a behavioral excess, describe below how you will control extraneous sources of reinforcement and how you could use extinction to decrease the behavior.

6. *Regardless* of whether the program you are designing deals with a behavioral excess, describe *two examples of each type* of punishment listed below. The examples you give should be ones you could apply in your current or a future self-management program.

- *Mild* physically aversive stimuli

- Reprimands

- Aversive activities

- Time-out

- Response cost

7. Describe why you could or could not use differential reinforcement and habit reversal in your program.

NOTE: If you will be submitting work sheets to your instructor or to a fellow student, make a copy of each sheet before submitting it.

Part Three

Methods of Changing Emotional Behavior and Associations

7 Behavioral Methods for Changing Respondent Behavior

Prologue

Child clinical psychologist Michael Rutter (1975) described the case of a 6-year-old boy named Martin who appeared to be a generally happy child with no psychological problems other than an extremely severe fear of dogs. He was so terrified of dogs that he couldn't go shopping or walking with his parents or on family outings, and he would run out to the road, heedless of traffic, to avoid encounters with dogs. If a dog came near,

> he screamed, cried, and ran away. The fear of dogs first started when Martin was a year old when he was repeatedly frightened by two very large and noisy hounds in the adjoining garden. The dogs never attacked Martin, but they would put their paws on top of the fence and snarl and bark at him. Martin would either stand still, screaming and terrified, or would rush into the house in tears. (p. 220)

Martin's parents protested, but the neighbors did not change the situation, which continued for a couple of years. The fear the child developed was very intense and persisted even 3 years after the situation with the dogs next door had ended. Martin's case is an example of a learned fear. It had become so maladaptive that it interfered with the boy's general functioning and required treatment. He received successful treatment with behavior therapy procedures like those we will discuss in this chapter.

Martin had learned his fear of dogs through respondent conditioning. In Chapter 1, we saw how John Watson and Rosalie Rayner (1920) demonstrated that an infant named "Little Albert" could learn to fear a gentle white rat. These researchers paired the rat, the *conditioned stimulus* (CS), with a loud noise, the *unconditioned stimulus* (US), that was already able to elicit in Albert an *unconditioned response* (UR) of fear. Martin's fear of dogs had become a *conditioned response* (CR) in real life in much the same way as Albert's fear had been conditioned in a laboratory. The present chapter examines the process and characteristics of respondent conditioning and describes behavioral methods based on respondent conditioning that are useful in changing respondent behaviors. We'll start with the process and characteristics of respondent conditioning in everyday life.

Respondent Conditioning in Real Life

Real life provides many opportunities for individuals to learn respondent behaviors, such as fears. For example, picture the following scene, which unfolded some years ago on a beautiful day at a European beach. Two parents were trying to accus-

Figure 7.1 Diagram of the likely elements in the respondent conditioning of fear in the example of a baby placed face down in seawater.

tom an infant to seawater, which was most inviting to them. The father walked into waist-deep water, holding the baby, who was perhaps 18 months old. He lowered the child, face down, into the water, producing at least the threat of difficult breathing. Although there was no actual danger, the baby was terrified and screamed and flailed about constantly during several of these dunkings, each lasting long enough for the child's skin to become flushed from the exhausting ordeal. After quite some time with no improvement in the infant's response, the father decided that either he or the child had had enough and left the water. I don't know whether this infant developed a fear of water, but the situation was surely one that could produce an association between fear and water, as Figure 7.1 illustrates.

What We Learn in the Respondent Conditioning Process

Examples like those we've seen show us how we can develop respondent behaviors, but they don't tell us what exactly we learn in the process. Current research and theory indicate that what we learn in respondent conditioning consists of two components. First, we learn an *association* between the CS and the US, based largely or solely on their occurring "contiguously," or close in time. The CS does not need to *cause* the US to happen for an association to form—the two stimuli must simply be paired in some way. Each time the stimuli occur together, the CS gains in its ability to elicit the CR. Some researchers believe that the association is based solely on the stimuli occurring together (Papini & Bitterman, 1990). But Robert Rescorla (1988; Rescorla & Wagner, 1972) has proposed another view. He has suggested that the association between CS and US also involves a *contingency*, an "if–then" relationship—thus when we learn a respondent behavior, we learn that if the CS occurs, the US probably will occur. This is why the CS functions as an antecedent signal, enabling us to decide whether the US is likely to occur. If a person repeatedly experiences a CS—a dog in Martin's case—and the CS always occurs with a US, such as barking or snarling, the CS would be a very reliable predictor of the US. As an antecedent signal, the dog would have a high degree of stimulus control—that is, it would elicit a fear response virtually always. But if the dog barked and snarled only occasionally, it would have less stimulus control and would be less likely to elicit fear. In general, CSs that are paired consistently with a US are more likely to become strong antecedents for the CR than CSs that are paired only sometimes with the US.

The second component of what we learn in respondent conditioning is a CS *evaluation,* such as degree to which we like or dislike the stimulus (Baeyens, Hermans, & Eelen, 1993; Davey, 1994; I. Martin & Levey, 1994). So, when Martin had his experiences with the neighbors' dogs, he surely evaluated them quite negatively. But not all respondent conditioning leads to negative evaluations. It's possible to like a CS more if it is associated with a very attractive US. For instance, a little girl may start to like the sound of a car pulling into the driveway if she learns that soon after she hears it, her father will come in the door and play with her, as he regularly has done. (Go to .)

Factors and Phenomena in Respondent Conditioning

Several factors and phenomena influence the development of respondent conditioning and the strength of the resulting respondent behavior. We have already discussed one of these factors, the *consistency* with which the CS and US are paired: CSs that are paired consistently with a US are more likely to elicit the CR than CSs that are paired only sometimes with the US. Another factor is obvious: the greater the *number of times the CS and US are paired,* the greater the ability of the CS to elicit the CR and the stronger the CR is likely to be (Kimble, 1961). In the development of Martin's fear, it's likely that the continued pairing of the neighbors' dogs (the CSs) with their threatening behavior (the US) of snarling and barking made it more likely that the dogs would elicit the boy's fearful CR and that the response would be

Close-Up 7.1
What's What in Respondent Conditioning

When students learn about respondent conditioning, they sometimes have difficulty distinguishing among its components, especially the CS and US. You can figure out what's what in an example of respondent conditioning by following three steps (Lutz, 1994):

1. Search the example for an overt or covert response made by the person or animal. Since the UR and CR are virtually identical, this response is the UR *and* CR.
2. Look for the antecedent stimulus that probably had the ability to elicit the response *before* the situation in the example occurred. This is the US. It often is a stimulus you'd expect to elicit the response "naturally"—that is,

automatically or without learning—but it can also be a learned antecedent with a high degree of stimulus control.
3. Now search the example for another stimulus (or more than one) that (a) occurred *before the response* and (b) probably did *not* have the ability to elicit the response before the situation occurred, but (c) seems to have *gained the ability* to do so in the example. This is the CS, and the response it now elicits is the CR. The CS usually occurs just before the US in respondent conditioning.

Go back to the case of Martin in the Prologue and use these steps to identify the US, UR, CS, and CR.

intense. Let's look at some other important factors and phenomena in respondent conditioning.

CS–US Timing and Intensity

In respondent conditioning, as in telling a joke, timing is a critical factor. The CS and the US typically must occur *close enough in time* to allow the individual to connect the two. This makes sense. Imagine someone shouting to a child "Watch out!" (the CS) just before a ball hits her in the head (the US). It wouldn't take very many repetitions to teach this little girl to take defensive action, such as ducking, in response to the CS alone. But she'd have a hard time learning the relationship if the ball hit her, say, 30 minutes after the warning. In general, respondent conditioning develops most quickly and strongly when the CS precedes the US by a fairly short amount of time, usually between a quarter-second and several seconds (Fitzgerald & Martin, 1971; Kimble, 1961).

The *intensities* of CS and US are also important in conditioning. Shouting "Watch out!" is a more intense CS than saying it in a moderate voice, and being hit hard is a more intense US than being tapped softly. Respondent conditioning develops more quickly and strongly when either or both of these stimuli are fairly strong rather than weak (Kimble, 1961; Lutz, 1994).

Relevance of the CS to the US

Have you ever gotten sick to your stomach after eating something? If so, you probably learned to associate that food as a CS for the US, becoming sick. Chances are, you learned this connection quickly, even though you may not have felt sick until hours after you'd eaten the food. And a single experience might have been enough to make you dislike the food you "blamed." Your newly acquired dislike of the food is the CR. This kind of learning is called **taste aversion**. Animals also learn quickly to associate foods they consumed with becoming sick and tend to avoid those foods in the future (Garcia, Ervin, & Koelling, 1966; Garcia, Hankins, & Rusiniak, 1974; Garcia & Koelling, 1966; Wilcoxin, Dragoin, & Kral, 1971). What's more, it's easier to learn to associate the taste of food (CS) with becoming sick (US) than with receiving electric shock (US). These findings indicate that some CS–US combinations are more easily related than others.

Why would this be? Some CS–US combinations consist of stimuli that are more "relevant" to each other, either because of prior learning or as a result of some innate tendency to associate them (Davey, 1992; Hugdahl & Öhman, 1977; Seligman, 1971). A study demonstrated the importance of CS–US relevance by presenting college student subjects with an aversive loud noise and vibration just once and telling them that this aversive event might occur shortly after the appearance of some of the pictures that were about to be projected on a screen (Honeybourne, Matchett, & Davey, 1993). When each picture was shown, the students estimated the likelihood that the aversive event would happen, but it never actually occurred. The estimates that the aversive event would happen were much higher when the pictures the students saw were of fear-relevant objects, such as a snake or a handgun, than when the pictures were of fear-irrelevant objects, such as a flower.

Overshadowing, Blocking, and Latent Inhibition

In real-life respondent conditioning, the US occurs in a context with many stimuli, any of which could become a CS. The example we described earlier of a father placing his infant face down in seawater had a threatening US for the baby that involved difficult breathing and unsteady physical support. And there were many stimulus elements of the context that could become CSs. Consider just the water—the baby could see, feel, hear (splashes), smell, and even taste it. Which of these elements will become a CS?

People tend to perceive one or more stimuli in a context as relatively prominent or noticeable, particularly when a stimulus is very intense or involves a sensory system the person relies on heavily. For instance, most people rely more on vision than on smell. In contexts with many stimuli, the most prominent stimulus probably will become the strongest CS, having the greatest control in eliciting the CR. This phenomenon is called **overshadowing** because one stimulus outweighs the others in importance (Kamin, 1969; Pavlov, 1927). In the example of the infant in seawater, the CS of *seeing* the water may overshadow other stimuli, such as smelling it. Once a strong CS has been established, it tends to "block" other stimuli from becoming signals (CSs) for that US in the future. So, if the infant's parents tried the same method again and again to accustom the child to seawater, the sight of the water might prevent other features of the water from becoming CSs. **Blocking** refers to the phenomenon in which an existing CS prevents other stimuli from becoming effective signals of the US (Halas & Eberhardt, 1987; Kamin, 1969). It may be that blocking occurs because the individual pays attention to the established CS and not the other stimuli or because the other stimuli are redundant—they simply offer no added predictive value to the existing CS.

One other phenomenon in respondent conditioning involves prior experience with potential CSs. In **latent inhibition**, prior experience with a potential CS in neutral circumstances—that is, without a US—makes later respondent conditioning involving that CS more difficult. For instance, if Martin had had prior experience with neutral or friendly dogs before encountering his neighbors' dogs, his fear would have been more difficult to condition. A study of the origins of fears found that adults who were afraid of dogs reported having had relatively little contact with dogs before their fear developed (Doogan & Thomas, 1992). This suggests the possibility that early nonfearful exposure to dogs might reduce the likelihood of fears developing when aversive encounters happen.

Discrimination and Generalization

When we discussed operant antecedents in Chapter 4, we saw that people learn to *discriminate* between different antecedent stimuli and respond differently toward them, even though the stimuli may be similar in some respects. The same process

Giving children pleasant experiences with potentially fearful situations, such as deep water, is likely to reduce the chances that they will develop fears if they have aversive encounters with those situations later.

happens in respondent conditioning: individuals learn to discriminate between a particular CS and other potential antecedents (Kimble, 1961). We can see this in Martin's case because he was afraid of dogs but not other animals, such as cats, which also have four legs, furry coats, and tails. He could discriminate between these animals and confine his fearful reactions to dogs.

We also saw in Chapter 4 that people's reactions to antecedents show *stimulus generalization*, whereby we tend to respond to antecedents other than the exact ones we experienced in conditioning. Stimulus generalization occurs with respondent behaviors, too. For instance, Martin was afraid of *all* dogs, not just the ones he encountered at home. The greater the similarity between a new antecedent stimulus and the actual CS the individual experienced in conditioning, the stronger the CR is likely to be (Kimble, 1961). Martin probably showed much more fear of dogs that looked like the neighbors' pets than with dogs much different in size and color.

Second-Order Conditioning

Imagine this scenario: Carla and her boyfriend Gene have a nasty fight and split up, ending the relationship they began 2 years ago when they entered college. The fight (a US) made them dislike (the UR and CR) each other very much. Then, several times, Carla sees Gene walking and talking happily with Robin on campus. Gene and Carla neither liked nor disliked Robin before they split up. How does

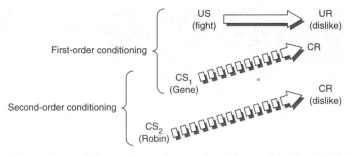

Figure 7.2   Comparison of first-order and second-order conditioning. Carla's disliking Gene (CS₁) developed in first-order conditioning, with their fight as the US. But her disliking Robin (CS₂) developed in second-order conditioning, building on her strong dislike of Gene.

Carla feel about Robin now? Most students answer that Carla probably dislikes Robin. Why? Because Robin is now paired with Gene, whom Carla dislikes.

But Gene is not a US, he's a CS. Robin was not paired with a US. When conditioning occurs with a US, it is called *first-order conditioning*. This is the kind of respondent conditioning we've stressed so far in this book. But respondent conditioning can develop by building from a strong CS, too, as Figure 7.2 illustrates. In **second-order conditioning**, a new CS gains the ability to elicit the CR by being paired with a CS that already elicits that respondent behavior (Rizley & Rescorla, 1972). Carla's dislike of Robin would be a result of second-order conditioning.

Students sometimes confuse second-order conditioning and blocking, which we discussed above, because both phenomena involve pairing an established CS and a potential CS. The difference between the two is subtle, but critical. In blocking, an established CS is paired with a potential CS *in the presence of the US*, and the potential CS does not develop the ability to elicit the CR. In second-order conditioning, an established CS and a potential CS are paired *without the US*, and the potential CS *does* develop the ability to elicit the CR.

Processes Underlying Conditioned Emotional Responses

Experience and biology play important roles in respondent conditioning. Because most of the research on these roles has studied the acquisition of emotions, our discussion of how experience and biology are involved in conditioning will center on the acquisition of fears. These respondent behaviors are examples of **conditioned emotional responses** (CERs, pronounced by spelling "c-e-r"). Some researchers distinguish between two categories of *fear*, defining a **phobia** as an intense and irrational fear of a specific thing, and **anxiety** as a fear that has a vague or unspecified source. Thus Martin's fear of dogs would be called a phobia, and the fear of contracting a rare fatal disease would be an anxiety. But these terms are often used interchangeably; in addition, the characteristic of vagueness or specificity is hard to assess, and distinctions among these terms don't seem to be useful in practice (Davison & Neale, 1994; Sarafino, 1986). We will use the term *fear* interchangeably with *phobia* and *anxiety*, selecting the two latter terms mainly when the vagueness or specificity is obvious.

The Role of Experience in CERs

Studies have shown that people can acquire CERs through direct or indirect respondent conditioning (Emmelkamp, Bouman, & Scholing, 1992; Milgrom et al., 1995; Rachman, 1991). Respondent conditioning is *direct* when the person actually experiences the CS and the US; it is *indirect* when the person acquires a CER through modeling or cognitive processes.

Analysis of interviews and surveys of people with fears suggests that in perhaps two-thirds or more cases, fears were acquired mainly through direct respondent conditioning (Doogan & Thomas, 1992; Merckelbach et al., 1992; Ost, 1987; Ost & Hugdahl, 1981; Wolpe, 1981). For instance, people reported having had negative experiences with the feared object—say, spiders—before the fear developed. But substantial proportions of these individuals also implicated modeling and verbal information they received as contributors to the development of their fears. Although these people's reports may have been inaccurate, since they were based on recollections of past events, some of which had occurred many years earlier, the proportions of individuals reporting direct and indirect sources of their fears have been similar across studies. Still, the factors that affect the way direct and indirect respondent conditioning lead to CERs are unclear. Most reports of indirect respondent conditioning have involved anecdotal evidence, and many people who have extremely frightening experiences—in war, for example—do not appear to develop long-lasting, severe fears (Rachman, 1991).

Biological Processes in CERs

Little research existed before the 1980s on the role of biological processes in people's development of CERs (Emmelkamp, Bouman, & Scholing, 1992). We will look at two biological processes in conditioning emotions that have been implicated since that time.

The first process involves *genetics*. Studies have compared the development of fears and anxieties in identical and same-sex fraternal twins. *Identical*, or "monozygotic," twins share exactly the same genetic inheritance because they result from the splitting of a single fertilized egg. *Fraternal*, or "dizygotic," twins arise from two separate eggs, each of which was fertilized by a separate sperm. If genetic factors are involved in the development of fears, researchers should find greater similarities in the fears of pairs of individuals who are identical twins than fraternal twins. These studies have generally found greater similarity in fears among identical than fraternal twins (Emmelkamp, Bouman, & Scholing, 1992). Such findings indicate that inborn, physiological factors may make some people more likely than others to develop fear reactions from their experiences. But we don't yet know how these physiological factors work, or indeed, what they are.

The other biological process pertains to *brain organization and function* in the storage and and use of memories of conditioned emotions. Current evidence suggests that when we learn something, such as a respondent or operant behavior, the brain stores information about this learning in at least two different memory systems with separate, but connected, physiological structures (Petri & Mishkin, 1994; Schacter, 1992; Squire, 1987). These systems are (1) *implicit or "nondeclarative" memory*, which refers to stored information about learned associations or procedures that is unavailable to our awareness, and (2) *explicit or "declarative" memory*, which refers to stored information we are aware of and can report, indicating that we know or have experienced something. Joseph LeDoux (1994) has described evidence that respondent conditioning of CERs usually produces memories of both types. He pointed out that we may store information from this conditioning

> within declarative memory, but it is kept there as a cold declarative fact. For example, if a person is injured in an automobile accident in which the horn gets stuck in the on position, he or she may later have a reaction when hearing the blare of car horns. The person may remember the details of the accident, such as where and when it occurred, who else was involved and how awful it was. . . . The person may also become tense, anxious and depressed, as the emotional memory is reactivated. (p. 57)

The reaction to horns results from the information in implicit, nondeclarative memory, but information about details of the accident is stored separately in explicit, declarative memory. According to LeDoux, this distinction may explain why some people's fears and anxieties respond to treatment temporarily or not at all. It may be that the partially successful treatment addressed one type of memory, but not the other. (Go to ✔ .)

Other Respondent Behaviors

Respondent conditioning is involved in many other behaviors people develop in real life. We will examine the role of conditioning in drug abuse and in coping with cancer chemotherapy.

Substance Use and Respondent Conditioning

Both respondent and operant forms of conditioning appear to lead to a person's continued and increasing use of mood altering *substances*, such as alcohol and narcotic drugs (heroin, etc.). Operant conditioning influences substance use in two ways. First, taking substances usually produces pleasant mood states that provide positive reinforcement for the behavior. Second, *not* taking the substance after having done so for a long time produces unpleasant "withdrawal" symptoms—such as anxiety, headache, and tremors—which can be removed by taking it again.

✔ Concept Check 7.1

• •

1. The association we learn in respondent conditioning is based largely on the CS and US occurring _____ .

2. In Martin's learning to fear dogs, the US, UR, CS, and CR were (a) _____ _____ , (b) _____ , (c) _____ , and (d) _____ , respectively. ⇔

3. Respondent conditioning develops most strongly and quickly when the CS precedes the US by _____ seconds.

4. An example of one CS overshadowing another at the time of a car accident (the US) might be _____ _____ . ⇔

5. Parents might use latent inhibition to reduce the likelihood that their child will learn to fear water by _____ _____ . ⇔

6. A person who is fearful of all flying insects after being stung by a bee is showing stimulus _____ .

7. People who can describe the circumstances under which they acquired a fear are using _____ memory.

_____

Answers: declarative
child pleasant early experiences with water. **6.** generalization **7.** explicit or
stronger CS than the rainy weather conditions at the accident **5.** giving the
2c. dogs **3.** fear **3.** 0.25 to several **4.** the sound of a horn being a
1. contiguously/close together in time **2a.** snarling and barking **2b.** fear

• •

Removing these symptoms provides negative reinforcement for using the substance.

In the context of substance use, respondent conditioning develops CSs, such as the sight of heroin or a bottle of liquor, that produce internal CRs like the unconditioned reactions of actually taking the substance (Niaura et al., 1988; Rohsenow et al., 1994). For instance, alcoholics who are shown their favorite liquor respond with strong cravings to drink and increased salivation and physiological arousal. Individuals who quit using a substance and then encounter antecedents like these have a difficult time resisting the temptation to start using it again.

Respondent conditioning also leads to increased substance use by inducing the phenomenon of *tolerance*, in which the body adapts to the substance, coming to require more and more of it to achieve the same effect. As a result, heroin addicts typically take doses of the drug that would kill individuals who had never or rarely used it. The body seems to acquire tolerance by trying to "protect" itself with physiological reactions that counteract the effects of the substance (Hinson, Poulos, & Cappell, 1982). But addicts sometimes die from their normal dose (normal, that is, in terms of amount and purity). Why would this be? Shephard Siegel and his colleagues (1982) reasoned that these deaths happen when the tolerance effect fails temporarily because the usual CSs that have elicited the protective reaction as a CR in the recent past are not there—if perhaps, the addict took heroin in a new environment. To test this hypothesis, the researchers injected rats with heroin every other day in a particular room until the animals had reached a high level of tolerance. On alternate days, the rats were injected with a sugar–water solution in a distinctly different room. Then the animals received a larger-than-usual dose of heroin; half of them were in the room where they had received heroin in the past, and half were in the room where they had gotten the sugar–water. If the "heroin room" was a CS that would elicit a protective CR, fewer rats would die from the heroin overdose given in this room than in the other room. The results confirmed this expectation: 32% of the "heroin room" rats died, compared with 64% of the other rats.

Chemotherapy Reactions and Respondent Conditioning

Many cancer patients receive chemotherapy treatment in which powerful drugs are administered orally or by injection to circulate through the body and kill cells that divide rapidly, as cancer cells typically do (Laszlo, 1987; C. J. Williams, 1990). One of the undesirable effects of chemotherapy is the severe nausea and vomiting many patients experience, which often produce two respondently conditioned reactions. One reaction is called *anticipatory nausea*, in which the drug is the US and nausea/vomiting is the UR and CR (Kvale et al., 1991; Taylor et al., 1992). By association, other related events, such as seeing the hospital or thinking about the procedure, become CSs and can then elicit nausea in the absence of the drug. The other reaction is called a *learned food aversion*, which is the same as taste aversion learning, discussed earlier—a food becomes distasteful because the person associates it as a CS with the US of becoming sick. Taste aversions can develop for foods eaten hours before the chemotherapy treatment and are more likely to be reported for foods with strong odors or tastes, such as chocolate and coffee, than for

 Close-Up 7.2
Preventing Learned Food Aversions

Cancer patients who develop learned aversions to foods they have always liked can become very demoralized by these experiences, feeling that they have suffered enough. Simply telling the patient why these aversions develop doesn't seem to stop them from occurring. Can behavioral methods be used to prevent cancer patients from learning to dislike foods they normally eat?

A promising approach to prevent a patient's normal foods from becoming disliked uses the phenomenon of *overshadowing*. The procedure is simple: the patient consumes a strongly flavored, unfamiliar food shortly before the chemotherapy session. Because it has been positioned as the most prominent item in the person's recent diet, the unfamiliar food probably will become the strongest CS if a taste aversion develops. In effect, this procedure makes this food a *scapegoat*, so that it "takes the blame" for the nausea. Studies using scapegoat candies and drinks with unusual, strong flavors, such as plum or coconut, have markedly reduced learned food aversions in adults and children who experienced nausea-producing events (I. L. Bernstein, 1991; Okifuji & Friedman, 1992).

milder foods (I. L. Bernstein, 1991). Strong odors or tastes are relatively intense CSs, making conditioning more likely. (Go to 🔍 .)

Preparing to Change a Respondent Behavior

Designing an intervention to change a respondent behavior requires procedures and data-gathering activities similar to those we've seen for changing operant behaviors. We need to assess the behavior and do a functional analysis of it before deciding exactly which methods to use and how to implement them.

Assessing Respondent Behaviors

For the most part, we can assess respondent behaviors by using the strategies and types of data covered in Chapter 3. Because most of the target behaviors addressed in interventions are CERs, we will focus our discussion of assessment methods on ways to measure fear. In measuring fear, we can use *direct assessment methods*—by observing the person's overt fearful behaviors, such as Martin's reluctance to approach a dog (the CS) or distress when one was present. Alternatively, we can use *indirect assessment methods*—by analyzing the data from self-reports, others' reports, or physiological measures of the person's reactions to the CS. Direct and indirect methods can be applied to collect various types of data that can reflect the presence or strength of the CER.

Frequency and *duration* data can be collected when it's important to know how often the fear CR occurs or how long it lasts when the CS is present. But the type of data most commonly used in interventions addressing CERs is *magnitude*—the degree or intensity of the CR. And two of the most frequently used measures of the magnitude of fear employ indirect assessment methods. *Physiological measures* assess internal events, such as heart rate, that are known to vary with outward signs and self-reports of fear. The greater the increase in heart rate when the CS appears, the stronger the fear is assumed to be. *Rating scales* assess the person's subjective feelings of fear. The higher the rating, the stronger the fear is assumed to be. In one common rating scale for the measurement of fear, the **subjective units of discomfort scale** (SUDS, which is pronounced as an acronym), the person is asked to assess fear experiences along a scale, usually ranging from 0 to 100 (Heimberg, 1990; Wolpe, 1973). The rating of 100 is usually defined something like "the worst fear you have ever experienced or can imagine experiencing," and each unit in the scale is called a "SUD." Thus a CR the person rates at 70 SUDs is subjectively much stronger than one rated at 20 SUDs. Because these are *subjective* ratings, we cannot assume that the same rating given by different people indicates that all raters experienced the same degree of discomfort. But we can assume that a person who gave the same rating to two CSs, such as taking an exam and giving a speech, experienced the same magnitude of fear in these two situations.

Functional Analyses of Respondent Behavior

Conducting a functional analysis is just as important in changing a respondent behavior as it is in changing an operant behavior. The A-B-C log and summary record form can help us identify and describe in detail the antecedents, behaviors, and consequences to address in a program to change a respondent behavior (Emmelkamp, Bouman, & Scholing, 1992).

Antecedents

The antecedents for a respondent behavior represent either the actual CSs conditioned through the individual's overt or covert experiences, or stimuli to which the CR has generalized. One approach for identifying problem CERs is to have individuals fill out questionnaires, such as the *Fear Inventory* in which they rate various situations, such as seeing lightning and being criticized, in terms of how disturbing each one is (Wolpe, 1973). Some instruments focus on assessing fears in children (R. J. Morris & Kratochwill, 1983).

But people's self-reports regarding how the antecedents came to elicit the CR are not necessarily useful in changing the behavior. It is much more critical to know specific recent antecedents for the behavior. A functional analysis of a CER, such as fear or anxiety, should try to answer the following questions about its antecedents (Emmelkamp, Bouman, & Scholing, 1992):

- Under what circumstances does the person's CER occur? These circumstances can include overt events or stimuli, such as certain places or people, or covert ones. We should identify a large number, say, two dozen or so, CSs related to the target respondent behavior that could elicit at least a weak CER.

- What factors about the individual's general life, such as being unemployed or disabled, or about the circumstances under which the CER occurs seem to affect how likely or strongly the behavior will be performed?

- What thoughts tend to precede the CER? Interviews can help to identify these thoughts in two ways. First, we can ask clear questions, such as "What was going through your mind?" or "What did you think might happen?" Second, we can have the person close his or her eyes, imagine instances in which the CER occurred, and speculate out loud about what the antecedent thoughts were.

Material later in this chapter and in the next one will describe several methods for changing respondent behaviors. Answers to the three questions about the antecedents will help us decide which methods to include in interventions we design and how to use them.

Behavior

The functional analysis should enable us to determine three characteristics about the respondent behavior we want to change (Emmelkamp, Bouman, &

Scholing, 1992). First, we should try to identify the person's bodily sensations and activities at the time of the CER. For example, does the person tremble, become fidgety, bite his or her nails, blush, or hyperventilate when the fear or anxiety occurs? Second, we should determine what avoidance behaviors the CER evokes. For instance, does the person procrastinate with respect to important behaviors, such as studying, or try to get out of them entirely? Does the person use mood-altering substances, such as alcohol, to reduce the fear or anxiety? Third, we may be able to identify related problem behaviors in the person's life. For example, anyone who uses alcohol excessively to reduce anxiety is likely to have social or employment difficulties as well.

Consequences

We saw in Chapter 1 that respondent and operant conditioning occur together in real life. In the case of CERs, the avoidance behaviors they evoke have consequences that can reinforce those behaviors. A functional analysis should allow us to identify the short-term and long-term consequences of avoidance behavior (Emmelkamp, Bouman, & Scholing, 1992). People often report that the avoidance behavior reduces the feelings of tension they experience in the CER, thereby providing negative reinforcement as a short-term consequence of the avoidance behavior. The long-term consequences of avoidance behavior usually are undesirable and affect the person's general functioning. For instance, a student who fears exams and then avoids studying may fail to learn important material, do poorly on tests, and flunk a course or miss graduating from school or college. On the other hand, some CERs have little or no impact on the person's life, and may not need to be addressed. Bostonians who are afraid of alligators probably are not affected very much by these fears.

Behavioral Methods to Reduce Respondent Behaviors

Interventions to change respondent behaviors generally address behavioral excesses, such as those resulting when individuals react fearfully or angrily too frequently, too strongly, or for too long. These programs are designed to reduce the respondent target behavior and help the person function more adaptively. We will examine several behavioral methods that help achieve these behavioral and outcome goals.

Extinction and Counterconditioning

Our discussions of operant and respondent conditioning have revealed many parallels in these two learning processes. For instance, stimulus generalization and discrimination take place in both types of learning. Moreover, these types of learning have several other phenomena in common, which can be applied to reduce unwanted respondent behaviors.

Extinction of Respondent Behavior

What do you suppose would have happened to Martin's fear of dogs if new neighbors had moved in next door with a very gentle, friendly dog? At first the child would have been very frightened, but eventually he would have learned that the new dog did not snarl and bark at him, and his fear would have begun to diminish. This example illustrates how extinction can take place with respondent behaviors in real life. In respondent conditioning, as in operant conditioning, the term **extinction** has two meanings: (1) a *procedure* or *condition* in which a CS is presented repeatedly *without the US* it had been paired with during conditioning and (2) a *process* in which the likelihood and vigor of the CR decrease when the US no longer occurs with the CS. Extinction probably plays a very substantial role in reducing respondent behaviors in everyday life. This is surely part of the reason children's fears tend to decline as they get older (Sarafino, 1986).

The process of extinguishing a respondent behavior tends to proceed gradually rather than rapidly, just as it does for operant behavior. For instance, an intervention using extinction procedures to reduce people's strong CERs to social situations found that SUDS ratings for feared social CSs declined by about 3.2% per treatment session (Turner et al., 1992). By the end of the 16 sessions in the intervention, the clients' SUDS ratings had declined by about 50%. Sometimes extinction methods are carried out by exposing the person to very intense CSs for prolonged periods of time—a technique called *flooding*. For instance, someone who is receiving flooding therapy for an intense fear of insects might be taken to the insectary at a zoo and persuaded to sit there surrounded by insects in glass enclosures for half an hour. This is a specialized variation of extinction that requires professional supervision, particularly during the early sessions of treatment (Stanley, 1992). We will examine flooding in detail in Chapter 14.

Another parallel to operant conditioning phenomena is the failure of extinction procedures to erase the memory of the original respondent learning (Bouton & Swartzentruber, 1991). Our memories retain at least part of what we learned in the original conditioning and in extinction. As a result, *spontaneous recovery*—the reappearance of an extinguished response—can take place after a respondent behavior has been extinguished. And if the CS and US are presented together again after extinction has been carried out for a prolonged period, the strength of the CR often returns very rapidly (Bouton & Swartzentruber, 1991). So, if Martin's fear of dogs were successfully eliminated with extinction procedures, and he later had a very negative encounter with a dog, his strong fear might return.

Respondent extinction seems to be a promising approach for treating substance abuse. You'll recall that when people use mood-altering substances, they develop CSs, such as the sight of liquor or the place where they usually drink, that produce internal CRs like the unconditioned reactions of actually taking the substance. Richard Blakey and Roger Baker (1980) applied extinction procedures with six male problem drinkers by having them repeatedly experience important CSs for their drinking, such as holding a can of beer, while not allowing them to drink. These sessions were carried out a few times per week for several weeks or months. Self-reports from most of the men suggested that their cravings for alcohol and drinking had decreased. More recent programs have had some success in treating substance abuse by applying respondent extinction alone or combining it with other behavioral or cognitive methods (Drummond & Glautier, 1994; Monti et al., 1993). These programs have provided stronger evidence for the usefulness of respondent extinction by assessing drinking in more objective ways, such as by having the subjects take breath tests and having family members confirm drinking data.

Counterconditioning

Another similarity in behavioral methods for changing respondent and operant behavior can be seen in the use of alternative responses. We've discussed how operant behavioral excesses can be reduced more effectively if an alternative response is reinforced. A similar effect is observed with respondent behaviors when we apply a technique called **counterconditioning**, in which the individual is trained to substitute a competing or incompatible behavior for the CR when the CS is present. Joseph Wolpe (1958, 1973) gave this technique the name "counterconditioning," based on the belief that it *reverses* a person's previous learning of fear in the following way: "If a response inhibiting anxiety can be made to occur in the presence of anxiety-provoking stimuli, it will weaken the bond between these stimuli and the anxiety" (1973, p. 17). Of course, since counterconditioning is conducted by presenting the CS without the US, extinction is part of the process.

We saw an example of counterconditioning in Chapter 1 in which Mary Cover Jones (1924) reduced a fear of rabbits a boy named Peter had developed. When this fear was first evaluated, the boy would cry if he spotted a rabbit far away and in a cage. The intervention took place over the next several weeks, with Peter receiving counterconditioning therapy once or twice a day. The procedure simply involved bringing the rabbit a little closer each time while Peter ate some favorite foods in the presence of an assistant he liked. Eating and being calm were the alternative responses. By the end of the intervention, Peter would ask for the rabbit and play with it.

In another example of this method, counterconditioning was applied to reduce a social fear of a 20-year-old female college student: she was afraid she would humiliate herself at a banquet she planned to attend, knowing that her ex-boyfriend also would be there—with a date (Ventis, 1973). The relationship had lasted 2 years, and he had ended it. To reduce her fear, the student was asked to imagine various scenes at the banquet, each ending in a mildly absurd event. For instance, she was asked to imagine herself there, waiting and watching for new arrivals, until the ex-boyfriend "entered, dressed in leotards." When she heard that last detail, she smiled and looked surprised, but then imagined the scene with a smile on her face. Her jolly reaction was the alternative response. Later, the student actually attended

✔️ Concept Check 7.2

● ●

1. Taking drugs to escape or avoid withdrawal symptoms provides _____ reinforcement for using the substance.
2. A cancer patient who becomes nauseated at the thought of the next chemotherapy treatment is experiencing _____ .
3. A food that might be a good candidate for a scapegoat to prevent learned food aversions to foods in an adult cancer patient's normal diet would be _____ _____ . ⇔
4. A common rating scale for the assessment of fears is called _____ .
5. To extinguish the fear of bees a child developed after being stung twice, you would need to present (a) _____ without (b) _____ . ⇔
6. An alternative response to replace fear or anger might be _____ . ⇔
_____ or laughter.

Answers: 4. SUDS/subjective units of discomfort scale   5a. bee   5b. the sting   6. calm
1. negative   2. anticipatory nausea   3. strong grape-flavored Kool-Aid

● ●

the banquet, reporting afterward that she had experienced only mild apprehension while there. A similar approach was applied successfully to countercondition a woman's anger toward her husband and child (R. E. Smith, 1973). (Go to ✔️ .)

Systematic Desensitization

The verb *to sensitize* means "to make someone highly responsive or susceptible to certain stimuli," and the prefix *de-* indicates removing, or doing the opposite of. So, a process of desensitization would remove a person's learned responsiveness, such as a CER, to a CS. Joseph Wolpe (1958, 1973) used his concept of countercondi-tioning as the basis in developing a technique to desensitize people's fears, which he described as proceeding in the following way:

> A physiological state inhibitory of anxiety is induced in the patient by means of muscle relaxation, and he is then exposed to a weak anxiety-arousing stimulus for a few seconds. If the exposure is repeated several times, the stimulus progressively loses its ability to evoke anxiety. Then successively "stronger" stimuli are introduced and similarly treated. (1973, p. 95)

This technique, called **systematic desensitization**, is designed to reduce a CER by presenting CSs that are successively more fear-arousing while the individual remains in a physiologically calm state, which is induced by having the person per-form relaxation exercises. It is called "systematic" because it is carried out as a gradual, step-by-step procedure. This procedure contains four important features:

- The person must remain very relaxed during the procedure.
- Each CS is presented briefly.
- The first CS presented is very mild, and the succeeding ones are progressively stronger antecedents for the CER.
- Each CS is desensitized before advancing to a stronger one.

Let's look at how these features are designed and carried out.

Relaxation Exercises

Relaxation is an alternative response to fear because people rarely, if ever, feel afraid and relaxed at the same time. To become very deeply relaxed, people need to receive training in specific techniques, such as *muscle relaxation exercises*, and practice them extensively. When doing these exercises, the people sit or lie down comfortably and then tense and relax each of the body's major muscle groups, one group at a time. They might start by tensing and relaxing the muscles in the hands and arms, then in the neck and shoulders, then in the abdomen, and so on. Doing the exercises produces a deeply relaxed feeling along with a calm physiological state, as reflected in reduced heart rate and blood pressure (Lichstein, 1988). After having practiced these exercises very frequently, people are usually able to induce relaxation more and more easily and quickly. Because several techniques are available to produce relaxation and they are also used frequently by themselves—that is, without desensitization—we will examine them in more detail later (in Chapter 8).

Constructing a Stimulus Hierarchy

The functional analysis should have identified a large number of CSs related to the respondent target behavior that could elicit at least a weak CR. These stimuli can be of three types:

- *In vivo*, or real-life events, objects, or people. For instance, for people who are very fearful of wasps, a CS might be an actual wasp flying nearby or in a capped jar.
- *Imaginal*, or covert representations of events, objects, or people, such as imagining a wasp is nearby.
- *Symbolic*, or overt representations of events, objects, or people, such as seeing a picture of a wasp.

One of the most important steps in using systematic desensitization is to pare these stimuli down to construct a **stimulus hierarchy**—a graded sequence of CSs that are rank-ordered in terms of the magnitude of the target behavior they are likely to elicit. Stimulus hierarchies commonly consist of between 10 and 15 rank-ordered stimuli.

Let's see how we would construct a stimulus hierarchy for a fear of fire a girl named Sue has developed. Suppose we had identified 20 *in vivo* CSs in our functional analysis of her fear. We would use five tasks to pare down these stimuli:

1. Write each CS on an index card, giving enough information to picture or create the stimulus in detail.

2. Have Sue give each CS a SUDS rating on a scale of 0 to 100.

3. Set up "anchor points"—a weak CS and the most intense CS—making sure that all the intense CSs represent reasonable situations that might be encountered in real life and are not very dangerous. In Sue's stimuli, seeing a matchbook several feet away is the weak anchor, rated at 5 SUDs, and poking burning logs with fireplace tools is the intense anchor, rated at 90 SUDs.

4. Rank-order the remaining index cards on the basis of the SUDS ratings. Among these CSs, Sue might have included for the hierarchy are a burning candle across the room, placing a pot on a stove with the gas burner flame lit, and walking to within 10 feet of a large fire in a fireplace.

5. Cull out five to ten stimuli, trying to equalize the step "sizes"—that is, the number of SUDs—between the stimuli we retain for the hierarchy.

To make the progression through the hierarchy *gradual*, the distances separating stimuli should be fairly consistent and not more than 10 SUDs (Wolpe, 1973). If the ratings of the original set of stimuli contain a large gap, the person should identify an intervening CS. Table 7.1 presents two example stimulus hierarchies, one with all in vivo CSs and one with a combination of symbolic, imaginal, and *in vivo* CSs.

Performing Desensitization

Once we've constructed the stimulus hierarchy, the procedure for desensitization is fairly straightforward. It starts by having the individual sit or lie down comfortably and perform the relaxation exercises. If the stimuli are imaginal, the person will be asked to picture each one as a scene and signal by raising a finger when the image is clearly formed (Wolpe, 1973). But if the stimuli are *in vivo* or symbolic, the person will need to experience each one—by approaching it, perhaps, or by looking at it. The procedure for desensitization usually lasts between 15 and 30 minutes of a therapy session, and only some of the stimuli are used in a single session.

Let's see how we would proceed to desensitize Sue's fear of fire. When she is completely relaxed, we'd start by presenting the weakest stimulus from the hierarchy: we would have her look at a matchbook several feet away for several seconds and then say, "Stop." She would look away or close her eyes and state in SUDs how much discomfort the activity had elicited. Her rating, say, "5," would end the first "trial" with that CS. We would immediately say "Go back to relaxing," and encourage Sue to do so for 20 to 30 seconds. Then we'd start the second trial with the same stimulus, repeating the same procedure. We would continue with additional trials until Sue reports *"0" on two successive trials*. Once this "success criterion" has been reached, we may advance to the next stimulus in the hierarchy. We would not advance to the next stimulus at any point in the desensitization process until this criterion has been met.

Table 7.1 *Examples of Stimulus Hierarchies with Hypothetical SUDS Ratings for a Fear of Heights and a Fear of Dating*

Heights: Stimulus hierarchy using all *in vivo* CSs:

1. Standing at an upper-floor window and looking out. (SUDS = 5)
2. Standing on a stepladder, 3 feet from the floor, to change a light bulb. (SUDS = 15)
3. Standing on a balcony near the railing, several stories above the ground. (SUDS = 25)
4. Walking on flat ground above a mountain cliff, 20 feet from the edge. (SUDS = 35)
5. Walking on flat ground above a mountain cliff, 5 feet from the edge (SUDS = 45)
6. Hiking on a steep trail. When cliffs are very near, there are guard rails (SUDS = 55)
7. Being a passenger in a car traveling at the speed limit on a narrow and winding mountain road. When cliffs occur, there are guard rails. (SUDS = 65)
8. Being on an extension ladder outside a house, cleaning a second-story window. (SUDS = 75)
9. Climbing up a 50-foot-high water tower, using a ladder with handrails. (SUDS = 85)
10. Standing on a moderately sloped roof of a house. (SUDS = 95)

Dating: Stimulus hierarchy using symbolic, imaginal, and *in vivo* CSs:

1. Looking at a photograph of an attractive prospective person to date. (SUDS = 3)
2. Imagining meeting the person in the photograph (item 1) at a party. (SUDS = 10)
3. Looking at a photograph of a couple on a date. (SUDS = 17)
4. Imagining being at a movie with several acquaintances and sitting next to one of them who could be a prospective date. (SUDS = 25)
5. Imagining exchanging phone numbers with an attractive person who could be a prospective date. (SUDS = 35)
6. Imagining calling the item 5 person to chat. (SUDS = 40)
7. Imagining accidentally meeting the item 5 person at a shopping mall and going for coffee together. (SUDS = 48)
8. Imagining calling the item 5 person for a date. (SUDS = 55)
9. Imagining being on a date with the item 5 person. (SUDS = 65)
10. Imagining a friend talking about helping to arrange a date with a mutual acquaintance who is an attractive person. (SUDS = 74)
11. Actually dialing the first several digits of the phone number of the attractive item 10 person, without completing the call. (SUDS = 80)
12. Dialing a number that always has a taped message, such as the phone at a movie theater, then talking as if the call had gone through to the attractive item 10 person and asking for a date. (SUDS = 85)
13. Imagining an "awkward silence" when conversing on a date with the item 10 person. (SUDS = 92)
14. Actually calling the item 10 person for a date. (SUDS = 98)

We would perform this same procedure for each CS, advancing through the hierarchy in sequence. Here are some guidelines to follow in desensitization (Sarafino, 1986; Wolpe, 1973):

THE FAR SIDE   By GARY LARSON

"Now relax.... Just like last week, I'm going
to hold the cape up for the count of 10. ...
When you start getting angry, I'll put it down."

Systematic desensitization has been
applied successfully with a variety of
conditioned emotional responses
(and types of clients!).

- Reducing a moderately strong fear is likely to take at least several sessions, and
  stronger fears may require many more.
- Each session should end on a positive note, either a stimulus should be successfully desensitized or very good progress on it should be made in that direction. If a success criterion is reached but there isn't enough time to complete
  another stimulus, save the item for the next session.
- The first stimulus used in each succeeding session should be the last one fully
  desensitized in the preceding session, and the success criterion should be
  repeated.

Finally, it is important to be flexible and willing to revise the procedure to meet the
individual's needs. Something may have happened in the person's life since the last
session to influence his or her reactions to the stimuli. (Go to 📖 .)

Effectiveness of Systematic Desensitization

Systematic desensitization is a well documented, highly effective method for
helping people overcome fears and other CERs (Borden, 1992; TFPDPP, 1993; G.

Case Study 7.1
Desensitizing a Boy's Fear of Loud Noises

• •

A bright 4-year-old boy developed an extreme fear in which loud sounds, such as a siren or airplane noise, would send him running in unpredictable directions, sometimes toward the source of the noise and sometimes away from it (as described in Tasto, 1969). His parents were concerned for three reasons. First, the fear was restricting the boy's social activities. Second, it could cause him to be killed or injured if he ran into the street when a noise occurred. Third, new CSs, such as rain, were beginning to develop because of their association to noises, such as thunder.

A stimulus hierarchy was constructed in which the strongest CS was a gun firing, and the weakest was a piece of paper being crunched. Intermediate CSs included a balloon breaking, thunder, and a board falling on the floor. The therapist taught the boy to perform relaxation exercises and then tried to desensitize the fear by having the boy *imagine* each stimulus. But the

boy did not report any fear to these stimuli during the sessions, and his real-life fears were not improving. So the therapist switched to *in vivo* stimuli, actually dropping a board to the floor and popping balloons.

The parents helped by having the boy practice relaxation exercises at home and presenting some of the stimuli. After the desensitization had progressed, the father got the boy to burst balloons by allowing him to keep coins that were inside them if he broke them. At first the balloons were only slightly inflated, but later the inflation—and noise—was increased. His father also took him to target practice—initially, the boy "would go quite a distance from his father, get relaxed, and signal his father to shoot. He gradually moved closer until he was shooting the gun himself." Follow-up reports from the parents 1 and 4 months after therapy indicated no recurrence of the boy's fear.

• •

T. Wilson, 1982). Not only does this method usually succeed in reducing fears by the end of treatment, but these improvements are durable. Follow up assessments taken for 2 years after treatment have found few recurrences in the fears (Paul, 1967; Rosen, Glasgow, & Barrera, 1977). What's more, many individuals who succeed in overcoming specific fears in treatment with systematic desensitization often report improvements in other areas of emotional functioning in their lives (Paul, 1967). Desensitization has also been used successfully in treating other anxiety-related problems, such as people's inability to urinate in public restrooms and compulsions to check repeatedly for such potentially harmful circumstances as doors left unlocked (McCracken & Larkin, 1991; Overholser, 1991).

In the case study of the boy who was afraid of loud noises, using imaginal CSs didn't work. Are imaginal CSs useful? Although desensitization with imaginal stimuli can reduce people's fears, several studies have shown that direct exposure to the feared object or situation results in greater fear reduction (Barlow et al., 1969; Crowe et al., 1972; Menzies & Clarke, 1993; Sherman, 1972; G. T. Wilson, 1982). In the research by David Barlow and his colleagues, female college students who were afraid of snakes were pretested for their fear with a "harmless boa constrictor" that was kept in a glass box with a wire mesh cover; then they were desensitized for their fear, and finally posttested with the snake. The pretests and posttests included two types of assessment: (1) a *behavioral test* that contained 17 acts, ranging from watching the snake in the cage 15 feet away to picking up the snake, and (2) a *physiological test* that measured galvanic skin responses while the snake was in the box at various distances away. Desensitization was carried out with the CSs in the stimulus hierarchy presented by either an imaginal or an *in vivo* procedure. Posttests conducted with the snake revealed that the individuals desensitized with the *in vivo* stimuli were able to perform more of the items in the behavioral test and showed much less physiological arousal to the snake than those desensitized with the imaginal stimuli, as depicted in Figure 7.3.

Some controversy exists over the importance of two features of the systematic desensitization procedure. One of these features is relaxation. Findings from some studies suggest that relaxation during sessions enhances the desensitization process, but other findings are contradictory (Kazdin & Wilcoxin, 1976). The second feature is the need to use relatively weak CSs in the stimulus hierarchy. A study compared the use of a full stimulus hierarchy with the use of only the strongest stimuli in the hierarchy in desensitizing college students' mathematics anxieties (Richardson & Suinn, 1973). The two approaches were equally successful in reducing the students' fears. Although there is some doubt about the importance of these features to the success of desensitization, the evidence against their use is not yet clear enough to warrant dropping them. Because relaxation exercises and full stimulus hierarchies don't seem to harm clients and may help the treatment process, it's probably best to include these features in systematic desensitization.

Vicarious Desensitization Through Modeling

A girl named Keisha was able to overcome her fear of cats by watching her parents play with one and later, with their encouragement, joining in and gradually contacting the cat. Notice that in this example the parents *modeled* fearless behavior for the child to watch. Modeling can be applied to desensitize fears in a *vicarious* manner. Keisha's parents reduced her fear with a method called **participant modeling** in which the fearful person watches someone else cope well in real-life, increasingly threatening situations; then the person is encouraged to join in and is guided toward more and more contact with the feared object (Bandura, 1975; Bandura, Jeffery, & Gajdos, 1975). Guiding toward contact usually involves verbal and physical prompts.

Studies of participant modeling have found it to be very successful in reducing fears and more effective than simply watching a filmed model cope with the feared situation (Borden, 1992; G. T. Wilson, 1982). Learning *how* to behave in fearful situations and *actually performing that behavior* in the modeling sessions seem to be critical components to overcoming fears. One study found that children who were asked to practice the coping behaviors they had seen in a video of children undergoing dental treatment were less disruptive in a subsequent dental visit than were other children who merely watched the video (Klingman et al., 1984). Other research findings indicate that the fear reduction produced through modeling can be fairly specific. For instance, a girl who was extremely afraid of dogs and cats was

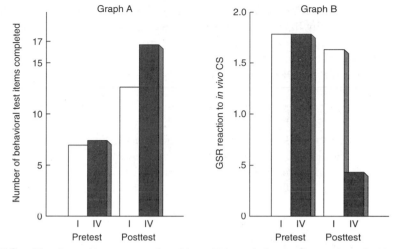

Figure 7.3   Number of items completed in a 17-item behavioral test (graph A) and Galvanic skin response (GSR, in graph B) with a real CS, a snake. The data are for snake-phobic adults before (pretest) and after (posttest) systematic desensitization to snakes conducted with imaginal (I) or *in vivo* (IV) CSs. High GSR scores indicate greater fear reactions. (Data from Barlow et al., 1969, Tables 1 and 2.)

treated first for her fear of dogs, which participant modeling decreased (Matson, 1983). But her fear of cats continued until it was specifically addressed.

Using Respondent-Based Techniques: Some Cautions

All the techniques we have examined to change respondent behavior feature ways to *reduce* the occurrence or magnitude of CERs, and these techniques are based on respondent conditioning processes and phenomena. But other techniques have been used with varying degrees of success to *increase* people's CERs—that is, to *sensitize* individuals to certain CSs by pairing these stimuli with *aversive* USs. These approaches are called *sensitization techniques* or *aversion therapy*. In an application of aversion therapy we discussed in Chapter 2, alcoholics take an emetic drug, which causes them to become nauseated and vomit when they consume alcohol. The nausea is the US, and alcohol-related stimuli, such as the taste of a drink or the sight of a bottle of liquor, become CSs for the CR of feeling nauseated. This approach is designed to impart negative sensitization to stimuli alcoholics ordinarily associate with drinking.

Some behavioral methods are potentially hazardous to an individual unless applied by a person having extensive professional training. Aversion therapy and flooding techniques, which we mentioned earlier, are examples of methods that are potentially hazardous. Do *not* try to apply them in your self-management program. Other methods, although perhaps not especially hazardous, require very special skills or circumstances that are accessible only to students who have received advanced graduate training. Taking this course will not give you sufficient training to use any of these techniques. We will classify all these techniques as *advanced, specialized techniques* and examine them together in Part V (Chapters 13–15) of this book. Virtually all the other methods we consider before Part V can be used in designing and carrying out a program to change your own behavior, but I caution you against trying to apply these methods to change someone else's behavior. Seemingly simple problems of others can be very complex, and changing their problem behaviors may require professional supervision. (Go to ✔ .)

Application Exercise

This application exercise has two main objectives. The first objective is to do a functional analysis and stimulus hierarchy for a CER. If your self-management project includes or focuses on reducing a CER, such as a fear or negative thoughts about yourself, the work sheets for this chapter and the next will identify and help you to plan the methods you can use in accomplishing your behavioral goals. For students whose self-management projects do not currently include a CER, the functional analysis will be hypothetical and relatively incomplete, but it will still have some

✔ Concept Check 7.3

1. Systematic desensitization is based on Wolpe's concept of _____ .
2. The alternative response to fear in systematic desensitization is _____ .
3. An example of a weak *in vivo* CS for a fear of flying might be _____
   _____ . ⇔
4. An example of a strong imaginal CS for a fear of flying might be _____
   _____ . ⇔
5. Rank-ordering CSs in a stimulus hierarchy is based on the fearful person's
   _____ ratings.
6. The success criterion for desensitizing a CS is _____
   _____ .
7. Having a fearful person gradually contact a fearful object or situation while watching someone else cope well with it is called _____ .

_____

Answers: **1.** counterconditioning **2.** relaxation **3.** calling an airline ticket agent for information **4.** picturing being on a bumpy flight **5.** SUDS **6.** "0" on two successive trials **7.** participant modeling value. It will promote an understanding of the concepts and procedures for changing respondent behaviors and make it possible to incorporate some of these procedures if it becomes desirable to include an unforeseen CER in a project. The second objective of this application exercise is to get you started on collecting baseline data for your project.

Tips on Using Respondent-Based Techniques

The following tips on using respondent-based techniques focus on using systematic desensitization to reduce problem CERs. These tips are applied by professionals when they design programs to change overt or covert respondent behaviors. You should consider them when you complete the design of your self-management program at the end of Chapter 9.

1. Make sure that all individuals directly involved in the program understand exactly what the procedures will be and what their purposes are. Emphasize that clinical research has shown that the techniques work very well in reducing problem CERs for the great majority of people.
2. The stimulus hierarchy must be personalized to the needs of the individual. For your self-management program, the hierarchy should be based on a functional analysis of the behavior and your SUDS ratings of all CSs it includes.
3. All CSs should be presented in ways that maximize how clearly and fully the person will experience them.
4. The stimulus hierarchy can contain imaginal CSs, especially for stimuli that cannot be presented in more concrete ways. Although desensitization with imaginal stimuli can reduce CERs, *in vivo* stimuli are more effective.
5. *In vivo* CSs with very high SUDS ratings should not be experienced unless another person is present.
6. Number the index cards that describe the CSs in their rank order and keep them with you to consult throughout each desensitization session.
7. Don't start the first desensitization session until the relaxation exercises have been practiced at least five times (preferably about ten); make sure the exercises produce deep relaxation and that deep relaxation is achieved within several minutes. See Chapter 8 for additional information about relaxation exercises.
8. Don't rush through the procedure. Make sure that each CS has been fully desensitized before moving on the the next. Some sessions may not get beyond one or two stimuli.
9. Don't make sessions too long. The desensitization procedure in a session should take, say, 20 minutes and should not exceed half an hour.
10. Desensitization sessions should take place at least once or twice a week, and they can be done as often as two or three times in any one day. Schedule between three and six sessions a week, if possible.

11. If you are conducting desensitization on yourself and experience too much discomfort with a newly introduced CS or a lot of difficulty relaxing during its presentation, withdraw the stimulus, practice relaxation for a couple of minutes, and try the CS again for a shorter time. If you still have difficulties, go back to the preceding CS, achieve the success criterion again, and advance once more to the problem CS. If the difficulties persist, stop the procedure and identify one or two intervening CSs that you can insert before the problem CS.

12. If you have tried the methods described in tip 11 and you appear unable to progress beyond that point in the hierarchy, discontinue the desensitization. If you still want to modify that behavior, consider seeking professional assistance.

The Next Steps in Your Program Design

The first task in this application exercise will be to identify a CER as the subject of a functional analysis we will perform. For students whose self-management projects *do not currently include a CER*, we will identify one to use for a functional analysis you will do *hypothetically* and *incompletely* just for practice. You won't collect data for it, but will answer questions *as if* this has been done. Then we will construct a stimulus hierarchy for the subject CER, address other issues about its antecedents, examine aspects of the behavior itself, and discuss the consequences this behavior produces.

After completing these tasks, we will finalize the format for your data sheet so that you can start collecting baseline data for the target behavior in your self-management project. Turn now to Work Sheet 7.1 to complete these tasks.

Summary

Children and adults learn many respondent behaviors, such as fears, from their experiences in everyday life. This learning includes an association between the CS and the US, as well as an evaluation (like/dislike) of the CS. Respondent conditioning develops most quickly and strongly when the CS and the US are paired consistently, frequently, and close enough in time to permit them to be associated. An exception to this rule is taste aversion learning, which develops very quickly even though the CS and US occur far apart in time.

Three important phenomena in respondent conditioning are (1) overshadowing, in which one CS outweighs others in being able to elicit the CR, (2) blocking, whereby an existing CS prevents other stimuli from becoming conditioned to a CR, and (3) latent inhibition, in which prior neutral experience with a CS makes it more difficult to associate it with a US in the future. People learn to discriminate between a particular CS and other stimuli that could serve as antecedents, and they also show stimulus generalization, responding to CSs that are not exactly the same as the one to which they were conditioned. People also learn respondent behavior through second-order conditioning, in which an established CS functions like a US in conditioning a new CS to a CR.

Many of the respondent behaviors people learn are conditioned emotional responses, such as anger and two types of fears: anxieties and phobias. Although we acquire conditioned emotional responses through direct and indirect experiences, biological processes are also important. Genetic factors appear to influence the development of fears, and people appear to store the memories of conditioned emotions in two different structures of the brain. Respondent conditioning is also important in the development of dependencies on mood altering substances, such as alcohol and drugs, and in cancer patients' acquisition of the responses of anticipatory nausea and food aversions when they receive nausea-producing chemotherapy.

Respondent behaviors can be measured with direct and indirect assessment methods, using data on frequency, duration, and magnitude. The magnitude of respondent behaviors can be assessed with physiological measures and rating scales, especially the subjective units of discomfort scale. Techniques that can reduce respondent behaviors include extinction, counterconditioning, systematic desensitization, and participant modeling. Systematic desensitization is a highly effective method for reducing fears and other emotional behaviors. It involves having the person become and remain relaxed while experiencing *in vivo*, imaginal, or symbolic CSs from a stimulus hierarchy. *In vivo* stimuli usually are more effective in reducing fears than imaginal or symbolic stimuli.

Key Terms and Review Questions

Key Terms

taste aversion	anxiety
overshadowing	subjective units of discomfort scale
blocking	extinction
latent inhibition	counterconditioning
second-order conditioning	systematic desensitization
conditioned emotional responses	stimulus hierarchy
phobia	participant modeling

Review Questions

1. Describe the associations and evaluations that occur in the respondent conditioning process.

2. How are CS–US intensity, and pairing consistency and timing, important in respondent conditioning?

3. Why are taste aversions learned so quickly even though the CS and US may occur far apart in time?

4. Define "overshadowing," "blocking," and "latent inhibition" and give an example of each phenomenon from an event that happened or might have happened in your own life.

5. Define "second-order conditioning" and describe the first- and second-order parts of an example of how it might have happened in your own life.

6. What are conditioned emotional responses? How are experience and biological processes involved in their development?

7. Describe the research by Siegel and his colleagues (1982) on tolerance effects and drug overdoses.

8. Why is overshadowing helpful in preventing learned food aversions in cancer patients who receive chemotherapy?

9. Define "extinction" in respondent conditioning and give an example of how it might be used to reduce a person's anger.

10. How are counterconditioning and systematic desensitization related?

11. Describe the steps in constructing a stimulus hierarchy.

12. Describe the procedure for conducting systematic desensitization.

13. What are imaginal and *in vivo* CSs, and how were they used in the case study on desensitizing a boy's fear of loud noises?

14. Describe the research by Barlow and his colleagues (1969). What do the results mean in designing stimulus hierarchies?

Related Readings

Borden, J. W. (1992). Behavioral treatment of simple phobia. In S. M. Turner, K. S. Calhoun, & H. E. Adams (Eds.), *Handbook of clinical behavior therapy* (2nd ed.). New York: Wiley.

Emmelkamp, P. M. G., Bouman, T. K., & Scholing, A. (1992). *Anxiety disorders: A practitioner's guide.* Chichester, UK: Wiley.

Morris, R. J., & Kratochwill, T. R. (1983). *Treating children's fears and phobias: A behavioral approach.* New York: Pergamon Press.

Rachman, S. (1991). Neo-conditioning and the classical theory of fear acquisition. *Clinical Psychological Review, 11,* 155–173.

Sarafino, E. P. (1986). *The fears of childhood: A guide to recognizing and reducing fearful states in children.* New York: Human Sciences Press.

Wolpe, J. (1973). *The practice of behavior therapy.* New York: Pergamon Press.

Name _____   Day & time
                                   class meets_____

Date _____

Chapter 7: Work Sheet 7.1

1. Your self-management target behavior(s): _____

2. Listed below are a variety of common CERs that create problems for adolescents and adults. You may add examples to this list if you wish. If the target behavior you have chosen for your self-management project is not a CER, look though the list and choose one you think you *might benefit from changing someday*, and *circle it* as a *hypothetical* CER you'll use for the tasks in this application exercise. If you have chosen a CER as the target behavior in your self-management project, skip to the next question.

- *Anger* at work, with family members or friends, when driving, or (specify) _____ .

- *Anxiety* in social situations, when performing or giving a speech, when studying, in tests, or (specify) _____ .

- *Fear* of animals or insects, heights, doctors or dentists, physical injury, or (specify) _____ .

- *Negative thoughts* about your appearance, your abilities, other people, or (specify) _____ .

3. If your target behavior is a CER, use your functional analysis and prior work sheets to answer the following questions; if you are using a hypothetical CER, just use your intuition. Describe the behavior itself. What are your bodily sensations and activities at the time of the CER? What avoidance behaviors, such as procrastination or substance use, does the CER evoke? What other problem behaviors in your life seem to be related to the CER?

4. What thoughts tend to precede the CER? To answer this, ask yourself "What was going through your mind?" or "What did you think might happen?"

5. How does your avoidance behavior provide negative reinforcement as a short-term consequence of the CER? Describe a couple of examples. How can you prevent this reinforcement? What are some long-term consequences of avoidance?

6. Construct a stimulus hierarchy of 10 to 15 CSs for the CER. Use the following steps. (a) Start by listing about 20 situations or variations of the antecedents that produce the CER, making sure they range from weak to strong CSs. (b) Give each one a SUDS rating on a scale of 0 to 100, where 100 means the CS would elicit the most severe reaction you have ever experienced or can imagine experiencing for this CER. (c) Set up "anchor points"—a weak CS and the most intense CS. (d) Cull out five to ten stimuli, trying to equalize the step "sizes"—that is, the number of SUDs—between the stimuli you retain for the hierarchy.

7. Refer back to Work Sheet 6.1 and compose a final draft of the data sheet you will use to assess the target behavior for your self-management project. If your target behavior is a CER, be sure to include a way to collect SUDS ratings. Start collecting baseline data as soon as you have any permission you may need from your instructor.

NOTE: If you will be submitting work sheets to your instructor or to a fellow student, make a copy of each sheet before submitting it.

8 Covert Behavioral Methods for Changing Respondent Behavior

Prologue

A 31-year-old divorced man named Dennis developed a severe anxiety condition called *panic disorder*: he experienced occasional, sudden, and irrational attacks that were characterized by intense physiological symptoms and feelings of impending doom. The attack that led to his seeking therapy occurred while he and his fiancée, Elaine, were Christmas shopping at a mall. Being in large crowds had been a problem for Dennis for years, and on that occasion he had an attack with classic symptoms of panic disorder. He suddenly became physically

> very sick. His hands began to tremble uncontrollably, his vision became blurred, and his body felt weak all over. He experienced a tremendous pressure on his chest and began to gasp for breath, sensing that he was about to smother. These dramatic physical symptoms were accompanied by an overwhelming sensation of apprehension. He was terrified but did not know why. Without saying anything to Elaine, he whirled and dashed from the store, seeking refuge in their car. . . . He continued to feel dizzy and short of breath for about 10 minutes more. (Oltmanns, Neale, & Davison, 1991, p. 17)

Dennis had left Elaine so suddenly that she was unaware he had gone, and she looked for him in stores for over an hour before finding him in the car. When he explained what had happened, she persuaded him to seek professional help.

Dennis's interviews with a therapist revealed that his first full-blown attack had occurred 7 years earlier when he and his wife were with some of her professional colleagues at a dinner theater. He didn't know what was happening and was terrified in his seat when others noticed, tried to help, and eventually took him to a lounge where he could lie down. Dennis did not seek medical treatment, deciding to attribute the attack to something he had eaten. But this and subsequent attacks, such as one while he was driving alone, had the effect of making him even more anxious than he had been. For instance, Dennis became less and less socially active and very frightened of driving in rush hour and on bridges for fear of having another attack in such dangerous circumstances. Being in social situations and driving had become CSs for intense feelings of anxiety, the CR.

This chapter, like the last one, concentrates on changing respondent behaviors that have become problems for individuals. But the techniques we will examine to produce these changes focus relatively heavily on covert behaviors, such as people's thoughts and imagery processes, rather than on overt conditioning or modeling processes. A major component of the successful treatment Dennis received was training in relaxation—the first category of *covert behavioral methods* we will discuss.

Relaxation Techniques

"Try to relax when hassles or pressures happen in your life," physicians often advise patients who have high blood pressure. Does this advice help? Probably not, and it may actually make the person's problem worse if he or she tries to relax without knowing how. Researchers demonstrated this possible effect with two groups of subjects who watched a videotape of physiologically arousing events (Suls, Sanders, & Labrecque, 1986). None of the subjects had been trained to relax, but some were asked simply to try to relax and keep their blood pressures low while they watched the TV and others were asked to respond as they normally would. The subjects who were asked to relax showed greater blood pressure increases during the videotape than the subjects who were given no such instructions. These findings suggest that people who have not been trained to relax may try too hard. Individuals who have received training in relaxation techniques are able to become psychologically and physiologically relaxed and can react less strongly when they experience arousing stimuli (Lichstein, 1988).

The term **relaxation** refers to a state of reduced psychological and physiological tension or arousal. Techniques to produce relaxation gained wide acceptance in psychological therapy through their inclusion in successful systematic desensitization treatments of emotional respondent behaviors, especially anxieties and phobias. In the 1970s, relaxation techniques became recognized as therapeutic tools that were effective in their own right as approaches in programs to treat a variety of psychological and medical problems, such as fears, asthma, high blood pressure, migraine and tension headache, and cancer chemotherapy reactions (Carlson & Hoyle, 1993; Lichstein, 1988).

"You've got to learn to relax."

Simply telling someone to relax is not likely to help very much.

People can use any of several techniques to achieve relaxation. Regardless of the particular methods used, a few points should be kept in mind (Lichstein, 1988; Moore, 1987; C. B. Taylor, 1978). First, the procedure should be carried out when the person is seated or reclining in a *quiet and comfortable setting*. It's usually best not to do relaxation exercises on a bed—the person should not be comfortable enough to fall asleep. Loosen any tight-fitting clothing. Second, sessions last between *10 and 30 minutes*, but the first ten sessions or so are likely to take more time than later sessions because people get better at inducing relaxation with practice. Third, it's typically a good idea to *set aside regular times* to practice the relaxation exercises once or twice a day as "homework" in a place that is *free of interruptions and distractions*. The place can be at home, in a library, or anywhere else these conditions can be assured. To assure that these conditions will exist, the person may need to plan ahead or negotiate with other people, such as roommates. Fourth, some people report that doing relaxation exercises leaves them relaxed but *alert*, making it hard to go to sleep. Therefore you may not want to use relaxation techniques within an hour or so of going to bed. Finally, the person should collect data rating the magnitude of his or her relaxation during sessions, using a data sheet like the one in Figure 8.1. We'll turn now to descriptions of three of the most commonly used types of relaxation techniques: progressive muscle relaxation, autogenic training, and meditation.

Progressive Muscle Relaxation

The approach we described briefly in Chapter 7 involved alternately tensing and relaxing separate muscle groups while resting comfortably. This technique, developed in the 1920s and 1930s by Edmund Jacobson (1938), is called **progressive muscle relaxation** or just *progressive relaxation*. Because the original technique was extremely detailed and dozens of hours sometimes were needed to train a person to relax, a shorter, easier-to-learn version of this technique was eventually developed by Douglas Bernstein and Thomas Borkovec (1973). This shorter version—or some variation of it—is what is meant by progressive muscle relaxation today (Lichstein, 1988). Studies with follow-up assessments have shown that the positive psychological and physiological effects of using progressive muscle relaxation continue, and may even get stronger, in the weeks and months after individuals receive training in the procedure (Carlson & Hoyle, 1993). Children just 3 or 4 years old can learn muscle relaxation techniques and apply them to reduce their anxieties during stressful events, such as receiving dental treatment (L. J. Siegel & Peterson, 1980).

Before we examine an actual *protocol*, or script, for performing progressive muscle relaxation, we will consider two aspects of the procedure that currently are controversial. First, it is not certain whether it is necessary or desirable to *tense* the muscles as part of the process. For instance, a recent study found evidence that alternating tensing and relaxing muscle groups may not be as effective in inducing deep physiological relaxation as procedures that omit the tensing phase (Lucic et al., 1991). But other researchers have reported contradictory results, indicating that having individuals tense their muscles is helpful *while they are being trained* in the technique (Lehrer, 1982). Tensing probably promotes learning the skill of relaxing by teaching the sub-

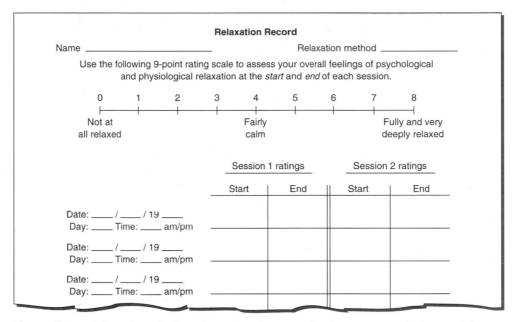

Figure 8.1 A data sheet for keeping relaxation records of progress made in practicing relaxation techniques.

ject to discriminate between relaxation and muscular tension. After people have mastered the skill, tensing the muscles can be eliminated (Moore, 1987).

The second controversial aspect of the progressive muscle relaxation procedure pertains to the value of using tape-recorded protocols during relaxation sessions. Many therapists either provide protocol tapes or advise clients to make tapes of the scripts that are used in relaxation exercises. Although these tapes are generally used for clients to practice relaxation as homework assignments, they have also been tried as a substitute for in-person training with a therapist. Studies have found that people can use taped protocols to learn how to induce relaxation without supervised training, but in-person training is more effective (Beiman, Israel, & Johnson, 1978; Lehrer, 1982). It may be that supervised training allows the therapist to notice difficulties and give corrective feedback. Other studies have shown that the beneficial effects of relaxation are greater when in-person training is conducted individually rather than in groups and that providing taped protocols for clients to use in practicing relaxation on their own appears to be very helpful (Carlson & Hoyle, 1993). Although clients tend to overstate their claimed amounts of homework practice with tapes, most appear to practice relaxation about as often as the therapist advises (C. B. Taylor et al., 1983).

Close-Up 8.1 contains a protocol you can use to carry out progressive muscle relaxation training based on information from several sources (Bernstein & Borkovec, 1973; Lichstein, 1988; NJNPI, 1972; C. B. Taylor, 1978). You'll notice that the tensing and relaxing progresses through a series of different muscle groups.

Breathing exercises are included, as well. If you want to use the protocol, make a tape recording of it, but do not say the numbering and time measurements (note that 7" and 30" mean 7 seconds and 30 seconds). Tensing phases should be about 7 (between 5 and 10) seconds long, and relaxation phases should be about 30 (between 20 and 45) seconds. When you tape the protocol, simply leave blank tape

 Close-Up 8.1
A Protocol for Progressive Muscle Relaxation

Please sit or lie back, get comfortable, and keep your eyes closed throughout these exercises. When I ask you to tense a certain set of muscles of your body, tense only those muscles, quickly make them *as tight as you can*, and keep them tight, noticing how tense they are. After several seconds, I will say "Now relax." And when I do, *release* those muscles immediately, letting them go completely limp. Keep them limp and relaxed for quite a while, *feeling* the relaxation *spread* through those muscles. Focus your attention on your sensations and think over and over to yourself something like, "I feel so peaceful, so wonderfully calm and beautifully relaxed. My whole body feels so warm and good. I'm so very relaxed, deeply relaxed." Keep relaxing until I say, "OK, stop," which will signal either the next exercise or the end of the session. We'll start with the muscles in your right hand.

1. Make a tight fist with your *right hand*. Squeeze it very tightly. Keep it tight and notice how it feels. . . . (7") Now relax. Release all that tension and let it flow out of those muscles so that your hand is limp. Feel how limp your hand feels. . . . (30") OK, stop.

2. Clench your *left hand* to make a tight fist. Squeeze it tightly, very tightly. Hold that tension and notice how it feels. . . . (7") Now relax. Release the tension and let your hand go limp. Focus on how relaxed your hand feels. . . . (30") OK, stop.

3. Bend your *right arm* to make your biceps very hard. Tighten those muscles and make them hard, like steel. Keep them tight and feel the tension. . . . (7") Now relax. Let your arm fall to your side and allow the tension to flow out. When your muscles seem

relaxed, see if you can relax them even more. . . . (30") OK, stop.

4. Bend your *left arm* and make your biceps very hard. Keep them very, very hard and feel the tightness. . . . (7") Now relax. Let your arm fall to your side. Feel the tension flowing out and the wonderful tingling sensation in your limp arm. . . . (30") OK, stop, and let's move to the muscles in your head.

5. Pull your *eyebrows* together very tightly, wrinkling your forehead and squinting your eyes. Hold that tension and study it. . . . (7") Now relax. Let your forehead relax and feel so comfortable. . . . (30") OK, stop.

6. Now scrunch up the lower part of your *face*, raising your cheeks, elongating your lips, wrinkling your nose, and squinting your eyes. Make all those muscles tight. . . . (7") Now relax, just totally relax. Feel the tension flow out of your lower face and down your neck. . . . (30") OK, stop.

7. Stretch the *back of your neck* by bending your head forward so your chin is very close to your chest. As you stretch those muscles, at the same time tighten the ones in the front of your neck. Concentrate on the two sets of muscles tugging against each other. . . . (7") Now relax. Just let go and feel the wonderful relaxation in your neck and how it flows downward to your shoulders. . . . (30") OK, stop.

8. Stretch the *front of your neck* by bending your head backward as far as you can. As you stretch those muscles, tighten the ones in the back of your neck. Notice how tight both sets of muscles are. . . . (7") Now relax. Let your neck muscles go limp, so limp that you think a breeze could move your head

for the amount of time you will use for each tensing or relaxing period. You may record the tape in your own voice or have someone else read the material. If possible, have someone who understands the purpose of the procedure supervise the first several sessions to provide feedback. We will discuss later how to shorten the procedure and leave out the tensing part of the process. (Go to 🔍 .)

---

back and forth. Notice how the tingling and warmth of the relaxation is spreading downward in your body. . . . (30") OK, stop, and let's try a breathing exercise.

9. Take a deep *breath* and hold it, feeling the pressure in your chest. . . . (7") Now relax and exhale slowly. When all the air is out, take another deep breath, hold it, and notice the pressure again. . . . (7") Now relax, exhale slowly, and say in your mind "relax and let go." When all the air is out, rest a moment and take one more deep breath—a very, very deep breath. Hold it, hold it. . . . (7") Now relax and exhale slowly, very slowly. And think about how the air flowing out is like letting out all your tensions, your anxieties, and your frustrations. Notice how peaceful and calm you feel. Just relax and breathe normally. . . . (30") OK, stop, and let's move our exercises to your shoulders.

10. Hunch your *shoulders* forward, squeezing them toward each other so that you can feel the muscles of your upper back stretch tightly. Notice how tight the muscles are between your shoulder blades, across the top of your shoulders, and in your chest. Hold that tightness. . . . (7") Now relax, and feel the relaxation spread from your neck, shoulders, and chest to your whole upper body, especially your back. . . . (30") OK, stop.

11. Move your *shoulders* upward toward your head, pushing them as far up as you can. Feel the tension in your neck and shoulder muscles. . . . (7") Now relax. Release the tension in those muscles, and let your shoulders sink back down. Think about how deeply and completely relaxed you're becoming. . . . (30") OK, stop.

12. Tighten your *stomach* muscles while pulling your shoulders back and arching your back backward. Suck in your stomach as far as you can and feel the tension as you keep your stomach muscles tight as a drum. . . . (7") Now relax. Feel completely relaxed. . . . (30") OK, stop.

13. Lift both your *legs* a few inches and curl your toes so that the muscles of your arches and calves are very tight. Hold that tightness. . . . (7") Now relax. Let your legs fall as their muscles go limp. Feel the tension flowing out and calmness spreading up toward your stomach. . . . (30") OK, stop.

14. Lift both your *legs* again, but this time tighten the muscles in your thighs and lower abdomen. Make the muscles as tight as a drum. Feel how tense they are. . . . (7") Now relax. Let your legs fall as the muscles in your legs and abdomen go limp. Feel the tingling and warm sensations of relaxation flow down your legs and up your trunk. . . . (30") OK, stop, and let's do another breathing exercise.

15. In this exercise, you'll take a series of *five deep breaths*, inhaling and exhaling very slowly. You'll notice that when your lungs reach their peak of fullness, they seem to relax almost on their own. Each time the peak is reached, tell yourself to "relax and let go" as you start to exhale. Go ahead and take those five deep breaths, and each time you exhale very slowly, think about how peaceful, calm, and wonderfully well you feel. . . . (100") OK, stop. Breathe normally again and enjoy your refreshing feeling of well-being and calm throughout your body as this relaxation session ends.

Autogenic Training

Another approach for helping people relax has them imagine being in a pleasant and peaceful scene and experiencing specific bodily sensations, such as their arms feeling warm or heavy. This relaxation technique is called **autogenic training** and was developed in Germany by Johannes Schultz (1957; Schultz & Luthe, 1969). The name "autogenic" reflects Schultz's view that the technique's psychological and physiological effects are self-produced: *auto-* means "self" and *-genic* means "produced by."

In the standard autogenic training procedure, the person listens to instructions from a therapist or on tape and tries to imagine the events described. The procedure starts by asking the person to (1) adopt a passive and relaxed attitude, (2) allow changes in his or her bodily processes to evolve naturally, and (3) choose a pleasant, peaceful scene, such as lying on the beach or sitting in a meadow on a beautiful, warm day. Then the training proceeds through a series of six phases, each with a theme regarding the type of sensation to imagine in the body. Of these themes, the two that are the most commonly used in therapy involve feeling *heaviness* and *warmth* in parts of the body (Lichstein, 1988). The instructions specify the parts of the body to focus on and what to feel—for instance:

> My left arm is heavy. . . . I'm at peace. . . . My left arm is heavy. . . . My left arm is heavy. . . . I'm at peace. . . . My left arm is heavy. . . . My left arm is heavy. . . . My left arm is heavy.

Each instruction like this one is read very slowly. The person repeats the instruction to himself or herself while focusing attention on that part of the body and then receives a rest period. This sequence of reading/repeating/resting with the same instruction is repeated three times for a total of about 5 minutes. This same procedure then moves to six other parts part of the body for 5 minutes each, still with the same theme. Covering the theme for all seven parts of the body takes about 35 minutes.

The next theme is warmth, and the instructions would include phrases like, "My abdomen is warm." Each of the six themes is covered in the same way we've seen, and the whole phase takes about 35 minutes. Because the complete, standard procedure for autogenic training is so time-consuming, researchers have developed versions in which the repetition, the timing of each instruction sequence, or the number of themes is reduced (Lichstein, 1988). These versions take less than half an hour to carry out. Although some evidence indicates that the shorter versions do induce relaxation, more research is needed to determine whether the relaxation they produce is as deep as that achieved with the standard procedure or progressive muscle relaxation. Since, however, autogenic training doesn't require the tensing and relaxing of muscles, it has a clear advantage over progressive muscle relaxation for many people, particularly those who suffer from medical conditions like severe arthritis or low back pain, which make movement painful or difficult.

Meditation

The third approach for helping people learn to relax uses various forms of **meditation**—the process of contemplating or focusing one's attention on an object, event, or idea. The practice of meditation derives from Eastern philosophy and religion, especially Buddhism, and is intended to help people recognize but become detached from their physical states, thoughts, and feelings (de Silva, 1984, 1990; Hart, 1987; Solé-Leris, 1986; Thera, 1979). Although an important function of meditation is to produce relaxation, or "tranquility," it has a broader purpose: *to develop a clear and mindful awareness*, or "insight," unencumbered by cognitive or emotional distortions, regarding the essence of each experience.

An example of how mindful awareness may help individuals detach experiences from cognitive and emotional distortions comes from research on people with chronic pain. Jon Kabat-Zinn (1982; Kabat-Zinn, Lipworth, & Burney, 1985) trained chronic pain patients to use meditation techniques to focus on painful sensations as they happened, rather than trying to block them out, and to separate the physical sensations from the cognitive and emotional reactions that accompany pain. The patients were trained to pay close attention to their sensations, including pain, without reacting toward them in any way. By doing this, they could become aware of the pain itself, unembellished by their thoughts or feelings about it. This training reduced the patients' reported physical and psychological discomfort. As Kabat-Zinn described the rationale in using meditation treatment for pain, the sensory signals "may be undiminished, but the emotional and cognitive components of the pain experience, the hurt, the suffering, are reduced" (1982, p. 35).

The relaxation component of meditation can be achieved by doing exercises to focus attention on a *meditation stimulus*, which may be one or more of the following:

- *A static visual object*—something pleasing and simple, such as a flower, a bowl, or a symmetrical design. If you use this type of stimulus to meditate, do not try to describe or evaluate the object; just try to see it as a whole and let its image rest in your awareness. Sometimes the objects seem to change or move, even though they are unchanging. Don't focus on these changes, but simply accept them passively.

- A *mantra*, or spoken sound—such as *om*, *shirim*, or *wen*—which you say softly over and over to yourself. The mantra can be a word, but the word should be neutral in emotional content.

- Your own *breathing*. For instance, breathe slowly and deeply through your nose in a natural, effortless manner and pay close attention to the air going into your nose as you inhale, and out of your nose as you exhale.

You may want to close your eyes if you're not using a visual object as your meditation stimulus. During meditation, your mind may sometimes wander to other thoughts. This is to be expected. When it happens, gently coax your attention back to the meditation stimulus, without getting intellectually or emotionally involved in the intrusive thoughts. Don't become annoyed with the thoughts or try to keep them out; if they happen, they happen. The stimulus will return.

Individuals who are being trained to use meditation as a relaxation technique are instructed to practice it once or twice a day in a quiet environment, sitting upright in a relaxed and comfortable position. Each meditation session takes about

20 minutes. Some psychologists and psychiatrists advocate meditation exercises to reduce reactions to stress. For example, Herbert Benson has developed a widely known meditation procedure that incorporates breathing and mantra meditation stimuli. Benson instructs individuals who want to reduce stress to

> relax all your muscles. . . . Become aware of your breathing. As you breathe out, say the word *one* silently to yourself. . . . Maintain a passive attitude and permit relaxation to occur at its own pace. Expect other thoughts. When these distracting thoughts occur, ignore them by thinking, "Oh well," and continue repeating, "One." (1984, p. 332)

According to Benson (1974, 1984, 1991), using meditation in this way increases people's ability to react in stressful situations by making a "relaxation response," which includes reduced physiological arousal, as an alternative to the CER they usually make. It is not clear to what extent this reduced physiological arousal develops in people from Western cultures who are trained to meditate (D. S. Holmes, 1984; Lichstein, 1988). Research has shown, however, that Buddhist monks in Southeast Asia can dramatically alter their body metabolism and brain electrical activity through meditation (Benson et al., 1990).

Regardless of whether we choose progressive muscle relaxation, autogenic training, or meditation as the standard technique for relaxation training, the procedure can be shortened to sessions 10 or 20 minutes in length after the technique has been mastered. This can be accomplished in progressive muscle relaxation by

Meditation should occur in a quiet environment, and the person should sit upright in a relaxed and comfortable position.

combining a few of the exercises, such as doing both hands or arms together, and eliminating the tensing phases of all muscle exercises you retain. Shortening autogenic training can be accomplished by using only the heaviness and warmth themes and combining parts of the body to which they are applied. Meditation sessions can be shortened simply by stopping sooner. There is one caution in shortening relaxation sessions: they should not become so brief that deep relaxation is not achieved. If a tape-recorded protocol is being used for a relaxation technique, a new tape should be made for the shortened version, leaving out all instructions that no longer apply.

Rapid Relaxation Induction

The relaxation techniques we've seen help individuals to be less easily aroused by CSs that elicit CERs in their lives, allowing them to be calmer and more clear-headed in the general style with which they approach potentially arousing antecedent events. But many people who have problems with emotional behaviors also need *an alternative, quick way* to induce some level of relaxation when troublesome CSs arise—for example, if they are about to give a speech in class. The alternative method is meant to supplement, not take the place of, deep relaxation.

The best way to develop an alternative procedure for rapid relaxation induction is by altering and shortening considerably the standard technique that has been mastered (Lichstein, 1988). There are four points to keep in mind in creating a rapid induction procedure. First, a rapid induction method is not a substitute for the standard procedure. The person should continue practicing the standard relaxation technique in 10- to 20-minute sessions at least a few times a week. Second, we should try to make sure that the person has mastered the standard relaxation technique on which the rapid method will be based. We can do this by reviewing the person's relaxation records and observing the person use the technique. Third, rapid induction methods generally do not result in relaxation as deep as can be obtained by the standard techniques. And fourth, rapid induction methods work best if the person can anticipate the need to use them by being aware of the antecedents that lead to the CER.

Useful Components for Rapid Relaxation Induction

When we design a rapid relaxation method, we can enhance its effectiveness by trying to incorporate three useful components: verbal cues for relaxation, breathing exercises, and cognitive images. The standard relaxation techniques include having the person make certain statements or sounds, which can serve as *verbal cues* for rapid relaxation. For instance, someone who says "Relax," "Feel calm," or a mantra, such as "om," in the standard procedure should use the same words or sounds softly or covertly as part of the rapid method.

Some standard relaxation techniques include *breathing exercises* that involve slowly inhaling and exhaling deep breaths. If we know before selecting the standard technique that we will want to use a rapid induction method, we should make sure the standard technique includes breathing exercises in which the person takes *deep* breaths and pays close attention to them. Sometimes deep breathing exercises can be added to a standard technique, thereby providing the opportunity to use breathing exercises in the rapid induction method you create. The deepness of the breathing is usually lessened to *moderately deep* for a rapid induction method because the deep breathing might be noticeable to others, who may interrupt the process or make it embarrassing to use (Lichstein, 1988).

The third useful component involves using clear and detailed *cognitive images* of pleasant or relaxing scenes, which are called **calm scenes** (NJNPI, 1972). One of the standard relaxation techniques, autogenic training, incorporates a pleasant scene for the individual to picture while doing imaginal exercises for six different themes, such as feelings of heaviness and warmth in parts of the body. But calm scenes can be used in the two other relaxation approaches, as well. In meditation, a calm scene could serve as a meditation stimulus in place of a static visual object. In progressive muscle relaxation, a calm scene could be added to the breathing exercises as a focal object during the time of relaxation. When using calm scenes with any of these standard approaches, it is helpful to include short, specific instructions, such as:

> With your eyes closed, picture yourself in your calm scene—the scene that makes you feel comfortable, peaceful, and relaxed. Experience the scene in all its details and with all your senses. Try to see aspects of the scene, hear them, smell them, and feel them on your body. As you picture this scene, you'll feel more and more deeply relaxed.

Using calm scenes in relaxation exercises requires that the person select *one scene* to employ whenever a scene is applied. Two of the most common themes or types of calm scene are lying on a beach and walking or sitting in a forest. Although the scene can have almost any theme, it:

- Should be one the person *has actually experienced* in the past, felt *very relaxed* in, and believes will *always help* him or her to feel relaxed and calm.
- Should be one the person *can imagine easily and clearly, with as many senses as possible.* For instance, in a scene of lying on the beach, one would try to see the water, sand, and clear blue sky; smell the water and hear it splashing; feel the warmth of the sun; and see and hear gulls or other sea birds.
- Should *not* be one that portrays or includes (1) the use of mood-altering substances, such as alcohol or drugs, and (2) someone with whom the person has or wants to have a strong emotional attachment. Although people we love usually make us feel calm and relaxed, such as when cuddling, if the relationship should change, becoming very distressing, the scene will is no longer be useful.

To be effective in a rapid induction method, the components chosen should be incorporated into the standard relaxation technique in which the person is originally trained. These components will be retained as the person learns to use the quicker method.

Creating A Rapid Induction Method: An Example

As an example of how we can create a rapid relaxation method, we'll use progressive muscle relaxation as the standard technique. Before moving toward creating a rapid relaxation method, the person should have practiced the full procedure for at least ten sessions, mastered it, shortened it to a 10- to 20-minute version, and practiced the shortened version for several sessions. The person should continue to practice that shortened version indefinitely.

We can create a rapid method of progressive muscle relaxation by introducing two intermediate steps, each of which involves making a new tape of a version that is further altered or shortened. These two tapes, based on the protocol of Close-Up 8.1, would contain the following components and modifications:

1. *Intermediate tape 1:* exercises numbered 1, 2, 6, 9, 10, 12, 14, and 15 from the protocol (without tensing), including calm scenes. Use this tape in place of the tape with the shortened version for at least five sessions.

2. *Intermediate tape 2:* exercises numbered 9, 10, 12, and 15 from the protocol, as used in intermediate tape 1, except for two changes: (a) deep breathing should be diminished to *moderately* deep breathing and (b) relaxation periods should be only *half as long* in each exercise. Use this tape in place of intermediate tape 1 for several sessions.

The final procedure inducing rapid relaxation has three steps: (1) take a moderately deep breath, (2) say a verbal cue softly or covertly while exhaling—for instance, "Relax. Feel nice and calm," and (3) think of the calm scene. This induction procedure does not have to be taped and is short enough to elicit a relaxation CR in a matter of seconds. (Go to ✔ .)

Covert Conditioning

The success of using imaginal procedures in relaxation and systematic desensitization techniques led psychologist Joseph Cautela (1966, 1993a) to develop an array of imagery-based conditioning methods called **covert conditioning**. Cautela refers to the methods as *covert* because the person is asked to imagine all components of the conditioning process—the antecedents, target behavior, and consequences. And he considers the methods to be forms of conditioning because he views them as private or internal respondent or operant behaviors.

The covert conditioning method called **covert sensitization** pairs in the person's imagination an existing antecedent, or CS, with aversive events that serve either as a US (in respondent conditioning) or as a punisher (in operant condi-

✓ **Concept Check 8.1**

• •

1. A medical condition for which relaxation techniques appears to be a useful component of treatment is _____ . ⇔

2. Alternately tensing and relaxing separate muscle groups while resting comfortably is called _____ .

3. The relaxation technique in which the individual imagines a pleasant scene and sensations in different parts of the body is called _____ .

4. The process of contemplating or focusing one's attention on an object, event, or idea is called _____ .

5. A static visual object you could use as a meditation stimulus in your own residence is _____ . ⇔

6. An example from the progressive muscle relaxation protocol of muscle groups you could combine to shorten the procedure is _____
_____ . ⇔

7. An example of a verbal cue you could incorporate from autogenic training into a rapid induction method is _____ . ⇔

8. A calm scene you might use in designing your own relaxation exercises is _____
_____ . ⇔

_____

Answers:

1. asthma/migraine headache   2. progressive muscle relaxation   3. autogenic training   4. meditation   5. a painting   6. tensing and relaxing both biceps together   7. "I'm at peace."   8. walking in Tuolumne Meadows in Yosemite National Park

• •

tioning). Cautela applied covert sensitization to help a 29-year-old nurse overcome her alcohol abuse problem by having her imagine various scenes. In one scene, she was asked to imagine that she had ordered and got her favorite drink. Then

> as you reach for the drink you start to feel sick to your stomach. As you hold the glass in your hand you feel yourself about to vomit. As you are just about to put the glass to your lips you vomit. It comes out your mouth all over the table and the floor. It is a real mess. (1966, p. 37)

In some scenes, she was told that she refused to take a drink, and she felt calm right away. In interviews after several sessions of covert sensitization and again 8 months later, the nurse reported having stopped drinking (the study did not include a procedure for validating the subject's reports).

A similar covert sensitization approach was used in another study, which had as its subjects men who were hospitalized for alcohol abuse (Ashem & Donner, 1968). Follow-up assessments 6 months later with confirmation by relatives revealed that 6 of the 15 men who received the treatment remained abstinent; but of an additional 8 men who did not get this treatment, none was abstinent. Other interventions incorporating covert sensitization have successfully reduced people's nail-biting (Daniels, 1974; Paquin, 1977) and sexually deviant behaviors, such as exhibitionism and excessive masturbation (Hayes, Brownell, & Barlow, 1978; Krop & Burgess, 1993).

Another covert conditioning method resembles *desensitization*, but Cautela refers to it as a **covert positive reinforcement** procedure. Here the person imagines performing a target behavior that is followed by a pleasant event. Dennis Upper (1993) applied this method in a program to help a young woman named Joan overcome her severe anxieties about sexual contact. The therapist and his client constructed a stimulus hierarchy of sexual situations and started the procedure with the least anxiety-provoking stimulus. For each stimulus,

> the client is asked to imagine herself performing the behavior, experiencing mild anxiety, and using relaxation or some other procedure for decreasing the anxiety, and then is asked to switch in imagination to a pleasant (that is, reinforcing) scene. (p. 239)

The reinforcing scene involved skiing, which Joan enjoyed doing very much.

Joseph Cautela (1993c) described another intervention using covert positive reinforcement to treat 6-year-old Alice's unusual phobia of buttons. This fear was so great that the little girl would not wear clothes with buttons or stay in the same room with people who wore buttons. Cautela treated the fear with a program that included teaching Alice relaxation exercises and presenting stories for her to imagine. In one story that portrayed a family outing at the beach, Alice and her sister Amy were digging in the sand and found a treasure chest that contained

> coins, necklaces, rings and bracelets! Also there are some beautiful buttons [Alice winces]. The buttons are so beautiful they look like jewelry. . . . and then your sister says, "Oh, I want to hold and look at the buttons." Your father gives her some beautiful buttons while you look at your gold-and-diamond ring. You're all so happy. (p. 129)

The therapy advanced through increasingly fear-provoking stories and even included some *in vivo* stimuli. Alice's fear eventually disappeared after about a dozen sessions, and she had no more problems with buttons thereafter.

As you think about covert conditioning procedures, you'll realize that virtually all learning processes and conditioning phenomena can take place covertly. For instance, the imaginal scene used in treating Alice's fear of buttons included *covert modeling*: sister Amy asked for and held some buttons that the girls' father had handed her. Scenes can also be designed to include covert instances of extinction, punishment, and negative reinforcement (Cautela, 1993a). Covert conditioning methods are probably not as effective in changing respondent behaviors as *in vivo* procedures—for instance, we saw in Chapter 7 that desensitization is more effective with *in vivo* stimuli than with imaginal ones. But covert methods may be especially useful when certain stimuli are too threatening or inconvenient to present in real life (Ascher, 1993). To enhance the success of covert procedures, Cautela (1993a) recommends having the person rate the clarity of the image and the pleasantness or aversiveness of the events on 5-point scales—the scale for image clarity could range from "not at all clear" to "very clear," for example. A scene would be applied only if the client gave high ratings for both the image's clarity and the event's pleasantness or aversiveness.

Cognitive-Behavioral Coping Techniques

Have you ever expected to be very frightened or anxious during an experience, such as giving a speech, only to find that you weren't? People often expect to be more fearful in fear-arousing situations than they turn out to be (Rachman, 1994). Cognitive processes and people's respondent behaviors are intimately linked, and each can affect the other. For instance, a man who was very frightened of developing cancer frequently examined his body,

> especially his skin. During these periods of elevated anxiety the natural and permanent patches of his skin appeared to him to have become significantly enlarged. When the anxiety subsided, however, he was able to estimate the size of these skin patches correctly. He experienced similar fluctuations in his estimations of the size of various bumps and lumps. (Rachman & Cuk, 1992, p. 584)

In such cases, the CER seems to produce *perceptual distortions*, thereby making the situation seem worse than it actually is.

An experiment to investigate the possibility of perceptual distortions during fearful experiences was conducted with individuals who either were or were not very fearful of snakes or spiders (Rachman & Cuk, 1992). The subjects watched one of two live harmless animals—a spider or a garter snake—in a glass enclosure and estimated its movement. Those who were fearful estimated that the creature showed far more movement toward them and made more efforts to leave the enclosure than the nonfearful subjects did. All subjects then saw a video in which a therapist used participant modeling to reduce a person's fear of a snake or spider. When the subjects were again asked to watch a spider or snake in the enclosure and estimate its movement, the estimates of both fearful and nonfearful subjects were far lower than before. These findings indicate that cognitive processes can exaggerate people's experience of a CS, almost certainly making these experiences more difficult.

But cognitive processes can also help people *reduce* the impact of a CS through the use of coping techniques. *Coping* refers to the use of cognitive and behavioral processes in attempting to manage experiences of emotionally arousing or stressful events in life. Psychologists have identified many coping techniques people commonly use (Cohen & Lazarus, 1979; Moos & Schaefer, 1986). These techniques often combine behavioral and cognitive methods, and are called *cognitive-behavioral coping techniques*. Some individuals seem to use these techniques more effectively than others do in managing their respondent behavior. Training individuals to use coping techniques can help them deal better with the antecedents to CERs, perhaps by making their perceptions more positive or by preventing fearful distortions from happening. Let's look at some cognitive–behavioral coping techniques that have been applied widely in interventions to change respondent behaviors.

Self-Statements

Suppose you were about to experience a painful medical procedure. Could you talk yourself into coping with this aversive situation? Many people say things like "Be brave—you can take it," or "It will hurt, but having this done will make you walk better." These sentences are examples of **self-statements**—things we say to ourselves, which can be either *positive* or *negative*. Both are examples of positive self-statements, with the former being a *coping statement*, and the latter a *reinterpretative statement* (Fernandez, 1986). Interventions to train individuals to use positive self-statements instead of negative ones appear to be very successful in reducing anxiety in a variety of situations, such as taking tests and speaking in public (Dush, Hirt, & Schroeder, 1983). Let's look at coping and reinterpretative statements more closely.

Coping Statements

Coping statements are things people say to themselves that emphasize their ability to tolerate unpleasant situations. When feeling anxious about a paper you're writing, you might say to yourself, "Relax—you're in control" or "It's hard, but you'll get through it." Coping self-statements like these help you tolerate the anxiety and keep working. Unfortunately, many students do the opposite, saying to themselves self-defeating things like "I'm not good at this," or "I'm gonna fail." People who make very frequent negative self-statements are likely to experience a lot of anxiety in stressful situations. (Go to .)

Close-Up 8.2
Age Differences in Fears and Using Self-Statements

As children get older, the things they fear tend to become less *concrete* and more *abstract*, particularly after about 5 years of age (Sarafino, 1986). During the middle childhood years, children become less afraid of tangible and immediate situations, such as noises and strange objects, and more afraid of imaginary creatures (ghosts and witches), the dark, and signs of fear in others. In later childhood, these fears tend to decline, and anxieties relating to school and social relations become increasingly common. At the other end of the life span, the most prominent fears of people in old age are that they or loved ones will die or become ill or injured (Liddell, Locker, & Burman, 1991).

These changes in fears reflect the different experiences and levels of cognitive development of people at different ages. The factors of experience and cognitive level also relate to the use of self-statements in the face of stressful events. For example, a study had 8- to 18-year-old students describe what they say to themselves when they are about to get an injection at a dental visit (J. M. Brown et al., 1986). Of children at age 8 or 9, over 62% reported making *negative* self-statements, such as "I'm scared" or "I want to run away," and less than 43% said they used *positive* self-statements, such as "Be brave" or "I can take this." In contrast, adolescents' self-statements were much more positive. Of the 16- to 18-year-olds, only 44% reported making negative self-statements and 86% reported using positive self-statements. These results show that children's cognitive coping skills improve with age and suggest that training young children to use positive self-statements would help them cope better with stressful events—a prediction that has been confirmed in research (Kanfer, Karoly, & Newman, 1975; L. J. Siegel & Peterson, 1980).

Reinterpretative Statements

Reinterpretative statements are declarations people make to themselves that redefine a situation by negating its unpleasant aspects or giving a reason to view it differently. Sometimes these positive self-statements simply try to put a good face on a bad situation—by noting that things could be worse, for example, or by making comparisons with those who are less well off, or predicting that something good will somehow result. For example, a woman with breast cancer remarked:

> What you do is put things into perspective. You find out that things like relationships are really the most important things you have—the people you know and your family—everything else is just way down the line. It's very strange that it takes something so serious to make you realize that. (S. E. Taylor, 1983, p. 1163)

Other reinterpretative statements can help those who "take things personally" to see events as having nonpersonal causes. For instance, a person who thinks, "She just snubbed me," when an aquaintance passes by without speaking could try to think, "What other reasons might explain this behavior?"

But reinterpretative statements must be declarations the person can *believe*. For instance, Dennis, the panic attack victim we discussed earlier, tried to cope with unfounded anxieties about his ability to sell insurance by using the following pep talk he tape-recorded and played in his car:

> Go out there and charm 'em, Dennis. You're the best damn salesman this company's ever had! They're gonna be putty in your hands, big fella. Flash that smile. . . . They'll love you! (Oltmanns, Neale, & Davison, 1991, p. 19)

Listening to this declaration made the tension worse. Even though Dennis really was a very successful agent, he didn't believe it. Hearing these flattering statements probably just reminded him of what he feared.

More believable reinterpretative statements were used in covert conditioning therapy with another man who had severe anxieties about his work performance. He was asked to imagine being at a business meeting and thinking, "I hope I don't do anything wrong at the meeting," followed by the reinterpretative statement, "I haven't in the past; there is no reason to believe that I will in the future." He was also asked to imagine thinking, "I know that I'm going to perspire at the meeting and everyone will notice," followed by "People are too self-absorbed to notice a subtle change in your appearance" (Ascher, 1993, p. 18). This therapy helped the executive cope better at business meetings.

Training to use positive self-statements can help young children cope with their fears, too. Researchers trained 5- and 6-year-old kindergartners who were afraid of the dark to make various self-statements to help them cope (Kanfer, Karoly, & Newman, 1975). The children were pretested in the dark by giving them a dimmer switch to use to turn on a light and increase its brightness and asking them to "Try to keep the room as dark as you can, for as long as you can." Then some of the children were taught to say, "I am a brave boy [girl]. I can take care of myself in the

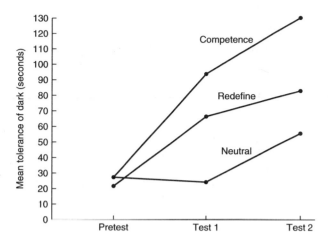

Figure 8.2 Mean duration (in seconds) of tolerance for being in darkness at a pretest and at two tests after children had received training in using self-statements that either expressed competence in coping with darkness, redefined the darkness situation, or were neutral (i.e., unrelated to darkness). (Adapted from Kanfer, Karoly, & Newman, 1975, Figure 1.)

dark." These statements reflected a sense of competence and ability to control the situation. Other children were taught to say, "The dark is a fun place to be. There are many good things in the dark," which might simply redefine the situation. And a third group of children were just told to recite, "Mary had a little lamb. Its fleece was white as snow." Upon retesting in the dark room two more times, all three groups improved in their ability to remain in the dark and use low illumination. Figure 8.2 shows that this improvement was greatest among the children who had been taught the competence self-statements and lowest by far among those who'd recited "Mary had a little lamb." These results highlight how important the *content* of self-statements can be in helping people cope.

Thought Stopping and Distraction

The last two cognitive–behavioral coping techniques we'll consider simply involve interrupting or diverting one's attention from antecedents that elicit overt or covert CERs.

Thought Stopping

"Stop!" the therapist shouted sharply as Phil described a depressing thought he often has about his ex-girlfriend. The therapist had asked Phil to describe the thought to permit the introduction of a simple procedure called **thought stopping** in which the word "stop" is said suddenly and emphatically soon after the person starts to describe or concentrate on an unwanted thought (Cautela & Wisocki, 1977; Wolpe, 1973). Individuals can apply thought stopping as a self-management technique by saying "stop" either aloud or very clearly in the mind as soon as the unwanted thought occurs.

Case Study 8.1

Thought Stopping and Self-Statements to Reduce Depressive Thoughts

• •

After Carol's boyfriend of 3 years left her for another woman, she began to have recurrent thoughts about him and about herself that made her depressed (as described in G. Martin, 1982). Although she was attractive and had good social skills, she would think such things as, "I feel that I am a failure. I feel ugly and useless. I keep thinking about not being able to 'keep a man,' and not being able to have a husband." Then she would cry, sometimes for long periods of time, even at her job as a secretary.

Carol was referred by a friend for therapy, which consisted of training her to use thought stopping and positive self-statements when the troublesome thoughts arose. She carried these techniques out in two steps: First she'd use thought stopping by closing her eyes, covertly yelling "Stop!" to herself, and counting to 10

silently. Then she'd take out a few photographs she had selected, read statements she had written on the back of each one, and consider the pictures for several seconds apiece. One picture, for example, showed Carol at the airport before leaving on a trip by herself. The message on the back said, "I'm my own boss. My life is ahead of me. I can do what I want to do."

Carol had been taught to evaluate "how bad" her days were in terms of the thoughts she experienced, using a 6-point rating scale in which 5 equaled a "very bad day" and 0 equaled a "very good day." Her average daily rating per week declined from slightly over 4 in baseline to under 1 after several weeks of therapy. A follow-up assessment 4 months later revealed no recurrence of problem thoughts about her ex-boyfriend.

• •

Although thought stopping has been used widely as a component in successful interventions to reduce respondent behavior, research demonstrating its utility by itself either has involved very few clients or has produced mixed results (Arrick, Voss, & Rimm, 1981; Hackman & McClean, 1975; R. S. Stern, Lipsedge, & Marks, 1973; Tryon, 1979). Thought stopping seems to be most useful in combination with other methods, such as replacing the unwanted thought with a positive self-statement immediately after one has said "stop." (Go to .)

Distraction

Distraction is a technique in which individuals shift their attention from a CS that elicits a CER to overt or covert stimuli that are unrelated to the CER. Distraction can be used for just a moment—perhaps by focusing on a picture on a wall as you receive an injection, or for a longer time—for example, by watching a TV show when feeling anxious about giving a speech you've practiced many times. All sorts of stimuli and activities can distract us from unpleasant antecedents to respondent behavior. In a study we considered earlier, one group of children coped with their fears of the dark by reciting "Mary had a little lamb." Probably the familiar verse served as a distraction. But as we saw, this activity was not nearly as effective as using self-statements. And distraction techniques tend to work best for momentary, mildly or moderately stressful experiences, rather than severe, recurrent, and long-lasting, ones (Greene, Seime, & Smith, 1991; McCaul & Malott, 1984). (Go to ✔ .)

✔ Concept Check 8.2

1. Imagery-based techniques that have individuals think about scenes of an existing CS being paired with an aversive US are called _____ .

2. A person who always avoided using elevators because of a phobia of enclosed spaces might benefit from a *covert extinction* procedure in which he or she imagined

_____

_____ . ⇔

3. A perceptual distortion a fearful dental patient might experience when getting an injection is _____

_____ . ⇔

4. "Relax—the traffic will let up eventually" is an example of a _____ statement.

5. When faced with a stressful experience, young children tend to make more (a) _____ self-statements than (b) _____ self-statements.

6. Saying "It could be worse" is an example of a _____ statement.

7. Thought stopping tends to be more useful when it is followed by a _____

_____ .

_____

Answers:

1. covert sensitization 2. riding an elevator safely and calmly 3. the needle seems to be larger than it is 4. coping 5a. negative 5b. positive 6. reinterpretative 7. positive self-statement.

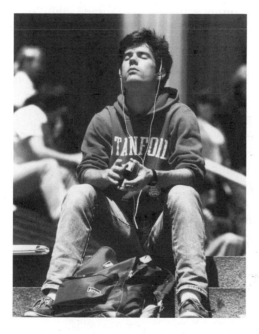

Listening to music can be used as a distraction technique to shift one's attention from overt or covert events that elicit anxiety or other conditioned emotional responses.

Application Exercise

The Chapter 7 work sheet activities set the stage for two important tasks we will do in this application exercise: (1) generating covert behavioral methods to reduce a CER and (2) completing your baseline data collection. For the first of these tasks, you'll use the material from Work Sheet 7.1, in which you selected an example CER, summarized the outcome of a functional analysis for it, and constructed a stimulus hierarchy that could be applied in a systematic desensitization procedure to reduce that respondent behavior. The second task will have you consult the baseline data you've collected if you are carrying out a self-management project. By now you should have collected data for at least a few days.

Tips on Using Covert Behavioral Methods

The following tips for using covert behavioral methods to change respondent behavior basically consolidate and recap recommendations presented in this chapter. Consider these tips when you design a self-management program to change a respondent behavior.

1. As a general rule, the procedures selected to change respondent behavior should use *in vivo* stimuli rather than imaginal ones whenever possible.
2. When considering which type of relaxation technique to use, consider whether any type would be uncomfortable to practice. For instance, someone suffering from muscle or joint pain might be uncomfortable using progressive muscle relaxation, and autogenic training with a warmth theme might not be appropriate for people suffering from certain forms of internal disorders, such as ulcers.
3. Learning a relaxation technique takes a lot of practice. You'll need to adhere very closely to a planned schedule of practice sessions. Try to establish a high priority for doing relaxation exercises, thereby diminishing the temptation to skip sessions because "I don't have the time."
4. Use tapes for practicing relaxation whenever possible.
5. If possible, relaxation exercises should be conducted in a quiet environment that is not brightly lit. This ideal cannot always be achieved, but do the exercises anyway. Earplugs may help.
6. The mind sometimes wanders during progressive muscle relaxation, autogenic training, or meditation sessions. Be aware that this happens, and simply bring the focus gently back to the technique.
7. Don't try to introduce a rapid relaxation method until you have completed at least ten sessions with the standard technique and mastered it.
8. Assess the degree to which you are relaxing during sessions. Decisions about how fast to progress in the training or whether to advance to a rapid method should be based on those data.

9. Select for your program a calm scene that doesn't include anyone to whom you are or want to be emotionally attached.

10. Rate the clarity of scenes you use in imaginal procedures, such as those needed in covert conditioning.

11. When developing new positive self-statements, select statements that are reasonable and believable.

12. Go through this chapter and the preceding one to consider all the methods described when you design a program to change respondent behavior.

The Next Steps in Your Program Design

The main steps we'll take toward designing your self-management program will relate to completing your baseline data collection. You are probably wondering when can you stop collecting baseline data. That is, how long should the baseline phase be? Baseline data gathering for self-management projects *usually takes about 2 weeks*, but there's no fixed answer to this question because it depends on your data. Let's see why.

You may have already noticed that your data can fluctuate from day to day, and sometimes the fluctuations are quite large. When large differences are charted, it's difficult to get a sense of the "normal level" of the behavior unless there is a fairly substantial amount of data. The baseline data you collect *must give you a clear picture of the normal level of the behavior*. For instance, a student of mine named Kelly wanted to decrease her cursing. The data for the number of times she cursed during 7 successive baseline days were as follows: 16, 23, 15, 5, 12, 9, and 14. What was her normal level of cursing for that period? It's hard to tell: was the 23 unusually high or the 5 unusually low? Clearly it was important to continue collecting data. You need to know the level at which you're starting your program so you can see how much, if any, improvement is made during the intervention.

You also need to consider whether the period during which you've collected baseline data is representative of your usual life. Suppose you wanted to increase the amount of time you spend exercising, and you usually exercise for 2 hours a week. But you were sick or injured during the first week of baseline. The data from week 1 would not represent your normal level of exercising. Most behaviors can be affected temporarily by unusual circumstances. If your target behavior is anger, having unusually great or exceptionally mild frustrations during the first week of baseline would make those data unrepresentative of your usual life. Similarly, if your target behavior is TV watching, having unusually large or small numbers of attractive shows to watch could make the data unrepresentative.

Baseline periods rarely elicit representative data in less than a week. Sometimes, however, your aim is to change a behavioral deficit with respect to a target behavior that has never occurred in the past. Exercising is a good example. I've had students ask, "Do I need to collect baseline data? I've never ever exercised in my life." Even then, it's a good idea to have a week's worth of data just for comparison purposes with intervention data. It certainly isn't difficult to "collect" data for a week if the behavior doesn't occur.

The tasks in this application exercise will begin with having you design covert behavioral techniques you could use to reduce the CER you used in Work Sheet 7.1. Then we will look at the baseline data you've collected thus far. Turn now to Work Sheet 8.1 and fill it out.

Summary

Relaxation is a state of diminished psychological and physiological tension. Relaxation techniques should be practiced in quiet settings with no interruptions. Progressive muscle relaxation uses a protocol for tensing and relaxing separate muscle groups. In autogenic training, individuals imagine a pleasant scene and the experience of certain bodily sensations, such as a heaviness in the limbs. Meditation involves focusing the attention on a meditation stimulus, which may be a static visual object, a mantra, or one's own breathing. Although sessions using these techniques usually take close to half an hour during training, they can be shortened to 10 or 20 minutes after mastery has been achieved. Breathing exercises and calm scenes generally should be included in relaxation techniques if rapid relaxation induction methods will be used.

Covert conditioning methods involve having individuals imagine scenes that include respondent and operant conditioning procedures. These methods include covert sensitization, in which the person imagines an existing CS followed by an aversive event, and covert positive reinforcement, which is like desensitization. Other covert conditioning methods include covert modeling, extinction, punishment, and negative reinforcement.

Self-statements can help or hinder our ability to cope with difficult events—they can be positive or negative self-statements. Coping statements emphasize our ability to tolerate troublesome events, and reinterpretative statements redefine the situation, making these events easier to face. Thought stopping and distraction are cognitive–behavioral coping techniques in which attention is interrupted or diverted from troublesome stimuli. Training in these coping techniques seems to help people reduce problem CERs.

Key Terms and Review Questions

Key Terms

relaxation   autogenic training
progressive muscle relaxation   meditation

calm scenes

covert conditioning

covert sensitization

covert positive reinforcement

self-statements

coping statements

reinterpretative statements

thought stopping

distraction

Review Questions

1. Near the beginning of the discussion of relaxation techniques, several guidelines were described. Describe three of those guidelines.

2. Define "progressive muscle relaxation" and discuss the pros and cons of including muscle tensing in the procedure.

3. Describe in a few sentences an overview of the procedure for conducting progressive muscle relaxation as outlined in the protocol of Close-Up 8.1.

4. What is autogenic training, and how is it similar to progressive muscle relaxation?

5. Describe the three types of meditation stimulus and how you might use each if you practiced meditation.

6. After a standard relaxation technique has been mastered, how might you go about shortening it?

7. What guidelines should you follow in selecting a calm scene?

8. Describe the three steps in the rapid relaxation induction method.

9. Define "covert sensitization" and give an example.

10. Describe the research by Rachman and Cuk (1992) showing how perceptual distortions occur when fearful stimuli are present.

11. Define "coping statements" and "reinterpretative statements," and give two examples of each.

12. How might you use distraction as a coping technique when a nurse draws a sample of blood from your arm?

Related Readings

Benson, H. (1974). Your innate asset for combating stress. *Harvard Business Review, 52,* 49–60.

Carlson, C. R., & Hoyle, R. H. (1993). Efficacy of abbreviated progressive muscle relaxation training: A quantitative review of behavioral medicine research. *Journal of Consulting and Clinical Psychology, 61,* 1059–1067.

Cautela, J. R., & Kearney, A. J. (Eds.). *Covert conditioning handbook.* Pacific Grove, CA: Brooks/Cole.

Hart, W. (1987). *The art of living: Vipassana meditation.* New York: HarperCollins.

Lichstein, K. L. (1988). *Clinical relaxation strategies.* New York: Wiley.

Name _____   Day & time
                                      class meets_____

Date _____

Chapter 8: Work Sheet 8.1

1. Your self-management target behavior(s): _____

2. Describe in detail a calm scene you think would work for you if you were to use relaxation techniques. Imagine it clearly and write down what the scene comprises.

3. Describe exactly where and when you could do relaxation exercises if you were to start doing them. Would you need to negotiate with other individuals to ensure a quiet environment with no interruptions?

4. Refer back to your answer to question 5 in Work Sheet 7.1 regarding the short-term consequences of the CER. Describe how you could use *covert extinction* to reduce that CER.

5. Refer back to your answer to question 4 in Work Sheet 7.1 regarding antecedent thoughts to the CER. Are any of them negative self-statements? What positive self-statements could you substitute?

6. Indicate the type of baseline data (frequency, duration, etc.) you are collecting for your self-management project and list the data you've collected to date.

7. Describe how much fluctuation these data show from day to day. Has it become easy to get a picture of the normal level of your target behavior?

8. Describe the degree to which the data you've collected reflect the target behavior in your usual life circumstances. How were the circumstances during this period similar to those in your usual life, and how were they different?

NOTE: If you will be submitting work sheets to your instructor or to a fellow student, make a copy of each sheet before submitting it.

Part Four

Program Design and Evaluation

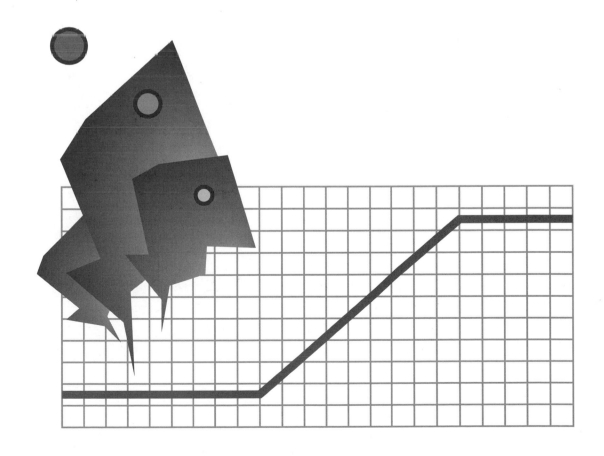

9 *Putting Techniques Together to Design a Program*

Prologue

Mr. W. had walked in his sleep four or five times a week since the age of 15 years; when he was 24 years old, he entered therapy with the goal of stopping this behavior (R. G. Meyer, 1975). Mrs. W. had tolerated her husband's sleepwalking in the past, complaining only if she was awakened by his fumbling around. But her view changed

> because during a recent act of sleepwalking he took down a shotgun, loaded it, and prepared to fire at imaginary burglars. Luckily, his wife's screaming woke him before he could fire. (p. 167)

She insisted that he get professional help immediately. In therapy, Mr. W. revealed that his sleepwalking was related to feelings of anxiety about taking tests and that he had become extremely anxious about an upcoming bar examination, which he had to pass to be licensed as a lawyer. A decision was made to disable the shotgun for the time being by dismantling the firing pin.

The therapist decided to stop Mr. W.'s sleepwalking by applying two behavioral methods, each focusing on a different aspect of the problem. One method focused on sleepwalking as an operant behavior. This method was punishment: the sound of a loud whistle when sleepwalking occurred. Because Mrs. W. was a light sleeper, the couple moved their furniture so the man would have to crawl over his wife to get out of bed. She would blow the whistle if she awoke and found him sleepwalking. The other method focused on the underlying respondent behavior of anxiety, which seemed to be an antecedent to sleepwalking. Systematic desensitization was applied to reduce Mr. W.'s test anxiety. He learned to practice relaxation exercises, helped in constructing a stimulus hierarchy of imaginal CSs, and received ten sessions of desensitization. This intervention combining two techniques was effective. Not only did it almost completely eliminate the sleepwalking, but Mr. W. was able to study better and passed the bar examination easily. Follow-up assessments revealed only four sleepwalking episodes during the next year.

Designing an intervention typically involves putting together several behavior modification techniques to form a program to change a target behavior. To maximize the program's effectiveness, the techniques it includes should be directed at all three *dimensions* of the problem behavior: the *target behavior* itself, its *antecedents*, and its *consequences*. In this chapter, we will describe how to select from and combine the techniques we've discussed thus far to design successful programs to change behavior. This material will be invaluable when you design a self-management program.

Combining Techniques for a Behavior Change Program

Behavior therapists recognize the need to combine appropriate techniques to maximize treatment effectiveness, and they tend to use several intervention techniques with each client (Swan & McDonald, 1978). If you think back to the techniques we've discussed in the preceding chapters, you'll notice that each one is useful in addressing a specific dimension of a problem behavior we may want to change. Interventions that combine techniques to address more than one dimension of a problem behavior are called **multidimensional programs** (Friedman, Campbell, & Evans, 1993). In designing an effective multidimensional program to change a behavior, we'll want to consider techniques to address the:

- *Antecedents*—perhaps by altering antecedent physical or social stimuli to reduce the likelihood of the problem behavior occurring.
- *Behavior*—for instance, by teaching a desirable, alternative response.
- *Consequences*—that is, by changing the existing consequences of the behavior through reinforcement, extinction, or punishment methods.

In addition to addressing the antecedents, behavior, and consequences, it is important to include procedures to maintain the newly acquired desirable behavior and to prevent the unwanted behavior from returning (Friedman, Campbell, & Evans, 1993). Chapter 11 will examine techniques for maintaining behavior changes over long periods of time. These techniques can be added to the program once the intervention is under way.

Identifying Possible Techniques to Use

Chapters 4 through 8 present all the basic techniques to consider using in designing a multidimensional program to change behavior. The starting point in the identification of techniques that might be appropriate for the program is the functional analysis we've performed. We would begin by asking two questions. First, does the target behavior involve operant behaviors, respondent behaviors, or both? Different techniques apply to different types of behavior. As we saw in the case of Mr. W.'s sleepwalking, an intervention can combine techniques that focus on each type of behavior when both types need to be addressed. The chapters in Part Two of this book describe methods to change operant behavior; Part Three covers methods to change respondent behavior.

The second question is: Is the program being designed to change a behavioral excess or a behavioral deficit? Once again, the answer will suggest different techniques for us to apply. For instance, reinforcement methods are extremely important to correct an operant behavioral deficit or to increase an alternative response; extinction and punishment procedures might be very useful in decreasing an operant behavioral excess. Bear in mind that keeping records, performing relaxation exercises, and the other activities a person does in self-management procedures are all behavioral deficits. It's often a good idea to reinforce those activities.

Once we've answered these questions, we can proceed with the task of designing the program as a problem-solving activity. The most efficient strategy to arrive at the best solution to a problem begins by *generating many alternative solutions* (D'Zurilla & Nezu, 1982; Nezu, Nezu, & Perri, 1989). Generating a large number of alternatives increases the likelihood that the most appropriate or most effective techniques will be considered for inclusion in the program. A good way to generate alternative solutions is to use the method of **brainstorming**, which has three rules:

- *Aim for quantity.* The more alternative solutions we produce, the more likely we'll be to have good ones from which to select.
- *Defer judgment.* When brainstorming, don't stop to evaluate any of the ideas generated, saying things like "I'll never make that technique work" or "I don't like the idea of . . . ." We'll evaluate the ideas later.
- *Start with strategies; then move to tactics.* Initial ideas can be general strategies, which can be refined later to specific tactics. If a strategy chosen is "use reinforcement," tactics might include using "tokens" and "activities as backup reinforcers."

Figure 9.1 presents a checklist of methods we've discussed in the preceding chapters. You can find those discussions by using the index at the end of the book. These materials can help in the brainstorming process and in selecting the techniques to use. The next step in designing a multidimensional program is to pick the most promising alternatives from the ones generated. Before we consider how to select techniques from these alternatives, let's look at some example programs.

Examples of Multidimensional Programs

To illustrate how various techniques to change behavior can be combined, we will examine a variety of multidimensional programs with very different goals and settings. Some programs have applied relatively broad resources with many clients, and others were designed for specific individuals.

Broad, Community-Based Programs

Community-based programs to change behavior are designed with the view that serious behavior problems, such as alcohol abuse, result from factors that operate in and are affected by the community in which the individual lives. This view suggests that it is preferable to treat substance abuse by rearranging these factors in the community rather than by trying to correct the problem in a hospital. Using this view, Nathan Azrin and his colleagues have designed the *community-reinforcement approach* to treat alcoholism (Azrin, 1976; Azrin et al., 1982, Hunt & Azrin, 1973; Sisson & Azrin, 1989). The program has evolved over the years, but some of its main enduring features have been:

- Daily doses of the emetic drug *disulfiram*. An emetic is a drug that produces nausea; disulfiram has this effect if the person drinks. Taking the drug is monitored and verbally reinforced by the person's spouse or other intimate individual.
- Marital counseling, job counseling, and participation in a program aimed at getting work.

CHECKLIST OF BEHAVIOR CHANGE METHODS

This checklist can be used to generate and select ideas in designing programs to change behavior. Use the index at the end of the book to find descriptions of the techniques listed. The techniques are separated on the basis of whether their most common uses are to manage the antecedents, the behavior, or the consequences. But some techniques may be directed toward managing more than one dimension of the behavior change process. If you use the checklist to design a program, you may want to make a photocopy of it and write *yes* or *no* in the spaces preceding the methods to indicate their potential usefulness.

Managing the Antecedents
_____ Differential reinforcement
_____ Prompting/fading
_____ Modeling
_____ Instructions
_____ Self-instructions/rules
_____ Altering antecedent chains
_____ Reducing/avoiding antecedents
_____ Narrowing antecedent control
_____ Cognitive strategies
_____ Systematic desensitization
_____ Participant modeling
_____ Self-statements
_____ Thought stopping
_____ Distraction

Managing the Behavior
_____ Subgoals
_____ Shaping
_____ Shortcuts to shaping
_____ Chaining
_____ Alternative responses
_____ Counterconditioning
_____ Relaxation techniques
_____ Covert conditioning

Managing the Consequences
_____ Positive reinforcement
_____ Tangible/consumable
_____ Activities
_____ Social reinforcers
_____ Feedback
_____ Tokens
_____ Covert reinforcers
_____ Negative reinforcement
_____ Extinction (operant/respondent)
_____ Reducing counterproductive reinforcers
_____ Lotteries/group contingencies
_____ Punishment
_____ Physically aversive stimuli
_____ Reprimands
_____ Aversive activities
_____ Time-out
_____ Response cost
_____ Differential reinforcement
_____ Habit reversal
_____ Self-monitoring/self-instruction

Figure 9.1 Checklist of behavior change methods.

- Reinforcers for taking the disulfiram and attending counseling sessions.
- Assistance in developing hobbies and recreational activities in which alcohol is not available.
- Training in refusing drinks when offered.
- Training in relaxation exercises and practice in ways of handling social problems that have led to drinking in the past.

If you examine this list carefully and look back at the checklist in Figure 9.1, you'll see that the program includes techniques directed at the antecedents, behavior,

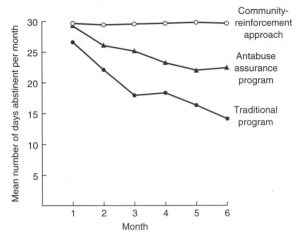

Figure 9.2   Mean number of days per month on which alcoholic clients who had received treatment with an emetic drug (disulfiram) did not drink during a 6-month follow-up period. The 41 clients received one of three treatments: the community-reinforcement approach (a multidimensional program that included the use of disulfiram), the antabuse assurance program (which focused only on having the client take disulfiram in the presence of a significant other at scheduled times and places), and the traditional program (which simply provided the client with disulfiram and instructions on how, when, and why it should be administered). (From Azrin et al., 1982, Figure 2.)

and consequences of drinking. Several interventions using the community-reinforcement approach have been used with high rates of success in maintaining sobriety (Tucker, Vuchinich, & Downey, 1992). Data from one of these interventions showing its success relative to other approaches are presented in Figure 9.2.

Classroom Programs

Multidimensional programs have been used extensively in classrooms to enhance students' academic learning and improve their social behavior and general conduct. One program was designed to improve the social skills of nine 8- and 9-year-old deaf children with language disabilities (Rasing & Duker, 1992). The program focused on increasing several specific behaviors, such as waiting to speak without interrupting someone; calling a hearing person's name once or twice in a moderate voice to get his or her attention; and providing help, praise, or comfort to someone. It also focused on reducing certain other behaviors, such as aggression, screaming, and teasing other people. The children's teachers were trained to implement a variety of behavioral methods for use in the program. These methods included providing (1) prompts for appropriate social behaviors, (2) verbal and modeled instruction regarding the specific behaviors to perform, (3) negative feedback and corrective instruction for inappropriate behaviors, and (4) immediate reinforcement for appropriate behaviors by means of praise and tokens, which the children could redeem for tangible and activity reinforcers. All the children showed

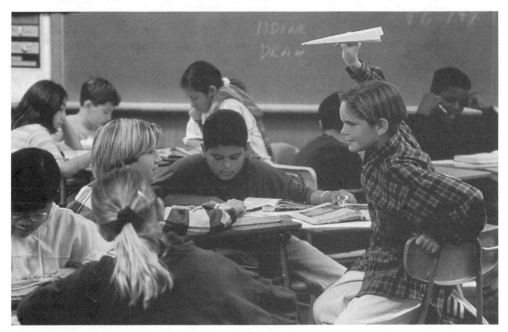

Classroom misconduct like that shown in this photo can be addressed effectively with multidimensional behavior modification programs.

substantial increases in the appropriate social behaviors and decreases in the inappropriate behaviors.

Interventions Implemented on an Individual Basis

A wide variety of operant and respondent target behaviors have been addressed very successfully with multidimensional programs. For example, a program to increase the operant behavior of dental flossing was conducted in the homes of four 7- to 11-year-old boys and girls (Dahlquist & Gil, 1986). In addition to providing each child with training in correct flossing procedures, the program included the following techniques. First, the intervention used prompts of two types: cards stating "Remember to Floss" were hung in the child's room, and a poster describing the steps in flossing was hung in the bathroom. Second, self-monitoring was used: each child had to record instances of flossing on a calendar in the bathroom and save used floss in a bag. Third, parents were trained to evaluate their child's flossing and give praise or corrective feedback. Fourth, the child received tangible reinforcers three times a week if his or her self-monitoring behavior and flossing quality met certain criteria. These criteria were low initially, but were increased periodically during the intervention.

Functional analyses of problem CERs often indicate that both respondent and operant behaviors need to be addressed. For example, a 9-year-old boy's fears relating to school resulted in his avoiding the classroom, either by refusing to go to school or by hiding, once there (Lazarus, Davison, & Polefka, 1965). The interven-

Case Study 9.1
A Multidimensional Program to Reduce a Fear of Upcoming Surgery

At 7 years of age, Robert had developed an intense fear of undergoing a scheduled surgical procedure to remove nonmalignant tumors from his legs and arms (as described in Friedman, Campbell, & Evans, 1993). The tumors, a recurrent condition that resulted from a rare disease called *osteochondroma*, were impairing his walking and the use of his left hand. Robert had undergone surgery to remove earlier tumors with no complications. But he vividly remembered the pain he had experienced during his recovery—and recalling one postoperative procedure provoked a great deal of anxiety: He was told that he would

> have "steel sutures" removed. He became highly agitated, making removal of the sutures more difficult and painful. Medical records reflect his level of pain, noting that "plain Tylenol is not holding him." The parents were very distressed about the amount of pain and finally requested a change in medications. This experience appeared to form the core of his current anxieties. (p. 243)

A multidimensional program was implemented to treat Robert's fear before he underwent the new round of surgery. The program included several components. First, the boy was trained to practice progressive muscle relaxation at home and to use the technique when he was afraid. Second, imaginal systematic desensitization was used to reduce fear of the surgical environment. Third, he was taught to use self-statements, such as using "Ninja powers" to "fight off scary thoughts" when he was afraid. Fourth, his parents were instructed to prompt his use of these fear reduction techniques. Fifth, the parents were instructed to praise Robert's brave behaviors and reduce their attention to his fearful acts. And sixth, he was promised a "Ninja-pizza" dinner and a trophy if he completed the surgery. This intervention markedly reduced the boy's fearful behavior in presurgical medical visits, at the time of surgery, and during the following year, when other medical procedures were done.

tion included the use of distraction techniques to divert the boy's attention on the way to school, *in vivo* desensitization for the school situation itself, and a variety of reinforcers for going to school and interacting with classmates. (Go to .)

Self-Management Programs

Self-management procedures are often applied as a part of behavior therapy interventions with a therapist (Swan & McDonald, 1978). For instance, the therapist might have the client practice relaxation techniques at home, keep self-monitoring records, or provide self-reinforcement for improvements in an operant behavior. In contrast, individuals who initiate, design, and conduct self-management projects to change personal behavior—for instance, as part of a college course—usually devise and implement almost all the techniques themselves. These projects typically are multidimensional programs that include about six to twelve different techniques (S. B. Hamilton, 1980).

A fine example of a self-management program was designed and conducted by a student of mine named Diane, the mother of a 2-year-old boy, who wanted to improve her parenting behaviors. She and her husband had decided before

Andrew was born that they would "take a non-violent, rational, and positive approach" toward parenting. But instead, Diane found that she was using more and more yelling and spanking to discipline the child. Her functional analysis of the problem revealed three antecedents to her behavior. First, she had such a hectic lifestyle that "being a mother, wife, student, and employee leaves me very little time to relax." Second, Diane's behavior of yelling at her son and spanking him usually occurred when she was in a hurry, especially when she was getting Andrew ready to go out. Third, her rush to get the child ready initiated a chain of events: Andrew would struggle against getting dressed or groomed; his mother would yell at him; he'd scream; she'd spank his hand; he'd cry; she'd try to ignore his crying; and he'd become infuriated and cry more. These encounters left Diane "feeling horrible."

Diane's program contained many different behavioral methods, some of which are listed:

1. Substituting the alternative responses of using calm explanations or brief time-out punishment in place of yelling and spanking when Andrew misbehaved.
2. Using self-instructions to prompt using these alternative responses.
3. Praising Andrew for behaviors that helped in the process of getting ready to go out.
4. Using thought stopping to replace negative self-statements, such as "Oh no, we're going to be late," with positive ones, such as "In the long run, it isn't worth it."
5. Meditating each morning before Andrew woke up.
6. Providing a system of reinforcers, with separate rewards for increasing her calm parenting behaviors while decreasing her yelling and spanking, praising Andrew's help, and practicing meditation.

By the end of the month-long intervention, Diane was using calm parenting 100% of the time in these interactions with Andrew, compared with only 25% of the time in baseline. She had stopped yelling and no longer spanked her little boy, and he rarely misbehaved when getting ready to go out.

Features of a Good Program

A "good program" to change behavior is not simply an intervention that succeeds. If someone makes a New Year's resolution to quit smoking and just stops "cold turkey," we cannot say that the person used a good program. We should be able to judge whether a program is good before it is even conducted. We would make this judgment on the basis of the processes used in designing it and the techniques it included. Smokers rarely succeed in quitting the first time they try, and most go back to smoking if they quit (Sarafino, 1994). As Mark Twain noted: "To cease smoking is the easiest thing I ever did; I ought to know because I've done it a thousand times." Smokers who quit and stay quit use better designed programs than those who don't succeed.

What Makes a Behavior Change Program Good?

First and foremost, a good behavior change program has been designed on the basis of data collected in a carefully done *functional analysis*. As such, the program should be *multidimensional*, containing techniques to address the behavior itself, its antecedents, and its consequences. If the program is designed to change more than one behavior, such as a person's diet and exercise patterns, each one probably should be addressed with separate methods, such as different reinforcers. Several other features will also increase the quality of the program (Kanfer & Grimm, 1980; McLaughlin, Burgess, & Sackville-West, 1982; Passman, 1977; Prue et al., 1980). A good program to change behavior should:

1. Identify and clearly specify the target behavior(s), alternative responses, behavioral goals, and subgoals.
2. Describe the rules or criteria that will determine what consequences will apply to the behaviors to be changed.
3. Try to involve the client as an active participant in designing and implementing the program.
4. Provide training and reinforcers for any staff or helpers the program may employ or enlist (teachers, friends, or relatives, and so on).
5. Assess the person's behavior carefully and arrange for some way to check that the data are accurate. When possible, enlist the help of more than one staff member or of a friend or relative to provide data to confirm those the client collects.
6. Use the data collected to provide feedback to the client regarding improvements in his or her behavior and progress toward goals.
7. Provide feedback to staff or helpers regarding their performance.
8. Allow for the possibility of making adjustments to the program if conditions change.
9. Later in the intervention, introduce techniques to increase the durability of the posttreatment behavior change and to improve the chances that the change will generalize to appropriate new environments.
10. Try to maximize the person's commitment to the program, as well as his or her motivation for carrying out the steps and achieving the behavioral goals.

Deciding Which Techniques to Use

The first consideration in selecting techniques to use in changing a behavior consists of deciding which ones are likely to be highly effective. Whenever possible, of course, choose the most effective methods for the type of problem to be addressed. For instance, when trying to increase an operant behavior, it is essential to include a strong system of reinforcers. When trying to reduce a fear with systematic desensitization, *in vivo* stimuli should be used in preference to imaginal ones if possible.

Another consideration in choosing techniques is practicality in terms of the time or effort they require and their financial cost. Some techniques are very economical of time and money. Shortcut methods for shaping or stimulus control are examples of very effective, economical techniques. Other methods are complicated or burdensome to implement, sometimes requiring tremendous amounts of time to carry out properly. Overcorrection punishment procedures, for example, tend to use up many hours (Kelly & Drabman, 1977). Time-consuming methods are often rejected if they would have to be implemented by paid staff or therapists, thereby adding to the cost of the intervention, or by friends or relatives, who may be unwilling or unable to give very much of their time. High expenses for materials, such as tangible reinforcers, may also influence our choice of specific methods in designing a given program.

Decisions to use punishment or other aversive procedures should be made very carefully in designing programs to change behavior. In most cases, aversive methods are rejected because the target behavior can be changed effectively with other methods. Using moderately or highly aversive procedures should be considered only as a last resort and only when the (1) behavior is very maladaptive, (2) intervention is carried out under professional supervision, (3) the program has gotten appropriate ethical approval, and (4) the procedure contains safeguards to protect the client. Punishment procedures that are only mildly unpleasant, such as covert punishment or some forms of time-out, are usually more acceptable, but a program that includes them should be approved by a professional or other supervisor. Keep in mind that one of the drawbacks of using aversive procedures is that they can reduce the person's motivation to participate in the program (G. T. Wilson et al., 1975; G. T. Wilson & Tracey, 1976). (Go to ✔ .)

✔ Concept Check 9.1

1. Interventions that contain techniques to address the antecedents, behavior, and consequences are called _____ programs.
2. A technique that could be useful for reducing a behavioral excess but not for changing a behavioral deficit might be _____ . ⇔
3. To generate alternative solutions in designing an intervention, it is helpful to use the method of _____ .
4. A component of the community-reinforcement approach to treating alcohol abuse that is directed at managing behavioral consequences is _____ _____ . ⇔
5. The first consideration in deciding to use a technique for a behavior change program is this: Is it likely to be _____ ?
6. Techniques that are moderately or highly _____ should be considered for a behavior change program only as a last resort.

Answers: 1. multidimensional 2. punishment/extinction 3. brainstorming 4. reinforcing the taking of disulfiram 5. highly effective 6. aversive

Motivational Factors to Consider

People who are highly motivated to change their behavior are more likely to participate successfully in interventions for making the change (Cautela & Upper, 1975; S. B. Hamilton, 1980; Kanfer & Grimm, 1980; Perri & Richards, 1977). Assessing a person's motivation to change is important in individual therapy, especially if he or she will be using self-management techniques, such as doing homework assignments that involve self-monitoring, covert conditioning, or relaxation exercises. A therapist can assess the client's motivation by using the *Scale of Motivation to Change Behavior* presented in Figure 9.3.

People's Readiness to Change

An important factor in people's motivation to change a behavior is their level of *self-efficacy*—the belief in one's ability to succeed at a specific task the person wants to

---

SCALE OF MOTIVATION TO CHANGE BEHAVIOR

Use the following questions to evaluate a client's motivation to change his or her behavior. On the basis of information from direct and indirect assessment methods, *rate* each item in the space preceding it, using a 5-point scale in which 0 = "not much or often," 2 = "fairly much or often," and 4 = "very much or often."

_____   How *often* has the client clearly stated he or she wants to change?

_____   How *much* strength in a desire to change do the client's verbal and gestural expressions suggest he or she may have?

_____   How *often* has the client canceled, delayed, or been late for therapy appointments?

_____   With how *much* care and regularity has the client kept requested records of his or her behavior and its antecedents and consequences?

_____   With how *much* care and regularity has the client completed therapy homework assignments, such as doing relaxation exercises or developing a list of feared stimuli?

_____   How *much* openness and cooperation has the client shown in answering questions in therapy sessions?

_____   How *much* attentiveness has the client shown during therapy sessions?

_____   **Total Score** (The total score reflects the client's overall motivation to change, but low ratings of individual items may suggest the need for specific efforts to address relevant factors.)

Figure 9.3   The Scale of Motivation to Change Behavior (based on material in Cautela & Upper, 1975). Although this scale is designed to assess client motivation in individual therapy, similar items could be rated in interventions of other types.

🔍 Close-Up 9.1
The Stages of Change Model

• •

The **stages of change model** is a theory that describes five *stages* through which people's motivation and intention to modify their behavior can progress (DiClemente et al., 1991; Prochaska & DiClemente, 1984; Prochaska, DiClemente, & Norcross, 1992). These stages are arranged from lowest to highest readiness to change:

1. *Precontemplation.* People in this stage are not seriously considering changing the behavior in question—smoking, for instance—at least during the next several months or so. These people may never have thought about changing or may have decided against it.
2. *Contemplation.* During this stage, people are aware that a problem exists and are seriously considering trying to change within the next several months. But they are not yet ready to make a commitment to take action.
3. *Preparation.* At this stage, individuals plan to pursue a behavioral goal, such as stopping

smoking, within the next month and have tried to reach that goal in the past year without being fully successful.
4. *Action.* This stage spans a period of time, usually 6 months, from the start of a successful effort to change a behavior.
5. *Maintenance.* People in this stage work to maintain the successful behavior changes they achieved.

According to the stages of change model, people who are currently in one stage show different behavioral and cognitive characteristics from people in other stages. For instance, people in the precontemplation stage regarding a behavior, such as smoking, are likely to have less self-efficacy than individuals at more advanced stages and to see more disadvantages than advantages to changing that behavior. People's own efforts or those of others to change the behavior are not very likely to succeed.

• •

do. In the case of changing a behavior, people need to believe they can carry out the necessary activities to achieve their behavioral goals. Self-efficacy is a critical element in people's "readiness" to begin and participate in self-management activities. The role of readiness to change behavior is the main focus of a motivational theory called the stages of change model. (Go to 🔍.)

Ways to Enhance Motivation to Change

What can be done to strengthen a person's motivation to participate in and complete an intervention to change a problem behavior? The intervention can contain provisions to help the person to acquire *realistic expectations* about the behavior change process, a *sense of commitment* to the program's goals, and *social support and supervision*.

Realistic Expectations

At the start of an intervention to change behavior, the person needs to develop realistic expectations about the procedures that will be used, the effort they will require, and how quickly and smoothly the progress toward the behavioral goal is likely to be (Kanfer & Grimm, 1980). One way to enhance motivation is to foster the realistic expectation that the burdensome requirements of the program will be temporary and brief. For example, it can be explained that the collection of detailed data for a functional analysis will be over in several days, and the amount of time needed to practice relaxation exercises will decrease after a week or two. In addition, the person should be informed that improvements in behavior are usually slower to emerge early in the intervention than later on, and that setbacks or lapses in progress are typical experiences. A **lapse** is an instance of backsliding—sort of a "mistake"—in the person's performance. For instance, a person who has stopped smoking might have a cigarette one day. People should expect to have occasional lapses, especially when they are trying to change habitual or lifestyle behaviors.

People's motivation to change a behavior can also be enhanced by letting them know about the program's provisions or techniques for reducing the usual temptations they experience as antecedents to the unwanted behavior. For instance, individuals who are trying to limit their intake of fattening foods might be advised to eat low-calorie foods either before going to a party or restaurant or early in a meal, thereby decreasing the temptation to have dessert. Other methods we've discussed for dealing with antecedents can also help. Because people who want to change their behavior often have doubts about their self-efficacy to deal with tempting antecedents, they need to know what techniques they can use and how to use them when temptations arise.

Another way to enhance people's motivation to participate in an intervention to change their behavior is to include in the program a provision called a **rule-release**, in which the person is exempted from restrictive rules of the program under certain *specific and limited conditions*. Rule-releases are especially useful when the program restricts behaviors the person enjoys, such as eating fattening foods, or requires behaviors the person doesn't enjoy, such as studying. A rule-release identifies *in advance* the specific conditions under which the restrictive rules won't apply. Some examples of rule-releases my students have used in programs to decrease calorie intake, reduce excessive drinking, and increase studying are:

- "I can have a dessert when I go out to dinner or to a party on Friday and Saturday nights. I can overeat on Thanksgiving Day."
- "I can drink beer at parties, and I can go to a maximum of two parties in any week. Beer is the only alcoholic beverage I can have."
- "I don't have to study on Thursday nights and on Saturdays."

The purpose of rule-releases is to eliminate the tendency to make negative self-statements, such as "I can never eat what I like" or "I never have time to enjoy myself." Statements like these demoralize people and decrease their motivation to adhere to the program. Rule-releases are not appropriate for all behaviors one might want to change, but they can be useful in some cases.

When designing rule-releases, two guidelines should be kept in mind. First, the release from the program's rules must be *guaranteed*—whereas reinforcers are contingent on the person's behavior, rule-releases never are. So, in the last example of a rule-release listed above, no matter how little a student, Sylvia, studied during the week, Thursday nights and Saturdays would be free. The consequences Sylvia's program provided to increase her studying applied to all other times. Second, rule-releases should *not include lapses.* That is, they should not be drafted to allow an unwanted behavior whenever the antecedents for backsliding are very strong. For example, a person who is trying to stick to an exercise routine should not have a rule-release that says, "I don't have to exercise if I have too much work to do." Rule-releases must describe conditions that are predetermined, specific, and limited.

A Sense of Commitment to Change

Having a sense of commitment to the goals of a behavior change program increases the person's motivation to adhere to it. One way to increase commitment to a program is to have people simply state to others the goals they want to achieve and the actions they intend to take to reach those goals. Research has found that asking people to state verbally or in writing what they will do increases the likelihood that they will do it (Griffin & Watson, 1978; Kulik & Carlino, 1987; Ward & Ware, 1990). Writing out one's intentions makes the commitment more formal and concrete, as illustrated in the following *commitment statement* written and signed by a student named Christine:

> I plan to exercise more, and will eventually walk 2 miles five times a week and do 20 minutes of aerobics three times a week. I am committed to changing my behavior to reach the goal I've chosen and will work hard to carry out the program.

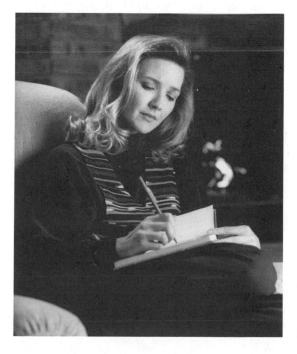

Writing a commitment statement encourages the person to complete a behavior change program successfully.

Making a public commitment that describes the behavioral goals and consequences may be especially important when the person will self-administer reinforcement (Hayes et al., 1985). It may be that having others know the contingencies makes the person more careful in judging whether reinforcers have been earned.

Another simple approach individuals can use to increase their commitment to a behavior change program consists of writing out a list of *pros and cons*—the advantages of changing and the disadvantages of not changing. Long-term and short-term advantages and disadvantages should be included. The list of pros and cons can be posted on a wall to serve as a prompt or written on a card and kept handy to consult when temptations arise.

People's commitment to completing a behavior change intervention can also be enhanced by having them invest a great deal of effort and/or money in the program: doing a functional analysis represents a substantial investment of time, for example, and sometimes it is necessary to buy equipment to carry out a program. When tempted to lapse, the person can reflect on how much he or she has already invested. Probably a better approach for many people is to deposit items of value—such as clothing, jewelry, or money—with a friend or relative (Wysocki et al., 1979). The person must then earn these items back by performing activities required in the program. Whatever is not earned back can be given away. For instance, leftover money could go to a charity the person respects to some degree, but ordinarily would not support.

Social Support and Supervision

Interventions appear to be more effective in changing behavior if the person receives social support and supervision for performing activities in the program (Passman, 1977). For instance, a study of married cigarette smokers found that those who quit and did not smoke again during the next 6 months reported greater helpfulness on the part of their spouses in the effort to quit than did smokers who either never quit or quit but returned to smoking later (Mermelstein, Lichtenstein, & McIntyre, 1983). Other studies have shown that individuals who attempt to carry out a self-management program using only a manual, without supervision of any kind, are unlikely to follow the program or succeed in changing their behavior (Marshall, Presse, & Andrews, 1976; Zeiss, 1978). Having someone with training in behavior management programs to consult with, even for a few minutes a week by telephone, appears to improve people's motivation and success in carrying out the program.

Assembling Materials for the Program

Before starting an intervention, we'll need to prepare and assemble all the materials we plan to use in carrying out the program. These materials may include data sheets, supplies or equipment for performing the behavior, and reinforcers. In addition, it's often useful to formalize the elements of the program into a *behavioral contract*, which is sometimes called a "contingency contract."

Developing a Behavioral Contract

A **behavioral contract** is a formal, written and signed agreement that states explicitly what the target behavior is, the conditions under which it should or should not be performed, and the consequences for proper behavior and lapses. In other words, a behavioral contract describes the behavior and the antecedents and consequences that will apply (DeRisi & Butz, 1975; Homme, 1971; O'Banion & Whaley, 1981; Stuart, 1971).

The agreement generally is made between and signed by at least *two parties*: the *person* whose behavior is to change and a *mediator*—an individual who can and will monitor the behavior and dispense the consequences. The mediator can be the person's therapist, teacher, coworker, friend, or relative. In some cases more than one mediator is involved; and in self-management programs, the two parties may be the same person. The contract should indicate the roles of all parties, and each one should sign. From this description we can state that a good behavioral contract contains or clearly describes the following elements:

1. Target behaviors and antecedents, specifying the behaviors, the occasions when they should or should not be performed, and behavioral improvements that may be required. The reasons for the intervention and the behavioral goals can be indicated. Rule-releases should be clearly specified.

2. Monitoring process, including who will observe the behavior, the type of data to be collected, and how these data will be recorded and made available to determine the consequences.

3. Consequences, which ideally should include immediate and delayed reinforcers for meeting the terms of the contract, as well as penalties for not doing so. Penalties usually take the form of time-out or response cost punishment. The contract should specify who will dispense the consequences, and when.

4. Bonus rewards for high-level, consistent compliance with the terms of the contract.

5. A schedule to review the person's progress, the rate at which reinforcement has been given, and any problems that may need to be addressed.

6. Signatures of all parties.

The terms of the agreement are negotiated by the parties, not simply imposed on the person by someone who has power. The terms can also be adjusted if any of the parties discovers problems or flaws when trying to carry out the agreement. A new contract can be negotiated when the current one expires. The sample behavioral contracts in Figures 9.4 and 9.5 illustrate that these agreements can vary in complexity.

BEHAVIORAL CONTRACT

Between Dick and his roommate Bob

Date: _____

1. *Target behaviors and antecedents:* Dick's anxieties about taking tests in college have impaired his performance. As a part of an intervention he helped design to reduce his test anxiety to manageable levels, he must practice progressive muscle relaxation for 30 minutes each morning for 2 weeks, after which the sessions will be shortened to 10 minutes each.

2. *Monitoring process:* Bob will serve as the mediator, observing and keeping records of Dick's frequency of doing relaxation exercises.

3. *Consequences:* If Dick does his exercises for the day, he will earn a token and be allowed to watch TV that night. When he has earned five tokens, he can rent a video-tape of his choosing to watch with Bob. If Dick does not do the exercises on any day, he must pay Bob one dollar that night.

4. *Bonus reward:* If Dick does the relaxation exercises at least six mornings in a given week, Bob will do some of Dick's housekeeping chores for half an hour next week.

5. *Schedule for reviewing progress:* Every Sunday with Bob.

6. *Signatures:* By signing below, I agree to follow the terms of this contract for a period of 4 weeks, beginning today.

Dick _____

Bob _____

Figure 9.4   Sample of a fairly simple behavioral contract to encourage a young man to perform progressive muscle relaxation exercises.

You can see in Figure 9.5 that agreements can involve more than one behavior, more than one mediator, and several reinforcers. In addition, agreements can designate separate reinforcers for different behaviors. For example, a contract Richard Stuart (1971) helped develop for a delinquent 16-year-old girl named Candy and her parents stated that (1) Candy could go out one weekend evening until 11:30 P.M. and would not have to account for her whereabouts if she maintained "a weekly average of 'B' in the academic ratings of all her classes" and (2) she could go out in the afternoon on weekend days and holidays if she "completed all household chores *before* leaving" and agreed to call her parents once while she was out.

Negotiating the Terms of a Behavioral Contract

Behavioral contracts generally provide for outcomes that are wanted by all parties. In Candy's case, she wanted some freedom to socialize with friends, and her parents wanted her delinquent behavior to decrease and her performance of schoolwork and household chores to improve. In the case of Dick and Bob, whose

---

BEHAVIORAL CONTRACT

Between Jo and Her Teacher and Mother
Date: _____

1. *Target behaviors and antecedents:* Jo has refused to go to school for the past 3 weeks, and when she was going she often failed to do her homework, claiming she forgot to take home the books she needed. Her five target behaviors involve: (a) not fussing at home when getting ready to go to school, (b) arriving at school each day on time, (c) attending all classes as scheduled, (d) taking home all her books, and (e) submitting acceptable homework on time.

2. *Monitoring process:* Jo's mother will observe and keep records of Jo's getting ready for school and bringing home her books. Her teacher will observe the three in-school behaviors and at the end of each day initial on a card any of the three listed behaviors she performed acceptably.

3. *Consequences:* At the end of each school day that Jo earns two or more initialings on her card, she may feed the class hamster or choose a book for the teacher to read to the class on the next school day. She will take the card home. Jo's mother will review with her each day's card and records regarding Jo's fussing and bringing home books. When Jo has accumulated ten acceptably performed behaviors, she may choose one of the following rewards: (a) have a friend over to play, (b) a candy bar, (c) first choice of what to watch on TV for an hour that night, (d) help her mother make cookies, (e) take some homemade cookies as a treat for her class. If Jo's records show fewer than three acceptably performed behaviors on any school day, she cannot have her usual snack before bedtime. Rule-release: If Jo is clearly ill (e.g., has a fever), these rules are suspended until she is well.

4. *Bonus rewards:* If Jo's records show all five behaviors performed acceptably on each of three school days in one calendar week, she may choose a videotape for her mother to rent and watch it that night.

5. *Schedule for reviewing progress:* Every day with her teacher at school and with her mother at home. Teacher and mother will talk on the phone every Friday.

6. *Signatures:* By signing below, I agree to follow the terms of this contract for a period of 8 weeks, beginning tomorrow.

Jo _____

Mother _____

Teacher _____

Figure 9.5 Sample of a moderately complex behavioral contract to help an 8-year-old girl reduce school-related behavior problems.

contract appears in Figure 9.4, the young men were good friends, and Bob wanted to help.

Because the conditions of the agreement affect all parties, each should have a say in the contract's provisions (Kanfer & Grimm, 1980; O'Banion & Whaley, 1981).

Being a mediator is an imposition: it takes time and effort, and often there is no pay. Thus a mediator's motivation to follow the agreement will depend on provisions the contract contains. Sometimes it's useful to include provisions for reinforcing the mediator's activities. The motivation of the person whose behavior is the main subject of the contract is also critical to the success of the program. To maximize this person's motivation and behavior change, he or she should have a say in which reinforcers the program will use and the criteria for earning them. Standards imposed by others lead to smaller changes in behavior than standards the person has helped to develop (Dickerson & Creedon, 1981; Lovitt & Curtiss, 1969). The parties to a contract usually negotiate to reach an agreement they think is fair and reasonable for them to follow. Having a therapist supervise the negotiations can help in developing a contract that contains few flaws and will achieve what each party wants.

An intervention to improve the homework performance of four 9- to 11-year-old students employed negotiated behavioral contracts between each child and one of his or her parents (D. L. Miller & Kelley, 1994). Two types of negotiation occurred throughout the intervention. First, for each homework assignment, the parent and child negotiated the division of the task into "challenging, yet attainable" goals for the child to complete. Each party would suggest a goal and then the two would work out a compromise, which was recorded. For instance, it might be agreed that the child should complete five math problems in the next 10 minutes. Second, each week the parent and child negotiated the rewards for the child's bringing home the needed homework materials and achieving the goals they agreed upon for each assignment. For these negotiations, the parent was to

> identify several rewards from which the child could choose and to change the rewards occasionally to prevent the child from becoming bored with reward choices. Rewards were different for each child and included special snacks, small amounts of money (e.g., 25 cents), stickers, and late bedtime as daily rewards, and renting a videotape, having a friend spend the night, or a trip to a shopping mall as weekly rewards. (p. 78)

The parents received instructions on listening carefully to the child's views, offering a variety of solutions, avoiding criticism, and being willing to compromise. All four of the children showed substantial improvements in their homework performance during the intervention.

Benefits of Using Behavioral Contracts

Using behavioral contracts to formalize the procedures to change behavior has several advantages. First, a contract ensures that the parties know what their roles are and what the conditions of the program are, thereby minimizing disagreements and errors in execution. Second, having all parties sign the contract enhances everyone's commitment to fulfilling the roles. Third, putting the conditions in writing makes it easier for the parties to see how much progress is being made in changing the target behavior and how close the program is to meeting its goals. Fourth, negotiating a contract increases the likelihood that the program will contain elements that will lead to success. Fifth, negotiating a contract and structuring difficult interpersonal relationships may help to improve the way the parties interact. And sixth, using a contract enables each party to estimate more clearly the costs in time and money for participating in the program.

Preparing Other Program Materials

To carry out a program to change behavior, we must prepare and assemble all materials *in advance* of their use (Homme, 1971). At least a week's supply of all data sheets and other forms we may need should always be available. Reinforcers we plan to use must be available as soon as they are scheduled to be given. Don't run out and have to delay a reinforcer or make a substitution. A variety of materials may be necessary for the person to perform the target behaviors or other program activities. For instance, if the target behavior involves a child's homework assignments from school, all books and stationery items must be ready to use at each study session. If the behavior involves household chores, the cleaning materials and equipment must be available when needed. If the person will be doing relaxation exercises, any taped protocols should be ready when needed. We must plan for and anticipate all items we'll need for all aspects, phases, and procedures of the intervention. (Go to ✔ .)

✔ Concept Check 9.2

1. The motivational theory that focuses on people's readiness to change their behavior is called the _____ .

2. Cigarette smokers who realize they should quit for health reasons and are thinking about ways to do it, but have not yet decided when they might start are probably in the _____ stage of readiness to change.

3. An instance of backsliding for a program's target behavior is called a(n) _____ .

4. An example of a rule-release you might use in a program to reduce TV watching is: _____ . ⇔

5. A formal written agreement describing the target behavior and the antecedents and consequences that will apply in an intervention is called a(n) _____

_____ .

6. An example of materials that should be assembled before starting an intervention is _____ . ⇔

Answers:

1. stages of change model 2. contemplation 3. lapse 4. "I can watch any amount of TV on Saturdays" 5. behavioral contract 6. data sheets/ reinforcers

Application Exercise

We are now ready for you to select the techniques you'll use in your self-management project and finalize your program design. These are the objectives of this application exercise. To achieve these objectives, you'll need to consult your earlier work sheets, your functional analysis, and most of the preceding chapters. Once you've completed your design, gotten any needed approvals, and assembled the required materials, you will be able to start your intervention.

Tips on Designing a Program

Selecting the techniques you'll use and putting them together are the most critical tasks in designing a program to change behavior. Do these tasks very carefully. Research has identified several factors that can help in this process (Charlop et al., 1988; Gross & Drabman, 1982; S. B. Hamilton, 1980; Heffernan & Richards, 1981; Perri & Richards, 1977). These factors are included in the following tips on designing a program.

1. Use techniques to address the target behavior itself as well as its antecedents and consequences.
2. If more than one target behavior is involved in the program, and you want to be sure that each one improves, use separate reinforcers and behavioral criteria for each.
3. Use at least six techniques from Figure 9.1 for each behavior, but note that using more than about ten different techniques usually doesn't add much to a program's effectiveness.
4. In assessing the behavior, try to have some way to confirm the accuracy of the data you collect. Although it is best to have a second observer make independent assessments at the same time, this ideal is not always possible. A useful but less precise approach is to have someone who has many opportunities to observe the behavior make assessments of it at convenient times, to permit you to compare the second set of data with your own.
5. Make sure that each instance of the desired behavior receives some form of reinforcer immediately, even if it's just a covert or token reinforcer, and that at least one relatively more powerful reinforcer is given each day the behavior meets the criterion you've set. The criterion can become more rigorous during the intervention if you feel that doing so would help the program achieve its behavioral goals.
6. It may be useful to vary the specific reinforcers or punishers if it seems likely that they will become "boring" or in some other way less powerful.
7. It's usually a good idea to provide reinforcers for performing the self-management activities, such as keeping records carefully or doing relaxation exercises.

8. Estimate the likely costs of the program in time and money and adjust the design if its costs would be higher than is feasible.

9. Make lists of the responsibilities and activities of each party involved in carrying out the program and set a schedule for reviewing progress and discussing any problems that may arise.

10. Examine all the tips listed in the application exercises of Chapters 3 to 8 and incorporate those recommendations into your design.

The Next Steps in Your Program Design

We will do several tasks in this application exercise. We will begin by specifying once again your target behavior(s) and your goal(s) for your self-management project. Then you'll list the short-term and long-term pros and cons for the project and write a commitment statement. After that, you will select the techniques you'll use in the program, describe these techniques briefly, and write a behavioral contract for changing your behavior. Last, you'll list the materials you'll need to carry out the project and assemble them before starting the intervention.

Some of you may need to obtain feedback on program design from your instructor or fellow students before beginning the intervention. If so, wait to start until you have the needed feedback. For now, turn to Work Sheet 9.1 to complete the tasks described above.

Summary

Interventions can direct techniques at each of the three dimensions of a problem behavior—the behavior itself, its antecedents, and its consequences. Multidimensional programs address more than one dimension of the problem behavior. When designing a multidimensional program, it's usually a good idea to generate many alternative solutions by using the brainstorming method. Multidimensional programs have been applied to treat alcoholism, to correct classroom conduct problems, to teach children self-help skills, to improve parents' skills in disciplining their children, and to reduce children's fears. "Good" behavior change programs usually are multidimensional and contain features to ensure that the program is carried out carefully, provides ways to collect and use accurate data effectively, and motivates all involved parties.

Highly motivated individuals are more likely to participate in interventions to change their behavior, and to be successful. People's motivation and readiness to participate in a behavior change program are likely to be fairly high if they have high levels of self-efficacy. According to the stages of change model, readiness to change can progress through five stages: precontemplation, contemplation, preparation, action, and maintenance. One way to enhance people's motivation to change their behavior is to make sure that they have realistic expectations about the procedures to be used, the effort required, and the progress likely to be seen. For instance, they should be aware that lapses are likely to occur. Additional motivation enhancers include providing rule-releases in the program design, using techniques to increase the person's sense of commitment, and making sure that the person has sufficient social support and supervision for completing the intervention.

A behavioral contract is a negotiated agreement that describes the conditions of the intervention. It describes the target behaviors and antecedents, the monitoring process, the consequences, the bonus reward(s), and a schedule for reviewing progress in the intervention. It also contains the signatures of all parties. All materials to be used in the program, including any behavioral contracts, should be prepared and assembled before the intervention begins.

Key Terms and Review Questions

Key Terms

multidimensional programs   lapse
brainstorming   rule-release
stages of change model   behavioral contract

Review Questions

1. What are multidimensional programs?

2. Describe the three rules to use when applying the brainstorming method.

3. Outline the community-reinforcement approach to treating alcoholism, and illustrate the multiple dimensions of this program.

4. Describe the multidimensional program used by Friedman, Campbell, and Evans (1993) to reduce the fear of surgery of a boy named Robert.

5. List several characteristics of a good behavior modification program.

6. What factors go into deciding which techniques to use in a program to change behavior?

7. Describe the stages of change model, using examples related to increasing a person's exercising.

8. Define "lapse" and give two examples.

9. Define "rule-release" and give two examples.

10. What two guidelines should you keep in mind when designing a rule-release?

11. What is a behavioral contract, and what six elements should it have?

12. Describe four benefits of using behavioral contracts.

Related Readings

DeRisi, W. J., & Butz, G. (1975). *Writing behavioral contracts: A case simulation practice manual.* Champaign, IL: Research Press.

Hamilton, S. B. (1980). Instructionally-based training in self-control: Behavior-specific and generalized outcomes resulting from student-implemented self-modification projects. *Teaching of Psychology, 7,* 140–145.

Heffernan, T., & Richards, C. S. (1981). Self-control of study behavior: Identification and evaluation of natural methods. *Journal of Counseling Psychology, 28,* 361–364.

Kanfer, F. H., & Grimm, L. G. (1980). Managing clinical change: A process model of therapy. *Behavior Modification, 4,* 419–444.

Stuart, R. B. (1971). Behavioral contracting within the families of delinquents. *Journal of Behavior Therapy and Experimental Psychiatry, 2,* 1–11.

Name _____

Date _____

Day & time
class meets_____

Chapter 9: Work Sheet 9.1

1. Refer back to earlier Work Sheets to write a clear description of your target behavior(s) and your outcome and behavioral goal(s). If your program will use sub-goals, what will they be?

2. Make a list of the short-term and long-term advantages of changing your target behavior(s) and disadvantages of not doing so. Use this list to make a card to carry with you or a poster to hang prominently.

3. Write a commitment statement modeled after the one presented on page 291 for your self-management program and sign it.

4. Use the checklist of behavior change methods in Figure 9.1 and the brainstorming method to identify techniques you might use. Then select from those the ones you will use and describe briefly how you will use them.

5. Negotiate and draft below an outline of a behavioral contract to cover all or some aspects of your self-management program. On a separate sheet of paper, type up the agreement (see Figures 9.4 and 9.5). All parties involved should sign it.

6. Make a list of the materials you'll need to carry out your self-management project.

NOTE: If you will be submitting work sheets to your instructor or to a fellow student, make a copy of each sheet before submitting it.

10 *Organizing and Using Data*

Prologue

Try to picture the work schedule of a creative person, such as a famous novelist. Do you imagine this person sitting down to write when he or she feels inspired with a great idea? And if no rush of inspiration exists on a particular day, the novelist simply does something else? You might believe, as many people do, that people can't be creative "on call" or at will because creativity happens spontaneously. If you believe this, you may also feel we can't set behavioral goals for creativity—it happens when it happens.

Maybe these beliefs hold true for some authors, but many famous novelists work on a regular schedule, keep track of how much they produce, and set behavioral goals and subgoals for their work (Wallace & Pear, 1977). For example, when American novelist Ernest Hemingway was interviewed, he revealed how he kept

> track of his daily progress—"so as not to kid myself"—on a large chart. . . .
> The numbers on the chart showing the daily output of words differ from 450,
> 575, 462, 1250, back to 512, the higher figures on days Hemingway puts
> in extra work so he won't feel guilty spending the following day fishing on
> the Gulf Stream. (Plimpton, 1963, p. 219)

Looking at these data, you can see that Hemingway paced himself at about 500 words a day, plus or minus, say, 50 or so.

Other great authors have used similar self-monitoring methods to set numerical writing goals and stick to them. The nineteenth-century British novelist Anthony Trollope reported in his autobiography that he

> allotted myself so many pages a week. The average number has been about
> 40. It has been placed as low as 20, and has risen to 112. And as a page
> is an ambiguous term, my page has been made to contain 250 words. . . . I
> have had every word counted as I went. (Trollope, 1946, p. 117)

Clearly this author kept close track of his progress. Trollope worked at a fairly steady pace and at perhaps twice Hemingway's rate in pages. He felt that falling below his writing goals for a week or more was "a blister to my eye" and "a sorrow to my heart." He noted in his autobiography that others had chided him for keeping data to motivate his writing, saying it was "beneath the notice of a man of genius." But Trollope knew he would not have been nearly as productive otherwise.

Data serve many useful functions. They make a permanent record of what currently exists and what has occurred in the past. By comparing current and past data, we can clarify our understanding of the whole situation, and we can tell precisely how much change has taken place over time. We have seen in earlier chapters that using data in these ways enables us to assess a target behavior and tell whether an intervention has changed it. The present chapter examines how to use and organize data to enhance their usefulness in evaluating and improving programs to change behavior. This material is especially relevant if you are currently conducting a self-management program.

Ways to Use and Organize Data

You can't really know a target behavior very clearly or fully until you've assessed it by collecting data. The data you collect provide more detailed and accurate information about the behavior than you've ever had before. This information is most useful when you know what to look for and how to organize it.

What the Data Tell You

Data tell you the current status and history of **variables**—or characteristics of people, objects, or events that can *vary* or change. Behavior is a variable, and its antecedents and consequences are variables, too. The data we collect on variables can clarify different issues or concerns at different points in planning and conducting a program to change a target behavior.

When we do a functional analysis, the data tell us what antecedents and consequences are associated with the target behavior. By seeing these connections, we can choose the most appropriate techniques to use in a program to change the behavior. Baseline data give us a representative picture of the extent or severity of the problem behavior before the intervention begins. Sometimes these data will tell us that the behavior is not as serious a problem as we had believed. Without these data, we might have implemented a program for a behavior that didn't really need to be changed. But the main role of baseline data is to give a reference point for comparisons during the intervention phase. Data collected during the intervention tell us how well the behavior change program is working.

Organizing Data

To find out what collected data can tell you about a behavior and whether it is changing, you'll need to organize the data in a way that presents a clear picture. Obviously, you'll need to organize the data in chronological order to see whether the behavior has changed over time. Other approaches to organizing data are also used, but the need for them may be less obvious. Choosing approaches to organize data entails consideration of characteristics of the data and awareness of what you are trying to find out about the behavior. We'll begin looking at ways to organize data by considering how arithmetic calculations can help.

Using Arithmetic Calculations

Suppose the data we collected in a behavior change program fluctuated quite a lot from one observation or time block to the next. For instance, suppose the data pertained to cursing behavior, and they were as follows for 14 successive days: 38, 9, 3, 22, 7, 40, 21, 31, 5, 9, 23, 4, 39, and 8. How much did the person curse overall? Did the target behavior decrease over time? It's hard to tell, isn't it? The picture these data present is not at all clear because they vary so much.

When the collected data vary a great deal, we can clarify the picture they present by calculating the average, or **mean**, value for a set of data. To calculate the mean, add up the scores and divide the total by the number of scores you added up. In the cursing data, the overall total is 259, which, when divided by 14, gives a mean of 18.5 instances of cursing per day. In the first and second weeks, the means are 20 and 17, respectively. Cursing occurred frequently and decreased somewhat from the first to the second week. Calculating the mean organizes the data by smoothing out the record to estimate the general level of the behavior. Probably the most common approach for calculating means involves grouping the data by weeks, as we just did. This is because many behaviors fluctuate by the day of the week. A person might curse very frequently on, say, Mondays and Thursdays, and rarely on Sundays.

Suppose a different problem exists in your data: you want to compare a person's behavior for two time periods or circumstances, but the *opportunities* to perform the behavior were different for the two sets of data. For instance, suppose an intervention was implemented to reduce a clerk's impatient behavior toward indecisive customers. To check the progress of the program, you decide to compare the frequencies of impatient behaviors in the baseline week and the first week of intervention. These data were 12 and 4, respectively. This drop might suggest that the clerk's behavior had improved; but in fact, the number of indecisive customers who came into the store when the clerk was on duty had dropped sharply, from 30 to 10, in those weeks.

How can you clarify whether the clerk's behavior improved? You can solve this problem by comparing percentages, as we discussed in Chapter 3. Percentages organize data by combining instances of when the behavior did and did not occur when it ordinarily would or should have, thereby taking into account opportunities for the behavior to occur. By calculating a percentage, you can find out *how much* the behavior occurred *in proportion to the opportunities* for it to occur. To calculate a *percentage*, divide the data representing the behavior's instances of occurrence by the opportunities to occur in the corresponding time period or circumstances, and multiply by 100. In our example, you would separate the sets of data—that is, baseline and intervention. For each set, divide the number of behaviors by the corresponding number of indecisive customers the clerk served, and then multiply by 100. Doing this with the data already discussed reveals that the clerk was impatient with 40% of indecisive customers in baseline and also in the first week of intervention. Thus the target behavior had not improved.

Whenever we design a behavior change program and think the opportunities to perform the behavior might fluctuate across the time periods or circumstances we will want to compare, we must collect data on the opportunities to perform the behavior. Without such information, we won't be able to calculate percentages. Many of my students have used percentages to evaluate the behavioral improvements they've made in their self-management projects. For instance, in projects to increase the amount of studying they do, students often find that the opportunities to study—that is, amount of time available after excluding necessary commitments, such as attending class or working—varies widely for different days and different weeks. These students have been able to calculate the daily percentages of available time they used for studying because they first collected data on amount of time available and duration of studying for each day.

Calculating means and percentages can also be useful in comparing data that cover unequal lengths of time. For example, we may want to compare the target behavior during 2 weeks of baseline and 4 weeks of intervention.

Using Tables

A **table** is a systematic arrangement of data in rows and columns for easy reference. By organizing the data visually, a table gives a whole picture, so we can see patterns and make comparisons plainly and quickly. The data in tables are usually numerical, and the rows and columns can be divided on the basis of any variable we want to examine, such as different periods of time or different types of antecedents, behaviors, or consequences. Table 10.1 presents an example of tabular data compiled by a student named Tom for the baseline phase of his self-management project to achieve a gradual reduction in cigarette smoking.

Notice four features about this table. First, not only do you get a sense of how much Tom smoked, but you can see that he smoked more on weekends than during the week. This is an example of how tables can help you to see patterns and make comparisons. Second, this array of data is called "Table" and has been given a number that reflects the order in which it was first mentioned in the text material. Third, the text material refers to Tom's tabular material by number ("Table 10.1

Table 10.1 *Frequency of Cigarette Smoking Each Day for 2 Weeks of Baseline*

Day of Week	Weeks	
	One	Two
Monday	19	15
Tuesday	16	17
Wednesday	16	18
Thursday	17	16
Friday	17	17
Saturday	24	25
Sunday	21	20

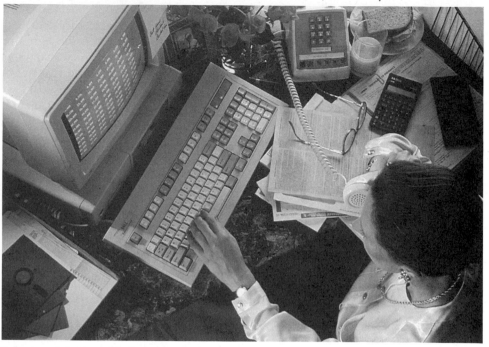

Entering data in a table—on paper or in a computer—organizes the data visually and enables us to see patterns more easily.

presents . . ."). Fourth, the table has a descriptive title. A table should always have a number and a title, and the associated text material should mention the table by number at least once.

A quotation in the Prologue to this chapter revealed Hemingway's self-monitoring technique: the famous author said he recorded in a "chart" the number of words he had written each day. The term *chart* has a very broad meaning—it can be a table, a graph, a diagram, a map, or just a sheet of paper that has a grid printed on it. As a result, "chart" is rarely used in scientific papers.

Graphing Your Data

A **graph** is a drawing that depicts variations within a set of data, typically showing how one variable changed with changes in another variable. Throughout this book, we have used graphs to illustrate the effectiveness of different interventions in changing behavior. Data collection and precise records are essential parts of the scientific method and of assessments of programs to change behavior. A graph that is constructed in a careful and direct way provides the clearest picture of any changes that occurred in the target behavior over time, indicating, as well, when particular techniques were applied.

Types of Graph

Graphs can take several forms, and we will discuss three: line graphs, bar graphs, and cumulative graphs. Each of these graphs is constructed with a *horizontal axis*, or "abscissa," and a *vertical axis*, or "ordinate." In graphs of data from behavior change programs, the vertical axis typically represents a measure of behavior, such as frequency or duration, and the horizontal axis represents another variable, such as chronological time or the type of procedure applied.

Line graphs use straight lines to connect successive data points that represent the intersects of plotted values for the variables scaled along the horizontal and vertical axes. Line graphs are the most commonly used format for presenting the effects of programs to change behavior, and the horizontal axis almost always scales chronological time, spanning baseline and intervention phases of a program. That axis is usually divided into and labeled to indicate periods in which intervention techniques were used or not used. Figure 10.1 illustrates a line graph based on data from the self-management project mentioned above, conducted by a student named Tom to reduce his cigarette smoking; each data point reflects the number of cigarettes smoked on a given day. Tom hadn't quit entirely by the end of the semester, but you can see that his smoking declined markedly: the mean number of cigarettes smoked per day was 18.43 in baseline and 5.14 in the last week shown in the graph. Tom planned to continue the program after the semester ended. In

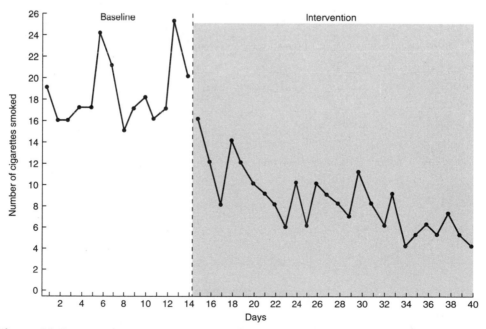

Figure 10.1 Illustration of a line graph. The data are from a self-management project conducted by Tom, a student who wanted to quit smoking.

Figure 10.2   Illustration of a bar graph showing the magnitude of fear response (mean heart rate in beats per minute, hypothetical data) of clients who had received either systematic desensitization therapy or psychoanalytic therapy for their fear. For the purposes of this graph, high heart rate reflects high fear.

some programs, the horizontal axis of a line graph covers several phases, to indicate, for instance, that two or more intervention techniques are used in sequence.

Bar graphs use vertically arranged rectangles to represent data points scaled along the vertical axis. The rectangles, or "bars," are usually spaced along and extend up from the horizontal axis to the appropriate point represented on the vertical axis. The bar graph illustrated in Figure 10.2 shows that each bar reflects the behavior of individuals categorized by the groups or circumstances in which they were assessed. Sometimes the rectangles in bar graphs are arranged horizontally instead of vertically. If so, the axes are switched, and the measure of behavior runs along the horizontal axis, with the categories spaced along the vertical axis.

Cumulative graphs, or *cumulative records*, are line graphs in which the measure of behavior accumulates across units scaled along the horizontal axis. Figure 10.3

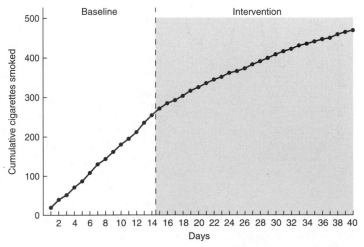

Figure 10.3   Cumulative graph of Tom's data for cigarette smoking. Compare this graph with the one in Figure 10.1, which plots the same data.

gives an example of a cumulative graph, using Tom's data on cigarette smoking again. Notice how the number of cigarettes smoked on any day is added to the preceding total. For instance, we know from Figure 10.1 that on the first two days of baseline, Tom smoked 19 and 16 cigarettes, respectively. Thus on the cumulative graph, the data point for the second day reflects the total, 35. Because the data accumulate, the graph is smoother and the line can never turn downward. If the number of responses declines, the graph just goes up by a smaller amount. And if no responses occur on a particular day, the line would not go up at all—it would parallel the horizontal axis. The *steeper the slope* of the line, the *higher the response rate.* In Figure 10.3, the slope of the line is steeper for the baseline data than for the intervention data. This means that the number of cigarettes smoked per day was greater in baseline than intervention. If Tom had quit smoking entirely, the line would have stopped going up. (Go to 🔍 .)

Making a Graph

Graphs can be prepared by hand or with computer graphics programs. When preparing a graph by hand, it's a good idea to use graph paper and a ruler to make

Close-Up 10.1
Which Type of Graph Should You Use?

In considering when to use line, bar, and cumulative graphs, we can start with the rule of thumb for selecting between line and bar graphs. Line graphs usually are appropriate when the variable arranged along the horizontal axis is *continuous*—that is, when values along the bottom (or top) scale represent a numerical progression of number, amount, or degree. Chronological time is a continuous variable, and graphs of data from behavior change programs typically scale this variable along the horizontal axis in graphs to show how the target behavior changed across time in the baseline and intervention phases. As a result, the line graph is the most commonly used type of graph to represent data from programs to change behavior. Other continuous variables that can be scaled along the horizontal axis of a line graph are age, income, and the amount of a particular medication or therapy a person received.

Bar graphs should be used when the variable represented along the horizontal axis involves *discrete*, or separate, categories, rather than a progression of numerical values. As we saw in Figure 10.2, the *type* of therapy individuals receive is an example of a discrete variable—systematic desensitization and psychoanalytic therapy are separate approaches to therapy and are not related to each other as part of a progression. Other discrete variables for which bar graphs are appropriate are gender, college major, religion, and political party affiliation.

Cumulative graphs are used occasionally in programs to change behavior. They are most useful when the *rate* of responding or the *total* number of responses must be monitored constantly as critical aspects of the behavior. For instance, a therapist might need to monitor constantly the self-injurious behaviors of an autistic child to see how many of these responses the child has made and to find out whether the response rate is reduced when different behavioral methods are introduced. Changes in response rates and totals show up more clearly and quickly on cumulative graphs than on other graphs.

all lines neat and straight. Start by making a sketch of what the graph will look like, including all labels it will have and a caption, which describes what the graph contains. In a report or book, each graph is numbered and referred to as a "figure." The figure number, which also appears in the caption, reflects the order in which the graph is mentioned in the text. The text material should refer at least once to each figure by number (for instance, "Figure 1 presents . . ."). Label each axis clearly with measurement units and a name that communicates the nature of what the axis represents. A well-planned and attractively prepared figure:

- Is easy to read and understand.
- Contains only essential information and leaves out visually distracting detail.
- Creates a clear and fair picture of what the data indicate.
- Uses distinct geometric forms, such as circles or squares, for data points. Don't use color to distinguish different sets of data.

Use the figures contained in this book as models. We'll use the remainder of this section to describe the preparation of a line graph because it is the type of graph most commonly used in behavior change programs.

The *vertical axis* will represent a measure of the behavior. Make this axis about 4 to 6 inches long. To create a scale for the vertical axis, find the largest and smallest values of the data you collected. If the smallest value is much higher than zero, you may break the axis with double slash marks, as was done in Figure 10.2, and start the scale at a value that is a little lower than the smallest value you collected. Divide up the remainder of the axis into equal segments to reflect units of the scale, which should accommodate the largest and smallest values you collected. The *horizontal axis* typically will represent chronological time, usually in units of days or weeks. Each baseline and intervention phase is plotted separately and chronologically along this axis. If you're using days and the data fluctuate so widely from one day to the next across most of the graph that it's difficult to see that the behavior is increasing or decreasing, consider combining data from successive days and plotting means. As we saw earlier, organizing data in this way will smooth out the plot and create a clearer picture of the change that has occurred.

Using Graphs

Graphs can be used in two ways. First, you can use graphs to assess the effectiveness of an intervention. This assessment is done simply by visual inspection—a procedure called **graphic analysis**. You would examine the graph to see whether the behavior changed substantially when intervention techniques were implemented. If the changes shown in the graph are very pronounced, you would conclude that the intervention has affected the behavior. If the changes are not very clear, you would conclude that the program has not been effective. Although there is no widely accepted, specific criterion for deciding whether the changes are or are not pronounced enough, these evaluations require the use of rigorous standards. Only very

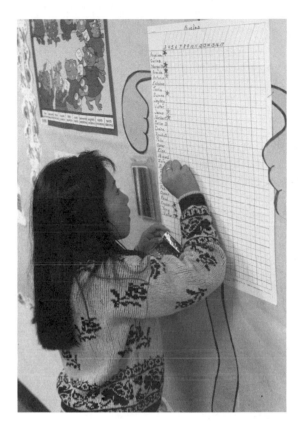

Having students post records of their behavior provides reinforcement when they perform well and enhances their motivation to improve more.

clear and marked changes should be accepted as reflecting a successful intervention.

The second way graphs can be used is to provide feedback as reinforcement and enhance motivation to improve the target behavior. For instance, teachers can post a graph of children's conduct or academic performance so that everyone can see how much progress has been made. Seeing concrete evidence of improvement can be reinforcing for everyone who wants the behavior to change. This approach can be very reinforcing and motivating in self-management programs, too. If you try to change your own behavior, consider starting a graph when you begin the intervention, with the idea of adding data points each day. Display the graph where you can see it, especially if it can serve as a reminder to monitor, record, and regulate your behavior. Depending on what your target behavior is, you might want to post the graph on the refrigerator or food cabinet, above your desk, on the door to your room or closet, in your medicine chest, or on your alarm clock. If the behavior is not highly personal, display the graph where others can see it and tell them about your project. Sharing project information seems to help improve the target behavior (McKenzie & Rushall, 1974). My students tell me that their friends and family members almost always want to help when they know about the project. (Go to ✔ .)

✔ Concept Check 10.1

1. An example of a variable you have used in doing the application exercises in this book is _____. ⇔
2. The arithmetic approach to use when data fluctuate a great deal from day to day is to calculate the _____ .
3. If the opportunity to perform the target behavior varies a lot from day to day, you can take opportunities into account by calculating a(n) _____ .
4. You can organize numerical data visually by constructing a(n) _____ .
5. The most common type of graph used in evaluating behavior changes is the _____ graph.
6. If a person made 10 responses on the first day of baseline, 10 on the second day, and 5 on the third, the value of the data point for the third day in a cumulative graph would be _____ .
7. The type of graph you should use if the horizontal axis represents a discrete variable is the _____ graph.
8. Assessment of the success of an intervention by visually inspecting a graph is called _____ .

Answers:

1. a target behavior. 2. mean 3. percentage 4. table 5. line 6. 25 7. bar 8. graphic analysis

Is the Program Working?

As soon as we begin the intervention phase of a program to change a behavior, we'll be wondering whether the program is working. After about a week or so, we should try to find out. As we shall see, such determinations are based mainly on inspecting the data to see how much progress has been made, but other approaches can help you make this judgment, too.

Ways to Assess a Program's Progress

Three approaches can be used to determine how well a program is working. First, we can interview individuals who must deal with the behavioral problem on a day-to-day basis (D. M. Baer, Wolf, & Risley, 1968). These people may include the person himself or herself, as well as his or her teachers, parents, or coworkers. Have they noticed any change at all? Are they pleased with any changes they've seen? Second, we can consult experts and research literature on the particular behavioral problem we're trying to change. From these sources, we can estimate how much change might reasonably be expected in the time since the intervention began.

The third and most critical approach is to conduct a graphic analysis of the data. We saw earlier that a graphic analysis is done by visually inspecting a graph of

Figure 10.4 Illustration of data used to assess the effectiveness of a program to reduce nail-biting. The data are from a self-management project conducted by a student named Jennelle. The two open-circle data points represent the means for the two time periods being compared: baseline and the first 8 days of intervention. The trend lines for these periods are represented by dashes.

the data to judge whether it depicts pronounced changes in the behavior that can be attributed to an intervention. This judgment involves assessing two *trends*—or general patterns of change in the behavior over time—shown in the data. One trend reflects any improvement in behavior from *baseline to intervention*, and the second trend reflects the extent to which the behavior has continued to *improve across time during the intervention.*

To see how to assess these trends in a graphic analysis, we will use the data graphed in Figure 10.4. These data are from a self-management program conducted by a student named Jennelle to reduce her nail-biting. At the end of 8 days of intervention, Jennelle did a graphic analysis to assess whether her program was working. An assessment is fairly obvious just by looking at the graph: nail-biting frequency had dropped after baseline, but hadn't declined very much after the first day of the intervention. We'll see later how Jennelle used this assessment.

A graphic analysis to determine whether a program is working can be made even clearer by carrying out three procedures. First, calculate the means for the baseline and intervention data you want to compare. In Jennelle's data, the mean frequencies of nail-biting were 9.62 for baseline and 4.25 for the first 8 days of the intervention. Second, mark each of those means on the graph with a data point placed halfway across the corresponding time period, using a geometric form that is different from any other forms you've used in the graph—Figure 10.4 uses small open circles, one at day 11 (halfway across the 21 days of baseline) and one between days 25 and 26 (halfway across the first 8 days of intervention). Third, for each time period you're comparing, draw a **trend line**—that is, a straight line that best "fits" or represents all the data points in a time period. Each trend line should pass through or very near the data point for the corresponding mean; draw trend lines very lightly in pencil initially, in case examination indicates that change is necessary. Positioned correctly, a trend line will appear to carve the data points in half, with about the same number of points above and below it. Then use a ruler to darken the line, making it distinctly different from any other lines in the graph, perhaps by using short dashes, as in Figure 10.4.

If Jennelle's nail-biting had been declining across time during the intervention, the trend line for those data would slope sharply downward. As you can see, the line slopes only slightly. Analysis of the two trends in the graph suggests that the program had helped but might benefit from some adjustments to improve its effectiveness. The graph reveals that Jennelle revised her intervention after the eighth day, and her nail-biting declined more sharply thereafter.

Problems in Graphic Analyses

Trends in the data you collect when conducting programs to change behavior will not always be as clear as Jennelle's, thereby making graphics more difficult to interpret. Three fairly common generic problems in the data can result in trends that are hard to evaluate. These problems are *excessive variability, a decreasing baseline trend* (for a behavioral excess), and an *increasing baseline trend* (for a behavioral deficit). Each type of problem is illustrated with three graphs in Figure 10.5, using hypothetical data for 1 week of baseline and 1 week of intervention. Let's look at these problems by analyzing the three graphs. As we do this, you'll see that the problems illustrated in the graphs are compounded when data are collected for an insufficient amount of time.

Figure 10.5a presents data for a program to reduce the frequency of a person's anger episodes. The excessive variability in the baseline data makes it difficult to decide whether any real change has occurred thus far in the intervention phase, even though the trend lines suggest that the number of anger episodes per day has declined. This difficulty exists because the baseline data are very unstable, containing sharp fluctuations. Is the declining trend in anger frequency depicted in the intervention data just an extension of the baseline fluctuations, or has the behavior really decreased? Perhaps, instead, the high variability was an unusual circumstance. In this case, collecting baseline data for at least another week might have helped to stabilize the data. As we saw earlier, it may also be possible to stabilize the data by averaging them across days. But to ensure that enough averages can be plotted to show a trend, this approach usually requires more than seven data points.

In Figure 10.5b, the data represent a person's frequency of gossiping. Notice that the baseline data for this behavioral excess show a clear decreasing trend that existed before the intervention was introduced to reduce the gossiping behavior. Is the decrease in gossiping after baseline due to the intervention, or is it just a continuation of the existing trend? If the declining trend during the intervention phase had been much sharper than the trend in baseline, we could assume that the difference resulted from the intervention. But the two trends in this graph are very similar. As a result, we can't determine whether the program is working or whether the decreasing trends in both phases are due to some other factor, such as a temporary change in the person's general social experiences. Again, collecting baseline

(a)

(b)

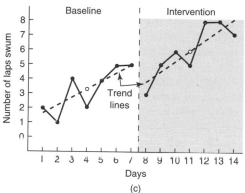

(c)

Figure 10.5 Graphs illustrating three types of problem data: (a) excessive variability, (b) decreasing baseline trend for a behavioral excess, and (c) increasing baseline trend for a behavioral deficit. The means (open circles) and trend lines (dashes) for each set of data (hypothetical) are plotted. These graphs assume that the evaluations of whether the programs were working were undertaken 1 week after the start of the intervention.

data for another week might have clarified the situation—in this case, a reversal might have appeared in the baseline trend.

Figure 10.5c presents data for a program to increase the number of laps a person swims in a pool each day. The problem is similar to the one we just saw for the gossiping data. For the swimming program, however, the baseline data for this behavioral deficit depict a clear increasing trend before the introduction of the intervention to increase swimming. Once again, the trends in both phases are not very different, so we can't tell whether the program is working or whether some other factor is responsible for the increases in swimming in both phases.

In general, whenever baseline data show excessive variability or an increasing or decreasing trend in relation to the behavioral goal, we should consider delaying the start of the intervention and collecting additional baseline data.

Troubleshooting and Improving a Program

Each program to change behavior is unique and is designed to meet the needs of a specific individual whose problem behaviors, prior learning experiences, and cur-

Case Study 10.1
Revising Monica's Dietary Program

Monica was a student of mine who designed and conducted a self-management program to reduce her daily consumption of junk food snacks, such as cookies and ice cream, in favor of healthy snacks, such as fruits and vegetables. Although the initial design was very good and included techniques that were directed at the snacking behavior itself and its antecedents and consequences, Monica found that the program wasn't working as well as she wanted. Both target behaviors had improved moderately from baseline to intervention, but showed no improvements in more than a week of her intervention.

Monica decided to revise her intervention in three ways. One change she made was to use the technique of narrowing antecedent control by deciding:

"If I'm going to eat junk food, it has to be at a table made for eating." Dining room tables

or tables in cafeterias would be examples. I allowed myself to eat healthy snacks anywhere at all. This strategy helped eliminate eating unhealthy goodies while driving, studying in the student center, watching TV, or just hanging out being bored.

She also introduced using the strategy of "cool" cognitions to reperceive junk foods as neutral items when they tempted her. Finally, she increased the amount of the monetary reward she would "earn" if she ate no junk food on a given day. By the end of Monica's month-long intervention, her daily junk food intake had declined to less than one-third of its baseline value. Also, her daily consumption of healthy snacks had increased substantially, and she was now eating healthy snacks about three times as much as junk food snacks.

rent life situations are typically different from those other people. As a result, conducting an intervention is an experiment or test of the program design, which may contain flaws that impair its effectiveness. In addition, new circumstances can arise that affect the target behavior. This is why, starting after about a week of the intervention, we assess whether a program is working. The graph of Jennelle's data (Figure 10.4) showed that this student revised her program after seeing that her nail-biting had not decreased much during the first 8 days of her intervention. Her revision was fairly simple: she deposited with a friend a large amount of money, which she would earn back and use to shop for items she wanted if she achieved her behavioral goal. Once that revision was in place, Jennelle's nail-biting began to decline. Problems in the initial designs of programs are common. When a program isn't working, we must find out why and make improvements. (Go to .)

Discovering Why a Program Isn't Working

There are several reasons why programs to change behavior may not be as effective as they could be. For one thing, sometimes programs are designed without doing a careful functional analysis of the target behavior, its antecedents, and its consequences. In the absence of data from a functional analysis, the program design is likely to be based on misperceptions or misunderstandings of the factors that control the target behavior. This leads to incorrect choices of intervention techniques and improperly established rules for their use.

Another reason why programs do not attain maximal effectiveness lies in the techniques they include, which may not be the best ones available, or alternatively, may not be powerful enough. The use of less-than-optimal techniques is a fairly common problem that usually can be corrected easily. For instance, both Jennelle and Monica initially used reinforcement systems that were not powerful enough to elicit the desired progress. Making the reinforcers more powerful enhanced the success of the students' programs. It's hard to know in advance how many reinforcers to use, what types should be selected, and how much reward value each should have to maximize the success of a behavior change program. Skill in choosing and designing optimally effective techniques improves with experience.

Finally, the individuals who administer program techniques may not implement them carefully enough or rigorously enough. This may happen partly because many of the techniques of behavior modification are commonly used in everyday life, but usually in a haphazard manner and for behaviors that have not been carefully defined. Parents and teachers apply reinforcers and punishers to influence children's behavior, but these adults typically do not apply consequences consistently and immediately for every correct instance of a behavior they want to change. Sometimes adults fail to apply consequences consistently or immediately because the target behavior is not well defined. It is also true, however, that people tend to fall back into their habitual ways of doing things, and that carrying out procedures haphazardly is easier than implementing them carefully and rigorously. It takes a lot of time, effort, motivation, and training to carry out a behavior change program effectively.

How to Improve a Program

To improve a program that is not as effective as it could be, we need to ascertain how the intervention has been conducted, determine what problems have impaired its success, and decide what to do about these problems. These activities begin with the process of *troubleshooting*—that is, investigating to find problems—for all aspects of the existing program (DeRisi & Butz, 1975; D. L. Holmes, 1977).

Troubleshooting the Program

One of the first steps in troubleshooting is to answer the diagnostic questions listed below concerning program design and execution. Answers are written down for *only the questions that pertain* to the way the program was actually designed or conducted. The questions are categorized under headings that indicate the dimensions to which the techniques apply or the procedures the program has involved.

Methods of Managing the Antecedents   Examine the effectiveness of methods for the management of the antecedents of the target behavior by answering the following questions about methods the program has been using:

1. Were the prompts, modeling, or instructions used in the intervention (a) noticed by the person and (b) effective?
2. Were there difficulties in trying to alter chains, reduce or avoid antecedents, or narrow antecedent control?
3. Were the CSs in the stimulus hierarchy for desensitization (a) applied effectively and (b) appropriately spaced?

Methods of Managing the Behavior   Examine the effectiveness of methods directed toward managing the behavior by answering the following questions about methods the program has been using:

1. Was the target behavior defined clearly for the person?
2. Were the shaping steps appropriate to the skills and abilities of the person?
3. Did the person lack any prerequisite skills for learning the new behavior?
4. Was the person able to use the relaxation techniques effectively?
5. When covert conditioning was used, was the person able to form clear images of the scenes?
6. Were the alternative responses used in the program appropriate and effective?

Methods of Managing the Consequences   Examine the effectiveness of methods to manage the consequences of the target behavior by answering the following questions about methods the program has been using:

1. Did the reinforcers lose some of their appeal or become undermined by external factors, such as other people providing stronger, counterproductive reinforcers?
2. Were some reinforcers provided immediately after appropriate behaviors, and were these rewards given frequently and in small amounts?
3. Were any punishers functioning as reinforcers—that is, did they seem to maintain a behavioral excess instead of decreasing it?
4. Were there difficulties in implementing extinction procedures for positive or negative reinforcement in an effort to decrease undesirable behavior?
5. Did lottery or group contingency procedures for administering reinforcers lead to any difficulties?

Procedural Aspects of the Program   Examine various procedural aspects of the program by answering the following questions:

1. Were assessment methods performed correctly, and were data calculated or charted without errors?
2. Was it possible to verify the accuracy of the data?
3. Was the data collection process overly difficult, complex, or time-consuming?
4. Were the program's techniques or procedures, such as reinforcement, implemented correctly and as planned?

5. Were all mediators or program administrators using the techniques in the same way?

6. Was the behavioral contract appropriately negotiated, and were its terms clear and fair?

7. Did some unexpected outside factor interfere with the program or disrupt it?

8. Were there reasons to suspect that motivational problems or a lack of training hampered the performance of the individuals who administered the techniques?

Correcting the Program

To decide how to correct problems you may have discovered in your self-management program by troubleshooting, use your written answers to the questions above to stimulate your rethinking of decisions you made in the application exercise for Chapter 9. You will probably find it useful to consult the functional analysis materials, relevant sections of this text, and the checklist of behavior change methods (Figure 9.1). If you found problems with the program's system of reinforcers, you may find it useful to consult the Preferred Items and Experiences Questionnaire (Figure 5.2) to decide how to improve your design.

Once you have decided how to revise the program's design, make sure you have the materials you'll need to incorporate the new methods into the intervention. Begin the revised program as soon as possible, and reevaluate progress after several days by conducting another graphic analysis. Chances are, one revision is all you'll need to do to troubleshoot an initial design that did not work as well as you expected. The need to revise a program shouldn't be construed as indicating a "failure" in the design. It is a positive and reasonable step toward fine-tuning the program's effectiveness. (Go to ✔ .)

✔ Concept Check 10.2

• •

1. A general pattern of change in a behavior over time is called a(n) _____ .

2. A trend line is a straight graph line that best _____ the data points within a time period.

3. An example of a set of data showing excessive variability for 5 days might be _____ _____ . ⇔

4. An example of a set of data showing a decreasing baseline trend for 5 days might be _____ . ⇔

5. One revision Monica made to her dietary program was to introduce _____ _____ .

6. Answering diagnostic questions to find problems in the way a program was actually conducted is part of the process of _____ .

_____

Answers: **1.** trend **2.** fits/represents **3.** 9, 2, 0, 7, 3 **4.** 9, 8, 6, 6, 5 **5.** narrowing antecedent control/"cool" cognitions/stronger reinforcer. **6.** troubleshooting

• •

Application Exercise

This application exercise has three main objectives: to encourage you to use the methods we've examined to organize your data, to give you practice in graphing your data, and to provide a framework for assessing whether your program is working. If you will not be collecting data for your project, make up 7 days of baseline data and 7 days of intervention data for this application exercise. Make the data appropriate for the hypothetical project you have used in prior work sheets. Before working toward the objectives, let's look at some pointers you can use.

Tips on Using Data and Improving Programs

As you read and carry out the tasks of this application exercise, you'll want to keep in mind the following helpful tips on using data and improving programs.

1. Transfer data from your data sheets to a table on a regular basis, daily if possible. Don't throw away your rough notes until you have checked to be sure that no errors were made in this process.
2. Look for problems in the data, such as excessive variability and increasing or decreasing baseline trends.
3. Make sure that all final versions of tables and graphs you construct are neat and accurate. Don't draw any lines freehand—use a ruler.
4. Keep track of any unusual circumstances, such as sickness, that may have affected your performance. If necessary, add footnotes to the graph to explain anomalous data.
5. When constructing a graph, sketch it out freehand on scratch paper first to see what it will look like. Redraw it until it is clear, uncluttered, and appropriately proportioned.
6. When composing the final version of a graph, label trend lines (if any), baseline and intervention phases, and points at which revisions were introduced to the intervention.
7. After the intervention has been in force for about a week, do a full graphic analysis with trend lines. Troubleshoot and make revisions, if needed.
8. When troubleshooting a program, write down all answers to relevant diagnostic questions and all ideas you may have about improving the program.
9. Add data points to the graph periodically and evaluate the progress being made each week.

The Next Steps in Your Program Design

The tasks you will do in this application exercise will enable you to decide whether your program is working, and, if not, what revisions to the design might be helpful.

We will begin by having you organize your baseline data, putting them in a table and calculating weekly means. Then you will construct a graph of your baseline and intervention data, conduct a graphic analysis, and summarize your findings. If necessary, you will troubleshoot your program. Turn now to Work Sheet 10.1 to complete these tasks.

Summary

Data in a program of behavior modification provide a record of variables related to the target behavior and clarify whether and how much the behavior has changed. Several methods for organizing data can clarify the picture data present. A mean combines data into an average and is an especially useful way of organizing data that vary a great deal from one collection instance to the next. A percentage is a useful way of organizing data when the opportunities to perform the behavior differ for two or more sets of data. Transferring data to a table organizes the data visually, allowing us to see patterns.

Data can also be presented in line graphs, bar graphs, and cumulative graphs. Line graphs are the most commonly used way of presenting data from programs of behavior modification because the horizontal axis typically scales units of chronological time, such as days or weeks, which are continuous variables. The most common way of determining whether a behavior change program is working is to inspect graphs of the data, using a process called graphic analysis. We can improve the clarity of the data subjected to graphic analysis by computing means for the baseline and intervention data we want to compare and then drawing trend lines to represent the general pattern of change in the behavior over time.

When a graphic analysis indicates that a given intervention is not changing behavior as effectively as it should be, we will need to revise the program. This process begins with troubleshooting the program by answering diagnostic questions about design and administration. This information is then used in deciding what revisions to make.

Key Terms and Review Questions

Key Terms

variables	bar graphs
mean	cumulative graphs
table	graphic analysis
graph	trend line
line graphs	

Review Questions

1. Define "variables" and give three examples.

2. Two arithmetic ways to organize data involve calculating the *mean* and the *percentage*. Define both terms and indicate when these calculations are useful.

3. What is a data table, and how is it useful?

4. Describe the axes used when presenting graphical data for a behavior change program.

5. What are line graphs, bar graphs, and cumulative graphs? How are they similar and different?

6. Describe how to decide when line graphs are more appropriate than bar graphs, and vice versa.

7. Describe how to construct a line graph.

8. Describe in detail how to do a graphic analysis using trend lines.

9. Draw graphs of the three problems in the data that can make interpreting a graphic analysis very difficult.

10. Write a hypothetical account of the troubleshooting process Monica (in Case Study 10.1) might have used in revising her dietary program.

Related Readings

American Psychological Association (1994). *Publication manual* (4th ed.). Washington, DC: Author.

DeRisi, W. J., & Butz, G. (1975). *Writing behavioral contracts: A case simulation practice manual.* Champaign, IL: Research Press.

Name _____

Date _____

Day & time
class meets_____

Chapter 10: Work Sheet 10.1

1. Compose a table of your *baseline* data, using Table 10.1 as a model. If you find that this model does not fit the way you feel your data should be organized, you may want to change the structure of the table.

2. On the accompanying grid, construct a graph of your data for baseline and the first week or so of intervention, plotting days along the horizontal axis. If you are trying to change *more than one target behavior* or if you are collecting *more than one type of data* (for example, frequency and magnitude), make separate graphs on other sheets of graph paper. Do a graphic analysis by calculating the means and drawing trend lines for the baseline and intervention data.

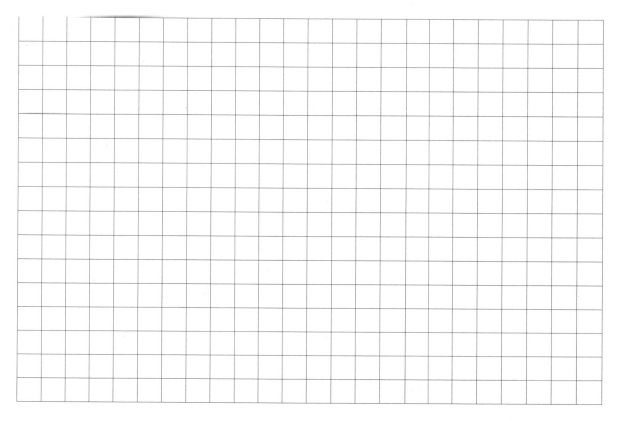

3. Do your data show excessive variability, a decreasing baseline trend for a behavioral excess, or an increasing baseline trend for a behavioral deficit? Is any of these features of your data severe enough to cause problems in interpreting whether your program is working? If so, what can you do about it?

4. When you can interpret your data, write a description of your analysis of whether your program is working.

5. If you judged that your program is not working as well as it should, troubleshoot the program. In the space provided, write the answers to the diagnostic questions and your plans for revising the program.

NOTE: If you will be submitting work sheets to your instructor or to a fellow student, make a copy of each sheet before submitting it.

11 *Maintaining Behavior Changes*

Prologue

Imagine that you had been one of the therapists in the following intervention to train eight autistic 4- to 13-year-old children to perform basic classroom behaviors, such as looking at the teacher and imitating the teacher's actions when requested (Koegel & Rincover, 1974). Students must be able to do these things if they are to learn in a classroom. But the autistic children in this study had very poor basic classroom skills: four of them were mute, and four could only echo words they heard others say; all had extremely low IQs. In an effort to teach several basic classroom skills, the therapists worked on a one-to-one basis with the children, using a training procedure in which

> responses were shaped by first rewarding the child for establishing eye contact with the teacher until the child would consistently (90% correct trials for three consecutive days) look at the teacher for a period of at least 5 seconds when the teacher commanded, "Look at me." Then, nonverbal imitation was gradually established by prompting and reinforcing copying behaviors until the subject could consistently imitate. . . . Imitation was then used as a prompt to teach other nonverbal responses to instructions. For example, the teacher would say, "Touch your nose" and prompt the correct response by saying "Do this" and modelling the correct response. The prompts were then faded. (p. 47)

After 2 to 4 weeks of this training, all the children were able to perform the skills correctly at least 80% of the time. Then came the crucial test to see whether the children would use these skills when the situation was more like a classroom setting—that is, when they were tested with all eight children present in the same room, instead of alone. The average correct responding when alone—nearly 89%—dropped to about 28% when the entire group was present.

If you had spent weeks in one-to-one training of basic classroom behaviors, only to have the skills fall apart when the children were in the same room, you'd probably be very discouraged. Why didn't these behaviors generalize to the group situation? What can we do to increase the likelihood that the behaviors we train will be maintained in and generalize to other appropriate situations? These are the issues we will examine in this chapter.

Will the Behavior Changes Last?

A student named Kevin conducted a self-management project to increase exercising and decrease eating high-fat foods as a permanent lifestyle change. A few months later, he stopped by to tell me that he had stuck to the program and felt great about having done so. Another student, Jane, chose to do a self-management project one spring semester to lose about 11 pounds so she would fit into a size 8 bridesmaid's gown for her sister's wedding in May. Jane's was a short-term goal, and she succeeded in losing the weight, but she gained it right back by the fall semester. Short-term goals can be of value, but behavior change programs are usually undertaken with long-lasting goals in mind. We have seen that programs consisting of behavioral and cognitive methods can succeed in changing behavior. But will the change last?

Relapses in Behavior

Even when the goal of an intervention is to produce a permanent improvement in the person's behavior and he or she agrees with the goal, the behavior sometimes regresses after the intervention has ended. You undoubtedly know individuals who seemed to have succeeded in stopping smoking or in reducing their intake of fattening foods, but went back to the old habits. Falling back to one's former, full-blown pattern of an undesired behavior is called a **relapse**. We saw in Chapter 9 that a *lapse* is an instance of backsliding—a relatively isolated or temporary regression to the former behavior. People often can bounce back from a lapse fairly easily if they know that backsliding is common and should be expected. Relapses are especially likely to occur when the person is not very committed to changing the target behavior and when changes in his or her lifestyle or longstanding habits are called for. Let's look at a few different examples of postimprovement relapses.

The first example comes from an intervention to improve the feeding skills of a profoundly retarded 6-year-old girl (O'Brien, Bugle, & Azrin, 1972). Before the intervention began, the child ate without utensils, using her hands to grasp some food, crush it, and put it in her mouth. As you might imagine, her feeding was both unsightly and messy. The intervention used two main techniques to teach the little girl to eat with a spoon: (1) physical guidance prompts, in which the teacher held and moved the girl's hand through the feeding movements, and (2) interruption–extinction, in which the teacher stopped an incorrect response, such as trying to eat with the hands, and prevented reinforcement by cleaning the food from the girl's hands so she couldn't eat it. When physical guidance was used, the guidance was withheld for the next response following a correctly performed, guided response in order to assess her skill in independent feeding with a spoon. Figure 11.1 shows that the girl's performance in using a spoon to eat improved greatly when the interruption–extinction method was added to the physical guidance but dropped sharply when the intervention techniques were withdrawn in the reversal phase. Even though the girl had learned how to eat with a spoon, she did not continue to eat properly when the intervention ended.

O. Ivar Lovaas and his coworkers (1973) conducted a program in which 20 developmentally disabled children received intensive individual training to reduce undesirable behaviors, such as engaging in self-stimulation, and to increase desirable behaviors, such as using speech, playing with other children, and performing self-care activities. The program applied behavioral methods over many months

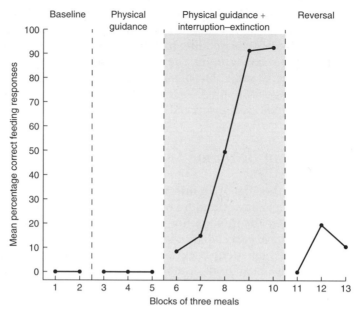

Figure 11.1   Percentage of correctly performed feeding responses by a profoundly retarded child during four phases of the training program. The mean percentages were calculated across three meals. All data plotted are for feeding responses the child performed independently. During phases in which physical guidance was used, the guidance was withheld for some responses to assess independent feeding. (Based on data abstracted from O'Brien, Bugle, & Azrin, 1972, Figure 1.)

and succeeded in improving the target behaviors in all the children, some of whom showed very large gains. Then, 1 to 4 years after discharge from the program, each child was revisited for follow-up assessment. These evaluations revealed that the environment *after* an intervention is crucial to maintaining such children's behavioral improvements. Some of the children went to live at home upon leaving the program, and their parents received training in behavioral methods. These children's behaviors continued to improve. Those who could not be placed at home, however, went to institutions, where they received basically custodial care with no behavioral methods, and their behavior relapsed.

Interventions have tried to prevent or reduce juvenile delinquency in problem adolescents by using behavioral methods to increase performance of socially and academically desirable behaviors and decrease performance of activities that lead to social, academic, and legal problems. In some of these interventions, youths with problem behaviors have attended separate classes in a public school, and their teachers and parents have administered token reinforcement systems (Heaton & Safer, 1982; Safer, Heaton, & Parker, 1981). Other interventions have housed the youths in community-based group homes while they attended public schools. Behavioral methods with token reinforcers were administered mainly by trained supervisors at the group home, with feedback from teachers regarding school performance

(Fixsen et al., 1978; Phillips et al., 1973; Wolf, Braukmann, & Ramp, 1987). Although each of these programs has produced impressive improvements in the youths' target behaviors during the many months in which the intervention was in effect and for about a year after it ended, the behavioral improvements achieved by many of the participants were lost after a couple of years. Relapse seems very likely if problem adolescents are returned to their original life circumstances without continued treatment or support to encourage them to maintain the improved behaviors.

Why Relapses Occur

Have you ever had an experience like this one? I bought a new refrigerator with a special bin on the door to store a gallon milk container, and months later I found myself sometimes looking for milk on a shelf in the body of the refrigerator or starting to return the container to its former place, as I had done for years with the old appliance. Automatic or habitual behaviors die hard. Why? We continue to perform the obsolete behaviors even though we know the correct actions partly because we have learned the old behaviors so thoroughly. In addition, the antecedent cues and chain of responses, such as opening the door and thinking "Get milk," are much the same as they had been. If we then were to perform the old behavior and often receive reinforcement as a consequence, we may revert to the old habit entirely. This account describes some of the factors that can lead to relapses.

The strength of the old behavior and the circumstance of encountering antecedents to that behavior are important factors in determining whether a

Being in a group with other cigarette smokers presents strong social temptations for ex-smokers to return to smoking.

relapse will happen after a behavioral excess has been reduced. People who have succeeded in stopping smoking or drinking for a few weeks or longer may return to the habit again if they do not or cannot control the associated antecedents. For instance, individuals frequently report having gone back to smoking because they had experienced high levels of frustration or stress or strong social temptations to smoke, all of which are common antecedents for smoking (Shiffman, 1986).

And behavioral relapses happen for many other reasons. Some of these reasons relate to the strength or persistence of responses the program tried to enhance. These behaviors can include alternative responses used in the intervention and new behaviors that were trained to address behavioral deficits, as in the program discussed earlier for training a retarded girl to eat with a spoon. The stronger or more persistent these behaviors are, the less likely relapses become. Other factors that can lead to relapses involve cognitive processes—for example, a diminution in the person's sense of self-efficacy for being able to maintain the behavior change. The remainder of this chapter concentrates on methods programs can include to maintain behavior changes and overcome the many factors that can lead to relapses. (Go to 🔍 .)

Thinning and Delaying Reinforcement

To prevent a relapse, we need to apply methods that will enable the improved behavior to persist after the intervention ends. We saw in Chapter 5 that one way to maintain a behavior change involves *thinning* (sometimes called "fading" or "leaning") the schedule of reinforcement used in the program. Once a target behavior has been learned and well established under a *continuous reinforcement* (CRF) schedule, we can thin the schedule by gradually reducing the rate at which the behavior is reinforced. Thinning the reinforcement schedule makes the consequences for the behavior more like the conditions people experience in everyday life. For instance, when you place a phone call, sometimes you reach the party and sometimes you don't. When you do a good job in your chores at home or at work, sometimes you are praised and sometimes you're not. Behavior changes produced in an intervention are likely to receive *intermittent* or *partial reinforcement* in the person's daily life.

The reason for decreasing reinforcement *gradually* rather than suddenly is to guard against deterioration of the behavior. If reinforcement is reduced too quickly, the person may not be sufficiently motivated to continue responding appropriately. Thus the behavior may decline rapidly, necessitating the introduction of a CRF schedule again to reestablish the behavior. How gradual should the thinning be? As with the gradual processes of shaping a behavior and fading prompts, there are no fixed rules. Sometimes the reinforcement schedule can be thinned very quickly, and other times the process takes weeks (Sulzer & Mayer, 1972). It seems reasonable to assume that thinning can progress rapidly for individuals who understand the need to reduce the rate of reinforcement and have some control—perhaps through negotiations for a behavioral contract—over how quickly these reductions take place.

Close-Up 11.1
Relapse and the Abstinence Violation Effect

One way by which cognitive processes may lead to a relapse has been described by G. Alan Marlatt and his colleagues (Marlatt & Gordon, 1980; Marlatt & Parks, 1982). As we consider the course of events these processes follow in producing a relapse, we will use an example of a man named Victor, who had stopped drinking alcohol. According to Marlatt, the course of events leading to a relapse starts with the experience of a high-risk antecedent situation:

1. *High-risk situation.* Victor encounters two tempting antecedents for drinking—he was feeling upset by events at his job and was invited to go to a bar.

2. *Poor coping with the risk.* He decides to accept the invitation, promising himself he will only drink nonalcoholic beverages.

3. *Negative self-statements and thoughts.* At the bar, Victor begins to feel a strong craving for a drink. He begins to doubt his self-efficacy, thinking "It's no use—the booze is gonna win." And he thinks about how good a drink would taste and make him feel.

4. *Lapse.* He orders a drink and starts to consume it, rationalizing that "With the day I've had, who could blame me." (He'll find out who: himself!)

5. *Perceived violation of abstinence rule.* Because Victor believed the slogan, "You are always only one drink away from a drunk," he had been committed to the rule of *total abstinence*: he would never drink again, ever. Now he starts to realize he has violated that rule. He feels guilty, blames himself for the transgression, and concludes that ordering the drink was a sign of personal failure: "I don't have enough willpower to control my drinking. I'm really just an alcoholic after all." This series of thoughts and feelings is called the **abstinence violation effect** and can precipitate a full relapse. Strictly speaking, the abstinence violation effect applies when the person is committed to a rule of total abstinence, but violating less severe rules can have similar effects sometimes.

6. *Increased likelihood of relapse.* Once Victor felt weak-willed and powerless to resist that first drink, his ability to resist subsequent drinks was greatly reduced that night. The abstinence violation effect carried over into the next day, and he drank several drinks again. A relapse had begun.

Programs to change behavior often need to include techniques to prevent such cognitive events from undermining the gains the person has made, leading to a relapse.

Probably the most common approach for thinning a schedule of reinforcement is to reduce the percentage or *ratio* of correct responses that receive rewards. In a CRF schedule, 100% of correct responses receive reinforcement. Beth Sulzer and G. Roy Mayer conducted a program to teach a child to name various items in a set of objects. They thinned the reinforcement schedule, starting

> by *skipping* reinforcement for about one correct response out of four. As time went by, more and more trials went unreinforced until eventually the child had to label the whole set before the . . . reinforcer was delivered. (1972, p. 109)

This thinning process began by reducing reinforcement to about three of every four correct responses, or 75%, by skipping one reward. When the schedule was thinned to 50%, the child had to name two objects correctly to get a reinforcer. Gradually, the child had to name more and more objects correctly for each instance of reinforcement.

Other strategies can be used in thinning reinforcement schedules. For example, one intervention trained children to identify and request nutritious snacks, such as fruit, to receive reinforcers of various types on a CRF schedule (R. A. Baer et al., 1987). In the process of thinning, the children continued to get reinforcement on a CRF schedule on days when rewards were made available, but the percentage of *days* when rewards were available was reduced from 100% of the days to 67%, and then 33%. A reinforcement schedule also can be thinned by decreasing the frequency of behavior assessment. For instance, an intervention was conducted to discourage a boy from stealing the belongings of other students in his classroom (Rosen & Rosen, 1983). Initially, token reinforcers and punishers were administered by assessing his stealing behavior every 15 minutes, but this schedule was thinned by increasing the *interval* between assessments to once every 2 hours.

Decreasing the rate of reinforcement is a very flexible process that can progress at different speeds and follow different strategies. To determine whether the thinning procedure we are using is advancing too quickly, we monitor the person's performance carefully and frequently. If the behavior seems to be regressing, we may be reducing the reinforcement rate too quickly, hence may need to slow the pace. Choosing a strategy for thinning reinforcement should be based on and coordinated with the intermittent reinforcement schedule we plan to use in the program.

Types of Intermittent Reinforcement Schedule

When a reinforcement schedule is thinned, only some instances of the behavior will be reinforced, and the schedule of reinforcement is *intermittent* or *partial*. The rule specifying the circumstances under which some instances of the behavior will be reinforced is called an **intermittent reinforcement schedule** or *partial reinforcement schedule*. For example, a rule in my everyday life specifies that every other Friday during the academic year, I will be paid for my work as a college instructor. Although the rules governing intermittent reinforcement schedules in our everyday lives are sometimes stated or clear, most often they are not. The matrix in Figure 11.2 outlines the four basic intermittent reinforcement schedules—the two described in the top row are *ratio schedules*, and two in the bottom row are *interval schedules*. Let's examine these types of reinforcement schedule.

Ratio Schedules

In **ratio schedules**, the rule for administering each instance of reinforcement is based on *the number of correct responses* made since the last reinforcer was given. This rule can describe one of two *patterns*: the number of responses required for reinforcement can be *fixed*, or constant, for every instance of reinforcement, or it can be *variable*, changing from one instance to the next.

RESPONSE OR TIME PATTERN

		Fixed	Variable
Response or time criterion	Ratio	**Fixed-Ratio (FR):** Rule based on a constant number of responses per instance of reinforcement.	**Variable-Ratio (VR):** Rule based on a varying number of responses per instance of reinforcement.
	Interval	**Fixed-Interval (FI):** Rule based on a constant amount of time elapsing since the last instance of reinforcement.	**Variable-Interval (VI):** Rule based on a varying amount of time elapsing since the last instance of reinforcement.

Figure 11.2 Fixed-ratio, variable-ratio, fixed-interval, and variable-interval intermittent reinforcement schedules: the four basic types. Each reinforcement schedule is defined by a rule based on two factors: (1) the response or time *criterion* (the number of responses or elapsed time) since the last instance of reinforcement, and (2) the response or time *pattern* (fixed or variable) required for the criterion.

In a **fixed-ratio** (FR) schedule of reinforcement, the criterion for receiving each instance of reinforcement is performance by the individual of a constant number of correct responses. Typically, the reinforcer is given immediately after the individual makes the last response in the fixed criterion. An everyday example of a fixed-ratio schedule is the practice of factories to pay employees on a piecework basis—a garment worker might have to sew five pullover shirts to earn one dollar. In this example, the ratio of the number of responses (shirts sewn) for each dollar is 5:1, which is abbreviated as FR 5. Note that an FR 1 schedule is a CRF schedule, but it isn't intermittent. People's rate of responding for fixed-ratio intermittent reinforcement usually is very high because the more rapidly they respond, the more rewards they'll get.

The process of thinning reinforcement to a fixed-ratio schedule was used in an intervention to improve a boy's arithmetic skills by providing praise, such as "Good work," for correctly solved math problems (Kirby & Shields, 1972). The number of correct math problems required to earn a statement of praise was doubled every couple of days, until an FR 16 schedule had been reached. In fixed-ratio schedules, the rule governing the timing of reinforcements is often stated explicitly or is easy for the person to detect after many instances of reward. Even though people with impaired intellectual abilities may not notice the pattern or understand it when told, some form of knowledge of the arrangement seems to affect their behavior.

In a **variable-ratio** (VR) schedule, the rule governing the timing of reinforcements calls for an unspecified and changing number of correct responses for each instance of the reward. As with fixed-ratio schedules, the reinforcer is typically given immediately after the individual has made the last response in the varying criterion. Thus, for a series of six instances of reinforcement, the person might be required to perform the following numbers of responses: 4, 12, 23, 8, 11, and 2, respectively. This is an example of a VR 10 schedule because the *average* number of responses required for reinforcement is 10. Notice that the required number of responses varies from one instance of reinforcement to the next. Variable-ratio schedules keep the person guessing about whether or when a payoff will happen because instances of reinforcement are unpredictable. But responding at a rapid rate increases the frequency of reward. As a result, people usually respond at high rates for variable-ratio reinforcement.

Gambling pays off on variable-ratio schedules. In playing a slot machine for a few hours, for instance, the number of times you would need to perform the chain of dropping a coin into the slot and pulling the lever varies from one jackpot to the next—the machine is programmed to ensure this. Another everyday example of a behavior being reinforced on a variable-ratio schedule is found in telemarketing: telephoning people to sell products or services, with a commission earned for each sale. The number of calls the person will need to make before selling something will vary from one sale to the next.

Interval Schedules

In **interval schedules**, the rule for administering each instance of reinforcement is based on *the elapsed time* since the last reinforcer. A reinforcer is given for the *first correct response* following some period of time since the occurrence of the last reinforcement. In other words, reinforcement is not available for a period of time after each reward is given. But when reinforcement becomes available again, the first correct response is reinforced. As with ratio schedules, the specific rule for an interval schedule can describe one of two *patterns*: the amount of time during which reinforcement is not available can be *fixed*, or constant, for every instance of reinforcement, or it can be *variable*, changing from one instance to the next. Refer back to Figure 11.2 to compare interval and ratio schedules. Thinning reinforcement to an interval schedule is generally done by gradually extending the time when reward is not available.

A **fixed-interval** (FI) schedule makes reinforcement unavailable for a constant amount of time after each instance of reinforcement. The first correct response the individual makes after that time has elapsed is reinforced immediately. Because the time period is fixed, people and animals usually can learn to predict fairly accurately when reinforcement will be available again. It appears that they learn to respond slowly or not at all early in the interval and to increase the rate of responding toward the end of the interval.

There are many examples of fixed-interval schedules in everyday life. For instance, checking my mail is rewarded on a fixed-interval schedule because it is delivered at the same time every weekday (getting mail I want is a reward). Going to campus every other Friday is rewarded too: I get my salary. These are examples of FR 24-hours (or 1-day) and FR 2-weeks schedules. Notice that with interval schedules the abbreviation must specify the time units, such as seconds, minutes, or hours. Another everyday example of a fixed-interval schedule entails watching TV. If you are watching a show you enjoy and are not interested in the commercials, reinforcement for looking at the TV is not available during the time commercials are aired. Because commercial interruptions tend to have a standard duration, you can leave the room or engage in some other activity for about that amount of time and start looking at the TV again toward the end of the interval.

In a **variable-interval** (VI) schedule, the rule governing when the reinforcer will not be available involves an unspecified and a changing amount of elapsed time after each instance of the reward. As with fixed-interval schedules, the reinforcer is typically given immediately after the individual has made a single correct response after the appropriate amount of time elapsed. Thus for a series of, say, six instances of reinforcement, the reward might be unavailable for following amounts of time: 4, 12, 23, 8, 11, and 2 minutes, respectively. This would be an example of a VI 10-minutes schedule because the *average* time that reinforcement was unavailable is 10 minutes. Variable-interval schedules, like variable-ratio schedules, make instances of reinforcement unpredictable and keep the person guessing about whether or when a payoff will happen. But in variable-interval schedules, responding at a consistently rapid rate will not speed up the reinforcement. As a result, people tend to respond at a steady, moderate rate when this type of schedule is in effect.

Montrose Wolf and his colleagues (1970) used a variable-interval reinforcement schedule in an intervention to increase grade schoolers' sitting in their seats in class. The teacher set a kitchen timer for varying amounts of time on a VI 20-minutes schedule and provided token reinforcement for students who were in their seats when the timer sounded. An everyday example of a variable-interval schedule can be seen in grilling steaks on a barbecue. The amount of time needed to cook steak to the desired doneness can vary a lot, depending on how hot the coals are, how cold the meat was before it went onto the grill, and how thick the steak is. Another everyday behavior that is reinforced on a variable-interval schedule is looking to see when a red traffic light turns green. If you arrive at an unfamiliar traffic signal after the light has turned red, you don't know when to expect it to change. So of course you look at it; but looking at it a lot won't make it turn green faster! When it finally turns green, looking at it is reinforced by being able to proceed.

Although most intermittent reinforcement schedules from everyday life probably fit into the four basic types, not all do. For instance, the so-called *duration schedules* require that the person engage in the target behavior for certain amounts of time before being reinforced. Being paid an hourly wage is an example because work behavior is required during each hour. Sometimes interval schedules have an extra requirement: namely, the person must respond within a certain amount of time after reinforcement becomes available or lose the chance. This added requirement is called a *limited hold* because reinforcer availability is "held" for a limited time. Consider a train that has a regular, fixed-interval, schedule. The "limited hold" aspect of the rule is that the train will wait at the station for only a limited amount of time.

Other everyday reinforcement schedules involve combinations of the types we've discussed. For example, taking full advantage of weekly department store sales requires that you arrive when the store opens, and arriving much earlier probably won't matter. So far, this is just a fixed-interval schedule. Once you're in the store, a variable-ratio schedule will apply: the number of rummaging behaviors you'll need to perform in finding items you want at bargain prices will vary from one item to the next.

Effects of Intermittent Reinforcement Schedules

So far, we have described the effects of intermittent reinforcement on behavior rather broadly. We will look next at the effects of the four basic intermittent reinforcement schedules in more detail, examining them first while the schedules are in force (as they are during an intervention) and then after reinforcement has been discontinued (as is the case when the intervention is over).

Effects of Schedules During an Intervention

In our discussion of the effects of various schedules of reinforcement on behavior during interventions, we will assume that the target responses have progressed to the point of being well established and that the reinforcement schedules have been thinned. In general, all intermittent reinforcement schedules produce higher rates of responding than CRF schedules do while they are in force.

Ratio Schedules   Ratio schedules produce very high rates of responding, and response rates are somewhat higher under variable-ratio than fixed-ratio reinforcement schedules, as Figure 11.3 illustrates. The two cumulative graphs present hypo-

Figure 11.3   Illustration of hypothetical *cumulative graphs* of the number of words a child might read correctly in interventions using (a) a fixed-ratio (FR 20) reinforcement schedule and (b) a variable-ratio (VR 20) reinforcement schedule. The arrowheads pointing at the plotted lines indicate instances of reinforcement.

thetical data contrasting the usual kinds of effects of fixed- and variable-ratio schedules, as might be found in an intervention to increase a child's performance in reading words from a list. Notice three features of these graphs. First, the two reinforcement schedules are equated for the average number of responses, 20, required for reinforcement. By equating the two schedule types in this way, we can compare the effects without being concerned that one schedule provided more reinforcement than the other. Second, although the slope is steep in both cases, the variable-ratio graph is somewhat steeper than the fixed-ratio graph. In cumulative graphs, the steeper the slope, the higher the response rate. Third, individuals receiving reinforcement on fixed-ratio schedules tend to pause briefly in their responding, usually just after obtaining the reward. These **postreinforcement pauses** tend to be longer when many responses are required for each reward than when few responses are required. Although it's tempting to conclude that these pauses result because the individual is using the reinforcer, such as eating a food reward, there are two reasons to think that other factors must be involved. First, the pauses don't happen with variable-ratio schedules. Second, pauses also occur with reinforcers of other types, such as praise and money. It's as if the individual sees completing each fixed number of responses for a reward as a "goal" and "takes a break" after achieving each one.

Research using ratio schedules has shown that increasing the number of responses required for each instance of reinforcement increases people's response rates, within limits (Schroeder, 1972; Stephens et al., 1975). But at some point, the number of responses may become too large, and the behavior may begin to deteriorate. This effect is called **ratio strain** because the ratio of responses to reinforcement has become so large that the behavior isn't reinforced enough to be maintained (L. K. Miller, 1980). Although we can't predict the point at which ratio strain will happen, it appears to depend on several factors, such as the reward value, how gradually the thinning procedures advanced, and how much effort the response requires. Still, individuals will often perform at very high rates for fairly modest reinforcers. For instance, researchers used variable-ratio token reinforcement to increase exercising on a stationary bicycle on the part of obese and nonobese 11-year-old boys (De Luca & Holborn, 1992). The backup reinforcers included a kite, a model car, a flashlight, and comic books. The schedule of reinforcement was thinned for each boy to at least a VR 100 schedule, in which one point was earned for every 100 pedal revolutions on the bicycle, with no deterioration in the behavior. What's more, when the 30-minute exercise sessions were over, the boys often asked to be allowed to continue exercising to "get more points."

Interval Schedules   As Figure 11.4 illustrates, interval schedules produce moderately high response rates that are stronger and more constant with variable-interval schedules than with fixed-interval. Like the graphs for ratio schedules, these two cumulative graphs present hypothetical data contrasting the usual kinds of effect found with fixed- and variable-interval schedules. In this case, the intervention involves increasing the number of arithmetic problems a teenager completed in half-hour sessions. Notice that the two reinforcement schedules are equated for the

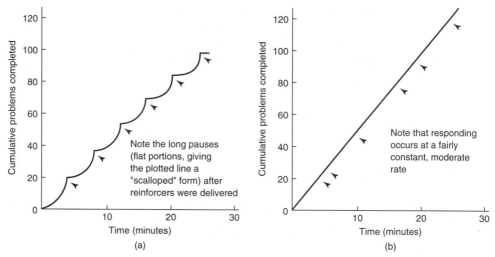

Figure 11.4   Illustration of *cumulative graphs* of the number of arithmetic problems a teenager might complete in interventions using (a) a fixed-interval (FI 4-minutes) reinforcement schedule and (b) a variable-interval (VI 4-minutes) reinforcement schedule. Arrowheads indicate instances of reinforcement.

average interval length, 4 minutes, when reinforcement is not available. Once again, equating the two schedule types in this way enables us to compare effects without being concerned that one schedule provided more reinforcement than the other.

An important phenomenon tends to occur with fixed-interval schedules. As the cumulative record in Figure 11.4a shows, fixed-interval schedules produce a prolonged pause in responding after each instance of reinforcement, causing the curve on the graph to resemble a series of *scallops*, or arcs. These pauses occur because the individual learns that the response will not lead to reinforcement soon after a reward was received. But after a while, responding begins to accelerate because the end of the interval is approaching and reinforcement will be available again. These pauses have the obvious effect of slowing down the rate of responding, thereby making variable intervals preferable to fixed. Although variable-interval schedules don't produce response rates that are as high as those associated with ratio schedules, they have a practical advantage for use in certain settings, especially in classrooms: administering the schedule doesn't require us to keep track of all instances of the target behavior. Simultaneously and continuously keeping track of the behavior of more than one person is difficult and time-consuming. (Go to 🔍 .)

Effects of Schedules After the Intervention Ends

When an intervention ends and the reinforcement given in the behavior change program is discontinued, the everyday life of the person may provide little

Q Close-Up 11.2
Cognitive Factors and Intermittent Reinforcement Effects

••

The effects and phenomena relating to intermittent reinforcement and behavior were shown originally with animals—especially pigeons and rats—as subjects in research. Later, the principles developed from this research were applied toward changing human behavior. But we now know that the effects of intermittent schedules of reinforcement are not always the same for animals and humans (Baron & Galizio, 1983; Lowe, 1979). One of the clearest differences is that humans who are being reinforced under a fixed-interval schedule sometimes don't show the prolonged pauses in responding after reinforcement that are usually found with this schedule. Why should this be?

The answer almost certainly involves the greater cognitive abilities of humans. People often try to figure out the rules governing their experiences and to verbalize these rules in regulating their behaviors (Baron & Galizio, 1983; Michael, 1987). But the rules figured out are not necessarily correct—and when people decide on

the wrong rule, their response patterns are likely follow the rule they believe exists rather than the actual rule. Three lines of evidence support the view that cognitive factors can affect people's performance under intermittent reinforcement. First, the cumulative graphs of children under fixed-interval reinforcement schedules show less and less scalloping as the subjects get older and their cognitive and verbal skills develop (Bentall, Lowe, & Beasty, 1985; C. F. Lowe, Beasty, & Bentall, 1983). Second, when adults are prevented from using verbal instructions to regulate a target behavior—for example, by having them subtract numbers in their heads—cumulative graphs of their behavior under fixed-interval reinforcement show very pronounced scalloping (Laties & Weiss, 1963). Third, simply giving adults rate-related instructions, such as to "go fast" or "go slow," can greatly affect their response rates in operant tasks with various reinforcement schedules (Catania, Matthews, & Shimoff, 1982; Hayes et al., 1986).

••

or no reinforcement for the target behavior. If this happens, ratio strain or extinction may cause a relapse in the behavior. We saw in Chapter 6 that giving reinforcement on an intermittent schedule rather than a CRF schedule makes the behavior more persistent, more resistant to extinction. This effect has been found with animals and humans (Kazdin & Polster, 1973; Kimble, 1961; Lewis, 1960; Lewis & Duncan, 1956). In general, behaviors that have been reinforced on variable schedules rather than on their fixed counterparts appear to be especially resistant to extinction (Shaw, 1987). To maintain a behavioral change and prevent a relapse, interventions should reinforce the target behavior on an intermittent schedule of reinforcement.

A reanalysis by John Nevin (1988) of data from several studies conducted with animals has raised some controversy regarding the impact of intermittent reinforcement schedules on extinction. According to this reanalysis, resistance to extinction may be *greater* after CRF than after intermittent reinforcement schedules when the behavior involves a "free operant" response—that is, a behavior one can engage in freely, with few or no constraints on the opportunity to act. Probably most behaviors people perform would qualify as free operant responses. On the basis of this reanalysis, some researchers (for example, Epstein, 1992) have recommended that interventions to change most problem operant behaviors in humans use CRF rather than intermittent reinforcement schedules. But applying this recommendation at this time seems premature. A large body of research supports using intermittent reinforcement to promote the persistence of free operant behavior, and Nevin's compelling reanalysis was conducted on only a small number of studies, all of which used rats or pigeons as subjects. To justify changing the current practice of using intermittent schedules to prevent relapses, we would need much more evidence, particularly with human subjects.

Delaying Reinforcement

Reinforcement in everyday life often is delayed. For instance, when you turn in a fine job on an essay exam or a paper, you may not get your A grade for several days or longer. Although immediate reinforcement is important in learning to perform new behaviors, once the behavior has been well established, the delay before reinforcement occurs can be increased without impairing performance. In fact, some evidence indicates that gradually delaying reinforcement of a behavior that is well established can enhance its persistence after an intervention has come to an end (Dunlap & Plienis, 1988; Fowler & Baer, 1981). To use delayed reinforcement in an intervention, wait until the behavior is well established, increase delays gradually, and monitor the person's performance carefully to make sure that improvements in the behavior are not lost. (Go to ✔ .)

Promoting Natural Reinforcement

One of the best ways to prevent relapses is to make sure the target behavior receives reinforcement in the person's everyday environment. **Natural reinforcers** are rewards people receive in their usual life situations. In contrast to the programmed reinforcers used in interventions, natural reinforcers happen spontaneously as a normal part of daily life. Enjoying a TV show is a natural reinforcer for turning on the set, selecting the proper channel, and sitting there to watch. Other examples of natural reinforcers include obtaining needed information by reading some material, receiving praise for good work in school or on a job, absorbing continuous feedback from your senses that your movements in performing a motor action are correct, and having someone laugh at a joke you tell. Interventions generally teach behaviors and skills that are expected to produce natural reinforcers in the person's everyday life.

Behaviors a person acquires in an intervention surely were not sufficiently reinforced in his or her everyday life in the past. If the behaviors had been reinforced, the person would have been performing them already, and the intervention wouldn't have been needed. Studies examining the occurrence of natural reinforcement in daily life have found that desirable behaviors often don't produce the kinds of consequence that would support or maintain them. For instance, observations in elementary and high schools have found that teachers tend to use more reprimands

✓ Concept Check 11.1

1. Regressing into a full-blown pattern of unwanted behavior is called a(n) _____ .
2. In the series of cognitive events leading a person to return to smoking after quitting, a high-risk situation might be _____
   _____ . ⇔
3. Thinning is recommended after a behavior has been well established under a(n) _____ schedule.
4. An everyday example of a variable-ratio schedule that doesn't involve gambling or selling products might be _____
   _____ . ⇔
5. The abbreviation for a reinforcement schedule in which the reward is unavailable for 2 minutes after each reinforcer is given would be _____ .
6. The reinforcement schedule that produces the highest response rate is the _____
   _____ schedule.
7. Temporary halts in responding after receiving rewards are called
   _____ _____ .
8. People don't always show prolonged pauses after reinforcement under a fixed-interval schedule as animals do; this is probably because people's _____
   _____ abilities are different from those of animals.

_____
Answers:

pauses **8.** cognitive/verbal
tances for dates **5.** FI 2-minutes **6.** variable-ratio **7.** postreinforcement
1. relapse **2.** someone offering a cigarette **3.** CRF **4.** asking new acquain-

than praise with their students (Thomas et al., 1978; M. A. White, 1975). If a person whose behavior has been improved in an intervention is returned to an environment that does not reinforce the improved behavior, the gains will be lost.

The importance of natural reinforcers in preventing relapses can be seen in people who have quit smoking. Researchers have found that the efforts to abstain of individuals who continue not to smoke after quitting receive more reinforcement and less punishment from their spouses than the efforts of individuals who relapse (Mermelstein, Lichtenstein, & McIntyre, 1983). Because natural reinforcement of the improved behavior is so important in maintaining it, behavior change programs should include procedures that promote its occurrence and effects. Let's see how this can be done.

Applying Natural-like Reinforcers

Ending an intervention involves a transition to naturally occurring reinforcers. A behavior change program can help a person to make this transition by applying natural-like reinforcers in the intervention. For instance, social reinforcers, such as praise, are among the most common types of reinforcer in daily life. Deliberately programming and applying social reinforcers in an intervention is likely to ease the per-

Being praised for one's good work is a natural reinforcer people often experience in daily life.

son's transition to his or her natural environment. This is one reason for the frequent inclusion in behavior change programs of social reinforcers in the techniques used to address the consequences of target behaviors. For example, programs to improve the social behaviors of children have had more mature classmates model, initiate, and praise appropriate social behavior, such as smiling and inviting another child to play (Cooke & Apolloni, 1976; Strain, Shores, & Timm, 1977). To the extent that these positive social behaviors become part of the mutual interactions of the children in class, the behaviors will be maintained by natural reinforcement (Fowler, 1988).

Assessing and Increasing Natural Reinforcement

A critical step in promoting the occurrence of natural reinforcement for the improved behavior is to assess the person's everyday environment for two characteristics. First, the natural environment should provide opportunities to perform the changed behavior so that it can be reinforced (Horner, Williams, & Knobbe, 1985). This is especially important for maintaining alternative responses and newly trained responses to correct behavioral deficits. Second, the environment must provide sufficient natural reinforcement to maintain the target behavior. These characteristics can be assessed in several ways—for example, by doing a functional analysis of the behavior during or soon after the process of ending the intervention (Durand & Carr, 1991; Favell & Reid, 1988; Kohler & Greenwood, 1986). If these assessments indicate that the person's current environment is not likely to maintain the behavior, efforts should be made to modify the environment. One of the best ways to increase the opportunities for the person to perform the changed behavior consists of instructing other people, such as parents and teachers, to make sure these opportunities occur. For instance, teachers of children whose social behaviors have been improved can schedule classroom activities and provide materials that encourage rather than constrain the desired behaviors.

There are basically two approaches for increasing the occurrence of natural reinforcement in the everyday life of someone whose behavior has been changed in an intervention. First, we can train the person to seek out or *recruit* natural reinforcement. Because individuals often fail to get the feedback and praise they need to maintain appropriate behavior, it may be useful to teach them appropriate ways to elicit the reinforcement they need. This approach was used in an intervention to improve the work skills of three mentally retarded individuals in a sheltered workshop (Hildebrand et al., 1990). Training these workers to recognize when they had reached a productivity goal and then ask their supervisors to give them feedback increased the production rates of two of the subjects.

The second approach for increasing natural reinforcement after an intervention involves training others in the person's everyday life to watch for the behavior and reinforce it. Anyone with whom the person has contact regularly can assist in such monitoring and reinforcement, but usually family members and teachers are selected. We can mention three examples. First, programs to improve classroom conduct have included procedures to train teachers in the regular use of token reinforcement in the classroom (Walker & Buckley, 1972; Walker, Hops, & Johnson, 1975). Second, an intervention to improve autistic children's speaking and self-care skills trained the parents in behavioral techniques (Lovaas et al., 1973). Third, a program to reduce a man's pain behaviors suffered a setback because the family reinforced unwanted behaviors that had been virtually eliminated; it was then necessary to train the family to ignore pain complaints and praise motor activities, to prevent resumption of the old patterns (Kallman, Hersen, & O'Toole, 1975). In each of these interventions, training to change the behavior of people in the person's natural environment helped the improved behavior persist.

Calvin and Hobbes   by Bill Watterson

Some individuals may need to recruit natural reinforcement in their daily lives when they perform desirable behaviors.

Promoting Generalization of the Behavior

To assure that a person's improved behavior will persist after an intervention, behavior change programs should include steps to help the response generalize to the antecedents likely to be encountered in everyday life. We saw in Chapter 4 that when individuals learn to perform behaviors in association with specific antecedents, they also tend to make those responses to stimuli that are similar to the antecedents they have learned. This phenomenon is called *stimulus generalization.* Although there are many other forms of generalization (see J. S. Allen et al., 1991), we will focus on eliciting the behavior in a variety of appropriate situations that were not explicitly trained in the intervention.

How well do improved behaviors generalize to everyday appropriate situations? Some behavior change programs have assessed the occurrence of target behaviors in nontrained situations without having included specific steps to promote generalization. Sometimes the behavior did generalize—for example, it occurred in non-trained settings or with different antecedent cues (D. M. Baer, Peterson, & Sherman, 1967; McNeil et al., 1991; Stokes & Baer, 1976). But in other programs, the behavior did not generalize (Guevremont, Osnes, & Stokes, 1988; Hersen, Eisler, & Miller, 1974). Interventions can use several techniques to promote generalization (Landrum & Lloyd, 1992; Stokes & Baer, 1977; Stokes & Osnes, 1988, 1989). Let's see what these techniques are.

Training with Everyday Antecedents

Interventions often occur in settings and with antecedent stimuli that are very different from those the person will need to know how to handle if he or she is to perform the target behavior in everyday life. For instance, the settings in therapists' offices and psychiatric hospitals are quite different from those in clients' natural environments. The greater the differences between intervention and natural settings, the less likely it is that the behavior will generalize. As a result, programs to change behavior need to ensure that training occurs under conditions as similar as possible to those in the person's usual environment (Favell & Reid, 1988; Landrum & Lloyd, 1992; Stokes & Osnes, 1989).

There are three ways of making the intervention and natural conditions similar, thereby promoting generalization of the target behavior. One approach involves fading any prompts used in training a behavior that will not be available in the person's everyday environment. The second way involves conducting some or all of the intervention training in the person's natural environment. For example, a program to improve the strained communication patterns of parents and their adolescent children initially provided training in therapists' offices (Serna at al., 1991). Although the families learned the skills and could demonstrate them when assessed in the office settings, they didn't use skills effectively at home until training was moved to the home situation. Other studies with different behaviors and subjects have also found that carrying out training in settings like those in which the behavior is expected to occur promotes generalization to those situations (Corte, Wolfe, & Locke, 1971; Stark et al., 1986).

In the third approach for making the intervention and natural conditions similar to promote generalization of the target behavior, aspects of the everyday environment are brought into the therapy setting. An intervention used this approach to get autistic children to generalize to the classroom situation appropriate behaviors they were taught individually in a different room (Koegel & Rincover, 1974). These behaviors included looking at the teacher and imitating the teacher's actions upon request. To promote generalization, the training conditions were changed to resemble a classroom more closely by gradually adding other children to the intervention sessions. This procedure was very effective in getting the autistic children to generalize the target behaviors to the classroom. (Go to 📖 .)

Widening Stimulus Control

Another reason for the failure of people's improved behaviors to generalize to everyday life is the tendency of some behaviors to become associated with too small a range of antecedent stimuli in the intervention. For example, suppose a child receives training in naming objects, but only one teacher and one set of materials are used. The stimulus control exerted by that teacher and that set of materials may become very strong because these discriminative stimuli (S^Ds) have been associated with reinforcement frequently and consistently, but other stimuli have not. As a

 Case Study 11.1
Getting Alice to Speak Up in Class

Alice was a very withdrawn, mildly retarded 15-year-old girl who almost never spoke at a level others could hear (as described in Jackson & Wallace, 1974). A program was undertaken to induce Alice to speak up by using tokens to reinforce her when she read words at acceptable loudness levels while sitting inside an enclosed booth in a laboratory. Although the intervention succeeded in the therapy setting, Alice still spoke too softly in the classroom as determined by assessment each day of the intervention. To promote generalization of audible speech, the therapists caused the therapy setting to seem more and more like the classroom by making the following changes during the next 15 training sessions:

1. Two classmates were brought into the laboratory to study silently several feet away from the booth and out of Alice's view while she read words.

2. The side of Alice's booth was opened part way, reducing her privacy.

3. The side of the booth was removed, exposing the teenager to the two classmates who studied silently.

4. The teacher and five students conducted a study period in the laboratory while Alice read words in the booth, still with the side removed.

These steps to promote generalization succeeded. Classroom assessments soon showed Alice speaking at normal loudness levels.

result, the child may respond correctly only when these S^Ds are present and not when other teachers or materials are used. Programs can avoid this kind of problem and promote generalization of the behavior by taking steps to widen stimulus control.

The basic approach to the widening of stimulus control involves incorporating into the intervention a range of antecedent stimuli. More than one teacher can be used, for example, or several sets of materials, multiple activities, or different settings for training. The effects of using this approach were tested in a study of ways to increase the positive comments students made to one another at a residential home for delinquent and disturbed teenagers (Emshoff, Redd, & Davidson, 1976). All the students in the study received token and social reinforcers for making positive comments to a peer during seven 30-minute sessions. Half of the students experienced these sessions with varying antecedent stimuli (trainers, locations, time during the day) and activities (at dinner, for example, or while playing cards, word games, or Ping-Pong). For the remaining students, the sessions always occurred with the same trainer, location, time of day, and activity (Ping-Pong).

To test whether generalization was greater when training was carried out with varied antecedents, positive comments were assessed during other home activities, such as watching TV. Not only did the students who received training with varied antecedents show far more generalization of the behavior to other home activities, but during follow-up assessments in the 3 weeks after the intervention ended, their positive comments continued to occur at higher rates than those with constant antecedents. Other studies with different behaviors and subjects have also found high levels of generalization when the interventions used varied antecedent stimuli (Poche, Brouwer, & Swearingen, 1981; Stokes, Baer, & Jackson, 1974).

The approach of using a range of antecedent stimuli to widen stimulus control has been refined and formalized into a procedure called *general case training* (Albin & Horner, 1988; Horner, Eberhard, & Sheehan, 1986). General case training begins with the specification of the exact situations in which the behavior should occur after the program has ended, as well as the extent to which antecedent stimuli and the person's behavior can be allowed to vary. The next step is to identify a series of teaching examples that sample the full range of stimulus and response variations within each situation in which the behavior should be performed. Finally, one teaches the examples. Studies that have tested the general case training approach have found not only that it promotes the generalization of target behaviors, but it is more effective in promoting generalization than several other commonly used approaches (Ducharme & Feldman, 1992; Horner, Eberhard, & Sheehan, 1986; Neef et al., 1990).

Enhancing Self-Regulation Skills

According to Frederick Kanfer and Laurence Grimm (1980), therapy using behavior change techniques procedes through a series of phases, the last of which focuses on the generalization and maintenance of treatment gains as the culmination of the therapy process, since the overall goal is to help the client become his or her own therapist by extending treatment gains beyond the time limits of therapy and to problems that may occur after termination. (p. 436)

Some research suggests that enhancing individuals' abilities to direct and modulate their own target behavior—their *self-regulation* skills—tends to promote generalization of that behavior to everyday life.

In one study, emotionally disturbed adolescents were trained to increase their on-task behavior in the classroom and decrease socially undesirable behavior, such as fighting and cursing (Ninness et al., 1991). The behavior change program included modeling, reinforcement, and self-management techniques. After 5 weeks of training, the students' classroom conduct had improved substantially, and the improvement generalized to between-class periods when the students were asked to apply the self-management skills, such as self-monitoring, they had learned. In another study, adults and adolescents received participant modeling treatment to reduce their fear of snakes (Bandura, Jeffery, & Gajdos, 1975). Some of them spent an additional hour on their own handling the snake. Follow-up assessments revealed that compared with individuals who received participant modeling alone, those who spent time with the snake on their own reported greater reductions in a number of other, nontreated fears. These results suggest that interventions that give individuals opportunities to self-regulate their behavior promote generalization.

One additional point should be made about promoting the generalization and persistence of improved behavior: the techniques we've examined can be used in combination. One example of a program that combined these techniques was aimed at improving institutionalized adolescents' social skills, such as waiting to ask for materials and not interrupting others (Foxx, Faw, & Weber, 1991). This program faded the prompts that were used in training, widened stimulus control by training for a variety of social antecedents the teenagers were likely to encounter, thinned the monetary reinforcement given for attendance and performance at training sessions, and used some self-management techniques, such as self-monitoring.

Posttreatment Programs

Many people think of emotional and behavioral problems in the same framework they use in thinking about infectious illnesses: when you're sick, you become cured—free of the infection—by killing the microorganisms that caused the illness. Emotional and behavioral problems don't really conform to this view, however, partly because they usually result mainly from our learning, and we remember what we've learned. Even after an unwanted operant or respondent behavior has been extinguished and replaced, we retain the memory of the behavior (Bouton & Swartzentruber, 1991; LeDoux, 1994). This means there's always some risk of relapsing into the unwanted behavior. If we recognize this and prepare for the possible return of the behavior, it may be possible to head off a relapse.

There are two main approaches for heading off relapses, and each involves some form of posttreatment program. In one approach, the person participates in a **booster program**—that is, a set of additional intervention phases or sessions to shore up or refresh the original program's effects. These phases or sessions usually are similar to the original ones, and the person may need to participate in them periodically, perhaps every few months. Stan Paine and his colleagues (1982) used a booster program to refresh the training socially withdrawn school children received in an intervention that reinforced social behaviors with tokens. Because the children's improved social behavior tended to decline after the original training, the intervention was reintroduced three times as separate phases, with reversal phases in between. Across successive intervention phases, the children lost less and less of the improved behavior during the reversal phases and continued to show social behaviors that were within the normal range after the booster program ended. Other booster programs also have been successful, enhancing the maintenance of such new habits such as assertiveness, reduced drinking, and improved classroom conduct (Baggs & Spence, 1990; Connors, Tarbox, & Faillace, 1992; Maletzky, 1974).

The second approach, called the **relapse prevention method**, is based on G. Alan Marlatt's view that relapses develop through a series of cognitive events that often accompany the occurrence of a lapse. We saw earlier that these events lead to the abstinence violation effect, in which feelings of guilt and reduced self-efficacy after a lapse can precipitate a relapse (Marlatt & Gordon, 1980; Marlatt & Parks, 1982). The relapse prevention approach is basically a self-management program that is supervised by a therapist. A typical program consists of having the person take the following steps:

1. *Learn to identify high-risk situations* by generating a list and descriptions of antecedent conditions in which lapses are most likely to occur.

2. *Acquire competent and specific coping skills* through training in specific behaviors and thought patterns that will enable the person to deal with high-risk situations and avoid lapses.

3. *Practice effective coping skills in high-risk situations* under a therapist's supervision. For example, a problem drinker might go with his or her therapist to a bar and practice ways to avoid drinking.

Although the relapse prevention method was developed originally to address the high relapse rates often seen among participants in programs to reduce substance abuse, it has been applied to other behavior problems, too. (Go to ✔ .)

Application Exercise

Programs to change behavior should include techniques to help maintain behavior changes produced in the intervention. In this application exercise, we will generate

✓ Concept Check 11.2

• •

1. A natural reinforcer people might receive after starting an exercise program and becoming more physically fit is _____ . ⇔

2. One way to promote the generalization of the training given to institutionalized alcoholics to enhance their ability to refuse drinks at a party might be to _____
_____ . ⇔

3. The formal procedure for widening stimulus control is called _____
_____ .

4. If you provided treatment phases or sessions after an intervention had ended, you'd be using a(n) _____ to head off a relapse.

5. The first step in the relapse prevention approach is to have the person _____
_____ .

_____

Answers: case training   **4.** booster program   **5.** learn to identify high-risk situations
1. compliments   **2.** simulate a party atmosphere during training   **3.** general

• •

a set of methods you may want to include in your self-management program to maintain the changes it produces.

Tips on Maintaining Behavior Changes

We have discussed several ways in which interventions can help individuals maintain behavior changes when the intervention is over. Here are some tips to consider for your self-management program.

1. Try to focus interventions on target behaviors that will be useful in your natural environment, thereby leading to posttreatment reinforcement.

2. Train the target behavior(s) with a variety of antecedent stimuli that are likely to be encountered in the natural environment. If possible, start the training with simple tasks—for example, beginning with antecedents that are easy to discriminate—and then progress to harder ones.

3. Monitor the behavior very carefully upon fading prompts, thinning reinforcement, or introducing other procedural changes.

4. Thin the reinforcement gradually, preferably with the goal of establishing a variable schedule.

5. Assess the likelihood of natural reinforcement for the target behavior(s) before the intervention ends.

6. Make sure you will have opportunities to perform the target behavior in your everyday life.

The Next Steps in Your Program Design

Doing the tasks in this application exercise will enable you to add techniques to your program design to help maintain behavior changes. You probably won't have time to include the techniques in the intervention before the end of this course, but you can continue your self-management project after the course has ended and introduce them at that time. In the tasks presented in Work Sheet 11.1, you will develop plans for methods you can use later.

Summary

Although some behavior changes produced in interventions are permanent, other changes are not. Relapses in behavior are not unusual. They occur partly because as a rule, the former behavior has been learned very thoroughly and the likelihood of encountering the old antecedent cues and chains again often is high. Sometimes the behavioral improvements the intervention produced are not learned strongly enough. And cognitive factors can lead to a relapse. For example, encountering a high-risk situation may lead to a lapse, which in turn can lead to the abstinence violation effect, a series of negative thoughts and feelings; and this constellation of events can precipitate a relapse.

Thinning the reinforcement to an intermittent reinforcement schedule tends to make the behavior more persistent. In ratio schedules, the occurrence of reinforcement is based on the number of correct responses made. For each instance of reinforcement, a fixed-ratio (FR) schedule requires a constant number of responses, but in a variable-ratio (VR) schedule, the required number of responses is unspecified and changing. In interval schedules, rewards are given following the first correct response after an interval of time has elapsed. For each instance of reinforcement, a fixed-interval (FI) schedule sets a constant length of time during which the reward is not available, but a variable-interval (VI) schedule makes rewards unavailable for an unspecified and changing period of time. While reinforcement schedules are in force, ratio schedules produce very high rates of response, especially if the schedule uses variable ratio reinforcement. Fixed-ratio schedules produce post-reinforcement pauses in responding. If the number of responses required for each instance of reinforcement becomes too large, there may be deterioration in the behavior due to ratio strain. Interval schedules produce moderate response rates, with cumulative graphs of responses showing a scalloping pattern. The presence of scalloping in the graphs of human subjects appears to be affected by cognitive factors.

Natural reinforcers occur as a normal part of everyday life and can play an important role in maintaining changes in behavior. Before an intervention ends, the person's natural environment should be assessed to determine whether natural reinforcers are likely to maintain behavior or whether they will need to be enhanced. To help prevent relapses, programs can promote generalization of the behavior by conducting training with everyday antecedents and with a variety of stimuli and situations. Booster programs and relapse prevention methods are post-treatment approaches for maintaining behavior changes.

Key Terms and Review Questions

Key Terms

relapse

abstinence violation effect

intermittent reinforcement schedule

ratio schedules

fixed-ratio

variable-ratio

interval schedules

fixed-interval

variable-interval

postreinforcement pauses

ratio strain

natural reinforcers

booster program

relapse prevention method

Review Questions

1. How are relapses different from lapses? Why do relapses occur?

2. Define "intermittent reinforcement schedules," and describe how ratio and interval schedules differ.

3. What is an FR schedule? Give an example from your everyday life that doesn't involve piecework.

4. What is a VR schedule, and how is it different from an FR schedule?

5. Explain what an FI schedule is, and give two examples from everyday life that are not in the text.

6. Explain what a VI schedule is, and give two examples from everyday life that are not in the text.

7. What are duration schedules, and how are they different from interval schedules?

8. Describe the effects of ratio schedules of reinforcement on behavior.

9. Describe the effects of interval schedules of reinforcement on behavior.

10. What is ratio strain?

11. How are natural reinforcers important in maintaining a behavior change?

12. Describe how interventions can promote generalization of the target behavior.

13. Describe the research by Emshoff, Redd, and Davidson (1976) on generalization. What do the results mean?

14. Describe the two main approaches for heading off relapses after an intervention ends.

Related Readings

Horner, R. H., Dunlap, G., & Koegel, R. L. (Eds.) (1988). *Generalization and maintenance: Lifestyle changes in applied settings*. Baltimore: Paul H. Brookes.

Landrum, T. J., & Lloyd, J. W. (1992). Generalization in social behavior research with children and youth who have emotional or behavioral disorders. *Behavior Modification, 16,* 593–616.

Marlatt, G. A., & Parks, G. A. (1982). Self-management of addictive behaviors. In P. Karoly & F. H. Kanfer (Eds.), *Self-management and behavior change: From theory to practice*. New York: Pergamon Press.

Stokes, T. F., & Osnes, P. G. (1989). An operant pursuit of generalization. *Behavior Therapy, 20,* 337–355.

Name _____   Day & time
                                    class meets_____
Date _____

Chapter 11: Work Sheet 11.1

1. Describe specifically how you might thin the reinforcement you have designed for your program after using a CRF schedule. Indicate what the steps will be and what final reinforcement schedule you would like to reach before discontinuing the program.

2. Estimate the number of opportunities per week you're likely to have to perform the target behavior(s) upon completion of the intervention. Your functional analysis and baseline data may help. If you don't expect many opportunities, what can you do to increase them?

3. Describe some natural reinforcers you're likely to encounter for performing the target behavior(s) in your everyday life. Do you think they'll be sufficient to maintain the behavior? Are these reinforcers the same ones you've received for those behaviors before? If so, why didn't they maintain the behavior then?

4. Look back though the material in this chapter on promoting generalization of the behavior. Describe specifically how you could apply two of these techniques to your program.

5. Describe how you could apply a booster program or a relapse prevention program to maintain your improved behavior and prevent a relapse.

NOTE: If you will be submitting work sheets to your instructor or to a fellow student, make a copy of each sheet before submitting it.

12

Research Methods in Behavior Modification

Prologue

Each semester, students in Mrs. Quinn's fifth-grade classes try to improve their public speaking skills by giving short speeches. In one semester, a boy named Cassius was doing poorly in the first week of these activities, performing at a much lower level than any of his classmates. Because Mrs. Quinn wanted very much to have all her students do well, she met with the boy individually to provide training in several areas. The teacher identified certain behavioral deficits in the way her student introduced and ended his speeches—for instance, his failure to smile or look at the audience—and trained him in doing these things. And she addressed another deficit by giving Cassius a few specific rules for organizing speeches, such as "Present an overview first" and "Cover the topics in the stated order." Mrs. Quinn's techniques included verbal prompts, modeling, and token and praise reinforcers. After just three individual sessions in the first week, the grades Cassius received on his classroom speeches were higher than the class average.

Did the student's improved grades result from the intervention techniques Mrs. Quinn used? Although it's very tempting to think that they did, other factors might have been responsible. For instance, maybe Cassius started out with good speaking skills, but illness or difficulties at home impaired his performance in the first week and ended soon after. Or maybe his speeches improved because his parents helped him compose them. Or maybe he hadn't done any preparation for his speeches in the first week but became motivated to work on them in the second week because of the individual attention he was getting. And maybe the boy's performance didn't really improve at all, but the teacher perceived better skills because she believed her methods would work. Since in this case the improved grades could have resulted from any of these reasons and many others, the question of whether the intervention produced the changes cannot be answered with certainty.

In evaluating the success of a program to change behavior, we can have two purposes in mind. First, we are likely to want to know whether the behavior has changed. We saw in Chapter 10 that we can do a graphic analysis to make such a determination. Second, we may want to know *why* the behavior changed. Research in behavior modification is designed to demonstrate unambiguously that changes in the behavior resulted from the intervention's techniques, rather than from some other factors. This chapter focuses on this second purpose and describes various research methods used in demonstrating that the techniques in the intervention, rather than other factors, were responsible for any changes we observe in the behavior.

Accuracy of the Data

To evaluate clearly whether behavior changes have occurred and, if so, why, we must have data that accurately reflect the status of the behavior. Problems of several types can reduce the accuracy of the data collected in a program of behavior modification.

Sources of Data Inaccuracies

Suppose Vera is trying to control her weight, but the bathroom scale she uses to monitor her progress gives widely different readings, even when her true weight hasn't changed. For instance, when she got on and off the scale three times in row without doing anything to change her true weight, the scale read 148, 153, and 145. Because the scale doesn't give the same reading each time the same poundage is weighed, Vera's weight data are *unreliable*. The source of these inaccuracies lies in the measuring instrument—the scale. If the data vary unpredictably, there isn't any good way to decide which reading is correct. Sometimes people in everyday life simply decide that the correct reading is the one that pleases them. Beth Sulzer and G. Roy Mayer (1972) described how a dieting woman they knew would get on and off her unreliable scale repeatedly until the reading pleased her. Then she would walk away smiling and thinking, "The diet is working." Deluding oneself doesn't make the data any more accurate. Of course, measurement accuracy is never perfect, but variations from the true reading should be very slight or rare. Whenever possible, unreliable instruments should be replaced or corrected.

Assessments of behavior can be unreliable, too. Indirect assessment methods can lead to inaccuracies in assessing behavioral changes for at least three reasons. First, some indirect assessments measure the outcomes of behavior, not the target behavior itself. For example, part of an intervention to reduce cash register shortages resulting from theft or careless change-counting by store cashiers consisted of assessing discrepancies between sales receipts and cash in the register (Marholin & Gray, 1976). While the intervention was in force, these discrepancies decreased. But this doesn't necessarily mean that accidental or deliberate change-counting errors had been reduced. As the researchers noted, it may be

> that the victim became the customer instead of the employer; i.e., the employees resorted to short-changing the customer rather than taking money directly from the cash register. Another possibility is that the cashiers may have increasingly been underringing sales. (pp. 28–29)

Given the procedures used in this intervention, the underlying target behavior may not be reflected in the data collected. Second, when indirect assessment methods involve rating scales or questionnaires, the data are likely to be unreliable if the questions or labels they use can be interpreted in different ways. Third, data from self-report instruments depend on people's memories, which can be faulty. Reports about a specific event can vary from one assessment to another because what people remember about it can change.

Direct assessment methods of behavior can produce unreliable data for several reasons. For one thing, as we saw in Chapter 3, people's behavior can be affected by *reactivity;* that is, actions may change when individuals know they are being observed (C. G. Baum, Forehand, & Zegiob, 1979; Monette, Sullivan, & DeJong, 1990). These effects often are temporary, perhaps occurring during just a few initial observations, and they tend to disappear as the person becomes accustomed to being observed. When reactivity occurs, the assessments will either over- or underestimate the behavior during those observations, making the data less reliable across time periods. As an example, reactivity may reduce a behavioral excess during baseline, but disappear by the time the intervention starts. If there is reason to think reactivity has been occurring, it is usually a good idea to keep collecting baseline data until the data stabilize.

Three other problems can lead to unreliable data (Hawkins & Dotson, 1975; Sulzer & Mayer, 1972). First, the *definition of the target behavior* may be unclear. When the operative definition is stated vaguely or incompletely, it is hard for an observer to be sure whether or to what extent the behavior occurred. Second, the *observer* may not have received enough training and practice or be sufficiently motivated to watch for the behavior carefully and to detect and record the behavior accurately. Third, *detectability* may be impaired because the behavior is very subtle or because distractions or other factors interfere with the observation process. Although we can reduce many of these problems by clarifying the definitions of behaviors, providing sufficient training, and removing distractions, we may not eliminate them entirely. As a result, it is often important to assess the reliability of the data.

Assessing Data Reliability

Assessing the accuracy of data collected should begin while observers are being trained and should continue throughout baseline and intervention phases of behavior change programs. The general approach for assessing data accuracy involves evaluating the degree of consistency in the records collected by two or more observers, and the degree of consistency it reveals is called **interobserver reliability** (or *interrater reliability* or *interobserver agreement*). Observer consistency or reliability is not exactly the same as accuracy, but data are more likely to be reliable if they are accurate. To assess interobserver reliability, you must have the observers collect data simultaneously for the same behaviors. You must also make sure the observers record their data independently, without being able to tell what data are being recorded by any other observer at any given time. Although there several ways to evaluate the consistency of the data different observers have collected, two methods are especially common (Foster & Cone, 1986).

In the *session totals method* of assessing interobserver reliability, all the data collected by each of two observers in an observation session or period are added, the smaller total is divided by the larger, and a percentage of agreement or consistency is obtained by multiplying by 100. For example, suppose Todd and Kim observed and recorded a worker's frequency of complimenting customers for an entire day at work. Todd recorded 40 acts of complimenting, and Kim recorded 36. You would divide 36 by 40 (which equals 0.90), and multiply by 100, which yields 90% agreement. What does this percentage mean?

Interobserver reliability evaluated with the session totals method should be interpreted with caution. Although the percentage gives us a sense of the extent of overall agreement for the amount of complimenting Todd and Kim observed the worker perform, it does not mean that they both recorded the same 36 compliments, with Todd seeing 4 additional instances that Kim missed. It is possible that

Two or more observers may not always agree on what they have just experienced. To ensure that observers' assessments of behavior are dependable, researchers use procedures to evaluate interobserver reliability.

Todd was mistaken about the 4 extra ones. And it is possible that the worker actually made 50 compliments, and only 30 of them were seen by both Todd and Kim. Still, a percentage as high as 90% gives us reason to believe that the total number of acts recorded is a reliable estimate of the actual behavior, even though the observers may have disagreed on some individual instances.

The Todd and Kim example used frequency data. But the session totals method can also be used with other types of data, such as duration or magnitude. For instance, Tim Wysocki and his colleagues (1979) used this method to compare the total points awarded by observers to 12 individuals for the intensity and duration of their exercising. As an example, someone who ran a mile in about 9 minutes got

4.0 points, and someone who swam 200 yards in 4 minutes got 1.5 points. To calculate the percentage of agreement, the smaller number of points given by two observers for an individual's exercising was divided by the larger and multiplied by 100. Across all individuals, agreements ranged from about 83% to 100%. In this study, interobserver reliability evaluations with two observers were done for about one-fourth of the observations. Assessing data reliability on only some of the possible observations is a fairly common practice, but to get a representative sample of the behavior, the number of observations should be both substantial and distributed evenly over the duration of the study.

The second commonly used approach for assessing interobserver reliability is the *interval recording method*. We saw in Chapter 3 that in interval recording, only one instance of the target behavior is recorded for each particular, specified time interval in an extended observation period, even if many more instances occurred. Let's suppose that Todd and Kim collected their data on the worker's complimenting by using the strategy of interval recording. They watched the worker for 30 minutes and, if an instance of complimenting a customer occurred during each 15-second interval, the observers were supposed to record it. Their records might agree that complimenting occurred in some intervals and disagree with respect to others. To calculate the interobserver reliability with the interval recording method, the number of intervals for which Todd and Kim agreed that a compliment occurred would be divided by the total number of intervals in which their records agreed and disagreed. Suppose that for eight of the intervals, both observers said the worker complimented customers in each interval, but for two intervals there was disagreement (Todd's records saying complimenting occurred in one of the intervals and Kim's saying complimenting occurred in another interval). You would calculate the percentage of agreement by dividing 8 (agree intervals) by 10 (agree + disagree intervals) and multiplying by 100, yielding 80% agreement.

At this point you may be wondering why all the intervals in which Todd and Kim recorded no complimenting are not included in the analysis. After all, they both seemed to agree that the behavior did *not* occur in those intervals. Many researchers do not like to include data for nonoccurrences of the behavior, however, because these data are more likely to be faulty or inaccurate than data for occurrences (Foster & Cone, 1986; Hawkins & Dotson, 1975). For instance, both records might show no complimenting even though it actually occurred if both observers missed seeing it because of a distraction in the environment. By including inaccurate records in assessing interobserver reliability, you would be biasing the evaluation. As a result, the interval recording method generally excludes nonoccurrence data. One exception to this rule occurs when the target is a behavioral excess, such as an emotional reaction, and you need to determine whether the observers agree that the behavior no longer occurs when the antecedent cues are present (Foster & Cone, 1986). In this case, you would use nonoccurrences in place of occurrences in the calculations.

Four additional points can be stated about assessing data accuracy. First, some evidence indicates that letting observers know their records will be checked against those of other observers appears to increase their accuracy (Foster & Cone, 1986). Second, methods that call for the calculation of interobserver reliability can be

✔️ **Concept Check 12.1**

1. An outcome measure of dieting behavior that uses an indirect assessment method is _____ . ⇔
2. A temporary factor that can produce unreliable data in initial observations is called _____ .
3. The degree of consistency in the data collected by two or more observers is called _____ .
4. If you examined two observers' data and divided the smaller number of responses by the larger number of responses they recorded, you'd be using the _____ _____ method of assessing interobserver reliability.
5. The minimum level of reliability that is generally considered acceptable is _____%.

Answers:　1. weight　2. reactivity　3. interobserver reliability　4. session totals　5. 80

used in training observers before they begin to collect data. In one study, observers received training until they showed 90% agreement during three consecutive observation periods (Zohn & Bornstein, 1980). Third, the general rule of thumb is that 80% agreement is the minimum acceptable level of reliability (Sulzer & Mayer, 1972). Fourth, interobserver reliability can be used to assess data accuracy in self-management programs, too, by having one or more observers collect data on the person's behavior to compare against the person's self-monitoring records.

Collecting reliable data is essential in evaluating changes in behavior. Without reliable data, research projects start out with weak foundations and produce ambiguous results that can have more than one plausible interpretation. When research is well designed and conducted, one interpretation of why the changes occurred is clearly more convincing than any other. Research designs can take many different forms, but the most commonly used designs in evaluating behavior changes can be classified into two categories: *intrasubject* research, which focuses on behavioral changes in individual subjects across time, and *group-based* research, which examines changes or differences in behavior across categories or sets of individuals. Sometimes research is conducted simply to determine *whether and to what extent an intervention has changed behavior*, and sometimes it is conducted *to isolate the cause of the change*. The purpose of the research is a major consideration in deciding which type of research design to use. (Go to ✔️ .)

Intrasubject Research

Research using **intrasubject designs**, or *single-subject designs*, examines changes in the behavior of individual subjects across time, while interventions are either in effect or absent (Hilliard, 1993; Monette, Sullivan, & DeJong, 1990). Sometimes intrasubject research is conducted with more than one subject, but the data collected for the target behaviors are typically evaluated for each subject separately, using graphic analysis methods. We will see that there are several types of intrasubject design, and researchers name and describe some of these designs by using the first two letters of the alphabet to signify different phases of the research. The letter *A* indicates a baseline or reversal phase in which the intevention was absent, and the letter *B* symbolizes a phase in which a specific form of intervention was in effect. Other letters, such as *C* or *D*, sometimes are used to indicate phases in which intervention techniques different from those in *B* were in effect.

"AB" Designs

The **AB design** is the simplest type of intrasubject research, consisting of one baseline phase and one intervention phase. We saw an example of an AB design earlier in the program used by Mrs. Quinn to improve the public speaking skills of a student named Cassius. As we noted in that discussion, we cannot determine whether the teacher's intervention was responsible for the boy's improved grades. This is because having just one baseline and one intervention phase doesn't allow us to rule out factors in the person's life other than the intervention that may actually be responsible for behavior changes observed. As a result, the AB design may be useful when the purpose of research is simply to determine the extent to which the behavior changed, but it is less than ideal when we want to isolate the cause of the change.

Drew Erhardt and Bruce Baker (1990) used an AB design to evaluate changes in two 5-year-old hyperactive children after their parents began a training program in behavior modification techniques. The parents were trained in methods of identifying and defining target behaviors, collecting data, determining relevant antecedents and consequences, and applying various types of reinforcement for appropriate behavior. Although the target behaviors observed for each child were somewhat different, noncompliance with adult requests was targeted as a problem behavior for both children. Noncompliance declined modestly and continued to fluctuate for both children across the several weeks of the intervention. Even though this study does not allow us to isolate the causes of the behavior changes, its outcome is important because it provides preliminary evidence that parent training in behavioral methods may be useful in treatment programs for hyperactive children.

Reversal Designs: "ABA" or "ABAB"

Reversal designs involve a series of phases in which an intervention is alternatively present and absent. Two types of reversal design are commonly used. The **ABA design** consists of three phases: baseline, intervention, and reversal—that is, the intervention is withdrawn to reinstate the baseline conditions. The reversal phase allows us to see whether the behavioral changes that occurred during intervention will revert toward baseline levels when the intervention is withdrawn. The **ABAB design** contains four phases: baseline, intervention, reversal, and intervention. By reinstating the intervention, we have another opportunity to observe whether the behavior changes in reponse to the same intervention. Reversal designs have a distinct advantage over AB designs—they can demonstrate increases and decreases in the behavior that correspond to the presence and absence of the intervention. Because these corresponding increases and decreases would be unlikely to result from factors other than the conditions in the research, they provide strong evidence that the intervention *caused* the behavior to change. As a result, reversal designs not only show changes in the behavior, but they indicate why the changes occurred.

To illustrate intrasubject research using an ABAB design, we will describe an intervention to reduce the excessive, loud, and abusive statements of a 58-year-old institutionalized retarded woman named Ruth (Bostow & Bailey, 1969). Her tirades tended to focus on demands for various items, such as articles of clothing or significant objects that she frequently dropped but couldn't retrieve from her wheelchair. Ruth's verbal excesses were particularly severe at mealtimes: she would scream violently when she wanted her meal tray delivered, her tray removed when she was finished, and so on. To reduce the frequency of Ruth's outbursts, the intervention applied two techniques: (1) time out punishment, which involved wheeling the patient to a corner of the room when outbursts occurred and leaving her there for 2 minutes, and (2) differential reinforcement of other behavior (DRO), in which she would receive reinforcers for *not* having an outburst for certain periods of time. The researchers monitored Ruth's outbursts by using a tape recorder that had a device to activate it only when a sufficiently loud noise occurred. As Figure 12.1 shows, the frequency of Ruth's loud vocalizations dropped sharply during both times the intervention was in force and returned to baseline levels during the reversal phase. These data clearly indicate that the combined consequences of time-out and DRO caused the undesirable outbursts to decrease. (Go to 🔍 .)

Multiple-Baseline Designs

Research using **multiple-baseline designs** basically conduct more than one AB design, with all baselines starting together and proceeding simultaneously for a while. Each baseline period continues for a different length of time before the intervention begins. As a result, multiple-baseline designs have three important characteristics. First, there are no reversal phases. This feature makes multiple-baseline designs useful when the behavior change is permanent or when withdrawing the intervention is undesirable. Second, introduction of the intervention is staggered across the separate AB designs. Third, a baseline phase in at least one AB design can overlap an intervention phase in at least one other design. You can see this overlap in the following multiple-baseline design with three AB designs, where

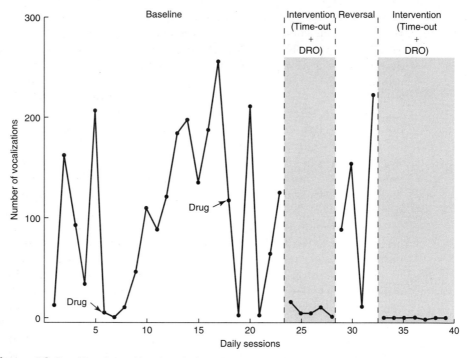

Figure 12.1 Number of loud verbal outbursts (vocalizations) made by a retarded woman named Ruth in each 1-hour observation session in the baseline and intervention phases of a program using the ABAB design. The intervention consisted of time-out punishment for outbursts and differential reinforcement of other behavior (DRO). On two occasions during the baseline phase (labeled "Drug"), Ruth was given a tranquilizer because her tirades had been so extreme. (From Bostow & Bailey, 1969, Figure 1.)

each letter represents a period of time—say, one day—in either the baseline phase (A) or the intervention phase (B):

AB Design #1: **A, B, B, B**

AB Design #2: **A, A, B, B**

AB Design #3: **A, A, A, B**

This overlap enables us to compare the target behavior in baseline with the behavior in the intervention simultaneously within and across designs. The effect of the intervention on the behavior can then be seen by making comparisons with baseline data after the introduction of each intervention phase. Information so obtained reveals how the intervention selectively affects the target behavior in each AB design. Multiple-baseline designs can be carried out across different *behaviors,* individual *subjects,* or *situations.*

🔍 Close-Up 12.1
Problems in Using Reversal Designs

••

Using reversal designs can present two problems for researchers. First, the effect of the intervention may not be fully or substantially reversible. That is, when the intervention is withdrawn, the behavior sometimes does not or cannot revert toward baseline levels. Under such conditions, our ability to interpret the results unambiguously is impaired because we cannot be certain why the behavior changed during the first intervention phase. For example, the target behavior may fail to regress if it has been changed permanently by the original intervention phase, as might occur if the person learned a skill that he or she finds useful in a variety of settings. For example, tennis players who learn effective strategies for performing excellent forehand and backhand strokes are not likely to stop using these strategies just because their trainers stop reinforcing the related behavior.

If we think that the target behavior we plan to change could not be expected to regress when the intervention is withdrawn, we do not use a reversal design. But it is not always possible to predict that an intervention will produce a quick and permanent change in a behavior. For instance, an intervention consisting only of punishment with mild electric shock was used to reduce a 14-year-old boy's frequent and chronic cough (Creer, Chai, & Hoffman, 1977). The cough had become so severe that classmates ridiculed the boy, and he was expelled from school at the request of his teachers. Various therapies had been administered without success, and the boy and his parents agreed to try the shock. The researchers planned to use an ABAB design. During the 1-hour baseline period, the boy coughed 22 times. In intervention, the boy's

> only cough in what was to be the initial . . . intervention phase was followed immediately by a mild (5 mA) electric shock of 1 second duration to the forearm. . . . Because the boy did not cough again for the remainder of the hour or the next 2 hours, a reversal procedure could not be instituted. (p. 108)

The boy returned to school the next day and experienced no recurrence of the chronic cough in follow-up assessments over a 2 1/2–year period.

The second problem researchers can face in using reversal designs is that it may be undesirable or unethical to withdraw an intervention that appears to have produced a beneficial effect. Suppose, for example, that an intervention successfully reduced severe self-injurious behaviors in autistic children. It would not be desirable or ethically appropriate for the researcher to withdraw the treatment to meet the needs of a research design. Fortunately, other intrasubject research designs that do not involve reversal phases may be selected for use in such situations.

••

Multiple Baselines Across Behaviors

The **multiple-baseline, across-behaviors** research design uses separate AB designs for each of two or more different *behaviors* for a single individual in a particular setting. In using this research design, we would monitor simultaneously two or more different behaviors—for instance, a factory worker's frequency of arriving to work on time (determined daily), the number of items made, and the amount of time spent in idle conversation—starting in baseline. Once the baseline data had stabilized for each behavior, we would apply the intervention techniques, such as token reinforcement, to *one* of them. Soon we should see in our graph that this first behavior has changed. When the change is clear, we would apply the intervention to the next behavior, and so on. Because the *only* behavior that changes at any given time is the one newly exposed to the intervention, we could infer with strong certainty that applying the techniques caused the change.

A multiple-baseline, across-behaviors design was used to examine the effects of an intervention to reduce the certainty or conviction a 29-year-old male psychiatric patient expressed regarding three delusional beliefs he had (Lowe & Chadwick, 1990). For more than 2 years, he had held the beliefs that:

- He was to be married to a woman called Amanda, with whom he had not been in contact for many years, who supposedly was reading his mind and controlling many of the things that happened to him.
- He had been Jesus Christ in a prior life.
- He had been Leonardo da Vinci in a prior life. (p. 466)

A therapist met with him once a week for 90 minutes, during which time the patient rated his conviction regarding each belief on a 0–100% scale. The intervention, which involved logical discussions of the likelihood of each belief being true, was introduced first for the belief about Amanda, then the belief about Jesus, and then the belief about Leonardo. Figure 12.2 depicts the results of this study and the sequencing of the intervention's introduction for each belief. Notice four aspects in the graph. First, the baseline phases started together but lasted for different amounts of time. Second, the man's conviction ratings for the Jesus and Leonardo beliefs were unchanged while the Amanda belief ratings declined. Third, his ratings for the Jesus belief did not diminish until it was subjected to the intervention. Fourth, his ratings for the Leonardo belief began to decline in baseline, paralleling his Jesus ratings. This change probably resulted from response generalization because the Jesus and Leonardo beliefs were so similar. The effects of the intervention would have been clearer if the Leonardo belief had not begun to change in baseline. Although these results indicate that the man's *ratings* of his beliefs changed as a result of the intervention, the actual extent to which he believed his delusional ideas may not have changed, of course.

The target behaviors of research using multiple-baseline, across-behavior designs can vary in the degree to which the behaviors are related or unrelated. Thus, studies have examined the effects of interventions on articulation errors in producing *th* and *z* sounds (Bailey et al., 1971), classroom behaviors of being out of one's seat and making inappropriate statements or sounds (Calhoun & Lima, 1977), and sleeping problems of a child who would not go to sleep on time and insisted on entering her sister's bed (Ronen, 1991). Some of these studies examined several behaviors, not just the two listed, and each specific behavior was observed in a baseline phase and an intervention phase.

Multiple Baselines Across Subjects

The **multiple-baseline, across-subjects** research design uses separate AB designs for each of two or more individual *subjects* for a particular behavior in a particular

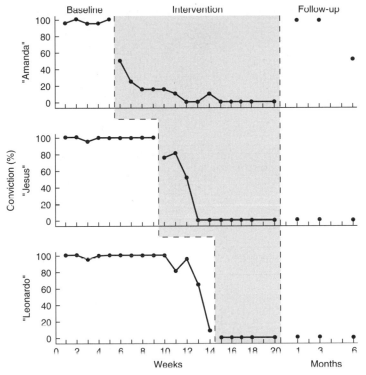

Figure 12.2   Conviction ratings by a psychiatric patient regarding his three delusional beliefs about Amanda, Jesus Christ, and Leonardo da Vinci. The percentages express the degree of certainty he reported for each of the three beliefs. The intervention involved logical discussions of the likelihood of each belief being true. (From C. F. Lowe & Chadwick, 1990, Figure 1.)

setting. In this design, each subject receives a baseline phase and an intervention phase for the same target behavior. Once the baseline data have stabilized for each subject, the intervention is applied to *one* of these individuals. When graphed data indicate that the behavior has changed for this subject, the intervention is applied to the next subject, and so on. Because the *only* subject whose behavior changes at any given time is the person newly exposed to the intervention, we can infer with strong certainty that applying the intervention techniques caused the change.

A study used a multiple-baseline, across-subjects design to examine the effects of an intervention to prevent infection with the human immunodeficiency virus (HIV) among hospital nurses (DeVries, Burnette, & Redmon, 1991). The target behavior was wearing rubber gloves in hospital activities that present a high probability of contact with a patient's body fluids. Wearing gloves reduces the risk of becoming infected with HIV. The intervention, consisting of biweekly performance feedback and encouragement to wear gloves in these high-risk activities, was introduced with one nurse first, then another nurse, and so on. Figure 12.3 illustrates

Figure 12.3 Percentage of occasions on which four nurses wore rubber gloves during 16 consecutive 10-hour shifts when contact with a patient's body fluids was likely. The intervention in this multiple-baseline, across-subjects design involved feedback about the nurses' recent use of gloves and encouragement to wear them more often. Arrows indicate points at which feedback was given by a nurse specializing in the control of the spread of infection in hospitals. (From DeVries, Burnette, & Redmon, 1991, Figure 1.)

the design and results of this study. Notice that the target behavior improved in each nurse only after the intervention was introduced, which indicates that the feedback caused the behavior to change.

Multiple Baselines Across Situations

The **multiple-baseline, across-situations** research design uses separate AB designs for each of two or more different *situations* for a single individual and a specific behavior. In this design the subject receives a baseline phase and an intervention phase in each of two or more situations—for example, in different places or with different people present. As with the other multiple-baseline designs, the baselines in all situations begin at much the same time. Once the baseline data have stabilized in each situation, the intervention is applied in *one* of them. When the change is clear on a graph, the intervention is applied in the next situation, and so on. Because the behavior *only* changes at any given time in the situation with the newly presented intervention, we can conclude that applying the techniques caused the change.

Jack James (1981) conducted a study using a multiple-baseline, across-situations design to test the effects of an intervention of brief (2-second) time-out punishment procedures on a young man's stuttering. In both the baseline and intervention phases, the client talked while a tape recorder was running in one of five situations: in the laboratory talking alone, in the laboratory conversing with a researcher, at home talking with an adult, on the telephone talking with an adult, and in various business settings talking with clerks or agents. The results demonstrated that stuttering decreased in each situation, but only when the time-out consequences were applied there.

We hinted earlier at a potential problem in using multiple-baseline designs: a target behavior may begin to change during a baseline phase, before the intervention has been introduced. This occurred in the study we saw earlier on reducing a patient's ratings of his delusional beliefs—that is, when his conviction regarding one belief (having been Leonardo da Vinci in a past life) began to decline in baseline, paralleling the decline in another belief rating that was currently receiving the intervention. When this happens, we can't be certain why the untreated behavior has begun to decline. Although the study on delusional beliefs used a multiple-baseline, across-behaviors design, similar problems can arise in other multiple-baseline designs. In the multiple-baseline, across-subjects design, changes in the target behavior for the person receiving the intervention may lead to changes in the behavior of other individuals. And in the multiple-baseline, across-situations design, changes in the person's behavior in the situation featuring the introduction of the intervention may lead to changes when the person is in other situations still lacking the intervention. But, even though some potential exists for these problems to arise, they do not seem to be very common.

Changing-Criterion Designs

Another useful approach for demonstrating that intervention techniques have caused changes in a behavior is the **changing-criterion design**. As the name implies, the criterion for successful performance changes over time, usually becoming more rigorous. For instance, when we start the intervention, we may require a fairly lax level of performance for receiving a reward. After the behavior has stabilized at that level, we may raise the criterion to a higher level—and when the behavior stabilizes again, we may raise the criterion again, and so on. If the behavior increases or decreases in accordance with each change in the criterion, we can conclude that the reward is responsible for the behavioral changes.

Rayleen De Luca and Stephen Holborn (1992) used a changing-criterion design to study the effects of a token reinforcement system on 11-year-old obese

Figure 12.4   Mean (average) number of revolutions per minute pedaled on a stationary bicycle by two boys, Paul, who was obese, and Shawn, who was not obese. (Data for four other boys in this study, not included here, showed similar patterns.) A changing-criterion design was used, with each increased criterion (dashed horizontal lines) being set at 15% above the average pedaling rate the boy had achieved in the preceding phase. After the initial baseline phase, token reinforcement was given on increasingly rigorous variable-ratio (VR) schedules. The BL phase is a reversal baseline phase. (From DeLuca & Holborn, 1992, Figure 1.)

and nonobese boys who were supposed to exercise on a stationary bicycle. Once each boy's pedaling rate had stabilized in baseline, the researchers began to reinforce pedaling on a variable-ratio schedule in each 30-minute exercise session. The number of pedaling revolutions required for each instance of reinforcement at the start of the intervention for each boy was set roughly 15% above his average rate in baseline. So, if a boy had pedaled in baseline at the rate of 70 revolutions per minute, the intervention began by requiring an average rate of 80 revolutions per minute. Each subsequent increased criterion for reinforcement was set at 15% above the average pedaling rate achieved in the preceding phase. Whenever a boy earned "a point" token while pedaling, a bell would ring and a light would go on, announcing the success. The tokens could be exchanged later for backup rewards.

Figure 12.4 shows the data for two of the six boys in the exercise bicycle study. Notice how their pedaling increased in accordance with each increase in the criterion for reinforcement. This pattern occurred for all six boys. Although the reversal (BL) phase was not necessary in the design, the corresponding decrease in performance makes the effects of the reinforcement clearer. Other researchers have used changing-criterion designs to study the effects of consequences introduced for meeting or not meeting specific criteria for smoking fewer and fewer cigarettes (Axelrod et al., 1974; Belles & Bradlyn, 1987).

Alternating-Treatment Designs

Alternating-treatment designs (also called *simultaneous-treatment* or *multielement designs*) examine the effects of two or more treatments, each of which is conducted within the same intervention phase with the same person. Although both treatments are applied in the same phase, they are separated in time and alternated. Thus each treatment might be applied on different days or at different times during the day throughout the intervention phase. By examining graphs of the data, we can determine whether one treatment is consistently more effective than another in changing the person's target behavior.

An example of an alternating-treatment design was provided by Frank Kohler and Charles Greenwood (1990), who examined the tutoring behaviors of school children after they had been trained in two tutoring procedures to help classmates in spelling. The *standard tutoring procedure* involved having the tutor give the student feedback and token reinforcers for correct spellings and provide corrective feedback when a word was misspelled. The *modified tutoring procedure* had the tutor use praise and token reinforcers for correct spelling and present corrective feedback as soon as a student gave an incorrect letter in a word. During the intervention phase, the tutors were told which procedure to apply in each tutoring session. The 10-minute tutoring sessions in all phases were observed for instances of a type of tutoring behavior called "help," which involved spelling a word *more than once* during corrective feedback for an error. The training the tutors received had them spell the word only once. Figure 12.5 presents the number of help behaviors per tutoring session by Karen, one of the tutors. Notice that she rarely performed help behaviors in baseline and during the intervention phase when the instructions were to use the standard tutoring procedure. But her help behaviors occurred very frequently

Figure 12.5   Number of "help" behaviors per 10-minute tutoring session by a tutor named Karen, as examined in an alternating-treatment design. Help behaviors were assessed in baseline, under two different tutoring procedures in the intervention phase, and later, when Karen could use the tutoring procedure of her choice. (Data for two other tutors, not included here, showed similar patterns.) (From Kohler & Greenwood, 1990, Figure 2.)

when she was told to use the modified tutoring procedure during intervention. In the "choice" phase, the tutors were allowed to use the procedure of their choice, and she continued to use help behaviors.

Alternating-treatment designs have two principal advantages. First, as in some other designs, no reversal phases are needed. Second, two or more treatments can be compared to see whether one is more effective than another. But a problem can arise in alternating-treatment designs that cannot happen with other designs: the effects of the treatments may "interact"—for example, if a person receives two treatments, the effect of one of the treatments may be influenced by its being contrasted with the second treatment (Barlow & Hayes, 1979; Hains & Baer, 1989). If only one of these treatments had been implemented during the intervention, its effects on behavior might have been different. (Go to ✔ .)

Group-Based Research

Most research on learning and psychology is *group-based*, with observations taken on large numbers of individuals, instead of just one or a few. In group-based research, the data for the subjects are combined, rather than examined separately.

✔ Concept Check 12.2

1. Studies that examine changes in the behavior of individual subjects across time are examples of _____ designs.
2. Isolating the causes of changes in behavior is especially difficult in intrasubject research when a(n) _____ design is used.
3. A preschool child's behavior that might not regress when a reversal phase is in effect is _____
   _____ . ⇔
4. Research that begins an intervention to improve three different job skills in a single individual at work would be using a(n) _____
   _____ design.
5. A potential problem with multiple-baseline designs is that the behavior may begin to change during _____ .
6. In a changing-criterion design seeking to determine the effects of rewards on lifting weights in an exercise program, you might change the criterion by requiring more _____ . ⇔

Answers:

1 intrasubject 2. AB 3. learning to play with other children 4. multiple-baseline, across-behaviors 5. baseline, before the intervention 6. weight/repetitions

Combining data is usually accomplished by computing the average, or *mean*, across the subjects. These means are then compared. Keep in mind, however, that the behavior of any specific individual in a group of subjects may be very different from the *average* response across the group. Still, research with many subjects is very useful in showing effects that may apply to a wide range of individuals and can be conducted as within-subjects designs and between-subjects designs.

Within-Subjects Designs

We saw in Chapter 1 that *within-subjects designs* test many individuals in more than one condition of the study. The data collected for all subjects are combined for each condition, and then the combined data are compared. In research conducted to examine the effects of methods for changing behavior, these designs are generally structured like intrasubject designs, with all subjects being observed in each phase of the design. As with intrasubject designs, the success of the methods in changing behavior is usually evaluated by doing a graphic analysis. Let's see how this approach works.

Dennis Upper (1973) performed a study using a within-subjects design with 30 patients in a psychiatric hospital. A token system had already been established in a ward of the hospital to reinforce self-care and sociable behaviors, but the patients had been violating ward rules that were not part of the reinforcement program. The rule violations included spitting on the walls or floor, sleeping in unauthorized areas, engaging in indecent exposure, and stealing. To decrease rule violations, consequences of obeying the rules were added to the existing token system: the patients earned 15 tokens each day for not violating any of the specified rules, but those who violated rules were fined from 3 to 15 of those possible tokens per infraction, depending on its severity. Patients who lost more than 15 of those tokens had to pay tokens they had earned under the original token system. This study had an AB design structure, with a baseline phase and an intervention phase, but the data were combined across all 30 subjects by calculating the *average* number of tokens per patient that the members of the group lost as fines for their violations. Figure 12.6 shows that the average fines for each week declined markedly across the 8 intervention weeks.

Within-subjects designs can follow the structure used in any of the intrasubject designs we have considered. For instance, a study used a within-subjects design that was structured like an ABAB design to examine the effects of a peer tutoring program to improve low-performing students' arithmetic skills (Pigott, Fantuzzo, & Clement, 1986). The peer tutoring intervention greatly increased the students' average number of correctly calculated arithmetic problems compared with their averages for baseline and reversal phases. Also, Elizabeth Barton and her colleagues (1970) used a multiple-baseline, across-behaviors design to examine the effects of a time-out intervention on undesirable mealtime behaviors of 16 retarded individuals. Each target behavior (stealing food, eating with fingers, and so on) improved across the group of subjects when the intervention was applied to it.

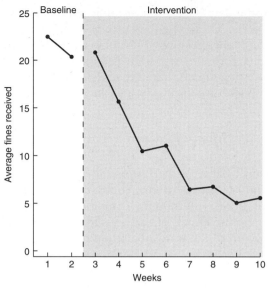

Figure 12.6   Average number of tokens taken per week in fines from 30 psychiatric patients during baseline and intervention phases for infractions of ward rules. (Data from Upper, 1973, Table 2.)

Between-Subjects Designs

Between-subjects designs involve collecting data on the behavior of many subjects who are separated into two or more groups. The data for all subjects in each group are then combined by calculating the mean score, and the groups' means are compared to determine whether there is any substantial difference. To evaluate whether two or more means differ, researchers compute complex statistics to use in evaluating the "significance" of the difference. A *significant difference* indicates that given the pattern of data in each of the groups, the difference in the mean scores is sufficiently great that it probably is not attributable to chance or accident. Keep in mind that the term "significant" describes a mathematical concept and doesn't mean "important." It is possible to find a statistically significant difference in the data for two or more groups even if the problem being studied is trivial.

Separating the subjects into groups can be accomplished in more than one way, and the method chosen can determine whether the research is viewed as an *experiment* or as a *quasi-experiment*.

Experiments

An **experiment** is a controlled study in which the researcher manipulates—that is, determines or controls the level of—a variable to examine its effect on another variable. The manipulated variable is called the *independent variable*; the other variable is called the *dependent variable* because its value is expected to *depend* on the manipulated level of the independent variable. In behavior modification research, the independent variable is typically an intervention or behavior change technique, and the dependent variable is the target behavior.

Our description of experiments will focus on the simplest and very commonly used form that has two groups of subjects: one group receives the intervention and is called the *experimental group*; the other group does not receive the intervention and is called the *control group*. By administering the intervention to one group but not the other, the researcher is manipulating the independent variable. To separate the subjects into these two experimental sectors, the researcher assigns the individuals *randomly* to one group or the other. The term "random" means that the assignment of each individual is determined by chance alone. One way to assign the subjects randomly is to write each name on a card, shuffle the deck thoroughly, and draw cards from the deck without looking. The first name drawn would be assigned to one group, the second name to the other group, and so on. This process distributes personal characteristics of the subjects in an unbiased manner and tends to produce groups that, overall, are very similar with respect to their abilities and other characteristics that might affect their performance in the research. As a result, these characteristics usually will have about the same impact on the subjects' behavior in each group, thereby making the independent variable responsible for, or the *cause* of, any differences observed in the dependent variable. Because in experiments researchers manipulate the independent variable while controlling other variables that are not being studied, such as personal characteristics of the subjects, *cause–effect* relationships between variables can be discovered.

Thomas Burling and his colleagues (1991) conducted an experiment with a between-subjects design to assess the effects of an intervention to induce pregnant women to stop smoking for their own health and that of their babies. The 139 women in the study, outpatients at a medical clinic, were randomly assigned to two groups. Seventy women were assigned to the experimental group and received standard prenatal care, including antismoking information, plus additional antismoking materials and a personal letter stating that "abnormalities in the chemistry of your blood . . . pose a risk to both you and your unborn child. This abnormality will disappear if you stop smoking." The 69 women in the control group received only the standard prenatal care. Although most of the women in both groups did not quit smoking, the number of subjects who quit was significantly greater in the experimental group than in the control group.

Another experiment using a between-subjects design was performed by Nathan Azrin and Alan Peterson (1990) to test the effects of an intervention to reduce motor and vocal tics in patients with a neurological disease called Tourette's syndrome. The intervention applied the method of habit reversal, which consists of several techniques, such as competing response practice and relaxation training. The subjects, recruited through newspaper articles and an association for people with Tourette's syndrome, were randomly assigned to the experimental group and a *waiting-list control* group, with five subjects in each. Waiting-list control groups are frequently used in clinical research; for these subjects, the intervention is postponed until it has been shown to be clearly successful in the experimental group. Statistical analyses were carried out on data collected in the 3 months when the habit reversal treatment was in effect for the experimental group, but not the control group. These analyses revealed that subjects in the experimental group had significantly fewer tics per month than the subjects in the control group.

Quasi-Experiments

Sometimes researchers who perform studies with between-subjects designs, are unable to randomly assign subjects to groups. Random assignment may not be feasible for many reasons. For instance, a researcher may want to see how changes in the living environments at a nursing home would affect the residents' behavior. To randomly assign the subjects to the changed environments would require relocating the residents to different living quarters—a procedure that is unlikely to be strategically or ethically acceptable. Or a researcher examining the role of an existing variable may use the variable itself to categorize subjects into one of two or more groups: male and female adults, for example, or delinquent and nondelinquent teenagers. Studies of this type are called **quasi-experiments**—they "look" like experiments because they have separate groups of subjects, but they are not: the variable that forms the groups—such as gender or living quarters—is not manipulated, and the subjects who participate in the study cannot be randomly assigned to the groups (C. J. Goodwin, 1995; Monette, Sullivan, & DeJong, 1990). As a result, we cannot arrive at cause–effect conclusions from the data, even if the behavioral differences between the groups are huge.

Quasi-experiments are very common in psychological research. For instance, many studies have been done to determine whether meditation techniques enable individuals to achieve states of profound rest. In the typical between-subjects design, subjects are selected and assigned to two groups: experienced meditators and nonmeditators. The subjects' physiological arousal is then assessed while the meditators practice meditation and the nonmeditators simply try to rest. Reviews of these studies have revealed no consistent differences in blood pressure, heart rate, or respiration rate between the meditating and the resting subjects (D. S. Holmes, 1984; Lichstein, 1988). But the quasi-experimental nature of these studies leaves open the possibility that the failure to find consistent differences in arousal may be due to other differences between individuals who do and do not meditate.

Evaluating the Resulting Changes in Behavior

Researchers assessing the effects of intervention techniques on behavior have two main goals. First, they want to know whether the techniques they applied were responsible for the changes in the subjects' target behaviors. This goal was an important focus of the research designs we have just considered. Second, researchers want to evaluate the effectiveness of the techniques. An enormous variety of interventions have been tested in clinical research, some using behavior modification techniques and some using other approaches. Not all interventions have been effective, and occasionally they seem to have made behavioral or emotional problems worse (Bangert-Drowns, 1988; Shaffer et al., 1990). In our efforts to evaluate interventions and the behavioral changes they produce, we need to consider more than whether prominent graphical or statistical differences were found between conditions when the intervention was present than when it was absent. We also need to evaluate interventions on the basis of several other perspectives or dimensions.

Dimensions of Evaluation

In addition to graphical or statistical differences, three dimensions are commonly used to evaluate the effectiveness and usefulness of intervention techniques. These dimensions consider the *generalization and durability* of the behavioral changes in the person's natural environment, the *amount and importance of the changes* to the person's everyday life and functioning, and the *costs and benefits* of the intervention.

Generalization and Durability of the Changes

For a behavior change intervention to be viewed as effective and useful, the improved behavior must generalize to the person's natural environment, and it must be durable. Thus someone who has mastered a relaxation technique and learned to use a rapid relaxation induction method must be able to apply these skills as the need arises in everyday anxiety-provoking situations. Similarly, someone who has learned how to avoid antecedents that lead to an unwanted behavior, such as smoking or drinking, must continue to use these skills in his or her usual environment. We considered the importance of generalization and durability in Chapter 11 and described methods programs can use to enhance these outcomes.

When ending an intervention, it is often a good idea to phase it out, by thinning reinforcement schedules, for example, or by withdrawing some techniques earlier than others. Gradually withdrawing behavior change techniques offers two potential benefits. First, it tends to promote generalization and durability of the improved behavior. Second, the target behavior can be monitored during this process to assess the degree to which each component of the program is critical for maintaining the behavior after the intervention has ended (Rusch & Kazdin, 1981). To evaluate the durability of a behavioral change, the program must conduct follow-up assessments periodically. Collecting follow-up data will indicate any deterioration in the behavior improved by the intervention. If deterioration is revealed, a posttreatment program may be needed to maintain the behavior.

Amount and Importance of the Changes

The *amount of change* an intervention produces in the person's problem behavior and the *importance of the changes* to the person's everyday life and functioning are critical factors in evaluating a program's effectiveness. These factors can be assessed by considering two outcomes of the behavior change: its clinical significance and its social validity.

The concept of **clinical significance** refers to the degree to which the change in behavior is *meaningful* to the person's life and functioning, where a meaningful change is one that is large and brings the behavior into the *normal range* (N. S. Jacobson, Follette, & Revenstorf, 1984; Speer, 1992). As an example, let's consider the hypothetical case of an 8-year-old boy who stutters, on average, about 10% of the syllables he speaks. Suppose that an intervention reduces the child's stuttering to 6% of his spoken syllables. This would be a large change, but the behavior would not yet be in the normal range. Now suppose that the intervention were continued or strengthened and reduced his stuttering to 3% of his spoken syllables. This level would represent a clinically significant change because it is large *and* the behavior is within the normal range (Gagnon & Ladouceur, 1992). Determining the normal range can be accomplished in two ways. First, prior research may have identified a *norm* for the behavior—that is, its usual level among a large population of individuals of the same age and gender (Trull, Neitzel, & Main, 1988). Second, the researcher may identify and test a control group to assess their average level of the behavior (Dush, Hirt, & Schroeder, 1983).

The second outcome of behavior change that indicates the amount or importance of the change is its **social validity**—that is, the utility and adaptiveness of the change for the person's everyday functioning. According to Montrose Wolf (1978), a behavior change program can be evaluated for social validity by collecting data to answer three questions:

- Are the behavioral goals of the program desired by society and appropriate for the person's life?

- Are the person and significant individuals in his or her life—such as relatives, teachers, or coworkers—satisfied with the amount and utility of the behavioral changes the program has produced?

- Are the treatment techniques and procedures acceptable to the person, significant individuals in his or her life, and the community at large?

Answers to these questions can be obtained in several ways. For instance, we can ask for assessments from relevant individuals—the person and people who, because they have frequent contact with him or her, might be affected by the behavioral changes the program produces (Schwartz & Baer, 1991). We can also have independent judges evaluate the person's behavior after the intervention (Fawcett & Miller, 1975). And we can examine measures of the outcome that show a clear social impact of the changes, such as reductions in the person's drug use or arrests for criminal activity following an intervention to modify delinquent behavior (Bank et

Case Study 12.1

Assessing Social Validity in Reducing a Boy's Tics

Hugh had developed multiple tics at the age of 3 and was 11 years old when he entered a behavioral treatment program to correct this problem (as described in Finney et al., 1983). In the recent months prior to beginning the program, there had been an increase in the frequency and intensity of four tics: head-shaking, head-jerking, mouth-grimacing, and eye-blinking. The intervention, which was based on the habit reversal technique, produced dramatic reductions in each of these tics within several weeks, and follow-up assessments indicated that these decreases were maintained over the next year.

People commonly seek treatment for tics because of the social embarrassment produced by bizarre motor behavior. To evaluate the pro-

gram within a social validity framework, the researchers made videotapes of Hugh during baseline and intervention phases of the treatment. These tapes were rated by two groups of judges: 12 teachers from a junior high school and 36 graduate students in pediatric fields, such as nursing and special education. The judges did not know Hugh; they were chosen because they had regular contact with children of Hugh's age. When the panel rated Hugh's tics, using a 7-point scale (1 = not distracting; 7 = very distracting), the average ratings were as follows: about 6.5 for the baseline tapes and 1.6 for the intervention tapes. This assessment of social validity suggests that Hugh's tics became far less embarrassing as a result of this treatment.

al., 1991). By evaluating the clinical significance and social validity of behavioral changes, we can get a sense of the degree to which the intervention has made a real difference in the lives of the subject, as well as others who are affected by the outcomes of the program. (Go to .)

Costs and Benefits in Producing the Changes

Finally, we can evaluate the effectiveness of an intervention by assessing its **cost–benefit ratio**, or the extent to which the costs of providing the treatment are outweighed by the money saved in the long run (Jospe, Shueman, & Troy, 1991; Kaplan, 1989). In medical settings, for example, studies have shown that providing behavioral interventions to reduce anxiety enables surgery patients to recover more quickly and use less medication than patients who do not receive these interventions (Sarafino, 1994). The financial savings in medical costs far exceed the costs of administering these interventions.

Composing a Report

After an intervention has been completed, the professionals who supervised the project usually write a report to describe the target behavior(s), intervention techniques, and outcomes of the program. Often, these reports are published in professional journals; in other cases, they are kept on file in counseling offices or institutions. The outcomes of the program are presented graphically, showing data

✓ Concept Check 12.3

1. Studies that test many individuals in more than one condition use _____ _____ designs.

2. An independent variable that might be used in a between-subjects design in behavior modification is _____ . ⇔

3. An example you have seen in everyday life of a person being randomly chosen might be _____ . ⇔

4. A group of subjects in an experiment for whom treatment is postponed is called a _____ group.

5. A norm for infant or child motor development might describe the age at which most children _____ _____ . ⇔

6. Determining whether an intervention's treatment procedures are acceptable to the person can be part of an evaluation of a program's _____ .

_____

Answers: 1. within-subjects 2. schedule of reinforcement 3. a lottery drawing 4. waiting-list control 5. start to walk without being supported 6. social validity

from baseline and intervention phases, and in words. When possible, the outcomes should provide data on follow-up assessments, too. (Go to ✓ .)

Application Exercise

This application exercise has two main objectives: you are to learn how to calculate interobserver reliability and to apply hypothetically some of the information on research designs to your self-modification project, to help you understand how these designs are conducted.

Tips on Doing Behavior Modification Research

Some of the research methods used in behavior modification are unique to this field, but other methods are used widely in psychology and other disciplines. Let's look at some tips on doing research in behavior modification.

1. It's important to use more than one observer to collect data on a target behavior; moreover, the observers should work simultaneously and independently. Try to have simultaneous recording for as much of the data as possible—at least 25% is desirable.

2. Let observers know that other observers will be collecting data simultaneously as a check on accuracy.

3. It's important to have a practice period for collecting data before the actual records for research will be collected. Not only is training provided for the observers, but the person under observation has an opportunity to adapt to being watched, thereby reducing subsequent reactivity.

4. Before moving from one phase to another, wait for the behavior to stabilize—or reach a fairly constant level—if possible.

5. When planning to do a research project, consider whether the target behavior is likely to regress if a reversal phase is introduced. If you have reason to suspect that there will be no regression, use a research design other than ABA or ABAB.

Research Designs and Your Self-Management Program

The tasks in this application exercise are designed to help you understand how to use different types of research design and check the accuracy of the data you collect. Turn now to Work Sheet 12.1 to complete these tasks.

Summary

Collecting accurate data is critical in evaluating the success of behavior modification programs, but inaccuracies can be introduced for many reasons. One way to assess the accuracy of collected data is to have a second observer collect data simultaneously and independently from the primary observer and compare the two sets of records. The degree to which the records agree is called interobserver reliability.

Research using intrasubject designs examines behavioral changes over time in one subject at a time, while interventions are either in force or absent. Intrasubject designs include the AB, ABA, and ABAB types. The AB designs, which consist of a baseline phase and an intervention phase, do not indicate unequivocally whether the intervention caused changes in the behavior. Reversal designs yield stronger evidence than AB designs for cause–effect links between interventions and changes in behavior, but only for target behaviors that regress upon introduction of a reversal phase.

Multiple-baseline designs start baselines simultaneously but begin the interventions in sequence, thereby showing patterns of change in the behavior that correspond to the introduction of the intervention. Such approaches can be applied as three different designs: multiple baselines across behaviors, multiple baselines across subjects, and multiple baselines across situations. In changing-criterion designs, the criterion for success changes, generally by becoming increasingly rigorous. We can conclude that the intervention is responsible for behavioral changes if the behavior increases or decreases in accordance with criterion changes.

Alternating-treatment designs allow the comparison of two or more treatments presented in the same intervention phase.

Group-based research collects data on many subjects and then combines and compares the data by computing means, or averages. Within-subjects designs test each individual in more than one condition of the study, and between-subjects designs separate the subjects into groups. Between-subjects designs are called experiments when an independent variable is manipulated, subjects are randomly assigned to experimental and control groups, and changes in the dependent variable are assessed. Quasi-experiments use or select for an existing variable, which becomes the basis for categorizing the subjects into groups. Because true experiments manipulate the independent variable and equate the groups through random assignment, they can yield cause–effect conclusions about the link between variations in the independent and dependent variables.

Behavior change programs can be evaluated on the basis of graphical or statistical comparisons of the behavior and three other dimensions. First, the improved behavior should generalize to the person's everyday environment, and it should be durable. Second, the amount and importance of the change in behavior should be substantial, which can be evaluated by assessing the clinical significance of the change and the social validity of the program and its outcomes. Third, programs should strive to have a favorable cost–benefit ratio, demonstrating that in the long run, the intervention saves more money than it costs.

Key Terms and Review Questions

Key Terms

interobserver reliability	multiple baselines across situations
intrasubject designs	changing-criterion designs
AB design	alternating-treatment designs
reversal designs	experiment
ABA design	quasi-experiments
ABAB design	clinical significance
multiple-baseline designs	social validity
multiple baselines across behaviors	cost–benefit ratio
multiple baselines across subjects	

Review Questions

1. Describe four sources of inaccuracies in recording data on behavior.

2. Define the concept of interobserver reliability.

3. In calculating interobserver reliability, how are the session totals and interval recording methods different?

4. What are intrasubject designs, and how are they different from group-based designs?

5. Define "ABAB designs," and indicate why they can be superior to AB designs.

6. Describe the two problems associated with the use of reversal designs, and include the research by Creer, Chai, and Hoffman (1977) as an example.

7. Define "multiple-baseline designs," and indicate how they can be carried out across subjects and situations.

8. Describe the research design and results of C. F. Lowe and Chadwick (1990).

9. Define "changing-criterion designs" and give an example of how this research approach might be used in an intervention to improve a child's spelling skills.

10. How are experiments and quasi-experiments different?

11. Define "clinical significance."

12. Describe the three types of question by which one can assess the social validity of a behavior change program.

Related Readings

Monette, D. R., Sullivan, T. J., & DeJong, C. R. (1990). *Applied social research: Tool for the human services* (2nd ed.). Fort Worth, TX: Holt, Rinehart & Winston.

Schwartz, I. S., & Baer, D. M. (1991). Social validity assessments: Is current practice state of the art? *Journal of Applied Behavior Analysis, 24,* 189–204

Wolery, M., & Gast, D. L. (1990). Re-framing the debate: Finding middle ground and defining the role of social validity. In A. C. Repp & N. N. Singh (Eds.), *Perspectives on the use of nonaversive and aversive interventions for persons with developmental disabilities.* Sycamore, IL: Sycamore.

Wolf, M. M. (1978). Social validity: The case for subjective measurement or how applied behavior analysis is finding its heart. *Journal of Applied Behavior Analysis, 11,* 203–214.

Name _____   Day & time
                                    class meets_____
Date _____

Chapter 12: Work Sheet 12.1

1. In an intervention to reduce a girl's physical aggression against classmates, two observers recorded how often she hit other children during a 30-minute period on the playground. One observer recorded 40 hits, and the other recorded 50. Calculate the interobserver reliability for these frequency data and indicate whether the level of agreement you find is acceptable.

2. What kind of design is the project you've been doing, actually or hypothetically, for the application exercises? From the data this project might collect, would you be able to conclude that the intervention caused any changes in the behavior? Why?

3. Suppose you wanted to conduct the self-management project as a multiple-baseline, across-situations design. Indicate what the situations might be and exactly how you would carry out the design.

4. Suppose you wanted to conduct the self-management project as a changing-criterion design. Describe the criteria you might use and tell exactly how you would carry out the design.

5. Describe when, where, and how you might conduct follow-up assessments of the target behavior in your (actual or hypothetical) self-management project.

6. Describe specifically how you might assess various aspects of the social validity of your self-management program.

NOTE: If you will be submitting work sheets to your instructor or to a fellow student, make a copy of each before submitting it.

Part Five

Advanced and Specialized Methods in Behavior Modification

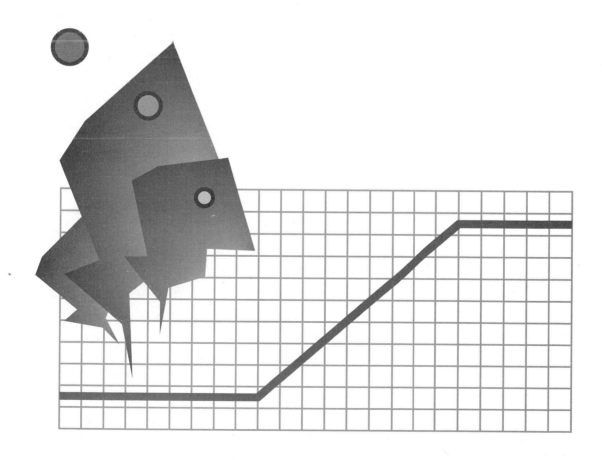

13 *Token Economies*

Prologue

Located in Mexico about 175 miles south of the Arizona border is a private community called Comunidad los Horcones (Rohter, 1989). Its approximately 40 adult and child residents have constructed a set of social rules and consequences to build and maintain a society based on cooperation and equality, rather than competition and discrimination. The community is self-supporting and sustains itself by farming and by providing educational programs for children from a nearby city. The entire community shares the money these activities bring in and engages in discussion and democratic vote to arrive at decisions about how to spend their income.

One of the community's founders, Juan Robinson, had studied psychology and read B. F. Skinner's (1948) *Walden Two*. This novel by the famous behaviorist describes a utopian society that used operant conditioning principles to create an environment that promoted positive social conduct and relationships. To achieve these goals for los Horcones, Juan and his fellow residents have used democratic procedures to develop a detailed code of behavior that applies to all residents and all major facets of life in their community. The code for children, for instance, has 24 categories of outcome goals that include about 150 specific, defined behaviors. By behaving in accordance with the code—for example, by performing the work needed for the community to function, individual residents earn token reinforcers. As you might guess, the token reinforcement system applied at los Horcones is very complex.

In the present chapter and the next two, we shift our attention from methods that can be used fairly easily in many different everyday situations to *techniques that are more advanced and specialized* in their application. You will see that these techniques are relatively *specialized* with respect to appropriate settings for their use and more *advanced* with regard to the skills needed to carry them out effectively. Training in an undergraduate course on principles of behavior change is not sufficient to develop the needed skills to design programs using these methods. Individuals who use or directly supervise the use of these methods typically have graduate degrees. This chapter introduces you to complex systems of token reinforcement called *token economies*.

The Token Economy Approach

In discussing programs that have applied token reinforcement, we've seen that tokens used as reinforcers have several advantages over rewards of some other types. For instance, the tokens can be given immediately after a desirable behavior to bridge the delay between performing the behavior and getting the tangible, consumable, or activity reinforcer that has been earned. Token reinforcers can also be applied more easily than other rewards with groups of individuals, and since a variety of attractive backup reinforcers is possible, the reward value of the tokens is likely to remain high. Advantages like these have made token reinforcers very popular in behavior change programs.

This chapter focuses on the token economy approach in providing consequences for people's behavior. What is a token economy, and what makes it different from the token reinforcement approaches we've seen so far? A **token economy** is a method of using a complex system of consequences that is typically applied with groups of individuals for a wide range of target behaviors (Ayllon & Azrin, 1968b). Token economies differ from other token systems in three ways. Compared with other token systems, token economies generally:

- Try to change the behaviors of groups of people, rather than just one person.
- Attempt to change relatively wide ranges of target behaviors.
- Use relatively complex systems of consequences for those behaviors.

Although these characteristics help to define "token economies," there are no definite criteria by which to determine whether a program qualifies as a token economy. The number of people included in the intervention, the range of behavior to be changed, and the complexity of the system of consequences can vary.

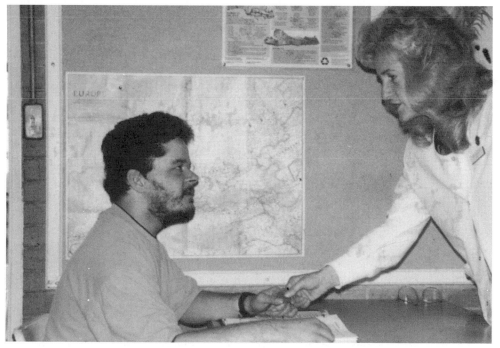

This man is receiving a token for good performance. He will be able to exchange the token for a backup reinforcer later.

Usual Settings for Token Economies

One of the earliest recorded instances of using a token economy approach occurred in a nineteenth-century prison (Pitts, 1976). Alexander Meconochie, a captain in the British Royal Navy, was placed in charge of

> one of the worst British penal colonies, Norfolk Island, located about 1000 miles off the coast of Australia. The inmates were two-time losers, having committed major crimes in both England and Australia. (p. 146)

To control the inmates' behavior, the captain implemented a point system by which the prisoners could earn their way out of the penal colony by performing appropriate tasks and social behaviors. The number of points one needed depended on the seriousness of the crimes he had committed. Meconochie had a motivational rationale for using this approach: "When a man keeps the key of his own prison, he is soon persuaded to fit it into the lock." Even though this approach seemed to be successful in controlling the behavior of the Norfolk Island prisoners, Meconochie's superiors criticized it and recalled him to England.

Because token economies are usually implemented to change the behaviors of groups of individuals, they are applied mainly in organizational or institutional settings. Token economies have been used in a great variety of settings, including classrooms for normal students of all ages, classrooms and institutions for mentally retarded people, hospitals for psychiatric patients and drug abusers, group homes for teenagers who have committed antisocial acts and are at risk of becoming delinquents, and work settings to enhance job performance (Kazdin, 1985). Los Horcones, described at the beginning of this chapter, is one of several similar communities in such locations as Kansas, Michigan, Virginia, and Canada that have been established with token economies to structure social behaviors (Rohter, 1989).

What's Needed to Start a Token Economy

Starting a token economy requires that several tasks be completed in advance. One of the main steps is deciding on the target behaviors the behavior modification program will try to change. Decisions about which behaviors to include will depend on the types of problem behavior the group appears to have, the specific needs of individual group members, and the needs of the organization or institution in which the program will be implemented. If the individuals in the group are very similar in their problem behaviors and personal characteristics, the target behaviors and rules about them can apply broadly to all members of the group. Having similar individuals in the group is a fairly common circumstance, as might be expected from the examples of settings just mentioned. For instance, each mentally retarded child is likely to have many behavioral deficits and excesses that are like those displayed by other mentally retarded children, and many of these problems are likely to be different from those found among children in regular classrooms.

The staff worker (left) in a token economy store greets a client who wants to exchange the tokens he earned for items displayed on the counters.

Once the target behaviors have been identified, they must be defined carefully and in detail so that the members of the group and the staff who administer the program will know exactly what the behaviors are and can determine reliably whether they occurred. At that point, four tasks should be initiated. First, functional analyses should be conducted to ascertain the antecedents and consequences that seem to be involved in each of the behaviors. Second, because token economies usually require several staff members to administer the program, these individuals must be recruited. Third, the staff must receive extensive training in identifying the target behaviors, using methods to reduce the antecedents and consequences that have promoted inappropriate behaviors in the past, recording data, and administering the token system. Fourth, the staff must collect baseline data. Let's see what the next steps would be if we wanted to set up a token economy and implement it.

Setting Up and Implementing a Token Economy

After the functional analyses have been conducted, all the materials, equipment, and facilities that will be needed to implement the token economy can be lined up while the baseline data are being collected. ("Materials and equipment" might include a supply of tokens, data sheets to record each person's behaviors and tokens earned, behavioral contracts, backup reinforcers, and timing devices.) Token economies in large institutions often have a special room, set up like a store, where tokens can be exchanged for tangible or consumable backup reinforcers; in smaller token economies, the store may be kept in a cabinet or large box. Any special facilities, such as a store, will need to be set up in advance. To assemble all these materials, it will be necessary to plan various features of the program, starting with the "tokens" themselves.

The Tokens: Choosing Them and Monitoring Their Use

Tokens can take many different forms. For instance, they can be poker chips, stars or stamps attached to a chart, check marks in a table, data entries in logs that are like bankbooks, or specially printed paper money. Tokens can be color-coded to reflect some important dimension, such as their value or the type of behavior for which they were earned. Because tokens function like money, they serve as points or credits toward the exchange cost for backup reinforcers. Sometimes tokens are specifically designed to operate timers or automatic dispensers. For example, Leonard Jason (1985) used coinlike tokens in a program that had TV watching as an activity backup reinforcer for several behaviors, such as doing chores or homework. A timer was connected to the TV set, and each token activated the timer for 30 minutes.

Ideally, tokens should have certain practical characteristics: they should be durable, convenient to store and handle, easy to carry around and dispense, and difficult to steal or counterfeit. Stealing tokens can be a major problem in some settings, and programs must be designed to prevent or strongly discourage this behavior. It is also a good idea to provide some way for each person to store the tokens he or she earns, such as in a purse or wallet. (Go to ▧ .)

Backup Reinforcers and Punishers

Making decisions about which backup reinforcers and punishers to include in a token economy program can be accomplished by using the principles and strategies we discussed in Chapters 5 and 6. To identify potentially strong backup reinforcers, we can use two approaches: direct assessment methods, such as observing the person's preferences in naturalistic or structured tests, and indirect assessment methods, such as asking probing questions in an interview or using a questionnaire, like the Preferred Items and Experiences Questionnaire (see Figure 5.2). The larger the variety of reinforcers available for exchange in the token system, the greater the chance that the tokens will maintain their effectiveness and provide strong reinforcement for all individuals under the token economy. A related issue to keep in mind is that reinforcement in a token economy is more effective when individuals

Case Study 13.1
Not-So-Funny Money

Because token economies are usually carried out with groups of people, presenting a single person as a case study might be misleading. So the "case" in this case study box is a type of token that was nicely designed by Daniel Logan (1970) to serve in a token economy at a psychiatric hospital. The tokens were printed "paper money" receipts that could not be easily counterfeited, or redeemed, if stolen, partly because each one had to be filled out by a staff member, as shown in Figure 13.1. Each money receipt

was color-coded according to broad classes of behavior. Money bearing the labels "Self-Care," "Ward Work," and "Social Contact" was printed in different colors to facilitate easy recognition and quick sorting. The money was also stamped according to the

denomination (1 cent, 5 cents, and 10 cents). (p. 183)

The space labeled *Task* on the receipt was filled in by staff to indicate the specific behavior that was reinforced, such as "emptying the trash" or "playing checkers."

The receipts had other advantages, too. Because of the information staff wrote on them, the receipts were worth saving as records of behavior. That is, when patients exchange the receipt tokens for the backup reinforcers, they can be sorted and stored according to denominations and re-sorted by color to see quickly which classes of behavior are being reinforced. Sorting can also be done by the specific behavior or by the issuing staff member (to determine the kinds of behaviors each staff member has been rewarding).

Figure 13.1 Sample of the "paper money" receipts used in a token economy. (Based on information in Logan, 1970.)

can select their reinforcers from an array of items rather than having items assigned to them (Karraker, 1977).

A type of punishment that often dovetails easily into token economies is response cost, in which the person pays fines, in tokens, for instances of misbehavior. Although problems can arise if a person runs out of points or credits to lose, the reinforcement system can be designed to provide enough credits for appropriate behavior so that the person will almost always have enough to cover any amount of misbehavior he or she performs. Some research findings suggest that earning and losing tokens—that is, reward and punishment methods—may be equally effective in changing behavior (Sullivan & O'Leary, 1990).

Managing the Consequences

Once we have decided what reinforcers and punishers to include in the program, we will need to keep a large supply of backup reinforcers available and devise a system for managing the distribution of consequences. To manage the consequences effectively, we should follow a few important guidelines and decide certain critical questions in advance.

Guidelines for Administering Tokens

Four general guidelines should be followed in managing all token economy programs. First, specify clearly to everyone involved the behavioral criteria for earning tokens and the exchange rates for backup reinforcers. Post the criteria and rates prominently, if possible. Second, be sure to award tokens as soon as possible after the desired behavior occurs. Third, use natural reinforcers, such as praise, in conjunction with dispensing tokens. Fourth, keep careful and accurate records of the target behaviors performed and the reinforcers dispensed.

Who Will Administer Consequences?

Who will deliver and keep track of the token credits each person has earned or lost and the backup reinforcers or punishers received? The person or persons bearing these responsibilities will need to monitor the target behaviors and record data carefully, and deliver tokens promptly. Administration usually is handled by staff members of the organization or institution—for example, attendants, teachers, or supervisors. When more than one staff member is involved simultaneously in administering consequences, be sure each one has a separate role in the process and knows what that role is (Ayllon & Azrin, 1968b). Otherwise administrators may duplicate each other's actions or fail to act, thinking that the other staff member will do it, or already has. If we decide to include self-management procedures in a token economy, each person may administer the consequences to himself or herself, but there must be methods for checking the accuracy of the data and the judgments the participant make (Hundert & Batstone, 1978; McLaughlin, Burgess, & Sackville-West, 1982).

How Many Tokens Will a Behavior Earn?

The goal in deciding how many tokens a behavior will earn is to maximize each person's performance of the target behaviors. When making decisions about the number of tokens a behavior will earn, we will want to take a few factors into account. First, the laws of supply and demand are relevant (Ayllon & Azrin, 1968b). Behaviors or chores that are less attractive than others—perhaps because they are relatively time-consuming, strenuous, anxiety-arousing, or tedious to do—may require more tokens to enhance the reward value of the reinforcer. And there is a fairness issue, too. People tend to feel that they deserve more pay for the less attractive behaviors. So, for example, in a token economy in which college students earned tokens for doing chores in their residence, the number of tokens each student received for completing a task was directly related to the amount of time the chore took per week to do (S. P. Johnson et al., 1991).

Three other factors are also considered when deciding on the number of tokens to give for a behavior. First, individuals with lesser abilities to learn or perform the needed behaviors may be given more tokens per behavior to equalize the potential for getting backup reinforcers. Second, it is sometimes useful to reinforce the behavior with more tokens in the first few days of a person's participation in a token economy than later on in the program. Third, after the behaviors have become established, the schedule of reinforcement can be thinned to an intermittent schedule (W. C. Stainback et al., 1973).

What Will the Exchange Rates Be?

Decisions about the number of tokens needed to buy each backup reinforcer depend on four factors. First, these decisions are tied to the number of tokens individuals can earn for each behavior. If the number of tokens earned per behavior is small, the cost of the backup reinforcers should be low—and vice versa. Second, some reinforcers cost the program money to buy, and the number of tokens needed to get a particular reinforcer should be related to the monetary cost of that item. Third, the laws of supply and demand may apply again. That is, some reinforcers are in greater demand than others; those with high demand and low supply can cost more than those with low demand and high supply. This factor may apply especially well to activity reinforcers, such as going into town. Suppose several individuals like to go to town and often choose that as a backup reinforcer, but there are only five seats in the car regularly used for the trip. Thus the high demand and low supply for this reinforcer may provide a rationale for making its cost higher than that of an activity with an unlimited supply. Fourth, some backup reinforcers may have more therapeutic relevance than others, and charging a relatively small number of tokens for these reinforcers can encourage individuals to choose them. For example, going on a shopping trip might cost only a few tokens because the participants may learn valuable skills from that experience.

How Often Will Backup Reinforcers Be Available?

Another decision to be made in implementing a token economy concerns the availability of the backup reinforcers—that is, how often and when tokens can be redeemed for backup reinforcers. A factor here is the intellectual ability of the people in the token economy. Very young children and low functioning individuals, such as the mentally retarded, probably will need to have the backup reinforcers available at least twice a day, especially when they enter the program. For other children, the token exchanges for backup reinforcers

> should probably take place once or twice each day during the first three or four days of a token economy. In this way the children are made aware of the real value of the tokens shortly after receiving them. (Stainback et al., 1973).

After the first few days, reinforcer availability should be reduced gradually toward the goal of allowing the children to redeem their tokens infrequently, such as only once a week. In general, regardless of the age of the individuals in a token economy, the greater their cognitive abilities, the more quickly the availability of backup reinforcers can be reduced. The frequency with which tokens can be redeemed should be based on the characteristics of the recipients and on the rate that maintains the target behavior best.

Will the Program Use Group or Individual Contingencies?

Like most other reinforcement programs, token economies can use group or individual contingencies for administering reinforcers. When a token economy uses a group contingency, tokens are given on the basis of the group's performance as a whole. With an individual contingency, tokens are given to each person based on his or her own performance. As we discussed in Chapter 5, group contingencies have the advantages of being relatively easy to administer and having built-in incentives to prevent group members from reinforcing one another's inappropriate behaviors. But negative peer pressure tactics, such as threats, seem to be more likely to happen with group than with individual contingencies, especially when the consequences include group punishment if behavioral criteria are not met. Keep in mind that a program can be a hybrid, in which some behaviors are rewarded with group contingencies and others with individual contingencies.

Phasing Out the Program

Although token economies are sometimes used just to maintain appropriate conduct or high performance while people are in organizational and institutional settings, they can also be applied in programs with broader, long-term goals. For instance, the goals of token economies in psychiatric hospitals may involve helping individuals to function better in natural environments, outside the institution. The methods we discussed in Chapter 11 for maintaining improved behavior after an intervention ends can help achieve these long-term goals. One of these approaches involved using natural reinforcers, such as praise and feedback, along with tokens. Later in the program, the natural reinforcers can gradually replace the tokens.

Other approaches for maintaining improved behavior after an intervention has ended include thinning and delaying reinforcement. These methods can be implemented by:

- Decreasing the number of tokens each target behavior earns.
- Decreasing the number of target behaviors that earn tokens.
- Increasing the number of tokens required to buy backup reinforcers.
- Increasing the delays between receiving tokens and having opportunities to redeem them for backup reinforcers.

✓ Concept Check 13.1

1. A behavior change program designed to change a wide range of behaviors in groups of individuals by using a complex system of reinforcers is called a _____ _____ .

2. An example of the materials or equipment to be obtained and set up before starting a token economy is _____ . ⇔

3. An example of tokens that could be used in a token reinforcement program is _____ . ⇔

4. A type of punishment that can fit into a token economy especially easily is _____ _____ .

5. To equalize the potential for getting backup reinforcers among individuals who differ in their abilities to perform the target behaviors, those with lesser abilities can be given _____ per behavior.

6. People who are likely to need opportunities to exchange tokens for backup reinforcers very frequently are likely to be individuals with lesser _____ _____ abilities.

_____

Answers: 5. more tokens 6. cognitive/intellectual

1. token economy 2. backup reinforcers 3. poker chips 4. response cost

These approaches can be used separately or in combination, but it is not yet clear which method or combination of techniques will enhance maintenance of behaviors best. (Go to ✓ .)

An Example Token Economy: Achievement Place

Now that we have seen the general features of token economies and how they are set up and implemented, we will examine in some detail a fine example of a token economy program to see how one functions. This token economy, called Achievement Place, was developed in Kansas in the 1960s and 1970s by Elery Phillips (1968) and several colleagues, particularly Montrose Wolf and Dean Fixsen (Phillips et al., 1971, 1973).

The Purpose and Structure of Achievement Place

Achievement Place was designed as a residential token economy program for juvenile boys who were classified as "predelinquent." The term *predelinquent* reflects the belief that a given juvenile's home life and record of minor offenses, such as petty thefts and fighting, indicated the likelihood that he or she would become a habitual lawbreaker if no corrective action were taken. The purpose of Achievement Place was to rehabilitate the boys who were placed in the program by the courts, to prevent them from becoming delinquents. The approach this program developed became a model for over 200 other programs to prevent delinquency in the United States, including *Boys' Town* (Fixsen et al., 1978; Wolf, Braukmann, & Ramp, 1987). Although most of these programs have been for boys, many have been for girls. The average age at *entry* into and *exit* from these programs have been 14.1 and 15.0, respectively, for boys, and 14.8 and 15.4 for girls (Kirigin et al., 1982).

Achievement Place was set up in a large house and received predelinquent boys from the local community. The house served as the residence for several boys at a time and a pair of *teaching parents*, who supervised the program. The boys continued to go to their usual schools, and their teachers completed brief "report cards" daily. Each day the boys could earn or lose points based on the performance of spe-

Table 13.1   *Some Target Behaviors in the Achievement Place Program and the Number of Points Each One Earned or Lost*

Behaviors That Earned Points	Points
1. Watching news on TV or reading the newspaper	300 per day
2. Cleaning and maintaining neatness in one's room	500 per day
3. Keeping one's person neat and clean	500 per day
4. Reading books	5–10 per page
5. Aiding house-parents in various household tasks	20–1000 per task
6. Doing dishes	500–1000 per meal
7. Being well dressed for an evening meal	100–500 per meal
8. Performing homework	500 per day
9. Obtaining desirable grades on school report cards	500–1000 per grade
10. Turning out lights when not in use	25 per light

Behaviors That Lost Points	Points
1. Failing grades on the report card	500–1000 per grade
2. Speaking aggressively	20–50 per response
3. Forgetting to wash hands before meals	100–300 per meal
4. Arguing	300 per response
5. Disobeying	100–1000 per response
6. Being late	10 per minute
7. Displaying poor manners	50–100 per response
8. Engaging in poor posture	50–100 per response
9. Using poor grammar	20–50 per response
10. Stealing, lying, or cheating	10,000 per response

Source: Phillips (1968), Table 2.

cific social, academic, and everyday living behaviors both at the house and in school. Whenever points were earned or lost, the behavior and the number of points were recorded on an index card each boy carried with him. Table 13.1 describes some of the target behaviors in the program and the number of points earned or lost. The backup reinforcers—or "privileges," as they were called—were mainly activities, such as being allowed to go downtown, and consumable items, such as snacks, that would be naturally available in most teenagers' everyday lives.

An important feature of this program was a gradual transition toward self-regulation. This transition was made by having the boys advance through three levels or phases of the program. When a boy entered the program, he started on a *daily point system* in which the points he earned were tallied at the end of each day and could be exchanged for privileges to be received on the following day. This arrangement allowed the newcomer to learn how the system worked and the value of earning tokens. As soon as a boy could function with less structure, he advanced to the second level, the *weekly point system*, in which his points were tallied for a full week and exchanged for reinforcers he would receive for the following week. In the last level in the program called the *merit system*, the point system was phased out and the privileges became freely available as long as improved social, academic, and everyday living behaviors were maintained with social reinforcement alone. Boys were placed on the merit system only if their behavior was consistently good and they appeared to be almost ready to leave Achievement Place and return home.

The token economy for the daily and weekly point systems was designed so that boys who performed all the target behaviors and lost few points in fines could expect to earn essentially all the privileges available. Table 13.2 lists the privileges the boys could earn at Achievement Place and the number of points needed to purchase each one on the daily and weekly point systems. The privileges called "basics"

Table 13.2 *Privileges (Backup Reinforcers) That Could Be Earned at Achievement Place and the Numbers of Points Needed to Purchase Them on the Daily and Weekly Point Systems*

Privileges	Price in Points	
	Weekly System	Daily System
Basics (hobbies and games)	3000	400
Snacks	1000	150
TV	1000	150
Allowance (per $1.00)	2000	300
Permission to leave Achievement Place (home, downtown, sports events)	3000	*
Bonds (savings for gifts, special clothing, etc.)	1000	150
Special privileges	Variable	*

*Not available.
Source: Phillips et al. (1971), Table 1.

were exchanged as a package that included the use of a telephone, a radio, the recreation room, and tools. The number of points needed to purchase each privilege stayed fairly constant but could change occasionally if the reward value varied. For example, watching TV cost more tokens during the winter than in other seasons. Various "special privileges" could be available. One special privilege the boys could buy at an auction each week was the opportunity to serve as *manager*—the person with authority to assign chores and award tokens to the other boys under his supervision. The manager's behavior earned or lost points for him, depending on how well the other boys performed their household chores and everyday living behaviors, such as brushing their teeth and getting up on time in the morning.

A Day in One's Life at Achievement Place

Because the boys lived in a house with two "teaching parents," and the social structure and activities were like those of a family, the Achievement Place approach came to be known as the *teaching-family model*. The daily routine was designed to be like the routines of most families. As Elery Phillips (1968) has described, the boys got up at a standard time in the morning, showered and dressed, and cleaned their rooms. Then,

> after breakfast, some of the boys had kitchen clean-up duties before leaving for
> school. After school the boys returned home and prepared their homework, after

The seven youths in this photo were residents at Achievement Place who were voting on an issue during a daily "family conference." The teaching parents and their young daughter are seated to the right in the foreground.

which they could watch TV, play games, or engage in other recreational activities if these privileges had been earned via the token economy. Some boys were assigned kitchen clean-up duties after the evening meal. (p. 214)

A "family conference" was held each evening to enable the boys and the teaching parents to discuss the day's events, the manager's performance, and any problems with the token economy program (Phillips et al., 1973). These conferences gave the boys chances to contribute to and learn from the way the program was administered. During the rest of the evening, the boys could engage in individual and group recreational activities before going to bed at a standard time.

How Effective Is the Achievement Place Approach?

Studies have shown that the Achievement Place approach is very effective in improving a wide variety of behaviors while predelinquent juveniles are in the program and for a year or so after it ends. For instance, a 2-year follow-up study found that compared with boys who had been placed either in a large institution for delinquents or on probation, Achievement Place boys had fewer by far police and court contacts, greater school attendance, and higher grades (Fixsen et al., 1978).

Another study compared the effects of group homes of two types: 13 homes that followed the teaching family model and 9 homes that used other approaches to prevent delinquency (Kirigin et al., 1982). The court and police records of each boy or girl were examined for instances of alleged criminal offenses during the intervention period and for the year before and the year after the group home intervention. The *rate* of offenses was then determined by taking the average number of offenses per month. The researchers then compared the rates of offenses for the three periods—before, during, and after intervention. For the juveniles in the homes using the teaching-family model, the rate of offenses dropped by about half during the intervention and did not increase in the subsequent year. For those in the homes using other approaches, the rate of offenses *increased* sharply during the intervention and dropped in the subsequent year to the same rate as that of the teaching-family homes. Thus the teaching-family homes were much more effective in controlling delinquent behaviors while the juveniles were in group homes, but the two types of programs did not differ in being able to prevent delinquency in the subsequent year.

Despite the success of the teaching-family model for improving the behavior of predelinquent juveniles while they are in the program and for the year after, it is now clear that the improvements charted are often lost after a couple of years (Wolf, Braukmann, & Ramp, 1987). In addition, the rate of criminal offenses for these juveniles after the intervention is, on average, still well above national norms for individuals of matching ages.

The failure of short-term interventions to prevent delinquency fully and durably should not be very surprising. Juveniles who complete a teaching-family program typically are returned to the same environment that reinforced antisocial behavior in the past. Little encouragement exists in that environment for behaviors of the kind that were reinforced at the group home. The solution to the problem of maintaining the gains interventions produce in predelinquent juveniles may be to provide longer-term contact with environments that support positive social behavior, perhaps by having trained foster parents supervise these teens throughout adolescence (Wolf, Braukmann, & Ramp, 1987).

Other Settings for Token Economies

Three of the many other settings in which token economies have been used successfully are school classrooms, places of employment, and institutions for psychiatric and developmentally disabled individuals. We will look briefly at some representative interventions and the target behaviors they addressed.

Token Economies in Classrooms

The use of rewards to influence classroom behavior has a long history. Your parents and grandparents probably remember teachers who gave "stars" to students for academic achievement and extra recess time to children who had "been good." And these reinforcers are still used today. Rewards like these, which generally are not exchanged for backup reinforcers, basically give social reinforcement or feedback. But using tokens as reinforcers in schools has a shorter history. It began in the 1960s and has continued in many regular and special education classrooms since then, usually in programs conducted to improve students' general conduct and academic performance. Some of these programs qualify as token economies because they addressed several target behaviors and used fairly complex reinforcement systems.

One early example of a token economy applied in a school setting was carried out in a special education classroom with mildly and moderately retarded 8- to 14-year-olds (Birnbrauer et al., 1972). Although token and social reinforcement were given mainly for correct performance on academic assignments, such as vocabulary and arithmetic tasks, the students also could earn tokens for being cooperative or doing an extra activity. Reprimands and time-out were used as punishment for disruptive behaviors. The tokens were marks the teacher put in squares that divided up sheets of paper in a student's "mark book" folder. At the end of the daily token economy class, the students could exchange fully marked sheets for backup reinforcers (balloons, trinkets, pencils, etc.). Sheets that had any squares unmarked could be carried over to the next day. In some cases a child would save up sheets to buy a special, relatively expensive item that was included as a backup reinforcer specifically for him or her. After the students had spent more than 3 months in the token economy, the token reinforcement was suspended for more than 3 weeks. Only a third of the children continued to perform well during that time, but the higher performance levels returned when the token economy was reinstated.

Another token economy program was applied for a full academic year in an entire elementary school, spanning from kindergarten through sixth grade (Boegli & Wasik, 1978). The target behaviors differed somewhat for the younger and older children, but in all cases they called for being at assigned areas on time, having needed supplies and books for the day's activities, talking or moving about quietly so as not to disturb people, helping others, and successfully completing assigned work. Tokens for appropriate behaviors could be distributed by all teachers and all other staff of the school, including librarians and aides, all of whom were trained in the token economy method. Token exchanges could occur at various times during any day, but they were always supervised by the child's teacher, and children could save their tokens across days if they wished. Sometimes auctions were held in which the children could bid on various items, such as musical recordings, magazines, comic books, toys, and jewelry donated by parents and merchants. Data analyses revealed decreases in student disruptions and suspensions, and the students' scores on reading and mathematics achievement tests showed greater improvements during the year of the program than during the preceding year.

Token Economies at Worksites

The owner of a company that manufactures egg cartons in Massachussetts introduced a token economy to improve several behaviors, but the focus was on absenteeism and discipline problems (Nelton, 1988). The point system worked in this way: each employee would earn 25 points for excellent attendance for an entire

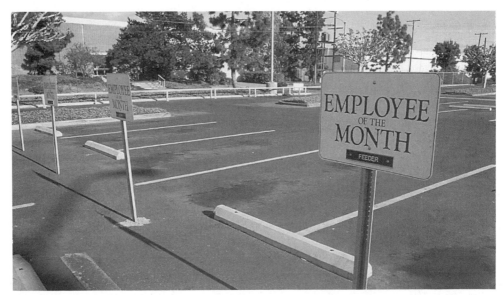

Worksite token economies might use convenient parking spaces as backup reinforcers.

year, 20 points for having no formal disciplinary action for a year, and 15 points for having no injuries requiring an absence in a year. Points could also be earned for submitting suggestions that improved safety or reduced costs and lose points for being absent from work. When workers accumulated 100 points, they became members of the company's "100 Club" and were awarded a jacket with the name of the club and company logo printed on it. Although this backup reinforcer is quite limited and may seem a bit corny, individuals who received it seemed quite proud.

A more complex worksite token economy was introduced at two open-pit mines to improve worker safety in the hazardous jobs associated with mining (Fox, Hopkins, & Anger, 1987). Each year hundreds of mining workers are killed and many thousands are injured in the United States. The two mines that received the intervention had very poor safety records, with the numbers of days workers lost due to work-related injuries being several times higher than the national mining average. The tokens were trading stamps that were awarded monthly with paychecks and could be redeemed at stores for hundreds of different items, including a spice rack, bowling ball, gas-fired barbecue grill, and microwave oven. Workers received the tokens mainly for not having had any injuries requiring a physician's care in the prior month, but tokens could also be earned for safety suggestions. The token economy divided the workers into four groups on the basis of how hazardous their jobs were. Although injuries had occurred in all job groups, most injuries were in jobs associated with the use and maintenance of heavy machinery. The more hazardous the job, the more tokens a worker received for avoiding injury. What's more, a group contingency was added so that all workers under the same supervisor got tokens if none of those workers was injured during a month. As Figure 13.2 depicts, the rates of work-related injuries dropped after the token economies were introduced and remained relatively low at both mines during the many years the interventions remained in effect.

Token Economies in Institutional Settings

The structure and usefulness of the token economy approach for changing behavior was first described by Teodoro Ayllon and Nathan Azrin (1968b), based on the program they applied in a psychiatric hospital. In this groundbreaking program, patients could earn tokens for a variety of activities and chores, such as helping to serve meals or clean the kitchen, gathering clothes to be laundered, and performing personal hygiene tasks. The tokens were specially made metal coins that "could not be obtained outside the ward" (p. 222). The patients could exchange the tokens for two types of backup reinforcers (1) candies, magazines, or other items at a "store" on the ward and (2) opportunities to watch movies or TV programs, choose the people to dine with, and attend extra religious services. (We'll see later that some of these reinforcers cannot be used in hospitals today because of legal or ethical concerns.) After this program provided a model structure for a token economy and demonstrated that this approach could be implemented successfully in psychiatric settings, token economies were used in other psychiatric hospitals and in institutions of many other types (Glynn, 1990; Welch & Gist, 1974).

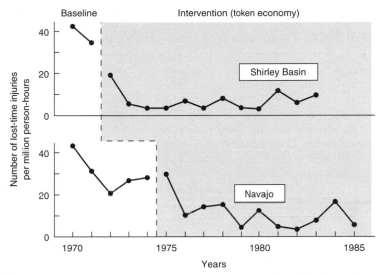

Figure 13.2   Baseline and intervention rates of serious work-related injuries, as reflected in the yearly number of injuries, per million person-hours worked, that resulted in the loss of 1 or more days from work. The token economies were studied with a variation of a multiple-baseline, across-subjects design, comparing employees at two open-pit mines: the Shirley Basin uranium mine in Wyoming and the Navajo coal mine in Arizona. (From Fox, Hopkins, & Anger, 1987, Figure 2.)

A long-term and extensive research project was undertaken to compare the effectiveness of a token economy program with two other commonly used approaches for treating about 100 institutionalized psychiatric patients (Paul & Lentz, 1977). The researchers randomly assigned the patients to the three treatment approaches and evaluated several outcome measures over several years. The token economy was very carefully designed and applied, and included many different backup reinforcers for a wide range of socially relevant behaviors. The patients who were treated with the token economy program showed greater improvements in their behaviors in the institution, were released sooner, adjusted better to living outside the institution, and used less medication to control their psychological functioning than the patients who were treated with the two other approaches. But despite the clear effectiveness of the token economy approach in treating psychiatric patients, it has not been widely adopted in mental hospitals. (Go to 🔍 .)

Benefits and Problems of Token Economies

The token economy has been clearly established as an effective treatment approach for changing problem behaviors (TFPDPP, 1993). People tend to perform a program's target behaviors at high rates when the token economy is in effect. But these

Close-Up 13.1
Why Are Token Economies Not Used Widely with Psychiatric Patients?

Token reinforcement approaches have been successful and widely adopted for changing problem behavior in many different settings. Given the success of token economies in treating psychiatric patients, why are they not used widely in mental hospitals in the United States? Shirley Glynn (1990), a token economy researcher, has offered five reasons:

- *Staff resistance.* The staff working in mental hospitals may resist using token economies because of the intensive supervision and monitoring these approaches require and for philosophical reasons—some, for example, may view reinforcers as "bribes."

- *Economic factors.* The immediate costs of back-up reinforcers and extra staff needed to carry out a token economy may preclude the use of this approach, despite the likelihood of a favorable cost–benefit ratio in the long run.

- *Reduced length of hospitalization.* Token economies often take several months or longer to achieve success with psychiatric patients. Because of cost-containment policies at most institutions, however, patients remain in hospitals only for short stays, returning periodically when they relapse.

- *Emphasis toward community-based treatment.* Coinciding with having patients stay in hospitals for brief periods has been an emphasis on outpatient treatment. Although there are some advantages to outpatient treatment, token economies are harder to supervise and appear to be less effective in correcting problem behaviors in psychiatric patients when administered on an outpatient basis.

- *Legal/ethical concerns.* Legal rulings and ethical concerns have had the effect of restricting the types of backup reinforcer that can be used with psychiatric patients. In some states, for instance, institutions are required to give free access to personal property, cheerful furnishings, television, and so on. Also, using some backup reinforcers, such as cigarettes, raises ethical issues: An item may be highly effective as a reinforcer, but is it right for program administrators to ignore known negative health effects of its use? Although these constraints do not prevent token economies from being used, they make it more difficult to apply powerful reinforcers to change behavior in institutions.

gains are often temporary if the program is discontinued, or when individuals are released from an institution that uses a token economy. Although the loss of these gains is an important problem, the real question should be whether improved behaviors can be maintained better after interventions with token economies than with other approaches. As we have seen in programs with predelinquent adolescents and psychiatric patients, token economies are at least as effective and are sometimes more effective than other approaches in maintaining improved behaviors.

Not all behavioral improvements are likely to be lost when a token economy ends. For instance, children who acquire new academic skills in classroom token economies are likely to retain these skills, especially if the skills are useful—that is, reinforced—in other classes or outside the academic environment. Skills in reading or arithmetic usually are useful in many situations children encounter. In contrast, improvements in general conduct or lifestyle behaviors may be harder to maintain after a token economy has been phased out because the natural environment may not reinforce the new behaviors.

One solution to this problem may be simply to continue the token economy. But the feasibility of continuing a program, especially if it is expensive to run, will surely depend on its cost–benefit ratio, and it will be necessary to demonstrate that the savings can be realized fairly soon. For example, the token economies applied to increase worker safety in mining jobs continued for many years. By maintaining safety behaviors, industries with hazardous jobs can save money in the costs of insurance and absenteeism. These savings often can offset the costs of running an effective program to change behavior.

Sometimes token economies are criticized as being "demeaning" to participants, especially if they are adults who should be able to control their behavior on their own. If this criticism is correct, assessments of the program's social validity by the participants and others should indicate dissatisfaction with the methods it used. But this does not seem to be a problem. For instance, evaluations of satisfaction were taken with 7-point rating scales, where a 7 reflected high satisfaction. Predelinquent teenagers who received interventions in group homes gave ratings that averaged 6.5 out of 7 points for the homes using the teaching-family model and only 5.0 points for the homes using other approaches (Kirigin et al., 1982). Perhaps token economy participants realize that the system is not very different from the idea of earning pay for working or grades for studying. Perhaps they also realize that any "demeaning" aspects to the program, if such exist, are easily offset by the sense of self-esteem and pride to be gained from improving personal problem behaviors. (Go to ✔ .)

✔ Concept Check 13.2

. . . .

1. In the Achievement Place program, the last level toward self-regulation is called the _____ system.
2. A likely task of an Achievement Place manager might be to have other boys _____ _____ . ⇔
3. The rate of criminal offenses of juveniles after receiving a teaching-family intervention in a group home is _____ than the national norms for teens.
4. In the token economy applied at the two mines, workers received token reinforcers mainly for _____ .
5. A backup reinforcer one may *not* be allowed to use with patients in institutions is _____ . ⇔
6. An improved behavior that might be relatively difficult to maintain after a token economy ends is _____ _____ . ⇔

Answers:
1. merit 2. clean bathrooms 3. higher 4. not having injuries 5. watching TV 6. obeying rules

. . . .

Application Exercise

In this application exercise and the ones in the remaining chapters, our focus will be restricted to helping you understand the material you have just read. The sections entitled "Tips on . . ." and "The Next Steps in Your Program Design" are no longer used because you will not be applying the information in these chapters to enhance the design or execution of your self-management program. Work Sheet 13.1 contains tasks to clarify the processes involved in designing and carrying out a token economy. This work sheet and the remaining ones will be easier to complete if you fill them out soon after doing the reading.

Summary

A token economy is a complex system of consequences that is usually applied to change a wide range of behaviors in groups of people. Token economies have been used mainly in organizational and institutional settings, such as classrooms for normal students, institutions for mentally retarded people and psychiatric patients, group homes for predelinquent teenagers, and worksites. They have also been applied to structure and encourage positive social conduct in private communities.

Starting a token economy requires that many detailed decisions be made; in addition, staff must be trained, and baseline data collected. Setting up a token economy is a very complex process. It involves choosing the tokens, the backup reinforcers, and the punishers to be used. And it involves assigning one or more persons to administer consequences, as well as establishing the number of tokens a behavior will earn, the exchange availability and rates for reinforcers, and whether individual or group contingencies will be used. Phasing out a token economy can promote the maintenance of the improved behavior by using natural reinforcers and by thinning and delaying reinforcement.

Achievement Place was designed as a residential token economy in which "teaching parents" supervised the behavior of predelinquent juveniles. This approach is called the teaching-family model, and it features a gradual transition toward self-regulation by progression through three levels: the daily point system, the weekly point system, and the merit system. Although the teaching-family model appears to be more effective than other group home approaches in reducing antisocial behavior while the juveniles are in the program, the gains are often lost by the teenagers 2 years after being returned to their home environments.

Token economies have been applied successfully to improve classroom conduct and academic achievement, in worksites to improve job performance and safety, and in psychiatric hospitals. Because improved behaviors often are not maintained after people leave the program, it may be necessary to continue the system in some form to prevent relapses.

Key Terms and Review Questions

Key Terms

token economy   Achievement Place

Review Questions

1. What is a token economy, and how is it different from other token reinforcement systems?

2. Describe the steps that need to be completed before a token economy can start to function.

3. What kinds of token are there?

4. State the four general guidelines for administering tokens.

5. What issues do you need to consider when deciding who will administer consequences in a token economy?

6. Describe the factors to consider when deciding how many tokens to give for target behaviors.

7. Describe the factors to consider when deciding on the exchange rate for back-up reinforcers.

8. How can token economies be phased out while enhancing the likelihood that desirable behaviors will be maintained when participants have left the program?

9. Describe the levels of transition Achievement Place provides toward self-regulation.

10. Describe the study by Kirigin et al. (1982) comparing the outcomes of group homes using the teaching-family model with homes using other approaches.

11. Describe the study by Fox, Hopkins, and Anger (1987) on applying token economies to improve worker safety in mining.

12. Describe the research by Paul and Lentz (1977) comparing a token economy with other approaches in treating psychiatric patients.

13. Discuss why token economies are not used widely with psychiatric patients.

Related Readings

Ayllon, T., & Azrin, N. H. (1968b). *The token economy: A motivational system for therapy and rehabilitation.* Englewood Cliffs, NJ: Prentice-Hall.

Glynn, S. M. (1990). Token economy approaches for psychiatric patients: Progress and pitfalls over 25 years. *Behavior Modification, 14,* 383–407.

Phillips, E. L. (1968). Achievement Place: Token reinforcement procedures in a home-style rehabilitation setting for "pre-delinquent" boys. *Journal of Applied Behavior Analysis, 1,* 213–223.

Stainback, W. C., Payne, J. S., Stainback, S. B., & Payne, R. A. (1973). *Establishing a token economy in the classroom.* Columbus, OH: Charles E. Merrill.

Wolf, M. M., Braukmann, C. J., & Ramp, K. A. (1987). Serious delinquent behavior as part of a significantly handicapping condition: Cures and supportive environments. *Journal of Applied Behavior Analysis, 20,* 347–359.

Name _____   Day & time
                                      class meets_____
Date _____

Chapter 13: Work Sheet 13.1

A major source of food poisoning in restaurants is the failure of food servers to wash their hands after they have touched a contaminated object. Almost *any object can be contaminated* with bacteria that cause food poisoning. If food servers get these bacteria on their hands and then touch a customer's food, the customer may ingest the bacteria and become sick. Suppose you, as the owner of a fast-food restaurant, want to apply a token economy to reduce the chances of employees transmitting these bacteria. To design the program, answer the following questions.

1. Hand washing is the behavior to focus on, but under exactly what circumstances should the target behavior occur?

2. What will you use as tokens, and why is this a good choice?

3. List a wide variety of backup reinforcers and punishers you could use.

4. What will be the rules for administering the tokens and backup reinforcers, and who will do it?

5. How many tokens will each appropriate instance of hand washing earn?

6. What will the exchange rates be for the backup reinforcers you listed in item 3?

7. How often will backup reinforcers be available?

8. Describe how you could include both individual and group contingencies in the token economy.

NOTE: If you will be submitting work sheets to your instructor or to a fellow student, make a copy of each sheet before submitting it.

14 *Advanced Behavioral Methods for Therapy*

Prologue

When getting on an escalator, does it ever occur to you that the moving hand rail might move too fast and pull you forward, making you trip and fall? This idea formed part of one female college student's phobia when she entered therapy (Nesbitt, 1973). Her fear of riding on escalators had developed several years earlier: she had ridden on one of the familiar people-movers with relatives without difficulty, but when the family were about to board the escalator later to descend, she said she was afraid because of the apparent height. The relatives may have thought the young woman was "being silly," so they forced her onto the escalator. After that experience, however, she avoided escalators, and always took the stairs or elevator instead. If anyone she was with suggested taking an escalator, she bluntly refused.

On one occasion, this woman approached an escalator unexpectedly while shopping and became so overcome by anxiety that she nearly vomited. Because of the problems she experienced with escalators, she had tried, before entering therapy, to reduce her fear

> by attempting, in the company of friends, to get on an escalator. On those occasions when she could bring herself to stand at the foot of the escalator, she would not step on for fear that by holding on to the hand rail she would be pulled downward and so miss her step. (p. 405)

The therapist helped her overcome her fear in one very intense session in which she had to ride on a department store escalator repeatedly with him. Getting her to board the escalator the first time required a great deal of coaxing and "a little physical force." Once on board, the client held onto the therapist's shirt tightly, said she felt she'd vomit, and seemed on the verge of crying. The next escalator ride was somewhat easier. After nearly half an hour of riding escalators continuously, she could ride on her own comfortably. Months later, she reported rarely experiencing anxiety when on escalators.

As you read about this fear reduction method, you probably noticed how different it was from methods discussed earlier in which individuals encounter fearful stimuli gradually. You may have thought that it was a good idea for the therapist to be there in case the client "freaked out." Experienced therapists usually are able to gauge how anxious a client feels and can help prevent the person from feeling overwhelmed.

This chapter examines behavioral methods that require professional supervision. Although in most cases supervision is necessary throughout all applications of the techniques, some methods may need professional supervision mainly in early sessions or to provide training for clients who will use the techniques in self-management programs. The first behavioral method we will examine is biofeedback, which clients usually can apply in self-management programs after training by a professional.

Biofeedback

Perhaps you have had the following experience: after lying down for a long while, you stood up quickly and then felt light-headed or dizzy. You were dizzy because by standing up too quickly, you failed to allow your blood pressure to develop the force necessary to pump enough blood to your brain to accommodate the sudden change in bodily orientation. When you go from a lying position to standing, gravity retards the flow of blood in the veins that feed the heart. If you stand quickly, the biological feedback mechanism that controls blood pressure in your body may not keep up with your fast change in posture (McClintic, 1985; R. M. Stern & Ray, 1980). Now, suppose you had some way of telling how much blood your brain was getting. If you had this feedback about your physiological processes, you might be able to alter them and avoid, for example, getting dizzy. Receiving information about the status of our bodily functions is the basis of biofeedback.

What Is Biofeedback?

Biofeedback is a technique in which an electrical/mechanical device monitors the status or changes of a person's physiological processes, such as heart rate or muscle tension, and immediately reports that information back to the individual. This feedback allows the person *to gain voluntary control over these bodily processes* through operant conditioning. If, for instance, we were to use biofeedback to lower your blood pressure and the device reports that the pressure has just decreased a bit, this information reinforces whatever you had done to accomplish this decrease.

Measuring blood pressure provides a clear and familiar example of how biofeedback devices work. You've surely seen a physician or nurse apply the basic device, called a sphygmomanometer, to measure someone's blood pressure. A cuff wrapped around the person's arm is filled with air until it is tight enough to stop the blood from flowing through the main artery in the arm (AMA, 1989). The cuff is then slowly deflated so that the medical worker can hear through a stethoscope the first beat forcing its way along the main artery as the blood flow overcomes the pressure in the cuff. The cuff pressure at that first beat can be seen on a gauge and indicates the person's maximum (called "systolic") blood pressure at that time, which occurs when the heart contracts to pump the blood. The medical worker continues deflating the cuff until the beating sound has disappeared. The pressure shown on the gauge at this time reflects the resting (diastolic) pressure in the artery while the heart chambers fill with blood between contractions. Blood pressure biofeedback sessions can be conducted in several different ways (Olson & Kroon, 1987). In one approach, many sphygmomanometer readings may be taken, with the person receiving each pressure reading. Some devices can inflate and deflate the cuff and take readings automatically (I. B. Goldstein, Jamner, & Shapiro, 1992).

Biofeedback information can take many different forms. For instance, the level of physiological functioning can be reflected by high or low numbers on a gauge, pitches of tones produced by an audio speaker, degrees of loudness of a tone from

One way to assess a person's physiological state is to use sensors that wrap around fingers. This approach can be used in measuring heart rate (pulse) or skin temperature, for instance.

a speaker, or degrees of brightness of a light. Status and functioning can be measured for many different physiological processes, enabling the use of biofeedback on each process (Olson, 1987; Peek, 1987). For some body functions, such as heart rate or temperature, measurements can be taken continuously, without having to cycle through a procedure. There are specific names for biofeedback techniques for different physiological processes, such as *blood pressure* (BP). Some of the other commonly used types of biofeedback are:

- *Heart rate* (HR), or heartbeats per minute.
- *Galvanic skin response* (GSR—also called electrodermal activity, EDA), which measures sweat gland activity by testing how readily the skin conducts minute levels of electricity. Sweaty skin conducts more readily than dry skin.
- *Electroencephalograph* (EEG), which assesses electrical activity in the brain.
- *Electromyograph* (EMG), which measures muscle tension by assessing the electrical activity of muscles when they contract.
- *Skin temperature*, which measures the flow of blood, which is warm, in part of the body, such as a foot or hand, by assessing the skin temperature in that region of the body.

Note that all these measures are indirect. They are taken on the outside of the body or just below the skin to reflect changes deeper in the body, such as brain activity, and sometimes the measure allows us only to *infer* internal changes, as we do when we assume that skin temperature changes mean that blood flow changes have occurred.

Learning to regulate one's bodily processes with biofeedback usually requires training. The customary training incorporates a shaping procedure in which tiny physiological changes in the desired direction are reinforced initially: as the training progresses, larger and larger changes are required for reinforcement. Although clients are usually encouraged to practice biofeedback techniques at home when they receive training, some evidence indicates that doing so may not help individuals learn to apply the methods any better or faster (Blanchard et al., 1991).

Biofeedback Applications

As we will soon see, biofeedback techniques have been applied successfully to produce many medical and psychological benefits for people. Because of such successes, "miracle" cures for all sorts of problems have been advertised by biofeedback therapists and commercial companies, sometimes despite the scarcity or absence of good evidence that the techniques are effective. For instance, one company advertised tape recordings entitled "Let your cancer disappear with image rehearsal and biofeedback," "Image rehearsal and biofeedback to let your joints be normal and comfortable if you have arthritis," and "Feel wonderful without the urge to drink alcohol excessively with image rehearsal and biofeedback" (R. M. Stern & Ray, 1980, p. v). We will look at several effective biofeedback applications. (Go to .)

Close-Up 14.1
"Mind Control" with EEG Biofeedback?

In the early 1970s, the findings of research on EEG biofeedback seemed to suggest that training to increase a specific type of brain electrical activity, called *alpha brain waves*, enabled individuals to achieve an "alpha experience" of deep relaxation and well-being (Olson & Schwartz, 1987; R. M. Stern & Ray, 1980). Alpha waves are a normal component of wakeful brain activity that tend to increase during certain conditions, such as while daydreaming or meditating. The news media quickly publicized the findings about biofeedback, and many people rushed to get training or to buy equipment with instructions that would permit them to achieve that experience, and with it, some level of "mind control."

The idea of being able to control one's own mind to decrease feelings of anxiety and increase feelings of relaxation through EEG biofeedback is quite intriguing. But research results have not supported this possibility (Olson & Schwartz, 1987; White & Tursky, 1982). For instance, studies have shown that people who receive training to increase alpha activity are likely to report that they have had the "alpha experience" only if they were told it would happen (Plotkin, 1976). EEG training to increase alpha wave activity does not seem to help people to reduce their anxiety or to experience feelings of relaxation and well-being.

Biofeedback and Epilepsy

Epilepsy is a neurological condition marked by recurrent, sudden seizures that result from electrical disturbances in the brain (EFA, 1990). In the most severe form of epileptic seizure, called a *grand mal attack*, the person loses consciousness and has muscle spasms. EEG biofeedback has been used successfully with many patients in helping them learn to control their brain electrical activity and reduce their seizures (L. H. Goldstein, 1990; Sterman, 1986). The general approach in using EEG biofeedback with epileptics involves training the patient to increase or decrease certain kinds of brain wave activity in specific areas of the brain. If the person can gain some measure of control over these brain waves in the areas of the brain where the disturbances occur, seizures should diminish. Although not all patients benefit from this approach, many do. One problem in using biofeedback to reduce seizures is the lack of a good way to predict which patients will benefit from the approach and which will not. This is an important consideration because the procedure is costly, requiring many hours of individually supervised training with expensive equipment.

Biofeedback and Hypertension

Hypertension is the medical condition of having high blood pressure consistently over several weeks or more. Medical treatment for hypertension usually includes having the person use prescription drugs and make lifestyle changes, such as exercising and making dietary changes designed to lower weight. BP biofeedback is a useful supplement to medical treatment. It appears to help people control their blood pressure, thereby enabling them to use less medication (McCaffrey & Blanchard, 1985; Olson & Kroon, 1987). The drugs used in treating hypertension can cause side effects, such as increased blood sugar levels or feelings of weakness or confusion, that some patients can tolerate only with great difficulty. Using behavioral methods may be especially useful in helping these people to reduce their blood pressures while minimizing the use of drugs.

Biofeedback and Anxiety

In earlier chapters, we have discussed how anxiety and other conditioned emotional responses can be reduced through procedures that relax the muscles, particularly by using progressive muscle relaxation techniques. Because EMG biofeedback can help people learn to relax specific muscle groups, studies have investigated the utility of this form of biofeedback in treating anxiety. Most of these studies have focused on applying biofeedback to reduce tension in the *frontalis*—a large, rectangular sheet of muscle that spans most of the forehead. These studies focused on tension in this muscle because some evidence suggests a link between frontalis relaxation and general body relaxation (Surwit & Keefe, 1978). Robert Gatchel (1982) has reviewed the research using EMG biofeedback and concluded that although the procedure is effective in reducing anxiety, it is not more effective than other, more easily administered relaxation methods, such as progressive muscle relaxation.

Biofeedback and Chronic Headache

Two biofeedback approaches have been used for treating patients who suffer from severe and chronic headaches (Andrasik, Blake, & McCarran, 1986). One approach is used with *muscle-contraction* (or "tension") *headaches*, which seem to result from persistent contraction of the head and neck muscles; patients receive EMG biofeedback training to control the tension in specific muscle groups, such as those in the scalp and neck. The other approach is used with *migraine headaches*, which appear to result from the constriction and dilation of blood vessels inside and outside the skull. Patients with migraine headaches receive temperature biofeedback training to help them control the constriction and dilation of arteries in the head. Research has shown that biofeedback methods and relaxation methods are about equally effective in reducing chronic headache, and using both methods together can be more effective than using either one alone, at least for some patients (Andrasik, Blake, & McCarran, 1986; Holroyd & Penzien, 1985). What's more, the results of several follow-up studies have shown that treating chronic headache with relaxation techniques or with relaxation and biofeedback methods together provides durable relief for at least 2 years (Blanchard, 1987). The data from one study with five yearly follow-up assessments are presented in Figure 14.1 (Blanchard et al., 1987).

This woman is receiving EMG biofeedback with sounds delivered through the earphones to reflect the level of muscle tension in her forehead.

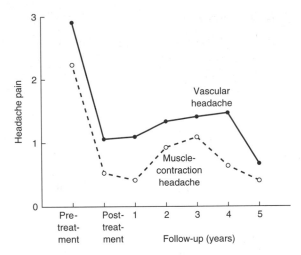

Figure 14.1   Mean ratings of headache pain for muscle-contraction and vascular (migraine, often with muscle-contraction) headache patients who completed treatment with either progressive muscle relaxation or both relaxation and biofeedback. The graph plots patients' ratings at pretreatment, posttreatment, and follow-up years 1 through 5. (Data from Blanchard et al., 1987, Table 1.)

Biofeedback and Neuromuscular Disorders

Neuromuscular disorders are medical conditions affecting the muscles and the nerves that carry information directing the muscles to move. Some neuromuscular disorders involve paralysis, which may have resulted from a spinal cord injury or a stroke that damages the brain, and other disorders cause the muscles to become rigid or have spasms. Such conditions have been treated successfully with EMG biofeedback (Brudny, 1982; Fogel, 1987; Krebs, 1987). The procedure involves monitoring muscles in the affected body parts, such as the legs, with electronic equipment sensitive enough to detect tiny changes in muscular function. In the case of patients with paralysis of part of the body, the paralysis cannot be total, as happens when the spinal cord is completely severed. For patients whose muscles are incompletely paralyzed—that is, the nerves are damaged, but the spinal cord is not severed—EMG biofeedback is conducted by showing the patient that the muscle has tensed a bit and encouraging him or her to tense it more and more, thereby

After this police officer had recovered from a gunshot wound, he received EMG biofeedback to improve the muscle control in his hand and arm.

gradually increasing its strength. For patients with rigid muscles, the feedback focuses on relaxing the muscles. Patients with muscle spasms focus on trying to get the EMG pattern to match that of normal muscle action.

Methods Using Intense and Prolonged Exposure

Several methods have been developed to reduce people's fears. Some methods, such as systematic desensitization, proceed very gradually in exposing a person to fearful situations, to minimize the degree of fear experienced. Other techniques take a very different approach: they deliberately expose the person to high levels of fear while preventing the possibility of escape or avoidance behaviors. The purpose of this approach is to extinguish the escape or avoidance behaviors the person has relied on in the past when the fear was aroused. Because these methods are designed to arouse high anxiety, they are called **anxiety-induction therapies**. There are two basic types: flooding and implosive therapy.

Flooding

At the beginning of this chapter, we considered the case of a woman who was afraid of escalators. Her therapist helped her overcome this fear by accompanying her as she rode up and down on a department store escalator for about half an hour. This treatment is an example of a technique called **flooding** (or *response prevention*) in which the person is exposed to a highly feared situation for prolonged periods of time under the direction of a therapist. In flooding, the therapist tries to prevent the person from using avoidance or escape responses to reduce anxiety; relaxation exercises usually are not included. In effect, since negative reinforcement is prevented, flooding is an extinction procedure. Therapists typically explain to their clients the rationale for having to experience the highly feared situation intensely for prolonged periods without avoiding or escaping. Upon receiving this explanation, clients know what to expect, can make an informed consent to participate in the treatment approach, and have an opportunity to become committed to trying hard to tolerate emotionally difficult periods in the treatment. When the source of a fear is fairly specific, such as escalators, it is often possible to complete flooding treatment in one session. But when the source is broad, complex, or vague, as it is in the case of most social anxieties, many sessions may be needed to present a wide range of possible CSs.

Flooding Procedures

In our example of the woman who was afraid of escalators, the initial boarding of the moving stairway was very difficult. And once she was on board the first time, the woman appeared very frightened. It is not unusual for clients to be highly emotional in the early stages of flooding procedures, but these reactions decrease with exposure. Still, some clients are not able to tolerate extremely intense initial exposures, and a therapist may need to present the feared situation somewhat gradually, advancing through a short stimulus hierarchy that contains several fear-arousing situations (Borden, 1992). Requiring an initial exposure that is too threatening may lead the client to drop out of treatment and retain the fear. Obviously, the therapist should make certain that exposure to the feared situation (the CS) will *not* be accompanied by an unpleasant US. For instance, a client who is fearful of dogs should not be exposed to a dog that might bite.

Fearful situations in flooding can be presented *in vivo*—that is, in real life, as in the therapy for the fear of escalators—or as scenes in the person's imagination. Sometimes *in vivo* presentations can be more complicated than the escalator example to set up. In one case, a woman had developed an *obsessive–compulsive disorder*, a condition characterized by an extreme preoccupation (or "obsession") with anxiety-provoking ideas or events and a compulsion to perform maladaptive rituals to reduce the anxiety. This woman had developed an idea she found very distressing, namely, that objects associated with death were "contaminated" with death (Meyer, Robertson, & Tatlow, 1975). After her father died, for example, she took a suitcase of his belongings to her apartment. Because of her idea that the dead man's personal things were contaminated, she carefully washed the suitcase, placed it in the back of a closet, and took a bath. These actions made her feel better, and she never touched the suitcase again. Other items she thought were contaminated were pictures of dead people, newspaper articles about death, and her fiancé, whose ex-wife had died recently. The successful *in vivo* flooding treatment included a visit to a hospital mortuary, in the company of a therapist, in which she had to touch a dead body.

Research comparing *in vivo* and imaginal flooding procedures has found that both methods can successfully reduce many different anxieties and phobias, and neither approach is clearly more effective than the other (Borden, 1992; James, 1986; Mathews et al., 1976). Imaginal procedures can be used when it is difficult or impossible to present feared situations in their real-life form, and this is an important advantage. For example, it may be difficult to use real-life stimuli when a person is afraid of flying in airplanes, especially if the fear is greatest under flight conditions of turbulence or when strange noises occur. And it is impossible to present *in vivo* stimuli to reduce the fears individuals develop with respect to extremely traumatic events, such as wars, natural disasters, or rape. (Go to 📖 .)

Effectiveness of Flooding

Research has shown that flooding is a highly effective technique for reducing a wide variety of anxiety and phobic conditions (TFPDPP, 1993; Trull, Nietzel, & Main, 1988). Flooding is about as effective as systematic desensitization, but imaginal flooding appears to be more effective than imaginal desensitization (Marshall et al., 1977; G. T. Wilson, 1982).

Case Study 14.1
Imaginal Flooding for War Trauma
....

Joseph was a 6 1/2-year-old Lebanese boy who had experienced a bomb blast; he was referred for therapy by his teacher because he had developed frequent temper outbursts, memory problems, and inattention behaviors in class (as described in Saigh, 1986). Interviews and clinical assessments revealed that the child showed similar behavior problems at home, had trauma-related nightmares, and was very depressed. Imaginal flooding was applied to reduce his emotional condition.

The therapy Joseph received combined a flooding procedure with relaxation, using progressive muscle relaxation exercises and a calm scene of being on a beach. (As we saw earlier, using relaxation with flooding is unusual.) Each session began with relaxation exercises and then focused mainly on flooding one of several trauma-related

scenes, two of which were: "hearing a loud explosion and seeing injured people and debris" and "being led away from the site against background calls for help and automobile horns." Joseph had assessed each of the trauma-related scenes on a subjective units of discomfort scale (SUDS) as being extremely uncomfortable to imagine. No mild or moderately strong CSs were used. During the flooding procedure, he was asked to imagine a traumatic scene in great detail for over 20 minutes and give it a SUDS rating every minute. The remainder of the session was spent briefly imagining the other traumatic scenes and doing more relaxation exercises. The SUDS ratings Joseph gave were reduced dramatically in about three sessions for each traumatic scene. Follow-up assessments made during the 6 months after treatment showed only mild discomfort for any of the scenes.

....

A recent study examined the success of a combination of *in vivo* and imaginal flooding in treating social phobics—individuals who suffer extreme levels of anxiety in social situations (Turner, Beidel, & Jacob, 1994). People with social phobias experience strong physiological symptoms, such as trembling, heart palpitations, and sweating, when experiencing social situations that others do not find particularly distressing. This study compared the effects of three treatment conditions: (1) flooding therapy, (2) drug therapy in which clients took a commonly prescribed drug (atenolol) for helping social phobics cope with social situations, and (3) a *placebo* condition in which clients took inert tablets they thought were atenolol. All three treatment conditions were administered for 3 months, and the effects were assessed, for example, by having the clients fill out psychological tests measuring their anxiety and asking them to speak for 10 minutes to an audience of three individuals. The results showed that flooding was generally more effective than the drug and placebo conditions in reducing the clients' anxiety problems and maintaining their gains in the 6 months after the treatment ended. For example, Figure 14.2 shows that the mean length of the speeches given by clients increased much more for those who received flooding therapy than for those in the two other treatment conditions.

Studies have also examined two important questions about using flooding techniques. First, is it necessary for a therapist to accompany clients when they are exposed to the fearful situations? The outcome of research on this question indicates that the success of flooding is not enhanced by having therapists present for most of their clients' exposures to highly fearful situations (Al-Kubaisy et al., 1992).

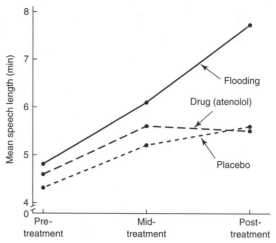

Figure 14.2   Mean speech length in minutes at pretreatment, midtreatment, and posttreatment assessments for socially phobic clients under three treatment conditions: flooding therapy, drug (atenolol) therapy, and placebo drug therapy (clients took inert tablets that were described as atenolol). At each assessment, the clients were asked to give a 10-minute speech. As a social comparison, normal (nonphobic) individuals who were assessed in the same manner spoke for an average of 8.1 minutes. (Data from Turner, Beidel, & Jacob, 1994, Table 3.)

It may be important for therapists to be present during the most fearful encounters, but their main roles in flooding therapy involve assessing the problem, designing the treatment, instructing the client on how to perform flooding, and monitoring progress. Second, how safe is flooding? When anxiety-induction therapies were originally described, many therapists were concerned about the possibility of serious side effects, perhaps making clients' conditions worse, rather than better. But a survey of therapists who had used anxiety-induction therapies with clients in the intervening years revealed that the procedures are quite safe, with negative outcomes being reported in only 9 out of nearly 3500 cases (Shipley & Boudewyns, 1980).

Implosive Therapy

Implosive therapy is a variation of imaginal flooding in which a person is asked to imagine scenes that include unrealistic, exaggerated, or physically damaging events that are unlikely to happen in real life (Morganstern, 1973; Stampfl & Levis, 1967). When Thomas Stampfl developed this technique, he wanted to address unrealistic beliefs that often seem to underlie or maintain people's anxieties. So, for instance, the following scenes have been used in implosive therapy:

- A client with an extreme fear of heights imagined being on a roof garden atop a 40-story building, leaning against a wall that collapses, and falling down to the street (Crowe et al., 1972).

✔ Concept Check 14.1

1. Biofeedback involves giving individuals information about the _____ _____ in their physiological systems.
2. Receiving information about the status or changes in muscle tension is called _____ _____ biofeedback.
3. EEG training to increase _____ wave brain activity does not seem to help reduce anxiety.
4. A medical condition for which biofeedback training can be helpful is _____ _____. ⇔
5. An example of a fear for which *in vivo* flooding would be difficult or impossible to conduct is the fear of _____. ↔
6. Having clients who are afraid of elevators imagine they are in one that is plunging down 20 stories is an example of _____ therapy.

_____

Answers:

1. status or changes 2. electromyograph (EMG) 3. alpha 4. neuromuscular disorders/headache/epilepsy/hypertension 5. being mugged or shot 6. implosive

• A person with a phobia of spiders imagined a spider having crawled on "your face and that it starts biting your cheek and chewing your eyes" (Marshall et al., 1977).

• A client with a phobia of snakes imagined being bitten and slithered on by a large, slimy snake (Mealiea & Nawas, 1971).

Although several studies have shown that implosive therapy can reduce people's anxiety and phobic conditions, flooding techniques without including unrealistic aversive events are at least as effective as implosive therapy (Marshall et al., 1977; Morganstern, 1973; G. T. Wilson, 1982). Having clients imagine exaggerated or physically damaging events does not appear to reduce their fears any faster than comparable techniques. (Go to ✔ .)

Specialized Modeling Applications

We have seen in earlier chapters that modeling is a straightforward and very useful method for changing operant and respondent behaviors. In efforts to change operant behaviors, modeling serves as a shortcut stimulus control technique for the demonstration of how the responses are to be performed. In changing respondent behaviors, modeling shows adaptive behaviors that can be applied in fearful situations and enables the fear to become desensitized vicariously. We will examine a few ways in which modeling has been applied in specialized settings and circumstances.

Training Professional Skills

Modeling is often applied in training specific skills professionals need to use in their work (Dowrick & Jesdale, 1991). Videotapes are commonly employed to present the modeled professional skills. For instance, videotapes have been developed to show health care workers in hospitals how to handle such psychiatric emergencies as incoming patients who threaten to kill themselves. Other tapes have been developed for training graduate students to serve as teaching assistants and for training counselors in skills needed to mediate divorces. Research investigating the effectiveness of videotaped modeling in training professional skills has shown that this approach is often more effective than live *role-playing*—that is, having two or more individuals enact interpersonal scenes.

Sometimes the videotapes used in professional training are designed around a story or high interest issue to arouse the interest of the viewer. But there is a danger in doing this: some research findings indicate that "modeling videotapes purposely designed to maintain high viewer interest may cause so much attention to be focused on the issue presented that the modeled behaviors themselves may be overlooked" (Dowrick & Jesdale, 1991, p. 69). So, for example, in a videotape on the handling of psychiatric emergencies, the story of why a person wants to commit suicide may be so absorbing that the viewer doesn't notice the modeled skills for preventing suicide.

Assertion Training

Being *assertive* involves speaking up and reacting openly around people, expressing both positive and negative opinions and feelings. **Assertion training** refers to programs of behavioral methods that train individuals to be assertive in appropriate and adaptive ways. Assertiveness need not be accompanied by inconsiderate or aggressive behavior. One view of the ways appropriate and adaptive assertion differs from aggression is that assertion involves

> expressing thoughts, feelings, and beliefs in direct, honest, and appropriate ways which respect the rights of other people. In contrast, aggression involves self-expression which is characterized by violating others' rights and demeaning others in an attempt to achieve one's own objectives. (Lange & Jakubowski, 1976, pp. 38–39)

Although assertion training can be applied to tone down people's excessive assertive behaviors, it is generally used with individuals who are unassertive. People may fail to assert themselves for many reasons. For instance, they may not know what to say, may fear something awful will happen if they speak up, or may believe that being assertive is not proper in many situations.

Types and Assessment of Assertion

Individuals who are relatively assertive are not likely to be assertive in all situations. One factor that can influence whether people will be assertive is the type of assertion a given situation calls for (Christoff & Kelly, 1985; Lange & Jakubowski, 1976). Four common types of assertive behavior are:

- *Refusing others' requests*—being able to say no when others ask you to do them a favor or service, especially when the request is unreasonable. For instance, if a friend asks you to run an errand that would make you late for an appointment, you might say, "I'm sorry, I can't do that right now because I'd be late for my exam. I could do it later, if that would help."

- *Standing up for one's rights*—being able to object when you think your rights are being abridged or that someone is cheating you. Say you've been waiting for service in a store and another customer comes in and gets the clerk's attention. You might say, "I suppose you didn't notice, but I was here first."

- *Voicing one's opinions or feelings*—being able to express positive or negative ideas or judgments. For instance, you might express your liking or admiration for someone by saying, "That answer you gave in class was really insightful." Or, you might express a political or moral viewpoint to others with the knowledge that those in the group disagree strongly.

- *Expressing one's desires or requests*—being able to voice your needs or goals to others. For example, you might ask someone for help or suggest doing some activity you would enjoy.

Some people have an easy time showing some types of assertion, such as voicing their opinions, but have difficulty showing other types of assertion, such as saying no. Other people have problems showing any assertion at all. In some cases, being assertive is difficult only in certain situations or with certain people.

Therapists usually assess a client's assertiveness on the basis of interviews and one or both of two other measures. One measure involves observing the client either in real assertion situations or in simulated situations, using a *role-playing* method. The second measure has the client fill out a questionnaire that measures assertion. On some questionnaires clients rate the degree to which each of many different assertive behaviors describes the way they react in everyday life. For instance, clients might rate statements such as "I speak up easily when I am in a group" on a 5-point scale (0 = never and 4 = always). Two instruments that use this approach are the Assertion Inventory (Gambrill & Richey, 1975) and the College Self-Expression Scale (Galassi et al., 1974). Other questionnaires have clients predict from several possible responses how they would react to very specific situations. For example, the Conflict Resolution Inventory (McFall & Lillesand, 1970, 1971) presents 35 hypothetical situations in which the respondent receives a request, such as:

> A slight acquaintance of yours asks to borrow $5 until next week. You have the money, but you would have to postpone buying something you wanted until the loan was repaid.

The respondent chooses from five statements ranging from "I would *refuse* and would not feel uncomfortable about doing so" to "I would *not refuse* because it seems to be a reasonable request."

Assertion Training Techniques

Modeling plays a critical role in assertion training programs (Hersen et al., 1979; McFall & Twentyman, 1973). Although modeling procedures are usually carried out *overtly* in individual therapy or in group therapy sessions, they can be very effective when applied *covertly*, too. In *overt* modeling, the therapist, another client, or some other person models assertive behavior live or on videotape for scenarios in which assertion would be appropriate or adaptive. After each scenario, the client is asked to imitate the observed behavior and receives feedback on his or her performance. The client's acting out the behavior is called **behavior rehearsal**. This procedure is carried out for a variety of everyday scenarios, and the client may also be asked to demonstrate how he or she would react in situations that were not specifically modeled.

In *covert* modeling, the therapist describes the full scenario and has the client visualize the appropriate assertive behavior in his or her imagination (Cautela, 1993a). The individual performing the behavior in the scene can be the client or some other person. The therapist instructs the client on the assertive behavior to visualize and indicates appropriate features. For instance, if the client is the assertive person in the scene, the therapist might state (Hersen et al., 1979, p. 372):

- You must be looking directly at the person to whom you are speaking.
- You should respond promptly to the other person.

After this client acts out a response in a behavior rehearsal procedure, she will receive feedback on her performance.

- Talk long enough to ensure that the person fully understands what you are saying.
- Be sure that your tone of voice reflects how you feel about the situation.

The client is asked to relax and imagine the complete scene. When the client signals, such as by raising a finger, that the imagery is clear, the therapist describes a positive consequence for the client to imagine as an outcome of the assertive interaction.

A few other points can be made about assertion training. First, the therapy typically includes *homework assignments* designed to permit clients to engage in overt and covert assertive behaviors. Often these assignments are arranged in a hierarchy, beginning with easy assertive situations and advancing gradually to more difficult ones. For instance, in a restaurant, a very unassertive client might start by simply asking a waiter for a menu, then asking the waiter to repeat a description of some food, and then requesting a service, such as bringing a fork, that the waiter should have done already. Second, assertion training tries to be realistic in preparing clients for events in which being assertive doesn't work. (Suppose a client requests a favor and receives a refusal.) Modeling and role-playing are used in teaching clients how to deal with these situations. Last, although many clients appear to relapse into unassertiveness after successful assertion training, research has found that those who receive monthly booster sessions are much more likely to maintain their gains and to improve further than clients who receive no booster sessions (Baggs & Spence, 1990).

Reducing Anxiety in Medical Patients

Videotaped modeling is a very effective method for reducing patients' anxieties before, during, and after frightening medical treatments, such as surgery or invasive dental work (Parrish & Babbitt, 1991). Reducing patients' anxieties is important for humane reasons, but it can have two other desirable effects: (1) it tends to increase the likelihood that patients will cooperate with and not disrupt the medical procedures, and (2) it tends to decrease the amount of time patients spend in the hospital to recover and the amount of medication they take while there (Sarafino, 1994).

Preparing Patients for Nonsurgical Procedures

Many medical procedures that don't involve surgery are very difficult to undergo, sometimes because they produce pain or discomfort. *Endoscopy*, which is used in diagnosing ulcers and other disorders of the digestive tract, is one such procedure. The most aversive aspect of an endoscopic examination is that a long, flexible, fiberoptic tube, almost half an inch in diameter, must be passed through the patient's mouth and down to the stomach or intestine. This tube, which transmits images of the interior lining, remains in the digestive tract for about 15 to 30 minutes. The person receives tranquilizing medication and has had the throat swabbed with a local anesthetic, but he or she is awake throughout the procedure.

Videotaped modeling has been applied in research to show patients who were awaiting endoscopic examinations what the procedure consists of and how to reduce their anxiety (Shipley et al., 1978). The tape was 18 minutes long and showed an adult

> patient actually receiving an endoscopy. The patient in the tape showed an "average" amount of distress during the examination, gagging several times and requiring a moderate amount of "calming talk" by the nurse. (p. 502)

Some patients saw the tape three times before having the procedure themselves, other patients saw it only once, and other patients saw a different videotape that was not related to having any medical procedure. After each endoscopy, the physicians and nurses rated the degree of anxiety each patient showed during the procedure, without knowing which videotape condition the patient had experienced. The findings indicated that seeing the videotape of the endoscopy just once reduced the patients' signs of anxiety substantially, and seeing it three times reduced their anxiety even more.

Preparing Patients for Surgical Procedures

The application of videotaped and filmed modeling to reduce anxieties prior to undergoing surgery has focused mainly on pediatric patients (Parrish & Babbitt, 1991). Barbara Melamed and Lawrence Siegel (1975) conducted an experiment with 4- to 12-year-old hospital patients who were scheduled for elective surgery, such as tonsillectomies. The researchers assigned the children to two groups, matching them for age, sex, race, and type of operation. One group saw a film that was relevant to having surgery, and the other group saw a film about a boy who goes on a nature trip in the country. The film "Ethan Has an Operation" portrays the hospital experience of a 7-year-old boy,

> showing various events that most children encounter when hospitalized for elective surgery from the time of admission to time of discharge including the child's orientation to the hospital ward and medical personnel such as the surgeon and anesthesiologist; having a blood test and exposure to standard hospital equipment; separation from the mother; and scenes in the operating and recovery rooms. . . . Both the child's behavior and verbal remarks exemplify the behavior of a coping model so that while he exhibits some anxiety and apprehension, he is able to overcome his initial fears and complete each event in a successful and nonanxious manner. (p. 514)

To assess the emotional adjustment of the children in the two groups the evening before surgery and at a follow-up visit about 3 weeks after the operation, the researchers used measures of three types: the children's hand sweating, questionnaire self-reports of fear, and ratings by trained observers of the emotional behaviors displayed.

The results with all three measures revealed that the children who saw the film about Ethan's operation experienced less anxiety before and after surgery than those who saw the irrelevant film. Several studies have found similar benefits in using video presentations to reduce children's medical fears (Parrish & Babbitt, 1991). But other studies have discovered that the effects of video preparation for surgery may depend on the age and prior medical experiences of the child (Sarafino, 1994). Still, video preparations for surgery are usually helpful and appear to be cost-effective: a study of children hospitalized for elective surgery found that those who received video preparation recovered more quickly than those who did not get the preparation (Pinto & Hollandsworth, 1989). The savings due to earlier release from the hospital amounted to several times the cost of providing the preparation.

Aversion Therapy

The powerful 1971 science fiction movie *A Clockwork Orange* portrayed an extremely violent young man who was convicted of a vicious crime and underwent a grotesque form of therapy to reduce his violent behavior: his eyelids were propped open with splints and then he was forced to watch violent scenes projected on a screen while becoming nauseated from the effects of an emetic drug. After many of these sessions, he could no longer bear the idea of aggression and became so meek that he could not defend himself when he was released to his original environment. This movie presents some interesting and compelling concerns about the use of aversive techniques in behavior therapy. It has been known for some time, however, that the effects these techniques produce on behavior are far weaker than those portrayed in the movie and that the techniques are not very effective when applied to individuals against their will (Barlow, 1978). Nevertheless, aversive therapeutic techniques can be helpful under certain circumstances in programs to change behavior.

In **aversion therapy**, an unpleasant or painful stimulus is introduced while the client engages overtly or covertly in an undesirable behavior. The aversive stimulus is generally terminated as soon as the person stops the behavior. This procedure may be repeated over and over again within each of many therapy sessions. The purpose in using this therapy approach is to have the client begin to associate the behavior or its antecedents with the aversive stimulus, through respondent conditioning, so that performing that response becomes unpleasant. Thus, the procedure is a form of *counterconditioning*, in which the attractiveness of inappropriate behavior or stimuli is reduced and replaced with unpleasantness.

Aversion therapy procedures can apply almost any stimulus the client finds unpleasant or painful, including nausea-producing drugs, disgusting odors, feelings of humiliation, and painful (but not dangerous) electric shock. When electric shock is used, the level of shock is determined individually for each client by starting with a low voltage and increasing it to a level that is very uncomfortable or somewhat painful to that person (Barlow, 1978). An advantage in using shock is that it can be turned on and off exactly as needed. The technique of aversive therapy was developed mainly as a way of modifying behaviors that produce powerful reinforcers, as occur in smoking cigarettes and drinking alcohol.

Aversion Therapy in Stopping Smoking

Aversion therapy to help people stop smoking has applied stimuli of three main types: electric shock, imagined negative scenes, and cigarette smoke itself. When electric shock is used, the therapist first determines the appropriate voltage to be used and then pairs the shock with smoking plus stimuli associated with smoking. When imagined negative scenes are used, the client thinks about a sequence of negative events, such as getting ready to smoke but becoming nauseated and vomiting.

Cigarette smoke can be made into an unpleasant stimulus in several ways. One way, called *rapid smoking*, requires the person to take a puff, or "drag," of a cigarette every several seconds while concentrating on the unpleasant sensations the smoke produces (Tiffany, Martin, & Baker, 1986). In *satiation*, the person doubles or triples his or her usual smoking rate at home for some period of time. Using cigarette smoke as an unpleasant stimulus in aversion therapy for controlling smoking appears to be more effective than imagined scenes or electric shock (Kamarck & Lichtenstein, 1985; Lichtenstein & Mermelstein, 1984). Stopping smoking is hard to do. For some smokers, aversion therapy techniques may be useful as a first step in a treatment program for quitting.

Aversion Therapy in Stopping Drinking

Like quitting smoking, stopping excessive drinking is difficult. Using aversive therapy may help. In aversion therapy to help people stop drinking, two main types of unpleasant stimulus have been used—electric shock and nausea-producing drugs—but electric shock has not been a very successful aversive stimulus in stopping problem drinking (Miller & Hester, 1980).

A much more effective aversion therapy strategy has been to have the person take an *emetic drug*, such as *emetine*, that induces nausea when alcohol is consumed. In a typical half-hour session, the person first receives an injection of emetine and then repeatedly drinks an alcoholic beverage, each time quickly becoming nauseated and vomiting (W. R. Miller & Hester, 1980). The person undergoes several of these sessions, typically as an inpatient in a hospital, and receives booster sessions periodically after discharge. A study of hundreds of problem drinkers who received emetine therapy revealed that 63% of the men and women remained abstinent during the 12 months after treatment, and half of these individuals remained abstinent for the next 2 years (Wiens & Menustik, 1983). Although the effectiveness of emetive therapy is far from ideal, it is high for this type of problem behavior. Other studies using emetine in aversion therapy for alcohol abuse have also demonstrated high rates of success (Elkins, 1991; W. R. Miller & Hester, 1980).

Despite the success aversion therapy has had in modifying various behaviors, it is not widely used for at least three reasons (Wilson, 1991). First, there are important ethical concerns associated with the use of aversive stimuli in treatment, par-

✔ Concept Check 14.2

....

1. The therapy method of having two or more people enact interpersonal scenes is called _____ .

2. As an example of being unassertive, someone might want to _____ _____ but does not speak up. ⇔

3. A client's practicing a behavior that someone modeled is called _____ .

4. An example of a nonsurgical medical procedure (other than endoscopy) for which patients might benefit by having their anxieties reduced through the method of videotaped modeling is _____ . ⇔

5. Using videotaped modeling to reduce children's anxieties about prospective surgery is known to be cost-effective because the children _____ _____ .

6. The approach of applying an unpleasant or painful stimulus while the client engages in an undesirable behavior is called _____ .

_____

Answers: 1. role-playing   2. compliment a friend/suggest changing the TV channel others are watching   3. behavior rehearsal   4. childbirth/dental work   5. recover and leave the hospital sooner   6. aversion therapy

....

ticularly when research has not yet demonstrated a clear superiority of aversion therapy over other approaches for changing such target behaviors as drinking. Second, aversion therapy can be more expensive to carry out than other approaches of behavior modification, especially if the treatment must be done in a hospital or under the continual supervision of a therapist. Third, some evidence indicates that clients who receive aversive therapy are more likely to drop out of treatment or fail to administer the aversive stimulus at home—by not taking emetine, for example (G. T. Wilson, Leaf, & Nathan, 1975; G. T. Wilson & Tracey, 1976). (Go to ✔ .)

Application Exercise

This application exercise is designed to have you apply the concepts on specialized behavioral methods you've just read about. Turn to Work Sheet 14.1 and complete the tasks dealing with biofeedback, intense and prolonged exposure methods, modeling, and aversion therapy.

Summary

This chapter describes specialized behavioral methods that typically require professional supervision. In the technique of biofeedback, an electrical/mechanical device monitors the status of changes in a person's physiological processes. The device immediately reports that information to the person, enabling him or her to apply the principles of operant conditioning to gain voluntary control over those internal processes. Training in biofeedback can be given for a wide variety of physiological systems, using such measures as blood pressure, heart rate, muscle tension, and skin temperature. This technique has been used in treating epilepsy, hypertension, anxiety, chronic headache, and certain neuromuscular disorders.

Anxiety-induction therapies are designed to arouse high levels of fear while preventing the client from escaping or avoiding the fearful situations presented. In flooding, a person experiences intense, prolonged exposure to feared situations under the direction of a therapist. The exposure can be *in vivo* or imagined, and both modes are highly effective in reducing strong fears and obsessive–compulsive behaviors. Implosive therapy is an imaginal procedure to reduce fears by means of having a person picture exaggerated events that are unlikely to happen in real life. The exaggerated scenes used in this anxiety-induction therapy method do not seem to make the technique more effective than imaginal flooding.

Modeling techniques have been applied in specialized ways and settings to train workers in professional skills, to help people be more assertive, and to help individuals cope well with frightening medical procedures. In assertion training, clients are helped to become more appropriately and adaptively assertive in daily life by learning to stand up for their rights, to identify and refuse unreasonable requests, and so on. This training often involves overt and covert modeling, behavior rehearsal, role-playing, and homework assignments. Using videotaped modeling to reduce fears of surgical and diagnostic procedures increases the likelihood that medical patients will cooperate with and not disrupt the procedures, and decreases patients' recovery time, length of hospital stay, or both.

Aversion therapy is a specialized technique in which an unpleasant or painful stimulus is applied while the client engages overtly or covertly in an undesirable target behavior. This therapy method was developed as a way of reducing problem behaviors that produce powerful reinforcers. Aversion therapy has shown some success in helping people stop smoking cigarettes and drinking excessively.

Key Terms and Review Questions

Key Terms

biofeedback
anxiety-induction therapies
flooding
implosive therapy

assertion training
behavior rehearsal
aversion therapy

Review Questions

1. What is biofeedback and what can it enable the user to do?

2. Describe four different types of biofeedback.

3. Discuss the usefulness of biofeedback training on alpha brain waves.

4. Describe how a physical therapist might use biofeedback to help a patient gain strength in her legs after a few months of being unable to walk as a result of an injury that damaged (but did not sever) the spinal cord.

5. Define the basic approach of anxiety-induction therapies.

6. Describe how a therapist might use imaginal flooding to help a man overcome his extreme fear of going outside at night, a phobia he developed after being mugged and assaulted one evening.

7. What is implosive therapy, and how useful is its feature of including exaggerated events in its scenes?

8. Define "being assertive," and give one example each of three different types of assertive behavior.

9. What is assertion training, and what techniques does it include?

10. Describe the methods a therapist could use to assess a client's assertiveness.

11. Describe the research by Melamed and Siegel (1975) on reducing anxiety in children who are awaiting surgery.

12. What is aversion therapy, and what is its general obective?

13. Describe the types of unpleasant stimulus that have been used in aversive therapy to help people stop smoking.

Related Readings

Bandura, A. (1969). *Principles of behavior modification*. New York: Holt, Rinehart & Winston.

Barlow, D. H. (1978). Aversive procedures. In W. S. Agras (Ed.), *Behavior modification: Principles and clinical applications* (2nd ed.). Boston: Little, Brown.

Dowrick, P. W. (Ed.)(1991). *Practical guide to using video in the behavioral sciences*. New York: Wiley.

Schwartz, M. S. (Ed.)(1987). *Biofeedback: A practitioner's guide*. New York: Guilford.

Name _____   Day & time
                                   class meets_____
Date _____

Chapter 14: Work Sheet 14.1

1. *Asthma* is a respiratory condition whose symptoms include recurrent episodes of impaired breathing that results when tissue inflammation causes the airways to narrow, develop spasms, and produce mucus. Biofeedback devices can be used to measure the flow of air in the airways (Sarafino, 1995a). Suppose you were a therapist and wanted to use biofeedback to help a 7-year-old boy control his breathing better when he starts to have an asthma attack. Describe how you think the procedure would be conducted.

2. Describe a scene that might be used in implosive therapy for a young California woman's phobia for earthquakes.

3. Describe an assertion training scenario that clients might role-play in groups.

4. Describe a homework assignment a therapist might give to a 35-year-old man who is receiving assertion training for dealing with a bullying supervisor at his place of employment.

5. Describe an imagined negative scene that could be used as an unpleasant stimulus in aversion therapy to help someone stop smoking.

NOTE: If you will be submitting work sheets to your instructor or to a fellow student, make a copy of each sheet before submitting it.

15

Cognitive–Behavioral Therapies

What Are Cognitive–Behavioral Therapies?

Why Cognitive Processes Can Be Important

Historical Roots of Cognitive–Behavioral Therapy

Cognitive Restructuring Approaches

Rational–Emotive Therapy

Cognitive Therapy

Cognitive Skills Training Approaches

Stress Inoculation Training

Problem–Solving Training

Combined Therapy Approaches

Application Exercise

Prologue

Joseph Cautela (1993b) has described the case of client who didn't seem to be trying very hard to overcome his intense fear of flying. The man was not picturing very well the scenes he was asked to imagine, and he hadn't been listening to the tapes the therapist had asked him to use at home. So Cautela tried to find out why.

The therapist asked the man if he believed the behavior therapy techniques would work, and the client said he was sure they would because the friend who had recommended Cautela had overcome the same fear. So the therapist asked the client what would happen if he didn't have his fear, and the man replied that he would be promoted at work. At first Cautela thought the promotion would be an incentive for overcoming the fear, and said so, but the ensuing conversation indicated otherwise. The client responded to the idea that the promotion should be a motivator by saying,

> "Yeah, I guess so." I [Cautela] said, "What would the promotion mean to your job description?" He replied that he would have to fly more often. I said, "O.K., then we should get on with it." Then I asked what was wrong with flying a lot. He looked surprised and said, "Well, some of my co-workers who got promoted and flew a lot ended up getting heart attacks." I asked him if he was afraid of dying if he got promoted. He said, "Yes, I guess that's it." (p. 157)

Understanding the antecedent beliefs associated with the fear enabled the therapist and client to continue with appropriate procedures and to succeed in overcoming the problem at hand. Ultimately, the man was able to fly without being afraid.

This example illustrates how cognitive processes can influence the problem behaviors people develop. The way we perceive and think about events in everyday life has a strong impact on how we behave and what we feel. Because of the role cognitive processes can play in initiating and maintaining people's behavior, the techniques used in therapy often include cognitive methods to modify people's thought processes. This chapter focuses on therapy approaches that include cognitive methods in helping people change their overt and covert behavior.

What Are Cognitive–Behavioral Therapies?

The term **cognitive–behavioral therapy** refers to a broad class of therapy approaches to changing overt and covert behaviors by the application of both cognitive and behavioral methods (Dobson & Block, 1988). We examined the individual cognitive–behavioral techniques of self-statements, thought stopping, and distraction in Chapter 8. These techniques are often used in cognitive–behavioral therapy.

According to Donald Meichenbaum (1986), all cognitive–behavioral therapies share several characteristics. For instance, they provide a good deal of structure to the therapy process, and they enlist the clients as active participants in that process by, for example, giving them homework assignments. What's more, all cognitive–behavioral therapies apply to some degree procedures that can help clients to:

- Understand the nature of the problems they entered therapy to overcome.
- See their usual patterns of "automatic" thoughts, beliefs, and feelings as events that can be questioned and tested rather than as facts.
- Try out different overt and covert behaviors, then review their outcomes as "evidence" to disconfirm incorrect expectations and beliefs held previously.
- Learn new skills and strategies that promote self-regulation of overt and covert social, cognitive, and emotional behaviors.

The various forms of cognitive–behavioral therapy differ in the extent to which they emphasize each of these characteristics.

Sometimes cognitive–behavioral therapies are called *cognitive-behavior therapies* or simply *cognitive therapies*, and many psychologists use these names interchangeably (Davison & Neale, 1994; Dobson & Block, 1988; Kazdin, 1978). The terms for these forms of therapy have not yet been standardized. In fact, one form of cognitive–behavioral therapy is named "cognitive therapy," as we shall see.

Why Cognitive Processes Can Be Important

Several lines of evidence illustrate the role cognitive processes can play in problem behaviors and indicate why therapy approaches may find it helpful to address those processes (J. M. G. Williams et al., 1988). An example comes from the case of the man who was afraid of flying, which opened this chapter. Cautela's client was not participating fully in his therapy because he believed two things: first, that he would have to fly often if he overcame his fear, and second, that flying a lot causes heart attacks—which was his own incorrect deduction, based on his observation that other individuals who had flown a lot got heart attacks (Cautela, 1993b). This case provides clinical evidence that such beliefs may need to be addressed because they have the potential to prevent clients from cooperating in therapy.

Research has shown that cognitive processes are involved in or related to the development of several clinical disorders, such as depression and anxiety (Stein & Young, 1992). Let's consider *depression*. Clinical depression is much more than just feeling sad—when a person's sadness is severe, frequent, and long-lasting, it becomes a psychological disorder. In addition to having a generally unhappy mood, clinically depressed people typically feel *hopeless* and *pessimistic* about the future and have *low self-esteem*, often blaming themselves for the stressful, negative events they experience (Rosenhan & Seligman, 1984). These characteristics involve cognitive processes, such as thinking and believing, that can also lead individuals to thoughts

A teenage boy who is feeling depressed. When people are clinically depressed, their sadness is severe, frequent, and long-lasting.

or attempts of suicide. Studies of depressed adults and children have found that feelings of hopelessness are more closely related to whether people consider or attempt suicide than are other characteristics of depression, such as the degree of sadness they feel (Beck, Kovacs, & Weissman, 1975; Kazdin et al., 1983).

In the cognitive process called *attribution*, people try to identify causes or make judgments regarding their own or others' actions, motives, feelings, or intentions. The attributions individuals make can affect their behavior. Kenneth Dodge (1993) has described a large body of evidence showing a link between attributional patterns and physical aggressiveness. For instance, studies have shown that highly aggressive boys appear to be *biased* toward making *hostile attributions*—that is, they are far more likely than are boys who are not very aggressive to interpret an accidental event, such as being bumped in a crowded mall, as having been intentional and motivated by hostility. What's more, the results of several studies indicate that having this bias leads individuals to develop aggressive behavior problems in childhood and to commit violent crimes in the future. This means that individuals with this attributional bias are more likely to perceive a nonaggressive accident as hostile, hence to respond aggressively.

Another line of evidence showing a role of cognitive processes in behavior has to do with expectations and fear. Gerry Kent (1985) had dental patients fill out a brief anxiety scale while waiting for their dental appointments. They were then asked to rate the pain they expected to experience during the dental treatment. After their appointments, the patients rated the pain they actually experienced, and rated it again by mail 3 months later. The ratings suggested that anxiety had played a role in the subjects' expectations of pain and in their memories of it 3 months later. For the patients with high dental anxiety, the ratings for the pain they expected *and* the pain they remembered months later were four times as high as their ratings of the pain they experienced (the ratings given right after the appointments). In contrast, the low-anxiety patients' ratings of expected and remembered pain were less than twice as high as their ratings of the pain they experienced. These findings suggest that high-anxiety patients' memories of pain are determined far more by what they expect than by what they actually experience.

One other line of evidence illustrating why it can be useful to consider and address cognitive processes in programs to change behavior relates to the organization and function of brain structures. As we saw in Chapter 7, the results of research on memory and physiology support the view that the human memory system consists of two parts (Petri & Mishkin, 1994; Schacter, 1992; Squire, 1987). When we learn an operant or respondent behavior, we appear to store information about this learning in at least two different memory systems with separate, but linked, physiological structures. One of these systems, called *implicit* or *nondeclarative memory*, stores the basic associations for these learned behaviors. These associations link antecedents and behaviors—connecting, for example, a CS and a CR in a person's fear—but we are unaware of and cannot describe them. Nevertheless, associations stored in implicit, nondeclarative memory seem to trigger our habitual and emotional reactions to antecedents. In contrast, *explicit* or *declarative memory* contains factual information and details that we are aware of and can describe. If we know what antecedents trigger our behaviors, it's presumably because this knowledge is stored as factual information in explicit, declarative memory. So, for example, this information enables us to know that we are afraid of something and to describe how we acquired the fear. Presumably, then, we use our explicit or declarative memory systems in our cognitive processes when we think or have expectations about our fears. The distinction between these two memory systems may have important implications for therapy insofar as it offers an explanation of why some people's fears either do not respond to therapy or relapse after successful treatment (LeDoux, 1994). That is, a therapy that failed to eliminate a fear may have addressed the fear representation in only one memory system, leaving the other largely intact.

Historical Roots of Cognitive–Behavioral Therapy

The idea that altering the way people think about events in their lives can change their behavior has a long history that has been documented in ancient Buddhist and Greek writings (de Silva, 1984; M. J. Mahoney, 1993). For instance, Buddhist writings describe the case of a woman named Kisa Gotami who suffered intense grief after her infant son had died. She would not allow anyone to take his body from her and carried it around as she roamed the streets asking people if they knew of a remedy to bring him back to life. One man directed her to consult Siddhartha Gautama, the founder of Buddhism, whose followers often call "the Buddha," who suggested that she bring back to him some white mustard seeds from any house that had not experienced death. The bereaved mother went to a great many houses without success, and then

> began to realize what the Buddha had meant. She realized that death comes to all, that she was not the only one to have lost a child. When she returned to the

 ## Close-Up 15.1
Intellectual Capacity and Cognitive Methods

• •

For theoretical and intuitive reasons, we might expect that the effectiveness of cognitive methods in changing behavior would depend on the client's intellectual capacity or development, even if we excluded individuals who are developmentally disabled (Braswell & Kendall, 1988; Garfield, 1986). Is this expectation correct?

Researchers have examined the question in two ways. First, researchers conducted a meta-analysis for the results of over 60 studies that examined the effectiveness of cognitive–behavioral therapy with children at different levels of cognitive development (Durlak, Fuhrman, & Lampman, 1991). The children's problems varied, but each child showed substantial behavioral or social maladjustment. To examine the role of cognitive development in the success of cognitive–behavioral therapy, the analysis assumed that the children's developmental levels were higher among older children than among younger children. The researchers separated the children into three age groups—about 6 years, 9 years, and 12 years of age—and then compared the groups at the end of therapy to assess relative degrees of improvement. The analysis revealed that the children in each age group showed at least a moderate degree of improvement, but the oldest group improved far more than the two younger groups, which did not differ. These results suggest that older, more cognitively advanced children are likely to benefit more

from cognitive–behavioral therapy than are younger, less cognitively advanced children.

The second way researchers have examined the role of intellectual capacity in the success of cognitive–behavioral therapy involves seeing whether the degree of improvement resulting from treatment is related to the intelligence of the person treated. One study used this approach with 106 adult clients who were being treated for depression and anxiety disorders (Haaga et al., 1991). The researchers assessed each client's disorder and intelligence with appropriate and widely used standardized tests at the start of the therapy process. The intelligence of the subjects was in the "high average" range. The clients then received an average of about 20 cognitive–behavioral therapy sessions. The final session included a reassessment of the client's disorder, to permit the derivation of an improvement score by taking the original assessment of the disorder into account. No relationship was found between intelligence and improvement scores for clients with depression or with anxiety disorders.

An overview of these studies suggests that the intellectual skills people generally acquire in childhood play an important role in the likely success of cognitive–behavioral therapy for them, but having greater than normal intellectual skills in adulthood does not enhance the success of cognitive–behavioral treatment.

• •

monastery, the Buddha asked: "Have you got the mustard seed?" "No," she replied, "nor shall I try to find it anymore. In every village and every household, the dead are more than the living. My grief had made me blind. Now I understand." (de Silva, 1984, p. 673)

The approach used in this example enabled this woman to perceive her situation differently and, by doing so, change her behavior.

As we discussed in Chapter 1, the field of behavior therapy developed in the second half of the twentieth century. In the first decade or so of its development, behavior therapy treatments focused almost exclusively on applying behavioral methods. But by the early 1970s, behavior therapy had begun to incorporate a variety of cognitive methods as well (Dobson & Block, 1988; Kazdin, 1978; M. J. Mahoney, 1993). The introduction of cognitive methods in behavior therapy came about for at least two reasons. First, many behavior therapists had come to the conclusion that behavioral methods were too limited in scope and impact, hence appropriate and effective only for certain kinds or aspects of clients' problems. Second, the focus of psychology as a whole had begun to move toward a cognitive orientation for the understanding and explanation of human behavior. By the end of the 1980s, the application of cognitive methods had become widespread in behavior therapy and well established in research.

Not all experts in behavior modification techniques believe that the growth of the cognitive perspective has benefited the field. Some researchers believe that theories incorporating cognitive factors are stated too vaguely to be of scientific value (Lee, 1992). Others have argued that the role of cognitive processes is limited and has been overstated both in the development and maintenance of behavioral problems, such as phobias and anxieties, and in the treatment of these problems (Latimer & Sweet, 1984; Sweet & Loizeaux, 1991; Wolpe, 1993). Still, a good deal of evidence exists to indicate that some cognitive–behavioral therapies are useful in treating problems of certain kinds, such as clinical depression, some chronic pain disorders, and some forms of anxiety (TFPDPP, 1993). Indeed, the effectiveness of these methods usually can be assessed by measuring overt behaviors, and this is one reason for the acceptance by behavior therapists of cognitive methods in their treatment approaches. (Go to 🔍 .)

Cognitive Restructuring Approaches

Some cognitive–behavioral therapies focus on *reducing an excess of covert behaviors*: maladaptive or "dysfunctional" thought patterns. These therapies try to reduce these thoughts through the process of **cognitive restructuring** in which methods are applied to alter the way clients perceive and think about events in their lives, thereby enabling them to modify problem behaviors and emotions. For example, cognitive restructuring methods might be used to help depressed clients think about their life circumstances in more hopeful and less negativistic ways. Two widely applied types of cognitive–behavioral therapy that stress the use of cognitive restructuring approaches are *rational–emotive therapy* and *cognitive therapy* (Dobson & Block, 1988).

Rational–Emotive Therapy

Albert Ellis (1962, 1977, 1987, 1993) developed the cognitive restructuring approach called **rational–emotive therapy** (RET) in the 1950s, from the premise that emotional difficulties often arise from faulty and irrational thinking. These thinking processes lead individuals to have unrealistic misperceptions, interpretations, and attributions about the experiences they have and the people they know. Ellis devised the following terms to describe some commonly used irrational ways of thinking:

- *Awfulizing*—for example, "It's *awful* if I get less than an A on a test."
- *Can't-stand-itis*—as in, "I *can't stand* getting turned down when I ask for a date."
- *Musterbating*—for instance, "People I like *must* like me, or I'm worthless."

Suppose a man we'll call Alex has the strong belief, "Candice absolutely, really, really *must* like me," but she doesn't care for him. He is likely to exaggerate the situation with unrealistic ideas, such as "She hates me," "It's *awful* and I *can't stand* it if she hates me," and "I'm worthless if she hates me." These thoughts exaggerate the person's negative view of the situation and are upsetting. The main purpose of RET is to change thoughts and beliefs of this nature.

The Process of Rational–Emotive Therapy

A bright 8-year-old boy named Robert had become terrified of going to school because he was afraid of not doing well and having others think he was incompetent. Part of the treatment he received used rational–emotive therapy, which involved discussions to alter his beliefs and the way he perceived events in school. In one session with his therapist, Robert described how terrible he felt when he answered incorrectly on a test. The therapist had Robert imagine his teacher returning to him a test on which he had made a mistake and asked him what thoughts he would have at that moment. The following dialogue ensued (Oltmanns, Neale, & Davison, 1991, p. 281):

Robert (forehead furrowed): Oy, I made a mistake. She thinks I'm a jerk, a dope. She doesn't like me anymore. I can't stand this.

Therapist: Hmm, that's heavy stuff, little friend. Is that what you'd really think to yourself?

Robert: Well, I think so. I give myself a hard time when I make a mistake, and I'm sure other people think I'm a jerk.

Therapist: Do *you* think other people are jerks when they make mistakes?

Robert: Well, sometimes I do. I mean, if you're careful about what you do, won't you always be right?

Therapist: I don't think so. I make lots of mistakes, but I don't think I'm a jerk for doing that. That's part of being a human being. Aren't you one of those? (Pokes Robert playfully in the ribs.)

Robert (laughs in spite of himself): Yah, I guess so. I'm sure no angel!

The dialogue continued to point out that even if Robert's teacher was displeased that he made a mistake, that wouldn't make him a "total jerk." After all, he usually performs well in school and behaves nicely with other children. The purpose of this kind of dialogue is to *dispute* irrational beliefs and disprove them.

RET is often applied when clients have severe problems with anxiety, anger, and depression. The procedures used in RET focus on several aspects or stages of the client's thought processes, using Ellis's (1977) A-B-C-D-E paradigm. Table 15.1 illustrates the basic outline of this paradigm by using the case of a woman we'll call Sue, a therapy client who is upset at having been fired from a job. Therapists who use RET vary in the style they use in disputing clients' beliefs. Some try to lead clients gently toward discovering alternative ways of thinking, as Robert's therapist did. Others, like Ellis himself, are much more direct and forceful, arguing with clients

Table 15.1 *Illustration of Ellis's A-B-C-D-E Paradigm for Rational Emotive Therapy*

- **A** stands for the *activating* experience, the event Sue describes as having precipitated her upset: Her boss said, "I've warned you time and again about your lateness and sloppy work. I don't want you to work here anymore. You're fired."
- **B** refers to the *beliefs* and thoughts that go through the person's mind in response to A. These thoughts may be rational, as in, "I guess I deserved being fired. I need to be more responsible and careful about my work." But Sue focused on irrational beliefs, thinking, "I can't do anything right. I wish I had behaved better; that was a good job. I'm totally worthless and useless. I can't stand myself, and I can't bear facing people and telling them I was fired."
- **C** symbolizes the emotional and behavioral *consequences* of feelings of disappointment and a determination to improve in her next job. But Sue's consequences were inappropriate—she felt depressed, ashamed, and helpless, and has not tried to find a new job in the several months since being fired.
- **D** refers to the *disputing* of irrational beliefs that goes on in therapy. It includes discriminating between valid ideas, such as "I wish I had behaved better," and irrational ones, such as "I'm totally worthless." Irrational beliefs are critically and logically examined in RET so that they can be disproven.
- **E** stands for the therapy's *effect*, which consists of a restructured belief system and philosophy. With this effect, Sue should be able to cope with her world more sensibly in the future.

Source: Sarafino (1994) Table 5.2.

and teasing them about their beliefs, describing their ideas as "nutty," and so on (see Ellis & Dryden, 1987, pp. 143–149). An important feature of RET is that it includes homework assignments, such as having the client read some materials about irrational beliefs, engage in making positive self-statements, or do relaxation exercises.

How Effective Is Rational–Emotive Therapy?

Dozens of studies have been conducted to assess the effectiveness of RET for treating a variety of behavioral and emotional disorders (Engels, Garnefski, & Diekstra, 1993; Gossette & O'Brien, 1993; Haaga & Davison, 1989, 1993; Lyons & Woods, 1991). An overview of this research suggests five conclusions. First, RET appears to be an effective therapy for certain disorders, such as anxieties, producing clear improvements over baseline or in comparison to the no-treatment condition. Second, RET is not superior to and is often less effective than other treatment approaches, such as systematic desensitization, for treating phobias and anxieties. Third, little evidence exists regarding the durability of improvements produced by RET, since few studies have incorporated long-term, follow-up assessments. Fourth, many studies of RET have been poorly designed or reported, making their results ambiguous. For instance, some studies did not report the numbers of clients who dropped out of treatment and other studies did not indicate or define exactly the therapy techniques used. Fifth, research is lacking with regard to the specific aspects or components of RET that are effective. RET often applies a variety of cognitive and behavioral methods, and the style of disputing clients' beliefs can vary greatly. Are certain methods or styles more effective than others?

Cognitive Therapy

Cognitive therapy, a cognitive restructuring approach for treating behavioral and emotional disorders, was developed by Aaron Beck independently of but at about the same time as RET (1967, 1976, 1993; Beck et al., 1990; DeRubeis & Beck, 1988). Like RET, cognitive therapy is based on the view that emotional disorders develop because of faulty and negativistic thought patterns that must be altered in treatment.

The fundamental cognitive therapy concept called **schema**, refers to a basic cognitive structure or unit of knowledge that serves to organize individuals' experiences and affect their perceptions, interpretations, and attributions of everyday events. Schemata (the plural form of schema) can be thought of as "core beliefs." We all have schemata to organize our knowledge of the world. In people who develop emotional problems, however, these core beliefs tend to become **automatic thoughts**—erroneous and maladaptive thought patterns that occur habitually and frequently. Clients generally report that these thoughts seem to arise "automatically," like "reflexes." For instance, someone with a schema of personal incompetence will tend to expect failure in many situations, particularly ones that resemble situations in which the schema was learned. Cognitive therapy attempts to discover what the automatic thoughts are, point them out to the client, and change them.

According to Beck, individuals who develop emotional disorders engage in erroneous and maladaptive thought patterns excessively. Their automatic thoughts can contain any of several types of cognitive errors, including:

- *Dichotomous thinking* (thinking in absolute, all-or-none terms). For instance, people are either saints or sinners; objects are either perfect or defective.
- *Overgeneralization* (arriving at a sweeping conclusion or general rule on the basis of one or a few events and applying the conclusion in judging other people or events). For example, a mother who discovers her son has stolen something might decide that she is a terrible and useless mother or that her child is evil.
- *Arbitrary inference* (drawing a specific conclusion from insufficient, ambiguous, or contrary evidence). For instance, a worker might interpret his boss's bad mood as meaning that the supervisor is unhappy with his performance when in fact she is preoccupied with a personal matter.
- *Magnification* (greatly exaggerating the meaning or impact of an event). For example, a student who receives a B on a test may define the grade as a "catastrophe."

Beck believes that people who become clinically depressed develop a *negative triad*—three clusters of schemata that involve erroneous, negative views of the *self,* the *world,* and the *future.*

The Process of Cognitive Therapy

Although cognitive therapy and RET both try to alter the client's incorrect thought patterns, the procedures they use differ in several ways. We will consider two of the clearest ways in which they differ. First, the treatment in cognitive therapy is more clearly a *collaborative effort* between therapist and client than it is in RET. That is, therapist and client in cognitive therapy actively share in the effort to discover and change automatic thoughts. The therapist tries to build a trusting relationship early in therapy and then guides the client toward discovering and examining the cognitive errors that underlie the person's maladaptive thought patterns. Although some degree of collaboration occurs in RET, the focus on shared effort is more pronounced in cognitive therapy.

Second, cognitive therapy uses a *hypothesis testing* technique. Once the therapist and client have discovered an erroneous belief or thought, they treat it as a hypothesis rather than a fact and go about trying to test its validity. They question the belief in terms of (1) the evidence for and against it, (2) alternative explanations for or ways of looking at specific situations or feelings, and (3) the actual implications the belief might carry if it were basically true. They also seek hard evidence regarding the belief by making observations in real-life situations. Suppose a male client is attracted to a female classmate in college but believes she dislikes him because she rarely looks at or talks to him. The therapist and client would devise an actual test of this belief—perhaps by having the client keep track of how often the young lady looked at or talked to other male classmates. If she didn't look at or talk to most or all other males in class, this pattern of behavior would constitute evidence that the client's belief is unwarranted.

We can see how hypothesis testing might be used by looking at an example of dialogue from a cognitive therapy session with a 33-year-old client named Sharon who had low self-esteem. Sharon was depressed, she believed she was "fat and ugly," and thought she had mannerisms that were "peculiar and annoying" to others. In the dialogue, the therapist asked:

> *Therapist:* . . . what evidence do you have that all this is true? That you are ugly, awkward? Or that it is not true? What data do you have?
>
> *Sharon:* Comparing myself to people that I consider to be extremely attractive and finding myself lacking.
>
> *Therapist:* So if you look at that beautiful person, you're less?
>
> *Sharon:* Yeah.
>
> *Therapist:* Or if I look at that *perfect* person, I'm less. Is that what you're saying? . . .
>
> *Sharon:* Yeah. I always pick out, of course, the most attractive person and probably a person who spends 3 hours a day on grooming and appearance, clothes shopping, and I only compare myself to them. I don't compare myself to the run-of-the-mill—I have begun to try to contradict all this stuff. . . .
>
> *Therapist:* I would like to hear some of that.
>
> *Sharon:* Well, I have done very well this whole week. I'm a lot less depressed. I have done a couple of really tough dysfunctional thought analyses, which I feel I have made very good progress on, and . . . I find myself contradicting the negative thoughts almost automatically, especially the ones I have written out. I have enjoyed what I have been doing this week. (Freeman, 1990, p. 83)

Cognitive therapy typically entails homework assignments. A client may be asked to list and analyze maladaptive or "dysfunctional" thoughts or to collect data to test a hypothesis (Freeman, 1990; Thase & Wright, 1991). These assignments can also include the solo application of various behavioral methods—having the client do relaxation exercises, for example.

How Effective Is Cognitive Therapy?

Cognitive therapy was originally developed as a treatment for depression. Research has shown that cognitive therapy is a clearly effective and durable approach for treating this disorder (Craighead, Evans, & Robins, 1992; DeRubeis & Beck, 1988; Dobson, 1989; Hollon, Shelton, & Davis, 1993; Robins & Hayes, 1993; TFPDPP, 1993). For most clients, cognitive therapy is at least as effective in reducing depression and maintaining improved emotional functioning as other forms of psychological therapy and various drugs therapies. Studies with follow-up assessments 1 and 2 years after cognitive therapy for depression have reported low rates of relapse. About one-third of depressed clients do not improve substantially with cognitive therapy, however. Some evidence indicates that clients who are least likely to improve in cognitive therapy are those who have very severe initial levels of depression, serious family problems, and additional psychological disorders.

Since the 1970s, cognitive therapy has expanded its scope to treating a wide variety of emotional problems, such as anxiety, panic, and eating disorders (A. T. Beck, 1993; A. T. Beck et al., 1990). Although relatively few studies have been done to evaluate the effectiveness of cognitive therapy in treating these disorders, existing research indicates that it is a very promising approach (Chambless & Gillis, 1993; G. T. Wilson & Fairburn, 1993). Still, as with RET, research is lacking with regard to the aspects or components of cognitive therapy that are effective. Cognitive therapy typically applies a variety of cognitive and behavioral methods. Which methods are responsible for the effectiveness of cognitive therapy? (Go to ✔ .)

✔ Concept Check 15.1

• •

1. A characteristic of clinical depression in addition to feeling unhappy is _____ _____ ↩

2. The cognitive process by which people try to identify causes of events in their lives is called _____ .

3. Information that explicit, declarative memory might include about one of our fears is: _____ _____ . ⇔

4. The effectiveness of cognitive–behavioral therapy with children appears to increase as children become _____ _____ .

5. _____ processes in therapy alter the way clients perceive and think about events in their lives.

6. In RET, "It would be awful if I applied for a job and didn't get it" is an example of an irrational thought pattern called _____ .

7. In cognitive therapy, erroneous and maladaptive thought patterns that arise habitually are called _____ .

8. Having a client collect data in everyday situations to disconfirm a maladaptive belief is an example of the _____ technique.

9. Cognitive therapy is most clearly effective for treating the psychological disorder called _____ .

Answers: 1. feeling hopeless/pessimistic 2. attribution 3. when the fear started/how strong the fear is 4. older or more cognitively advanced 5. cognitive restructuring 6. awfulizing 7. automatic thoughts 8. hypothesis testing 9. depression

• •

Cognitive Skills Training Approaches

We have just seen that cognitive–behavioral therapies in which cognitive restructuring methods are the main techniques applied focus on reducing an excess of maladaptive covert behaviors—thought patterns that maintain the client's emotional problems. Other cognitive–behavioral therapies take a different approach, trying *to correct a deficit of adaptive covert behaviors* by training clients in *cognitive skills* they don't yet possess or use. By trying to correct cognitive deficits in clients, therapists hope to enable them to apply the new skills to reduce overt and covert emotional difficulties. We will discuss two widely applied types of cognitive–behavioral therapy that focus on training clients in adaptive cognitive skills. These approaches are *stress inoculation training* and *problem-solving training* (Dobson & Block, 1988).

Stress Inoculation Training

People encounter many stressful circumstances, ranging from major serious events, such as the death of a close family member or being fired from a job, to everyday hassles, such as being late for an appointment or misplacing important items. We often can't control whether these circumstances occur, but we can learn cognitive skills to help us cope with or adjust to them. When we cannot cope well with stress, we tend to feel anxious, angry, or depressed. Frequently, people who enter therapy for anxiety, anger, and depressive disorders lack important cognitive skills to help them cope with stress. Donald Meichenbaum developed a therapy procedure called **stress inoculation training** that is designed to teach clients cognitive skills to help them cope with the stressful events they experience (Meichenbaum, 1977; Meichenbaum & Cameron, 1983; Meichenbaum & Deffenbacher, 1988).

The Process of Stress Inoculation Training

The term "inoculate" designates the use of procedures that can enable individuals to defend themselves from disease. Stress inoculation training is designed to give clients self-defense skills that can be deployed during stressful experiences. This form of therapy teaches coping skills and has clients practice them in training programs that proceed through three phases.

In the first phase, called *conceptualization,* clients discuss their past stressful experiences to learn about the nature of stress and how people react to it. These discussions can be conducted on an individual basis or in groups. They consider such questions as:

- Under what specific circumstances do you experience stress?
- What have you done in the past to reduce your stress, and what do you believe could be done instead?
- What seems to make the problem worse or better?

They also try to identify antecedents for the problem behavior. In the following dialogue, a therapist leads a highly anxious client to see the need for determining which situations do and do not make him anxious and encourages him to collect related data.

> *Therapist:* Any notions about how we might be able to better figure this out?
>
> *Client:* I suppose I could keep track . . . you know, make some notes or something about when I get really uptight and when I just get upset.
>
> *Therapist:* Keep track? How might you do that?
>
> *Client:* Well I could get a notebook, and, you know, write down what I was feeling.
>
> *Therapist:* That sounds like a really good idea. You could get a notebook and write down what you were feeling and the situation you were in at the time. (Meichenbaum & Deffenbacher, 1988)

You may have recognized that the therapist was getting the client to conduct part of a functional analysis of his anxiety.

In the second phase of stress inoculation training, *skills acquisition and rehearsal*, clients learn specific behavioral and cognitive coping skills, such as relaxation, systematic desensitization, self-statements, and coping statements. Some statements clients might learn to help them cope with stress are:

- "Easy does it. Getting upset won't help."
- "These are some anxiety cues I knew I could experience. They should remind me to use the coping skills I learned."
- "Stay cool and relax. If I need to, I can use my calm scene to help."

Other skills may depend on the individual's problems and personal circumstances. Thus, clients might learn communication skills, or study skills, or parenting techniques, and so on. The clients practice their newly learned skills under the therapist's supervision.

In the third phase, called *application and follow-through*, stress inoculation training helps clients make the transition to using the learned coping skills in the natural environment. To achieve this transition, clients respond to stress-provoking events that are introduced in the therapy setting in a graded sequence, as in a stimulus hierarchy. Various events are used in an effort to promote generalization of the skills to a variety of real-world situations. Clients also receive homework assignments that expose them to increasingly stressful situations in their everyday lives. Follow-up sessions are held periodically during the subsequent year or so, as part of an effort to prevent relapse.

How Effective Is Stress Inoculation Training?

The methods used in stress inoculation training are well thought out and include a number of well-established techniques, such as relaxation, systematic

desensitization, and modeling. Most studies of the effectiveness of stress inoculation training have been done with clients who had anxiety or stress problems
(Meichenbaum & Deffenbacher, 1988). These studies have generally found that
stress inoculation training reduces anxiety and stress and is at least as effective as
less comprehensive programs, such as those that train clients only in systematic
desensitization or cognitive coping skills. Other studies have applied stress inoculation training successfully in helping police officers and abusive parents control
their anger (Nomellini & Katz, 1983; Novaco, 1976, 1977). Although stress inoculation training is a very promising cognitive–behavioral therapy for emotional problems, more evidence is needed to demonstrate its value relative to other treatment
approaches.

Problem-Solving Training

Another approach that offers training in adaptive cognitive skills is designed to
help clients solve problems. In this context, a "problem" is a life circumstance that
requires one or more effective, adaptive responses that the person is unable to perform because he or she does not know what to do or how to do it (D'Zurilla, 1988;
D'Zurilla & Goldfried, 1971). Suppose, for instance, you had deadlines to meet for
college exams and papers and didn't know how you were going to find the time to
do it all. You'd be faced with a problem.

As a rule, people who do not know how to solve most of their everyday problems become extremely anxious, frustrated, and depressed. **Problem-solving training** is a form of cognitive–behavioral therapy in which clients learn a strategy for
identifying, discovering, or inventing effective or adaptive ways of addressing problems they face in everyday life. This form of therapy can be used to reduce clients'
emotional disorders or simply to improve their adaptive social functioning
(D'Zurilla, 1988; Nezu, Nezu, & Perri, 1989).

The Process of Problem-Solving Training

There are two widely used therapy approaches for providing problem-solving
training, and each one teaches clients a stepwise strategy for solving problems
(D'Zurilla, 1988; Spivack & Shure, 1974, 1982).The problem-solving training
approach developed by Thomas D'Zurilla and Marvin Goldfried (1971; D'Zurilla,
1988), which we will examine, teaches clients a five-step strategy for solving problems.

In the first step in this problem-solving strategy, *problem orientation*, individuals
develop a general mind-set to be alert to or watchful for problems that arise. To
deal with problems effectively, we must first know they exist. Training clients in
problem orientation begins by encouraging them to notice problems and helping
them to realize that problems are both normal and inevitable. Clients are also
taught ways to stop themselves from taking the easy way out and doing nothing, or
from acting impulsively. For instance, they might be taught to use self-statements

such as "OK, slow down and think." Then they learn to proceed calmly and cautiously in addressing the problems they find.

Problem definition and formulation is the second step in the strategy for solving a problem. This step involves defining the problem in concrete, clear terms, rather than in vague, abstract terms. You may have noticed that this process is essentially the same as defining a target behavior in a behavior change program. Clients tend to describe their problems in very general or vague terms, such as "I get upset by my roommate's attitude." By looking more carefully at the roommate's behavior, we might find out that the "attitude" is actually inferred from very specific, concrete behaviors, such as leaving the kitchen a mess and failing to do chores around the shared apartment. It's these behavioral deficits in the roommate that are upsetting.

The third step in solving a problem is the *generation of alternative solutions.* Once the behavior has been clearly defined, the client should make a list of possible solutions by using the process of *brainstorming*, which we considered in Chapter 9. The purpose of brainstorming is to identify as many alternative solutions as possible, even if some are not very good. For instance, in trying to deal with the problem of a roommate who is messy and doesn't do her chores, the client might come up with these alternatives:

- Yell at her louder and more often.
- Ignore the situation, to see if she will eventually realize how useful it would be to clean her messes.
- Enlist the pressure of other roommates against her.
- Reinforce her for cleaning up and doing her chores, perhaps using praise or suggesting an activity she likes to do.
- Punish her by dumping the kitchen mess on her bed.
- Hang pictures of pigs around the apartment.
- Find another apartment.

As you can imagine, the list of alternative solutions can be quite long and may contain some very creative ideas.

In the fourth step, called *decision making*, the client examines the list of alternatives and eliminates those that are clearly not acceptable. "Finding another apartment" would be unacceptable, for example, if it would involve breaking a lease for the current apartment. Then the client would try to assess the short-term and long-term consequences of each alternative to the roommate and herself. Using these factors, she would be able to select the alternatives that seem most likely to provide the best solution. During the earlier sessions of therapy, she and the therapist would have made decisions together; later, the client becomes able to make decisions more and more on her own.

The last step in problem solving is called *solution implementation and verification.* When the solution has been in effect for a while, the client tries to evaluate its success. If the problem seems to have been solved—say, if the roommate is no longer messy and does her chores—nothing more needs to be done. If the problem continues to exist, the client can choose other alternative solutions from the existing list or generate additional alternatives. Sometimes it is necessary to back up to the step of problem definition and formulation to redefine the problem. (Go to .)

How Effective Is Problem-Solving Training?

The rationale for applying problem-solving training to improve clients' functioning in everyday life situations and to reduce their emotional difficulties has a good deal of intuitive appeal. Evidence indicates that depression and anxiety dis-

Case Study 15.1
Problem-Solving Training for Neglectful Parents

Three mothers who were judged by welfare authorities to be "child neglectful" were referred for treatment. Problem-solving training was applied, and a multiple-baseline, across-subjects design was used to assess treatment effects (Dawson et al., 1986). All three mothers were in their twenties, were receiving public assistance, and had no more than a tenth-grade education; one mother was currently married. The women had been brought to the attention of authorities for different reasons. One mother had abandoned her 5-year-old asthmatic son with an unwilling caretaker for 3 days. The second had to give up her two children, aged 3 and 5, to foster care because of past child abandonment. The third mother, who had four young children, had failed to provide her epileptic son with needed medication and had left the children unattended in potentially dangerous conditions and with unsuitable caretakers, including a relative who was multiply handicapped.

Part of the problem-solving training involved discussing a variety of vignettes in which a mother is faced with a problem in child care. The vignettes were based on actual difficulties these parents had experienced in the past. For example:

You and your mother have an argument on the phone. She tells you that you can just forget about bringing your children over tonight for her to babysit while you go out with your boyfriend (husband). It's 5:00 P.M. You don't

have any money to hire a babysitter. The story ends with you and your boyfriend (husband) going out for the evening. (p. 213)

Each mother was asked to define the problem in each vignette, generate possible solutions, describe the pros and cons of each solution, and choose the best one. Then the problem-solving performances were rated qualitatively.

Before the intervention began, about eight 60–90 minute baseline sessions were conducted with vignettes. The problem-solving performance ratings revealed poor problem-solving skills in baseline, but the ratings began to improve for each mother as soon as the intervention was introduced, reaching over four times the baseline levels for the last six intervention sessions. Other assessments indicated that the effects of problem-solving training generalized to the home situation and were long-lasting. Ratings by social workers of each mother's parenting performance at home revealed substantial improvements by the end of the intervention. What's more, follow-up evaluations 15 months later showed continued success of the training. Although two mothers had moved and were no longer available for testing on the vignettes, they had regained full custody of their children and had no further reports of neglect. The mother who was available for testing continued to demonstrate high levels of skill in problem solving.

orders are linked to inability to solve everyday problems (D'Zurilla, 1988; Nezu, Nezu, & Perri, 1989). In addition, problem-solving strategies appear to be very easy for adults and children to learn, often being mastered in a single session, particularly by adults. For instance, the neglectful mothers in Case Study 15.1 showed improved skills in the very first session of the intervention (Dawson et al., 1986). And an adult client who was being treated for severe anxiety learned a problem-solving strategy in a single 1 hour session (Mayo & Norton, 1980). This client also provides a good example of the link between anxiety and lack of problem-solving skills: being a mother and a student, she experienced problems in child care that made her very anxious about meeting her classes and tests

> because she was unable to identify effective strategies which would alter the problematic situations. For example, if her babysitter called saying she couldn't care for the baby the next day, [the client] would become very anxious and would have difficulty identifying solutions which would allow her to attend class. (p. 288)

Studies have found that problem-solving training produces beneficial effects for clients with depression and anxiety disorders and for clients with difficulties in their general functioning, such as those doing poorly in school and those who are undecided about career goals (D'Zurilla, 1988). And some research results suggest that the improvements from problem-solving training carry over into clients' natural environments and are durable, at least for adults. But other research indicates that these effects sometimes are variable, do not generalize well, and may not be long-lasting for children (Nelson & Carson, 1988; Yu et al., 1986). Few studies have compared problem-solving training with other forms of therapy. As a result, the relative effectiveness of this treatment modality is not clear.

Combined Therapy Approaches

Therapists often find that each client who enters therapy has problems that have many different dimensions or aspects. As a result, one particular technique may not be sufficient in designing a treatment for any given person, and the most effective therapy may draw on many different techniques. We saw in discussing the approaches of cognitive restructuring and cognitive skills training that therapy programs are usually multidimensional, using a variety of behavioral and cognitive methods. Programs that have combined various therapy approaches can be seen in the following examples.

- A program combining several techniques successfully treated two girls whose anxieties about being separated from their parents was reflected in the children's refusals to sleep in their own beds (Ollendick, Hagopian, & Huntzinger, 1991). The program consisted of behavioral methods, such as reinforcement and extinction, and "self-control training" with cognitive methods, such as training in relaxation exercises, problem-solving strategies, and using positive

Figure 15.1   Data for two girls, 10-year-old Mary and 8-year-old Lucy, showing the number of nights per week each girl spent in her own bed, rather than with her parents, and the levels of anxiety (the STAIC scores, where high scores reflect high anxiety) reported by each girl when thinking about being in her bed alone. Assessments in this multiple-baseline, across-subjects design were made in baseline (monitoring), self-control training (SCT), SCT plus reinforcement, and follow-up phases. (From Ollendick, Hagopian, & Huntzinger, 1991, Figure 1.)

self-statements. As Figure 15.1 shows, self-control training by itself was not very effective, but the combined treatment was.

- An intervention that combined stress inoculation and problem-solving training was moderately successful in improving anger control among junior high school delinquents (Feindler, Marriott, & Iwata, 1984).

- A program provided treatment for highly aggressive, antisocial children and their parents by using one or both of two approaches: problem-solving training and parent management training, which consisted of teaching the parents how to use behavioral methods, such as reinforcement, shaping, and time-out (Kazdin, Siegel, & Bass, 1992). Although each form of training improved the children's behavior, combining the two approaches produced even greater improvements and placed a larger proportion of the children in the normal range for aggressive and antisocial behavior.

In an effort to promote the use of multidimensional approaches in therapy, Arnold Lazarus (1981) introduced the concept of **multimodal therapy**, in which the therapist identifies certain dimensions or parts of the client's problems and chooses appropriate techniques for each one. A therapist using multimodal therapy would consider several dimensions of the client's problems, four of which are: *behavior*, such as excessive eating; *affect*, for instance, severe anxiety or depression; *cognitions*, such as irrational thoughts; and *interpersonal relationships*, for example, hostile behavior. The therapy would then be tailored to the client's specific problems.

Most of us are probably tempted to believe that behavior change programs that combine techniques known to be individually effective will produce greater behavioral improvements than each technique applied by itself. Although there are many examples of interventions that support this belief, there are also examples that contradict it. For instance, a number of studies have found that the addition of cognitive methods to behavioral methods in treating emotional problems does not necessarily increase the effectiveness of the therapy (Sweet & Loizeaux, 1991). What's more, one study found that combining two behavior therapy approaches, each of which had been successful in prior interventions for treating eating disorders, was far less effective in reducing disordered eating patterns than using one method by itself (Agras et al., 1989). Whether combining particular therapy methods produces more effective treatment than each one singly for a specific disorder is an empirical issue that must be tested in research. (Go to ✔.)

✔ Concept Check 15.2

1. The first phase in stress inoculation training is called _____ _____ .

2. If stress inoculation training were being used to help clients control their anger, a coping statement they might be trained to apply in their lives is _____ . ⇔

3. A life circumstance that requires a response that the person is unable to perform because of a lack of cognitive skills is called a _____ .

4. The first step in the problem-solving treatment outlined by D'Zurilla and Goldfried is called _____ .

5. In the case study about the three neglectful mothers, an alternative solution that might have been proposed for the vignette about not having a babysitter might be to _____ . ⇔

6. The treatment approach in which the therapist identifies different dimensions of a client's problem and chooses methods to address each one is called _____ .

Answers: 1. conceptualization 2. "Stay cool." 3. problem 4. problem orientation 5. take the children with them 6. multimodal therapy

Application Exercise

In this application exercise, you will complete tasks that apply information about the different cognitive–behavioral therapies described in this chapter. Turn to Work Sheet 15.1 and fill it out.

Summary

Cognitive–behavioral therapy is a broad class of therapeutic approaches for the modification of overt and covert behaviors through the use of behavioral and cognitive methods. These forms of therapy are based on the view that cognitive processes play an important role in behavioral and emotional problems, such as excessive aggression, anxiety, and depression. The idea that modifying people's thoughts and beliefs can help change their behaviors and emotions has a long history. Research has shown that the success of cognitive methods improves with children's age, but having greater than normal intelligence in adulthood does not enhance the success of these methods.

Cognitive restructuring approaches are designed to reduce the client's excess of covert behaviors. One of these approaches, called rational–emotive therapy (RET), uses discussion to dispute irrational thought patterns that have been termed awfulizing, can't-stand-itis, and musterbating. Cognitive therapy is based on the view that each schema a person develops to organize his or her experiences forms a "core belief." Schemata can give rise to automatic thoughts, which are erroneous and maladaptive patterns of thinking that seem to maintain emotional and behavioral problems. There are several types of automatic thoughts, including dichotomous thinking, overgeneralization, arbitrary inference, and magnification. Cognitive therapy uses a more collaborative process than RET to change thought patterns and has clients subject their automatic thoughts to hypothesis testing. Studies have found that both RET and cognitive therapy are promising approaches for treating anxiety disorders, and cognitive therapy is clearly effective in reducing depression.

Cognitive skills training approaches attempt to correct clients' deficits in adaptive covert behaviors. Stress inoculation training attempts to teach clients cognitive skills to help them cope with stress. The training has three phases: conceptualization, skills acquisition and rehearsal, and application and follow-through. Problem-solving training attempts to teach clients a strategy for solving everyday problems. One widely used problem-solving strategy involves five steps: problem orientation, problem definition and formulation, generation of alternative solutions, decision making, and solution implementation and verification. Both stress inoculation training and problem-solving training seem to be effective in helping people to improve their behavioral and emotional functioning.

More research is needed to demonstrate the effectiveness of cognitive–behavioral therapies, particularly with respect to whether they are more effective than other therapy approaches. Many therapy programs combine different therapy approaches, often with improved effectiveness. Multimodal therapy is a cognitive–behavioral therapy approach in which the therapist chooses a variety of behavioral and cognitive methods to ensure that each dimension of the client's problems will be addressed.

Key Terms and Review Questions

Key Terms

cognitive–behavioral therapy
cognitive restructuring
rational–emotive therapy
cognitive therapy
schema

automatic thoughts
stress inoculation training
problem-solving training
multimodal therapy

Review Questions

1. What is cognitive–behavioral therapy, and what characteristics do all these approaches share to some degree?

2. Describe two reasons for assuming that cognitive processes can be important in overt and covert behavior.

3. Discuss the role of intellectual capacity and development in the success of cognitive methods.

4. What is cognitive restructuring?

5. Describe two examples each of the irrational thoughts Ellis calls awfulizing, can't-stand-itis, and musterbating.

6. What are schemata and automatic thoughts? Give an example of how a schema forms the basis of automatic thoughts.

7. Describe two examples each of overgeneralization and arbitrary inference.

8. What is hypothesis testing in cognitive therapy?

9. Discuss whether RET and cognitive therapy are effective therapies.

10. How are cognitive skills training approaches different from cognitive restructuring?

11. Describe the three phases of stress inoculation training and give an example of each.

12. Describe the five-step strategy in D'Zurilla and Goldfried's approach to problem-solving training.

13. Describe how problem-solving training was used to increase the parenting skills of three neglectful mothers.

14. Discuss whether stress inoculation training and problem-solving training are effective therapies.

15. What is multimodal therapy?

Related Readings

Beck, A. T., Freeman, A., & Associates (1990). *Cognitive therapy of personality disorders.* New York: Guilford.

Dobson, K. S. (1988) (Ed.). *Handbook of cognitive–behavioral therapies.* New York: Guilford.

Ellis, A., & Dryden, W. (1987). *The practice of rational–emotive therapy.* New York: Springer.

Meichenbaum, D., & Cameron, R. (1983). Stress inoculation training: Toward a general paradigm for training coping skills. In D. Meichenbaum & M. E. Jaremko (Eds.), *Stress reduction and prevention.* New York: Plenum Press.

Nezu, A. M., Nezu, C. M., & Perri, M. G. (1989). *Problem-solving therapy for depression: Theory, research, and clinical guidelines.* New York: Wiley.

Name _____   Day & time
                                      class meets_____
Date _____

Chapter 15: Work Sheet 15.1

1. Give one example each of *awfulizing* and *musterbating* that might be voiced by a depressed woman who thought she was very overweight. Describe the dialogue a RET therapist might have with her to alter her thinking.

2. Suppose you were a therapist using cognitive therapy with a psychiatric patient who was in good physical health but believed his muscles no longer had the strength to allow him to walk. You have decided to use *hypothesis testing* to alter this belief. Describe, or write out, the dialogue that might result.

3. Describe the self-statements a very fearful person might be trained to use in stress inoculation training designed to help cope with a painful dental procedure.

4. Imagine this scene: you are driving at night alone in an unfamiliar neighborhood of a big city far from home when you have a flat tire, and a thunderstorm has just started. You do not have a phone in the car. Brainstorm to generate a list of about *ten* alternative solutions to this problem, without being concerned about practicality. The goal in brainstorming is to generate as many possibilities as you can.

NOTE: If you will be submitting work sheets to your instructor or to a fellow student, make a copy of each sheet before submitting it.

Part Six

Present and Future Issues for Behavior Modification

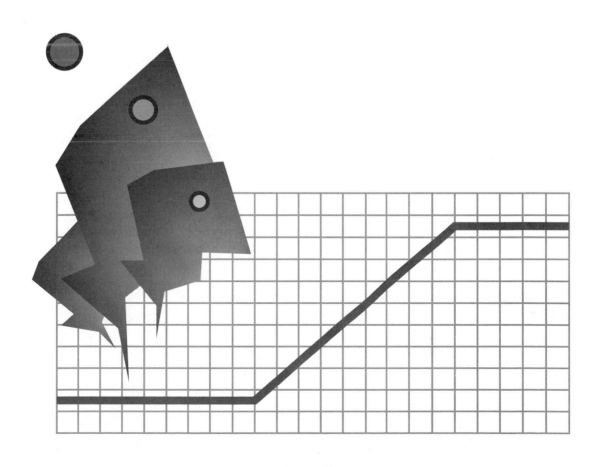

16

Current Concerns and Future Challenges

Prologue

Suppose this book were recorded on a computer compact disk—a CD-ROM—and you could glance through all the behavior change examples it described. As you reviewed the examples, you might notice that lots of decisions needed to be made to carry out the interventions: What will the target behaviors be? What behavioral goals will the program try to achieve? Which techniques will the program use? For the most part, you'd see these decisions as pretty straightforward and noncontroversial. But this isn't always the case.

Let's consider the case of a schizophrenic patient named Margaret (Oltmanns, Neale, & Davison, 1991). Schizophrenia is characterized by pervasively disordered thinking, perception, attention, and affect. Among the many clinical symptoms commonly displayed by schizophrenic patients are *hallucinations* (such as hearing nonexistent voices) and *delusions*, or beliefs that are contrary to reality. For example, Margaret claimed that she heard "two saints" talking about her and that her thoughts were being monitored by security personnel. Because of such cognitive and emotional disturbances, schizophrenic patients typically have very poor social and occupational skills.

Suppose you were a therapist and wanted to improve Margaret's ability to function in society and, perhaps to make it possible for her to hold a job. Obviously, you'd have to stop some of her symptoms, especially the cognitive disturbances. Today there is a way of doing that: have the patient take antipsychotic drugs regularly, on a long-term basis, as prescribed by a physician. But these drugs frequently have the serious and often irreversible long-term effect of causing a motor disorder called *tardive dyskinesia*, which is characterized by trembling and lip-smacking. Now we have a dilemma: Would it be acceptable to risk development of this motor disorder by having Margaret take an antipsychotic drug for a period long enough to permit some gains to be made in her social and occupational skills?

As we are about to see in this chapter, efforts to change behavior can present dilemmas of many different types to therapists and other professionals. After we have considered some of these dilemmas, we will examine ethical and legal issues in behavior modification therapy and research. Then we will consider some important challenges the discipline faces for the future.

Dilemmas in Efforts to Change Behavior

The dilemmas therapists and other professionals often face in their efforts to change behavior can be classified into two categories: those that pertain to the behavior change goals and those that pertain to the behavior change methods of the intervention.

Are the Behavior Change Goals Acceptable?

Most interventions involve target behaviors and behavioral goals that almost everyone would agree are appropriate and useful. Few people would deny the desirability of improving children's academic performance, reducing excessively disruptive classroom conduct, decreasing severely aggressive behavior, reducing serious anxiety problems, eliminating self-injurious behavior among autistic children, and increasing behaviors that promote health and fitness. **Goal acceptability** refers to the degree to which an intervention's outcome goals and behavioral goals are fair, appropriate, and reasonable. What factors determine the acceptability of behavior change goals?

Deciding Whether Behavior Change Goals Are Acceptable

We are likely to think the goals of a behavior change program are acceptable if they meet two broad *goal acceptability criteria*. First, the goals should have a high degree of *social validity*—that is, they should be desired by society and appropriate for the person's life (Wolf, 1978). Second, the goals should involve a *clinically significant* improvement that we can realistically hope to achieve. We can evaluate whether the goals of a behavior change program meet these criteria by answering several relevant questions:

- Is achieving the goals a likely prospect?
- Will achieving the goals greatly improve the person's general adaptive functioning—by, for example, enabling him or her to socialize more effectively?
- Will achieving the goals greatly decrease the likelihood of physical or psychological harm to the person, such as from self-injurious behavior?
- Will achieving the goals greatly reduce the likelihood that the person will physically or psychologically harm someone else—for example, a spouse or a child?
- Will achieving the goals greatly decrease reasonable difficulties other people experience with the person's behavior?
- Will achieving the goals bring the target behavior to a normal level for the person's age and gender?

An affirmative answer to one or more of these questions suggests that the behavior change goals are likely to be acceptable. But a "no" to the first question severely limits the acceptability of the goals. Keep in mind that these are not the only criteria societies have invoked in deciding whether a program's behavior change goals were acceptable, and sometimes these other criteria have led to strong controversies. (Go to 🔍 .)

Examples of Dilemmas in Behavior Change Goals

Occasionally social and moral questions regarding the behavior change goals in therapy make the choice of goals controversial. We will look at three very differ-

Close-Up 16.1
Trying to Make Gays Straight

Society's criteria for the acceptability of behavior change goals are profoundly affected by current beliefs. This can be seen in the history of efforts to change the sexual orientation of gay males and females (lesbians), based on the belief that being a homosexual is a "wrong," learned "choice" that can be changed.

What Causes Homosexuality?
Two of the most widely believed views on the development of homosexuality propose that people become gay because of the experiences they have. One theory is based on respondent conditioning: homosexual preference is learned through conditioning. A person might acquire such conditioning if a same-sex person (the CS) were paired with the individual's sexual arousal (the US) through seduction or sexual exploration. The other theory is based on the Freudian psychodynamic view that parent–child relationships determine sexual orientation. For instance, in this view males become gay because their fathers are detached and ineffectual, providing a poor role model, and their mothers are dominating and overprotective. But extensive research on the upbringing and experiences of homosexuals has failed to find much support for either of these theories (Bell, Weinberg, & Hammersmith, 1981; Garnets & Kimmel, 1991; Storms, 1983).

Rather, research has revealed three critical findings. First, the parent–child relationships experienced by homosexuals and heterosexuals while growing up are not very different. Second, although siblings share the same parents, who might in fact consist of an ineffectual father and dominating mother, one child who turns out to be gay will not necessarily have gay siblings. Third, gay men and women very often report being able to trace homosexual feelings to their childhood years, long before they ever had sexual relations or even knew what sex was. What's more, recent but tentative evidence suggests a substantial influence of biological factors in the development of homosexuality (Byne, 1994; LeVay & Hamer, 1994).

The Failure of "Conversion" Therapies
Many different *conversion therapies* have been designed and applied to change sexual preference from gay to heterosexual (Haldeman, 1994). Some of these therapies follow psychodynamic procedures; others use behavioral methods, mainly involving aversion therapy; and others use fundamentalist Christian programs of "reorientation counseling." In aversion therapy methods, electric shock or other aversive stimuli have been paired with sexually arousing photographs or thoughts (Barlow, 1978). Research on conversion therapies has shown that *none of these therapies is effective in changing sexual orientation,* even among individuals who want very much to change (Haldeman, 1994). Perhaps this should not be surprising. After all, would you expect conversion therapy to be effective in changing people's sexual preferences from *heter*osexual to *homo*sexual?

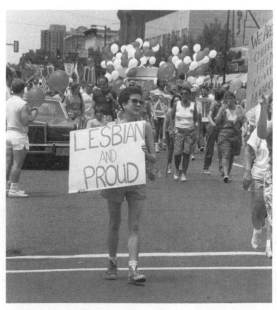

A gay pride parade in Minneapolis. Research indicates that therapy to change one's sexual orientation is usually ineffective.

In his clinical practice, Gerald Davison is a prominent clinical psychologist who had pioneered the use of behavioral methods to try to change sexual orientation. In 1976, 3 years after the American Psychiatric Association had declared that homosexuality would no longer be considered an illness, he wrote an article questioning the effectiveness of conversion therapy and detailing ethical objections to applying those therapies. The American Medical Association arrived at a similar conclusion in 1994 and recommended against the use of conversion therapies. These forms of therapy clearly do not meet the acceptability criteria outlined earlier for behavior change goals.

ent examples in which choosing the goals of therapy might present dilemmas for many people. We will express each dilemma as a question.

The first dilemma is: Should therapy programs pursue the goal of making children's sex-role behaviors consistent with traditional concepts of masculinity or femininity? George Rekers and O. Ivar Lovaas (1974) designed a program of behavioral methods to be applied by the parents of a 5-year-old boy named Kraig whose behaviors were highly effeminate. Kraig liked to cross-dress, use cosmetics, walk and talk in a feminine manner, and take the role of the mother when playing house with a neighbor girl; he engaged in virtually no masculine, rough-and-tumble behaviors. Kraig's parents were concerned because the child was becoming more and more socially isolated and ridiculed, and they feared that he was on the path to sexually deviant behavior in adulthood.

The therapists trained Kraig's parents to provide social and token reinforcers for masculine behaviors and to ignore feminine behaviors, which the parents had inadvertently reinforced in the past. The program succeeded in stopping the boy's feminine behaviors and increasing his masculine behaviors, and these changes were maintained at a follow-up assessment 3 years later.

Other psychologists, however, have criticized the goals of the program of Rekers and Lovaas, saying that by promoting overly strict adherence to social stereotypes, one may in fact impair psychological health (Nordyke et al., 1977; Winkler, 1977). In this case, for instance, Kraig stopped playing with dolls entirely and no longer chose little girls as playmates. Promoting highly traditional sex-role behavior to the exclusion of other gender behaviors is a value-laden course of action that many people today would argue benefits neither the client nor society.

The second dilemma is: Should a therapy program pursue the goal of helping obese individuals achieve normal weight levels by dieting? Considerable evidence indicates that obesity—that is, being more than 20% overweight for one's gender, height, and frame size—puts individuals at high risk of developing and dying from heart disease, hypertension, and diabetes (Sarafino, 1994). This evidence has provided the basis for the development of weight control programs in many nations to promote health. But researchers Kelly Brownell and Judith Rodin (1994) have described a controversy about the value of dieting that developed around 1990 when an antidieting movement formed. This movement claims that (1) diets almost always fail, (2) genetic factors make permanent weight reduction impossible for many people, and (3) obese people who do manage to lose weight and keep it off do not necessarily live longer.

Many people believe that boys benefit from engaging in nontraditional sex-role behavior, such as playing with dolls.

Although the foregoing claims are extreme, they are not entirely wrong. For instance, most people who lose weight do not manage to keep it off for more than a year. But many succeed; and behavioral methods are more effective than other treatments in helping people lose weight and keep it off. Is it worth pursuing in therapy the goal of losing weight if many people fail? Would the goal be worth pursuing if people who kept the weight off didn't live very much longer than they otherwise would have?

The third dilemma is: Should a therapy program pursue the goal of decreasing children's extremely oppositional and aggressive behavior if doing so requires getting them to play alone much of the time? Robert Wahler and James Fox (1980) applied behavioral methods with four 5- to 8-year-old boys to reduce their problem behaviors, which included failing to comply with requests, teasing other people, temper tantrums, destroying property, fighting, and hitting their parents. After the baseline phase, each child experienced more than one type of intervention in separate phases lasting a few weeks each. In the *solitary play* intervention, being reinforced required that the child play alone, quietly, and without interacting with others in any way. In the *cooperative play* intervention, being reinforced required that the child play with family members in a cooperative manner, with no rule violations. During the phases in which the different interventions were applied, the children's social behaviors were observed at home in 30-minute sessions with no encouragement given for play behavior. These observations were to serve in assessing whether the effects of the interventions carried over into the children's general social behavior.

The data revealed that the children's oppositional behavior decreased during solitary play phases, but not during cooperative play phases. In addition, all other social interactions decreased during solitary play phases, too. The researchers concluded that treatment approaches emphasizing solitary behaviors may be more effective in reducing oppositional behavior than approaches stressing appropriate social interaction. They also pointed out that critics might feel that encouraging oppositional children simply to become less sociable is not an acceptable way of correcting the behavior problem.

Dilemmas are often hard to resolve. When we arrive at a resolution, we do so on the basis of our value systems. For example, you may believe that making a child less sociable is too high a "price to pay" for being able to decrease oppositional behavior as effectively as possible. If so, your value system differs from that of Wahler and Fox, who argued that encouraging social interaction at high rates is "questionable in value to the developing child" (p. 38).

Are the Behavior Change Treatments Acceptable?

Another issue of importance in therapy is popular acceptability of the behavior change treatments. **Treatment acceptability** refers to the extent to which the client and the community consider the methods of a behavior change program to be *fair, appropriate, and reasonable* for the circumstances (Kazdin, French, & Sherick, 1981; Wolf, 1978). Treatment acceptability is part of the assessment of social validity, in which the goals, procedures, and outcomes of interventions are evaluated. Evaluating treatment acceptability is important for two principal reasons: to protect clients' rights, and to make the intervention agreeable to clients, thereby encouraging them to participate fully in their treatment (Singh, Lloyd, & Kendall, 1990; Wacker et al., 1990b).

Treatments Involving Aversive Stimuli

Probably the greatest concerns regarding treatment acceptability relate to methods that apply physically aversive stimuli, either as punishers or as USs in aversion therapy. As we have seen in earlier chapters, procedures using physically aversive stimuli should be avoided whenever possible. When aversive stimuli are used as punishers, the degree of their severity or restrictiveness should be as mild as possible while still allowing the intervention to succeed in reducing the unwanted behavior. Two useful procedures can be used to protect clients from harm and safeguard their rights (G. Green, 1990). First, the therapist should identify an appropriate professional committee that can review the plan to use aversive methods and seek their approval. Second, the therapist should describe the aversive methods to the client or guardian fully and seek consent to use those methods.

Careful scrutiny regarding the use of aversive stimuli has been applied to programs for improving the behaviors and skills of children, particularly those who are developmentally disabled (Singh, Lloyd, & Kendall, 1990). In some cases, advocacy groups and professional organizations have issued policy statements to guide or restrict the use of punishment techniques of certain types. Unfortunately, the recommendations of these organizations often are contradictory. For instance, the Association for Persons with Severe Handicaps opposes all uses of painful stimuli with handicapped individuals, but the American Psychological Association Division on Mental Retardation and Developmental Disabilities takes the position that painful stimuli may be used under very restricted circumstances, as exemplified by a behavior that is harmful to the client or others and has not been reduced by alternative treatments. When contradictory recommendations exist, which ones should therapists follow? In practice, most probably, therapists simply follow the recommendations of the organization with the closest match to their own value systems or beliefs.

Dilemmas often arise when therapists recognize that nonpunitive treatments have failed to decrease a potentially harmful behavior and physically aversive punishment may be the only alternative to doing nothing. In such instances, it is helpful to consider whether the ends justify the means. Israel Goldiamond (1974) has described a very thought-provoking case. A little girl in an institution was made to wear a padded football helmet and had her hands tied to her crib to protect her from self-injurious head-banging behavior. In efforts to take off the helmet, she would toss her head violently and pull her hair out whenever she got the chance. Her head was constantly bruised and bald. Eventually the child was placed in a different program in which punishment was introduced for these self-injurious behaviors. The punishment consisted of the therapist shouting "Don't!" and administering a sharp slap on the cheek. After fewer than a dozen instances of this punishment method, the self-injurious behavior stopped, the helmet was removed, the child's hair began to grow back, and her social behaviors began to improve. When the original institution and the girl's parents learned of the slapping, however, they removed her from the new program and returned her to the institution, where her behavior regressed and she was again restrained in a crib and required to wear a helmet. We can now ask ourselves two questions: Was using physical punishment acceptable in this case? Was it acceptable to return the child to the original treatment conditions?

Sometimes schools and psychiatric institutions place restrictions on the use of aversive procedures that are not painful but are *intrusive,* or forced on individuals without their permission. For instance, some schools have taken the position that intrusive punishers may only be used in response to the most severe forms of behavior. There are three problems with this position. First, there is no standard criterion for classifying methods with regard to intrusiveness. Second, the position may be interpreted so restrictively that no punishers of any kind would be permitted. Third, the effect of limiting the application of punishers to extreme behaviors may be to diminish drastically the effectiveness of otherwise useful punishers. (Go to 🖼 .)

Case Study 16.1

A Dilemma in Using Intrusive Punishment Only for Extreme Behaviors

An 11-year-old retarded boy named Cory was a student in a school that would permit the use of intrusive punishment only as a consequence of performing extreme acts of aggression or property destruction, which Cory did often (as described in Grace, Kahng, & Fisher, 1994). To test the effects of following the school's restriction, the researchers applied a nonpainful punishment technique during different phases of the intervention. In this punishment, which the school defined as "intrusive," Cory's arms were crossed across his chest, and he was guided to a seated position on the floor and held there for 3 minutes.

During some phases of the intervention, the therapist applied this punishment technique only after Cory had performed very severe aggressive or destructive acts, such as forcefully striking another person or throwing furniture. In other phases, the therapist used the technique after very severe acts *and* moderately severe acts, such as shoving someone or pushing objects off a table. Cory's aggressive and destructive behaviors in these different phases were compared. Punishing *both* the very severe and moderately severe acts resulted in an almost total elimination of Cory's aggressive and destructive behaviors. Punishing only the very severe acts was much less successful in decreasing his aggressive and destructive behaviors.

Assessing Treatment Acceptability

Treatment acceptability is assessed by having individuals fill out rating scales to evaluate the methods applied in interventions (Elliott, 1988). Several rating instruments have been developed for this purpose and are becoming more and more widely used. The assessment can be filled out by clients, relatives or friends of clients, teachers or coworkers of clients, hospital staff, and members of the general community (Schwartz & Baer, 1991). Because the assessments can accommodate multiple purposes, the purpose contemplated determines whose judgments will be sought. Thus, we would have clients rate proposed treatment methods if we wanted to know whether people would participate fully in their own therapy, and we would ask teachers or hospital staff to do the rating if we wanted to predict how motivated they would be to learn new techniques and administer them carefully.

The idea of assessing treatment acceptability may seem simple on the surface, but the factors affecting the ratings are actually very complex. The ratings people give depend on the exact wording used in describing the treatments, tending to be higher if a rationale for the method is given and the rater has a good understanding of the treatment procedures (Elliott, 1988). Ratings of treatment acceptability also tend to be higher when the behavior problem in question is very severe, there are few undesirable side effects from the treatment, the methods involve reinforcement rather than punishment, and the cost in time and effort is low (O'Brien & Karsh, 1990; Wacker et al., 1990b). Acceptability ratings also tend to be higher when the therapist has obtained the consent of the client or guardian, as well as approval from an appropriate committee (see later) to use the techniques. (Go to ✔.)

✔ Concept Check 16.1

....

1. When behavior change goals involve clinically significant improvement and have a high degree of social validity, they meet the two main _____ criteria.

2. A finding that disconfirms the psychodynamic view of the causes of homosexuality is that the parent–child relationships of homosexuals and heterosexuals when growing up are _____ .

3. All types of _____ therapy to change clients' sexual preferences appear to be ineffective.

4. A claim that the antidieting movement makes to argue against dieting is that _____ _____ . ⇔

5. The extent to which client and community consider the methods of a behavior change program to be fair, appropriate, and reasonable is called _____ _____ .

6. One way therapists can take action to protect clients from harm and safeguard their rights is to _____ .

7. An example of a potentially intrusive punisher is _____ . ⇔

_____

Answers: 7. time-out

1. goal acceptability   2. not very different   3. conversion   4. diets almost always fail   5. treatment acceptability   6. obtain each client's consent

....

Ethical and Legal Issues in Therapy and Research

Many different ethical concerns and issues can emerge when psychology professionals conduct therapy, diagnostic assessments, and research; and improper actions regarding some ethical issues can make professionals subject to legal action. Professionals engaged in therapy, assessments, and research try to carry out these activities at a high level of competence, and they take measures to protect the rights and safety of clients and subjects. An important mechanism that is available to protect clients and subjects is the *institutional review board* (or other review committee). In the United States, the federal Department of Health and Human Services requires all institutions receiving direct or indirect funding from the government to establish an institutional review board for the evaluation of proposals for conducting research, to ensure that clients and subjects will be protected from harm. These committees consist of at least five individuals who are not connected to the therapy or research in question and can represent the views of significant and relevant elements of society, such as the general community, child welfare groups, and the fields of medicine and law. What's more, major professional organizations have developed guidelines as standards of general professional conduct and as rules to guide the process of conducting therapy and research. We will examine some of the current guidelines for professionals who study or apply principles of behavior change.

General Principles for Psychologists

The American Psychological Association (APA, 1992) has developed a detailed set of ethical principles and codes of conduct to guide the behavior of psychologists in nearly all facets of their work. For instance, there are specific standards for explaining to the client the results of diagnostic assessments and for maintaining confidentiality. These guidelines begin with the following set of general principles.

- *Competence.* Psychologists should carry out their work competently, recognizing the limits of their abilities and providing only services they are sufficiently trained to administer properly.
- *Integrity.* Psychologists should strive to be honest and fair toward others and in presenting descriptions of their qualifications and activities.
- *Professional and scientific responsibility.* Psychologists should consult with colleagues and other professionals to prevent unethical conduct and to serve the interests of clients, students, or others who receive their services.
- *Respect for people's rights and dignity.* Psychologists should respect the rights to privacy, confidentiality, and autonomy and should be aware of cultural and individual differences, particularly those related to "age, gender, race, ethnicity, national origin, religion, sexual orientation, disability, language, and socioeconomic status."
- *Concern for others' welfare.* Psychologists should promote the welfare of clients, students, or others who receive or are affected by their services by trying to prevent them from harm or exploitation.
- *Social responsibility.* Psychologists should exercise professional responsibility to the larger community and to society by trying to reduce human suffering, prevent the misuse of their work, and promote enactment of laws and social policies that benefit their clients and the public.

More specific guidelines have been established to guide the way in which professionals conduct therapy and research.

Ethical Safeguards in Therapy

Various groups and organizations have issued specific guidelines to protect clients from harm in therapy processes. We will examine the guidelines for therapy developed by the Association for Advancement of Behavior Therapy (AABT) and the APA.

The AABT published in a 1977 issue of their journal, *Behavior Therapy*, an extensive set of questions therapists and others can consider when evaluating the ethical standards of an intervention. Table 16.1 presents these questions, along with an introductory explanation and factors to consider for each question. Keep in mind that the questions were designed to apply broadly to professionals who provide human services of all types, not just those who conduct behavior therapy. As you examine these questions, you may notice that some touch on topics we have considered at various points in this book. Other questions cover issues we've not mentioned before that are also important, such as the possibility of coercion to participate in therapy. If a therapist is planning or conducting an intervention, he or she should try to answer each question in the list. Answering *no* to any of these questions suggests that the program contains one or more features that may be ethically questionable. In such a case, revisions generally are in order.

In the 1970s, the APA commissioned a committee to develop detailed guidelines that would be specific to the practice of behavior modification in therapy and several other settings, such as schools and prisons (Stolz & Associates, 1978). Some of the issues this committee addressed were:

> How and by whom are problems to be defined and goals set? Does the psychologist serve established power structures in modifying an individual's behavior, or is the psychologist obligated primarily (or exclusively) to the interests of the person whose behavior is being changed? Can the psychologist ethically serve both the power structure and the target individual? (pp. 1–2)

Although the committee's recommendations were designed specifically with the practice of behavior modification in mind, they apply to psychologists using intervention methods of all types. These recommendations were separated into eight issues, as follows.

1. *Identification of the client.* From the psychologist's point of view, the term *client* can have two meanings: (a) the person whose behavior is the target for change and (b) the psychologist's employer, such as the person, institution, or community that pays the psychologist's salary or fee. In many therapy settings with adult clients, these two roles are filled by one person. When different individuals or entities fill these roles, the rights of the person whose behavior is to change must be protected from abuses that may be perpetrated, perhaps unwittingly, by the individual who controls the purse strings. (In this book, the term *client* has been reserved for the person whose behavior is to change, unless specifically clarified otherwise.)

2. *Definition of the problem and selection of the goals.* When considering changing a person's behavior, the psychologist must determine whether a problem exists, what it might be, and what behavioral goals would be appropriate. Various people may have input into these decisions, and they may reach conflicting conclusions, as in the dilemmas we posed earlier. Although the recommendations do not specify how to resolve such disagreements, they suggest that having all parties describe their values openly would help. As an addendum to these recommendations, the

Table 16.1   *Questions for Evaluating Interventions*

The eight questions listed below were developed by a committee of the AABT for professionals to consider when evaluating therapeutic interventions in all types of human service. In these questions, the term "client" refers to the individual whose behavior is to be changed, but a guardian may be substituted if the client cannot understand the issues to be considered; "therapist" refers to the professional in charge of providing the treatment. Ideal interventions generally allow clients maximum involvement in planning and carrying out the treatment while taking into account societal pressures on the clients, the therapists, and the therapists' employers. Although ideal interventions would receive *yes* answers for all eight questions, exceptions to this rule are possible while still maintaining high ethical standards. As you examine these questions, assume that the evaluation is being conducted after the intervention has already begun.

1. *Have the client and therapist considered the goals of treatment adequately?* An answer of yes is based on whether (a) the goals were made explicit to the client, preferably in writing, (b) the therapist had the client restate the goals orally or in writing, (c) the therapist and client agreed on the goals, (d) the immediate interests of or benefits for the client are consistent with his or her long-term interests, and (e) the interests of the client are compatible with those of other relevant individuals.

2. *Has the therapist examined the choice of treatment methods adequately?* A yes answer is based on whether (a) the published literature indicates that the methods in the intervention are the best ones for treating the client's problem, (b) the methods used are consistent with the accepted therapeutic practice, (c) the client was informed of alternative methods and their relative advantages and disadvantages, and (d) for treatment methods that are professionally, legally, or societally controversial, the therapist obtained approval through an ethical review by independent professionals.

3. *Is the client participating in treatment voluntarily?* Answering yes involves considering whether the client (a) is being coerced to participate, (b) was offered a choice of methods and therapists if the treatment was legally man-

dated, and (c) can withdraw from therapy without penalties beyond the loss of costs incurred for the treatment received.

4. *If some person or agency is legally empowered to arrange for treatment, have the interests of the client been considered adequately?* An answer of yes is based on whether (a) the client, although subordinated legally, was told of the treatment objectives and has had some input into the choices of treatment methods, (b) the empowered person or agency has discussed the goals and methods with the therapist and approved them, and (c) efforts were undertaken to make the interests of the client and those of the empowered person or agency compatible when their interests were in conflict.

5. *Does the intervention include procedures to assess treatment effectiveness?* A yes answer is based on whether (a) the intervention includes methods to assess the client's problem quantitatively and chart its progress and (b) the client has access to these assessments during treatment.

6. *Is the confidentiality of the therapeutic relationship adequately protected?* An answer of yes is based on whether (a) the client's records are accessible only to authorized individuals and (b) the client knows who has access to those records.

7. *Has the therapist referred the client to other professionals when necessary?* A yes answer is based on whether the client (a) was informed that he or she would receive a referral to another therapist if dissatisfied with the treatment and (b) received an appropriate referral if the treatment was unsuccessful.

8. *Is the therapist qualified to perform the treatment?* Answering yes depends on whether (a) the therapist has had appropriate training or experience in treating problems like those of the client, (b) the client was informed of any deficits in the therapist's qualifications, (c) an unqualified professional referred the client to or obtained careful supervision from a therapist who is qualified, and (d) the client was informed that a professional providing treatment was doing so under the supervision of a qualified therapist if such a circumstance existed.

Source: AABT, 1977.

1992 APA guidelines suggest that institutional review boards or other ethical review committees might be contacted to help resolve disagreements.

3. *Selection of the intervention method.* Psychologists should choose the most effective methods that present the least possible restriction and intrusiveness, and the fewest unpleasant side effects (or none). For instance, whenever possible, positive reinforcement approaches should be chosen in preference to punishment or other methods that use aversive stimuli. If neither reinforcement nor mild punishment changes the behavior, it may be necessary to apply stronger forms of punishment.

4. *Accountability.* Psychologists have the responsibility to produce satisfactory therapy outcomes and to document the intervention's success. Being accountable requires that reliable data on the behavior be collected and available for the client to examine.

5. *Evaluation of the quality of the psychologist and the intervention.* Performing any type of psychological therapy requires that the professional who is supervising the intervention have appropriate training and certification in clinical or counseling psychology. But procedures specifically for assessing skills in applying behavior modification techniques are lacking. Although a professional organization called the Association for Behavior Analysis has developed some guidelines to assess these skills, there are currently no generally accepted or used standards or processes for accrediting behavior modification skills.

6. *Record keeping and confidentiality.* All interventions should include procedures for keeping accurate and up-to-date records. Although clients and their guardians must have access to those records, psychologists should exercise great discretion in disclosing information about clients to anyone else. The 1992 APA guidelines also recommend that psychologists discuss the issue of confidentiality with clients and indicate its limits.

7. *Protection of the client's rights.* Three mechanisms should be used to protect the rights of clients. First, in many settings, an institutional review board or other ethical review committee should oversee and evaluate the ethics of an intervention. Second, the social validity of the treatment methods should be assessed during and at the end of therapy. Third, psychologists who provide therapy are expected to obtain from clients or guardians **informed consent—** that is, approval to carry out the planned procedures based on a knowledge of what the procedures will be and the positive and negative effects that may result. The 1992 APA guidelines clarify the process of informed consent by indicating that the individuals giving consent (a) should have the cognitive capacities to do so, (b) should have received relevant information concerning the techniques to be used, and (c) should be permitted to decline freely and without undue influence. When clients are legally incapable of giving informed consent, therapists should still try to explain the procedures to them in simple terms, request their consent, and consider their preferences as well as possible. When the client is a child, informed consent must be obtained from the parent or guardian before treatment begins.

8. *Assessment of the place of research in therapeutic settings.* Conducting therapy and doing research are complementary processes that often occur simultaneously. But the goals and methods of research should not take precedence over the progress of therapy or the rights of clients. So, for example, a research design used during therapy should not include a reversal phase if withdrawing treatment would impede the client's progress.

Ethical Safeguards in Research

The APA has also developed guidelines to safeguard individuals' rights and to protect from harm those who serve as subjects in research (APA, 1982, 1992). These guidelines parallel and are similar to those used in therapy. Ethical safeguards in research reflect eight principles:

1. All individuals, regardless of age or other characteristics, have rights that supersede those of the researcher.

2. The researcher should (a) inform the subject of all features of the research that may affect his or her willingness to participate and (b) answer the subject's questions in terms that are appropriate to his or her abilities to comprehend.

3. *Informed consent* should be obtained from the subject, if possible. If the subject is a child, informed consent should be obtained, preferably in writing, from his or her parents or from individuals who can reasonably act *in loco parentis*, (teachers or directors of institutions, for example). Individuals giving consent should be informed of all features of the research that may affect their willingness to consent.

4. The researcher should respect the subject's freedom to choose *not* to participate in the research or to discontinue participation at any time without undue coercion to reconsider such decisions.

5. The researcher should not use any procedure that may harm the subject physically or psychologically. When harm seems possible, the researcher must consult an institutional review board for guidance and approval. This often means that the research will need to be postponed and redesigned or abandoned.

6. Concealing important information from subjects or deceiving them should be avoided whenever possible. If such procedures are contemplated, the researcher must consult an institutional review board, demonstrate that alternative procedures are not feasible, and show that the research outcome will have considerable scientific or applied value. If the use of concealment or deception is allowed, the researcher must *debrief* the subjects to correct misconceptions, preferably as soon as their participation has been completed. This is done by describing the purpose of the research and explaining the need for deception (which may then be self-evident).

7. The researcher should keep confidential all information obtained about participants, unless the participants have agreed in advance to the open use of the information.

8. When research procedures result in unforeseen undesirable circumstances for the participant, the researcher should take immediate action to correct these circumstances, compensating, as well, for any long-term effects the subject may experience.

Future Challenges for Behavior Modification

We've covered a lot of ground in our examination of principles of behavior change, and we've seen that these principles have great potential for benefiting both societies and individuals. You now have a clear picture of what these principles are and how they can be applied successfully to change your own and others' behaviors. We've seen that the techniques of behavior modification are highly effective and produce obvious improvements in behavior fairly quickly, sometimes in just a few sessions. And we've seen that these techniques can be applied in a wide variety of settings to change almost any problem behavior. These techniques are generally at least as effective as other approaches in changing behavior. It should be clear that behavior modification methods possess many very significant strengths, but there are some limitations, too (Goldfried & Castonguay, 1993). In the remainder of this chapter, we will look at a few challenges the discipline faces for the future.

Improving the Effectiveness of Behavior Modification

Despite the clear success of behavioral and cognitive methods in changing behavior, some important challenges remain for the future. One way to improve the success of behavior modification techiques is to enhance the care with which interventions are designed and implemented. For instance, many professionals who design behavior change programs use "intuitive" processes in choosing treatment methods rather than doing thorough functional analyses (Lennox et al., 1988). In addition, staff members who administer interventions may become lax in applying the techniques if they are not carefully and periodically trained and monitored in their efforts (Harchik et al., 1992).

Not only are behavior modification techniques useful in correcting behavioral problems that already exist, they have shown some promise in the *prevention* of human suffering and problem behaviors, too. For example, interventions have been conducted with some degree of success in preventing teenagers from developing unhealthful addictive behaviors, such as smoking cigarettes or using drugs (Botvin et al., 1990; Flay et al., 1989; Murray et al., 1989). Some behavioral and cognitive methods were designed specifically to prevent future behavior problems by training individuals in skills to help them function better in everyday life. Self-management methods in general and stress inoculation training and problem-solving training approaches all qualify as preventive methods. Although some tentative evidence suggests that behavior modification programs may be useful in efforts to prevent medical and psychological problems, much more research is needed to demonstrate these effects convincingly.

We have seen that *relapse* is an important obstacle to the success of programs to change behavior. Behavior modification interventions typically do change problem behaviors while the programs are in effect, but behavior sometimes regresses after the programs have ended. Although some progress has been made in developing methods to reduce the likelihood of relapse, the problem remains as a critical challenge for the future.

Another challenge for the future will be to justify application of behavior modification in relation to its financial costs (D. M. Baer, Wolf, & Risley, 1987; Yates, 1994). Research needs to be conducted to demonstrate a favorable *cost–benefit ratio*—that is, the extent to which providing the intervention saves more money in the long run than it costs (Jospe, Shueman, & Troy, 1991; Kaplan, 1989). These "bottom line" issues often are used in deciding whether to apply certain procedures or whether insurance will pay for an intervention. Many behavior modification interventions have the potential to produce far more financial benefits than costs. Earlier in the book, for instance, we considered research findings indicating that hospital patients who receive help in coping with medical procedures recover more quickly and use less medication than those who don't receive such help. But most therapeutic techniques known to be effective have not yet been subjected to cost–benefit analyses (Yates, 1994).

Integrating Therapy Approaches

Because of the central role of research and data in behavior modification, many of the professionals who use behavioral and cognitive methods have been willing to consider using new techniques that are demonstrably effective in changing behavior. In the first decade or so of the discipline, behavior modification research and therapy tended to apply a single technique, such as reinforcement, by itself. Then the discipline began to combine different behavioral methods, and soon behavioral and cognitive methods were used in the same interventions.

By the 1970s, therapists had become increasingly eclectic in their orientations (Swan & MacDonald, 1978). These changes marked the beginning of a movement to integrate therapy approaches from widely different theoretical bases, such as medicine and psychoanalysis (G. T. Wilson, 1990). A chief factor that has led to an integration of therapy approaches is the development of research-based support for the effectiveness of many different methods of therapy (Beitman, Goldfried, & Norcross, 1989; M. L. Smith & Glass, 1977). One of the most common forms of integration with behavior therapy is the use of medication, for example, in treating anxiety disorders, depression, and hyperactivity (Emmelkamp, Bouman, & Scholing, 1992; Roth et al., 1982; Satterfield, Satterfield, & Cantwell, 1981; Simons et al., 1986). Psychologists cannot prescribe medication, but they often provide therapy in conjunction with professionals who can—that is, medical doctors (physicians and psychiatrists). The value of integrating therapy approaches is a very controversial issue at this time, and the speed and direction it will take are currently unclear.

Enhancing the "Image" of Behavior Modification

The early years of behavior modification were rocky in terms of public and professional acceptance of its approach. The field received very sharp criticism for two of its defining characteristics. First, its philosophical foundations seemed to reject the role of cognitive and biological processes in behavior. Second, the techniques it used seemed simplistic, cold, and impersonal. For instance, a great deal of the early research and application involved the use of punishment, sometimes using intense, physically aversive stimuli with developmentally disabled children. We have seen in this book that the field of behavior modification has evolved, discarding and replacing unacceptable and untenable features with perspectives and methods that are more consistent with the mainstream of psychological thought.

The negative impact of the early characteristics of behavior modification on its image continued at least until the 1980s (O'Leary, 1984). The extent of people's biases against the use of behavioral methods was shown in a fascinating study (Woolfolk, Woolfolk, & Wilson, 1977). Undergraduate and graduate students at a large state university watched a videotape in which a teacher of children in a special education class used reinforcement techniques, including social and token reinforcers. Before watching the tape, half of the university-educated subjects were

✔ Concept Check 16.2

1. Committees mandated by the U.S. Department of Health and Human Services to review the ethics of research are called _____ .
2. The APA recommends that psychologists recognize the limits of their abilities and provide only services in which they are well trained. This recommendation is part of the general principle called _____ .
3. A question the AABT recommends professionals ask in evaluating the ethics of an intervention is _____
_____ . ⇔
4. A client's approval for therapy to proceed after learning what the procedures will be is called _____ .
5. Whenever possible, researchers should avoid using _____ . ⇔
6. A common form of integration with behavior therapy is the use of _____
_____ in treating anxiety and depression.

_____

Answers: voluntary? **4.** informed consent **5.** deception **6.** medication
1. institutional review boards **2.** competence **3.** Is the client's participation

told they would see a teacher using *behavior modification* techniques with her students and half were told that the teacher would be using *humanistic psychology* teaching methods. The subjects were then asked to rate the teacher and her methods. As you may suspect, the subjects who were told that the techniques were humanistic rated the teacher much more favorably than the subjects who were told that the techniques were behavioral. Members of the group that had been told that the methods were "humanistic" also gave the methods higher ratings on a scale that assessed their likelihood of promoting academic and emotional growth.

Since the early 1980s, professionals who use behavior modification techniques have been working to correct the negative image of the field. One strategy they have used has been to challenge incorrect statements and misconceptions about behavior modification that have appeared in the news media (O'Leary, 1984). Another approach for enhancing the image of behavior modification has been to publicize the wide acceptance and use accorded the techniques within the field of psychology. As the field of behavior modification has evolved since the 1970s, its image probably has been improving. (Go to ✔ .)

Application Exercise

I hope you have enjoyed reading this book and that you will find it useful to refer to in the future when and if:

- You are working as a professional to help people change their behavior.
- You try to maintain and improve further the behavioral gains you achieved in the self-management program you designed.
- You decide to change another behavior by designing a new a self-management project.

The application exercises throughout the book were designed to help you develop the skills to be able to take on these activities successfully. For this last application exercise, we will consider several ethical issues. Turn to Work Sheet 16.1 and complete the questions.

Summary

Although most behavior change interventions involve outcome goals and behavioral goals that are generally acknowledged to be desirable, sometimes questions arise about the acceptability of certain goals for behavior change programs. An intervention's goals are likely to be viewed favorably if they meet two goal acceptability criteria: the goals should have a high degree of social validity, and they should propose achieving a clinically significant improvement. Although psychologists have used conversion therapies in efforts to change the sexual preference of homosexuals, these efforts have not been successful and the behavioral goals do not meet the acceptability criteria.

Treatment acceptability refers to assessments of the fairness, appropriateness, and reasonableness of the behavior change methods. Using physically aversive stimuli in interventions presents problems for treatment acceptability and should be avoided whenever possible. If aversive stimuli are used, their severity and restrictiveness should be as mild as possible, while still allowing the program to succeed in changing the target behavior. Treatment acceptability can be assessed by having individuals fill out rating scales.

Because many ethical concerns can arise in the course of conducting psychological therapy and research, institutional review boards or other review committees can be used to examine the plans and protect the rights of clients and research subjects. The APA and the AABT have developed principles to guide the behavior of psychologists in research and therapy activities. These guidelines discuss broad issues, such as competence and integrity, and outline codes of conduct in very specific activities, such as selecting intervention methods and maintaining confidentiality. Clients' rights in therapy can be protected with three mechanisms: (1) using institutional review boards, (2) assessing the social validity of the treatment, and (3) obtaining informed consent from client or guardian. Ethical safeguards are also applied to protect the rights of subjects in research.

Several challenges remain for the future of behavior modification. They include improving the effectiveness of behavioral and cognitive methods, integrating effective approaches from other disciplines into behavior therapy, and enhancing the image of behavior modification.

Key Terms and Review Questions

Key Terms

goal acceptability   treatment acceptability
informed consent

Review Questions

1. What two acceptability criteria apply toward deciding whether behavior change goals are acceptable?

2. Describe the questions one should ask in deciding whether behavior change goals are acceptable.

3. Describe the evidence against the view that homosexuality is caused by children's experiences with their parents.

4. Pick one of the three dilemmas in behavior change goals discussed in the chapter, and present two arguments for and against the goals.

5. Define "treatment acceptability."

6. Describe the case study of Cory and discuss the meaning of the outcome of the intervention for policies on using punishment.

7. What is an institutional review board?

8. Describe four of the APA's general principles of ethics for psychologists.

9. Describe how you might use the AABT questions in Table 16.1 to judge the ethics of therapy.

10. Discuss the three mechanisms for protecting the rights of clients in therapy.

11. Describe the ethical guidelines for doing psychological research.

12. Describe the research by Woolfolk, Woolfolk, and Wilson (1977) on the public image of behavior modification.

Related Readings

APA (American Psychological Association)(1982). *Ethical principles in the conduct of research with human participants.* Washington, DC: Author.

APA (American Psychological Association)(1992). Ethical principles of psychologists and code of conduct. *American Psychologist, 47,* 1597–1611.

Stolz, S. B., & Associates (1978). *Ethical issues in behavior modification.* San Francisco: Jossey-Bass.

Name _____   Day & time
                                       class meets_____

Date _____

Chapter 16: Work Sheet 16.1

1. Describe how you would go about evaluating the self-management project you designed in earlier work sheets with regard to the acceptability of its behavioral goals.

2. Describe your views about the treatment acceptability of the use of physical punishment (slapping) with the girl who had been physically restrained in an institution (her hands had been tied, and she had been made to wear a helmet).

3. Imagine that you were a member of an institutional review board that was asked to assess the ethics of an intervention to reduce the aggressive behavior of Cory, the retarded boy described in Case Study 16.1 The proposed program is multidimensional, with methods directed at the behavior itself and its antecedents and consequences, and will include the use of reinforcers and punishers. Describe exactly how you would evaluate the ethics of the program.

Glossary

A-B-C log   A chronological record of each instance of the target behavior, along with the antecedents and consequences that accompanied it.

AB design   Intrasubject research involving one baseline phase and one intervention phase.

ABA design   A reversal design consisting of three phases: baseline, intervention, and reversal (baseline).

ABAB design   A reversal design consisting of four phases: baseline, intervention, reversal (baseline), and intervention.

abstinence violation effect   A cognitive process: a lapse leads the individual to feel guilt and reduced self-efficacy, which then precipitate a relapse.

Achievement Place   A residental token economy program for predelinquent teenagers in which live-in teaching parents supervised the behavior and administration of reinforcers.

altering antecedent chains   Techniques designed to modify the chain of events that set the occasion for an undesirable behavior to occur, thereby reducing the likelihood of its occurrence.

alternating-treatment designs   A type of intrasubject research design in which two or more treatments are conducted during the same intervention phase to compare their effectiveness. Also called *simultaneous-treatment* or *multielement designs*.

alternative responses   Behaviors that interfere or compete with other responses, making the other responses unlikely to occur. Also called *competing responses*.

antecedents   Cues that precede and set the occasion for particular behaviors.

anxiety   A fear with vague or unspecified sources.

anxiety-induction therapies   Treatment approaches aimed at reducing phobias and anxieties by exposing the client to intense levels of the CS for prolonged periods of time under the supervision of a therapist.

assertion training   Programs using modeling and other behavior modification techniques to train clients in using more appropriately or adaptively assertive behavior in social situations.

autogenic training   A technique designed to induce psychological and physical calm: the person imagines being in a pleasant scene and experiencing certain calming body sensations.

automatic thoughts   In cognitive therapy, habitual erroneous and maladaptive thought patterns that arise from inappropriate schemata; found frequently in individuals with emotional problems.

aversion therapy   A treatment approach aimed at reducing an operant or respondent behavior by associating it with a highly unpleasant stimulus.

avoidance conditioning   Learning a behavior that prevents the occurrence of an aversive circumstance.

backward chaining   A method for teaching a chain of behavior by having the person master one link at a time, starting with the last link and adding each new one in the reverse sequence of the chain.

bar graphs   Diagrams that use rectangles to represent data points to show how one variable changes with another.

baseline   A term referring to a period of time before an intervention is introduced *or* to the data collected during such a period.

behavior   Any measurable response a person makes; can be overt or covert.

behavior modification   A discipline that focuses on using principles of learning and cognition to understand and change behavior.

behavior rehearsal   A technique used with modeling: clients perform the modeled behavior and receive feedback on the performance.

behavioral contract   A formal agreement in a behavior change program describing the target behavior explicitly; states where and when the target behavior should or should not be performed and what the consequences will be in either case.

behavioral deficit   An appropriate behavior that the person does not perform often enough, long enough, well enough, or strongly enough.

behavioral excess   An inappropriate response that the person performs too often, too strongly, or for too long.

behavioral goal   The desired level of the target behavior to be reached by the end of a behavior change program.

behavioral medicine   An interdisciplinary field developed to study the connections between behavior and health, emphasizing behavior modification perspectives.

behavioral methods   Behavior modification techniques that apply principles of operant conditioning, respondent conditioning, and modeling, especially toward altering overt behaviors.

behavioral subgoals   Specific intermediate levels of the target behavior to be achieved in the process of reaching a behavioral goal.

behaviorism   The school of thought that stresses the study of observable, measurable responses and proposes that behavior can be explained mainly by principles of learning, especially operant and respondent conditioning.

biofeedback   A technique that enables individuals to regulate the functioning of their physiological systems by providing moment-to-moment information about the status of each system.

blocking   A respondent conditioning phenomenon: having learned a CS as a signal for a particular US makes it difficult to learn a new CS for that US.

booster program   A program to maintain improved behaviors introduced after an intervention has ended; consists of periodic sessions of the intervention methods to refresh the effects of the original intervention.

brainstorming   A strategy for generating alternative solutions to solve a problem without concern for their quality or practicality.

calm scenes   Cognitive images of pleasant events that are relaxing.

chain   A sequence of operant responses that leads to a consequence.

changing-criterion design   A type of intrasubject research design in which the effect of an intervention is examined by altering the standards for correct performance periodically and noting whether the behavior matches the new standards.

classical conditioning   See *respondent conditioning*.

clinical significance   The meaningfulness (significance) of an intervention's success in modifying a person's behavior in everyday life; a highly meaningful change is one that is large and brings the behavior into the normal range.

cognition   Covert events, particularly thinking and reasoning.

cognitive methods   Behavior modification techniques that are used to change people's thought processes in order to modify associated overt and covert behaviors.

cognitive restructuring   A type of approach used by some cognitive–behavioral therapies: behavioral excesses of thinking maladaptive thoughts are reduced by altering the way clients perceive or think about events in their lives.

cognitive therapy   A cognitive restructuring treatment approach that engages clients and therapists in a collaborative effort of hypothesis testing as a method of changing clients' maladaptive automatic thoughts.

cognitive–behavioral therapy   Treatment approaches that use both cognitive and behavioral methods to change overt and covert behaviors.

computer-assisted instruction (CAI)   A form of programmed instruction in which a series of questions or problems is presented on a computer, which can provide immediate feedback regarding the individual's answers and give examples and explanations of concepts.

conditioned emotional responses (CERs)   Respondent behaviors that reflect emotions, such as fear and anger.

conditioned reinforcers   Consequences that developed their ability to strengthen behavior by way of conditioning, typically by being associated with established reinforcers. Also called *secondary reinforcers*.

conditioned response (CR)   A specific behavior that can be elicited by a conditioned stimulus as a result of prior learning.

conditioned stimulus (CS)   An event that has gained the ability to elicit a specific response through repeated pairing with a stimulus that already elicits that response.

continuous recording   A measurement strategy of keeping records of a target behavior by recording data on all instances of its occurrence in a specified time period.

continuous reinforcement (CRF)   A schedule of reinforcement in which a reinforcer is given after each and every instance of the correct response.

coping statements   Positive self-statements that emphasize the maker's ability to handle difficult situations.

cost–benefit ratio   An assessment of the extent to which the cost of treatment is exceeded by the amount of money it saves in the long run.

counterconditioning   A respondent learning process in which the person substitutes a competing or incompatible response for a previously learned CR when the CS is present.

covert conditioning   An array of imagery-based techniques in which a behavior is learned by imagining the components of operant or respondent conditioning events.

covert positive reinforcement   A covert conditioning technique that is used to reduce fear by having people imagine first performing the feared behavior (the CR) and then experiencing a pleasant event.

covert sensitization   A covert conditioning technique in which a person learns to dislike an existing positive CS or to suppress a liked behavior by associating an aversive stimulus with either of these events in imagined respondent or operant conditioning situations.

cumulative graphs   Line graphs in which the measure of one variable accumulates across units scaled along the horizontal axis. Also called *cumulative records*.

differential reinforcement   A discrimination learning process in which making a specific response to one stimulus is reinforced consistently, but making the same response to another stimulus is not reinforced.

differential reinforcement of incompatible behavior (DRI)   Delivering reinforcers contingent on the performance of an alternative response to an undesirable target behavior.

differential reinforcement of low rates of responding (DRL)   Delivering reinforcers contingent on the performance of an undesirable target behavior at a rate that is below a certain level.

differential reinforcement of other behavior (DRO)   Delivering reinforcers contingent on the nonperformance of an undesirable target behavior during a certain time period.

direct assessment methods   Measuring behavior in a straightforward manner, usually by observing it directly.

discrimination learning   Learning to distinguish between and respond differently toward different stimuli.

discriminative stimulus (S^D)   A stimulus that has been associated as an antecedent for a specific reinforced response.

distraction   A technique in which attention is shifted from stressful overt or covert events to other stimuli.

duration   A measure of behavior that assesses the length of time an instance of the target response lasts.

emetic therapy   A behavior modification approach for reducing alcohol abuse by having clients take a drug that induces nausea if they drink alcohol while the emetic is present in the system.

escape conditioning   Learning a behavior that reduces or eliminates an existing aversive circumstance.

experiment   A type of group-based research in which subjects are randomly assigned to different conditions and the researcher manipulates the independent variable to determine its effect on a dependent variable.

extinction (in operant conditioning)   The process or procedure in which a previously reinforced behavior no longer receives reinforcement, making it less likely to occur in the future.

extinction (in respondent conditioning)   The process or procedure in which the CS occurs repeatedly without the US it was paired with, making the CR less likely to occur in the future.

extinction burst   A temporary increase in the frequency or magnitude of a response that sometimes occurs soon after an extinction procedure has been introduced.

fading   The process of gradually removing or changing a prompt to decrease reliance on it.

fixed-interval (FI)   A type of interval reinforcement schedule in which the time period after each reinforcer has been given and reinforcement is no longer available remains constant from one instance of reward to the next. The first correct response made after that period of time has elapsed is reinforced. See also *variable-interval*.

fixed-ratio (FR)   A type of ratio reinforcement schedule in which the number of correct responses that must be made for each instance of reward remains constant. See also *variable ratio*.

flooding   An anxiety-induction therapy in which exposure is given to one or more CSs based on a real-life feared situation; exposure can be *in vivo* or imaginal. Also called *response prevention.*

forward chaining   A method for teaching a chain of behavior by having the person master one link at a time, starting with the first link and adding each following one in the appropriate sequence.

frequency   A measure of behavior that assesses how often the target response occurs.

functional analysis   A procedure for assessing the connections between the target behavior and its antecedents and consequences.

goal acceptability   The extent to which the outcome goals or behavioral goals of a behavior change program are fair, appropriate, and reasonable.

graph   A diagram that generally shows how one variable changes as a function of another variable.

graphic analysis   A procedure used in examining graphs of data from behavior change programs to evaluate whether the program succeeded in changing the behavior substantially.

group contingency   A procedure for administering reinforcers in which the behavior of all members of a group determines the consequences they receive.

habit reversal   An array of methods designed to decrease operant behaviors, especially responses that are habitual or automatic, such as motor tics. The methods include competing response practice and training to make the person aware of the behavior's occurrence.

health psychology   A field of psychology introduced to study biopsychosocial processes in the development, prevention, and treatment of illness.

implosive therapy   An anxiety-induction therapy in which clients imagine highly exaggerated, unrealistic, or physically damaging events related to their fears or anxieties.

indirect assessment methods   Behavior measurements that use abstract or roundabout approaches, rather than observing responses directly.

informed consent   Approval of procedures contemplated for use in therapy or research, given by the participants and/or their guardians after they have been told what procedures have been planned and any negative effects that might result.

intermittent reinforcement schedule   A type of reinforcement schedule in which only some instances of a behavior are reinforced. Also called *partial reinforcement.*

interobserver reliability   An assessment of the degree to which the data from two or more observers agree regarding the occurrence of a target behavior. Also called *interrater reliability* or *interobserver agreement.*

interval recording   A measurement strategy in which observation periods are divided into fairly short intervals of equal length and a record is kept of whether the target behavior occurred in each interval.

interval schedules   Schedules of reinforcement in which delivery of each instance of reward is based on a rule that involves a period of time after the administration of each reinforcer during which reinforcement is no longer available. The first correct response made after that period of time has elapsed is reinforced.

instructions   Oral or written description of how to perform a behavior.

intrasubject designs   A type of research approach that examines changes in behavior for one individual at a time while an intervention is either in effect or absent. Also called *single-subject designs.*

lapse   An instance of backsliding—that is, performing an unwanted behavior—after having started or completed a program to improve that behavior.

latent inhibition   A respondent conditioning phenomenon in which prior experience with a specific stimulus in neutral circumstances retards the subsequent learning of that stimulus as a CS for a US.

learning   A relatively permanent change in behavioral tendency as a result of experience.

line graphs   Diagrams that use straight lines connecting data points to show changes of one variable in relation to another.

lottery   A procedure for administering reinforcers by entering all eligible individuals in a drawing to win one or more prizes.

magnitude   A measure of behavior that assesses its intensity, degree, or size.

mean   The arithmetic average for a set of data.

meditation   A technique designed to induce psychological and physical calm by having the person focus attention on a meditation stimulus, such as an object, event, or idea.

modeling   Learning a behavior by watching another individual perform it. Also called *observational learning, social learning,* and *vicarious learning.*

multidimensional programs   Behavior change programs that combine several methods to address a problem behavior, its antecedents, and its consequences.

multielement designs   See *alternating treatment designs.*

multimodal therapy   A treatment approach that selects and employs various cognitive and behavioral methods to address several dimensions of a client's problems.

multiple baselines across behaviors   A type of multiple-baseline design in which each AB design examines the effects of the intervention on *a different behavior* for a single individual in a particular situation.

multiple baselines across situations   A type of multiple-baseline design in which each AB design examines the effects of the intervention on a particular behavior in *a different situation* for a single individual.

multiple baselines across subjects   A type of multiple-baseline design in which each AB design examines the effects of the intervention on a particular behavior in a particular setting for *a different individual.*

multiple-baseline designs   Intrasubject research designs featuring two or more AB designs, with all baseline phases starting simultaneously but continuing for different lengths of time.

narrowing   Limiting a target behavior to a relatively small range of antecedent conditions.

natural reinforcers   Unprogrammed rewards people receive as a natural part of everyday life.

negative practice   Deliberately performing a behavior repeatedly and paying close attention to the sensations it produces.

negative punishment   A process in which subtracting or reducing a stimulus or condition suppresses the behavior on which it is contingent.

negative reinforcement   A process in which subtracting or reducing a stimulus as a consequence of a behavior strengthens that behavior.

observational learning   See *modeling*.

operant conditioning   A form of learning in which behavior can be changed by its consequences.

organizational behavior management   An approach for improving employee behavior and functioning by applying behavior modification techniques in employment settings.

outcome goals   Broad or abstracted results to be achieved in a behavior change program.

overcorrection   A punishment procedure in which when an undesirable behavior occurs, the person is obliged to engage in activities that correct (see *restitution*) and/or are the opposite of the misbehavior (see *positive practice*).

overshadowing   A respondent conditioning phenomenon in which one of multiple CSs outweighs the others in the ability to elicit the CR.

participant modeling   A fear reduction technique in which a fearful individual watches a therapist or other person engage in a feared activity and is encouraged and guided to join in the activity.

personalized system of instruction (PSI)   A method of teaching in which the course material is divided into a series of units; students study and take tests at their own pace and receive immediate feedback on their performance.

phobia   Intense and irrational fear, usually of a specific object or condition.

pinpointing   Translating broad or vague descriptions of people's behavior into specific, objective, and measurable responses.

physically aversive stimuli   Punishers that cause physical discomfort, pain, or other unpleasant sensations.

positive practice   A component of the overcorrection method of punishment in which the misbehaving person must engage repeatedly in a response that is the opposite of the misbehavior.

positive punishment   A process in which adding or introducing an aversive event suppresses the behavior on which it is contingent.

positive reinforcement   A process in which adding or introducing a consequence for a behavior strengthens that behavior.

postreinforcement pauses Brief pauses in responding, often seen after each instance of reward when reinforcement is on a fixed-ratio schedule.

Premack principle The idea that activities that are high-probability behaviors for a particular individual can reinforce responses that occur less frequently.

primary reinforcers See *unconditioned reinforcers.*

problem-solving training A cognitive–behavioral treatment approach that trains clients in a strategy for identifying and dealing with life circumstances that require actions based on effective decision-making processes.

programmed instruction A self-teaching process in which individuals learn material by working at their own pace through a series of questions or problems; the program provides immediate feedback for answers.

progressive muscle relaxation A technique designed to induce psychological and physical calm by having the person alternately tense and relax separate muscle groups. Also called *progressive relaxation.*

prompt An antecedent that reminds the person to perform a behavior or helps him or her learn how to perform it.

psychosomatic medicine A field of study introduced to examine the relationships between symptoms of illness and the emotions of the patient.

punishment A process whereby a consequence of an operant response suppresses that behavior.

quasi-experiments Research designs that have different groups of subjects and "look" like experiments but do not manipulate an independent variable or randomly assign subjects to conditions, hence are not "true experiments."

ratio schedules Schedules of reinforcement in which delivery of each instance of reward is determined by a rule that specifies the number of correct responses that must have been made since the last reinforcer was given.

ratio strain Deterioration of a behavior when the number of responses required in a ratio schedule of reinforcement becomes too large.

rational–emotive therapy (RET) A cognitive restructuring treatment approach in which a therapist challenges clients' irrational beliefs and trains them to substitute thoughts that are more adaptive and rational.

reactivity The tendency for behavior to change when people know they are being watched.

reinforcement A process whereby a consequence of an operant response strengthens that behavior.

reinforcer sampling A procedure for enhancing the effectiveness of a reinforcer by presenting a small or brief sample of the reinforcing consequence before a target behavior is performed.

reinterpretative statements Positive self-statements that redefine a difficult situation by nullifying its unpleasant aspects or providing reasons for seeing it differently.

relapse A return to a former level of an undesirable behavior.

relapse prevention method   A self-management program that individuals are taught as part of an intervention, to help them maintain their improved behavior by learning how to identify and deal effectively with situations that tend to lead to relapses.

relaxation   A psychological and physical state of calm.

reprimands   Verbal statements expressing strong criticism of behavior.

respondent conditioning   A learning process in which a stimulus gains the ability to elicit a particular response by being paired repeatedly with an unconditioned stimulus that already elicits that response. Also called *classical conditioning*.

response   See its synonym: *behavior*.

response cost   A punishment procedure in which the misbehaving person loses a valued item or privilege.

response generalization   A phenomenon in which modifying a target behavior leads to similar changes in another response that was not specifically addressed in the behavior change program.

response prevention   See *flooding*.

restitution   A component of the overcorrection method of punishment in which the misbehaving person must correct or restore the environmental situation, often to a better condition than had existed before the misbehavior.

reversal designs   Intrasubject research formats with a series of phases that involve alternations in the presence and absence of the intervention.

rule-release   A provision in a behavior change program that allows for exemption from its restrictive rules during certain predefined, limited conditions.

S-delta (S^Δ)   A stimulus that has been associated consistently with nonreinforcement of a specific response.

schedule of reinforcement   A rule that determines which instances of a response will result in a reinforcer.

schema (plural = *schemata*)   In cognitive therapy, a cognitive structure that organizes one's knowledge and affects one's perceptions and interpretations of everyday experiences.

second-order conditioning   A respondent conditioning phenomenon in which a new CS gains the ability to produce a CR by becoming associated with an existing CS that already elicits that response.

secondary reinforcers   See *conditioned reinforcers*.

self-control   The ability to exercise restraint over our own emotions, impulses, or desires. (Sometimes used interchangeably with *self-regulation*.)

self-efficacy   People's beliefs about their ability to succeed at performing a particular behavior they want to do.

self-instruction   An antecedent statement people make to themselves that guides, directs, or describes the behavior they will perform.

self-management   The application of behavioral or cognitive methods to change one's own behavior.

self-monitoring   Assessing one's own target behaviors.

self-regulation   The ability to direct and modulate one's own responses to result in appropriate behavior.

self-statements   Things people say to themselves either overtly (aloud) or covertly to influence their overt or covert behaviors.

shaping   A process or procedure in which a new behavior becomes increasingly well developed when the criteria for being reinforced for successive instances of the response become increasingly rigorous.

simultaneous-treatment designs   See *alternating treatment designs.*

single-subject designs   See *intrasubject designs.*

social learning   See *modeling.*

social validity   An evaluation by the client and individuals in his or her life of the social utility and adaptiveness of any changes in behavior produced by an intervention.

spontaneous recovery   The reappearance of a previously extinguished behavior. If extinction continues, the response is weak and temporary.

stages of change model   A theory that incorporates motivations and intentions to describe five stages in people's readiness to change their behavior.

stimulus control   The ability of an antecedent stimulus to affect the performance of a specific behavior.

stimulus generalization   The tendency to perform a learned behavior in response to an antecedent stimulus or condition that is similar but not identical to the actual discriminative stimulus for that behavior.

stimulus hierarchy   A series of CSs that are rank-ordered in terms of the degree of fear each one arouses.

stress inoculation training   A cognitive–behavioral treatment approach that focuses on teaching specific skills clients can use in coping with stressful experiences in their everyday lives.

subjective units of discomfort scale (SUDS)   A scale a fearful person can use to rate the feelings of fear aroused by particular CSs.

systematic desensitization   A respondent conditioning technique for reducing fear by presenting increasingly strong CSs and replacing the CR with a calm response.

summary record   A form that when filled out using the A-B-C log data, organizes and summarizes the data, allowing patterns to be seen in the relationships among the antecedents, behavior, and consequences.

table   A chart that systematically arranges a set of data in rows and columns.

target behaviors   The responses to be changed in a behavior modification intervention.

task analysis   A process used in identifying the component responses and required sequences that make up a complex action.

taste aversion   A specific form of learning in which the taste of a liked food becomes disliked very easily through respondent conditioning, even though CS and US are separated by a substantial period of time.

thinning   Gradually reducing the rate at which a behavior is reinforced.

thought stopping   A technique in which individuals interrupt disturbing thoughts by saying "Stop" emphatically, either aloud or covertly.

time sampling   A measurement strategy in which observation periods are divided into subperiods of equal length; a record is kept of occurrences of the target behavior during a short interval at the start of each subperiod.

time-out   A form of punishment in which the misbehaving person's reinforcing environment is converted or moved to one that is less reinforcing.

token economy   A method that uses a complex system of consequences, with tokens as reinforcers, to modify a wide range of behaviors in groups of individuals.

tokens   Symbolic rewards that can serve as conditioned reinforcers by being traded for and associated with already established, backup reinforcers.

total-task presentation   A method for teaching a chain of behavior by having the person learn all the links together as a complete sequence.

treatment acceptability   The extent to which the treatment methods in a behavior change program are considered by the client and the community to be fair, appropriate, and reasonable.

trend line   A "best fitting" straight line applied in a graph to represent the overall or general changes in one variable across a set of data points plotted as a function of another variable.

unconditioned reinforcers   Consequences that have the ability to strengthen behavior with little or no prior learning. Also called *primary reinforcers.*

unconditioned response (UR)   A specific behavior made automatically to a particular stimulus.

unconditioned stimulus (US)   A specific event that elicits a particular response automatically.

urine alarm apparatus   A device that applies operant and respondent conditioning principles to eliminate the release of urine during sleep or at other inappropriate times.

variable-interval (VI)   A type of interval reinforcement schedule in which the time period during which reinforcement is no longer available changes and is unspecified from one instance of reward to the next. The first correct response made after each period of time has elapsed is reinforced. See also *fixed-interval.*

variable-ratio (VR)   A type of ratio reinforcement schedule in which the number of correct responses that must be made for each instance of reward changes and is unspecified from one instance to the next. See also *fixed-ratio.*

variables   Any characteristics of people, events, or objects that can change.

References

AABT (Association for Advancement of Behavior Therapy) (1977). Ethical issues for human services. *Behavior Therapy, 8,* v–vi.

Acker, L. E., Goldwater, B. C., & Agnew, J. L. (1990). Sidney Slug: A computer simulation for teaching shaping without an animal laboratory. *Teaching of Psychology, 17,* 130–132.

Ackerman, M. D., & Carey, M. P. (in press). Psychology's role on the assessment of erectile dysfunction: Historical precedents, current knowledge, and methods. *Journal of Consulting and Clinical Psychology.*

Ackerman, M. D., D'Attilio, J. P., Antoni, M. H., Weinstein, D., Rhamy, R. K., & Politano, V. A. (1991). The predictive significance of patient-reported sexual functioning in RigiScan sleep evaluations. *Journal of Urology, 146,* 1559–1563.

Ackerman, M. D., D'Atillio, J. P., Antoni, M. H., Rhamy, R. K., Weinstein, D., & Politano, V. A. (1993). Patient-reported erectile dysfunction: A cross-validation study. *Archives of Sexual Behavior, 22,* 603–618.

Agras, W. S., Schneider, J. A., Arnow, B., Raeburn, S. D., & Telch, C. F. (1989). Cognitive–behavioral and response prevention treatments for bulimia nervosa. *Journal of Consulting and Clinical Psychology, 57,* 215–221.

Albin, R. W., & Horner, R. H. (1988). Generalization with precision. In R. H. Horner, G. Dunlap, & R. L. Koegel (Eds.), *Generalization and maintenance: Life-style changes in applied settings.* Baltimore: Paul H. Brookes.

Alexander, R. N., Corbett, T. F., & Smigel, J. (1976). The effects of individual and group consequences on school attendance and curfew violations with predelinquent adolescents. *Journal of Applied Behavior Analysis, 9,* 221–226.

Al-Kubaisy, T., Marks, I. M., Logsdail, S., Marks, M. P., Lovell, K., Sungur, M., & Araya, R. (1992). Role of exposure homework in phobia reduction: A controlled study. *Behavior Therapy, 23,* 599–621.

Allen, J. S., Tarnowski, K. J., Simonian, S. J., Elliott, D., & Drabman, R. S. (1991). The generalization map revisited: Assessment of generalized treatment effects in child and adolescent behavior therapy. *Behavior Therapy, 22,* 393–405.

Allen, K. D., Loiben, T., Allen, S. J., & Stanley, R. T. (1992). Dentist-implemented contingent escape for management of disruptive child behavior. *Journal of Applied Behavior Analysis, 25,* 629–636.

Allen, K. D., & Stokes, T. F. (1987). Use of escape and reward in the management of young children during dental treatment. *Journal of Applied Behavior Analysis, 20,* 381–390.

Allen, L. D., & Iwata, B. A. (1980). Reinforcing exercise maintenance: Using existing high-rate activities. *Behavior Modification, 4,* 337–354.

Allison, J. (1989). The nature of reinforcement. In S. B. Klein & R. R. Mowrer (Eds.), *Contemporary learning theories: Instrumental conditioning and the impact of biological constraints on learning.* Hillsdale, NJ: Erlbaum.

Altman, K., Haavik, S., & Cook, J. W. (1978). Punishment of self-injurious behavior in natural settings using contingent aromatic ammonia. *Behaviour Research and Therapy, 16,* 85–96.

AMA (American Medical Association) (1989). *The American Medical Association Encyclopedia of Medicine.* New York: Random House.

Anderson, K. O., & Masur, F. T. (1983). Psychological preparation for invasive medical and dental procedures. *Journal of Behavioral Medicine, 6,* 1–40.

Andrasik, F., Blake, D. D., & McCarran, M. S. (1986). A biobehavioral analysis of pediatric headache. In N. A. Krasnegor, J. D. Arasteh, & M. F. Cataldo (Eds.), *Child health behavior: A behavioral pediatrics perspective.* New York: Wiley.

APA (American Psychological Association) (1982). *Ethical principles in the conduct of research with human participants.* Washington, DC: Author.

APA (American Psychological Association) (1992). Ethical principles of psychologists and code of conduct. *American Psychologist, 47,* 1597–1611.

Arrick, M. C., Voss, J., & Rimm, D. C. (1981). The relative efficacy of thought-stopping and covert assertion. *Behaviour Research and Therapy, 19,* 17–24.

Asbell, B. (1984, February 26). Writers' workshop at age 5. *New York Times Magazine,* pp. 55–72.

Ascher, L. M. (1993). Treating recursive anxiety with covert conditioning. In J. R. Cautela & A. J. Kearney (Eds.), *Covert conditioning handbook.* Pacific Grove, CA: Brooks/Cole.

Ash, D. W., & Holding, D. H. (1990). Backward versus forward chaining in the acquisition of a keyboard skill. *Human Factors, 32,* 139–146.

Ashem, B., & Donner, L. (1968). Covert sensitization with alcoholics: A controlled replication. *Behaviour Research and Therapy, 6,* 7–12.

Aubuchon, P., Haber, J. D., & Adams, H. E. (1983). Can migraine headaches be modified by operant pain techniques? *Journal of Behavior Therapy and Experimental Psychiatry, 16,* 261–263.

Axelrod, S. (1990). Myths that (mis)guide our profession. In A. C. Repp & N. N. Singh (Eds.), *Perspectives on the use of nonaversive and aversive interventions for persons with developmental disabilities.* Sycamore, IL: Sycamore.

Axelrod, S., Brantner, J. P., & Meddock, T. D., (1978). Overcorrection: A review and critical analysis. *Journal of Special Education, 12,* 367–391.

Axelrod, S., Hall, R. V., Weis, L., & Rohrer, S. (1974). Use of self-imposed contingencies to reduce the frequency of smoking behavior. In M. J. Mahoney & C. E. Thoresen (Eds.), *Self-control: Power to the person.* Monterey, CA: Brooks/Cole.

Ayllon, T. , & Azrin, N. H. (1968a). Reinforcer sampling: A technique for increasing the behavior of mental patients. *Journal of Applied Behavior Analysis, 1,* 13–20.

Ayllon, T., & Azrin, N. H. (1968b). *The token economy: A motivational system for therapy and rehabilitation.* Englewood Cliffs, NJ: Prentice-Hall.

Ayllon, T., & Michael, J. (1959). The psychiatric nurse as a behavioral engineer. *Journal of the Experimental Analysis of Behavior, 2,* 323–334.

Azrin, N. H. (1976). Improvements in the community-reinforcement approach to alcoholism. *Behaviour Research and Therapy, 14,* 339–348.

Azrin, N. H., & Foxx, R. M. (1971). A rapid method of toilet training the institutionalized retarded. *Journal of Applied Behavior Analysis, 4,* 89–99.

Azrin, N. H., & Holz, W. C. (1966). Punishment. In W. K. Honig (Ed.), *Operant behavior: Areas of research and application.* New York: Appleton.

Azrin, N. H., Hontos, P. T., & Besalel-Azrin, V. (1979). Elimination of enuresis without a conditioning apparatus: An extension by office instruction of the child and parents. *Behavior Therapy, 10,* 14–19.

Azrin, N. H., & Nunn, R. G. (1973). Habit-reversal: A method of eliminating nervous habits and tics. *Behaviour Research and Therapy, 11,* 619–628.

Azrin, N. H., Nunn, R. G., & Frantz, S. E. (1980). Habit reversal vs. negative practice treatment of nervous tics. *Behavior Therapy, 11,* 169–178.

Azrin, N. H., & Peterson, A. L. (1990). Treatment of Tourette syndrome by habit reversal: A waiting-list control group comparison. *Behavior Therapy, 21,* 305–318.

Azrin, N. H., & Powell, J. (1969). Behavioral engineering: The use of response priming to improve prescribed self-medication. *Journal of Applied Behavior Analysis, 2,* 39–42.

Azrin, N. H., & Powers, M. A. (1975). Eliminating classroom disturbances of emotionally disturbed children by positive practice procedures. *Behavior Therapy, 6,* 525–534.

Azrin, N. H., Sisson, R. W., Meyers, R., & Godley, M. (1982). Alcoholism treatment by disulfiram and community reinforcement therapy. *Journal of Behavior Therapy and Experimental Psychiatry, 13,* 105–112.

Azrin, N. H., & Thienes, P. M. (1978). Rapid elimination of enuresis by intensive learning without a conditioning apparatus. *Behavior Therapy, 9,* 342–354.

Azrin, N. H., & Wesolowski, M. D. (1974). Theft reversal: An overcorrection procedure for eliminating stealing by retarded persons. *Journal of Applied Behavior Analysis, 7,* 577–581.

Azrin, N. H., & Wesolowski, M. D. (1975). The use of positive practice to eliminate persistent floor sprawling by profoundly retarded adults. *Behavior Therapy, 6,* 627–631.

Baer, D. M., Peterson, R. F., & Sherman, J. A. (1967). The development of imitation by reinforcing behavioral similarity to a model. *Journal of the Experimental Analysis of Behavior, 10,* 405–416.

Baer, D. M., Wolf, M. M., & Risley, T. R. (1968). Some current dimensions of applied behavior analysis. *Journal of Applied Behavior Analysis, 1,* 91–97.

Baer, D. M., Wolf, M. M., & Risley, T. R. (1987). Some still-current dimensions of applied behavior analysis. *Journal of Applied Behavior Analysis, 20,* 313–327.

Baer, R. A., Blount, R. L., Detrich, R., & Stokes, T. F. (1987). Using intermittent reinforcement to program maintenance of verbal/nonverbal correspondence. *Journal of Applied Behavior Analysis, 20,* 179–184.

Baeyens, F., Hermans, D., & Eelen, P. (1993). The role of CS–US contingency in human evaluative conditioning. *Behaviour Research and Therapy, 31,* 731–737.

Baggs, K., & Spence, S. H. (1990). Effectiveness of booster sessions in the maintenance and enhancement of treatment gains following assertion training. *Journal of Consulting and Clinical Psychology, 58,* 845–854.

Bailey, J. S., Timbers, G. D., Phillips, E. L., & Wolf, M. M. (1971). Modification of articulation errors of pre-delinquents by their peers. *Journal of Applied Behavior Analysis, 4,* 265–281.

Baldwin, J. D., & Baldwin, J. I. (1981). *Beyond sociobiology.* New York: Elsevier.

Ballard, K. D., & Glynn, T. (1975). Behavioral management in story writing with elementary school children. *Journal of Applied Behavior Analysis, 8,* 387–398.

Bandura, A. (1965). Vicarious processes: A case of no-trial learning. In L. Berkowitz (Ed.), *Advances in experimental social psychology* (Vol. 2). New York: Academic Press.

Bandura, A. (1969). *Principles of behavior modification.* New York: Holt, Rinehart & Winston.

Bandura, A. (1975). Effecting change through participant modeling. In J. D. Krumboltz & C. E. Thoresen (Eds.), *Counseling methods.* New York: Holt, Rinehart & Winston.

Bandura, A. (1977). Self-efficacy: Toward a unifying theory of behavioral change. *Psychological Review, 84,* 191–215.

Bandura, A. (1986). *Social foundations of thought and action: A social–cognitive theory.* Englewood Cliffs, NJ: Prentice-Hall.

Bandura, A., Jeffery, R. W., & Gajdos, E. (1975). Generalizing change through participant modeling with self-directed mastery. *Behaviour Research and Therapy, 13,* 141–152.

Bangert-Drowns, R. (1988). The effects of school-based substance abuse education—A meta-analysis. *Journal of Drug Education, 18,* 243–264.

Bank, L., Marlowe, J. H., Reid, J. B., Patterson, G. R., & Weinrott, M. R. (1991). A comparative evaluation of parent-training interventions for families of chronic delinquents. *Journal of Abnormal Child Psychology, 19,* 15–33.

Barlow, D. H. (1978). Aversive procedures. In W. S. Agras (Ed.), *Behavior modification: Principles and clinical applications* (2nd ed.). Boston: Little, Brown.

Barlow, D. H., & Hayes, S. C. (1979). Alternating treatments design: One strategy for comparing the effects of two treatments in a single subject. *Journal of Applied Behavior Analysis, 12,* 199–210.

Barlow, D. H., Leitenberg, H., Agras, W. S., & Wincze, J. P. (1969). The transfer gap in systematic desensitization: An analogue study. *Behaviour Research and Therapy, 7,* 191–196.

Baron, A., & Galizio, M. (1983). Instructional control of human operant behavior. *Psychological Record, 33,* 495–520.

Barrera, F. J., & Teodoro, G. M. (1990). Flash bonding or cold fusion? A case analysis of Gentle Teaching. In A. C. Repp & N. N. Singh (Eds.), *Perspectives on the use of nonaversive and aversive interventions for persons with developmental disabilities.* Sycamore, IL: Sycamore.

Barrera, M., & Glasgow, R. E. (1976). Design and evaluation of a personalized instruction course in behavioral self-control. *Teaching of Psychology, 3,* 81–84.

Barrish, H. H., Saunders, M., & Wolf, M. M. (1969). Good behavior game: Effects of individual contingencies for group consequences on disruptive behavior in a classroom. *Journal of Applied Behavior Analysis, 2,* 119–124.

Barton, E. J., & Osborne, J. G. (1978). The development of classroom sharing by a teacher using positive practice. *Behavior Modification, 2,* 231–250.

Barton, E. S., Guess, D., Garcia, E., & Baer, D. M. (1970). Improvement of retardates' mealtime behaviors by timeout procedures using multiple-baseline techniques. *Journal of Applied Behavior Analysis, 3,* 77–84.

Baum, C. G., Forehand, R., & Zegiob, L. E. (1979). A review of observer reactivity in adult-child interactions. *Journal of Behavioral Assessment, 1,* 167–178.

Baum, W. M. (1994). *Understanding behaviorism: Science, behavior, and culture.* New York: HarperCollins.

Beck, A. T. (1967). *Depression: Clinical, experimental, and theoretical aspects.* New York: Harper & Row.

Beck, A. T. (1976). *Cognitive therapy and the emotional disorders.* New York: International Universities Press.

Beck, A. T. (1993). Cognitive therapy: Past, present, and future. *Journal of Consulting and Clinical Psychology, 61,* 194–198.

Beck, A. T., Freeman, A., & Associates. (1990). *Cognitive therapy of personality disorders.* New York: Guilford.

Beck, A. T., Kovacs, M., & Weissman, A. (1975). Hopelessness and suicidal behavior: An overview. *Journal of the American Medical Association, 234,* 1146–1149.

Beck, A. T., Ward, C. H., Mendelson, M., Mock, J. E., & Erbaugh, J. K. (1961). An inventory for measuring depression. *Archives of General Psychiatry, 4,* 561–571.

Beck, J. G. (1992). Behavioral approaches to sexual dysfunction. In S. M. Turner, K. S. Calhoun, & H. E. Adams (Eds.), *Handbook of clinical behavior therapy* (2nd ed.). New York: Wiley.

Becker, W. C., Madsen, C. H., Arnold, C. R., & Thomas, D. R. (1972). The contingent use of teacher attention and praise in reducing classroom behavior problems. In K. D. O'Leary & S. G. O'Leary (Eds.), *Classroom management: The successful use of behavior modification.* New York: Pergamon Press.

Beiman, I., Israel, E., & Johnson, S. A. (1978). During training and posttraining effects of live and taped extended progressive relaxation, self-relaxation, and electromyogram biofeedback. *Journal of Consulting and Clinical Psychology, 46,* 314–321.

Beitman, B. D., Goldfried, M. R., & Norcross, J. C. (1989). The movement toward integrating the psychotherapies: An overview. *American Journal of Psychiatry, 146,* 138–147.

Bell, A. P., Weinberg, M. S., & Hammersmith, S. K. (1981). *Sexual preference: Its development in men and women.* Bloomington: Indiana University Press.

Bellack, A. S., & Hersen, M. (Eds.) (1990). *Handbook of comparative treatments for adult disorders.* New York: Wiley.

Belles, D., & Bradlyn, A. S. (1987). The use of the changing criterion design in achieving controlled smoking in a heavy smoker: A controlled case study. *Journal of Behavior Therapy and Experimental Psychiatry, 18,* 77–82.

Benson, H. (1974). Your innate asset for combating stress. *Harvard Business Review, 52,* 49–60.

Benson, H. (1984). The relaxation response and stress. In J. D. Matarazzo, S. M. Weiss, J. A. Herd, N. E. Miller, & S. M. Weiss (Eds.), *Behavioral health: A handbook of health enhancement and disease prevention.* New York: Wiley.

Benson, H. (1991). Mind/body interactions including Tibetan studies. In The Dalai Lama, H. Benson, R. A. F. Thurman, H. E. Gardner, & D. Goleman (Eds.), *Mindscience: An East–West dialogue.* Boston: Wisdom.

Benson, H., Malhotra, M. S., Goldman, R. F., Jacobs, G. D., & Hopkins, P. J. (1990). Three case reports of the metabolic and electroencephalographic changes during advanced Buddhist meditation techniques. *Behavioral Medicine, 16,* 90–94.

Bentall, R. P., Lowe, C. G., & Beasty, A. (1985). The role of verbal behavior in human learning: II. Developmental differences. *Journal of Applied Behavior Analysis, 43,* 165–181.

Bernstein, D. A., & Borkovec, T. D. (1973). *Progressive relaxation training: A manual for the helping professions.* Champaign, IL: Research Press.

Bernstein, D. A., Borkovec, T. D., & Coles, M. G. H. (1986). Assessment of anxiety. In A. R. Ciminero, K. S. Calhoun, & H. E. Adams, (Eds.), *Handbook of behavioral assessment* (2nd ed.). New York: Wiley.

Bernstein, I. L. (1991). Aversion conditioning in response to cancer and cancer treatment. *Clinical Psychology Review, 11,* 185–191.

Bierman, K. L., Miller, C. L., & Stabb, S. D. (1987). Improving the social behavior and peer acceptance of rejected boys: Effects of social skill training with instructions and prohibitions. *Journal of Consulting and Clinical Psychology, 55,* 194–200.

Billings, D. C., & Wasik, B. H. (1985). Self-instructional training with preschoolers: An attempt to replicate. *Journal of Applied Behavior Analysis, 18,* 61–67.

Birnbrauer, J. S., Wolf, M. M., Kidder, J. D., & Tague, C. E. (1972). Classroom behavior of retarded pupils with token reinforcement. In K. D. O'Leary & S. G. O'Leary (Eds.), *Classroom management: The successful use of behavior modification.* New York: Pergamon Press.

Blakey, R., & Baker, R. (1980). An exposure approach to alcohol abuse. *Behaviour Research and Therapy, 18,* 319–325.

Blampied, N. M., & Kahan, E. (1992). Acceptability of alternative punishments. *Behavior Modification, 16,* 400–413.

Blanchard, E. B. (1987). Long-term effects of behavioral treatment of chronic headache. *Behavior Therapy, 18,* 375–385.

Blanchard, E. B., Applebaum, K. A., Guarnieri, P., Morrill, B., & Dentinger, M. P. (1987). Five year prospective follow-up on the treatment of chronic headache with biofeedback and/or relaxation. *Headache, 27,* 580–583.

Blanchard, E. B., Nicholson, N. L., Radnitz, C. L., Steffek, B. D., Applebaum, K. A., & Dentinger, M. P. (1991). The role of home practice in thermal biofeedback. *Journal of Consulting and Clinical Psychology, 59,* 507–512.

Boegli, R. G., & Wasik, B. H. (1978). Use of the token economy system to intervene on a school-wide level. *Psychology in the Schools, 15,* 72–78.

Borden, J. W. (1992). Behavioral treatment of simple phobia. In S. M. Turner, K. S. Calhoun, & H. E. Adams (Eds.), *Handbook of clinical behavior therapy* (2nd ed.). New York: Wiley.

Borkovec, T. D., Wilkinson, L., Folensbee, R., & Lerman, C. (1983). Stimulus control applications to the treatment of worry. *Behaviour Research and Therapy, 21,* 247–251.

Bornstein, P. H., Hamilton, S. B., & Bornstein, M. T. (1986). Self-monitoring procedures. In A. R. Ciminero, K. S. Calhoun, & H. E. Adams (Eds.,), *Handbook of behavioral assessment* (2nd ed.). New York: Wiley.

Bornstein, P. H., & Quevillon, R. P. (1976). The effects of a self-instructional package on overactive preschool boys. *Journal of Applied Behavior Analysis, 9,* 179–188.

Bostow, D. E., & Bailey, J. B. (1969). Modification of severe disruptive and aggressive behavior using brief timeout and reinforcement procedures. *Journal of Applied Behavior Analysis, 2,* 31–37.

Botvin, G. J., Baker, E., Dusenbury, L., Tortu, S., & Botvin, E. M. (1990). Preventing adolescent drug use through a multimodal cognitive–behavioral approach: Results of a 3-year study. *Journal of Consulting and Clinical Psychology, 58,* 437–446.

Bouton, M. E., & Swartzentruber, D. (1991). Sources of relapse after extinction in Pavlovian and instrumental learning. *Clinical Psychology Review, 11,* 123–140.

Brantner, J. P., & Doherty, M. A. (1983). A review of timeout: A conceptual and methodological analysis. In S. Axelrod & J. Apsche (Eds.), *The effects of punishment on human behavior.* New York: Academic Press.

Braswell, L., & Kendall, P. C. (1988). Cognitive–behavioral methods with children. In K. S. Dobson (Ed.), *Handbook of cognitive behavioral therapies.* New York: Guilford.

Brigham, T. (1982). Self-management: A radical behavioral perspective. In P. Karoly & F. H. Kanfer (Eds.), *Self-management and behavior change: From theory to practice.* New York: Pergamon Press.

Broden, M., Bruce, C., Mitchell, M. A., Carter, V., & Hall, R. V. (1972). Effects of teacher attention on attending behavior of two boys at adjacent desks. In K. D. O'Leary & S. G. O'Leary (Eds.), *Classroom management: The successful use of behavior modification.* New York: Pergamon Press.

Brown, J. M., O'Keeffe, J., Sanders, S. H., & Baker, B. (1986). Developmental changes in children's cognition to stressful and painful situations. *Journal of Pediatric Psychology, 11,* 343-357.

Brown, P. L. (1982). *Managing behavior on the job.* New York: Wiley.

Brownell, K. D., & Rodin, J. (1994). The dieting maelstrom: Is it possible and advisable to lose weight? *American Psychologist, 49,* 781–791.

Brudny, J. (1982). Biofeedback in chronic neurological cases: Therapeutic electromyography. In L. White & B. Tursky (Eds.), *Clinical biofeedback: Efficacy and mechanisms.* New York: Guilford.

Bryant, L. E., & Budd, K. S. (1982). Self-instructional training to increase independent work performance in preschoolers. *Journal of Applied Behavior Analysis, 15,* 259–271.

Burgess, R. L., & Richardson, R. A. (1984). Coercive interpersonal contingencies as a determinant of child maltreatment: Implications for treatment and prevention. In R. F. Dangel & R. A. Polster (Eds.), *Parent training: Foundations of research and practice.* New York: Guilford.

Burling, T. A., Bigelow, G. E., Robinson, J. C., & Mead, A. M. (1991). Smoking during pregnancy: Reduction via objective assessment and directive advice. *Behavior Therapy, 22,* 31–40.

Butler, R. A. (1954). Incentive conditions which influence visual exploration. *Journal of Experimental Psychology, 48,* 19–23.

Byne, W. (1994). The biological evidence challenged. *Scientific American, 270*(5), 50–55.

Calhoun, K. S., & Lima, P. P. (1977). Effects of varying schedules of timeout on high- and low-rate behaviors. *Journal of Behavior Therapy and Experimental Psychiatry, 8,* 189–194.

Campbell, B. A., & Kraeling, D. (1953). Response strength as a function of drive level and amount of drive reduction. *Journal of Experimental Psychology, 45,* 97–101.

Cantwell, D. P., & Baker, L. (1984). Research concerning families of children with autism. In E. Schopler & G. B. Mesibov (Eds.), *The effects of autism on the family.* New York: Plenum Press.

Carey, R. G., & Bucher, B. (1981). Identifying the educative and suppressive effects of positive practice and restitutional overcorrection. *Journal of Applied Behavioral Analysis, 14,* 71–80.

Carey, R. G., & Bucher, B. D. (1986). Positive practice overcorrection: Effects of reinforcing correct performance. *Behavior Modification, 10,* 73–92.

Carlson, C. R., & Hoyle, R. H. (1993). Efficacy of abbreviated progressive muscle relaxation training: A quantitative review of behavioral medicine research. *Journal of Consulting and Clinical Psychology, 61,* 1059–1067.

Carlson, C. S., Arnold, C. R., Becker, W. C., & Madsen, C. H. (1968). The elimination of tantrum behavior in a child in an elementary classroom. *Behaviour Research and Therapy, 6,* 117–119.

Carr, E. G. (1988). Functional equivalence as a mechanism of response generalization. In R. H. Horner, G. Dunlap, & R. L. Koegel (Eds.), *Generalization and maintenance: Life-style changes in applied settings.* Baltimore: Paul H. Brookes.

Carr, E. G., & Durand, V. M. (1985). Reducing behavior problems through functional communication training. *Journal of Applied Behavior Analysis, 18,* 111–126.

Carr, E. G., Taylor, J. C., & Robinson, S. (1991). The effects of severe behavior problems in children on the teaching behavior of adults. *Journal of Applied Behavior Analysis, 24,* 523–525.

Carson, T. P. (1986). Assessment of depression. In A. R. Ciminero, K. S. Calhoun, & H. E. Adams (Eds.,), *Handbook of behavioral assessment* (2nd ed.). New York: Wiley.

Carter, N., Holmström, A., Simpanen, M., & Melin, L. (1988). Theft reduction in a grocery store through product identification and graphing of losses for employees. *Journal of Applied Behavior Analysis, 21,* 385–389.

Catania, A. C., Matthews, B. A., & Shimoff, E. (1982). Instructed versus shaped human behavior: Interactions with nonverbal responding. *Journal of Applied Behavior Analysis, 38,* 233–248.

Caudill, B. D., & Lipscomb, T. R. (1980). Modeling influences on alcoholics' rates of alcohol consumption. *Journal of Applied Behavior Analysis, 13,* 355–365.

Cautela, J. R. (1966). Treatment of compulsive behavior by covert sensitization. *Psychological Record, 16,* 33–41.

Cautela, J. R. (1981). *Behavior analysis forms for clinical intervention* (Vol. 2). Champaign, IL: Research Press.

Cautela, J. R. (1993a). Covert conditioning: Assumptions and procedures. In J. R. Cautela & A. J. Kearney (Eds.), *Covert conditioning handbook.* Pacific Grove, CA: Brooks/Cole.

Cautela, J. R. (1993b). Insight in behavior therapy. *Journal of Behavior Therapy and Experimental Psychiatry, 24,* 155–159.

Cautela, J. R. (1993c). The use of covert conditioning in the treatment of a severe childhood phobia. In J. R. Cautela & A. J. Kearney (Eds.), *Covert conditioning handbook.* Pacific Grove, CA: Brooks/Cole.

Cautela, J. R., & Kastenbaum, R. (1967). A reinforcement survey schedule for use in therapy, training, and research. *Psychological Reports, 20,* 1115–1130.

Cautela, J. R., & Upper, D. (1975). The process of individual behavior therapy. In M. Hersen & R. M. Miller (Eds.), *Progress in behavior modification* (Vol. 1). New York: Academic Press.

Cautela, J. R., & Wisocki, P. A. (1977). The thought stopping procedure: Description, application, and learning theory interpretations. *Psychological Record, 2,* 255–264.

Chambless, D. L., & Gillis, M. M. (1993). Cognitive therapy of anxiety disorders. *Journal of Consulting and Clinical Psychology, 61,* 248–260.

Charlop, M. H., Burgio, L. D., Iwata, B. A., & Ivancic, M. T. (1988). Stimulus variation as a means of enhancing punishment effects. *Journal of Applied Behavior Analysis, 21,* 89–95.

Christoff, K. A., & Kelly, J. A. (1985). A behavioral approach to social skills training. In L. L'Abate & M. A. Milan (Eds.), *Handbook of social skills training and research.* New York: Wiley.

Christophersen, E. R., Arnold, C. M., Hill, D. W., & Quilitch, H. R. (1972). The home point system: Token reinforcement procedures for application by parents of children with behavior problems. *Journal of Applied Behavior Analysis, 5,* 485–497.

Chung, S.-H. (1965). Effects of delayed reinforcement in a concurrent situation. *Journal of the Experimental Analysis of Behavior, 8,* 439–444.

Ciminero, A. R. (1986). Behavioral assessment: An overview. In A. R. Ciminero, K. S. Calhoun, & H. E. Adams (Eds.), *Handbook of behavioral assessment* (2nd ed.). New York: Wiley.

Clark, H. B., Greene, B. F., Macrae, J. W., McNees, M. P., Davis, J. L., & Risley, T. R. (1977). A parent advice package for family shopping trips: Development and evaluation. *Journal of Applied Behavior Analysis, 10,* 605–624.

Clark, H. B., Rowbury, T., Baer, A. M., & Baer, D. M. (1973). Timeout as a punishing stimulus in continuous and intermittent schedules. *Journal of Applied Behavior Analysis, 6,* 443–455.

Cohen, F., & Lazarus, R. S. (1979). Coping with the stresses of illness. In G. C. Stone, F. Cohen, & N. E. Adler (Eds.), *Health psychology—A handbook.* San Francisco: Jossey Bass.

Cohen, R., De James, P., Nocera, B., & Ramberger, M. (1980). Application of a simple self-instruction procedure on adults' exercise and studying: Two case reports. *Psychological Reports, 46,* 443–451.

Conger, J. C., & Conger, A. J. (1986). Assessment of social skills. In A. R. Ciminero, K. S. Calhoun, & H. E. Adams (Eds.), *Handbook of behavioral assessment* (2nd ed.). New York: Wiley.

Connors, G. J., Tarbox, A. R., & Faillace, L. A. (1992). Achieving and maintaining gains among problem drinkers: Process and outcome results. *Behavior Therapy, 23,* 449–474.

Cook, J. W., Altman, K., Shaw, J., & Blaylock, M. (1978). Use of contingent lemon juice to eliminate public masturbation. *Behaviour Research and Therapy, 16,* 131–134.

Cook, P. S., Petersen, R. C., & Moore, D. T. (1990). *Alcohol, tobacco, and other drugs may harm the unborn.* Rockville, MD: U.S. Department of Health and Human Services.

Cooke, T. P., & Apolloni, T. (1976). Developing positive social–emotional behaviors: A study of training and generalization effects. *Journal of Applied Behavior Analysis, 9,* 65–78.

Cooper, L. J., Wacker, D. P., Thursby, D., Plagmann, L. A., Harding, J., Millard, T., & Derby, M. (1992). Analysis of the effects of task preferences, task demands, and adult attention on child behavior in outpatient and classroom settings. *Journal of Applied Behavior Analysis, 25,* 823–840.

Correa, E. I., & Sutker, P. B. (1986). Assessment of alcohol and drug behaviors. In A. R. Ciminero, K. S. Calhoun, & H. E. Adams (Eds,), *Handbook of behavioral assessment* (2nd ed.). New York: Wiley.

Corte, H. E., Wolfe, M. M., & Locke, B. J. (1971). A comparison of procedures for eliminating self-injurious behavior of retarded adolescents. *Journal of Applied Behavior Analysis, 4,* 201–213.

Craighead, W. E., Evans, D. D., & Robins, C. J. (1992). Unipolar depression. In S. M. Turner, K. S. Calhoun, & H. E. Adams (Eds.), *Handbook of clinical behavior therapy* (2nd ed.). New York: Wiley.

Creer, T. L., Chai, H., & Hoffman, A. (1977). A single application of an aversive stimulus to eliminate chronic cough. *Journal of Behavior Therapy and Experimental Psychiatry, 8,* 107–109.

Crespi, L. P. (1942). Quantitative variation of incentive and performance in the white rat. *American Journal of Psychology, 55,* 467–517.

Crowe, M. J., Marks, I. M., Agras, W. S., & Leitenberg, H. (1972). Time-limited desensitization, implosion and shaping for phobic patients: A crossover study. *Behaviour Research and Therapy, 10,* 319–328.

Cunningham, C. E., & Linscheid, T. R. (1976). Elimination of chronic infant ruminating by electric shock. *Behavior Therapy, 7,* 231–234.

Dahlquist, L. M., & Gil, K. M. (1986). Using parents to maintain improved dental flossing skills in children. *Journal of Applied Behavior Analysis, 19,* 255–260.

Daniels, L. K. (1974). Rapid extinction of nail biting by covert sensitization: A case study. *Journal of Behavior Therapy and Experimental Psychiatry, 5,* 91–92.

Dasen, P. R., & Heron, A. (1981). Cross-cultural tests of Piaget's theory. In H. C. Triandis & A. Heron (Eds.), *Handbook of cross-cultural psychology: Developmental psychology* (Vol. 4). Boston: Allyn & Bacon.

Davey, G. C. L., (1992). An expectancy model of laboratory preparedness effects. *Journal of Experimental Psychology: General,* 121, 24–40.

Davey, G. C. L. (1994). Is evaluative conditioning a qualitatively distinct form of classical conditioning? *Behaviour Research and Therapy, 32,* 291–299.

Davison, G. C. (1976). Homosexuality: The ethical challenge. *Journal of Consulting and Clinical Psychology, 44,* 157–162.

Davison, G. C., & Neale, J. M. (1994). *Abnormal psychology* (6th ed.). New York: Wiley.

Dawson, B., de Armas, A., McGrath, M. L., & Kelly, J. A. (1986). Cognitive problem-solving training to improve the child-care judgment of child neglectful parents. *Journal of Family Violence, 3,* 209–221.

Deitz, S. M., & Malone, L. W. (1985). On terms: Stimulus control terminology. *Behavior Analyst, 8,* 259–264.

Deitz, S. M., Repp, A. C., & Deitz, D. E. D. (1976). Reducing inappropriate classroom behaviour of retarded students through three procedures of differential reinforcement. *Journal of Mental Deficiency Research, 20,* 155–170.

De Luca, R. V., & Holborn, S. W. (1992). Effects of a variable-ratio reinforcement schedule with changing criteria on exercise in obese and nonobese boys. *Journal of Applied Behavior Analysis, 25,* 671–679.

Demchak, M. (1990). Response prompting and fading methods: A review. *American Journal on Mental Retardation, 6,* 603–615.

DeRicco, D. A., & Niemann, J. E. (1980). In vivo effects of peer modeling on drinking rate. *Journal of Applied Behavior Analysis, 13,* 149–152.

DeRisi, W. J., & Butz, G. (1975). *Writing behavioral contracts: A case simulation practice manual.* Champaign, IL: Research Press.

DeRubeis, R. J., & Beck, A. T. (1988). Cognitive therapy. In K. S. Dobson (Ed.), *Handbook of cognitive–behavioral therapies.* New York: Guilford.

de Silva, P. (1984). Buddhism and behavior modification. *Behaviour Research and Therapy, 6,* 661–678.

de Silva, P. (1990). Buddhist psychology: A review of theory and practice. *Current Psychology: Research and Reviews, 9,* 236–254.

DeVries, J. E., Burnette, M. M., & Redmon, W. K. (1991). AIDS prevention: Improving nurses' compliance with glove wearing through performance feedback. *Journal of Applied Behavior Analysis, 24,* 705–711.

Dickerson, E. A., & Creedon, C. F. (1981). Self-selection of standards by children: The relative effectiveness of pupil-selected and teacher-selected standards of performance. *Journal of Applied Behavior Analysis, 14,* 425–433.

Dickinson, A. M. (1989). The detrimental effects of extrinsic reinforcement on "intrinsic motivation." *Behavior Analyst, 12,* 1–15.

DiClemente, C. C., Prochaska, J. O., Fairhurst, S. K., Velicer, W. F., Velasquez, M. M., & Rossi, J. S. (1991). The process of smoking cessation: An analysis of precontemplation, contemplation, and preparation stages of change. *Journal of Consulting and Clinical Psychology, 59,* 295–304.

DiClemente, C. C., Prochaska, J. O., & Gilbertini, M. (1985). Self-efficacy and the stages of change of smoking. *Cognitive Therapy and Research, 9,* 181–200.

Dobson, K. S. (1989). A meta-analysis of the efficacy of cognitive therapy for depression. *Journal of Consulting and Clinical Psychology, 57,* 414–419.

Dobson, K. S., & Block, L. (1988). Historical and philosophical bases of the cognitive–behavioral therapies. In K. S. Dobson (Ed.), *Handbook of cognitive–behavioral therapies.* New York: Guilford.

Dodge, K. A. (1993). Social–cognitive mechanisms in the development of conduct disorder and depression. *Annual Review of Psychology, 44,* 559–584.

Dodge, K. A., & Frame, C. L. (1982). Social cognitive biases and deficits in aggressive boys. *Child Development, 53,* 620–635.

Doleys, D. M. (1977). Behavioral treatments for nocturnal enuresis in children: A review of the recent literature. *Psychological Bulletin, 84,* 30–54.

Doleys, D. M., Wells, K. C., Hobbs, S. A., Roberts, M. W., & Cartelli, L. M. (1976). The effects of social punishment on noncompliance: A comparison with timeout and positive practice. *Journal of Applied Behavior Analysis, 9,* 471–482.

Donahue, J. A., Gillis, J. H., & King, K. (1980). Behavior modification in sport and physical education: A review. *Journal of Sport Psychology, 2,* 311–328.

Donnellan, A. M., & LaVigna, G. W. (1990). Myths about punishment. In A. C. Repp & N. N. Singh (Eds.), *Perspectives on the use of nonaversive and aversive interventions for persons with developmental disabilities.* Sycamore, IL: Sycamore.

Doogan, S., & Thomas, G. V. (1992). Origins of fear of dogs in adults and children: The role of conditioning processes and prior familiarity with dogs. *Behaviour Research and Therapy, 30,* 387–394.

Dorsey, M. F., Iwata, B. A., Ong, P., & McSween, T. E. (1980). Treatment of self-injurious behavior using a water mist: Initial response suppression and generalization. *Journal of Applied Behavior Analysis, 13,* 343–353.

Dougherty, B. S., Fowler, S. A., & Paine, S. C. (1985). The use of peer monitors to reduce negative interaction during recess. *Journal of Applied Behavior Analysis, 18,* 141–153.

Dowrick, P. W. (1991). Analyzing and documenting. In P. W. Dowrick (Ed.), *Practical guide to using video in the behavioral sciences.* New York: Wiley.

Dowrick, P. W., & Jesdale, D. C. (1991). Modeling. In P. W. Dowrick (Ed.), *Practical guide to using video in the behavioral sciences.* New York: Wiley.

Drummond, D. C., & Glautier, S. (1994). A controlled trial of cue-exposure treatment in alcohol dependence. *Journal of Consulting and Clinical Psychology, 62,* 809–818.

Ducharme, J. M., & Feldman, M. A. (1992). Comparison of staff training strategies to promote generalized teaching skills. *Journal of Applied Behavior Analysis, 25,* 165–179.

Dunlap, G., & Plienis, A. J. (1988). Generalization and maintenance of unsupervised responding via remote contingencies. In R. H. Horner, G. Dunlap, & R. L. Koegel (Eds.), *Generalization and maintenance: Life-style changes in applied settings.* Baltimore: Paul H. Brookes.

Durand, V. M., & Carr, E. G. (1991). Functional communication training to reduce challenging behavior: Maintenance and application in new settings. *Journal of Applied Behavior Analysis, 24,* 251–264.

Durlak, J. A., Fuhrman, T., & Lampman, C. (1991). Effectiveness of cognitive–behavior therapy for maladapting children: A meta-analysis. *Psychological Bulletin, 110,* 204–214.

Dush, D. M., Hirt, M. L., & Schroeder, H. (1983). Self-statement modification with adults: A meta-analysis. *Psychological Bulletin, 94,* 408–422.

D'Zurilla, T. J. (1988). Problem-solving therapies. In K. S. Dobson (Ed.), *Handbook of cognitive–behavioral therapies.* New York: Guilford.

D'Zurilla, T. J., & Goldfried, M. R. (1971). Problem solving and behavior modification. *Journal of Abnormal Psychology, 78,* 107–126.

D'Zurilla, T. J., & Nezu, A. (1982). Social problem solving in adults. In P. C. Kendall (Ed.), *Advances in cognitive–behavioral research and therapy* (Vol. 1). New York: Academic Press.

Edelbrock, C. (1984). Developmental considerations. In T. H. Ollendick & M. Hersen (Eds.). *Child behavioral assessment: Principles and procedures.* New York: Pergamon Press.

EFA (Epilepsy Foundation of America)(1990). *Epilepsy: You and your child.* Landover, MD: Author.

Eimas, P. D. (1970). Information processing in problem solving as a function of developmental level and stimulus saliency. *Developmental Psychology, 2,* 224–230.

Elkins, R. L. (1991). An appraisal of chemical aversion (emetic therapy) approaches to alcoholism treatment. *Behaviour Research and Therapy, 29,* 387–413.

Elliott, S. N. (1988). Acceptability of behavioral treatments: Review of variables that influence treatment selection. *Professional Psychology: Research and Practice, 19,* 68–80.

Ellis, A. (1962). *Reason and emotion in psychotherapy.* New York: Lyle Stewart.

Ellis, A. (1977). The basic clinical theory of rational–emotive therapy. In A. Ellis & R. Grieger (Eds.), *Handbook of rational–emotive therapy.* New York: Springer.

Ellis, A. (1987). The impossibility of achieving consistently good mental health. *American Psychologist, 42,* 364–375.

Ellis, A. (1993). Reflections on rational–emotive therapy. *Journal of Consulting and Clinical Psychology, 61,* 199–201.

Ellis, A., & Dryden, W. (1987). *The practice of rational–emotive therapy.* New York: Springer.

Emmelkamp, P. M. G., Bouman, T. K., & Scholing, A. (1992). *Anxiety disorders: A practitioner's guide.* Chichester, UK: Wiley.

Emshoff, J. G., Redd, W. H., & Davidson, W. S. (1976). Generalization training and the transfer of prosocial behavior in delinquent adolescents. *Journal of Behavior Therapy and Experimental Psychiatry, 7,* 141–144.

Engel, G. L. (1977) The need for a new medical model: A challenge for biomedicine. *Science, 196,* 129–136.

Engel, G. L. (1980). The clinical application of the biopsychosocial model. *American Journal of Psychiatry, 137,* 535–544.

Engels, G. I., Garnefski, N., & Diekstra, R. F. W. (1993). Efficacy of rational–emotive therapy: A quantitative analysis. *Journal of Consulting and Clinical Psychology, 61,* 1083–1090.

Epstein, L. H. (1992). Role of behavior theory in behavioral medicine. *Journal of Consulting and Clinical Psychology, 60,* 493–498.

Erhardt, D., & Baker, B. L. (1990). The effects of behavioral parent training on families with young hyperactive children. *Journal of Behavior Therapy and Experimental Psychiatry, 21,* 121–132.

Evans, I. M., & Nelson, R. O. (1986). Assessment of children. In A. R. Ciminero, K. S. Calhoun, & H. E. Adams (Eds.), *Handbook of behavioral assessment* (2nd ed.). New York: Wiley.

Fantuzzo, J. W., & Clement, P. W. (1981). Generalization of the effects of teacher- and self-administered token reinforcers to nontreated students. *Journal of Applied Behavior Analysis, 14,* 435–447.

Favell, J. E., McGimsey, J. F., & Jones, M. L. (1978). The use of physical restraint in the treatment of self-injury and as positive reinforcement. *Journal of Applied Behavior Analysis, 11,* 225–241.

Favell, J. E., & Reid, D. H. (1988). Generalizing and maintaining improvement in problem behavior. In R. H. Horner, G. Dunlap, & R. L. Koegel (Eds.), *Generalization and maintenance: Life-style changes in applied settings.* Baltimore. Paul H. Brooks.

Fawcett, S. B., & Miller, L. K. (1975). Training public-speaking behavior: An experimental analysis and social validation. *Journal of Applied Behavior Analysis, 8,* 125–135.

Feeney, E. J. (1972, November). Performance audit, feedback and positive reinforcement. *Training and Development Journal,* pp. 8–13.

Feindler, E. L., Marriott, S. A., & Iwata, M. (1984). Group anger control training for junior high school delinquents. *Cognitive Therapy and Research, 8,* 299–311.

Feldman, M. A., Case, L., Garrick, M., MacIntyre-Grande, W., Carnwell, J., & Sparks, B. (1992). Teaching child-care skills to mothers with developmental disabilities. *Journal of Applied Behavior Analysis, 25,* 205–215.

Fernandez, E. (1986). A classification system of cognitive coping strategies for pain. *Pain, 26,* 141–151.

Field, D. (1981). Can preschool children really learn to conserve? *Child Development, 52,* 326–334.

Finney, J. W., Rapoff, M. A., Hall, C. L., & Christophersen, E. R. (1983). Replication and social validation of habit reversal for tics. *Behavior Therapy, 14,* 116–126.

Fischer, J., & Nehs, R. (1978). Use of a commonly available chore to reduce a boy's rate of swearing. *Journal of Behavior Therapy and Experimental Psychiatry, 9,* 81–83.

Fiske, D. W., & Maddi, S. R. (1961). A conceptual framework. In D. W. Fiske & S. R. Maddi (Eds.), *Functions of varied experience.* Homewood, IL: Dorsey.

Fitzgerald, R. D., & Martin, G. K. (1971). Heart-rate conditioning in rats as a function of interstimulus interval. *Psychological Reports, 29,* 1103–1110.

Fixsen, D. L., Phillips, E. L., Baron, R. L., Coughlin, D. D., Daly, D. L., & Daly, P. B. (1978, November). The Boys' Town revolution. *Human Nature,* pp. 54–61.

Flaherty, C. F., & Caprio, M. (1976). Dissociation between instrumental and consummatory measures of incentive contrast. *American Journal of Psychology, 89,* 485–498.

Flay, B. R., Koepke, D., Thomson, S. J., Santi, S., Best, A., & Brown, K. S. (1989). Six-year follow-up of the first Waterloo school smoking prevention trial. *American Journal of Public Health, 79,* 1371-1376.

Flora, S. R. (1990). Undermining intrinsic interest from the standpoint of a behaviorist. *Psychological Record, 40,* 323–346.

Fogel, E. R. (1987). Biofeedback-assisted musculoskeletal therapy and neuromuscular re-education. In M. S. Schwartz (Ed.), *Biofeedback: A practitioner's guide.* New York: Guilford.

Foster, S. L., & Cone, J. D. (1986). Design and use of direct observation procedures. In A. R.

Ciminero, K. S. Calhoun, & H. E. Adams (Eds.), *Handbook of behavioral assessment* (2nd ed.). New York: Wiley.

Fowler, S. A. (1988). The effects of peer-mediated interventions on establishing, maintaining, and generalizing children's behavior changes. In R. H. Horner, G. Dunlap, & R. L. Koegel (Eds.), *Generalization and maintenance: Life-style changes in applied settings.* Baltimore: Paul H. Brookes.

Fowler, S. A., & Baer, D. M. (1981). "Do I have to be good all day?": The timing of delayed reinforcement as a factor in generalization. *Journal of Applied Behavior Analysis, 14,* 13–24.

Fowler, S. A., Dougherty, B. S., Kirby, K. C., & Kohler, F. W. (1986). Role reversals: An analysis of therapeutic effects achieved with disruptive boys during their appointments as peer monitors. *Journal of Applied Behavior Analysis, 19,* 437–444.

Fox, D. K., Hopkins, B. L., & Anger, W. K. (1987). The long-term effects of a token economy on safety performance in open-pit mining. *Journal of Applied Behavior Analysis, 20,* 215–224.

Foxx, R. M., & Azrin, N. H. (1972). Restitution: A method of eliminating aggressive–disruptive behaviors of retarded and brain damaged patients. *Behaviour Research and Therapy, 10,* 15–27.

Foxx, R. M., Faw, G. D., & Weber, G. (1991). Producing generalization of inpatient adolescents' social skills with significant adults in a natural environment. *Behavior Therapy, 22,* 85–99.

Foxx, R. M., & Schaeffer, M. H. (1981). A company-based lottery to reduce the personal driving of employees. *Journal of Applied Behavior Analysis, 14,* 273–285.

Foxx, R. M., & Shapiro, S. T. (1978). The timeout ribbon: A nonexclusionary timeout procedure. *Journal of Applied Behavior Analysis, 11,* 125–136.

France, K. G., & Hudson, S. M. (1990). Behavior management of infant sleep disturbance. *Journal of Applied Behavior Analysis, 23,* 91–98.

Frankel, F. (1993). A brief test of parental behavioral skills. *Journal of Behavior Therapy and Experimental Psychiatry, 24,* 227–231.

Franks, I. M., & Maile, L. J. (1991). The use of video in sport skill acquisition. In P. W. Dowrick (Ed.), *Practical guide to using video in the behavioral sciences.* New York: Wiley.

Frederiksen, L. W. (1975). Treatment of ruminative thinking by self-monitoring. *Journal of Behavior Therapy and Experimental Psychiatry, 6,* 258–259.

Frederiksen, L. W., Jenkins, J. O., Foy, D. W., & Eisler, R. M. (1976). Social skills training to modify abusive verbal outbursts in adults. *Journal of Applied Behavior Analysis, 9,* 117–125.

Frederiksen, L. W., & Lovett, S. B. (1980). Inside organizational behavior management: Perspectives on an emerging field. *Journal of Organizational Management, 2,* 193–203.

Freeman, A. (1990). Cognitive therapy. In A. S. Bellack & M. Hersen (Eds.), *Handbook of comparative treatments for adult disorders.* New York: Wiley.

Freud, S. (1933). *New introductory lectures in psychoanalysis* (W. J. H. Sprott, Trans.). New York: Norton.

Freud, S. (1949). *An outline of psychoanalysis* (J. Strachey, trans.). New York: Norton.

Friedman, A. G., Campbell, T. A., & Evans, I. M. (1993). Multi-dimensional child behavior therapy in the treatment of medically-related anxiety: A practical illustration. *Journal of Behavior Therapy and Experimental Psychiatry, 24,* 241–247.

Friedrich-Cofer, L., & Huston, A. C. (1986). Television violence and aggression: The debate continues. *Psychological Bulletin, 100,* 364–371.

Friman, P. C., & Altman, K. (1990). Parent use of DRI on high rate disruptive behavior: Direct and collateral benefits. *Research on Developmental Disabilities, 11,* 249–254.

Gagné, R. M. (1985). *The conditions of learning and theory of instruction* (4th ed.). New York: Holt, Rinehart & Winston.

Gagnon, M., & Ladouceur, R. (1992) Behavioral treatment of child stutterers: Replication and extension. *Behavior Therapy, 23,* 113–129.

Galassi, J. P., DeLo, J. S., Galassi, M. D., & Bastien, S. (1974). The College Self-Expression Scale: A measure of assertiveness. *Behavior Therapy, 5,* 165–171.

Gambrill, E. D., & Richey, C. A. (1975). An assertion inventory for use in assessment and research. *Behavior Therapy, 6,* 550–561.

Garcia, J., Ervin, F. R., & Koelling, R. A. (1966). Learning with prolonged delay of reinforcement. *Psychonomic Science, 5,* 121–122.

Garcia, J., Hankins, W. G., & Rusiniak, K. W. (1974). Behavioral regulation on the milieu interne in man and rat. *Science, 185,* 824–831.

Garcia, J., & Koelling, R. A. (1966). Relation of cue to consequence in avoidance learning. *Psychonomic Science, 1,* 123–124.

Garfield, S. L. (1986). Research on client variables in psychotherapy. In S. L. Garfield & A. E. Bergin (Eds.), *Handbook of psychotherapy and behavior change* (3rd ed.). New York: Wiley.

Garnets, L., & Kimmel, D. (1991). Lesbian and gay male dimensions in the psychological study of human diversity. In J. D. Goodchilds (Ed.), *Psychological perspectives on human diversity in America.* Washington, DC: American Psychological Association.

Gatchel, R. J. (1982). EMG biofeedback in anxiety reduction. In L. White & B. Tursky (Eds.), *Clinical biofeedback: Efficacy and mechanisms.* New York: Guilford.

Gelfand, D. M., Hartmann, D. P., Lamb, A. K., Smith, C. L., Mahan, M. A., & Paul, S. C. (1974). The effects of adult models and described alternatives on children's choice of behavior management techniques. *Child Development, 45,* 585–593.

Geller, E. S., Bruff, C. D., & Nimmer, J. G. (1985). "Flash for Life": Community-based prompting for safety belt promotion. *Journal of Applied Behavior Analysis, 18,* 309–314.

Gelman, R., & Baillargeon, R. (1983). A review of some Piagetian concepts. In P. H. Mussen (Ed.), *Handbook of child psychology* (4th ed., Vol. 3). New York: Wiley.

Gibson, E. J., & Levin, H. (1975). *The psychology of reading.* Cambridge, MA: MIT Press.

Glynn, S. M. (1990). Token economy approaches for psychiatric patients: Progress and pitfalls over 25 years. *Behavior Modification, 14,* 383–407.

Goetz, E. M., & Baer, D. M. (1973). Social control of form diversity and the emergence of new forms in children's blockbuilding. *Journal of Applied Behavior Analysis, 6,* 209–217.

Goldiamond, I. (1965). Self-control procedures in personal behavior problems. *Psychological Reports, 17,* 851–868.

Goldiamond, I. (1974). Toward a constructional approach to social problems: Ethical and constitutional issues raised by applied behavior analysis. *Behaviorism, 2,* 1–84.

Goldfried, M. R., & Castonguay, L. G. (1993). Behavior therapy: Redefining strengths and limitations. *Behavior Therapy, 24,* 505–526.

Goldstein, I. B., Jamner, L. D., & Shapiro, D. (1992). Ambulatory blood pressure and heart rate in healthy male paramedics during a workday and a nonworkday. *Health Psychology, 11,* 48–54.

Goldstein, L. H. (1990). Behavioural and cognitive–behavioural treatments for epilepsy: A progress review. *British Journal of Clinical Psychology, 29,* 257–269.

Goodman, W. (1994, March 20). A few scary pictures can go a long way. *New York Times,* pp. 28, 34.

Goodwin, C. J. (1995). *Research in psychology: Methods and design.* New York: Wiley.

Goodwin, D. W. (1986). Heredity and alcoholism. *Annals of Behavioral Medicine, 8*(2-3), 3-6.

Gormally, J., Black, S., Daston, S., & Rardin, D. (1982). The assessment of binge eating severity among obese persons. *Addictive Behaviors, 7,* 47–55.

Gossette, R. L., & O'Brien, R. M. (1993). Efficacy of rational–emotive therapy (RET) with children: A critical re-appraisal. *Journal of Behavior Therapy and Experimental Psychiatry, 24,* 15–25.

Grace, N. C., Kahng, S. W., & Fisher, W. W. (1994). Balancing social acceptability with treatment effectiveness of an intrusive procedure: A case report. *Journal of Applied Behavior Analysis, 27,* 171–172.

Green, C. W., Reid, D. H., Canipe, V. S., & Gardner, S. M. (1991). A conprehensive evaluation of reinforcer identification processes for persons with profound multiple handicaps. *Journal of Applied Behavior Analysis, 24,* 537–552.

Green, C. W., Reid, D. H., White, L. K., Halford, R. C., Brittain, D. P., & Gardner, S. M. (1988). Identifying reinforcers for persons with profound handicaps: Staff opinion versus systematic assessment of preferences. *Journal of Applied Behavior Analysis, 21,* 31–43.

Green, G. (1990). Least restrictive use of reductive procedures: Guidelines and competencies. In A. C. Repp & N. N. Singh (Eds.), *Perspectives on the use of nonaversive and aversive interventions for persons with developmental disabilities.* Sycamore, IL: Sycamore.

Greene, P. G., Seime, R. J., & Smith, M. E. (1991). Distraction and relaxation training in the treatment of anticipatory vomiting: A single subject intervention. *Journal of Behavior Therapy and Experimental Psychiatry, 22,* 285–290.

Greenspoon, J. (1955). The reinforcing effect of two spoken sounds on the frequency of two responses. *American Journal of Psychology, 68,* 409–416.

Greenwood, C. R., Carta, J. J., & Kamps, D. (1990). Teacher-mediated versus peer-mediated instruction: A review of educational advantages and disadvantages. In H. C. Foot, M. J. Morgan, & R. H. Shute (Eds.), *Children helping children.* Chichester: Wiley.

Greenwood, C. R., & Hops, H. (1981). Group-oriented contingencies and peer behavior change. In P. S. Strain (Ed.), *The utilization of classroom peers as behavior change agents.* New York: Plenum Press.

Greenwood, C. R., Hops, H., Delquadri, J., & Guild, J. (1974). Group contingencies for group consequences in classroom management: A further analysis. *Journal of Applied Behavior Analysis, 7,* 413–425.

Greer, R. D., & Polirstok, S. R. (1982). Collateral gains and short-term maintenance in reading and on-task responses by inner-city adolescents as a function of their use of social reinforcement while tutoring. *Journal of Applied Behavior Analysis, 15,* 123–139.

Griffen, A. K., Wolery, M., & Schuster, J. W. (1992). Triadic instruction of chained food preparation responses: Acquisition and observational learning. *Journal of Applied Behavior Analysis, 25,* 193–204.

Griffin, D. E., & Watson, D. L. (1978). A written, personal commitment from the student encourages better course work. *Teaching of Psychology, 5,* 155.

Groden, G. (1989). A guide for conducting a comprehensive behavioral analysis of a target behavior. *Journal of Behavior Therapy and Experimental Psychiatry, 20,* 163–169.

Gross, A. M. (1984). Behavioral interviewing. In T. H. Ollendick & M. Hersen (Eds.), *Child behavioral assessment: Principles and procedures.* New York: Pergamon Press.

Gross, A. M., & Drabman, R. S. (1982). Teaching self-recording, self-evaluation, and self-reward to nonclinic children and adolescents. In P. Karoly & F. H. Kanfer (Eds.), *Self-management and behavior change: From theory to practice.* New York: Pergamon Press.

Guess, D., Sailor, W., Rutherford, G., & Baer, D. M. (1968). An experimental analysis of linguistic development: The productive use of the plural morpheme. *Journal of Applied Behavior Analysis, 1,* 297–306.

Guess, D., Turnbull, H. R., & Helmstetter, E. (1990). Science, paradigms, and values: A response to Mulick. *American Journal on Mental Retardation, 95,* 157–163.

Guevremont, D. C., Osnes, P. G., & Stokes, T. F. (1988). The functional role of preschoolers' verbalizations in the generalization of self-instructional training. *Journal of Applied Behavior Analysis, 21,* 45–55.

Haaga, D. A. F., & Davison, G. C. (1989). Slow progress in rational–emotive therapy outcome research: Etiology and treatment. *Cognitive Therapy and Research, 13,* 493–508.

Haaga, D. A. F., & Davison, G. C. (1993). An appraisal of rational–emotive therapy. *Journal of Consulting and Clinical Psychology, 61,* 215–220.

Haaga, D. A. F., DeRubeis, R. J., Stewart, B. L., & Beck, A. T. (1991). Relationship of intelligence with cognitive therapy outcome. *Behaviour Research and Therapy, 29,* 277–281.

Hackman, A., & McClean, C. (1975). A comparison of flooding and thought stopping in the treatment of obsessional neurosis. *Behaviour Research and Therapy, 13,* 263–269.

Hains, A. H., & Baer, D. M. (1989). Interaction effects in multielement designs: Inevitable, desirable, and ignorable. *Journal of Applied Behavior Analysis, 22,* 57–69.

Halas, E. S., & Eberhardt, M. J. (1969). Blocking and appetitive reinforcement. *Bulletin of the Psychonomic Society, 25,* 121–123.

Haldeman, D. C. (1994). The practice and ethics of sexual orientation conversion therapy. *Journal of Consulting and Clinical Psychology, 62,* 221–227.

Hall, R. V., Axelrod, S., Foundopoulos, M., Shellman, J., Campbell, R. A., & Cranston, S. S. (1971). The effective use of punishment to modify behavior in the classroom. *Educational Technology, 11,* 24–26.

Hamilton, M., & Matson, J. L. (1992). Mental retardation. In S. M. Turner, K. S. Calhoun, & H. E. Adams (Eds.), *Handbook of clinical behavior therapy* (2nd ed.). New York: Wiley.

Hamilton, S. B. (1980). Instructionally-based training in self-control: Behavior-specific and generalized outcomes resulting from student-implemented self-modification projects. *Teaching of Psychology, 7,* 140–145.

Harchik, A. E., Sherman, J. A., Sheldon, J. B., & Strouse, M. C. (1992). Ongoing consultation as a method of improving performance of staff members in a group home. *Journal of Applied Behavior Analysis, 25,* 599–610.

Haring, T. G., & Kennedy, C. H. (1990). Contextual control of problem behavior in students with severe disabilities. *Journal of Applied Behavior Analysis, 23,* 235–243.

Harris, C. L., & McReynolds, W. T. (1977). Semantic cues and response contingencies in self-instructional control. *Journal of Behavior Therapy and Experimental Psychiatry, 8,* 15–17.

Harris, F. R., Wolf, M. M., & Baer, D. M. (1964). Effects of adult social reinforcement on child behavior. *Young Children, 20,* 8–17.

Harris, V. W., & Sherman, J. A. (1973). Use and analysis of the "good behavior game" to reduce disruptive classroom behavior. *Journal of Applied Behavior Analysis, 6,* 405–417.

Hart, W. (1987). *The art of living: Vipassana meditation.* New York: HarperCollins.

Hawkins, R. C., & Clement, P. F. (1980). Development and construct validation of a self-report measure of binge eating tendencies. *Addictive Behaviors, 5,* 219–226.

Hawkins, R. P., & Dotson, V. A. (1975). Reliability scores that delude: An Alice in Wonderland trip through the misleading characteristics of interobserver agreement scores in interval recording. In E. Ramp & G. Semb (Eds.), *Behavior analysis: Areas of research application*. Englewood Cliffs, NJ: Prentice-Hall.

Hayes, S. C., Brownell, K. D., & Barlow, D. H. (1978). The use of self-administered covert sensitization in the treatment of exhibitionism and sadism. *Behavior Therapy, 9,* 283–289.

Hayes, S. C., Brownstein, A. J., Zettle, R. D., Rosenfarb, I., & Korn, Z. (1986). Rule-governed behavior and sensitivity to changing consequences of responding. *Journal of Applied Behavior Analysis, 45,* 237–256.

Hayes, S. C., Rosenfarb, I., Wulfert, E., Munt, E. D., Korn, Z., & Zettle, R. D. (1985). Self-reinforcement effects: Artifact of social standard setting? *Journal of Applied Behavior Analysis, 18,* 201–214.

Heaton, R. C., & Safer, D. J. (1982). Secondary school outcome following a junior high school behavioral program. *Behavior Therapy, 13,* 226–231.

Heffernan, T., & Richards, C. S. (1981). Self-control of study behavior: Identification and evaluation of natural methods. *Journal of Counseling Psychology, 28,* 361–364.

Hegel, M. T., Ayllon, T., VanderPlate, C., & Spiro-Hawkins, H. (1986). A behavioral procedure for increasing compliance with self-exercise regimens in severely burn-injured patients. *Behaviour Research and Therapy, 24,* 521–528.

Heimberg, R. G. (1990). Cognitive behavior therapy. In A. S. Bellack & M. Hersen (Eds.), *Handbook of comparative treatments for adult disorders*. New York: Wiley.

Hermann, J. A., de Montes, A. I., Domínguez, B., Montes, F., & Hopkins, B. L. (1973). Effects of bonuses for punctuality on the tardiness of industrial workers. *Journal of Applied Behavior Analysis, 6,* 563–570.

Herrnstein, R. J. (1969). Method and theory in the study of avoidance. *Psychological Review, 76,* 49–69.

Hersen, M., Eisler, R. M., & Miller, P. M. (1974). An experimental analysis of generalization in assertive training. *Behaviour Research and Therapy, 12,* 295–310.

Hersen, M., Kazdin, A. E., Bellack, A. S., & Turner, S. M. (1979). Effects of live modeling, covert modeling, and rehearsal on assertiveness in psychiatric patients. *Behaviour Research and Therapy, 17,* 369–377.

Hildebrand, R. G., Martin, G. L., Furer, P., & Hazen, A. (1990). A recruitment-of-praise package to increase productivity levels of developmentally handicapped workers. *Behavior Modification, 14,* 97–113.

Hilliard, R. B. (1993). Single-case methodology in psychotherapy process and outcome research. *Journal of Consulting and Clinical Psychology, 61,* 373–380.

Hinson, R. E., Poulos, C. X., & Cappell, H. (1982). Effects of pentobarbital and cocaine in rats expecting pentobarbital. *Pharmacology Biochemistry and Behavior, 16,* 661–666.

Hollon, S. D., Shelton, R. C., & Davis, D. D. (1993). Cognitive therapy for depression: Conceptual issues and clinical efficacy. *Journal of Consulting and Clinical Psychology, 61,* 270–275.

Holmes, D. L. (1977). *Troubleshooting Checklist and Procedure*. (Materials produced by Eden Institute, Princeton, NJ.)

Holmes, D. S. (1984). Meditation and somatic arousal reduction. *American Psychologist, 39,* 1–10.

Holroyd, K. A., & Penzien, D. B. (1985). Client variables and the behavioral treatment of recurrent tension headache: A meta-analytic review. *Journal of Behavioral Medicine, 9,* 515–536.

Homme, L. E. (1965). Perspectives in psychology: XXIV. Control of overants, the operants of the mind. *Psychological Record, 15,* 501–511.

Homme, L. E. (1971). *How to use contingency contracting in the classroom.* Champaign, IL: Research Press.

Honeybourne, C., Matchett, G., & Davey, G. C. L. (1993). Expectancy models of laboratory preparedness effects: A UCS-expectancy bias in phylogenetic and ontogenetic fear-relevant stimuli. *Behavior Therapy, 24,* 253–264.

Hopkins, B. L., Conrad, R. J., Dangel, R. F., Fitch, H. G., Smith, M. J., & Anger, W. K. (1986). Behavioral technology for reducing occupational exposures to styrene. *Journal of Applied Behavior Analysis, 19,* 3–11.

Horan, J. J., & Johnson, R. G. (1971). Coverant conditioning through a self-management application of the Premack principle: Its effect on weight reduction. *Journal of Behavior Therapy and Experimental Psychiatry, 2,* 243–249.

Horner, R. H., Eberhard, J. M., & Sheehan, M. R. (1986). Teaching generalized table bussing: The importance of negative teaching examples. *Behavior Modification, 10,* 457–471.

Horner, R. A., Williams, J. A., & Knobbe, C. A. (1985). The effect of "opportunity to perform" on the maintenance of skills learned by high school students with severe handicaps. *Journal of the Association for Persons with Severe Handicaps, 10,* 172–175.

Houts, A. C., Berman, J. S., & Abramson, H. (1994). Effectiveness of psychological and pharmacological treatments for nocturnal enuresis. *Journal of Consulting and Clinical Psychology, 62,* 737–745.

Hugdahl, K., & Öhman, A. (1977). Effects of instruction on acquisition and extinction of electrodermal responses to fear-relevant stimuli. *Journal of Experimental Psychology: Human Learning and Memory, 3,* 608–618.

Hull, C. L. (1943). *Principles of behavior.* New York: Appleton-Century-Crofts.

Hundert, J., & Batstone, D. (1978). A practical procedure to maintain pupil's accurate self-rating in a classroom token program. *Behavior Modification, 2,* 93–112.

Hunt, G. M., & Azrin, N. H. (1973). A community-reinforcement approach to alcoholism. *Behaviour Research and Therapy, 11,* 91–104.

Hutchinson, R. R. (1977). By-products of aversive control. In W. K. Honig & J. E. R. Staddon (Eds.), *Handbook of operant behavior.* Englewood Cliffs, NJ: Prentice-Hall.

Isaacs, W., Thomas, J., & Goldiamond, I. (1960). Application of operant conditioning to reinstate verbal behavior in psychotics. *Journal of Speech and Hearing Disorders, 25,* 8–12.

Iwata, B. A., Dorsey, M. F., Slifer, K. J., Bauman, K. E., & Richman, G. S. (1982). Toward a functional analysis of self-injury. *Analysis and Intervention of Developmental Disabilities, 2,* 3–20.

Iwata, B. A., Pace, G. M., Cowdery, G. E., & Miltenberger, R. G. (1994). What makes extinction work: An analysis of procedural form and function. *Journal of Applied Behavior Analysis, 27,* 131–144.

Iwata, B. A., Pace, G. M., Kalsher, M. J., Cowdery, G. E., & Cataldo, M. F. (1990). Experimental analysis and extinction of self-injurious escape behavior. *Journal of Applied Behavior Analysis, 23,* 11–27.

Jackson, D. A., & Wallace, R. F. (1974). The modification and generalization of voice loudness in a fifteen-year-old retarded girl. *Journal of Applied Behavior Analysis, 7,* 461–471.

Jacobson, E. (1938). *Progressive relaxation* (2nd ed.). Chicago: University of Chicago Press.

Jacobson, N. S., Follette, W. C., & Revenstorf, D. (1984). Psychotherapy outcome research: Methods for reporting variability and evaluating clinical significance. *Behavior Therapy, 15,* 336–352.

James, J. E. (1981). Behavioral self-control of stuttering using time-out from speaking. *Journal of Applied Behavior Analysis, 14,* 25–37.

James, J. E. (1986). Review of the relative efficacy of imaginal and *in vivo* flooding in the treatment of clinical fear. *Behavioural Psychotherapy, 14,* 183–191.

Jason, L. A., Neal, A. M., & Marinakis, G. (1985). Altering contingencies to facilitate compliance with traffic light systems. *Journal of Applied Behavior Analysis, 18,* 95–100.

Jason, L. A. (1985). Using a token-actuated timer to reduce television viewing. *Journal of Applied Behavior Analysis, 18,* 269–272.

Jensen, B. J., & Haynes, S. N. (1986). Self-report questionnaires and inventories. In A. R. Ciminero, K. S. Calhoun, & H. E. Adams (Eds.), *Handbook of behavioral assessment* (2nd ed.). New York: Wiley.

Johnson, M. D., & Fawcett, S. B. (1994). Courteous service: Its assessment and modification in a human service organization. *Journal of Applied Behavior Analysis, 27,* 145–152.

Johnson, S. P., Welsh, T. M., Miller, L. K., & Altus, D. E. (1991). Participatory management: Maintaining staff performance in a university housing cooperative. *Journal of Applied Behavior Analysis, 24,* 119–127.

Johnson, W. G., Schlundt, D. G., Barclay, D. R., Carr-Nangle, R. E., & Engler, L. B. (1995). A naturalistic functional analysis of binge eating. *Behavior Therapy, 26,* 101–118.

Jones, L. J., Singh, N. N., & Kendall, K. A. (1990). Effects of Gentle Teaching and alternative treatments on self-injury. In A. C. Repp & N. N. Singh (Eds.), *Perspectives on the use of non-aversive and aversive interventions for persons with developmental disabilities.* Sycamore, IL: Sycamore.

Jones, M. C. (1924). The elimination of children's fears. *Journal of Experimental Psychology, 7,* 382–390.

Jones, R. T., Nelson, R. E., & Kazdin, A. E. (1977). The role of external variables in self-reinforcement. *Behavior Modification, 1,* 147–178.

Jordan, J., Singh, N. N., & Repp, A. C. (1989). An evaluation of gentle teaching and visual screening in the reduction of stereotypy. *Journal of Applied Behavior Analysis, 22,* 9–22.

Jospe, M., Shueman, S. A., & Troy, W. G. (1991). Quality assurance and the clinical health psychologist: A programmatic approach. In J. J. Sweet, R. H. Rozensky, & S. M. Tovian (Eds.), *Handbook of clinical psychology in medical settings.* New York: Plenum Press.

Kabat-Zinn, J. (1982). An outpatient program in behavioral medicine for chronic pain patients based on the practice of mindfulness meditation: Theoretical considerations and preliminary results. *General Hospital Psychiatry, 4,* 33–47.

Kabat-Zinn, J., Lipworth, L., & Burney, R. (1985). The clinical use of mindfulness meditation for the self-regulation of chronic pain. *Journal of Behavioral Medicine, 8,* 163–190.

Kallman, W. M., & Feuerstein, M. J. (1986). Psychophysiological procedures. In A. R. Ciminero, K. S. Calhoun, & H. E. Adams (Eds.), *Handbook of behavioral assessment* (2nd ed.). New York: Wiley.

Kallman, W. M., Hersen, M., & O'Toole, D. H. (1975). The use of social reinforcement in a case of conversion reaction. *Behavior Therapy, 6,* 411–413.

Kamarck, T. W., & Lichtenstein, E. (1985). Current trends in clinic-based smoking control. *Annals of Behavioral Medicine, 7(2),* 19–23.

Kamin, L. J. (1969). Predictability, surprise, attention, and conditioning. In B. A. Campbell & R. M. Church (Eds.), *Punishment and aversive behavior.* New York: Appleton-Century-Crofts.

Kanfer, F. H., & Grimm, L. G. (1980). Managing clinical change: A process model of therapy. *Behavior Modification, 4,* 419–444.

Kanfer, F. H., Karoly, P., & Newman, A. (1975). Reduction of children's fear of the dark by competence-related and situational treat-related verbal cues. *Journal of Consulting and Clinical Psychology, 43,* 251–258.

Kaplan, R. M. (1989). Health outcome models for policy analysis. *Health Psychology, 8,* 723–735.

Kaplan, R. M., Atkins, C. J., & Reinsch, S. (1984). Specific efficacy expectations mediate exercise compliance in patients with COPD. *Health Psychology, 3,* 223–242.

Karraker, R. J. (1977). Self versus teacher selected reinforcers in a token economy. *Exceptional Children, 43,* 454–455.

Kau, M. L., & Fischer, J. (1974). Self-modification of exercise behavior. *Journal of Behavior Therapy and Experimental Psychiatry, 5,* 213–214.

Kayser, J. E., Billingsley, F. F., & Neel, R. S. (1986). A comparison of in-context and traditional instruction approaches: Total task, single trial versus backward chaining, multiple trials. *Journal of the Association for the Severely Handicapped, 11,* 28–38.

Kazdin, A. E. (1971). The effect of response cost in suppressing behavior in a pre-psychotic retardate. *Journal of Behavior Therapy and Experimental Psychiatry, 2,* 137–140.

Kazdin, A. E. (1972). Response cost: The removal of conditioned reinforcers for therapeutic change. *Behavior Therapy, 3,* 533–546.

Kazdin, A. E. (1973). The effect of vicarious reinforcement on attentive behavior in the classroom. *Journal of Applied Behavior Analysis, 6,* 71–78.

Kazdin, A. E. (1978). *History of behavior modification: Experimental foundations of contemporary research.* Baltimore: University Park Press.

Kazdin, A. E. (1985). The token economy. In R. Turner & L. M. Asher (Eds.), *Evaluating behavior therapy outcome.* New York: Springer.

Kazdin, A. E., & Erickson, L. M. (1975). Developing responsiveness to instructions in severely and profoundly retarded residents. *Journal of Behavior Therapy and Experimental Psychiatry, 6,* 17–21.

Kazdin, A. E., French, N. H., & Sherick, R. B. (1981). Acceptability of alternative treatments for children: Evaluations by inpatient children, parents, and staff. *Journal of Consulting and Clinical Psychology, 49,* 900–907.

Kazdin, A. E., French, N. H., Unis, A. S., Esveldt-Dawson, K., & Sherick, R. B. (1983). Hopelessness, depression, and suicidal intent among psychiatrically disturbed inpatient children. *Journal of Consulting and Clinical Psychology, 51,* 504–510.

Kazdin, A. E., & Geesey, S. (1977). Simultaneous-treatment design comparisons of the effects of earning reinforcers for one's peers versus oneself. *Behavior Therapy, 8,* 682–693.

Kazdin, A. E., & Polster, R. (1973). Intermittent token reinforcement and response maintenance in extinction. *Behavior Therapy, 4,* 386–391.

Kazdin, A. E., Siegel, T. C., & Bass, D. (1992). Cognitive problem-solving skills training and parent management training in the treatment of antisocial behavior in children. *Journal of Consulting and Clinical Psychology, 60,* 733–747.

Kazdin, A. E., & Wilcoxon, L. A. (1976). Systematic desensitization and nonspecific treatment effects: A methodological evaluation. *Psychological Bulletin, 83,* 729–758.

Keller, F. S. (1968). "Good-bye teacher . . ." *Journal of Applied Behavior Analysis, 1,* 79–89.

Kelly, J. F., & Hake, D. F. (1970). An extinction-induced increase in an aggressive response with humans. *Journal of the Experimental Analysis of Behavior, 14,* 153–164.

Kelly, J. A., & Drabman, R. S. (1977). Overcorrection: An effective procedure that failed. *Journal of Clinical Child Psychology, 6,* 38–40.

Kelly, J. A., St. Lawrence, J. S., Hood, H. V., & Brasfield, T. L. (1989). Behavioral intervention to reduce AIDS risk activities. *Journal of Consulting and Clinical Psychology, 57,* 60–67.

Kempe, C. H. (1976). Child abuse and neglect. In N. B. Talbot (Ed.), *Raising children in modern America: Problems and prospective solutions.* Boston: Little, Brown.

Kent, G. (1985). Memory of dental pain. *Pain,* 187–194.

Kimble, G. A. (1961). *Hilgard and Marquis' conditioning and learning* (2nd ed.). New York: Appleton-Century-Crofts.

Kimble, G. A. (1993). A modest proposal for a minor revolution in the language of psychology. *Psychological Science, 4,* 253–255.

Kirby, F. D., & Shields, F. (1972). Modification of arithmetic response rate and attending behavior in a seventh-grade student. *Journal of Applied Behavior Analysis, 5,* 79–84.

Kirigin, K. A., Braukmann, C. J., Atwater, J. D., & Wolf, M. M. (1982). An evaluation of teaching-family (Achievement Place) group homes for juvenile offenders. *Journal of Applied Behavior Analysis, 15,* 1–16.

Klingman, A., Melamed, B. G., Cuthbert, M. I., & Hermecz, D. A. (1984). Effects of participant modeling on information acquisition and skill utilization. *Journal of Consulting and Clinical Psychology, 52,* 414–422.

Koegel, R. L., & Rincover, A. (1974). Treatment of psychotic children in a classroom environment: 1. Learning in a large group. *Journal of Applied Behavior Analysis, 7,* 45–59.

Kohler, F. W., & Greenwood, C. R. (1986). Toward a technology of generalization: The identification of natural contingencies of reinforcement. *Behavior Analyst, 9,* 19–26.

Kohler, F. W., & Greenwood, C. R. (1990). Effects of collateral peer supportive behaviors within the classwide peer tutoring program. *Journal of Applied Behavior Analysis, 23,* 307–322.

Kohler, F. W., & Strain, P. S. (1990). Peer assisted interventions: Early promises, notable achievements, and future aspirations. *Clinical Psychology Review, 10,* 441–452.

Komaki, J., Barwick, K. D., & Scott, L. R. (1978). A behavioral approach to occupational safety: Pinpointing and reinforcing safe performance in a food manufacturing plant. *Journal of Applied Psychology, 63,* 435–445.

Konarski, E. A., Johnson, M. R., Crowell, C. R., & Whitman, T. L. (1981). An alternative approach to reinforcement for applied researchers: Response deprivation. *Behavior Therapy, 12,* 653–666.

Krantz, P. J., & Risley, T. R. (1977). Behavioral ecology in the classroom. In K. D. O'Leary & S. G. O'Leary (Eds.), *Classroom management: The successful use of behavior modification* (2nd ed.). New York: Pergamon Press.

Krebs, D. E. (1987). Biofeedback in neuromuscular re-education and gait training. In M. S. Schwartz (Ed.), *Biofeedback: A practitioner's guide.* New York: Guilford.

Krop, H., & Burgess, D. (1993). Use of covert conditioning to treat excessive masturbation. In J. R. Cautela & A. J. Kearney (Eds.), *Covert conditioning handbook.* Pacific Grove, CA: Brooks/Cole.

Krumboltz, J. D., & Krumboltz, H. B. (1972). *Changing children's behavior.* Englewood Cliffs, NJ: Prentice-Hall.

Kulik, J. A., & Carlino, P. (1987). The effect of verbal commitment and treatment choice on medication compliance in a pediatric setting. *Journal of Behavioral Medicine, 10,* 367–376.

Kvale, G., Hugdahl, K., Asbjørnsen, A., Rosengren, B., & Lote, K. (1991). Anticipatory nausea and vomiting in cancer patients. *Journal of Consulting and Clinical Psychology, 59,* 894–898.

Lancioni, G. E. (1982). Normal children as tutors to teach social responses to withdrawn mentally retarded schoolmates: Training, maintenance, and generalization. *Journal of Applied Behavior Analysis, 15,* 17–40.

Landrum, T. J., & Lloyd, J. W. (1992). Generalization in social behavior research with children and youth who have emotional or behavioral disorders. *Behavior Modification, 16,* 593–616.

Lange, A. J., & Jakubowski, P. (1976). *Responsible assertive behavior.* Champaign, IL: Research Press.

Laszlo, J. (1987). *Understanding cancer.* New York: Harper & Row.

Laties, V. G., & Weiss, B. (1963). Effects of a concurrent task on fixed-interval responding in humans. *Journal of the Experimental Analysis of Behavior, 6,* 431–436.

Latimer, P. R., & Sweet, A. A. (1984). Cognitive versus behavioral procedures in cognitive–behavior therapy: A critical review of the evidence. *Journal of Behavior Therapy and Experimental Psychiatry, 15,* 9–22.

Lattal, K. A. (1969). Contingency management of toothbrushing behavior in a summer camp for children. *Journal of Applied Behavior Analysis, 2,* 195–198.

Lazarus, A. A. (1981). *Multimodal therapy.* New York: Guilford.

Lazarus, A. A., Davison, G. C., & Polefka, D. A. (1965). Classical and operant factors in the treatment of a school phobia. *Journal of Abnormal Psychology, 70,* 225–229.

LeDoux, J. E. (1994). Emotion, memory and the brain. *Scientific American, 270*(6), 50–57.

Lee, C. (1992). On cognitive theories and causation in human behavior. *Journal of Behavior Therapy and Experimental Psychiatry, 23,* 257–268.

Lehrer, P. M. (1982). How to relax and how not to relax: A re-evaluation of the work of Edmund Jacobson—I. *Behaviour Research and Therapy, 20,* 417–428.

Leitenberg, H., Burchard, J. D., Burchard, S. N., Fuller, E. J., & Lysaght, T. V. (1977). Using positive reinforcement to suppress behavior: Some experimental comparisons with sibling conflict. *Behavior Therapy, 8,* 168–182.

Lennox, D. B., Miltenberger, R. G., & Donnelly, D. R. (1987). Response interruption and DRL for the reduction of rapid eating. *Journal of Applied Behavior Analysis, 20,* 279–284.

Lennox, D. B., Miltenberger, R. G., Spengler, P., & Erfanian, N. (1988). Decelerative treatment practices with persons who have mental retardation: A review of five years of the literature. *American Journal of Mental Retardation, 1988,* 492–501.

Lepper, M. R., Greene, D., & Nisbett, R. E. (1973). Undermining children's intrinsic interest with extrinsic reward: A test of the "overjustification hypothesis." *Journal of Personality and Social Psychology, 28,* 129–137.

Lerman, D. C., & Iwata, B. A. (1995). Prevalence of the extinction burst and its attenuation during treatment. *Journal of Applied Behavior Analysis, 28,* 93–94.

LeVay, S., & Hamer, D. H. (1994). Evidence for a biological influence in male homosexuals. *Scientific American, 270*(5), 44–49.

Lewis, D. J. (1960). Partial reinforcement: A selective review of the literature since 1950. *Psychological Bulletin, 57,* 1–28.

Lewis, D. J., & Duncan, D. P. (1956). Effect of different percentages of money reward on extinction of a lever-pulling response. *Journal of Experimental Psychology, 52,* 23–27.

Lewis, D. J., & Duncan, D. P. (1957). Expectation and resistance to extinction of a lever-pulling response as functions of percentage of reinforcement and amount of reward. *Journal of Experimental Psychology, 54,* 115–120.

Lichstein, K. L. (1988). *Clinical relaxation strategies.* New York: Wiley.

Lichtenstein, E., & Mermelstein, R. J. (1984). Review of approaches to smoking treatment: Behavior modification strategies. In J. D. Matarazzo, S. M. Weiss, J. A. Herd, N. E. Miller, & S. M. Weiss (Eds.), *Behavioral health: A handbook of health enhancement and disease prevention.* New York: Wiley.

Liddell, A., Locker, D., & Burman, D. (1991). Self-reported fears (FSS-II) of subjects aged 50 years and over. *Behaviour Research and Therapy, 29,* 105–112.

Linscheid, T. R., Iwata, B. A., Ricketts, R. W., Williams, D. E., & Griffen, J. C. (1990). Clinical evaluation of the self-injurious behavior inhibiting system (SIBIS). *Journal of Applied Behavior Analysis, 23,* 53–78.

Linscheid, T. R., & Meinhold, P. (1990). The controversy over aversives: Basic operant research and the side effects of punishment. In A. C. Repp & N. N. Singh (Eds.), *Perspectives on the use of nonaversive and aversive interventions for persons with developmental disabilities.* Sycamore, IL: Sycamore.

Logan, D. L. (1970). A "paper money" token system as a recording aid in institutional settings. *Journal of Applied Behavior Analysis, 3,* 183–184.

Long, P., Forehand, R., Wierson, M., & Morgan, A. (1993). Does parent training with young noncompliant children have long-term effects? *Behaviour Research and Therapy, 32,* 101–107.

Lovaas, O. I. (1977). *The autistic child: Language development through behavior modification.* New York: Irvington.

Lovaas, O. I., Koegel, R., Simmons, J. Q., & Long, J. S. (1973). Some generalization and follow-up measures on autistic children in behavior therapy. *Journal of Applied Behavior Analysis, 6,* 131–166.

Lovaas, O. I., Newsom, C., & Hickman, C. (1987). Self-stimulatory behavior and perceptual reinforcement. *Journal of Applied Behavior Analysis, 20,* 45–68.

Lovaas, O. I., Schaeffer, B., & Simmons, J. Q. (1965). Building social behavior in autistic children by using electric shock. *Journal of Experimental Research in Personality, 1,* 99–109.

Lovaas, O. I., & Simmons, J. Q. (1969). Manipulation of self-destruction in three retarded children. *Journal of Applied Behavior Analysis, 2,* 143–157.

Lovitt, T. C., & Curtiss, K. A. (1969). Academic response rate as a function of teacher- and self-imposed contingencies. *Journal of Applied Behavior Analysis, 2,* 49–53.

Lowe, C. F. (1979). Determinants of human operant behaviour. In M. D. Zeiler & P. Harzem (Eds.), *Advances in analysis of behaviour: Vol. 1. Reinforcement and the organization of behaviour.* Chichester: Wiley.

Lowe, C. F., Beasty, A., & Bentall, R. P. (1983). The role of verbal behavior in human learning: Infant performance on fixed-interval schedules. *Journal of Applied Behavior Analysis, 39,* 157–164.

Lowe, C. F., & Chadwick, P. D. J. (1990). Verbal control of delusions. *Behavior Therapy, 21,* 461–479.

Lowe, K., & Lutzker, J. R. (1979). Increasing compliance to a medical regimen with a juvenile diabetic. *Behavior Therapy, 10,* 57–64.

Luce, S. C., Delquadri, J., & Hall, R. V. (1980). Contingent exercise: A mild but powerful procedure for suppressing inappropriate verbal and aggressive behavior. *Journal of Applied Behavior Analysis, 13,* 583–594.

Lucic, K. S., Steffen, J. J., Harrigan, J. A., & Stuebing, R. C. (1991). Progressive relaxation training: Muscle contraction before relaxation? *Behavior Therapy, 22,* 249–256.

Ludwig, T. D., & Geller, E. S. (1991). Improving the driving practices of pizza deliverers: Response generalization and moderating effects of driving history. *Journal of Applied Behavior Analysis, 24,* 31–44.

Luiselli, J. K. (1990). Recent developments in nonaversive treatment: A review of rationale, methods, and recommendations. In A. C. Repp & N. N. Singh (Eds.), *Perspectives on the use of nonaversive and aversive interventions for persons with developmental disabilities.* Sycamore, IL: Sycamore.

Luria, A. R. (1961). *The role of speech in the regulation of normal and abnormal behaviors.* New York: Liveright.

Luthans, F., & Kreitner, R. (1985). *Organizational behavior modification and beyond: An operant and social learning approach.* Glenview, IL: Scott, Foresman.

Lutz, J. (1994). *Introduction to learning and memory.* Pacific Grove, CA: Brooks/Cole.

Lyons, L. C., & Woods, P. J. (1991). The efficacy of rational–emotive therapy: A quantitative review of the outcome research. *Clinical Psychology Review, 11,* 357–369.

MacKenzie-Keating, S. E., & McDonald, L. (1990). Overcorrection: Reviewed, revisited and revised. *Behavior Analyst, 13,* 39–48.

Madsen, C. H., Becker, W. C., & Thomas, D. R. (1968). Rules, praise, and ignoring: Elements of elementary classroom control. *Journal of Applied Behavior Analysis, 1,* 139–150.

Madsen, C. H., Becker, W. C., Thomas, D. R., Koser, L., & Plager, E. (1970). An analysis of the reinforcing function of "sit down" commands. In R. K. Parker (Ed.), *Readings in educational psychology.* Boston: Allyn & Bacon.

Mahoney, K., Van Wagenen, & Meyerson, L. (1971). Toilet training of normal and retarded children. *Journal of Applied Behavior Analysis, 4,* 173–181.

Mahoney, M. J. (1977). Reflections on the cognitive-learning trend in psychotherapy. *American Psychologist, 32,* 5–13.

Mahoney, M. J. (1993). Introduction to special section: Theoretical developments in the cognitive psychotherapies. *Journal of Consulting and Clinical Psychology, 61,* 187–193.

Main, M., & George, C. (1985). Responses of abused and disadvantaged toddlers to distress in age-mates: A study in the day care setting. *Developmental Psychology, 21,* 407–412.

Malatesta, V. J., & Adams, H. E. (1986). Assessment of sexual behavior. In A. R. Ciminero, K. S. Calhoun, & H. E. Adams (Eds,), *Handbook of behavioral assessment* (2nd ed.). New York: Wiley.

Maletzky, B. M. (1974). Behavior recording as treatment: A brief note. *Behavior Therapy, 5,* 107–111.

Marholin, D., & Gray, D. (1976). Effects of group response-cost procedures on cash shortages in a small business. *Journal of Applied Behavior Analysis, 9,* 25–30.

Marholin, D., & Townsend, N. M. (1978). An experimental analysis of side effects and response maintenance of a modified overcorrection procedure: The case of the persistent twiddler. *Behavior Therapy, 9,* 383–390.

Marlatt, G. A., & Gordon, J. R. (1980). Determinants of relapse: Implications for the maintenance of behavior change. In P. O. Davidson & S. M. Davidson (Eds.), *Behavioral medicine: Changing health lifestyles.* New York: Brunner/Mazel.

Marlatt, G. A., & Parks, G. A. (1982). Self-management of addictive behaviors. In P. Karoly & F. H. Kanfer (Eds.), *Self-management and behavior change: From theory to practice.* New York: Pergamon Press.

Marshall, W. L., Gauthier, J., Christie, M. M., Currie, D. W., & Gordon, A. (1977). Flooding therapy: Effectiveness, stimulus characteristics, and the value of brief *in vivo* exposure. *Behaviour Research and Therapy, 15,* 79–87.

Marshall, W. L., Presse, L., & Andrews, W. R. (1976). A self-administered program for public speaking anxiety. *Behaviour Research and Therapy, 14,* 33–39.

Martin, G. (1982). Thought-stopping and stimulus control to decrease persistent disturbing thoughts. *Journal of Behavior Therapy and Experimental Psychiatry, 13,* 215–220.

Martin, I., & Levey, A. (1994). The evaluative response: Primitive but necessary. *Behaviour Research and Therapy, 32,* 301–305.

Mathews, A. M., Johnston, D. W., Lancashire, M., Munby, M., Shaw, P. M., & Gelder, M. G. (1976). Imaginal flooding and exposure to real phobic situations: Treatment outcome with agoraphobic patients. *British Journal of Psychiatry, 129,* 362–371.

Mathews, R. M., & Dix, M. (1992). Behavior change in the funny papers: Feedback to cartoonists on safety belt use. *Journal of Applied Behavior Analysis, 25,* 769–775.

Matson, J. L. (1983). Exploration of phobic behavior in a small child. *Journal of Behavior Therapy and Experimental Psychiatry, 14,* 257–259.

Matson, J. L., & Taras, M. E. (1989). A 20 year review of punishment and alternative methods to treat problem behaviors in developmentally delayed persons. *Research in Developmental Disabilities, 10,* 85–104.

Mayhew, G. L., & Harris, F. (1978). Some negative side effects of a punishment procedure for stereotyped behavior. *Journal of Behavior Therapy and Experimental Psychiatry, 9,* 245–251.

Mayo, L. L., & Norton, G. R. (1980). The use of problem solving to reduce examination and interpersonal anxiety. *Journal of Behavior Therapy and Experimental Psychiatry, 11,* 287–289.

McCaffrey, R. J., & Blanchard, E. B. (1985). Stress management approaches to the treatment of essential hypertension. *Annals of Behavioral Medicine, 7*(1), 5–12.

McCaul, K. D., & Malott, J. M. (1984). Distraction and coping with pain. *Psychological Bulletin, 95,* 516–533.

McClannahan, L. E., McGee, G. G., MacDuff, G. S., & Krantz, P. J. (1990). Assessing and improving child care: A personal appearance index for children with autism. *Journal of Applied Behavior Analysis, 23,* 469–482.

McClannahan, L. E., & Risley, T. R. (1975). Design of living environments for nursing-home residents: Increasing participation in recreational activities. *Journal of Applied Behavior Analysis, 8,* 261-268.

McClintic, J. R. (1985). *Physiology of the human body* (3rd ed.). New York: Wiley.

McConnell, J. V. (1990). Negative reinforcement and positive punishment. *Teaching of Psychology, 17,* 247–249.

McCracken, L. M., & Larkin, K. T. (1991). Treatment of paruresis with *in vivo* desensitization: A case report. *Journal of Behavior Therapy and Experimental Psychiatry, 22,* 57–62.

McFall, R. M., & Lillesand, D. B. (1970). *Conflict Resolution Inventory.* Unpublished manuscript.

McFall, R. M., & Lillesand, D. B. (1971). Behavior rehearsal with modeling and coaching in assertion training. *Journal of Abnormal Psycholology, 77,* 313–323.

McFall, R. M., & Twentyman, C. T. (1973). Four experiments on the relative contributions of rehearsal, modeling, and coaching to assertion training. *Journal of Abnormal Psychology, 81,* 199–218.

McGee, G. G., Almeida, M. C., Sulzer-Azaroff, B., & Feldman, R. S. (1992). Promoting reciprocal interactions via peer incidental teaching. *Journal of Applied Behavior Analysis, 25,* 117–126.

McGee, J. J., & Gonzalez, L. (1990). Gentle Teaching and the practice of human interdependence: A preliminary group study of 15 persons with severe behavioral disorders and their caregivers. In A. C. Repp & N. N. Singh (Eds.), *Perspectives on the use of nonaversive and aversive interventions for persons with developmental disabilities.* Sycamore, IL: Sycamore.

McGee, J. J., Menolascino, F. J., Hobbs, D. C., & Menousek, P. E. (1987). *Gentle Teaching: A nonaversive approach for helping persons with mental retardation.* New York: Human Sciences Press.

McKenzie, T. L., & Rushall, B. S. (1974). Effects of self-recording on attendance and performance in a competitive swimming training environment. *Journal of Applied Behavior Analysis, 7,* 199–206.

McLaughlin, T. F., Burgess, N., & Sackville-West, L. (1982). Effects of self-recording and self-recording + matching on academic performance. *Child Behavior Therapy, 3,* 17–27.

McMahon, R. J. (1984). Behavioral checklists and ratings scales. In T. H. Ollendick & M. Hersen (Eds.), *Child behavioral assessment: Principles and procedures.* New York: Pergamon Press.

McNeil, C. B., Eyberg, S., Eisenstadt, T. H., Newcomb, K., & Funderburk, B. (1991). Parent–child interaction therapy with behavior problem children: Generalization of treatment effects to the school setting. *Journal of Clinical Child Psychology, 20,* 140–151.

McReynolds, W. T., & Church, A. (1973). Self-control, study skills development and counseling approaches to the improvement of study behavior. *Behaviour Research and Therapy, 11,* 233–235.

Mealiea, W. L., & Nawas, M. M. (1971). The comparative effectiveness of systematic desensitization and implosive therapy in the treatment of snake phobia. *Journal of Behavior Therapy and Experimental Psychiatry, 2,* 85–94.

Meichenbaum, D. (1977). *Cognitive–behavior modification: An integrative approach.* New York: Plenum Press.

Meichenbaum, D. (1986). Cognitive–behavior modification. In F. H. Kanfer & A. P. Goldstein (Eds.), *Helping people change: A textbook of methods* (3rd ed.). New York: Pergamon Press.

Meichenbaum, D., & Cameron, R. (1983). Stress inoculation training: Toward a general paradigm for training coping skills. In D. Meichenbaum & M. E. Jaremko (Eds.), *Stress reduction and prevention.* New York: Plenum Press.

Meichenbaum, D., & Deffenbacher, J. L. (1988). Stress inoculation training. *Counseling Psychologist, 16,* 69–90.

Meichenbaum, D. H., & Goodman, J. (1971). Training impulsive children to talk to themselves: A means of developing self-control. *Journal of Abnormal Psychology, 77,* 115-126.

Melamed, B. G., & Siegel, L. J. (1975). Reduction of anxiety in children facing hospitalization and surgery by use of filmed modeling. *Journal of Consulting and Clinical Psychology, 43,* 511–521.

Melin, L., & Götestam, K. G. (1981). The effects of rearranging ward routines on communication and eating behaviors of psychogeriatric patients. *Journal of Applied Behavior Analysis, 14,* 47–51.

Menzies, R. G., & Clarke, J. C. (1993). A comparison of *in vivo* and vicarious exposure in the treatment of childhood water phobia. *Behaviour Research and Therapy, 31,* 9–15.

Merckelbach, H., Arntz, A., Arrindell, W. A., & de Jong, P. J. (1992). Pathways to spider phobia. *Behaviour Research and Therapy, 30,* 543–546.

Mermelstein, R., Lichtenstein, E., & McIntyre, K. (1983). Partner support and relapse in smoking-cessation programs. *Journal of Consulting and Clinical Psychology, 51,* 465–466.

Meyer, R. G. (1975). A behavioral treatment of sleepwalking associated with test anxiety. *Journal of Behavior Therapy and Experimental Psychiatry, 6,* 167–168.

Meyer, V., Robertson, J., & Tatlow, A. (1975). Home treatment of an obsessive–compulsive disorder by response prevention. *Journal of Behavior Therapy and Experimental Psychiatry, 6,* 37–38.

Michael, J. (1975). Positive and negative reinforcement, a distinction that is no longer necessary; or a better way to talk about bad things. *Behaviorism, 3,* 33–44.

Michael, J. (1982). Distinguishing between discriminative and motivational functions of stimuli. *Journal of the Experimental Analysis of Behavior, 37,* 149–155.

Michael, J. (1986). Repertoire-altering effects of remote contingencies. *Analysis of Verbal Behavior, 4,* 10–18.

Michael, J. (1987). Experimental analysis of human behavior symposium: Comments by the discussant. *Psychological Record, 37,* 37–42.

Milgrom, P., Mancl, L., King, B., & Weinstein, P. (1995). Origins of childhood dental fear. *Behaviour Research and Therapy, 33,* 313–319.

Miller, D. L., & Kelley, M. L. (1994). The use of goal setting and contingency contracting for improving children's homework performance. *Journal of Applied Behavior Analysis, 27,* 73–84.

Miller, L. K. (1980). *Principles of everyday behavior analysis* (2nd ed.). Pacific Grove, CA: Brooks/Cole.

Miller, P. W. (1972). The use of behavioral contracting in the treatment of alcoholism: A case report. *Behavior Therapy, 3,* 593–596.

Miller, W. R., & Hester, R. K. (1980). Treating the problem drinker: Modern approaches. In W. R. Miller (Ed.), *The addictive behaviors: Treatment of alcoholism, drug abuse, smoking, and obesity.* New York: Pergamon Press.

Miltenberger, R. G., Fuqua, R. W., & McKinley, T. (1985). Habit reversal with muscle tics: Replication and component analysis. *Behavior Therapy, 16,* 39–50.

Mischel, W. (1981). Metacognition and the rules of delay. In J. H. Flavell & L. Ross (Eds.), *Social cognitive development: Frontiers and possible futures.* Cambridge: Cambridge University Press.

Monette, D. R., Sullivan, T. .J., & DeJong, C. R. (1990). *Applied social research: Tool for the human services* (2nd ed.). Fort Worth, TX: Holt, Rinehart & Winston.

Monti, P. M., Rohsenow, D. J., Rubonis, A. V., Naiura, R. S., Sirota, A. D., Colby, S. M., Goddard, P., & Abrams, D. B. (1994). Cue exposure with coping skills treatment for male alcoholics: A preliminary investigation. *Journal of Consulting and Clinical Psychology, 61,* 1011–1019.

Moore, S. (1987). Relaxation training. In R. J. Corsini (Ed.), *Concise encyclopedia of psychology.* New York: Wiley.

Moos, R. H., & Schaefer, J. A. (1986). Life transitions and crises: A conceptual overview. In R. H. Moos (Ed.), *Coping with life crises: An integrated approach.* New York: Plenum Press.

Morganstern, K. P. (1973). Implosive therapy and flooding procedures. *Psychological Bulletin, 79,* 318–334.

Morokoff, P. J., & LoPiccolo, J. (1982). Self-management in the treatment of sexual dysfunction. In P. Karoly & F. H. Kanfer (Eds.), *Self-management and behavior change: From theory to practice*. New York: Pergamon Press.

Morris, E. K., & Redd, W. H. (1975). Children's performance and social preference for positive, negative, and mixed adult-child interactions. *Child Development, 46,* 525–531.

Morris, R. J., & Kratochwill, T. R. (1983). *Treating children's fears and phobias: A behavioral approach*. New York: Pergamon Press.

Mosley, T. H., Eisen, A. R., Bruce, B. K., Brantley, P. J., & Cocke, T. B. (1993). Contingent reinforcement for fluid compliance in a hemodialysis patient. *Journal of Behavior Therapy and Experimental Psychiatry, 24,* 77–81.

Mowrer, O. H. (1938). Apparatus for the study and treatment of enuresis. *American Journal of Psychology, 51,* 163–165.

Mowrer, O. H. (1947). On the dual nature of learning—A reinterpretation of "conditioning" and "problem solving." *Harvard Educational Review, 17,* 102–148.

Muehlenhard, C. L., Koralewski, M. A., Andrews, C. A., & Burdick, C. A. (1986). Verbal and nonverbal cues that convey interest in dating: Two studies. *Behavior Therapy, 17,* 404–419.

Murphy, H. A., Hutchison, J. M., & Bailey, J. S. (1983). Behavioral school psychology goes outdoors: The effects of organized games on playground aggression. *Journal of Applied Behavior Analysis, 16,* 29–35.

Murray, D. M., Pirie, P., Leupker, R. V., & Pallonen, U. (1989). Five- and six-year follow-up results from four seventh-grade smoking prevention strategies. *Journal of Behavioral Medicine, 12,* 207–218.

Murrell, M., Hardy, M., & Martin, G. L. (1974). Danny learns to match digits with the number of objects. *Special Education in Canada, 49,* 20–22.

Nakano, K. (1990). Operant self-control procedure in modifying Type A behavior. *Journal of Behavior Therapy and Experimental Psychiatry, 21,* 249–255.

Neef, N. A., Lensbower, J., Hockersmith, I., DePalma, V., & Gray, K. (1990). In vivo versus simulation training: An interactional analysis of range and type of training exemplars. *Journal of Applied Behavior Analysis, 23,* 447–458.

Neef, N. A., Mace, F. C., Shea, M. C., & Shade, D. (1992). Effects of reinforcer rate and reinforcer quality on time allocation: Extensions of matching theory to educational settings. *Journal of Applied Behavior Analysis, 25,* 691–699.

Nelson, G., & Carson, P. (1988). Evaluation of a social problem-solving skills program for third- and fourth-grade students. *American Journal of Community Psychology, 16,* 79–99.

Nelton, S. (1988, March). Motivating for success. *Nation's Business,* pp. 18–26.

Nesbitt, E. B. (1973). An escalator phobia overcome in one session of flooding *in vivo*. *Journal of Behavior Therapy and Experimental Psychiatry, 4,* 405–406.

Nevin, J. A. (1988). Behavioral momentum and the partial reinforcement effect. *Psychological Bulletin, 103,* 44–56.

Nezu, A. M., Nezu, C. M., & Perri, M. G. (1989). *Problem-solving therapy for depression: Theory, research, and clinical guidelines*. New York: Wiley.

Niaura, R. S., Rohsenow, D. J., Binkoff, J. A., Monti, P. M., Pedraza, M., & Abrams, D. B. (1988). Relevance of cue reactivity to understanding alcohol and smoking relapse. *Journal of Abnormal Psychology, 97,* 133–152.

Ninness, H. A. C., Fuerst, J., Rutherford, R. D., & Glenn, S. S. (1991). Effects of self-management training and reinforcement on the transfer of improved conduct in the absence of supervision. *Journal of Applied Behavior Analysis, 24,* 499–508.

NJNPI (New Jersey Neuro-Psychiatric Institute) (1972). *Behavior modification training program: Drug staff.* Princeton, NJ: Author.

Nomellini, S., & Katz, R. C. (1983). Effects of anger control training on abusive parents. *Cognitive Therapy and Research, 7,* 57–68.

Nordquist, V. M. (1971). The modification of a child's enuresis: Some response–response relationships. *Journal of Applied Behavior Analysis, 4,* 241–247.

Nordyke, N. S., Baer, D. M., Etzel, B. C., & LeBlanc, J. M. (1977). Implications of the stereotyping and modification of sex role. *Journal of Applied Behavior Analysis, 10,* 553–557.

Novaco, R. W. (1976). The functions and regulation of the arousal of anger. *American Journal of Psychiatry, 133,* 1124–1128.

Novaco, R. W. (1977). A stress inoculation approach to anger management in the training of law enforcement officers. *American Journal of Community Psychology, 5,* 327–346.

O'Banion, D. R., & Whaley, D. L. (1981). *Behavior contracting: Arranging contingencies of reinforcement.* New York: Springer.

O'Brien, F., Bugle, C., & Azrin, N. H. (1972). Training and maintaining a retarded child's proper eating. *Journal of Applied Behavior Analysis, 5,* 67–72.

O'Brien, S., & Karsh, K. G. (1990). Treatment acceptability: Consumer, therapist, and society. In A. C. Repp & N. N. Singh (Eds.), *Perspectives on the use of nonaversive and aversive interventions for persons with developmental disabilities.* Sycamore, IL: Sycamore.

O'Brien, T. P., Riner, L. S., & Budd, K. S. (1983). The effects of a child's self-evaluation program on compliance with parental instructions in the home. *Journal of Applied Behavior Analysis, 16,* 69–79.

Okifuji, A., & Friedman, A. G. (1992). Experimentally induced taste aversions in humans: Effects of overshadowing on acquisition. *Behaviour Research and Therapy, 30,* 23–32.

Olds, J., & Milner, P. (1954). Positive reinforcement produced by electrical stimulation of the septal area and other regions of the rat brain. *Journal of Comparative and Physiological Psychology, 47,* 419–427.

O'Leary, K. D. (1984). The image of behavior therapy: It is time to take a stand. *Behavior Therapy, 15,* 219–233.

O'Leary, K. D., Becker, W. C., Evans, M. B., & Saudargas, R. A. (1969). A token reinforcement program in a public school: A replication and systematic analysis. *Journal of Applied Behavior Analysis, 2,* 3–13.

Oliver, S. D., West, R. C., & Sloane, H. N. (1974). Some effects on human behavior of aversive events. *Behavior Therapy, 5,* 481–493.

Ollendick, T. H. (1983). Reliability and validity of the Revised Fear Survey Schedule for Children (FSSC-R). *Behaviour Research and Therapy, 21,* 685–692.

Ollendick, T. H., Hagopian, L. P., & Huntzinger, R. M. (1991). Cognitive–behavioral therapy with nighttime fearful children. *Journal of Behavior Therapy and Experimental Psychiatry, 22,* 113–121.

Ollendick, T. H., & Hersen, M. (1984). An overview of child behavioral assessment. In T. H. Ollendick & M. Hersen (Eds.), *Child behavioral assessment: Principles and procedures.* New York: Pergamon Press.

Ollendick, T. H., & Matson, J. L. (1978). Overcorrection: An overview. *Behavior Therapy, 9,* 830–842.

Olson, R. P. (1987). Definitions of biofeedback. In M. S. Schwartz (Ed.), *Biofeedback: A practitioner's guide.* New York: Guilford.

Olson, R. P., & Kroon, J. S. (1987). Biobehavioral treatments of essential hypertension. In M. S. Schwartz (Ed.), *Biofeedback: A practitioner's guide.* New York: Guilford.

Olson, R. P., & Schwartz, M. S. (1987). An historical perspective on the biofeedback field. In M. S. Schwartz (Ed.), *Biofeedback: A practitioner's guide.* New York: Guilford.

Oltmanns, T. F., Neale, J. M., & Davison, G. C. (1991). *Case studies in abnormal psychology* (3rd ed.). New York: Wiley.

O'Neill, H. K., Sandgren, A. K., McCaul, K. D., & Glasgow, R. E. (1987). Self-control strategies and maintenance of a dental hygiene regimen. *Journal of Compliance in Health Care, 2,* 85–89.

O'Neill, R. E., Horner, R. H., Albin, R. W., Storey, K., & Sprague, J. R. (1990). *Functional analysis of problem behavior: A practical assessment guide.* Sycamore, IL: Sycamore.

O'Reilly, M. F., Green, G., & Braunling-McMorrow, D. (1990). Self-administered written prompts to teach home accident prevention skills to adults with brain injuries. *Journal of Applied Behavior Analysis, 23,* 431–446.

Ormrod, J. E. (1990). *Human learning: Theories, principles, and educational applications.* New York: Macmillan.

Ost, L. G. (1987). Age of onset in different phobias. *Journal of Abnormal Psychology, 96,* 223–229.

Ost, L. G., & Hugdahl, K. (1981). Acquisition of phobias and anxiety response patterns in clinical patients. *Behaviour Research and Therapy, 19,* 439–447.

Overholser, J. C. (1991). Prompting and fading in the exposure treatment of compulsive checking. *Journal of Behavior Therapy and Experimental Psychiatry, 22,* 271–279.

Pace, G. M., Ivancic, M. T., Edwards, G. L., Iwata, B. A., & Page, T. J. (1985). Assessment of stimulus preference and reinforcer value with profoundly retarded individuals. *Journal of Applied Behavior Analysis, 18,* 249–255.

Paine, S. C., Hops, H., Walker, H. M., Greenwood, C. R., Fleischman, D. H., & Guild, J. J. (1982). Repeated treatment effects: A study of maintaining behavior change in socially withdrawn children. *Behavior Modification, 6,* 171–199.

Papini, M. R., & Bitterman, M. E. (1990). The role of contingency in classical conditioning. *Psychological Review, 97,* 396–403.

Paquin, M. J. (1977). The treatment of a nail-biting compulsion by covert sensitization in a poorly motivated client. *Journal of Behavior Therapy and Experimental Psychiatry, 8,* 181–183.

Parrish, J. M., & Babbitt, R. L. (1991). Video-mediated instruction in medical settings. In P. W. Dowrick (Ed.), *Practical guide to using video in the behavioral sciences.* New York: Wiley.

Parrish, J. M., Cataldo, M. F., Kolko, D. J., Neef, N. A., & Egel, A. L. (1986). Experimental analysis of response covariation among compliant and inappropriate behaviors. *Journal of Applied Behavior Analysis, 19,* 241–254.

Passman, R. H. (1977). The reduction of procrastinative behaviors in a college student despite the "contingency fulfillment problem": The use of external control in self-management techniques. *Behavior Therapy, 8,* 95–97.

Patterson, C. J., & Mischel, W. (1975). Plans to resist temptation. *Developmental Psychology, 11,* 369–378.

Patterson, G. R. (1982). *Coercive family processes.* Eugene, OR: Castalia Press.

Paul, G. L. (1967). Insight versus desensitization in psychotherapy two years after termination. *Journal of Consulting Psychology, 31,* 333–348.

Paul, G. L., & Lentz, R. J. (1977). *Psychosocial treatment of chronic mental patients: Milieu vs. social learning programs.* Cambridge, MA: Harvard University Press.

Pavlov, I. P. (1927). *Conditioned reflexes.* (G. V. Anrep, Trans.). New York: Oxford University Press.

Pawlicki, R. E., & Galotti, N. (1978). A tic-like behavior case study emanating from a self-directed behavior modification course. *Behavior Therapy, 9,* 671–672.

Pear, J. J., & Eldridge, G. D. (1984). The operant-respondent distinction: Future directions. *Journal of the Experimental Analysis of Behavior, 42,* 453–467.

Pedalino, E., & Gamboa, V. U. (1974). Behavior modification and absenteeism: Intervention in one industrial setting. *Journal of Applied Psychology, 59,* 694–698.

Peek, C. J. (1987). A primer of biofeedback instrumentation. In M. S. Schwartz (Ed.), *Biofeedback: A practitioner's guide.* New York: Guilford.

Perri, M. G., & Richards, C. S. (1977). An investigation of naturally occurring episodes of self-controlled behaviors. *Journal of Counseling Psychology, 24,* 178–183.

Petri, H. L., & Mishkin, M. (1994). Behaviorism, cognitivism and the neuropsychology of memory. *American Scientist, 82,* 30–37.

Phillips, E. L. (1968). Achievement Place: Token reinforcement procedures in a home-style rehabilitation setting for "pre-delinquent" boys. *Journal of Applied Behavior Analysis, 1,* 213–223.

Phillips, E. L., Phillips, E. A., Fixsen, D. L., & Wolf, M. M. (1971). Achievement Place: Modification of the behaviors of pre-delinquent boys within a token economy. *Journal of Applied Behavior Analysis, 4,* 45–59.

Phillips, E. L., Phillips, E. A., Fixsen, D. L., & Wolf, M. M. (1973, June). Achievement Place: Behavior shaping works for delinquents. *Psychology Today,* pp. 75–79.

Phillips, E. L., Phillips, E. A., Wolf, M. M., & Fixsen, D. L. (1973). Achievement Place: Development of the elected manager system. *Journal of Applied Behavior Analysis, 6,* 541–561.

Piaget, J. (1929). *The child's conception of the world.* (J. Tomlinson and A. Tomlinson, Trans.) London: Routledge & Kegan Paul.

Piaget, J. (1952). *The origins of intelligence* (M. Cook, Trans.). New York: International Universities Press. (Originally published 1936.)

Piaget, J. (1970). Piaget's theory. In P. H. Mussen (Ed.), *Carmichael's manual of child psychology* (3rd ed., Vol. 1). New York: Wiley.

Pigott, H. E., Fantuzzo, J. W., & Clement, P. W. (1986). The effects of reciprocal peer tutoring and group contingencies on the academic performance of elementary school children. *Journal of Applied Behavior Analysis, 19,* 93–98.

Piliavin, J. A., Dovidio, J. F., Gaertner, S. L., & Clark, R. D. (1981). Responsive bystanders: The process on intervention. In J. Grzelak & V. Derlega (Eds.), *Living with other people: Theory and research on cooperation and helping.* New York: Academic Press.

Pinkston, E. M., Reese, N. M., LeBlanc, J. M., & Baer, D. M. (1973). Independent control of a preschool child's aggression and peer interaction by contingent teacher attention. *Journal of Applied Behavior Analysis, 6,* 115–124.

Pinto, R. P., & Hollandsworth, J. G. (1989). Using videotaped modeling to prepare children psychologically for surgery: Influence of parents and costs versus benefits of providing preparation services. *Health Psychology, 8,* 79–95.

Pitts, C. E. (1976). Behavior modification—1787. *Journal of Applied Behavior Analysis, 9,* 146.

Plimpton, G. (1963). Ernest Hemingway. In G. Plimpton (Ed.), *Writers at work: The Paris Review interviews* (Second series). New York: Viking Press.

Plotkin, W. B. (1976). On the self-regulation of the occipital alpha rhythm: Control strategies, states of consciousness, and the role of physiological feedback. *Journal of Experimental Psychology, 105,* 66–99.

Poche, C., Brouwer, R., & Swearingen, M. (1981). Teaching self-protection to young children. *Journal of Applied Behavior Analysis, 14,* 169–176.

Polivy, J., & Thomsen, L. (1988). Dieting and other eating disorders. In E. A. Blechman & K. D. Brownell (Eds.), *Handbook of behavioral medicine for women.* New York: Pergamon Press.

Pomerleau, O. F., & Pomerleau, C. S. (1989). A biobehavioral perspective on smoking. In T. Ney & A. Gale (Eds.), *Smoking and human behavior.* New York: Wiley.

Porterfield, J. K., Herbert-Jackson, E., & Risley, T. R. (1976). Contingent observation: An effective and acceptable procedure for reducing disruptive behavior of young children in a group setting. *Journal of Applied Behavior Analysis, 9,* 55–64.

Powell, J., Martindale, A., & Kulp, S. (1975). An evaluation of time-sampled measures of behavior. *Journal of Applied Behavior Analysis, 8,* 463–469.

Premack, D. (1959). Toward empirical behavior laws: I. Positive reinforcement. *Psychological Review, 66,* 219–233.

Premack, D. (1965). Reinforcement theory. In D. Levine (Ed.), *Nebraska Symposium on Motivation.* Lincoln: University of Nebraska Press.

Prochaska, J. O., & DiClemente, C. C. (1984). *The transtheoretical approach: Crossing traditional boundaries of therapy.* Homewood, IL: Dow Jones/Irwin.

Prochaska, J. O., DiClemente, C. C., & Norcross, J. C. (1992). In search of how people change: Applications to addictive behaviors. *American Psychologist, 47,* 1102–1114.

Pruc, D. M., Krapfl, J. E., Noah, J. C., Cannon, S., & Maley, R. F. (1980). Managing the treatment activities of state hospital staff. *Journal of Organizational Behavior Management, 2,* 165–181.

Puder, R., Lacks, P., Bertelson, A. D., & Storandt, M. (1983). Short-term stimulus control treatment of insomnia in older adults. *Behavior Therapy, 14,* 424–429.

Rachman, S. (1991). Neo-conditioning and the classical theory of fear acquisition. *Clinical Psychological Review, 11,* 155–173.

Rachman, S. (1994). The overprediction of fear: A review. *Behaviour Research and Therapy, 32,* 683–690.

Rachman, S. & Cuk, M. (1992). Fearful distortions. *Behaviour Research and Therapy, 30,* 583–589.

Rapport, M. D., Murphy, H. A., & Bailey, J. S. (1982). Ritalin vs. response cost in the control of hyperactive children: A within-subject comparison. *Journal of Applied Behavior Analysis, 15,* 205–216.

Rasing, E. J., & Duker, P. C. (1992). Effects of a multifaceted training procedure on the acquisition and generalization of social behaviors in language-disabled deaf children. *Journal of Applied Behavior Analysis, 25,* 723–734.

Rathus, S. A. (1973). A 30-item schedule for assessing assertive behavior. *Behavior Therapy, 4,* 398–406.

Redd, W. H., & Birnbrauer, J. S. (1969). Adults as discriminative stimuli for different reinforcement contingencies with retarded children. *Journal of Experimental Child Psychology, 7,* 440–447.

Rekers, G. A., & Lovaas, O. I. (1974). Behavioral treatment of deviant sex-role behaviors in a male child. *Journal of Applied Behavior Analysis, 7,* 173–190.

Repp, A. C., Deitz, S. M., & Deitz, D. E. D. (1976). Reducing inappropriate behaviors in classrooms and in individual sessions through DRO schedules of reinforcement. *Mental Retardation, 14,* 11–15.

Repp, A. C., Felce, D., & Barton, L. E. (1988). Basing the treatment of stereotypic and self-injurious behaviors on hypotheses of their causes. *Journal of Applied Behavior Analysis, 21,* 281–289.

Rescorla, R. A. (1988). Pavlovian conditioning: It's not what you think it is. *American Psychologist, 43,* 151–160.

Rescorla, R. A., & Wagner, A. R. (1972). A theory of Pavlovian conditioning: Variations in the effectiveness of reinforcement and nonreinforcement. In A. H. Black & W. F. Prokasy (Eds.), *Classical conditioning II: Current research and theory.* New York: Appleton-Century-Crofts.

Richardson, F. C., & Suinn, R. M. (1973). A comparison of traditional systematic desensitization, accelerated massed desensitization, and anxiety management training in the treatment of mathematics anxiety. *Behavior Therapy, 4,* 212–218.

Rilling, M. (1977). Stimulus control and inhibitory processes. In W. K. Honig & J. E. R. Staddon (Eds.), *Handbook of operant behavior.* Englewood Cliffs, NJ: Prentice-Hall.

Rincover, A., & Devany, J. (1982). The application of sensory extinction procedures to self-injury. *Analysis and Intervention in Developmental Disabilities, 2,* 67–81.

Riordan, M. M., Iwata, B. A., Finney, J. W., Wohl, M. K., & Stanley, A. E. (1984). Behavioral assessment and treatment of chronic food refusal in handicapped children. *Journal of Applied Behavior Analysis, 17,* 327–341.

Rizley, R. C., & Rescorla, R. A. (1972). Associations in second-order conditioning and sensory preconditioning. *Journal of Comparative and Physiological Psychology, 81,* 1–11.

Roberts, M. W., Hatzenbuehler, L. C., & Bean, A. W. (1981). The effects of differential attention and time out on child noncompliance. *Behavior Therapy, 12,* 93–99.

Roberts, R. N., Nelson, R. O., & Olson, T. W. (1987). Self-instruction: An analysis of the differential effects of instruction and reinforcement. *Journal of Applied Behavior Analysis, 20,* 235–242.

Roberts, R. N., & Tharp, R. G. (1980). A naturalistic study of school children's private speech in an academic problem-solving task. *Cognitive Therapy and Research, 4,* 341–352.

Robins, C. J., & Hayes, A. M. (1993). An appraisal of cognitive therapy. *Journal of Consulting and Clinical Psychology, 61,* 205–214.

Rohsenow, D. J., Monti, P. M., Rubonis, A. V., Sirota, A. D., Niaura, R. S., Colby, S. M., Winschel, S. M., & Abrams, D. B. (1994). Cue reactivity as a predictor of drinking among male alcoholics. *Journal of Consulting and Clinical Psychology, 62,* 620–626.

Rohter, L. (1989, November 7). Isolated desert community lives by Skinner's precepts. *New York Times,* pp. C1, C8.

Rolider, A., Cummings, A., & Van Houten, R. (1991). Side effects of therapeutic punishment on academic performance and eye contact. *Journal of Applied Behavior Analysis, 24,* 763–773.

Rolider, A., & Van Houten, R. (1990). The role of reinforcement in reducing inappropriate behavior: Some myths and misconceptions. In A. C. Repp & N. N. Singh (Eds.), *Perspectives on the use of nonaversive and aversive interventions for persons with developmental disabilities.* Sycamore, IL: Sycamore.

Rollins, H. A., McCandless, B. R., Thompson, M., & Brassell, W. R. (1974). Project Success Environment: An extended application of contingency management in inner-city schools. *Journal of Educational Psychology, 66,* 167–178.

Ronen, T. (1991). Intervention package for treating sleep disorders in a four-year-old girl. *Journal of Behavior Therapy and Experimental Psychiatry, 22,* 141–148.

Rosen, G. M., Glasgow, R. E., & Barrera, M. (1977). A two-year follow-up on systematic desensitization with data pertaining to the external validity of laboratory fear assessment. *Journal of Consulting and Clinical Psychology, 45,* 1188–1189.

Rosen, H. S., & Rosen, L. A. (1983). Eliminating stealing: Use of stimulus control with an elementary student. *Behavior Modification, 7,* 56–63.

Rosenhan, D. L., & Seligman, M. E. P. (1984). *Abnormal psychology.* New York: Norton.

Roth, D., Bielski, R., Jones, M., Parker, W., & Osborn, G. (1982). A comparison of self-control therapy and combined self-control therapy and antidepressant medication in the treatment of depression. *Behavior Therapy, 13,* 133–144.

Rusch, F. R., & Kazdin, A. E. (1981). Toward a methodology of withdrawal designs for the assessment of response maintenance. *Journal of Applied Behavior Analysis, 14,* 131–140.

Rushall, B. S. (1993). The restoration of performance capacity by cognitive restructuring and covert positive reinforcement in an elite athlete. In J. R. Cautela & A. J. Kearney (Eds.), *Covert conditioning handbook.* Pacific Grove, CA: Brooks/Cole.

Rutter, M. (1975). *Helping troubled children.* New York: Plenum Press.

Safer, D. J., Heaton, R. C., & Parker, F. C. (1981). A behavioral program for disruptive junior high school students: Results and follow-up. *Journal of Abnormal Child Psychology, 9,* 483–494.

Saigh, P. A. (1986). *In vitro* flooding in the treatment of a 6-year-old boy's posttraumatic stress disorder. *Behaviour Research and Therapy, 6,* 685–688.

Sajwaj, T., Libet, J., & Agras, S. (1974). Lemon-juice therapy: The control of life-threatening rumination in a six-month old infant. *Journal of Applied Behavior Analysis, 7,* 557–563.

Sajwaj, T., Twardosz, S., & Burke, M. (1972). Side effects of extinction procedures in a remedial preschool. *Journal of Applied Behavior Analysis, 5,* 163–175.

Sanders, M. R., & Glynn, T. (1977). Functional analysis of a program for training high and low preference peers to modify disruptive classroom behavior. *Journal of Applied Behavior Analysis, 10,* 503.

Sanders, M. R., & Glynn, T. (1981). Training parents in behavioral self-management: An analysis of generalization and maintenance. *Journal of Applied Behavior Analysis, 14,* 223–227.

Santogrossi, D. A., O'Leary, K. D., Romanczyk, R. G., & Kaufman, K. F. (1973). Self-evaluation by adolescents in a psychiatric hospital school token program. *Journal of Applied Behavior Analysis, 6,* 277–287.

Sarafino, E. P. (1977). *LotPACA:* A lottery procedure for administering competitive awards. *Journal of Behavior Therapy and Experimental Psychiatry, 8,* 449–450.

Sarafino, E. P. (1984). Rewards and intrinsic interest. In R. J. Corsini (Ed.), *Encyclopedia of psychology* (Vol. 3). New York: Wiley.

Sarafino, E. P. (1985). Peer–peer interaction among infants and toddlers with extensive day-care experience. *Journal of Applied Developmental Psychology, 6,* 17–29.

Sarafino, E. P. (1986). *The fears of childhood: A guide to recognizing and reducing fearful states in children.* New York: Human Sciences Press.

Sarafino, E. P. (1994). *Health psychology: Biopsychosocial interactions* (2nd ed.). New York: Wiley.

Sarafino, E. P. (1995a). *Behavioral approaches in the treatment of asthma.* Paper submitted for publication.

Sarafino, E. P. (1995b). *The Preferred Items and Experiences Questionnaire (PIEQ) for Adolescents and Adults.* Unpublished manuscript.

Sarafino, E. P., & Armstrong, J. W. (1986). *Child and adolescent development* (2nd ed.). St. Paul, MN: West.

Sasso, G. M., Reimers, T. M., Cooper, L. J., Wacker, D., Berg, W., Steege, M., Kelly, L., & Allaire, A. (1992). Use of descriptive and experimental analyses to identify the functional properties of aberrant behavior in school settings. *Journal of Applied Behavior Analysis, 25,* 809–821.

Satterfield, J. H., Satterfield, B. T., & Cantwell, D. P. (1981). Three-year multimodality treatment study of 100 hyperactive boys. *Journal of Pediatrics, 98,* 650–655.

Scarr, S., & Kidd, K. K. (1983). Developmental behavior genetics. In P. H. Mussen (Ed.), *Handbook of child psychology* (4th ed., Vol. 2). New York: Wiley.

Schacter, D. L. (1992). Understanding implicit memory: A cognitive neuroscience approach. *American Psychologist, 47,* 559–569.

Schepis, M. M., Reid, D. H., & Fitzgerald, J. R. (1987). Group instruction with profoundly retarded persons: Acquisition, generalization, and maintenance of a remunerative work skill. *Journal of Applied Behavior Analysis, 20,* 97–105.

Schnelle, J. F. (1974). A brief report on invalidity of parent evaluations of behavior change. *Journal of Applied Behavior Analysis, 7,* 341–343.

Schreibman, L., Charlop, M. H., & Kurtz, P. F. (1992). Behavioral treatment for children with autism. In S. M. Turner, K. S. Calhoun, & H. E. Adams (Eds.), *Handbook of clinical behavior therapy* (2nd ed.). New York: Wiley.

Schroeder, S. R. (1972). Parametric effects of reinforcement frequency, amount of reinforcement, and required response force on sheltered workshop behavior. *Journal of Applied Behavior Analysis, 5,* 431–441.

Schultz, D. D. (1965). *Sensory restriction: Effects on behavior.* New York: Academic Press.

Schultz, J. H. (1957). Autogenous training. In J. H. Masserman & J. L. Moreno (Eds.), *Progress in psychotherapy* (Vol. 2). New York: Grune & Stratton.

Schultz, J. H., & Luthe, W. (1969). *Autogenic therapy: Vol. 1. Autogenic methods.* New York: Grune & Stratton.

Schwartz, I. S., & Baer, D. M. (1991). Social validity assessments: Is current practice state of the art? *Journal of Applied Behavior Analysis, 24,* 189–204.

Scott, R. W., Peters, R. D., Gillespie, W. J., Blanchard, E. B., Edmunson, E. D., & Young, L. D. (1973). The use of shaping and reinforcement in the operant acceleration and deceleration of heart rate. *Behaviour Research and Therapy, 11,* 179–185.

Seaman, J. E., Greene, B. F., & Watson-Perczel, M. (1986). A behavioral system for assessing and training cardiopulmonary resuscitation skills among emergency medical technicians. *Journal of Applied Behavior Analysis, 19,* 125–135.

Seaver, W. B., & Patterson, A. H. (1976). Decreasing fuel-oil consumption through feedback and social commendation. *Journal of Applied Behavior Analysis, 9,* 147–152.

Seligman, M. E. P. (1971). Phobias and preparedness. *Behavior Therapy, 2,* 307–320.

Seligman, M. E. P., & Johnston, J. C. (1973). A cognitive theory of avoidance learning. In F. J. McGuigan & D. B. Lumsden (Eds.), *Contemporary approaches to conditioning and learning.* Washington, DC: Winston.

Seligmann, J., Namuth, T., & Miller, M. (1994, May 23). Drowning on dry land. *Newsweek,* pp. 64–66.

Serna, L. A., Schumacker, J. B., Sherman, J. A., & Sheldon, J. B. (1991). In-home generalization of social interactions in families of adolescents with behavior problems. *Journal of Applied Behavior Analysis, 24,* 733–746.

Shaffer, D., Vieland, V., Garland, A., Rojas, M., Underwood, M., & Busner, C. (1990). Adolescent suicide attempters: Response to suicide-prevention programs. *Journal of the American Medical Association, 264,* 3151–3155.

Shaw, R. A. (1987). Reinforcement schedules. In R. J. Corsini (Ed.), *Concise encyclopedia of psychology* (Vol.3). New York: Wiley.

Sheffield, F. D., Roby, T. B., & Campbell, B. A. (1954). Drive reduction versus consummatory behavior as determinants of reinforcement. *Journal of Comparative and Physiological Psychology, 47,* 349–354.

Sheffield, F. D., Wulff, J. J., & Backer, R. (1951). Reward value of copulation without sex drive reduction. *Journal of Comparative and Physiological Psychology, 44,* 3–8.

Sherman, A. R. (1972). Real-life exposure as a primary therapeutic factor in the desensitization treatment of fear. *Journal of Abnormal Psychology, 79,* 19–28.

Shiffman, S. (1984). Coping with temptations to smoke. *Journal of Consulting and Clinical Psychology, 52,* 261–267.

Shiffman, S. (1986). A cluster-analytic classification of smoking relapse episodes. *Addictive Behaviors, 11,* 295–307.

Shipley, R. H., & Boudewyns, P. A. (1980). Flooding and implosive therapy: Are they harmful? *Behavior Therapy, 11,* 503–508.

Shipley, R. H., Butt, J. H., Horwitz, B., & Farbry, J. E. (1978). Preparation for a stressful medical procedure: Effect of amount of stimulus preexposure and coping style. *Journal of Consulting and Clinical Psychology, 46,* 499–507.

Sidman, M., & Tailby, W. (1982). Conditional discrimination vs. matching to sample: An expansion of the testing paradigm. *Journal of the Experimental Analysis of Behavior, 37,* 5–22.

Siegel, L. J., & Peterson, L. (1980). Stress reduction in young dental patients through coping skills and sensory information. *Journal of Consulting and Clinical Psychology, 48,* 785–787.

Siegel, P. S., & Foshee, J. G. (1953). The law of primary reinforcement in children. *Journal of Experimental Psychology, 45,* 12–14.

Siegel, S., Hinson, R. E., Krank, M. D., & McCully, J. (1982). Heroin "overdose" death: The contribution of drug-associated environmental cues. *Science, 216,* 436–437.

Simons, A. D., Murphy, G. E., Levine, J. L., & Wetzel, R. D. (1986). Cognitive therapy and pharmacotherapy for depression: Sustained improvement over one year. *Archives of General Psychiatry, 43,* 43–48.

Singh, N. N., Lloyd, J. W., & Kendall, K. A. (1990). Nonaversive and aversive interventions: Issues. In A. C. Repp & N. N. Singh (Eds.), *Perspectives on the use of nonaversive and aversive interventions for persons with developmental disabilities.* Sycamore, IL: Sycamore.

Singh, N. N., Watson, J. E., & Winton, A. S. W. (1986). Treating self-injury: Water mist spray versus facial screening or forced arm exercise. *Journal of Applied Behavior Analysis, 19,* 403–410.

Sisson, R. W., & Azrin, N. H. (1989). The community reinforcement approach. In R. K. Hester & W. R. Miller (Eds.), *Handbook of alcoholism treatment approaches: Effective alternatives.* New York: Pergamon Press.

Skinner, B. F. (1938). *The behavior of organisms.* New York: Appleton-Century-Crofts.

Skinner, B. F. (1948). *Walden Two.* New York: Macmillan.

Skinner, B. F. (1953). *Science and human behavior.* New York: Macmillan.

Skinner, B. F. (1954). The science of learning and the art of teaching. *Harvard Educational Review, 24,* 86–97.

Smith, B. M., Schumaker, J. B., Schaeffer, J., & Sherman, J. A. (1982). Increasing participation and improving the quality of discussions in seventh-grade social studies classes. *Journal of Applied Behavior Analysis, 15,* 97–110.

Smith, L. K. C., & Fowler, S. A. (1984). Positive peer pressure: The effects of peer monitoring on children's disruptive behavior. *Journal of Applied Behavior Analysis, 17,* 213–227.

Smith, M. L., & Glass, G. V. (1977). Meta-analysis of psychotherapy outcome studies. *American Psychologist, 32,* 752–760.

Smith, R. E. (1973). The use of humor in the counterconditioning of anger responses: A case study. *Behavior Therapy, 4,* 576–580.

Smith, T. (1990). When and when not to consider the use of aversive interventions in the behavioral treatment of autistic children. In A. C. Repp & N. N. Singh (Eds.), *Perspectives on the use of nonaversive and aversive interventions for persons with developmental disabilities.* Sycamore, IL: Sycamore.

Sobell, L. C., Toneatto, A., & Sobell, M. B. (1990). Behavior therapy. In A. S. Bellack & M. Hersen (Eds.), *Handbook of comparative treatments for adult disorders.* New York: Wiley.

Solé-Leris, A. (1986). *Tranquility and insight.* Boston: Shambhala.

Solnick, J. V., Rincover, A., & Peterson, C. R. (1977). Some determinants of the reinforcing and punishing effects of timeout. *Journal of Applied Behavior Analysis, 10,* 415–424.

Solomon, R. L., Kamin, L. J., & Wynne, L. C. (1953). Traumatic avoidance learning: The outcomes of several extinction procedures with dogs. *Journal of Abnormal and Social Psychology, 48,* 291–302.

Speer, D. C. (1992). Clinically significant change: Jacobson and Truax (1991) revisited. *Journal of Consulting and Clinical Psychology, 60,* 402–408.

Spiegel, T. A., Wadden, T. A., & Foster, G. D. (1991). Objective measurement of eating rate during behavioral treatment of obesity. *Behavior Therapy, 22,* 61–67.

Spivack, G., & Shure, M. B. (1974). *Social adjustment of young children: A cognitive approach to solving real-life problems.* San Francisco: Jossey-Bass.

Spivack, G., & Shure, M. B. (1982). The cognition of social adjustment: Interpersonal cognitive problem-solving thinking. In B. B. Lahey & A. E. Kazdin (Eds.), *Advances in clinical child psychology* (Vol. 5). New York: Plenum Press.

Spooner, F. (1984). Comparisons of backward chaining and total task presentation in training severely handicapped persons. *Education and Training of the Mentally Retarded, 19,* 15–22.

Squire, L. R. (1987). *Memory and the brain.* New York: Oxford University Press.

Stainback, W. C., Payne, J. S., Stainback, S. B., & Payne, R. A. (1973). *Establishing a token economy in the classroom.* Columbus, OH: Charles E. Merrill.

Stampfl, T. G., & Levis, D. J. (1967). Essentials of implosive therapy: A learning-theory-based psychodynamic behavioral therapy, *Journal of Abnormal Psychology, 72,* 496–503.

Stanley, M. A. (1992). Obsessive–compulsive disorder. In S. M. Turner, K. S. Calhoun, & H. E. Adams (Eds.), *Handbook of clinical behavior therapy* (2nd ed.). New York: Wiley.

Stark, L. J., Collins, F. L., Osnes, P. G., & Stokes, T. F. (1986). Using reinforcement and cueing to increase healthy snack food choices in preschoolers. *Journal of Applied Behavior Analysis, 19,* 367–379.

Stasiewicz, P. R., & Maisto, S. A. (1993). Two-factor avoidance theory: The role of negative affect in the maintenance of substance use and substance use disorder. *Behavior Therapy, 24,* 337–356.

Steege, M. W., Wacker, D. P., Cigrand, K. C., Berg, W. K., Novak, C. G., Reimers, T. M., Sasso, G. M., & DeRaad, A. (1990). Use of negative reinforcement in the treatment of self-injurious behavior. *Journal of Applied Behavior Analysis, 23,* 459–467.

Stein, D. J., & Young, J. E. (Eds.) (1992). *Cognitive science and clinical disorders.* San Diego, CA: Academic Press.

Stephens, C. E., Pear, J. J., Wray, L. D., & Jackson, G. C. (1975). Some effects of reinforcement schedules in teaching picture names to retarded children. *Journal of Applied Behavior Analysis, 8,* 435–447.

Sterman, M. B. (1986). Epilepsy and its treatment with EEG feedback therapy. *Annals of Behavioral Medicine, 8*(1), 21–25.

Stern, R. M., & Ray, W. J. (1980). *Biofeedback: Potential and limits.* Lincoln: University of Nebraska Press.

Stern, R. S., Lipsedge, M. S., & Marks, I. M. (1973). Obsessive ruminations: A controlled trial of thought-stopping techniques. *Behaviour Research and Therapy, 11,* 659–662.

Stokes, T. F., & Baer, D. M. (1976). Preschool peers as mutual generalization-facilitating agents. *Behavior Therapy, 7,* 549–556.

Stokes, T. F., & Baer, D. M. (1977). An implicit technology of generalization. *Journal of Applied Behavior Analysis, 10,* 349–367.

Stokes, T. F., Baer, D. M., & Jackson, R. L. (1974). Programming the generalization of a greeting response in four retarded children. *Journal of Applied Behavior Analysis, 7,* 599–610.

Stokes, T. F., & Osnes, P. G. (1988). The developing applied technology of generalization and maintenance. In R. H. Horner, G. Dunlap, & R. L. Koegel (Eds.), *Generalization and maintenance: Life-style changes in applied settings.* Baltimore: Paul H. Brookes.

Stokes, T. F., & Osnes, P. G. (1989). An operant pursuit of generalization. *Behavior Therapy, 20,* 337–355.

Stolz, S. B., & Associates (1978). *Ethical issues in behavior modification.* San Francisco: Jossey-Bass.

Storms, M. D. (1983). *Development of sexual orientation.* Washington, DC: American Psychological Association.

Strain, P. S., Shores, R. E., & Kerr, M. M. (1976). An experimental analysis of "spillover" effects on the social interaction of behaviorally handicapped preschool children. *Journal of Applied Behavior Analysis, 9,* 31–40.

Strain, P. S., Shores, R. E., & Timm, M. A. (1977). Effects of peer social initiations on the behavior of withdrawn preschool children. *Journal of Applied Behavior Analysis, 10,* 289–298.

Stuart, R. B. (1971). Behavioral contracting within the families of delinquents. *Journal of Behavior Therapy and Experimental Psychiatry, 2,* 1–11.

Sullivan, M. A., & O'Leary, S. G. (1990). Maintenance following reward and cost token programs. *Behavior Therapy, 21,* 139–149.

Suls, J., Sanders, G. S., & Labrecque, M. S. (1986). Attempting to control blood pressure without systematic instruction: When advice is counterproductive. *Journal of Behavioral Medicine, 9,* 567–576.

Sulzer, B., & Mayer, G. R. (1972). *Behavior modification procedures for school personnel.* Hinsdale, IL: Dryden.

Surwit, R. S., & Keefe, F. J. (1978). Frontalis EMG feedback training: An electronic panacea? *Behavior Therapy, 9,* 779–792.

Swain, J. J., Allard, G. B., & Holborn, S. W. (1982). The Good Toothbrushing Game: A school-based dental hygiene program for increasing the toothbrushing effectiveness of children. *Journal of Applied Behavior Analysis, 15,* 171–176.

Swan, G. E., & MacDonald, M. L. (1978). Behavior therapy in practice: A national survey of behavior therapists. *Behavior Therapy, 9,* 799–807.

Sweet, A. A., & Loizeaux, A. L. (1991). Behavioral and cognitive treatment methods: A critical comparative review. *Journal of Behavior Therapy and Experimental Psychiatry, 22,* 159–185.

Swizer, E. B., Deal, T. E., & Bailey, J. S. (1977). The reduction of stealing in second graders using a group contingency. *Journal of Applied Behavior Analysis, 10,* 267–272.

Tasto, D. L. (1969). Systematic desensitization, muscle relaxation and visual imagery in the counterconditioning of four-year-old phobic child. *Behaviour Research and Therapy, 7,* 409–411.

Taylor, C. B. (1978). Relaxation training and related techniques. In W. S. Agras (Ed.), *Behavior modification: Principles and clinical applications* (2nd ed.). Boston: Little, Brown.

Taylor, C. B., Agras, W. S., Schneider, J. A., & Allen, R. A. (1983). Adherence to instructions to practice relaxation exercises. *Journal of Consulting and Clinical Psychology, 51,* 952–953.

Taylor, K. L., Bovbjerg, D. H., Jacobsen, P. B., Redd, W. H., & Manne, S. L. (1992, March). *An experimental model of classically conditioned nausea during cancer chemotherapy.* Paper presented at the meeting of the Society of Behavioral Medicine, New York.

Taylor, S. E. (1983). Adjustment to threatening events: A theory of cognitive adaptation. *American Psychologist, 38,* 1161-1173.

TFPDPP (Task Force on Promotion and Dissemination of Psychological Procedures). (1993). *A report to the Division 12 Board, October 1993.* Washington, DC: American Psychological Association Division of Clinical Psychology.

Thase, M. E., & Wright, J. H. (1991). Cognitive behavior therapy manual for depressed inpatients: A treatment protocol outline. *Behavior Therapy, 22,* 579–595.

Thera, P. (1979). *Buddhist meditation: The way to inner calm and clarity.* Kandy, Sri Lanka: Buddhist Publication Society.

Thomas, J. D., Presland, I. E., Grant, M. D., & Glynn, T. L. (1978). Natural rates of teacher approval and disapproval in grade-7 classrooms. *Journal of Applied Behavior Analysis, 11,* 91–94.

Thorndike, E. L. (1898). Animal intelligence: An experimental study of the associative processes in animals. *Psychological Review Monograph Supplements, 2,* No. 8.

Thorndike, E. L. (1931). *Human learning.* New York: Century.

Tiffany, S. T., Martin, E. M., & Baker, T. B. (1986). Treatments for cigarette smoking: An evaluation of the contributions of aversion and counseling procedures. *Behaviour Research and Therapy, 24,* 437–452.

Timberlake, W., & Allison, J. (1974). Response deprivation: An empirical approach to instrumental performance. *Psychological Review, 81,* 146–164.

Todd, J. T., Morris, E. K., & Fenza, K. M. (1989). Temporal organization of extinction-induced responding in preschool children. *Psychological Record, 39,* 117–130.

Torgersen, S. (1983). Genetic factors in anxiety disorders. *Archives of General Psychiatry, 40,* 1085–1089.

Touchette, P. E., & Howard, J. S. (1984). Errorless learning: Reinforcement contingencies and stimulus control transfer in delayed prompting. *Journal of Applied Behavior Analysis, 17,* 175–188.

Tough, P. (1993, November 7). Into the pit. *New York Times Magazine,* pp. 52–54.

Trollope, A. (1946). *An autobiography.* London: Williams & Norgate. (Original work published 1883.)

Trull, T. J., Nietzel, M. T., & Main, A. (1988). The use of meta-analysis to assess the clinical significance of behavior therapy for agoraphobia. *Behavior Therapy, 19,* 527–538.

Tryon, G. S. (1979). A review and critique of thought stopping research. *Journal of Behavior Therapy and Experimental Psychiatry, 10,* 189–192.

Tucker, J. A., Vuchinich, R. E., & Downey, K. K. (1992). Substance abuse. In S. M. Turner, K. S. Calhoun, & H. E. Adams (Eds.), *Handbook of clinical behavior therapy* (2nd ed.). New York: Wiley.

Turkat, I. D. (1986). The behavioral interview. In A. R. Ciminero, K. S. Calhoun, & H. E. Adams (Eds.), *Handbook of behavioral assessment* (2nd ed.). New York: Wiley.

Turner, S. M., Beidel, D. C., & Jacob, R. G. (1994). Social phobia: A comparison of behavior therapy and atenolol. *Journal of Consulting and Clinical Psychology, 62,* 350–358.

Turner, S. M., Beidel, D. C., Long, P. J., & Greenhouse, J. (1992). Reduction of fear in social phobics: An examination of extinction patterns. *Behavior Therapy, 23,* 389–403.

Turner, S. M., Calhoun, K. S., & Adams, H. E. (Eds.) (1992). *Handbook of clinical behavioral therapy* (2nd ed.). New York: Wiley.

Upper, D. (1973). A "ticket" system for reducing ward rules violations on a token economy program. *Journal of Behavior Therapy and Experimental Psychiatry, 4,* 137–140.

Upper, D. (1993). The use of covert reinforcement and thought stopping in treating a young woman's sexual anxiety. In J. R. Cautela & A. J. Kearney (Eds.), *Covert conditioning handbook.* Pacific Grove, CA: Brooks/Cole.

Van Houten, R. (1983). Punishment: From the animal laboratory to the applied setting. In S. Axelrod & J. Apsche (Eds.), *The effects of punishment on human behavior.* New York: Academic Press.

Van Houten, R., Nau, P. A., MacKenzie-Keating, S. E., Sameoto, D., & Colavecchia, B. (1982). An analysis of some variables influencing the effectiveness of reprimands. *Journal of Applied Behavior Analysis, 15,* 65–83.

Van Houten, R., Nau, P., & Marini, Z. (1980). An analysis of public posting in reducing speeding behavior on an urban highway. *Journal of Applied Behavior Analysis, 13,* 383–395.

Vargas, J. M., & Adesso, V. J. (1976). A comparison of aversion therapies for nailbiting behavior. *Behavior Therapy, 7,* 322–329.

Venn, J. R., & Short, J. G. (1973). Vicarious classical conditioning of emotional responses in nursery school children. *Journal of Personality and Social Psychology, 28,* 249–255.

Ventis, W. L. (1973). Case history: The use of laughter as an alternative response in systematic desensitization. *Behavior Therapy, 4,* 120–122.

Vygotsky, L. (1962). *Thought and language.* Cambridge, MA: MIT Press.

Wacker, D., McMahon, C., Steege, M., Berg, W., Sasso, G., & Melloy, K. (1990). Applications of a sequential alternating treatments design. *Journal of Applied Behavior Analysis, 23,* 333–339.

Wacker, D., Steege, M., Northup, J., Reimers, T., Berg, W., & Sasso, G. (1990). Use of functional analysis and acceptability measures to assess and treat severe behavior problems: An outpatient clinic model. In A. C. Repp & N. N. Singh (Eds.), *Perspectives on the use of nonaversive and aversive interventions for persons with developmental disabilities.* Sycamore, IL: Sycamore.

Wahler, R. G. (1975). Some structural aspects of deviant child behavior. *Journal of Applied Behavior Analysis, 8,* 27–42.

Wahler, R. G., & Dumas, J. E. (1984). Changing the observational coding styles of insular and noninsular mothers: A step toward maintenance of parent training effects. In R. F. Dangel & R. A. Polster (Eds.), *Parent training: Foundations of research and practice.* New York: Guilford.

Wahler, R. G., & Fox, J. J. (1980). Solitary toy play and time out: A family treatment package for children with aggressive and oppositional behavior. *Journal of Applied Behavior Analysis, 13,* 23–39.

Wahler, R. G., & Fox, J. J. (1981). Setting events in applied behavior analysis: Toward a conceptual and methodological expansion. *Journal of Applied Behavior Analysis, 14,* 327–338.

Wahler, R. G., Winkel, G. H., Peterson, R. F., & Morrison, D. C. (1965). Mothers as behavior therapists for their own children. *Behaviour Research and Therapy, 3,* 113–124.

Walker, H. M., & Buckley, N. K. (1972). Programming generalization and maintenance of treatment effects across time and across settings. *Journal of Applied Behavior Analysis, 5,* 209–224.

Walker, H. M., Hops, H., & Johnson, S. M. (1975). Generalization and maintenance of classroom treatment effects. *Behavior Therapy, 6,* 188–200.

Wallace, I., & Pear, J. J. (1977). Self-control techniques of famous novelists. *Journal of Applied Behavior Analysis, 10,* 515–525.

Walters, G. C., & Grusec, J. E. (1977). *Punishment.* San Francisco: Freeman.

Ward, W. D., & Stare, S. W. (1990). The role of subject verbalization in generalized correspondence. *Journal of Applied Behavior Analysis, 23,* 129–136.

Wasik, B. H. (1970). The application of Premack's generalization on reinforcement to the management of classroom behavior. *Journal of Experimental Child Psychology, 10,* 33–43.

Watson, J. B. (1913). Psychology as the behaviorist views it. *Psychological Review, 20,* 158–177.

Watson, J. B. (1930). *Behaviorism.* New York: Norton.

Watson, J. B., & Rayner, R. (1920). Conditioned emotional reactions. *Journal of Experimental Psychology, 3,* 1–14.

Webster-Stratton, C. (1982a). The long-term effects of a videotape modeling parent-training program: Comparison of immediate and 1-year follow-up results. *Behavior Therapy, 13,* 702–714.

Webster-Stratton, C. (1982b). Teaching mothers through videotape modeling to change their children's behavior. *Journal of Pediatric Psychology, 7,* 279–294.

Weiner, H. (1970). Instructional control of human operant responding during extinction following fixed-ratio conditioning. *Journal of the Experimental Analysis of Behavior, 13,* 391–394.

Weiss, R. F., Cecil, J. S., & Frank, M. J. (1973). Steep delay of reinforcement gradient in escape conditioning with altruistic reinforcement. *Bulletin of the Psychonomic Society, 2,* 372–374.

Welch, M. W., & Gist, J. W. (1974). *The open token economy system: A handbook for a behavioral approach to rehabilitation.* Springfield, IL: Charles C. Thomas.

Weld, E. M., & Evans, I. M. (1990). Effects of part versus whole instructional strategies on skill acquisition and excess behavior. *American Journal of Mental Retardation, 94,* 377–386.

Whelan, J. P., Mahoney, M. J., & Meyers, A. W. (1991). Performance enhancement in sport: A cognitive behavioral domain. *Behavior Therapy, 22,* 307–327.

White, G. D., Nielsen, G., & Johnson, S. M. (1972). Timeout duration and the suppression of deviant behavior in children. *Journal of Applied Behavior Analysis, 5,* 111–120.

White, L., & Tursky, B. (1982). Stress and anxiety. In L. White & B. Tursky (Eds.), *Clinical biofeedback: Efficacy and mechanisms.* New York: Guilford.

White, M. A. (1975). Natural rates of teacher approval and disapproval in the classroom. *Journal of Applied Behavior Analysis, 8,* 367–372.

Whitman, T. L., Mercurio, J. R., & Caponigri, V. (1970). Development of social responses in two severely retarded children. *Journal of Applied Behavior Analysis, 3,* 133–138.

Wiens, A. N., & Menustik, C. E. (1983). Treatment outcome and patient characteristics in an aversion therapy program for alcoholism. *American Psychologist, 38,* 1089–1096.

Wilcoxin, H. C., Dragoin, W. B., & Kral, P. A. (1971). Illness-induced aversions in rat and quail: Relative salience of visual and gustatory cues. *Science, 171,* 826–828.

Williams, C. D. (1959). The elimination of tantrum behavior by extinction procedures. *Journal of Abnormal and Social Psychology, 59,* 269.

Williams, C. J. (1990). *Cancer biology and management: An introduction.* New York: Wiley.

Williams, J. M. G., Watts, F. N., MacLeod, C., & Mathews, A. (1988). *Cognitive psychology and emotional disorders.* New York: Wiley.

Williamson, D. A., Williamson, S. H., Watkins, P. C., & Hughes. H. H., (1992). Increasing cooperation among children using dependent group-oriented reinforcement contingencies. *Behavior Modification, 16,* 414–425.

Wilson, C. C., Robertson, S. J., Herlong, L. H., & Haynes, S. N. (1979). Vicarious effects of time-out in the modification of aggression in the classroom. *Behavior Modification, 3,* 97–111.

Wilson, G. T. (1982). Adult disorders. In G. T. Wilson & C. M. Franks (Eds.), *Contemporary behavior therapy: Conceptual and empirical foundations.* New York: Guilford.

Wilson, G. T. (1990). Clinical issues and strategies in the practice of behavior therapy. In C. M. Franks, G. T. Wilson, P. C. Kendall, & J. P. Foreyt (Eds.), *Review of behavior therapy: Theory and practice* (Vol. 2). New York: Guilford.

Wilson, G. T. (1991). Chemical aversion conditioning in the treatment of alcoholism: Further comments. *Behaviour Research and Therapy, 29,* 415–419.

Wilson, G. T., & Fairburn, C. G. (1993). Cognitive treatments for eating disorders. *Journal of Consulting and Clinical Psychology, 61,* 261–269.

Wilson, G. T., Leaf, R. C., & Nathan, P. E. (1975). The aversive control of excessive alcohol consumption by chronic alcoholics in the laboratory setting. *Journal of Applied Behavior Analysis, 8,* 13–26.

Wilson, G. T., & Tracey, D. A. (1976). An experimental analysis of aversive imagery versus electrical aversive conditioning in the treatment of chronic alcoholics. *Behaviour Research and Therapy, 14,* 41–51.

Wilson, W. H., & Simpson, G. M. (1990). Pharmacotherapy. In A. S. Bellack & M. Hersen (Eds.), *Handbook of comparative treatments for adult disorders.* New York: Wiley.

Wincze, J. P. (1977). Sexual deviance and dysfunction. In D. C. Rimm & J. W. Somervill (Eds.), *Abnormal psychology.* New York: Academic Press.

Winkler, R. C. (1977). What types of sex-role behavior should behavior modifiers promote? *Journal of Applied Behavior Analysis, 10,* 549–552.

Witryol, S. L. (1971). Incentives and learning in children. In H. W. Reese (Ed.), *Advances in child development and behavior* (Vol. 6). New York: Academic Press.

Wixted, J. T., Bellack, A. S., & Hersen, M. (1990). Behavior therapy. In A. S. Bellack & M. Hersen (Eds.), *Handbook of comparative treatments for adult disorders*. New York: Wiley.

Wolf, M. M. (1978). Social validity: The case for subjective measurement or how applied behavior analysis is finding its heart. *Journal of Applied Behavior Analysis, 11*, 203–214.

Wolf, M. M., Braukmann, C. J., & Ramp, K. A. (1987). Serious delinquent behavior as part of a significantly handicapping condition: Cures and supportive environments. *Journal of Applied Behavior Analysis, 20*, 347–359.

Wolf, M. M., Hanley, E. L., King, L. A., Lachowicz, J., & Giles, D. K. (1970). The timer-game: A variable interval contingency for the management of out-of-seat behavior. *Exceptional Children, 37*, 113–117.

Wolfe, D. A., Mendes, M. G., & Factor, D. (1984). A parent-administered program to reduce children's television viewing. *Journal of Applied Behavior Analysis, 17*, 267–272.

Wolpe, J. (1958). *Psychotherapy by reciprocal inhibition*. Stanford, CA: Stanford University Press.

Wolpe, J. (1973). *The practice of behavior therapy*. New York: Pergamon Press.

Wolpe, J. (1981). The dichotomy between directly conditioned and cognitively learned anxiety. *Journal of Behavior Therapy and Experimental Psychiatry, 12*, 35–42.

Wolpe, J. (1993). Commentary: The cognitivist oversell and comments on symposium contributions. *Journal of Behavior Therapy and Experimental Psychiatry, 24*, 141–147.

Wong, S. E., Terranova, M. D., Bowen, L., Zarate, R., Massel, H. K., & Liberman, R. P. (1987). Providing independent recreational activities to reduce stereotypic vocalizations in chronic schizophrenics. *Journal of Applied Behavior Analysis, 20*, 77–81.

Woolfolk, A. E., Woolfolk, R. L., & Wilson, G. T. (1977). A rose by any other name . . . : Labeling bias and attitudes toward behavior modification. *Journal of Consulting and Clinical Psychology, 45*, 184–191.

Wysocki, T., Hall, G., Iwata, B., & Riordan, M. (1979). Behavioral management of exercise: Contracting for aerobic points. *Journal of Applied Behavior Analysis, 12*, 55–64.

Yates, B. T. (1994). Toward the incorporation of costs, cost-effectiveness analysis, and cost-benefit analysis into clinical research. *Journal of Consulting and Clinical Psychology, 62*, 729–736.

Yu, D., Martin, G. L., Suthons, E., Koop, S., & Pallotta-Cornick, A. (1980). Comparisons of forward chaining and total task presentation formats to teach vocational skills to the retarded. *International Journal of Rehabilitation Research, 3*, 77–79.

Yu, P., Harris, G. E., Slovitz, B. L., & Franklin, L. (1986). A social problem-solving intervention for children at high risk for later psychopathology. *Journal of Clinical Child Psychology, 13*, 30–40.

Zeiss, R. I. (1978). Self-directed treatment for premature ejaculation. *Journal of Consulting and Clinical Psychology, 46*, 1234–1241.

Ziegler, S. G. (1987). Effects of stimulus cueing on the acquisition of groundstrokes by beginning tennis players. *Journal of Applied Behavior Analysis, 20*, 405–411.

Zifferblatt, S. M., Wilbur, C. S., & Pinsky, J. L. (1980). Changing cafeteria eating habits. *Journal of the American Dietetic Association, 76*, 15–20.

Zimmerman, E. H., & Zimmerman, J. (1962). The alteration of behavior in a special classroom situation. *Journal of the Experimental Analysis of Behavior, 5*, 59–60.

Zohn, C. J., & Bornstein, P. H. (1980). Self-monitoring of work performance with mentally retarded adults: Effects upon work productivity, work quality, and on-task behavior. *Mental Retardation, 18*, 19–25.

Source Notes

Figure 1.2: From E. P. Sarafino & J. W. Armstrong (1986). *Child and adolescent development* (2nd ed.). St. Paul, MN: West. Copyright © 1986 by Edward P. Sarafino and James W. Armstrong.

Figure 2.1: From E. P. Sarafino & J. W. Armstrong (1986). *Child and adolescent development* (2nd ed.). St. Paul, MN: West. Copyright © 1986 by Edward P. Sarafino and James W. Armstrong.

Figure 2.2: From N. H. Azrin, P. T. Hontos, & V. Besalel-Azrin (1979). Elimination of enuresis without a conditioning apparatus: An extension by office instruction of the child and parents. *Behavior Therapy*, 10, 14–19. Copyright © 1979 by the Association for Advancement of Behavior Therapy. Reprinted by permission of the publisher and the author.

Text quotation (Chapter 2, page 48): From T. F. Oltmanns, J. M. Neale, & G. C. Davison (1991). *Case studies in abnormal psychology* (3rd ed.). New York: Wiley. Copyright © 1991 by John Wiley & Sons, Inc. Reprinted by permission of John Wiley & Sons, Inc.

Table 3.1: From J. E. Seaman, B. F. Greene, & M. Watson-Perczel (1986). A behavioral system for assessing and training cardiopulmonary resuscitation skills among emergency medical technicians. *Journal of Applied Behavior Analysis*, 19, 125–135.

Copyright © by the Journal of Applied Behavior Analysis. Reprinted by permission of the publisher.

Figure 4.4: From E. P. Sarafino & J. W. Armstrong (1986). *Child and adolescent development* (2nd ed.). St. Paul, MN: West. Copyright © 1986 by Edward P. Sarafino and James W. Armstrong.

Figure 5.1: From F. R. Harris, M. M. Wolf, & D. M. Baer (1964). Effects of adult social reinforcement on child behavior. *Young Children*, 20, 8-17. Copyright © 1964 (October issue) by the National Association for the Education of Young Children (NAEYC). Reprinted with permission from NAEYC.

Figure 5.2: From E. P. Sarafino (1995, unpublished manuscript). *The Preferred Items and Experiences Questionnaire (PIEQ) for Adolescents and Adults.* Reprinted by permission of the author.

Figure 5.3: M. D. Johnson & S. B. Fawcett (1994). Courteous service: Its assessment and modification in a human service organization. *Journal of Applied Behavior Analysis*, 27, 145–152. Copyright © by the Journal of Applied Behavior Analysis. Reprinted by permission of the publisher.

Figure 6.3: From J. W. Cook, K. Altman, J. Shaw, & M. Blaylock (1978). Use of contingent lemon juice to eliminate public masturbation. *Behaviour Research and Therapy*, 16, 131–134. Copyright © 1978.

Reprinted with kind permission from Elsevier Science Ltd.

Figure 6.4: From N. H. Azrin & M. D. Wesolowski (1974). Theft reversal: An overcorrection procedure for eliminating stealing by retarded persons. *Journal of Applied Behavior Analysis*, 7, 577–581. Copyright © by the Journal of Applied Behavior Analysis. Reprinted by permission of the publisher.

Text quotation (Chapter 8, page 248): From T. F. Oltmanns, J. M. Neale, & G. C. Davison (1991). *Case studies in abnormal psychology* (3rd ed.). New York: Wiley. Copyright © 1991 by John Wiley & Sons, Inc. Reprinted by permission of John Wiley & Sons, Inc.

Text quotation (Chapter 8, page 264): From T. F. Oltmanns, J. M. Neale, & G. C. Davison (1991). *Case studies in abnormal psychology* (3rd ed.). New York: Wiley. Copyright © 1991 by John Wiley & Sons, Inc. Reprinted by permission of John Wiley & Sons, Inc.

Figure 8.2: From F. H. Kanfer, P. Karoly, & A. Newman (1975). Reduction of children's fear of the dark by competence-related and situational treat-related verbal cues. *Journal of Consulting and Clinical Psychology*, 43, 251–258. Copyright © 1975 by the American Psychological Association; reprinted with the permission of the author.

Figure 9.2: From N. H. Azrin, R. W. Sisson, R. Meyers, & M. Godley (1982). Alcoholism treatment by disulfiram and community reinforcement therapy. *Journal of Behavior Therapy and Experimental Psychiatry*, 13, 105–112. Copyright © 1982. Reprinted with kind permission from Elsevier Science Ltd.

Figure 12.1: From D. E. Bostow & J. B. Bailey (1969). Modification of severe disruptive and aggressive behavior using brief timeout and reinforcement procedures. *Journal of Applied Behavior Analysis*, 2, 31–37. Copyright © by the Journal of Applied Behavior Analysis. Reprinted by permission of the publisher.

Figure 12.2: From C. F. Lowe & P. D. J. Chadwick (1990). Verbal control of delusions. *Behavior Therapy*, 21, 461–479. Copyright © 1990 by the Association for Advancement of Behavior Therapy. Reprinted by permission of the publisher and the author.

Figure 12.3: From J. E. DeVries, M. M. Burnette, & W. K. Redmon. (1991). AIDS prevention: Improving nurses' compliance with glove wearing

through performance feedback. *Journal of Applied Behavior Analysis*, 24, 705–711. Copyright © by the Journal of Applied Behavior Analysis. Reprinted by permission of the publisher.

Figure 12.4: From R. V. De Luca & S. W. Holborn (1992). Effects of a variable-ratio reinforcement schedule with changing criteria on exercise in obese and nonobese boys. *Journal of Applied Behavior Analysis, 25*, 671–679. Copyright © by the Journal of Applied Behavior Analysis. Reprinted by permission of the publisher.

Figure 12.5: From F. W. Kohler & C. R. Greenwood (1990). Effects of collateral peer supportive behaviors within the classwide peer tutoring program. *Journal of Applied Behavior Analysis*, 23, 307–322. Copyright © by the Journal of Applied Behavior Analysis. Reprinted by permission of the publisher.

Table 13.1: From E. L. Phillips (1968). Achievement Place: Token reinforcement procedures in a home-style rehabilitation setting for "predelinquent" boys. *Journal of Applied Behavior Analysis, 1*, 213–223. Copyright © by the Journal of Applied Behavior Analysis. Reprinted by permission of the publisher.

Table 13.2: From E. L. Phillips, E. A. Phillips, D. L. Fixsen, M. M. Wolf (1971). Achievement Place: Modification of the behaviors of pre-delinquent boys within a token economy. *Journal of Applied Behavior Analysis, 4*, 45–59. Copyright © by the Journal of Applied Behavior Analysis. Reprinted by permission of the publisher.

Figure 13.2: From D. K. Fox, B. L. Hopkins, & W. K. Anger (1987). The long-term effects of a token economy on safety performance in open-pit mining. *Journal of Applied Behavior Analysis*, 20, 215–224. Copyright © by the Journal of Applied Behavior Analysis. Reprinted by permission of the publisher.

Text quotation (Chapter 15, page 452): From T. F. Oltmanns, J. M. Neale, & G. C. Davison (1991). *Case studies in abnormal psychology* (3rd ed.). New York: Wiley. Copyright © 1991 by John Wiley & Sons, Inc. Reprinted by permission of John Wiley & Sons, Inc.

Figure 15.1: From T. H. Ollendick, L. P. Hagopian, & R. M. Huntzinger (1991). Cognitive-behavioral therapy with nighttime fearful children. *Journal of Behavior Therapy and Experimental Psychiatry, 22*, 113–121. Copyright © 1991. Reprinted with kind permission from Elsevier Science Ltd.

Photo Credits

Source/Photo Researchers.   *Page 425:* Dan McCoy/Rainbow.   *Page 426:* Hank Morgan/Photo Researchers.   *Page 434:* Jean-Claude LeJeune/Stock, Boston.

Chapter 15
Page 448: Antman/The Image Works.

Chapter 16
Page 476: Michael Siluk/The Image Works.   *Page 478:* Susan Woog Wagner/Photo Researchers.

Author Index*

Citations in the text and in this index give only the name of the first author when authorship has more than three names.

Subject Index